CONTENTS

Foreword from the First Edition	v
Preface	vii
Table of Cases	xix
Table of Statutes	xxv
Table of Statutory Instruments	xxxi
Table of International Legislation	xxxiii
Table of Abbreviations	xxxv
Glossary	xxxvii

Chapter 1
An Introduction to the Family Court 1
Legal systems within the United Kingdom 1
What is the Family Court? 2
The structure of the Family Court 3
The relationship between the Family Court and the High Court 3
Appeals 4
Public law and private law children proceedings 5
The Family Procedure Rules 2010 6
    Transparency and confidentiality 6
Practice Directions and Guidance 7
CAFCASS/ CAFCASS CYMRU 7
HMCTS 8

Chapter 2
Introduction to Child Protection 9
Introduction 9
    Child protection and adoption 10
Children Act 1989 11
    Parental responsibility 11
    Welfare is paramount 11
    Child protection 12
    Care order and supervision order 12
    Emergency powers 14
Adoption and Children Act 2002 14
    Relationship between care proceedings and the adoption process 15
    Who can adopt? 16
    Intercountry adoption 16
Human Rights Act 1998 16

The UN Convention on the Rights of the Child	17
Statutory rules and government guidance	18
Wales	18
Family Justice Council	18
Wardship and the inherent jurisdiction of the High Court	19

Chapter 3
Parental Responsibility and Disputes between Parents — 21

Introduction	21
Who is a parent?	22
DNA testing	23
Parental responsibility	24
What is it?	24
Who has it?	25
Parental responsibility and the child: Gillick competence	26
Guardians and special guardians	28
Guardians	28
Special guardianship	29
Section 8 orders	30
Child arrangements orders: 'spends time with' orders	32
'Spends time with' orders and domestic abuse	34
Interim orders	35
Children and Adoption Act 2006	36
Shared 'lives with' orders	37
Specific issue and prohibited steps orders	38
Parenting plans	40
Removing a child from the jurisdiction	40
Section 8 orders: procedure	41
The application	41
The respondents	44
Welfare reports	44
The child as a party: guardians ad litem in private law proceedings	45

Chapter 4
Local Authorities and the Family — 47

Local authorities, children and families	47
Inter-agency working and local safeguarding partners	49
The provision of services	49
Services provided to all children	50
Children in need	51
Services for children in need	51
Children with special educational needs and disabilities	53
Young Carers	53
Accommodating children: local authority	54
Accommodation where the child has no parent or the parents consent: CA 1989, s 20	56
Local authority provision of accommodation	57
Accommodation for children in care	59

Child Protection and the Family Court – What You Need to Know

Third Edition

The Rt Hon Sir Andrew McFarlane,
President of the Family Division

Madeleine Reardon,
Barrister, One King's Bench Walk
Alexander Laing,
Barrister, Coram Chambers

Bloomsbury Professional
LONDON • DUBLIN • EDINBURGH • NEW YORK • NEW DELHI • SYDNEY

BLOOMSBURY PROFESSIONAL
Bloomsbury Publishing Plc
41–43 Boltro Road, Haywards Heath, RH16 1BJ, UK

BLOOMSBURY and the Diana logo are trademarks of Bloomsbury Publishing Plc
© Bloomsbury Professional Ltd 2019

All rights reserved. No part of this publication may be reproduced or transmitted in any form or by any means, electronic or mechanical, including photocopying, recording, or any information storage or retrieval system, without prior permission in writing from the publishers.

While every care has been taken to ensure the accuracy of this work, no responsibility for loss or damage occasioned to any person acting or refraining from action as a result of any statement in it can be accepted by the authors, editors or publishers.

All UK Government legislation and other public sector information used in the work is Crown Copyright ©. All House of Lords and House of Commons information used in the work is Parliamentary Copyright ©. This information is reused under the terms of the Open Government Licence v3.0 (http://www.nationalarchives.gov.uk/doc/open-government-licence/version/3) except where otherwise stated.

All Eur-lex material used in the work is © European Union,
http://eur-lex.europa.eu/, 1998–2019.

All efforts have been made to contact the publishers of other reproduced extracts and sources are acknowledged with the extracts. We welcome approaches from publishers and other copyright holders to discuss further acknowledgement or terms relating to reproduction of this material.

British Library Cataloguing-in-Publication Data

A catalogue record for this book is available from the British Library.

ISBN:	PB:	978-1-52650-597-2
	ePDF:	978-1-52650-595-8
	ePub:	978-1-52650-596-5

Typeset by Evolution Design & Digital Ltd (Kent)
Printed and bound by CPI Group (UK) Ltd, Croydon, CR0 4YY

To find out more about our authors and books visit www.bloomsburyprofessional.com.
Here you will find extracts, author information, details of forthcoming events and the option to sign up for our newsletters

FOREWORD FROM THE FIRST EDITION

(Originally published as Child Care and Adoption Law: A practical Guide)

All professionals working with children, whether teachers, social workers, nurses or doctors have at times to grapple with legal matters. This book is a simple and accessible guide. It explains the jargon, whether this is the categories of persons with parental responsibility, a section 8 order, hearsay evidence, or inherent jurisdiction.

The book comprises eight main sections; an introduction to child protection and adoption, 'from 999 call to adoption' as the authors put it; parental responsibilities and disputes between parents; local authorities and the family; referrals, assessments and emergency intervention; care and supervision orders; adoption; secure accommodation; and wardship.

The contents comprise the legal nuts and bolts of all these topics. The authors have managed to turn a dry subject (the law) into an explanation that requires no legal or specialist knowledge on the part of the reader. The text is helpfully broken up into small numbered elements, with numerous sub-headings, making it simple to look up, and follow, any topic. The book also contains some useful worked examples of problems, such as a 16-year-old boy in care, who has moved to a new foster family following the breakdown of a previous placement. The new foster parents lock him in his bedroom when he becomes drunk and abusive. Was locking the door lawful? What should happen next? For the answers, and for many other useful problem scenarios, read the book!

TIM DAVID
Professor of Child Health, University of Manchester
Honorary Consultant Paediatrician, Booth Hall Children's Hospital,
Manchester

PREFACE

The aim of this book can be simply stated. It is to provide a comprehensive overview of children law and the work of the family courts to those who are not specialist children lawyers. We hope that this text will be of value to all those who need to know the landscape of children law in order better to carry out their own specialist role, whether you are a lawyer in a related area, social worker, GP, paediatrician, psychologist, psychiatrist, teacher, safeguarding officer, child protection officer or member of the clergy. In addition, parents, prospective adopters and special guardians may be assisted by the route map that we have provided.

Publication of the first edition (*Child Care and Adoption Law: A Practical Guide*) in 2006 coincided with the moulding together of the general law relating to children with that of adoption following the implementation of the Adoption and Children Act 2002 in December 2005. This third edition is able not only to update the law and practice of the key areas covered in previous editions, but also to explain important changes in the law: special guardianship, radicalisation, adoption, international issues and the introduction of the Child Arrangements Programme for private law.

Jargon and acronyms appear only so that they may be explained. The text is not overburdened with references to case law; we have, however, explained the content of the key court decisions in their proper context. The aim throughout has been to present a description of the law in an uncomplicated and clear narrative. The law can only function effectively if it is readily understood by all who have to use it. Our hope is that this modest work will provide a plain-speaking guide for all those concerned with the protection of children and the family courts, whatever their specialist role or interest.

Andrew McFarlane

Madeleine Reardon

Alexander Laing
30 December 2018

Child Protection and the Family Court – What You Need to Know

Third Edition

Looked after children: care planning and reviews	60
Care plans for children subject to care orders: the role of the court	61
Types of accommodation for looked after children	62
Foster care	62
Relative and friend foster placements	63
Regulation of fostering services	63
Local authority foster parents	64
Approval of foster parents: the process	65
Agency foster parents	65
Emergency placements	66
Rights and duties of foster parents	66
Funding	67
Children's homes	68
Placement with parents	68
Placement with parents: assessment checklist	69
Accommodating children who are not looked after	71
Private fostering	71
Accommodation by voluntary organisations	74
Other informal arrangements	74
Leaving care	74
Eligible children	75
Relevant children	75
Responsibilities towards eligible and relevant children	76
Former relevant children	78
'Staying Put'	78

Chapter 5
Referrals, Assessments and Emergency Intervention   **79**

Introduction	79
The initial referral	80
The local authority's response	80
The child protection investigation: section 47	81
A court 'referral': section 37	83
Interim care or interim supervision orders	84
Appointment of a children's guardian	84
Further child protection measures	85
Child protection plans	85
The child protection conference	86
The initial child protection conference: key functions	87
The core group	87
Review conferences	87
Ongoing legal proceedings	88
Police protection: section 46	88
Police protection: key features	88
Duties of the officer taking the child into police protection	89
Duties of the designated officer	89
Emergency protection orders: section 44	90
Emergency protection orders: key features	90

Procedure	91
Without notice applications	92
Application for emergency protection orders: checklist	93
If application made without notice	93
If application made by telephone	93
Grounds	93
Effect of the order	94
Locating and removing the child	96
Contact	96
Exclusion requirement: section 44A	96
Medical examinations and assessments	97
Challenging an emergency protection order	97
Child assessment orders: section 43	98
Child assessment orders: key features	98
Procedure	99
Grounds for the order	100
Effect of the order	100
Recovery orders: section 50	100
Procedure	101
Effect of the order	101
Older children	102
Child safety orders and parenting orders	102

Chapter 6
Care and Supervision Orders — **105**

The orders available	105
Care orders	105
Supervision orders	106
The threshold criteria	107
Significant harm	107
'Likely to suffer'	108
The relevant date	109
'Attributable to parental care'	110
The standard expected of a reasonable parent	110
The child beyond parental control	111
The welfare checklist; the European Convention on Human Rights; a holistic analysis	111
The welfare checklist	111
The European Convention on Human Rights	112
A holistic welfare analysis	112
The birth family	113
Splitting siblings	114
Babies and young children	114
Older children	115
Very young parents	116
Physical and learning disabilities	116
The care plan	117
Care proceedings: application and procedure	117

The parties	117
Intervenors	118
Allocation of proceedings	119
The designated local authority	119
The role of the court	120
The Public Law Outline	120
Attendance of the media at hearings	121
Interim orders	122
Exclusion requirements	123
Fact-finding or split hearings	123
Assessments	125
The local authority's care plan	125
Parallel planning	126
Concurrent planning	126
Final order or interim order?	127
Withdrawing the application	127
Discharging the order	127
Representing the child	128
The role of the children's guardian	128
The role of the solicitor for the child	129
Evidence	130
Fundamental principles	130
Hearsay evidence	131
Interviewing children	132
Interviewing children: key checklist	133
Disclosure	134
Public interest immunity	134
Confidentiality and disclosure outside the proceedings	135
The role of the expert witness	138
Parental contact with children in care	140
Further issues	141
Serious allegations and the standard of proof	141
Human rights and the threshold criteria	142
Radicalisation	143
Uncertain perpetrators	144
Care or supervision order?	146

Chapter 7
Adoption — 147

What is adoption?	148
Intercountry adoption	149
Who can be adopted?	150
Who can adopt a child?	150
Adoption by a couple	150
Parent as an adopter	152
Step-parent adoption	152
Sole applicant	153
Previous applicants	154

The welfare of the child	154
The paramountcy principle	154
Ceasing to be a member of the original family and becoming an adopted person	155
Relationship which the child has with relatives and prospective adopters	157
Religion, race and culture	158
Whole range of powers and 'no order' principle	159
Whole range of powers available	159
'No order' principle	160
Parental consent	160
Overview	160
Consent to adoption	161
'Parent'	161
Guardian	162
Consent to placement for adoption	162
Advance consent to adoption	163
Consent to making of adoption order	164
Form and proof of consent	164
Intercountry adoptions: consent	164
The effect of giving consent	165
Placement for adoption or advance consent to adoption	165
Dispensing with parental consent	165
Grounds for dispensing with parental consent	165
Procedure for dispensing with consent	167
Adoption services	167
Prospective adopters	167
Advice and information	167
Assessment	168
Adoption Panel	168
Independent Review Mechanism	168
Matching and placement	169
The birth family	169
Counselling and support	169
Life story work	170
Access to confidential adoption information	170
Confidentiality	170
Registration and tracing natural family	170
Adopted Children Register	170
Going behind the adoption curtain: tracing the natural family	171
Person adopted before 30 December 2005	171
Person adopted after 30 December 2005	172
Adoption Contact Register	173
Placing a child for adoption	174
Background	174
'Placement for adoption'	175
Two routes to placement for adoption	175
Placement with parental consent	176
Placing a child under six weeks old	177

Form of consent	177
Advance consent to adoption	177
Consequences of parental consent to placement for adoption	178
Restrictions on changing name or removing from UK a child placed for adoption	179
Withdrawal of consent	179
Position of a father without parental responsibility	180
Placement under a placement order	180
Placement orders	180
Conditions for making a placement order	181
Local authority required to apply for a placement order	181
Status of child pending determination of placement order application	182
Consequences of a placement order	182
Revocation of a placement order	183
Care proceedings: how does a plan for adoption develop?	184
Contact on placement and after adoption	185
Contact arrangements when child is authorised for an adoption placement	185
Adoption agency power to refuse to allow contact	186
Application for s 26 contact order	187
Contact after an adoption order	188
Illegal placements and other prohibited steps	188
Applying for an adoption order	189
Consequences of an adoption order	190
Adoptions with an international element	191
Foreign child 'adopted' abroad	192
Foreign child brought into England and Wales for adoption	192
Facilitating the adoption abroad of a child from the UK	193
Convention adoptions	193

Chapter 8
Special Guardianship — **195**

Application and procedure	198
Special guardianship orders within care proceedings	200
Support services and financial support	201
Interaction with other orders	203
Variation and discharge	203

Chapter 9
Secure Accommodation and Deprivation of Liberty — **205**

Introduction	205
What is secure accommodation?	206
Secure accommodation: key features	206
Criteria for a secure accommodation order	208
Effect of a secure accommodation order	209
Secure accommodation without an order	209
Secure accommodation with an order	209
Age and other restrictions	209

Children looked after by the local authority	210
Children accommodated by the health or education authorities	211
Children who are charged or convicted of a criminal offence	212
Children who have been convicted	212
Children who have been charged and/or are on remand	212
Children detained under the Mental Health Act 1983	213
Procedure	213
Representation of the child	214
Challenging the order	214
The local authority's obligations	215
Educational provision	215
Review	215
Release	215
Deprivation of liberty	215
The inherent jurisdiction	216
Spotting a case in which there is a deprivation of liberty	216
Key points to remember	217
Procedure	217
Looking to the future	218

Chapter 10
Medical treatment and other complex issues: The High Court's Inherent Jurisdiction

	219
The High Court's inherent jurisdiction – introduction	219
Wardship	220
Effects of wardship	221
Common uses of the wardship jurisdiction	222
Medical treatment	222
Publicity	222
Protection from publicity: statute	222
Criminal proceedings: limitation of High Court's jurisdiction	224
Child abduction and forced marriage	224
Radicalisation	224
The inherent jurisdiction outside wardship	224
Medical treatment and terminal illness under the inherent jurisdiction	225
Terminal illness	226
Limitations on the use of the inherent jurisdiction with respect to children	227
Children in care	227
Procedure	229

Chapter 11
Challenging the local authority

	231
Introduction	232
Parental responsibility and consent	233
Independent reviewing officer	234
Making a complaint	237
Powers of the Secretary of State	237
Children's Commissioner	238

Local Government and Social Care Ombudsman	238
Judicial review	238
Appeals	239
Human Rights Act 1998	240
Article 6: Right to a fair trial	241
Article 8: Right to respect for private and family life	242
Applying the ECHR in domestic courts under the HRA 1998	243
Reference to the European Court of Human Rights	244

Appendix 1
Children Act 1989, ss 1–50   247

Appendix 2
Adoption and Children Act 2002, ss 1, 18–29, 42–52, 66–68, 83–95   371

Appendix 3
Family Procedure Rules 2010, parts 1, 12, 14, 25 and 30 and practice directions 12A, 12B, 12J, 25B, 25C   403

Appendix 4
Framework for the Assessment of Children in Need and Their Families   541

Appendix 5
Schedule of Items in Relation to the Exercise of Parental Responsibility   543

Appendix 6
Key Extracts from Important Judgments   545

Index   553

TABLE OF CASES

A

A v A (shared residence & contact) [2004] EWHC 142 (Fam), [2004] WLUK 76, [2004] 1 FLR 1195 — 3.13, 3.38, 3.56; App 5
A (a child) (adoption: agreement: procedure), Re [2000] 1 WLUK 860, [2001] 2 FLR 455, [2001] 2 FCR 174 — 7.68
A (a child) (adoption: removal), Re [2009] EWCA Civ 41, [2010] Fam 9, [2009] 2 FLR 597 — 7.196
A (a child) (change of residence), Re [2007] EWCA Civ 899, [2007] 6 WLUK 326, [2008] 1 FCR 599 — 3.39
A (a child) (residential assessment), Re [2009] EWHC 865 (Fam), [2009] 4 WLUK 311, [2009] 2 FLR 443 — 6.73
AMR (adoption: procedure), Re [1999] 6 WLUK 449, [1999] 2 FLR 807, [1999] 3 FCR 734 — 7.60
AS (secure accommodation order), Re [1999] 1 FLR 103, [1999] 2 FCR 749, [1999] Fam Law 20 — 9.34, 9.35
Airedale NHS Trust v Bland [1993] AC 789, [1993] 2 WLR 316, [1993] 1 FLR 1026 — 10.26

B

B v B (residence: condition limiting geographic area) [2004] 5 WLUK 278, [2004] 2 FLR 979, [2004] Fam Law 651 — 3.33
B (a child) (care proceedings: appeal), Re [2013] UKSC 33, [2013] 1 WLR 1911, [2013] 3 All ER 929 — 6.14, 6.29; 7.83; App 6
B (a child) (prohibited steps order), Re [2007] EWCA Civ 1055, [2007] 7 WLUK 684, [2008] 1 FLR 613 — 3.33
B (a child) (residence: second appeal), Re [2009] UKSC 5, [2009] 1 WLR 2496, [2010] 1 All ER 223 — 3.52
B (adoption order: jurisdiction to set aside), Re [1994] 4 WLUK 287, [1995] 1 FLR 1, [1994] 2 FCR 1297 — 7.46
B (care proceedings: notification of father without parental responsibility), Re [1999] 3 WLUK 252, [1999] 2 FLR 408, [1999] 2 FCR 391 — 6.48
B (children) (sexual abuse: standard of proof), Re [2008] UKHL 35, [2009] 1 AC 11, [2008] 2 FLR 141 — 6.16, 6.139
BR (proof of facts), Re [2015] EWFC 41, [2015] 5 WLUK 198 — 6.139
B-S (children) (adoption: leave to oppose), Re [2013] EWCA Civ 1146, [2014] 1 WLR 563, [2013] 9 WLUK 384 — 6.29; App 6
Barrett v Kirklees Metropolitan Council [2010] EWHC 467 (Admin), [2010] 3 WLUK 403, [2010] 2 FCR 153 — 8.18

C

C (a child) (care proceedings: dismissal or withdrawl) [2017] EWFC 37, [2018] 3 WLR 107, [2017] 6 WLUK 542 — 6.145
C (a child) (No 2) (application for public interest immunity), Re [2017] EWHC 692 (Fam), [2017] 3 WLUK 810, [2017] 2 FLR 1342 — 6.113
C (a child) (secure accommodation order: representation), Re [2001] EWCA Civ 458, [2001] 4 WLUK 65, [2001] 1 FCR 692 — 9.35
C (adoption: religious observance), Re [2002] 3 WLUK 832, [2002] 1 FLR 1119, [2002] Fam Law 497 — 7.44

C (a minor) (adoption order: conditions), Re [1989] AC 1, [1988] 2 WLR 474, [1988] 2 FLR 159 — 7.7

C (a minor) (adoption: parental agreement: contact), Re [1992] 11 WLUK 100, [1993] 2 FLR 260, [1994] 2 FCR 485 — 7.59

C (a minor) (detention for medical treatment), Re [1997] 2 FLR 180, [1997] 3 FCR 49, [1997] Fam Law 474 — 9.7; 10.12

C (a minor) (medical treatment: court's jurisdiction), Re [1997] 3 WLUK 94, [1997] 2 FLR 180, [1997] 3 FCR 49 — 3.20

C (a minor) (wardship: medical treatment) (No 1), Re [1990] Fam 26, [1989] 3 WLR 240, [1990] 1 FLR 252 — 10.26

C (disclosure), Re [1995] 12 WLUK 34, [1996] 1 FLR 797, [1996] 3 FCR 765 — 6.49, 6.115

C (sexual abuse: disclosure to landlords), Re [2002] EWHC 234 (Fam), [2002] 2 WLUK 394, [2002] 2 FLR 375 — 6.121

C (internal relocation), Re [2015] EWCA Civ 1305, [2016] Fam 253, [2017] 1 FLR 103 — 3.63

C & B (children) (care order: future harm), Re [2000] 3 WLUK 927, [2001] 1 FLR 611, [2000] 2 FCR 614 — 5.53; App 6

CE (a minor) (appointment of Guardian ad Litem), Re [1994] 7 WLUK 112, [1995] 1 FLR 26, [1995] 1 FCR 387 — 5.20

CT (a minor) (wardship: representation), Re [1994] Fam 49, [1993] 3 WLR 602, [1993] 2 FLR 278 — 10.5, 10.14

County Council v K [2005] EWHC 144 (Fam), [2005] 3 WLUK 291, [2005] 1 FLR 851 — 6.140

County Council v W (disclosure) [1996] 3 WLUK 150, [1997] 1 FLR 574, [1996] 3 FCR 728 — 6.121

D

D v D (children) (shared residence order) [2000] 11 WLUK 607, [2001] 1 FLR 495, [2001] 1 FCR 147 — 3.54, 3.56

D (a child) (care proceedings: adoption), Re [2016] EWFC 1, [2017] 4 WLR 55, [2017] 1 FLR 237 — 6.43

D (a child) (intractable contact dispute: publicity), Re [2004] EWHC 727 (Fam), [2004] 4 WLUK 50, [2004] 1 FLR 1226 — 3.44

D (care: natural parent presumption), Re [1998] 7 WLUK 383, [1999] 1 FLR 134, [1999] 2 FCR 118 — 6.33

D & K (children) (care plan: twin track planning), Re [2000] 1 WLR 642, [1999] 4 All ER 893, [1999] 2 FLR 872 — 7.49

DE (a child) (child under care order: injunction under Human Rights Act 1998), Re [2014] EWFC 6, [2015] Fam 145, [2014] 3 WLR 1733 — 6.4

DH (a minor) (child abuse), Re [1994] 1 WLUK 603, [1994] 1 FLR 679, [1994] 2 FCR 3 — 6.153

Down Lisburn Health & Social Services Trust v H [2006] UKHL 36, [2006] 7 WLUK 320, [2007] 1 FLR 121 — 7.173; App 6

E

E (a child) (family proceedings: evidence), Re [2016] EWCA Civ 473, [2016] 4 WLR 105, [2016] 5 WLUK 441 — 6.92

EC (disclosure of material), Re [1997] Fam 76, [1997] 2 WLR 322, [1996] 2 FLR 725 — 6.118

G

G (a child) (care proceedings: welfare evaluation), Re [2013] EWCA Civ 965, [2013] 7 WLUK 976, [2014] 1 FLR 670 — App 6

G (a child) (interim care order: residential assessment), Re [2005] UKHL 68, [2006] 1 AC 576, [2006] 1 FLR 601 — 6.73

G (a child) (special guardianship order: application to discharge), Re [2010] EWCA Civ 300, [2010] 2 WLUK 269, [2010] 2 FLR 696 — 8.23

Table of Cases xxi

Gillick v West Norfolk & Wisbech Area Health Authority [1986] AC 112,
  [1985] 3 WLR 830, [1985] 3 All ER 402 3.19; 5.69; 6.37; 10.12; 11.7
Glass v United Kingdom (Application 61827/00) [2004] 3 WLUK 240, [2004]
  1 FLR 1019, [2004] 1 FCR 553 10.24

H

H & A (children) (paternity: blood tests), Re [2002] EWCA Civ 383, [2002]
  3 WLUK 643, [2002] 1 FLR 1145 3.10
H (a child) (interim care order), Re [2002] EWCA Civ 1932, [2002] 12
  WLUK 336, [2003] 1 FCR 350 6.65
H (adoption: parental agreement), Re [1982] 3 FLR 386 7.7
H (a minor) (shared residence), Re [1992] 12 WLUK 2, [1994] 1 FLR 717,
  [1993] Fam Law 463 3.53
H (minors: prohibited steps order), Re [1995] 1 WLR 667, [1995] 4 All ER
  110, [1995] 1 FLR 638 3.60
Haringey LBC v C (a child) [2006] EWHC 1620 (Fam), [2006] 7 WLUK 538,
  [2007] 1 FLR 1035 7.46
Hewer v Bryant [1970] 1 QB 357, [1969] 3 WLR 425, [1969] 3 All ER 578 3.18

J

J (a child) (leave to issue application for residence order), Re [2002] EWCA
  Civ 1346, [2002] 7 WLUK 876, [2003] 1 FLR 114 6.47
J (a minor) (child in care: medical treatment), Re [1993] Fam 15, [1992] 3
  WLR 507, [1992] 2 FLR 165 10.26
J (a minor) (wardship: medical treatment), Re [1991] Fam 33, [1991] 2 WLR
  140, [1990] 3 All ER 930 10.10
J-M (a child) (contact proceedings: balance of harm), Re [2014] EWCA Civ
  434, [2014] 4 WLUK 291, [2015] 1 FLR 838 3.37
JS (a child) (disposal of body: prospective orders), Re [2016] EWHC 2859
  (Fam), [2017] 4 WLR 1, [2016] 11 WLUK 312 3.58
Johnasen v Norway (Application 17383/90) [1996] 8 WLUK 44, (1997)
  23 EHRR 33 App 6

K

K v K (children: permanent removal from jurisdiction) [2011] EWCA Civ 793,
  [2012] Fam 134, [2012] 2 FLR 880 3.63
K & T v Finland (Application 25702/94) [2001] 7 WLUK 313, [2001] 2 FLR
  707, (2001) 36 EHRR 255 App 6
K (minors) (wardship: criminal proceedings), Re [1988] Fam 1, [1987] 3 WLR
  1233, [1988] 1 FLR 435 10.17
KD (a minor) (ward: termination of access), Re [1988] 1 AC 806, [1988] 2
  WLR 398, [1988] 2 FLR 139 App 6
Kelly v BBC [2001] Fam 59, [2001] 2 WLR 253, [2001] 1 FLR 197 10.16
Kirklees Metropolitan District Council v S (contact to newborn babies) [2005]
  7 WLUK 124, [2006] 1 FLR 333, [2005] Fam Law 768 6.34

L

L (a child) (care: threshold criteria), Re [2006] 10 WLUK 670, [2007] 1 FLR
  2050, [2007] Fam Law 297 6.43; App 6
L (a child) (contact: domestic violence), Re; V (a child) (contact: domestic
  violence), Re [2001] Fam 260, [2001] 2 WLR 339, [2000] 2 FLR 334 3.43
L (an infant), Re [1968] P 119, [1967] 3 WLR 1645, [1968] 1 All ER 20 2.35; 10.1
Lancashire County Council v B (a child) (care orders: significant harm) [2000]
  2 AC 147, [2000] 2 WLR 590, [2000] 1 FLR 583 6.19, 6.149
Local Authority v GC; C (a child) (adoption: parental consent), Re [2008]
  EHWC 2555 (Fam), [2009] Fam 83, [2009] 1 FLR 299 7.133

M

M (a child) (refusal of medical treatment), Re [1999] 7 WLUK 336, [1999] 2 FLR 1097, [1999] 2 FCR 577	10.12
M (a minor) (adoption or residence order), Re [1997] 11 WLUK 320, [1998] 1 FLR 570, [1998] 1 FCR 165	7.36
M (a minor) (care order: threshold conditions), Re [1994] 2 AC 424, [1994] 3 WLR 558, [1994] 2 FLR 577	6.17
M (a minor) (secure accommodation order), Re [1995] Fam 108, [1995] 2 WLR 302, [1995] 3 All ER 407	9.13
M (care: challenging decisions by local authority), Re [2001] 6 WLUK 682, [2001] 2 FLR 1300, [2001] Fam Law 868	11.47
M (care order: parental responsibility), Re [1996] 3 WLUK 347, [1996] 2 FLR 84, [1996] 2 FCR 521	6.12
M (care proceedings: judicial review), Re [2003] EWHC 850 (Admin), [2003] 4 WLUK 465, [2003] 2 FLR 171	6.34
M (children), Re [2014] EWHC 667 (Fam), [2014] 3 WLUK 87	6.146
M (children) (residence), Re [2004] EWCA Civ 1574, [2004] 10 WLUK 336, [2005] 1 FLR 656	3.70
M (intractable contact dispute: interim care order), Re [2003] EWHC 1024 (Fam), [2003] 5 WLUK 464, [2003] 2 FLR 636	3.39
M (minors) (adoption), Re [1990] 3 WLUK 353, [1991] 1 FLR 458, [1990] FCR 785	7.68
M v Warwickshire CC [2007] EWCA Civ 1084, [2008] 1 WLR 991, [2008] 1 FLR 1093	7.155
M & N (twins: relinquished babies: parentage), Re [2017] EWFC 31, [2017] 5 WLUK 534, [2018] 1 FLR 293	7.59

N

N (a child) (contact: leave to defend & remove guardian), Re [2002] 9 WLUK 288, [2003] 1 FLR 652, [2003] Fam Law 154	3.20
N (a child) (leave to withdraw care proceedings), Re [1999] 9 WLUK 396, [2000] 1 FLR 134, [2000] 1 FCR 258	6.83
N (a child) (recognition of foreign adoption order), Re [2016] EWHC 3085 (Fam), [2018] Fam 117, [2018] 2 WLR 449	7.193
N (children) (adoption: jurisdiction), Re; J (children) (Brussels II revised: article 15), Re [2015] EWCA Civ 1112, [2016] 2 WLR 713, [2016] 1 All ER 1086	7.30, 7.44
NHS Trust v Y [2018] UKSC 46, [2018] 3 WLR 751, [2018] 7 WLUK 690	10.27
Northamptonshire County Council v Islington Borough Council [2001] Fam 364, [2000] 2 WLR 193, [1999] 2 FLR 881	6.54
North Yorkshire County Council v SA [2003] EWCA Civ 839, [2003] 7 WLUK 36, [2003] 2 FLR 849	6.150
Nottingham City Council v M [2016] EWHC 11 (Fam), [2016] 1 WLR 2995, [2016] 2 WLUK 549	6.36

O

O (minors) (care or supervision order), Re [1996] 4 WLUK 201, [1996] 2 FLR 755, [1997] 2 FCR 17	App 6

P

P (a child) (adoption order: leave to oppose making of adoption order), Re [2007] EWCA Civ 616, [2007] 1 WLR 2556, [2007] 2 FLR 1069	7.54
P (a child) (adoption: step-parent's application), Re [2014] EWCA Civ 1174, [2015] 1 WLR 2927, [2014] 8 WLUK 244	7.22
P (a child) (care & placement: evidential basis of Local Authority case), Re [2013] EWCA Civ 963, [2013] 7 WLUK 991, [2014] 1 FLR 824	App 6
P (by his litigation friend, the Official Solicitor) v Cheshire West & Chester Council; P & Q (by their litigation friend, the Official Solicitor) v Surrey County Council [2014] UKSC 19, [2014] AC 896, [2014] 2 WLR 642	9.45

P (children) (placement orders: parental consent), Re [2008] EWCA Civ 535,
[2009] PTSR 150, [2008] 2 FLR 625   7.78; App 6
PJ (adoption: practice on appeal), Re [1998] 5 WLUK 235, [1998] 2 FLR 252,
[1998] Fam Law 453   7.22
Payne v Payne [2001] EWCA Civ 166, [2001] Fam 473, [2001] 1 FLR 1052   3.63
Portsmouth NHS Trust v Wyatt [2004] EWHC 206, [2004] Fam Law 866,
[2005] 1 FLR 21   10.26

R

R (a child) (care proceedings: teenage pregnancy), Re [2000] 5 WLUK 742,
[2000] 2 FLR 660, [2000] 2 FCR 556   6.40
R (a minor) (medical treatment), Re; Camden LBC v R (a minor) (blood
transfusion) [1993] 5 WLUK 222, [1993] 2 FLR 757, [1993] 2 FCR 544   10.33
R (children) (care & placement orders: paternal grandparents), Re [2013]
EWCA Civ 1018, [2013] 7 WLUK 460, [2013] 3 FCR 599   App 6
R (children) (secure editing of documents), Re; J v E [2007] EWHC 876
(Fam), [2007] 1 WLR 1654, [2007] 2 FLR 759   6.120
R (a minor) (wardship: restrictions on publication), Re [1994] Fam 254,
[1994] 3 WLR 36, [1994] 2 FLR 637   10.18
R (on the application of Burke) v General Medical Council [2005] EWCA Civ
1003, [2006] QB 273, [2005] 3 WLR 1132   10.26
R (on the application of G) v Nottingham City Council [2008] EWHC 400
(Admin), [2008] 3 WLUK 67, [2008] 1 FLR 1668   6.36
R (on the application of L (a child) v Manchester City Council [2001] EWHC
Admin 707, [2001] 9 WLUK 415, [2002] 1 FLR 43   4.76
R (on the application of O) v LB Barking & Dagenham [2010] EWCA Civ
1101, [2011] 1 WLR 1283, [2011] 3 FCR 558   4.111
R (on the application of T) v LB Newham [2008] EWHC 2640 (Admin),
[2008] 11 WLUK 20, [2009] 1 FLR 311   4.62
R & H v United Kingdom (Application 35348/06) [2011] 5 WLUK 848,
[2011] 2 FLR 1236, (2012) 54 EHRR 2   App 6
Roddy (a child) (identification: restriction on publication), Re [2003] EWHC
2927 (Fam), [2003] 12 WLUK 125, [2004] 2 FLR 949   10.16

S

S, Re; Newcastle City Council v Z [2005] EWHC 1490 (Fam), [2005] 7
WLUK 250, [2007] 1 FLR 861   7.46
S (a child) (adoption order or special guardianship order), Re [2007] EWCA
Civ 54, [2007] 2 WLUK 129, [2007] 1 FLR 819   8.7
S (a child), Re [2014] EWCC B44 (Fam)   6.60
S (a child), Re; K v London Borough of Brent [2013] EWCA Civ 926, [2013]
7 WLUK 914, [2014] 2 FCR 62   App 6
S (a child) (residence order: condition) (No 2), Re [2002] EWCA Civ 1795,
[2002] 12 WLUK 70, [2003] 1 FCR 138   3.33
S (a child) (split hearing: fact finding), Re [2014] EWCA Civ 25, [2014] 1
WLUK 575, [2014] 1 FLR 1421   6.67
S (adult patient: sterilisation: patient's best interests), Re [2001] Fam 15,
[2000] 3 WLR 1288, [2000] 2 FLR 389   10.25
S (a minor) (medical treatment), Re [1993] 1 FLR 376   10.33
S (children) (care order: implementation of care plan), Re; W (care order:
adequacy of care plan), Re [2002] UKHL 10, [2002] 2 AC 291,
[2002] 1 FLR 815   11.46
S-B (children) (care proceedings: standard of proof), Re [2009] UKSC 17,
[2010] 1 AC 678, [2010] 2 WLR 238   6.16, 6.139, 6.149, 6.150; App 6
S (J) (a minor) (care or supervision order), Re [1993] 1 WLUK 629, [1993] 2
FLR 919, [1993] Fam Law 621   6.152
Soderbäck v Sweden [1998] 10 WLUK 514, [1999] 1 FLR 250, (2000) 29
EHRR 95   7.22

Storck v Germany (Application 61603/00) [2005] 6 WLUK 367, (2006) 43
  EHRR 6, [2005] MHLR 211 .... 9.44, 9.46

T

T v T (shared residence) [2010] EWCA Civ 1366, [2010] 12 WLUK 49,
  [2011] 1 FCR 267 .... App 6
T (a minor) (care order: conditions), Re [1994] 4 WLUK 283, [1994] 2 FLR
  423, [1994] Fam Law 558 .... 6.82
T (wardship: impact of police intelligence), Re [2009] EWHC 2440 (Fam),
  [2009] 10 WLUK 179, [2010] 1 FLR 1048 .... 6.113

V

V (a minor) (care or supervision order), Re [1994] 6 WLUK 125, [1996] 1
  FLR 776, [1996] 2 FCR 555 .... 6.152

W

W v Essex County Council [2001] 2 AC 592, [2000] 2 WLR 601, [2000]
  2 All ER 237 .... 4.75
W, Re; F (children), Re [2015] EWCA Civ 1300, [2015] 12 WLUK 621 .... 6.109
W (a child) (care proceedings: leave to apply), Re [2004] EWHC 3342 (Fam),
  [2004] 11 WLUK 308, [2005] 2 FLR 468 .... 6.47
W (a child) (designation of local authority) [2016] EWCA Civ 366, [2016] 4
  WLUK 388, [2017] 1 FLR 1511 .... 6.2, 6.54
W (a child) (secure accommodation order), Re [2016] EWCA Civ 804, [2016]
  4 WLR 159, [2016] 7 WLUK 801 .... 9.14
W (a minor) (secure accommodation order), Re [1993] 1 WLUK 747, [1993]
  1 FLR 692, [1993] 1 FCR 693, [1993] Fam Law 345 .... 9.18
W (children) (care proceedings: litigation capacity), Re [2008] EWHC 1188
  (Fam), [2008] 6 WLUK 426, [2010] 1 FLR 1176 .... 6.141
W (children) (direct contact), Re [2012] EWCA Civ 999, [2012] 7 WLUK
  768,
  [2013] 1 FLR 494 .... App 6
W (children) (family proceedings: evidence), Re [2010] UKSC 12, [2010] 1
  WLR 701, [2010] 2 All ER 418 .... 6.92
Wolverhampton Metropolitan Borough Council v DB (a minor) [1996] 11
  WLUK 324, [1997] 1 FLR 767, [1997] 1 FCR 618 .... 9.7

X

X Local Authority v B (Emergency Protection Orders) [2004] EWHC 2015
  (Fam), [2004] 8 WLUK 150, [2005] 1 FLR 341 .... 5.50
X (Emergency Protection Orders), Re; X (a child), Re [2006] 2 FLR 701 ..... 5.50

Y

YC v United Kingdom (Application 4547/10) [2012] 3 WLUK 395, [2012]
  2 FLR 332, (2012) 55 EHRR 967 .... App 6

Z

Z (children) (disclosure: criminal proceedings), Re [2003] EWHC 61 (Fam),
  [2003] 1 WLUK 579, [2003] 1 FLR 1194 .... 6.119

TABLE OF STATUTES

Administration of Justice Act 1960	
s 11, 12	10.13
Adoption Act 1976	
s 6	7.27
Adoption and Children Act 2002	1.22; 2.1, 2.2, 2.3, 2.19, 2.22, 2.23, 2.27, 2.31, 2.32; 3.15, 3.16, 3.28; 6.12, 6.32, 6.80; 7.3, 7.13, 7.31, 7.44, 7.47, 7.60, 7.86, 7.95, 7.119, 7.120, 7.121, 7.126, 7.158; 8.1, 8.15; 11.15; App 2
s 1	7.32, 7.39, 7.57, 7.150, 7.164, 7.166, 7.174; App 2
(1)	7.27, 7.69
(2)	7.27
(3)	7.28
(4)	7.29, 7.80
(c)	7.32, 7.33, 7.81
(f)	6.80; 7.32, 7.38, 7.39, 7.41, 7.81
(ii)	7.43
(iii)	7.69
(5)	7.30, 7.44
(6)	7.31, 7.47, 7.48, 7.51, 7.83, 7.159; App 6
(7)	7.27, 7.57
18	App 2
(1)	7.133
(3)	7.123
19	7.61, 7.64, 7.130, 7.137, 7.142, 7.143, 7.163; App 2
(1)	7.61, 7.127, 7.131
(a), (b)	7.129
(2)	7.62, 7.129
(3)	7.131
(4)	7.130
(5)	7.61
20	7.56, 7.66, 7.183; App 2
(1), (2)	7.64, 7.137
(3)	7.65, 7.138
(4)	7.139
(6)	7.66
21	7.158; App 2
(1)	7.148
(2), (3)	7.150
22	7.160; :App 2
(1)	7.151
(2)	7.131
(4)	7.153

Adoption and Children Act 2002—*continued*	
s 22(5)	7.152
(6)	7.154
23	App 2
24	8.23; App 2
25	3.15; 7.149; App 2
(2)	3.15
26	7.140, 7.165, 7.166, 7.167, 7.168, 7.169, 7.170, 7.171; App 2
(1)	7.163, 7.170
(2), (6)	7.163
27	7.163, 7.165, 7.168; App 2
(1)	7.166
(2), (3)	7.169
(4)	7.164
28	App 2
(1)	7.142
(2), (3)	7.143, 7.155
(4)	7.143
29	App 2
(1), (2)	7.155
(5)	7.155
30	7.72
31	7.72
(2)	7.144
32	7.72
(2)	7.144
33–41	7.72
42	7.25; App 2
(2)–(5)	7.16
43	App 2
44	7.25; App 2
45	App 2
46	App 2
(5)	7.11
47	7.183, 7.187; App 2
(2)(a)	7.56, 7.68
(b), (c)	7.56
(4)	7.141
(5)	7.73, 7.141, 7.142
(7)	7.73, 7.141
(8)	7.11
(8A)	7.11
48	7.26; App 2
49	7.10; App 2
(2), (3)	7.15, 7.24
50	3.17; 7.12, 7.13; App 2
(1)	7.14, 7.18

Adoption and Children Act 2002—*continued*		Adoption (Intercountry Aspects)	
s 50(2)	7.18	Act 1999	7.9
51	7.12; App 2	Anti-social Behaviour, Crime and	
(1)	7.25	Policing Act 2014	5.96
(2)	7.21		
(3), (3A)	7.25	British Nationality Act 1981	7.188
51A	7.174; App 2	s 1(5)	7.189
(5)	7.174		
51B	App 2	Care Standards Act 2000	4.55
52	7.61, 7.150; App 2	s 47	4.56
(1)	7.74, 7.79	Pt V (ss 72–78)	11.23
(b)	7.78; App 6	Child Abduction and Custody Act	
(3)	7.61, 7.66, 7.68, 7.133	1985	10.1
(4)	7.63, 7.65, 7.72, 7.138, 7.144	Children Act 1989	1.21, 1.22, 1.24;
(5)	7.56, 7.61, 7.67, 7.68, 7.128		2.1, 2.2, 2.3, 2.4, 2.6, 2.7,
(6)	7.58, 7.59, 7.128, 7.145		2.15, 2.17, 2.19, 2.23, 2.27,
(7)	7.70, 7.135		2.31, 2.32, 2.35, 2.36; 3.12,
(8)	7.144		3.18, 3.19, 3.30, 3.48, 3.53,
54	7.114		3.56; 4.4, 4.11, 4.16, 4.33,
55	7.3, 7.4, 7.196		4.39, 4.49, 4.89, 4.99;
56	7.111, 7.113		5.33, 5.90; 6.6, 6.10, 6.25,
57	7.111, 7.113		6.26, 6.99, 6.116; 7.19,
(1)	7.113		7.23, 7.29, 7.47, 7.58,
58, 59	7.111, 7.113		7.60, 7.170, 7.171, 7.187;
60	7.111, 7.113, 7.114		8.5; 10.1, 10.2, 10.3, 10.5,
61–65	7.111, 7.113		10.13, 10.30, 10.34; 11.2,
66	App 2		11.10, 11.22, 11.42; App 1
67	3.8, 3.15; 7.188, 7.193; App 2	Pt I (ss 1–7)	3.4; App 1
(2)	7.5, 7.21	s 1	1.19; 7.32, 7.174
(3)	7.21	(1)	2.6; 3.54; 9.13
68	App 2	(3)	2.6; 3.62; 6.9, 6.25; 7.38
74	7.6	(g)	App 6
77	7.102	(4)	5.52
(4)	7.103	(5)	6.25; 7.51, 7.159; App 6
79(5)	7.111	2(1)	3.15
(6)	7.104	(1A)	3.15
80	7.116	(2)(a)	3.15
(2), (3)	7.116	(3)	3.15
81(1)	7.117	3	App 6
83	7.195; App 2	(1)	3.12
84	7.196; App 2	(4)	3.14
85	7.196; App 2	(5)	3.21, 3.23; 11.6
86–91A	App 2	4	3.50; 7.58
92	App 2	(1)	7.58
(1)	7.176	(a)	3.15
(2)	7.175, 7176, 7.177	(b)	3.15; 7.58
93	App 2	(c)	3.15
94	App 2	4A	3.66; 6.131; 7.23
(1)	7.177	(1)	3.15, 3.17
95	7.178; App 2	4ZA(1)	3.15
144	7.144, 7.171	5	3.15, 3.24
(1)	7.60, 7.144	(1), (2)	3.26
(4)	3.17; 7.5, 7.12, 7.13	6(3A), (3B)	3.25
(5)	7.13	7	3.69, 3.70; 5.15
(6)	7.13	Pt II (ss 8–16A)	3.4; App 1
Sch 1	7.102	s 8	3.32, 3.33, 3.52, 3.58, 3.62, 3.64,
Sch 2	7.104		3.66, 3.68; 5.35, 5.40, 5.61; 7.155,
para 4	7.104		7.163, 7.171, 7.174, 7.190; 8.19

Children Act 1989—continued

s 9	3.30, 3.66
(1)	3.51; 10.33
(5)	3.30
(6)	3.32
10	3.30, 3.66
(7A)	8.21
(9)	3.67
11	3.30
(1)	7.58
(4)	3.53
(7)	3.33
11A–11P	3.48
12	3.30
12(1), (1A)	3.15
(2)	3.15; 4.88
13	3.30, 3.60, 3.62
(2)	3.56
14A	7.49; 8.9
(7)	8.9
(11)	8.12
14B	7.49
(1)	8.19
14C	7.49; 8.5
(1)(a)	3.15
(b)	3.28
14D	7.49
(5)	8.23
14E	7.49
14F	7.49; 8.16
14G	7.49
Pt III (ss 16B–30A)	2.7, 2.8, 2.9; 4.7, 4.15, 4.26; 6.1; 7.123, 7.153; App 1
s 17	2.8; 4.13, 4.25; 5.6
(6)	4.17
17ZA, 17ZB	4.24
17ZC	4.25
17ZD	4.22
(10)	4.22
18	4.16
20	2.8; 4.33, 4.38, 4.71; 9.5, 9.10, 9.22; 11.38
(1)	4.35; 9.20
(2)	4.36
(3)	4.37; 9.19
(5)	9.19
(7)	9.20
(8)	11.5
(9)	9.21; 11.5
22	4.69
(1)	9.20
(3), (3A)	4.28
(4), (5)	4.28, 4.44
22A, 22B	4.29
22C(2)	4.30
(5)	4.30
(6)	4.29, 4.30

Children Act 1989—continued

s 22C(7)	4.30
(8), (9)	4.31
(9A), (9B)	4.32; 7.125, 7.161
(C)	7.125
23	4.69
(4)	4.78
(6)	4.79
23A–24D!	4.105
23B	4.105, 4.108
23C	4.105, 4.110
23CA	4.111
23CZA	4.112
25	9.2, 9.3, 9.4, 9.7, 9.9, 9.10, 9.13, 9.20, 9.22, 9.23, 9.24, 9.25, 9.26, 9.27, 9.29, 9.34, 9.43
(4)	9.14
(6)	9.35
25B(1)	11.9
(3)	11.11
26	11.2
(3)	11.13, 11.14, 11.15, 11.17, 11.19
27	4.2
29	4.18
Pt IV (ss 31–42)	2.6, 2.7, 2.8, 2.10; 5.48, 5.72; 6.1, 6.28; 11.13; App 1
s 31	2.10, 2.11, 2.15; 4.40; 6.12; 7.131; 9.12
(1)	6.14
(2)	6.9, 6.19; 7.150, 7.151
(3)	6.3
(3A), (3B)	4.47; 6.74
(6)	6.45
(8)	6.2, 6.53
(9)	5.51
(10)	6.11
31A	4.43
32	6.60
(8)	6.60
33(3)	11.3
(a)	3.15
(b)	8.20
(6)	11.4
34	2.12; 5.35, 5.61; 6.136; 7.163, 7.171; 8.20; 10.32
(1)	6.131, 6.134
(4)	6.135
(6)	6.134
(11)	6.130
37	3.69; 5.14, 5.15, 5.16, 5.17, 5.18, 5.19, 5.20; 6.58
(2)	4.21
(3)	5.18
(4)	5.17, 5.18
38(1)	5.18
(2)	6.64

Children Act 1989—*continued*		Children Act 1989—*continued*	
s 38(3)	6.153	s 91(15)	6.85
(4)	5.18; 6.64	(17)	6.136
(6)	6.71, 6.72; 7.154	97(2)	10.13
38A	6.66	98(2)	6.121
39(4)	6.88	100	10.3, 10.31
41	5.20, 5.21, 5.45; 9.34	(2)(a)–(d)	10.31
(6)	6.89	(4)	10.33
(11)	6.100	(a), (b)	10.32
42(1)	6.112	101(2)(c)	10.21
(2)	6.100	105(1)	4.39
Pt V (ss 43–52)	2.7, 2.8, 2.17; 5.45; 11.13; App 1	(4)	9.20
		Sch 2	4.15
s 43	5.71, 5.72; 9.19	para 2	4.19
(5)	5.74	3	4.13
44	2.17; 5.38; 9.20	5	5.54; 6.66
(4)	5.55	6	4.19
(5)	5.56	7(a)(i)	4.15
(6)	5.61, 5.68	8	4.16
(8)	5.68	9	4.11
(14)	5.46	Pt II (paras 12–19)	6.132
44A	5.63	para 12A	4.62
45(5)	5.43	19B	4.102, 4.105
(7)	5.44	Sch 3	
46	2.17; 5.32, 5.33	para 6(1), (3)	6.7
(1)	5.33	8(2)(b)	6.7
(10)	5.35	9	6.53
47	5.4, 5.6, 5.8, 5.9, 5.10, 5.11, 5.12, 5.13, 5.22, 5.26, 5.37	Sch 7	4.60
		Sch 14	
(6)	5.13	para 4	7.58
48(1)	5.58	Sch 15	7.58
(3)	5.59	Children Act 2004	4.4, 4.5; 5.95
(11)	5.60	Pt 1 (ss 1–9)	11.23
(12)	5.59	Children and Adoption Act 2006	3.33, 3.47, 3.48
49	5.83		
(1)(b), (c)	5.92	Children and Families Act 2014	3.31, 3.35, 3.36, 3.53; 4.4; 6.60
50	5.83, 5.91		
(9)	5.90		
51	5.92	s 25	4.20
Pt VII (ss 59–62)	4.88	Children and Social Work Act 2017	4.4, 4.5; 6.80
s 60	5.95		
62	4.89	Children and Young Persons Act 1933	
(1)	4.95	s 39	10.13
(5)	4.96	Children (Leaving Care) Act 2000	4.1011
(6)	4.95	Children's Commissioner for Wales Act 2001	11.23
66	4.90		
67	4.93	Child Support Act 1991	6.117
68	4.93	Civil Evidence Act 1995	6.106
70	4.93	s 1(1)	6.105
80(1)	11.21	Civil Partnership Act 2004	
84	11.22	s 79	7.25
85	4.88	Crime and Disorder Act 1998	5.93; 6.58
(1), (4)	4.89	s 8	5.96
86	4.88	11	5.94
91(5A)	8.20	Crime and Courts Act 2013	1.4
(6)	5.47	Criminal Justice Act 2003	6.102
(7), (8)	3.19		
(14)	7.36, 7.49	Equality Act 2010	6.43

Family Law Act 1986		Legal Aid, Sentencing and	
s 38	10.9	Punishment of Offenders Act	
Family Law Act 1996	5.54	2012	3.3
Family Law Reform Act 1969		Legitimacy Act 1976	
s 20	3.9, 3.11	s 2	7.58
Family Law Reform Act 1987	. 7.58	Local Authority Social Services Act 1970	
s 4	7.58	s 7	2.32; 11.20
Female Genital Mutilation Act 2003	10.1	Local Government Act 1974	
Forced Marriage (Civil Protection)		s 26	11.26
Act 2007	10.1, 10.19	Local Government (Scotland) Act 1973	
		s 23	11.26
Human Fertilisation and Embryology			
Act 2008		Marriage Act 1949	7.188
s 33	3.5	Sch 1	3.8
35–37	3.7	Mental Capacity Act 2005	7.77; 10.1, 10.24
42–44	3.7	Mental Health Act 1983	9.2; 10.11
Human Rights Act 1998	2.3, 2.26, 2.27,	s 2, 3	9.29
	2.29; 3.37; 4.38; 6.28,	33	10.11
	6.30, 6.47; 9.39; 10.14,		
	10.15; 11.2, 11.30, 11.36,	Senior Courts Act 1981	
	11.37, 11.44, 11.45,	s 7	10.21
	11.46, 11.48	31	11.32
s 3(1)	11.37	41(2)	10.35
6	11.45	Sexual Offences Act 1956	
7	4.50; 11.11, 11.45	s 10, 11	3.8
8	6.4; 11.47	Sexual Offences Act 2003	7.188
		s 64, 65	7.6
Immigration Act 1971	7.188	Social Services and Well-being	
Interpretation Act 1978		(Wales) Act 2014	
Sch 1	7.15	s 119	9.10

TABLE OF STATUTORY INSTRUMENTS

Adopted Children and Adopted Contact Registers Regulations 2005, SI 2005/924		Care Leavers (England) Regulations 2010, SI 2010/2571—*continued*	
reg 2	7.102	reg 7	4.105
8	7.117	(2)	4.107
Access to Information (Post-Commencement Adoptions) (Wales) Regulations 2005, SI 2005/2689	7.111	8	4.105, 4.106
		9	4.105
		Care Planning, Placement and Case Review (England) Regulations 2010, SI 2010/959	4.4, 4.55, 4.58
Adoption Agencies Regulations 2005, SI 2005/389	7.86	reg 4	4.43
reg 14(3), (4)	7.145	(1)	4.42
19	7.160	(4), (5)	4.44
20	7.136	5, 6	6.75
31(1)(a)	7.99	9	4.43
Pt 6 (regs 35–38)	7.124	14	4.72
reg 35	7.99	15–17	4.80
(4)	7.133	18	4.80
47	7.164, 7.169	(1)	4.81
(2)	7.167	19, 20	4.80
Sch 5	7.99	22	4.61
		23	4.69
Adoption (Designation of Overseas Adoptions) Order 1973, SI 1973/19	7.193	24	4.54
		28	4.86
		33	4.45
		36	4.51
Adoption Information and Intermediary Services (Pre-Commencement Adoptions) Regulations 2005, SI 2005/890	7.104	45	11.10, 11.11
		Sch 1	4.44
		Sch 2	4.43
reg 4	7.105	Sch 3	4.85
7	7.108	Sch 7	4.45
8	7.109	Children Act 1989 Representations Procedure (England) Regulations 2006, SI 2006/1738	11.17
9	7.110		
10	7.107	reg 3	11.17
Sch 2	7.136	Children (Admissibility of Hearsay Evidence) Order 1993, SI 1993/621	6.104, 6.106
Adoption Information and Intermediary Services (Pre-Commencement Adoptions) (Wales) Regulations 2005, SI 2005/2701	7.104		
		Children and Family Court Advisory and Support Service (Reviewed Case Referral) Regulations 2004, SI 2004/2187	11.11
Adoption Support Services Regulations 2005, SI 2005/691	7.86		
Adoption with a Foreign Element Regulations 2005, SI 2005/392	7.11, 7.195	Children (Private Arrangements for Fostering) Regulations 2005, SI 2005/1533	4.88
		reg 7, 8	4.89
Care Leavers (England) Regulations 2010, SI 2010/2571		Sch 3	4.92
		Children's Commissioner for Wales Regulations 2001, SI 2001/2787	11.23
reg 3	4.103		
5, 6	4.105		

Children (Secure Accommodation) (No 2) Regulations 1991, SI 1991/2034		Family Procedure Rules 2010, SI 2010/2955—*continued*	
reg 2	9.30	PD 12J	3.40, 3.41, 3.42, 3.43, 3.45; App 3
Children (Secure Accommodation) Regulations 1991, SI 1991/1505		Pt 14 (rr 14.1–14.28)	1.21; 7.170, 7.179
		r 14.1, 14.2	App 3
reg 3	9.6	14.3	7.170; App 3
4	9.8, 9.19	(2)	7.172
5(1)	9.26	14.4–14.7	App 3
(2)(a)	9.10, 9.19	14.8	7.181; App 3
(b)	9.19	14.9	App 3
6(1)(a)	9.27	(2)	7.85
(2)	9.28	14.10	App 3
7	9.24	(1)(a)	7.135
10(1)	9.15	14.11–14.20	App 3
(3)	9.16	14.21	7.146; App 3
11, 12	9.18	14.22–14.28	App 3
13	9.17	PD 14E	6.116
15	9.40	PD 14C	7.184
Children's Homes (England) Regulations 2015, SI 2015/541	4.77	r 15.2	7.77
		Pt 16 (rr 16.1–16.39)	1.21
Civil Procedure Rules 1998, SI 1998/3132	1.20	r 16.4	3.71
Pt 52 (rr 52.1–52.29)	1.12	PD 16A	3.71
Disclosure of Adoption Information (Post-Commencement Adoptions) Regulations 2005, SI 2005/888		Pt 19 (rr 19.1–19.9)	7.146
		r 21.3	6.113
		Pt 25 (rr 25.1–25.20)	1.21; 6.124, 6.127; App 3
	7.111	PD 25B	App 3
reg 4	7.111	PD 25C	App 3
17	7.115	r 27.10	6.62
Emergency Protection Order (Transfer of Responsibilities) Regulations 1991, SI 1991/1414		27.11(2)(f)	6.62
		Pt 30 (rr 30.1–30.14)	1.12; App 3
		Fostering Services (England) Regulations 2011, SI 2011/581	4.54, 4.55, 4.59
reg 2	5.39		
Family Court (Composition and Distribution of Business) Rules 2014, SI 2014/840		reg 2(1)	4.58
		26	4.63
	1.8	27(5)	4.60
Family Procedure Rules 2010, SI 2010/2955	1.20, 1.26; App 3	Sch 5	4.61
		Independent Review of Determinations (Adoption and Fostering) Regulations 2009, SI 2009/395	
Pt 1 (rr 1.1–1.4)	App 3		
r 1.1	1.20; App 3		
1.2–1.4	App 3		4.62; 7.93
2.3	7.77	Local Authority Social Services and National Health Service Complaints (England) Regulations 2009, SI 2009/309	
4.4	6.46		
PD 5A	7.135		
Pt 12 (rr 12.1–12.75)	1.21; App 3		
r 12.1, 12.2	App 3		11.13, 11.19
12.3	3.68; 6.46; 9.31; App 3	Restriction on the Preparation of Adoption Reports Regulations 2005, SI 2005/1711	
12.4–12.15	App 3		
12.16	9.33; App 3		7.177
(4)–(6)	5.49	Supreme Court Rules 2009, SI 2009/1603	
12.17–12.71	App 3		
12.72	6.161; 10.13; App 3		1.13
12.73	1.21; 6.116; 10.13; App 3	Special Guardianship (Amendment) Regulations 2016, SI 2016/111	8.11
12.74, 12.75	6.116; 10.13; App 3		
PD 12A	6.60, 6.76; App 3	Special Guardianship Regulations 2005, SI 2005/1109	8.11
PD 12C	3.68		
PD 12E	5.49	Pt 2 (regs 3–20)	8.16
PD 12G	6.116, 6.117	Schedule	8.10

TABLE OF INTERNATIONAL LEGISLATION

European Convention on Human Rights (Rome, 4 November 1950)   2.26, 2.27, 2.28, 2.29; 9.4 7; 11.17, 11.36, 11.37, 11.38, 11.39, 11.44, 11.45, 11.46, 11.49
  art 2, 3   11.39
    5   9.2, 9.3, 9.35, 9.39, 9.42, 9.44, 9.47; 11.39
      (1)(d)   9.39
    6   2.28; 6.49, 6.65, 6.126; 11.39, 11.40, 11.41
    8   2.27, 2.28; 3.37; 6.47, 6.61, 6.65, 6.73, 6.142; 7.22, 7.83, 7.159; 10.15, 10.16; 11.39, 11.42; App 6
    8(2)   11.42
    10   6.61; 10.15, 10.16
    12, 14   11.39
Convention on Protection of Children and Co-operation in Respect of Intercountry Adoption (The Hague, 29 May 1993)   7.9, 7.193, 7.197
United Nations Convention on the Rights of the Child (New York, 20 November 1989)   2.30
  art 2, 3, 8, 11, 12, 16, 17, 19, 22, 24, 26–28, 31   2.30

TABLE OF ABBREVIATIONS

AA 1976	Adoption Act 1976
AAR 2005	Adoption Agencies Regulations 2005
ACA 2002	Adoption and Children Act 2002
ACACRR 2005	Adopted Children and Adoption Contact Registers Regulations 2005
AIIS(PC)R 2005	Adoption Information and Intermediary Services (Pre-Commencement Adoptions) Regulations 2005
ASBO	Anti-social Behaviour Order
CA 1989	Children Act 1989
CA 2004	Children Act 2004
CAA 2006	Children and Adoption Act 2006
CAFCASS	Children and Family Advisory Support Service
CDA 1998	Crime and Disorder Act 1998
CFA 2014	Children and Families Act 2014
C(PAF)R 2005	Children (Private Arrangements for Fostering) Regulations 2005
CPPCR(E)R 2010	Care Planning, Placement and Case Review (England) Regulations 2010
DAI(PCA)R 2005	Disclosure of Adoption Information (Post-Commencement Adoptions) Regulations 2005
ECHR	European Convention on Human Rights
ECtHR	European Court of Human Rights
FJC	Family Justice Council
FLRA 1969	Family Law Reform Act 1969
FLRA 1987	Family Law Reform Act 1987
FS(E)R 2011	Fostering Services (England) Regulations 2011
HFEA 2008	Human Fertilisation and Embryology Act 2008
HRA 1998	Human Rights Act 1998
ICS	Integrated Children's System
IRM	Independent Review Mechanism
IRO	Independent Reviewing Officer
LAC	Looked After Child
LAC Review	Looked After Child Review
LASSA 1970	Local Authority Social Services Act 1970
LASSNHSC(E)R 2009	Local Authority Social Services and National Health Service Complaints (England) Regulations 2009

OFSTED	Office for Standards in Education, Children's Services and Skills
UNRC	United Nations Convention on the Rights of the Child

GLOSSARY OF TERMS

Child Arrangements Programme / CAP:	the procedure that is followed in private children law cases
Child protection plan:	a plan written by a local authority with the aim to ensure that a child is safe from harm and prevent her from suffering further harm, promote the child's welfare and development and support the family to safeguard and promote the child's welfare
Domestic abuse:	any incident or pattern of incidents of controlling, coercive or threatening behaviour, violence or abuse between those aged 16 or over who are or have been intimate partners or family members regardless of gender or sexuality. This can encompass, but is not limited to, psychological, physical, sexual, financial, or emotional abuse. Domestic abuse also includes culturally specific forms of abuse including, but not limited to, forced marriage, honour-based violence, dowry-related abuse and transnational marriage abandonment
Domicile:	the country that a person treats as their permanent home, or lives in and has a substantial connection with
ECHR, Art 5:	the right to liberty and security
ECHR, Art 6:	the right to fair trial
ECHR, Art 8:	the right to respect for private and family life
Fact-finding hearing:	a trial to determine whether allegations are true or false
Habitual residence:	for children, the place which reflects some degree of integration by the child in a social and family environment
Inherent jurisdiction:	a power that High Court judges have which is traced from the Crown's ancient power to protect its subjects
Ordinary residence:	a legal concept meaning, in the context of the designation of local authorities, the place where a child has her settled home, not counting a school or other institution, a placement whilst accommodated by a local authority or under a supervision order, or under a youth rehabilitation order

Parental responsibility:	all the rights, duties, powers, responsibilities and authority which by law a parent of a child has in relation to the child and her property
Private children law:	disputes between parents or other individuals who have a relationship with the child
Public children law:	cases involving the interaction between the state (normally through local authorities) and the family, in connection with the protection and wellbeing of children
S 17 assessment:	an assessment under CA 1989, s 17 to determine whether the child is 'in need'
S 47 assessment:	an assessment under CA 1989, s 47 in cases where there is reasonable cause to suspect the child is suffering or likely to suffer significant harm or a local child has been taken into police protection or made subject to an emergency protection order
Threshold criteria:	the test in the CA 1989, s 31 (2) that must be met before the court can sanction state intervention in a family's life in the form of a care or supervision order
Wardship:	one part of the inherent jurisdiction, in which custody of a child is vested in the High Court and no important decision can be taken in the child's life without the court's consent
Welfare / disposal hearing:	a trial to determine which, if any, orders are in the child's best interests

CHAPTER 1

AN INTRODUCTION TO THE FAMILY COURT

Chapter summary

- Legal systems within the United Kingdom
- What is the Family Court?
- The structure of the Family Court
- The relationship between the Family Court and the High Court
- Appeals
- Public law and private law children proceedings
- The Family Procedure Rules 2010
- Practice Directions and Guidance
- CAFCASS/CAFCASS CYMRU
- HMCTS

LEGAL SYSTEMS WITHIN THE UNITED KINGDOM

1.1 The Family Court forms part of the jurisdiction (legal system) of England and Wales. England and Wales together form one jurisdiction. Northern Ireland and Scotland are separate jurisdictions; the law in Northern Ireland is similar to that in England and Wales, but the legal system in Scotland is very different.

1.2 Although Wales forms part of the same jurisdiction as England, social care functions are devolved to the Welsh Assembly. This means that local authorities in England and Wales will have different child protection responsibilities, and in some respect the courts in each country will be required to apply different law. Some of the main differences between English and Welsh law are highlighted throughout the text, but full coverage of both English and Welsh provisions is outside the scope of this book. Practitioners in Wales should have regard to the specific Welsh statutes and regulations where necessary, in particular if the case requires detailed knowledge of the local authority's social care functions.

WHAT IS THE FAMILY COURT?

1.3 The modern Family Court was created on 22 April 2014. Prior to that date, the majority of family cases were dealt with by lay magistrates or by the county courts within their civil jurisdiction, while the most complex cases (or those with an international element) were heard in the Family Division of the High Court.

1.4 The Family Court came into existence as a result of the Crime and Courts Act 2013, which created for the first time a unified court dedicated to hear family cases. The Family Court may sit at any place in England and Wales; in practice many hearings continue to take place in magistrates and county courts, although some areas have their own dedicated Family Court buildings. Within the Family Court cases may be allocated to a particular judge or level of judge, and to a geographical area.

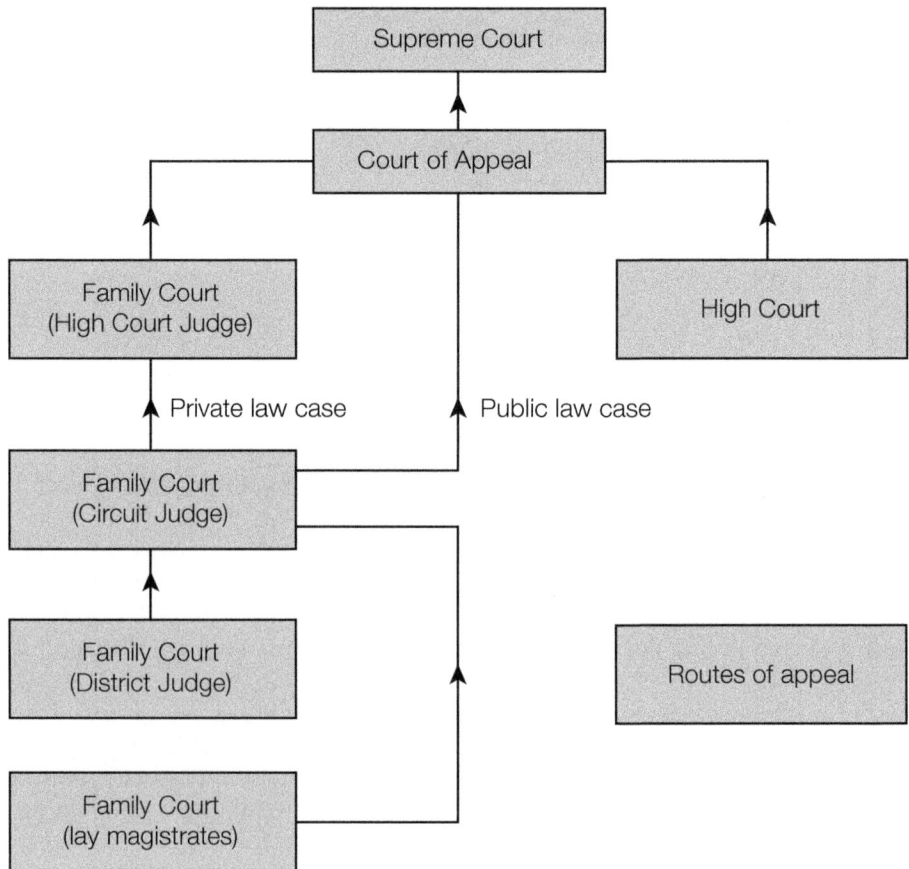

THE STRUCTURE OF THE FAMILY COURT

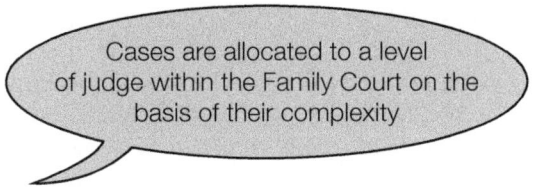

Cases are allocated to a level of judge within the Family Court on the basis of their complexity

1.5 The Family Court is one unified court with different levels of judge. The President of the Family Division is the head of the Family Court, and all High Court Family Division Judges are judges of the Family Court. The next two tiers of the judiciary are circuit judges, and then district judges. Lay justices (magistrates) may also hear family cases and are included within the definition of judges of the Family Court.

1.6 When a case is issued it will be allocated to an appropriate level of judge, based on the complexity and seriousness of the issues raised. A gatekeeping team, usually comprising a legal advisor (to lay justices) and a district judge, will consider the application on paper and make a provisional decision as to allocation. That decision will be reviewed at the first hearing and the court may re-allocate the case then or at any time thereafter if it considers it appropriate to do so.

1.7 Guidance on allocation is set out in two sets of President's Guidance on Allocation and Gatekeeping, the first covering public law proceedings and the second private law. In general terms, the Guidance provides for the more straightforward cases (in private and public law) to be allocated to lay justices, with cases involving, for example, allegations of serious physical or sexual abuse, or serious domestic abuse, being allocated to a district judge and cases involving conflicting expert evidence on a significant issue, or complex medical issues, being allocated to a circuit judge or High Court Judge.

THE RELATIONSHIP BETWEEN THE FAMILY COURT AND THE HIGH COURT

1.8 Some areas of work are reserved to the Family Division of the High Court and cannot be heard in the Family Court. These are set out in Guidance issued under the Family Court (Composition and Distribution of Business) Rules 2014, and fall into two categories: first, some types of international case, including child abduction cases; and secondly, cases involving the exercise by the High Court of its inherent jurisdiction relating to children[1].

---

[1] For the High Court's inherent jurisdiction, see **Ch 10**.

1.9 Additionally, the more complex family cases may be allocated to a Judge of High Court level sitting in the Family Court. These cases, however, remain within the Family Court and are not transferred to the High Court.

1.10 Because the jurisdiction of the High Court is, in theory at least, unlimited, while the jurisdiction of the Family Court is defined by statute, it is important that when a case is being heard by a High Court Judge there is clarity as to whether the Judge is sitting as a Judge of the Family Court, or as a Judge of the Family Division of the High Court; or simultaneously in both courts.

APPEALS

1.11 As a general rule, an appeal from a judge of the Family Court will lie to the next most senior level of judge. So, for example, an appeal from a district judge will be heard by a circuit judge. There are, however, a number of exceptions to this rule: appeals from lay justices do not lie to a district judge but to a circuit judge; and appeals from a circuit judge may lie to a High Court Judge or to the Court of Appeal, depending on the subject-matter of the case.

1.12 Appeals within the Family Court (ie appeals from one judge of the Family Court to another, higher level of judge within the Family Court) are governed by the Family Procedure Rules 2010, Pt 30. Appeals from a Judge of the High Court (whether sitting in the Family Court or the High Court), and appeals from circuit judges in public law proceedings, lie to the Court of Appeal and are governed by Civil Procedure Rules 1998 (CPR 1998), Pt 52.

1.13 Appeals from the Court of Appeal lie to the Supreme Court. These appeals are governed by the Rules of the Supreme Court 2009.

1.14 In most cases, other than when the appeal is from lay justices (or in some limited categories of case) permission to bring an appeal is required. Permission should be sought initially from the judge who made the order, and if it is refused then from the appeal court. The test for granting permission is that the court considers that the appeal has a real prospect of success[2], or there is some other compelling reason (for example, a novel point of law) why the appeal should be heard.

> the time limit for an appeal in most cases is 21 days from the date of the decision

---

[2] For the grounds for an appeal, see **Ch 11**.

1.15 The rules specify the time limit for making an application for permission to appeal. In most cases, this will be 21 days from the date of the decision of the lower court. This period may be extended (or reduced) by the court.

PUBLIC LAW AND PRIVATE LAW CHILDREN PROCEEDINGS

1.16 Cases relating to children may be characterised as either 'public law' or 'private law' proceedings. Public law proceedings are those which involve the state – usually, in children cases, local government in the form of the local authority. The classic example of a public law case is an application by the local authority for a care order in respect of a child. Private law cases will usually involve disputes between individuals: for example, a dispute between parents (or other holders of parental responsibility) about the living arrangements for a child.

> Private law cases involve disputes between individuals (usually, but not always, the child's parents). Public law cases involve disputes between the family and the state

1.17 The fundamental difference between public and private law proceedings is that before the court can make any public law orders (ie those which permit the state to intervene in the upbringing of a child), it must be satisfied that specified 'threshold' criteria are met. If that is not the case, the court has no power to make an order and the local authority cannot take any steps without the parents' consent.

1.18 The threshold criteria vary depending on the nature of the application (the threshold is higher if the local authority is seeking a permanent care or supervision order than if it is seeking a temporary order designed to secure the child's safety in the short term while investigations are carried out). As a minimum (for a child assessment order), the threshold criteria require the court to be satisfied that there is reasonable cause to suspect that the child may be suffering or likely to suffer significant harm. In order to make a final care order, the court must be satisfied on the balance of probabilities that the child is suffering, or is likely to suffer, significant harm[3].

1.19 Common to both types of children proceedings (but subject, in public law proceedings, to the threshold criteria being met) is the principle, set out in the Children Act 1989 (CA 1989), s 1, that in any decision relating to the upbringing

---

[3] For child assessment orders and other short-term protective orders, see **5.71**. For care orders, see **6.2**.

of a child, the child's welfare must be the court's paramount consideration. The welfare principle is discussed more fully at **6.25**.

THE FAMILY PROCEDURE RULES 2010

1.20 The procedure of the Family Court is governed by the Family Procedure Rules 2010 (FPR 2010), which are modelled on the CPR 1998 and provide one set of rules for all public and private law children cases, and adoption proceedings (as well as for other family proceedings, including divorce and financial remedy applications).

Rule 1.1 of the FPR 2010 is entitled the 'Overriding Objective'. It reads as follows:

(1) These rules are a new procedural code with the overriding objective of enabling the court to deal with cases justly, having regard to any welfare issues involved.

(2) Dealing with a case justly includes, so far as is practicable –
 (a) ensuring that it is dealt with expeditiously and fairly;
 (b) dealing with the case in ways which are proportionate to the nature, importance and complexity of the issues;
 (c) ensuring that the parties are on an equal footing;
 (d) saving expense; and
 (e) allotting to it an appropriate share of the court's resources, while taking into account the need to allot resources to other cases.

The Rules cover procedural issues including how to apply for an order, who the parties to a case will be, and how the court will manage and hear the case. There are timescales for certain types of case (in particular public law children proceedings, which must be heard within 26 weeks) and prescribed types of hearing, including in some types of proceedings dispute resolution hearings intended to assist the parties to reach an agreement if possible.

1.21 The rules governing CA 1989 proceedings are, for the most part, contained in Pt 12 of the FPR 2010. The rules for adoption proceedings are in Pt 14. Other important parts, for the purposes of children law, are Pt 25 which deals with the appointment and evidence of experts, Pt 16 which deals with the representation of children, and Pt 30 (appeals).

Transparency and confidentiality

1.22 Most cases under the CA 1989 and the Adoption and Children Act 2002 (ACA 2002) are heard in private, and there are restrictions within the Rules[4]

---

[4] Rule 12.73.

prohibiting the disclosure of material that is put before the court to those who are not connected with the case. Unless the court has permitted it, disclosure of information from the proceedings to anyone other than the limited categories of persons permitted by the Rules is likely to be a contempt of court, punishable by imprisonment.

1.23 Often where serious abuse is alleged, there will be a parallel police investigation and a consequent need to consider and control the flow of evidence between the care proceedings and the criminal investigation. In most circumstances it will be necessary to obtain the permission of the Family Court before disclosing information between the proceedings to the police.

1.24 In April 2009, following a public consultation, rules[5] were introduced permitting accredited media representatives to attend most CA 1989 hearings (but not adoption hearings) that would otherwise be heard in private, although the information that may be reported remains subject to restrictions.

1.25 In 2014 the then President of the Family Division issued Guidance on Publication of Judgments: Transparency in the Family Courts and the Court of Protection. The Guidance requires judges to publish (by putting a transcript on the legal website www.bailii.org) their judgments in certain specified categories of case, usually those which involve issues in which there is a legitimate public interest (such as cases in which the outcome is that a child is removed from her birth family and placed for adoption). In most cases the judgment will be anonymised, to protect the privacy of the family and in particular the children.

PRACTICE DIRECTIONS AND GUIDANCE

1.26 From time to time the President of the Family Division will issue Practice Directions designed to establish a unified practice in relation to the delivery of family justice across the jurisdiction of England and Wales. Practice Directions may supplement a particular provision of the FPR 2010 or be issued on a stand-alone basis.

CAFCASS/ CAFCASS CYMRU

1.27 CAFCASS (in Wales, CAFCASS Cymru) is the Children and Family Courts Advisory and Support Service. The need for a body to represent the voice of the child within court proceedings, separately and independently from the local authority and the parents, was identified in a number of public inquiries in the 1980s.[6] In public law proceedings, a CAFCASS officer (a professional social worker) will be appointed to represent the child, and will usually give instructions

---

[5] For the rules on media access to family proceedings, see **6.61**.
[6] Jasmine Beckford (1985); Tyra Henry (1987); Kimberley Carlile (1989); and Doreen Aston (1989).

to the child's solicitor. In private law proceedings, CAFCASS officers provide welfare reports to assist the court, and may also act as mediators between parents at 'conciliation' hearings. In a complex private law case, a CAFCASS officer may be appointed to act on behalf of the child.[7]

> CAFCASS officers will meet children and families and advise the court on welfare issues. They have been described as the 'eyes and ears' of the court

HMCTS

1.28 The administration of the Family Court is carried out by Her Majesty's Courts and Tribunals Service (HMCTS). Each court has a Court Manager who is responsible for the day to day operation of the court. The responsibilities of HMCTS include maintaining court files (electronic or paper), collecting fees, maintaining court buildings and infrastructure and supporting the judiciary.

---

[7] See **3.71**.

Chapter 2

INTRODUCTION TO CHILD PROTECTION

Chapter summary

- Introduction

- Children Act 1989

- Adoption and Children Act 2002

- Human Rights Act 1998

- The UN Convention on the Rights of the Child

- Statutory rules and government guidance

- Wales

- Family Justice Council

- Wardship and the inherent jurisdiction of the High Court

INTRODUCTION

2.1 The modern reformulation of the law relating to child protection and of the law relating to adoption took place some 13 years apart, but there are striking similarities to the gestation of each of these separate reforms. In each case proposals for reform had been developed over a period of years, but had failed to find a space in the government's legislative programme until a major scandal and ensuing public inquiry provided the political impetus for legislation. In the case of child protection the Review of Child Care Law began in 1984 and produced recommendations which the government adopted and produced as a White Paper[1] in 1987, but it was not until the Butler-Sloss Inquiry into child sexual abuse allegations in Cleveland[2] reported in July 1988 and recommended the 'urgent' implementation of these reforms that the issue was taken up as a government priority and led to the Children Act 1989 (CA 1989). Similarly the

---

[1] *The Law on Child Care and Family Services.*
[2] *Report of the Inquiry into Child Abuse in Cleveland 1987* (1988) Cm 412.

government Adoption Law Review was announced in 1989 and resulted in a detailed blueprint for reform in 1992. There followed a White Paper in 1993 and a draft Adoption Bill in 1996. Yet it was not until the publication of the Waterhouse Inquiry into abuse in residential children's homes in Wales in 2000 that the Prime Minister announced a review of adoption law by the Performance and Innovation Unit of the Cabinet Office, which resulted in a further White Paper[3] in December 2000 and in due course the passing of the Adoption and Children Act 2002 (ACA 2002).

2.2 The CA 1989 and the ACA 2002 are each wide-ranging and radical reforms of the previous law. The coming into force of the latter Act in December 2005 completed the process of reform and, for the first time, adoption law became fully compatible with the new law relating to children under the 1989 Act that had been in force since 1991. The two sets of provisions complement each other and provide a unified code, from '999 call to adoption', for the protection of children from abuse. The purpose of this Practitioner's Guide is to describe this code of law in plain, non-legal, terms so that all practitioners engaged in work with children may gain a ready understanding of the legal landscape and so that they may be better able to use the system to meet the needs of individual children.

Child protection and adoption

2.3 The following chapters look at individual aspects of the law relating to the protection of children, and adoption. In order to see these details in context, we will look first at the structure and themes of the legislation.

Child Protection: Key Sources

Statutes

✓ Children Act 1989

✓ Adoption and Children Act 2002

✓ Human Rights Act 1998

Guidance

✓ Working Together to Safeguard Children, Department for Education, 2018

---

[3] *Adoption: a new approach.*

CHILDREN ACT 1989

Parental responsibility

2.4 The CA 1989 covers both the private law (as between parents and family members) and public law (state involvement) relating to children. Central to both elements of the CA 1989 is the key concept of 'parental responsibility'.[4] Parental responsibility is the whole bundle of duties that a parent may have towards their child, together with the parallel powers and authority (previously 'parental rights') over him. A mother who gives birth to a child will have parental responsibility for her child from birth; a father, or a second female parent, may have it automatically (for example, because he or she is married to the mother, or named on the child's birth certificate) or may be able to acquire it by agreement or court order.

2.5 Much of the private law relating to children is concerned with the exercise, or control, of parental responsibility in circumstances where those who hold it may be in dispute with each other. In the context of child protection, a local authority will acquire parental responsibility, and the power to control the exercise of parental responsibility by anyone else, when a care order or an emergency protection order is made. If an adoption order is made, its principal effects will be that parental responsibility held by the natural parents will be extinguished and parental responsibility will be acquired by the adopters and that the child will be regarded as having been born to the adopters.

Welfare is paramount

2.6 A second key concept in the CA 1989, and one that is again common to both private and public law, is that the child's welfare must be the court's paramount consideration when determining any question with respect to the upbringing of a child.[5] This principle is fleshed out in a 'welfare checklist' which lists seven factors which, to a greater or lesser extent, are likely to be important in determining the 'welfare issue' in each case.[6] The paramountcy principle and the welfare checklist apply when a court is considering whether to make, vary or discharge a public law order under the CA 1989, Pt IV or a private law order under Pt II.[7]

> CA 1989, s1(1) reads: 'When a court determines any question with respect to (a) the upbringing of a child; or (b) the administration of a child's property or the application of any income arising from it, the child's welfare shall be the court's paramount consideration'

---

[4] Parental responsibility is more fully considered in **Ch 3**.
[5] CA 1989, s 1(1).
[6] Ibid, s 1(3); the full welfare checklist is set out at **6.26**.
[7] For the welfare principle in care proceedings, see **6.25**. For private law proceedings, see **3.52**.

Child protection

2.7 Moving away from principles which are common to both private and public law, the CA 1989 deals with issues of child protection in the following parts (groups of sections):

✓   Pt III: Local authority support for children and families (ss 17–30);

✓   Pt IV: Care and Supervision (ss 31–42);

✓   Pt V: Protection of Children (ss 43–52).

Subsequent parts of the CA 1989 make provision for many of the services provided for children (for example, children's homes, child minding and private fostering).

2.8 The structure of Parts III–V is set upon the premise that local authorities have a statutory duty to provide services for 'children in need' and their families.[8] The expectation within the legislation is that where a child is in need, the local authority for the area in which he lives will, without the need for court proceedings, make the necessary provision of services to meet his needs. In the first instance it is anticipated that those who have parental responsibility for the child will work in partnership with the local authority. A clear example of this process occurs where the parents and social services are agreed that the child should live away from home and be 'provided with accommodation' by the local authority.[9] To the lay observer the child will be being 'put into care', but the process is not one that involves court proceedings or a care order and is accomplished entirely upon a consensual basis.

2.9 In many cases where a child is in need, which might include the need to be protected from abuse, the whole process of child protection may be accomplished by agreement without resort to a court. However, where a local authority perceives the need to intervene in a family's care of a child in a way that is resisted (or is likely to be resisted) by those with parental responsibility, the case will move out of CA 1989, Pt III and into the territory of Pt IV with the local authority seeking public law orders (care order or supervision order) from the court in order to protect the child.

Care order and supervision order

2.10 The primary provision within Pt IV is s 31 which provides that a court may only make a care order or supervision order with respect to a child if it is satisfied:

---

[8]   CA 1989, s 17; see **4.13**.
[9]   Ibid, s 20.

(a) that the child concerned is suffering, or is likely to suffer, significant harm; and

(b) that the harm, or likelihood of harm, is attributable to:
   (i) the care given to him, or likely to be given to him if the order were not made, not being what it would be reasonable to expect a parent to give to him; or
   (ii) the child's being beyond parental control.

The criteria in s 31 (known as the 'threshold criteria') are the minimum circumstances which must be found to exist before the court can consider whether the state should be permitted to intervene compulsorily in family life.

2.11 If the circumstances are not found to be sufficient to satisfy s 31, the threshold is not crossed and the court does not have jurisdiction to consider whether the child's welfare requires that a care or supervision order be made. That this should be so can readily be understood by considering just how much power is given to a local authority if a care order is indeed made at the end of care proceedings. If a care order is granted a local authority is given parental responsibility for the child, together with the power to control the use of parental responsibility by any other person. Under a care order a local authority may, for example, keep a child in foster care for the remainder of her childhood. Further, the local authority may (subject to obtaining further orders from the court) use its status under a care order to move the child forward towards adoption and the permanent severing of the child's link with her natural family.

2.12 If a care order is made, save for the jurisdiction of the court under s 34 to regulate the degree of contact that the child has with any person, the responsibility for maintaining a care plan for the child, and for delivering that care, will be that of the local authority and not that of the court.

2.13 A supervision order, which like a care order requires the court to be satisfied that the threshold criteria are made out, is a lower level of state intervention under which the local authority does not acquire parental responsibility for the child. Under a supervision order the local authority is required to advise, assist and befriend the named child for a finite period of time (initially no more than a year).

2.14 An application for a care order ('care proceedings') may take a number of months to process from the date of the application being made to the court's final determination. During that time, evidence will be gathered and assessments made to inform the court about the need to protect the child and the plan that will best meet the child's needs. The question will therefore arise in each case as to the arrangements for the care of the child during the interim period. In some cases these arrangements will be agreed between the local authority and the parents without the need for a court order. In the event of a disagreement, or where there is a need for the local authority to have parental responsibility pending the final hearing, the court has the power to make an interim care order (or an interim supervision order).

2.15 In care proceedings the court has to consider two basic issues:

(i) are the threshold criteria (significant harm) in CA 1989, s 31 met in respect of the child?

if so the court has jurisdiction to make a care or supervision order and must ask:

(ii) taking the child's welfare as the paramount consideration, is any CA 1989 order required and, if so, which order is the most appropriate?

The principle that the child's welfare is paramount only applies to stage (ii). It is not uncommon for the court to conduct a 'split hearing' whereby the 'threshold' question and any necessary fact-finding are conducted at stage one, and the final 'welfare' stage is conducted at a later date after further time for consideration and assessment.

2.16 Applications for care and supervision orders are considered in more detail in **Chapter 6**.

Emergency powers

2.17 The final element in the structure of CA 1989 that directly relates to child protection is Pt V, which contains a range of provisions for the emergency, or short-term, protection of a child. The two central facilities provided by Pt V are the jurisdiction of the court to make an emergency protection order (s 44) and the power of the police to accommodate a child in a case of emergency (s 46). Where there is the need to provide short-term and immediate protection for a child, and there are no pending court care proceedings or interim care order, an application for an emergency protection order will often be the first application made to the court. The making of an emergency protection order will frequently be followed by the issue of an application for a care order and, within that, an application for an interim care order once the initial emergency protection order expires.

2.18 Applications for emergency protection orders are considered in **Chapter 5**.

ADOPTION AND CHILDREN ACT 2002

2.19 The law relating to adoption in England and Wales is entirely regulated by statute. Prior to 2006 the applicable law had last been fundamentally reformed nearly 30 years earlier, had become out of line with the modern approach to adoption work and did not dovetail easily in places with the CA 1989. Following a series of extensive reviews of adoption law, the ACA 2002 was passed and was brought into force on 30 December 2005. The ACA 2002, and the vast body of statutory instruments that underpin it, regulate all aspects of the adoption process and are described in **Chapter 7**.

2.20 In essence 'adoption' in English law is the process by which a child becomes regarded in law as the child of the adopter(s) and of no other person. Any parental responsibility that any person previously had for the child is extinguished by the adoption order and the child is regarded as if he had been born to the adopter(s). This state of affairs remains the case not just for the remainder of the child's childhood, but for life. The recognition, by Parliament and the courts, that adoption represents a significant interference with the child and her family's rights to respect for their private and family life is reflected in the statutory provisions and in the way in which these have been interpreted by the courts.[10]

2.21 An adoption order may only be made if at one or more key stages in the process each parent with parental responsibility for the child has either agreed to the child being adopted or has had their agreement to adoption dispensed with. The only grounds for dispensing with consent are either (a) that the parent is incapable of consenting or cannot be found or (b) that the child's welfare requires that consent be dispensed with. The child's welfare throughout his or her life is the court's paramount consideration and a specially tailored adoption 'welfare checklist' must be applied.

2.22 One innovation introduced by the ACA 2002 was to raise the step of 'placing a child for adoption' to that of a key stage in the process. A local authority, or adoption agency, may not place a child for adoption with prospective adopters unless they either have the consent of each parent with parental responsibility to do so, or they have obtained a 'placement order' from the court. This process replaces the previous scheme for obtaining an order 'freeing' the child for adoption.

Relationship between care proceedings and the adoption process

2.23 Whilst the legislation and procedure governing public law proceedings under the CA 1989 and that governing proceedings under the ACA 2002 are different and potentially free-standing, the reality in many cases is that there will be an overlap between the two processes. Where during the currency of care proceedings a local authority forms the opinion that the child should be adopted rather than rehabilitated back to her family, it may (and in some circumstances must) issue an application for a placement order which can then be consolidated with the care proceedings. Thus the court will have the power at the conclusion of the consolidated proceedings not only to grant a care order approving a care plan for adoption, but to go further and make a placement order. The effect of a

---

[10] See **6.29**.

placement order is substantial and may well limit the parents' ability to oppose any subsequent adoption application. The consolidated proceedings in such a case may therefore be the main and only full hearing of the issues not only about care but also about adoption and parental consent.

Who can adopt?

2.24 An adoption order may be made in favour of a couple, whether heterosexual or same-sex and whether married (or in a civil partnership) or not, or a single person. The adopters may be strangers to the child who have been selected by an adoption agency as substitute parents for a child who is in care. Many adoptions, however, involve members of the child's family, with the most obvious example being adoption by a step-parent in order to regularise relationships within a step-family.

Intercountry adoption

2.25 Intercountry adoption: the adoption of a child by adopters from a different country – is strictly controlled by both domestic law and international convention. This is to avoid exploitation of children and birth parents, and to ensure that the framework of international adoption is not used as a front for child trafficking. Any person intending to adopt a child from abroad must notify his or her local authority in advance so that full assessments can be carried out prior to the adopters being matched with the child. In some circumstances, bringing a child into or out of the UK for the purposes of adoption without complying with the relevant statutory provisions will constitute a criminal offence.

HUMAN RIGHTS ACT 1998

2.26 The Human Rights Act 1998 (HRA 1998) requires a court in England and Wales and any official body to act in a manner that is compatible with the European Convention on Human Rights (ECHR). In addition, where any aspect of English law falls to be interpreted, such interpretation must be compatible with the ECHR unless that goal is impossible to achieve (in which case a court may make a 'declaration of incompatibility' which triggers a referral of the incompatible provision before Parliament with the potential for repeal or reform).

2.27 The HRA 1998 and the ECHR are considered in **Chapter 10**. The ECHR affects all aspects of the state's intervention in the life of a child and family by care or adoption proceedings. Both the CA 1989 and the ACA 2002 were drawn up with the aim of compatibility with the ECHR. The key ECHR provision that is applicable to this field is Art 8 which requires respect for rights to family and private life. Put shortly, any step by the state (for example in the form of the social services or the court) to intervene in the life of a family will be in breach of Art 8, unless it can be shown that:

(a) the intervention is in accordance with the law;

(b) the intervention is to meet a legitimate need (for example the protection of the child);

(c) the intervention is necessary (in the sense of there being a pressing social need for it); and

(d) the level of proposed intervention is in proportion to the need to intervene.

Of these the latter two are the most influential and will dictate that the level of intervention justified to protect a child must be the least intrusive into the family's life with the child and for the shortest time that is necessary. Thus for example, where a supervision order is sufficient, that order, rather than the more intrusive care order, must be made. Another example is that, even where there is a care order, the aim should be for the child to be rehabilitated back to the family unless it is necessary to rule that option out and look for a long-term placement elsewhere.

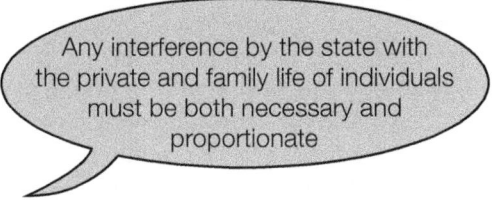

Any interference by the state with the private and family life of individuals must be both necessary and proportionate

2.28 The other ECHR article that is of particular relevance in this context is Art 6 which protects the right to a fair trial. Article 6 not only affects the trial process before the court, but a combination of Arts 6 and 8 mean that a family and child will have 'procedural rights' with respect to the manner in which the authorities involve them in any internal decision-making process before, during or after any court proceedings.

2.29 The family court must conduct its proceedings in a manner that is compatible with the ECHR. Any specific points relating to the impact of the ECHR should be raised within those proceedings, and will not normally be subject to a separate, free-standing application under the HRA 1998.

THE UN CONVENTION ON THE RIGHTS OF THE CHILD

2.30 The United Nations Convention on the Rights of the Child (UNCRC) was adopted in 1989 and has been ratified by 196 countries, including every member of the UN save for the US. It is a wide-ranging statement of children's human rights encompassing the following four key principles:

✓ the right of children to participate in decisions affecting them (Art 12);

✓ the right of children to protection and to prevention from harm (Arts 2, 3, 8, 11, 16, 19, 22 and 32–38);

- ✓ the right of children to provision of basic needs (Arts 17, 24, 26–28 and 31);
- ✓ the right of children for their best interests to be given priority.

Unlike the ECHR, the UNCRC is not incorporated into UK domestic law. The principles of the UNCRC are, however, at times referred to in court proceedings and have persuasive effect. Further, the UNCRC may be used as a tool to clarify and interpret the ECHR (which has been incorporated into domestic law).

STATUTORY RULES AND GOVERNMENT GUIDANCE

2.31 In addition to the main blocks of legislation contained within the CA 1989 and the ACA 2002, the law relating to child protection and adoption is regulated by a large body of statutory rules and regulations and government guidance. The statutory material makes detailed provision for various disparate topics from child minding to running a secure residential unit. Much of the engine room of the statutory scheme is in the rules and regulations.

2.32 In addition to the statutory material there is an additional layer of 'guidance' from central government. This 'guidance' is in fact binding upon local authorities by virtue of the Local Authority Social Services Act 1970, s 7. The guidance may take the form of substantial glossily published volumes (for example those accompanying the implementation of the CA 1989 and the ACA 2002) or more modestly presented circulars issued by the relevant government department (currently the Department for Education). Much of the guidance in force is available from the Department for Education website.[11]

WALES

2.33 Social care functions within Wales are devolved to the Welsh Assembly; consequently separate statutory rules and regulations and guidance are issued for Wales. Welsh law differs from English law in a number of important respects, particularly in relation to the local authority's obligations to provide support and services to children and families in its area.

FAMILY JUSTICE COUNCIL

2.34 The primary role of the Family Justice Council (FJC) is to promote an interdisciplinary approach to the needs of family justice, and through consultation and research, to monitor the effectiveness of the system and advise upon reforms necessary for continuous improvement. The FJC is chaired by the President of the Family Division and contains within its membership representatives from

---

[11] See www.education.gov.uk/.

all levels of the judiciary, local authorities, the medical profession, CAFCASS, barristers and solicitors. The work of the FJC is undertaken both at national level and at local level with each care centre having its own local FJC. The FJC's website contains further information.[12]

WARDSHIP AND THE INHERENT JURISDICTION OF THE HIGH COURT

2.35 This description of the law and procedure relating to child protection and adoption has thus far been largely based upon 'black letter law' set out in Acts of Parliament, regulations or statutory guidance. There is however a parallel jurisdiction relating to children which is available to the High Court in cases which call for judicial intervention, yet fall outside the statutory system. This jurisdiction, known as the 'inherent jurisdiction', derives from the ancient right and duty of the Crown as *parens patriae* (parent of the state) to take care of those who are not able to take care of themselves.[13] The High Court's jurisdiction to do right in respect of the affairs of children or vulnerable adults is, in theory, unlimited and unrestricted; however, the CA 1989 marks a clear boundary between the High Court's inherent jurisdiction and the statutory scheme for placing a child in care: a child may not be subject to both jurisdictions at the same time and the High Court may not place a child in care other than under the CA 1989 scheme.

> The High Court has an ancient power (belonging originally to the Crown) to take all necessary steps to protect those, including children, who are unable to protect themselves. However in modern times the exercise of this power is subject to the control of Parliament and is therefore limited by statute

2.36 Prior to the CA 1989 the inherent jurisdiction with respect to children was typically invoked through wardship proceedings, under which the child was made a 'ward of court'. Wardship still exists as an order available to the High Court, although its use is now much reduced. The principal effects of being a ward of court are that the court itself has parental responsibility for the child and no important step in the child's life may be taken without the prior permission of the High Court.

2.37 In modern times, the inherent jurisdiction of the High Court is now more frequently invoked, without resort to wardship, by way of a specific application

---

[12] See www.judiciary.gov.uk/about-the-judiciary/advisory-bodies/fjc.
[13] *Re L (An Infant)* [1968] 1 All ER 20.

based upon one aspect of parental responsibility. Examples of the type of issue that might justify the use of the inherent jurisdiction are where there is a dispute between parents and medical professionals about the medical treatment of a child, or where an injunction is sought to control press publicity. The jurisdiction is flexible and constantly adapting to modern needs. In recent years it has been used to achieve the return of young British nationals stranded abroad; and to make urgent orders to protect children who may be at risk of radicalisation or of being taken to join terrorist organisations overseas.

Chapter 3

PARENTAL RESPONSIBILITY AND DISPUTES BETWEEN PARENTS

Chapter summary

- Introduction
- Who is a parent?
- Parental responsibility
- Guardians and special guardians
- Section 8 orders
- Section 8 orders: procedure

INTRODUCTION

3.1 The law distinguishes between private and public disputes. Private law concerns disputes between private individuals or bodies; public law relates to the actions of the state in its various forms. The same distinction applies in family law. In children law, public law proceedings deal with the interaction between the state (through local authorities) and the family. At the heart of this area of law are applications for care (and similar) orders permitting the state's intervention in a family's life. The courts are also concerned with adoption, which often includes significant local authority involvement.

3.2 Private law proceedings address disputes between parents or other individuals who have a relationship with the child. It is important for social workers and other child protection professionals who deal mainly or exclusively with public law cases to have an understanding of the framework of private children law. Numerous public law cases start as a private law dispute between parents, during the course of whose proceedings it becomes evident that there is a need for local authority involvement. The question of parental responsibility for a child – who has it, how it is gained and what it means – is important too in public law cases and when working with a family more generally.

3.3 The Legal Aid, Sentencing and Punishment of Offenders Act 2012 removed legal aid from swathes of private children law. The effect has been stark. By September 2017, 36% of private children law cases involved no legal representation at all, with both the applicant and the respondent acting as litigants-in-person. The repercussions are felt across the family justice system: from delays in the court system caused by lack of familiarity with procedure and legal argument, to strongly expressed judicial concerns about the cross-examination of alleged victims by alleged perpetrators. The final report of the Bach Commission on Access to Justice opens with a warning, 'We live at a time when the rule of law is under attack... There is an urgent need to bring some areas of civil law back into the scope of legal aid, with a focus on early legal help in order to help prevent problems developing further down the track.'[1]

3.4 The central statutory provisions governing private children law disputes are contained in Pts I and II of the Children Act 1989 (CA 1989). On 22 April 2014, the Child Arrangements Programme (often shortened to 'CAP') was introduced to replace the Private Law Programme. The CAP sets out the process that governs applications made between separated parents and/or families. The CAP's focus is on avoiding, if possible, court proceedings and, if not, on streamlining their resolution. In particular, the emphasis on the pre-proceedings resolution of disputes is reflected in the introduction of the requirement for applicants to attend a mediation and information assessment meeting (known as a 'MIAM') before issuing proceedings, save in exceptional circumstances.

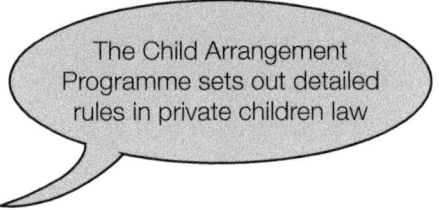

The Child Arrangement Programme sets out detailed rules in private children law

WHO IS A PARENT?

3.5 Under English common law, a woman who gives birth to a child is that child's mother. That is reinforced in cases involving assisted reproduction by s 33 of the Human Fertilisation and Embryology Act 2008 (HFEA 2008), irrespective of the country in which the woman was in at the time of the placing in her of the embryo or the sperm and eggs.

3.6 The position of the child's father is more complex. Where the child is born following a sexual relationship between a man and a woman, the man is the child's father for the purposes of the law.

---

[1] *The Right to Justice*, the Bach Commission, September 2017, quotes from the Foreword.

3.7 Where a heterosexual couple have together been involved in a course of assisted reproduction, the man will be treated as the father of any child conceived and born, regardless of whether or not he is the child's biological father. The man has the right to withdraw from the treatment at any time until an embryo is implanted, and if he does so he will not be treated in law as the child's father.[2] Since April 2009, it has been possible for a child born to two women undergoing treatment as a couple, whether or not they are in a marriage or civil partnership, to have two mothers (or, in the words of the statute, a mother and a second female 'parent of the child'). The provisions requiring the female partner to consent to the treatment mirror those that apply to heterosexual couples.[3] Children who are born by donor insemination of a single woman, or following the withdrawal of consent to treatment by the woman's partner, are treated in law as having no father or other female parent.

3.8 On the making of an adoption order, the child's adoptive parents become his legal parents and 'an adopted person is to be treated in law as if born as the child of the adopter or adopters': s 67 of the Adoption and Children Act 2002. The child's natural parents are stripped of all legal status in respect of the child and are legal strangers to her.[4]

DNA testing

3.9 Where the issue of a child's paternity arises during proceedings, it is very likely that the court will wish it to be determined with the highest possible degree of certainty. This tends to mean by DNA testing. Section 20 of the Family Law Reform Act 1969 (FLRA 1969) gives the court power in civil proceedings to direct that bodily tests should be carried out to establish whether or not a person is excluded from being a child's father. A sample cannot be taken from an adult without that person's consent, but the court may direct that a sample should be taken from a child if it considers that this would be in the child's best interests. The sample is generally one of saliva taken from a mouth swab, and any distress to the child is minimal.

3.10 In cases where paternity is in issue, it is very rare that a court will refuse to order DNA testing. In *Re H and A (Paternity: Blood Tests)*,[5] Thorpe LJ said that there were two points of principle to be drawn from the authorities on paternity testing. The first is that 'the interests of justice are best served by the ascertainment of truth'. The second is that 'the court should be furnished with the best available science and not confined to such unsatisfactory alternatives as presumptions and inferences'.

---

[2] HFEA 2008, ss 35–37.
[3] HFEA 2008, ss 42–44.
[4] Save for the purposes of Sch 1 to the Marriage Act 1949 and ss 10–11 of the Sexual Offences Act 1956 (incest and prohibited degrees of relationship). For these purposes, the adopted child retains her links to the natural family.
[5] *Re H and A (Paternity: Blood Tests)* [2002] EWCA Civ 383; [2002] 1 FLR 1145.

3.11 An adult has the right to withhold consent to the taking of a bodily sample and therefore a direction under s 20 of the FLRA 1969 should be phrased as a direction and not as an order. If he or she does refuse to submit to the sample, the court may draw inferences against him or her. This can cause problems: it is not entirely clear in which direction the inference should be drawn; and, in practice, where adults will not co-operate with testing, the child's paternity may remain unclear.

PARENTAL RESPONSIBILITY

What is it?

3.12 Parental responsibility was introduced as a new concept by the CA 1989. It is defined as:[6]

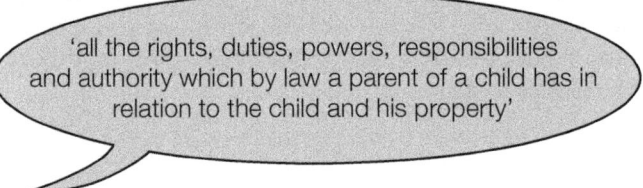

'all the rights, duties, powers, responsibilities and authority which by law a parent of a child has in relation to the child and his property'

3.13 Parental responsibility is a flexible concept. In most cases, two parents, each with parental responsibility, will have an equal say in the child's upbringing and an equal right to make important decisions in his life, even if only one of them lives with the child. Whether a decision is one (i) that a person with parental responsibility can take alone, (ii) on which those with parental responsibility must consult each other or (iii) about which those with parental responsibility must agree depends on the gravity of the decision. In *A v A*,[7] Wall J approved a schedule of issues drawn up and agreed by the parents and setting out which decisions each could take alone and which should only be taken in consultation with the other parent and/or with that parent's consent. The extent to which any person may exercise his parental responsibility may be shaped or restricted by order of the court, by the child's special guardian, or by a local authority holding a care order or a placement order in respect of the child.

3.14 Whether or not a person has parental responsibility does not affect his liability to maintain the child, or any rights which he may have to property inherited on the child's death.[8] An application to the Child Maintenance Service may be made against any parent, whether he has parental responsibility or not.

---

[6] CA 1989, s 3(1).
[7] *A v A (Shared Residence)* [2004] EWHC 142 (Fam); [2004] 1 FLR 1195.
[8] CA 1989, s 3(4).

Who has it?

3.15 Since the Adoption and Children Act 2002 (ACA 2002) came into force, the categories of persons with parental responsibility have been widened. The table below sets out the various persons or bodies who may have parental responsibility (PR) for a child, either for the duration of the child's minority or for a more limited period.

Relationship to child	**Circumstances in which PR held**	**Relevant law**
(Birth) mother	all circumstances, unless removed by adoption or by HFEA 2008, s 54	CA 1989, s 2(1), (2)(a)
Father	married to mother at child's birth or subsequently	CA 1989, s 2(1), (3)
Father	registered (or re-registered) as father on child's birth certificate after 1 December 2003	CA 1989, s 4(1)(a)
Father	who has entered into a PR agreement with mother	CA 1989, s 4(1)(b)
Father	who has been granted PR by the court	CA 1989, s 4(1)(c)
Father	with a child arrangement order (separate PR order must be made so that the father retains PR even if the residence order is discharged)	CA 1989, s 12(1)
Other female parent	who has undergone fertility treatment as part of a couple together with the mother, if she (a) is in a civil partnership or marriage with the mother, (b) is registered as other female parent on birth certificate, (c) has entered into a PR agreement with mother or (d) has been granted PR by court order, with or without a residence order	CA 1989, ss 2(1A), 4ZA(1), 12(1a)
Other 'lives with' order holder	for the duration of the child arrangement order	CA 1989, s 12(2)
Guardian	for the duration of appointment as guardian	CA 1989, s 5
Step-parent	who is married to or a civil partner of the child's parent and has entered into a PR agreement with all parents with PR or been granted PR by court order	CA 1989, s 4A(1)

Relationship to child	Circumstances in which PR held	Relevant law
Special guardian	for the duration of special guardianship order	CA 1989, s 14C(1)(a)
Prospective adopter	when the child is placed with him/her for adoption	ACA 2002, s 25(3)
Adoptive parent	on the making of an adoption order	ACA 2002, s 67
Local authority	holding a care order, or authorised to place the child for adoption	CA 1989, s 33(3)(a), ACA 2002, s 25

3.16 The ACA 2002 made it possible for the first time for a step-parent to be granted parental responsibility for a child. A step-parent may acquire parental responsibility by agreement of all other persons with parental responsibility, or by court order. This means that where a father has not acquired parental responsibility, a mother may at any time agree for her new husband to have parental responsibility, whether or not the child's father agrees.

3.17 A step-parent for the purposes of CA 1989, s 4A(1) means the spouse or civil partner of the child's parent. Unmarried partners cannot have parental responsibility for their partner's child (unless a 'lives with' child arrangements order, which carries with it parental responsibility, is made in their favour, or unless they adopt the child). Given that unmarried couples can adopt a child together,[9] and a very significant proportion of 'cohabitant' families include one or more stepchildren, this is perhaps a surprising omission.

Parental responsibility and the child: Gillick competence

3.18 It has long been recognised that a parent's influence over a child (whether or not it is given the formal title of parental responsibility) changes radically over the span of the child's minority. Well before the CA 1989 introduced the concept of parental responsibility, Lord Denning observed that the parental 'right' to the custody of a child is 'a dwindling right which the courts will hesitate to enforce against the wishes of the child, and the more so the older he is. It starts with the right of control and ends with little more than advice'.[10]

---

[9] ACA 2002, ss 50 and 144(4).
[10] *Hewer v Bryant* [1970] 1 QB 357.

> Parental decisions and older children:
> The older the child is, the more important her wishes are. A parent's 'right' 'starts with the right of control and [as a child older] ends with little more than advice'

3.19 In 1985, the House of Lords ruled by a majority of three to two against Victoria Gillick, a mother of four young girls who had sought to prevent her area health authority from providing them with contraceptive or abortion advice without her knowledge and consent.[11] It was held that children under the age of 16 had the capacity to consent, or to refuse to consent, to medical treatment once they reached an age 'of sufficient discretion to enable [them] to exercise a wise choice in [their] own interests'. The age at which a particular child will be capable of making a mature and considered decision will vary. Therefore, although the CA 1989 specifies that a parental responsibility order or agreement will last until the child is 18, unless brought to an end earlier,[12] in reality the 'rights' element at least of a parent's parental responsibility will carry decreasing weight as the child grows older.

3.20 The age at which the courts will consider that a child's views are determinative of the issue in question will vary according to the maturity of the child and, importantly, the nature of the decision that she is seeking to make. Where, for example, contact is regularly taking place and the only issue relates to the detail of the contact arrangements, most courts will give considerable weight to the views of relatively young children. Where the issue concerns serious medical treatment the age at which the child is to be treated as being capable of making his own decision will be much higher.[13] An 11-year-old boy has been refused permission, in a case where contact had broken down, to discharge his guardian and oppose a proposed plan for contact and therapy.[14] Coleridge J said that the essential question was not whether the child was capable of articulating instructions but whether he was of sufficient understanding to participate as a party, in the sense of being able to cope with all the ramifications of the proceedings and give considered instructions of sufficient objectivity.

---

[11] *Gillick v West Norfolk and Wisbech Area Health Authority* [1986] 1 FLR 224.
[12] CA 1989, s 91(7)–(8).
[13] The child's psychological condition will also be very relevant. A 16-year-old girl with anorexia nervosa has been compelled to undergo medical treatment against her wishes: *Re C* [1997] 2 FLR 180.
[14] *Re N* [2003] 1 FLR 652.

GUARDIANS AND SPECIAL GUARDIANS

3.21 Many adults are caring on a permanent basis for a child who is not their own. In most circumstances, it will be appropriate for those persons to have parental responsibility for the children they are bringing up, in order that they may make (or assist in making) arrangements and decisions for them over the course of their childhoods. Foster parents are the exception: while they are acting as foster parents they may not have parental responsibility for the child, and decisions regarding the child are made by the local authority, in consultation with the child's parent(s.) The fallback provision is contained in s 3(5) of the CA 1989, which is discussed below.

3.22 In some cases, a 'lives with' child arrangements order, which automatically confers parental responsibility on the named person with whom the child is to live, will be sufficient to ensure the child's stability and to enable the carer to take decisions regarding the child's upbringing. This will be particularly appropriate where the child's parents are not living with her, but play an ongoing role in her life. However, there are always cases where a child's parents play little or no part in her upbringing, because they have died or cannot be found, or because their particular situation means that their involvement with the child needs to be limited. In these cases, it may be appropriate for the child's carer to have sole or 'overriding'[15] parental responsibility for the child.

3.23 There are, of course, any number of wider family members, unmarried fathers and others (such as foster carers) who care for children for whom they do not have parental responsibility, whether because they are unaware of its availability, do not feel the need to acquire it or are not easily permitted it under the law. Section 3(5) of CA 1989 therefore provides that:

'A person who—

(a) does not have parental responsibility for a particular child; but
(b) has care of the child,

may (subject to the provisions of this Act) do what is reasonable in all the circumstances of the case for the purpose of safeguarding or promoting the child's welfare.'

Guardians

3.24 A parent with parental responsibility may appoint one or more persons as a guardian to care for his children in the event of the parent's death.[16] The appointment must (save in exceptional circumstances under wills) be in writing,

---

[15] A special guardianship order permits the special guardian to exercise parental responsibility to the exclusion of all other persons with parental responsibility (see **Ch 8** at **8.5** and **8.6**).
[16] The statutory provisions covering the appointment of guardians are set out in CA 1989, s 5.

dated and signed. The appointment will take effect on the death of the appointing parent if:

✓ the child then has no parent who has parental responsibility for her; or
✓ immediately before the appointing parent's death, there was a 'lives with' child arrangements order in that parent's favour (and not in favour of the other surviving parent) or the appointing person was the child's only (or last) surviving special guardian.

3.25 Guardianship may be disclaimed by the appointed guardian, revoked (by the appointing parent or guardian, or in certain specified circumstances[17]) or terminated by court order. An application to terminate the appointment of a guardian may only be made either by the child (with leave) or a person with parental responsibility. This means that a father without parental responsibility who finds that the mother has appointed another person as guardian cannot challenge this appointment unless he applies for and gains parental responsibility himself. The exception to this is that the court has the power, in family proceedings, to bring the appointment of a guardian to an end without an application.

3.26 The court may appoint a person as guardian of a child on that person's application, or in any family proceedings, if the court considers that the appointment should be made. It may do so only if:

✓ the child has no parent or special guardian with parental responsibility for him; or
✓ a parent with a 'lives with' child arrangements order has died while the order was in force, and any surviving parent did not also hold a 'lives with' child arrangements order.[18]

3.27 Once a person becomes a child's guardian, he has (in addition to parental responsibility) the same rights as a parent to consent or withhold consent to the child's adoption. If the child is made the subject of a care order, the guardian shares parental responsibility with the local authority in the same way as a parent and the local authority has the same duty to afford the guardian reasonable contact with the child.

Special guardianship

3.28 To meet the needs of those children who need a permanent parental figure, but who are not to be fostered or adopted, the ACA 2002 introduced the concept of special guardianship. Any person, other than the child's parent, may be a special guardian. A prospective special guardian must undergo a local authority assessment (which is very similar in structure to an assessment of

---

[17] Chiefly divorce or dissolution of a civil partnership: CA 1989, s 6(3A)–(3B).
[18] CA 1989, s 5(1)–(2).

prospective adopters) before the order can be made by the court. Once granted, a special guardianship order enables the special guardian to exercise parental responsibility for the child 'to the exclusion of any other person with parental responsibility for the child (apart from another special guardian)'.[19]

3.29 Special guardianship is discussed fully in **Chapter 8**.

SECTION 8 ORDERS

3.30 Section 8 is at the heart of the CA 1989's private law scheme. It gives the court power to determine a wide variety of issues that may arise in a child's life, from where and with whom she lives, to the name by which she is called, to where she goes to school. Section 8 orders fall into three categories, which between them cover the vast majority of issues that arise between parents. The three orders and their statutory definitions are set out below.

Order	Section 8 definition	Other key sections
Child arrangements order	an order regulating arrangements in relation to (a) with whom a child is to live (a 'lives with' order), spend time (a 'spends time with' order) or otherwise have contact and (b) when a child is to live, spend time or otherwise have contact with any person	CA 1989, s 9: restrictions on making s 8 orders CA 1989, s 10: the court's power to make s 8 orders – those who are entitled to make the application and those who need the court's leave CA 1989, s 11: ancillary provisions CA 1989, s 12: child arrangements orders and parental responsibility CA 1989, s 13: restrictions on removing a child from the jurisdiction or changing her name while a 'lives with' order is in force
Specific issue order	an order giving directions for the purposes of determining a specific question which has arisen, or may arise, in connection with any aspect of parental responsibility for a child	CA 1989, s 9 as above and particularly s 9(5): the court must not use its power to make a specific issue order or prohibited steps order with a view to achieving a result which could be

---

[19] CA 1989, s 14C(1)(b).

Order	Section 8 definition	Other key sections
		achieved by making a child arrangements order or a post-adoption contact order; or in any way which is denied to the High Court in exercising its inherent jurisdiction CA 1989, s 10 as above CA 1989, s 11 as above
Prohibited steps order	an order that no step which could be taken by a parent in meeting his parental responsibility for a child, and which is of a kind specified in the order, shall be taken by any person without the consent of the court	CA 1989, ss 9–11 as above

3.31 The Children and Families Act 2014 (CFA 2014) replaced 'contact' and 'residence' orders with 'spends time with' and 'lives with' orders as the two forms of child arrangements order. As with the previous move away from orders relating to 'custody' and 'care and control', the new language is intended to emphasise that parental responsibility will often remain joint and that each parent has an important role in raising and taking important decisions in relation to a child, irrespective of in whose home the child spends the majority of her time.

CONTACT ⟶ "SPENDS TIME WITH" ORDER
CUSTODY/ RESIDENCE ⟶ "LIVES WITH" ORDER

3.32 Section 8 orders may not, other than in exceptional circumstances, be made in respect of a child who has reached the age of 16, unless the order is simply varying or discharging a s 8 order already made. A 'lives with' order may be made to last until a child is 18; other s 8 orders may only be made to last beyond 16 only in exceptional circumstances.[20]

3.33 A section 8 order may have conditions attached, which must be complied with by any person who is named in the order as a person with whom the child is to live, spend time or otherwise have contact, who is a parent of the child or has parental responsibility for her, or with whom the child is living.[21] It is fairly common for conditions to be attached to a 'spends time with' order, and the

---

[20] Ibid, s 9(6) and (7).
[21] Ibid, s 11(7).

Children (Contact) and Adoption Act 2006 makes provision for the increased use of conditions to ensure that contact orders are complied with. Conditions attached to 'lives with' orders are rarer, but the courts have on occasion been prepared to impose conditions on where within England and Wales the resident parent may live, where it has been felt that absent such a condition the child's relationship with the other parent may be jeopardised.[22]

Child arrangements orders: 'spends time with' orders

3.34 A 'spends time with' order is directed to the person with whom the child lives and is a mandatory order requiring that person to make the child available to spend time with a named person. 'Spends time with' orders are, therefore, normally drafted so to permit the person in whose favour they are made to enforce them against the other party.

3.35 The CFA 2014 introduced a statutory presumption that the involvement of both parents in a child's life is beneficial.

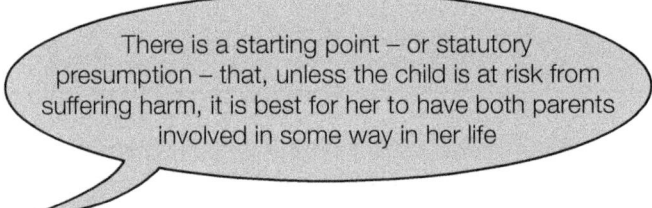

There is a starting point – or statutory presumption – that, unless the child is at risk from suffering harm, it is best for her to have both parents involved in some way in her life

However, this statutory presumption is significantly qualified. It provides that:

> '(2A) A court, in the circumstances mentioned in subsection 4(a) or (7), is as respects each parent within subsection (6)(a) to presume, unless the contrary is shown, that involvement of that parent in the life of the child concerned will further the child's welfare.
>
> (2B) In subsection (2A) "involvement" means involvement of some kind, either direct or indirect, but not any particular division of a child's time.
>
> …
>
> (6) In subsection (2A) "parent" means parent of the child concerned; and, for the purposes of that subsection, a parent of the child concerned—
>
> (a) is within this paragraph if that parent can be involved in the child's life in a way that does not put the child at risk of suffering harm; and
> (b) is to be treated as being within paragraph (a) unless there is some evidence before the court in the particular proceedings to suggest that involvement of

---

[22] *B v B (Residence: Condition Limiting Geographic Area)* [2004] 2 FLR 979; *Re S (Residence Order: Condition)* [2002] EWCA Civ 1795; [2003] 1 FCR 134; *Re B* [2007] EWCA Civ 1055; [2008] 1 FLR 613.

that parent in the child's life would put the child at risk of suffering harm whatever the form of involvement.'

3.36 Given that, previously, courts (and the CAFCASS officers who report for courts) were likely to take the view that, unless good reasons are shown, it is in a child's best interests to have the involvement of both parents in her life, the statutory presumption introduced by the CFA 2014 does not have a significant impact on the law.

3.37 Since the implementation of the Human Rights Act 1998 (HRA 1998), there has been considerable judicial discussion of the implications of Art 8 of the ECHR for 'spends time with' disputes. The European Court of Human Rights has confirmed that where there is a conflict between a child's rights and those of a parent, the child's rights will take priority. However, there is increasing recognition of the non-resident parent's right to a swift and fair determination of his application to spend time with his child, and, in tandem with that, an acknowledgement that complete refusals of direct contact and orders for only very limited direct contact lie at the very extremities of the court's powers. In short, it will only be in rare and exceptional cases that the court should order that there be no contact. Central to that is the positive obligation on the state (and therefore on the judge) to take measures to promote contact and to grapple with all available options and take all necessary steps before abandoning hope of achieving contact.[23]

3.38 At the same time, the courts are becoming more imaginative in the use of external resources to support fragile contact arrangements. In *A v A*,[24] a National Youth Advisory Service worker was commended for her tireless efforts to assist a family where the parents' mutual hostility meant that contact was hanging by a thread and the children's emotional welfare was at risk.

3.39 In difficult cases, where contact has broken down due to the hostility of one parent towards the other, the court should be ready to seek expert evidence on the reasons for the breakdown and any steps that might be taken to restore contact. Where one parent has influenced the child's views of the other to such an extent that it would not otherwise be possible for the child to have any relationship with the absent parent, the court may consider such robust solutions as a transfer of residence to the other parent,[25] or even a move to foster care.[26]

---

[23] *Re J-M (A Child)* [2015] 1 FLR 838, CA.
[24] *A v A (Shared Residence)* [2004] 1 FLR 1195.
[25] *Re A* [2007] EWCA Civ 899; [2008] 1 FCR 599.
[26] *Re M* [2003] EWHC 1024 (Fam); [2003] 2 FLR 636.

'Spends time with' orders and domestic abuse

3.40 Domestic abuse in private law disputes has, over the past few years, attracted significant attention. Central to the current law is the revised Family Procedure Rules 2010, PD 12J, which is the practice direction that addresses this area. The revised PD 12J applies to any family proceedings in the Family Court or the High Court in which an application is made for a child arrangements order, or in which any question arises about where a child should live, or about contact between a child and a parent or other family member.[27]

Practice Direction 12J
↓
Sets out the detailed rules where there is 'domestic abuse'

3.41 For the purposes of PD 12J, 'domestic abuse' includes

> 'any incident or pattern of incidents of controlling, coercive or threatening behaviour, violence or abuse between those aged 16 or over who are or have been intimate partners or family members regardless of gender or sexuality. This can encompass, but is not limited to, psychological, physical, sexual, financial, or emotional abuse. Domestic abuse also includes culturally specific forms of abuse including, but not limited to, forced marriage, honour-based violence, dowry-related abuse and transnational marriage abandonment.'[28]

3.42 There are two central principles. The first is that domestic abuse is harmful to children, whether they are subject to it, witness it, or live in a home in which it is perpetrated. PD 12J makes clear that, 'Children may suffer direct physical, psychological and/or emotional harm from living with domestic abuse, and may also suffer harm indirectly where the domestic abuse impairs the parenting capacity of either or both of their parents.' The second is that the court must, at all stages of the proceedings, and particularly at the first hearing (the First Hearing Dispute Resolution Appointment), consider whether domestic abuse is an issue and, if so, determine how it should be addressed.[29] As part of that, the court should consider, as soon as possible, whether a separate hearing (a 'fact-finding hearing') is required to determine the allegations of domestic abuse.[30]

3.43 In 2000, the Court of Appeal considered four cases where violence that had taken place within the family had been put forward as a reason for restricting or refusing the violent parent's contact with the children.[31] The court was assisted by a report prepared by Drs Claire Sturge and Danya Glaser,

---

[27] FPR 2010, PD 12J, para 1.
[28] Ibid, para 2.
[29] Ibid, paras 4 and 5.
[30] Ibid, para 16.
[31] *Re L; Re V; Re M; Re H* [2000] 2 FLR 334.

consultant child psychiatrists, which set out research findings on the effects on children of domestic violence. The experts felt that there needed to be greater awareness of the effect on children not only of being involved in violence but of being exposed to it. The Court of Appeal rejected the Sturge/Glaser report's recommendations that there should be a presumption against contact in cases where violence was proven to have taken place. However, the court emphasised the need to consider the risks to the child of contact and said that the court's priority must be to secure the safety and well-being of the child and the primary carer. This is reflected in the revised PD 12J, which provides not least that, in domestic abuse cases, 'When deciding the issue of child arrangements, the court should ensure that any order for contact will not expose the child to an unmanageable risk of harm and will be in the best interests of the child'.[32]

Interim orders

3.44 Interim orders, particularly in cases where there is a significant dispute of fact, pose real problems. On the one hand, as Munby J observed in *Re D*,[33] too often cases drift, suffering long delays, whilst CAFCASS or expert reports are ordered and awaited, and in the meantime the child's relationship with the absent parent is weakened. The answer in Munby J's view at that time was to 'grasp the nettle' in any case where there are factual disputes that might affect the outcome. In some cases, the courts should, his Lordship said, take a robust view of allegations made:

> 'Judges must resist the temptation to delay the evil day in the hope that perhaps the problem will go away. Judges must also resist the temptation to put contact "on hold", or to direct that it is supervised, pending investigation of the allegations. And allegations which could have been made at an earlier stage should be viewed with appropriate scepticism.'

3.45 On the other hand, given the increased recognition of the impact on children of domestic abuse, courts need to be cautious about making interim 'spends time with' orders prior to the determination of allegations. The revised PD 12J directs the court to focus very carefully on the possibility that an interim order may harm the child or the primary carer. The presumption is now in terms that:

> 'Where the court gives directions for a fact-finding hearing, or where disputed allegations of domestic abuse are otherwise undetermined, the court should not make an interim child arrangements order unless it is satisfied that it is in the interests of the child to do so and that the order would not expose the child or the other parent to an unmanageable risk of harm (bearing in mind the impact which domestic abuse against a parent can have on the emotional well-being of the

---

[32] FPR 2010, PD 12J, para 35.
[33] *Re D* (Intractable Contact Dispute: Publicity) [2004] EWHC 727 (Fam); [2004] 1 FLR 1226.

child, the safety of the other parent and the need to protect against domestic abuse including controlling or coercive behaviour).'[34]

3.46 In cases where an interim 'spends time with' order is made, the court must have careful regard to the arrangements that could be put in place (for example, the use of a contact centre and supervised contact) to ensure that the risk of any harm to the child and primary carer is minimised. If it is not appropriate for the child to see the parent against whom the allegations are made, the court should consider other forms of contact, such as telephone contact.[35]

Children and Adoption Act 2006

3.47 As discussed, there is increasing public awareness of domestic abuse. Part of that is concern about the use of the court system by abusers to continue a cycle of coercive and controlling behaviour. Reports by groups such as Women's Aid have stressed the extent to which domestic abuse remains a live and unresolved issue. At the same time, many are concerned about the difficulties that afflict non-resident parents (usually fathers) when attempting to secure a regular and meaningful role in their children's lives, with their plight highlighted by campaign groups such as Fathers for Justice and Families Need Fathers.

3.48 New provisions inserted into the CA 1989 by the Children and Adoption Act 2006, designed to support and enforce contact orders, came into force in December 2008. These included:[36]

✓ the power to impose an unpaid work requirement on a person who fails without reasonable excuse to comply with a contact order;

✓ the power in certain circumstances to order that a person should be compensated for financial loss incurred as a result of a breach of a contact order;

✓ contact activity directions and conditions: in conjunction with a contact order, the court may direct either or both parties to attend counselling or guidance programmes; programmes to address violent behaviour; or sessions providing information about mediation;

✓ the power to require CAFCASS to monitor compliance with either a contact order or a contact activity direction or condition, and to report back to the court;

---

[34] FPR 2010, PD 12J, para 25.
[35] Ibid, para 27.
[36] CA 1989, ss 11A–11P.

- all child arrangements orders made or varied after December 2008 must have a warning notice on them, setting out the consequences of not complying with the order.

3.49 In the decade since the introduction of these enforcement provisions, the use of contact activity directions in particular has grown, with courts often sending parents on courses to improve parental communication, most notably the separated parents' information programme. Nevertheless, for many parents caught up in private children law proceedings, particularly those to whom these amendments were intended to provide support, difficulties remain in securing and enforcing a meaningful and regular relationship with children.

3.50 A 'lives with' order is an order that determines with whom a child is to live. A 'lives with' order carries with it parental responsibility. If the order is made in favour of the child's father and he does not already have parental responsibility, the court must also make a parental responsibility order under *s 4* of the CA 1989, which will last until the child is 18 or until parental responsibility is removed by the court. If a 'lives with' order is made in favour of a non-parent, he or she will have parental responsibility only while the order remains in force.

3.51 No s 8 order can be made by a court in relation to a child who is in the care of a local authority, save for a 'lives with' child arrangements order.[37]

3.52 The principle that the child's welfare is paramount applies in 'lives with' disputes as it does in all s 8 of the CA 1989 applications. There is, for example, no presumption that the child should live with either parent, and no presumption in a dispute between a parent and a non-parent that the home offered by the parent should be preferred. In every case, the court must consider the child's welfare in the context of his particular circumstances and make the order that it considers to be in his best interests.[38]

Shared 'lives with' orders

3.53 The concept of 'shared residence' was flagged up explicitly in s 11(4) of the CA 1989, which provided, until the repeal of the provision by the CFA 2014, that 'where a residence order is made in favour of two or more persons who do not themselves all live together, the order may specify the periods during which the child is to live in the different households concerned'. However, in the years immediately following the CA 1989's implementation, the courts were reluctant to make shared residence orders other than in 'exceptional circumstances'. It was said in a number of cases that the benefit to the child of having a settled home outweighed any benefit of spending more time with the other parent,

---

[37] CA 1989, s 9(1).
[38] *Re B* [2009] UKSC 5.

and that having two competing homes would be likely in most circumstances to cause 'confusion and stress'.[39]

3.54 The 'exceptional circumstances' test applied until $D \ v \ D^{40}$ in 2001. There, the Court of Appeal held that all that was required for a shared residence order was that the making of the order should be in the child's interests, following the welfare checklist in CA 1989, s 1(3). The 'exceptional circumstances' test was to be applied no longer. Indeed, it was probably no longer necessary to show that there should be a 'positive benefit' to the child in the making of the order.

3.55 Now, there is a much greater willingness of courts to make shared 'lives with' orders. Such an order need not (and often does not) provide for a 50:50 split of the child's time between her parents. Indeed, as the popularity of the orders has risen, the variety of arrangements which may amount to a shared 'lives with' order has increased. It is now not at all unusual for a shared 'lives with' order to be made in the common situation where the child spends alternate weekends and perhaps some time during the week with one parent, and equal time with each parent during the holidays.

3.56 In $D \ v \ D$ the court referred for the first time to the psychological benefits, *from the parents' point of view*, of what was then called a shared 'residence' order. Since, there have been many more examples of shared residence orders being made to address a real or perceived power imbalance between the parents.[41] It seems that, although the CA 1989 concept of parental responsibility was intended to put parents on a level playing field, many still prefer the sense of equality that a shared 'lives with' order is thought to bring with it, as between the parents and also in the eyes of the schools, doctors and other agencies with whom the family is concerned. A shared 'lives with' order carries with it the additional advantage of automatic permission to remove the child for up to one month out of the jurisdiction.[42]

Specific issue and prohibited steps orders

3.57 Where parental responsibility is shared – or where a father without parental responsibility plays an active role in his child's life – disputes may arise about decisions on education, medical care and other aspects of the child's upbringing. The law is silent, where parental responsibility is shared, on who should have the final say. So, one or other parent will have to make an application to court.

3.58 Section 8 gives the court two options for controlling a parent's exercise of his parental responsibility: specific issue and prohibited steps orders. Specific

---

[39] See, eg, *Re H* [1994] 1 FLR 717.
[40] *D v D* (Shared Residence Order) [2001] 1 FLR 495.
[41] See eg *A v A* [2004] 1 FLR 1195.
[42] CA 1989, s 13(2). In practice, the approval of the other parent should always be sought, not least because it will likely impact on the time that the other parent is due to be spending with the child.

issue orders provide a general scheme for determining any issue that arises in connection with a child's upbringing. Issues that have been determined by the use of a specific issue order include:

- ✓ schooling;
- ✓ change of name;
- ✓ serious medical treatment;
- ✓ removing the child from the jurisdiction (see **3.62–3.63**);
- ✓ and, even for the cryo-preservation of a child's body.[43]

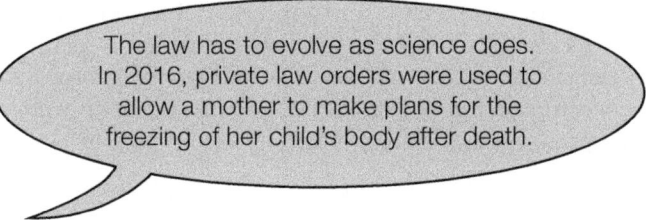

The law has to evolve as science does. In 2016, private law orders were used to allow a mother to make plans for the freezing of her child's body after death.

3.59 A prohibited steps order is a more focused order designed to prevent a person from taking a specified step. Again, prohibited steps orders are linked to parental responsibility, in that the step that might be taken must be one that could be taken by a parent 'in meeting his parental responsibility for a child'. However, prohibited steps orders may be made against any person, whether or not he is a parent of the child or in fact has parental responsibility, and whether or not he has notice of the proceedings or is present in court.[44]

3.60 Complications arise when one parent acts unilaterally without obtaining either the other parent's consent or a court order. The only statutory restriction on such actions is set out in CA 1989, s 13. Section 13 provides that:

'(1) Where a residence order is in force with respect to a child, no person may—

(a) cause the child to be known by a new surname; or
(b) remove him from the United Kingdom,

without the consent of every person who has parental responsibility for the child or the leave of the court.

(2) Subsection (1)(b) does not prevent the removal of a child, for a period of less than one month, by the person in whose favour the residence order is made.'

---

[43] *Re JS (Disposal of Body)* [2016] EWHC 2859 (Fam).
[44] *Re H* [1995] 1 FLR 638.

This does not mean that, where there is no 'lives with' order, a parent may simply change the child's name or take her out of the jurisdiction at will. Shared parental responsibility means that each parent has the right and duty to participate in decision-making for the child, and must consult the other in relation to any significant step in the child's life. As a rule of thumb, the more serious the decision, the more appropriate it is that both parents should be consulted and, if they do not agree, an application should be made to court.

Parenting plans

3.61 Separated parents may be encouraged, in court or in mediation, to draw up a parenting plan, which incorporates agreement on issues including discipline, medical and dental care, and education. Such a plan may reduce the need for either parent to apply to court for specific issue or prohibited steps orders. There are a number of online tools to help a parent draw up a parenting plan. When advising the court, CAFCASS will often recommend to separated parents that they make use of such a tool.

Removing a child from the jurisdiction

3.62 Applications to remove a child permanently from the jurisdiction may be made as an application for a specific issue order under CA 1989, s 8, or, if a 'lives with' order is in force, under CA 1989, s 13. Little will turn on the framework used in terms of the court's approach – although there is a technical distinction, in that the 'welfare checklist' (CA 1989, s 1(3)) applies to a s 8 application but not to a s 13 application.

3.63 In relocation cases, whether internal or external, the court must apply the welfare principle and the welfare checklist. That principle is the only one to be applied.[45] Whilst in most cases that will require the court to balance the loss to the child (usually a diminution in contact with the left-behind parent) with the impact on the child of the psychological harm likely to be caused to the resident parent by a refusal, the old legal principles espoused by *Payne v Payne*[46] have been moved away from, as has the near-sole focus on the resident parent's wishes to relocate.

---

[45] *K v K* (*Relocation: Shared Care Arrangement*) [2012] 2 FLR 880, CA and *Re C* (*Internal Relocation*) [2017] 1 FLR 103, CA.
[46] *Payne v Payne* [2001] EWCA Civ 166; [2001] 1 FLR 1052.

SECTION 8 ORDERS: PROCEDURE

The application

3.64 Proceedings are issued in the Family Court with an application for a s 8 order made on a Form C100. A Form C1A is provided in support in cases where domestic abuse or other harm is alleged.

3.65 A s 8 order may be made following an application or, within existing family proceedings, of the court's own motion. A local authority may not apply for a 'lives with' or 'spends time with' order and no court may make such an order in favour of a local authority.

3.66 Section 9 of the CA 1989 distinguishes between those who are entitled to apply for an order under s 8, and those who need the court's leave to apply. The restrictions in s 9 vary according to the order sought. Section 10 contains added restrictions on applications for s 8 orders. The provisions of ss 9 and 10 are summarised in the table below.

A. Order	B. Entitled to apply	C. May apply with leave	D. Prevented from applying
Child arrangements order	• any person who is entitled to apply for a specific issue order or prohibited steps order: see below • party to a marriage or civil partnership (whether or not subsisting) where the child is a child of the family • person with whom the child has lived for at least 3 years (need not be continuous)	• local authority foster parent who has the consent of the LA, is a relative of the child or has had the child living with him for at least 1 year • the child, if the court is satisfied he has sufficient understanding to make the application • any other person not excluded in column D	• local authority foster parents who do not meet one of the requirements in column C

A. Order	B. Entitled to apply	C. May apply with leave	D. Prevented from applying
	any person who has the consent of each of the persons named as persons with whom the child shall live under a 'lives with' order		
	where the child is in local authority care, has the consent of the LA		
	any person who has the consent of everyone who has parental responsibility for the child		
Child arrangements order: 'lives with' order	• person applying to vary or discharge an order made on his application or, in the case of a 'spends time with' order, a person named in the order		
	any non-parent or guardian who has parental responsibility by virtue of a 'spends time with' order		

A. Order	B. Entitled to apply	C. May apply with leave	D. Prevented from applying
	a local authority foster parent if the child has lived with him for at least 1 year		
	a relative if the child has lived with him for at least 1 year		
Specific issue order or prohibited steps order	• parent, guardian or special guardian	• local authority foster parent who has the consent of the LA, is a relative of the child or has had the child living with him for at least 1 year	• local authority foster parents who do not meet one of the requirements in column C
	• any step-parent who has acquired parental responsibility: CA 1989, s 4A	• the child, if the court is satisfied he has sufficient understanding to make the application	
	any person with a 'lives with' order in respect of the child		
	• person applying to vary or discharge an order made on his application or, in the case of a 'spends time with' order, a person named in the order	• any other person not excluded in column D	

3.67 When considering an application for leave to apply for a s 8 order, the court must, where the proposed applicant is not the subject child, apply the checklist in CA 1989, s 10(9). The factors that will be relevant to the application for leave include:

✓ the nature of the proposed application;

✓ the applicant's connection with the child;

✓ any risk there might be of the proposed application disrupting the child's life to such an extent that he would be harmed by it; and

✓ where the child is being looked after by a local authority:
 – the authority's plans for the child's future, and
 – the wishes and feelings of the child's parents.

The risk of disruption must be considered only in the context of the leave application. The court should not go on at the leave stage to consider whether the order sought would itself likely cause disruption to the child.

The respondents

3.68 The respondents to a s 8 application are set out in FPR 2010, r 12.3. The respondents are (i) every person with parental responsibility, (ii) every person with parental responsibility before the making of a care order and (iii) if an application to discharge or vary, the parties to that order. In addition, notice of proceedings on Form C6A is to be given to (i) the local authority, if accommodating the child, (ii) a person caring for the child or providing refuge, (iii) a person named in a court order that remains in force (unless irrelevant), (iv) a party to pending proceedings and (v) a person with whom the child has lived for three years.[47] Although the rules do not specifically provide for fathers without parental responsibility to be respondents, or even to be given notice of a s 8 application, in practice where an order is sought against, or affecting, a father without parental responsibility, he will be made a respondent to the proceedings.

Welfare reports

3.69 Sections 7 and 37 of the CA 1989 give the court power to direct in appropriate cases that an investigation should be carried out into welfare issues relating to the child, and that a report should be prepared, either by an officer of CAFCASS or by a local authority social worker. Reports ordered under s 37, in cases where a serious child protection issue has arisen, are dealt with in **Chapter 5** (see **5.14–5.17**). In most cases a CAFCASS report will be more appropriate. However, in cases where there has been some social services involvement with

---

[47] FPR 2010, PD 12C, para 3.1.

the family, albeit that the situation is not so serious as to warrant a full child protection investigation, a report from a social worker may be required.

3.70 The s 7 reporter has been described as the judge's 'eyes and ears'. She has a duty to visit the child and, where appropriate, ascertain as far as possible the child's views regarding the issues before the court. Although the recommendations of the reporter are by no means determinative, the judge must be prepared to justify a departure from those recommendations.[48]

The child as a party: guardians ad litem in private law proceedings

3.71 In an appropriate case, the child may herself be made a party to the proceedings. When done, a court will invite CAFCASS or an alternative agency (often the National Youth Advisory Service) to appoint a guardian ad litem under the FPR 2010, r 16.4. Cases which may be appropriate for the separate representation of children by a guardian include[49] those where:

- ✓ the CAFCASS officer is of the opinion that the child should be made a party;

- ✓ the child has interests which are inconsistent with or incapable of being represented by any of the adult parties;

- ✓ there is an intractable dispute over residence or contact, including where all contact has ceased, or where there is irrational but implacable hostility to contact or where the child may be suffering harm associated with the contact dispute;

- ✓ an older child is opposing a proposed course of action;

- ✓ the issues are unusually complex or there are international complications outside child abduction, in particular where it may be necessary for there to be discussions with overseas authorities or a foreign court;

- ✓ there are serious allegations of sexual, physical or other abuse in relation to the child;

- ✓ the proceedings concern more than one child and the children's welfare is in conflict;

- ✓ where there is a contested issue about scientific testing.

---

[48] *Re M* [2004] EWCA Civ 1574; [2005] 1 FLR 656.
[49] For a full list, see FPR 2010, PD 16A, para 7.1.

Chapter 4

LOCAL AUTHORITIES AND THE FAMILY

Chapter summary

- Local authorities, children and families
- The provision of services
- Children in need
- Accommodating children: local authority
- Looked after children: care planning and reviews
- Types of accommodation for looked after children
- Approval of foster parents: the process
- Placement with parents: assessment checklist
- Accommodating children who are not looked after
- Private fostering arrangements: duties of the local authority
- Leaving care

LOCAL AUTHORITIES, CHILDREN AND FAMILIES

4.1 From the day they are born, children begin to access a variety of services provided by the state. They, like their parents, are entitled to free health care. If they are part of a family with limited financial resources, they may be housed by the state. Their education, whether they are at state school, private school or being educated at home, is the responsibility of the local education authority. Some of these services are provided at a national level; others are the responsibility of the local city or county council or, in London, borough council.

4.2 Social services, like housing and education, are provided at a local level. The provision of social services for the children in its area is one of the broadest functions that a local authority carries out. Services provided range from nurseries and toddler groups to therapeutic residential units and adoption services. With such a broad responsibility, the local authority's social services functions often overlap with those of other local or national agencies, and the appropriate source of funding for a particular service is not always obvious. Section 27 of the Children Act 1989 (CA 1989) imposes a specific duty on local authorities to consider whether any other education, health, housing or other authority could assist it in carrying out its social services functions, and to request help if appropriate.

4.3 There is a division of responsibility within each local authority between adult services and children's services. Each local authority must appoint a director of children's services, who is responsible for children's education (other than further or higher education); and those aspects of children's health care for which the local authority is responsible on behalf of the NHS. The powers and duties of the director of children's services may be delegated to subcommittees or to individual officers of the local authority (for example, social workers or managers). It is no longer obligatory for the local authority to establish a social services committee, but in practice most local authorities have now created a children's services committee which carries out many of the functions of the director of children's services.

4.4 In this chapter, as in the rest of the book, the term 'local authority' means a local authority acting as a provider of children's social care, unless the context indicates otherwise.

Local Authority Responsibilities: Key Sources

Statutes

✓ Children Act 1989

✓ Children Act 2004

✓ Children and Families Act 2014

✓ Children and Social Work Act 2017

Regulations

✓ Care Planning, Placement and Case Review (England) Regulations 2010

> **Guidance**
>
> ✓ Children Act 1989 Guidance and Regulations 2015
>
> ✓ Working Together to Safeguard Children, Department for Education, 2018

Inter-agency working and local safeguarding partners

4.5 The Children Act 2004, as amended by the Children and Social Work Act 2017, requires the local authority to make arrangements to promote cooperation between itself and its local relevant partners to improve the wellbeing of children in its area. 'Relevant partners' include the police, probation, health services, schools and colleges, all of whom are also under a reciprocal duty to cooperate with the local authority. The local authority must also make arrangements to work together with any other person or body engaged in activities relating to children in the local area. This may include voluntary and faith organisations.

4.6 Government guidance[1] emphasises the importance of information-sharing between agencies, in order that practitioners are able to identify, assess and respond to safeguarding risks. All organisations should have arrangements in place that set out clearly the processes and principles for sharing information.

THE PROVISION OF SERVICES

4.7 The structure of local authority support services for children and families is set out in Pt III of the CA 1989. The local authority has the power and in some circumstances a duty to provide services of a different nature to:

✓ all children;

✓ children in need and their families and carers;

✓ children with special educational needs and disabilities; and

✓ young carers.

---

[1] Working Together to Safeguard Children, Department for Education, July 2018, para 23.

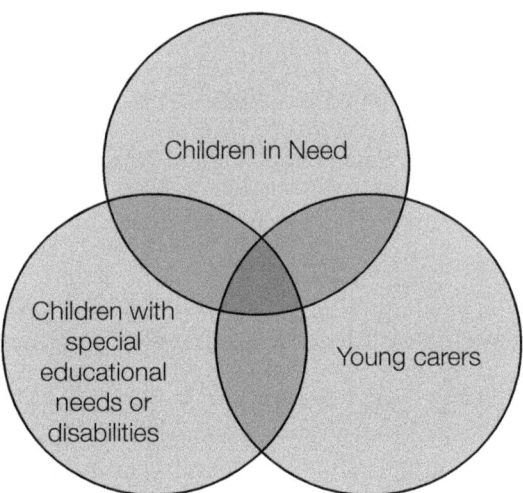

4.8 A child may fall within two or more of these categories at the same time. For example, a disabled child will automatically be a child in need by virtue of his disability, and a young carer may also have special educational needs. The legislation encourages local authorities to consider the child's needs as a whole, and where appropriate to carry out an integrated assessment of the child's needs for a variety of different services.

4.9 Where a statute imposes a duty upon the local authority, the local authority must act in accordance with that duty. Where a statute gives the local authority the power to provide a service, the local authority must exercise its discretion in deciding whether or not to exercise that power. If it exercises its discretion unreasonably, whether by acting or failing to act, it may be possible to challenge the decision by way of judicial review.

> There is a difference in local authority law between 'duties' and 'powers'. A local authority must act in accordance with its statutory duties. Where the statute confers a power, the local authority has a discretion in how it acts – but the discretion must be exercised reasonably

Services provided to all children

4.10 There are a number of different services that the local authority must or may ensure are available to all children and families in its area. The local authority may delegate the provision of these services to other agencies, including voluntary groups, but the responsibility remains with the local authority.

4.11 Each local authority has a duty under the CA 1989 to provide family centres for the use of families and children in its area.[2] Family centres vary in their nature and the kinds of services that they provide. The most basic simply provide a meeting place for families with children, with play and recreational facilities and some limited activities. Others may be staffed by trained workers who are available to provide counselling and other forms of therapeutic support for parents and families in crisis. Many family centres are set up and controlled by charities or local voluntary groups.

4.12 Local authorities may also provide a wide range of services including leisure facilities and after school and holiday care and activities.

CHILDREN IN NEED

4.13 A child in need is defined as a child:

- who is unlikely to achieve or maintain a reasonable standard of health or development without the provision of support services by the local authority;

- whose health or development is likely to be significantly impaired without the provision of such services; or

- who is disabled.[3]

In order to establish whether or not a child is a child in need, the local authority will carry out an assessment. This assessment may be carried out together with an assessment of the child's special educational needs or disabilities, or any other assessment of the child's needs which is being carried out.[4]

> A s 17 assessment is carried out to establish whether or not the child is a 'child in need'; and if so, what services should be provided to him

Services for children in need

4.14 The local authority must provide certain services to all children in its area who are in need and their families. 'Family' includes all persons with parental responsibility, and any person with whom the child is or has been living.

---

[2] CA 1989, Sch 2, para 9.
[3] Ibid, s 17.
[4] CA 1989, Sch 2, para 3.

4.15 The local authority has a general duty to safeguard and promote such a child's welfare, and, so far as is possible, to promote her upbringing by her family. This should be read in conjunction with the duty, imposed on the local authority by Sch 2 to the CA 1989,[5] to take reasonable steps to reduce the need to bring proceedings for care or supervision orders with respect to children within its area. The aim of Pt III of the CA 1989 is to encourage co-operation between parents and local authorities, so that the needs of the majority of children can be met by low-impact support services rather than by invoking the powers of the court.

4.16 The local authority must make what it considers to be 'appropriate' provision to ensure that the following services are available to children in need:

✓ advice, guidance and counselling;

✓ occupational, social, cultural or recreational activities;

✓ home help (which may include laundry facilities);

✓ facilities for, or assistance with, travelling to and from home for the purpose of taking advantage of any other service provided under the CA 1989 or of any similar service;

✓ assistance to enable the child and his family to have a holiday[6].

The local authority must also provide appropriate day care for children in need in their area who are aged five or under and not attending school. It must also make appropriate provision for children in need in its area who are attending school to be cared for outside school hours and in the holidays[7].

4.17 In addition, the local authority *may* provide:

✓ accommodation for the family; and

✓ assistance in kind or in cash.[8]

This section opens the door to the provision by a local authority via its social care budget of accommodation not just for a child but for a whole family. The question of when the responsibility for housing a family should be that of the social services department rather than the housing department is a difficult one and outside the scope of this book.

4.18 The local authority may charge for its services, other than for advice, guidance or counselling, but must have regard to the family's means and may only charge what it perceives to be a 'reasonable' sum.[9] Charges may not be imposed where the family is in receipt of certain means-tested benefits.

---

[5] Ibid, Sch 2, para 7(a)(i).
[6] Ibid, Sch 2, para 8.
[7] CA 1989, s 18.
[8] Ibid, s 17(6).
[9] Ibid, s 29.

Children with special educational needs and disabilities

4.19 A child is 'disabled' for the purposes of the legislation if he is blind, deaf or dumb, suffers from any mental disorder or is substantially and permanently handicapped by illness, injury or congenital deformity or any other prescribed disability. The local authority must keep a register of all disabled children in its area, and has a specific duty to provide services that will enable all such children to live as normal a life as possible and support those who are caring for them.[10] Such children automatically fall within the definition of children in need.

4.20 As well as children with disabilities, local authorities have a duty to identify all children and young people in its area who have or may have special educational needs. There is an overlap between the local authority's educational, health and social care responsibilities towards these children. Many of the services provided to such children will fall under the umbrella of the local authority's educational provision. Some, but not all, of these children will also be children in need. In order to ensure that the child's needs are considered as a whole, each local authority has a duty to ensure the integration of its educational, health care and social care provision for children with special educational needs or a disability where it thinks that this would promote their wellbeing, or improve the quality of the educational provision being made for them.[11]

4.21 A child with special educational needs may have an education, health and care ('EHC') plan. An EHC plan may specify any social care provision reasonably required by the learning difficulties or disabilities which result in the child having special educational needs.[12]

4.22 Parents of disabled children may be entitled to support from the local authority, and local authorities are under a duty to identify parent carers within their area who may have a need for support.[13] If it appears to the local authority that a parent carer may have needs for support, or upon a request by the parent carer, the local authority must carry out an assessment to establish whether there is a need for support and if so what the need is. In carrying out the assessment the local authority must have regard to the well-being of the parent carer, and the need to safeguard and promote the welfare of the disabled child and any other child in the family.[14]

Young Carers

4.23 Local authorities have a duty to take reasonable steps to identify young carers in their area who have needs for support. A 'young carer' is a

---

[10] Ibid, Sch 2, paras 2 and 6.
[11] Children and Families Act 2014, s 25.
[12] Ibid, s 37(2).
[13] CA 1989, s 17ZD.
[14] Ibid, s 17ZD(10).

person under the age of 18 who provides care for another person, other than by virtue of employment or as voluntary work (unless the local authority considers that the relationship between the young person and the person cared for is such that it would be appropriate for the young person to be regarded as a young carer). 'Care' includes both practical and emotional support.

4.24 Where a local authority considers that a young carer may have needs for support, or where the young carer or his parent have requested it, the local authority must carry out an assessment of the young carer's needs for support. The assessment must consider the extent to which the young carer is participating in education, training or recreation, and whether he is working or wishes to work. It must include an assessment of whether it is appropriate for the young carer to provide care in the light of the young carer's needs for support, other needs and wishes.[15]

4.25 The local authority must decide whether any support the young carer needs could be provided by the services the local authority may provide under CA 1989, s 17 to children in need.[16]

ACCOMMODATING CHILDREN: LOCAL AUTHORITY

4.26 The purpose of Pt III of the CA 1989 is to enable children to live at home and be cared for by their families wherever possible. Where this cannot be achieved the local authority must take responsibility for accommodating the child. The term 'looked after children' includes children who are living in local authority accommodation with their parents' consent, or because there is no person with parental responsibility for them. The term also includes children who have been placed in the care of the local authority by a court order. These children may in some circumstances remain living at home; but the local authority has parental responsibility for them and any placement at home is subject to regulation and will be closely monitored.

Children being looked after by a local authority	
Children being provided with accommodation	Children in care

4.27 As at March 2017 there were over 72,000 children looked after by local authorities in England,[17] a figure that has risen steadily since 2009. Of these, 76% were subject to care or placement orders, and 23% were accommodated

---

[15] CA 1989, s 17ZA and 17ZB.
[16] Ibid, s 17ZC.
[17] Department for Education.

voluntarily. Of this latter group, 4,500 (6% of all looked after children) were unaccompanied asylum-seeking children. The remaining 1% of looked after children were subject to short-term protective measures or remanded by the criminal courts to local authority accommodation.

4.28 The local authority has a general duty to safeguard and promote the welfare of every child it is looking after, and to make reasonable use of the services that are available in the area.[18] The duty includes in particular a duty to promote the child's educational achievement.[19] When a local authority makes any decision in relation to a child it is looking after it must, as far as reasonably practicable, consult the child, his parents, any other person with parental responsibility and any other person whose views the local authority considers relevant.[20] It must give due consideration to the wishes and feelings of these persons, and to the child's religious persuasion, racial origin and cultural and linguistic background.[21]

4.29 A local authority that is looking after a child, whether with the parents' consent or under a care order, has an obligation to provide the child with accommodation and to maintain the child.[22] The accommodation provided may be a placement with family or friends, a foster placement, or placement in a children's home.[23] Local authorities may also arrange for alternative accommodation, which may include supporting young people to live independently in rented accommodation or supported lodgings.[24]

4.30 Unless it would not be reasonably practicable or consistent with the child's welfare, the local authority must make arrangements for the child to live with a parent, a person with parental responsibility or a person with whom the child was living before coming into care.[25] Failing that, the local authority must place the child in the placement which is the most appropriate available, giving preference to a placement with any relative, friend or other person connected with the child.[26] In some cases this may involve the person in question becoming approved as a local authority foster carer.

4.31 So far as is reasonably practicable, the local authority must ensure that the child's placement allows her to live hear her home, does not disrupt her education or training, is suitable for any needs arising out of a disability and

---

[18] CA 1989, s 22(3).
[19] Ibid, s 22(3A).
[20] Ibid, s 22(4).
[21] Ibid, s 22(5).
[22] CA 1989, s 22A and 22B.
[23] Ibid, s 22C(6).
[24] Ibid, s 22C(6) and The Children Act 1989 Guidance and Regulations 2015, vol 2, para 3.3.
[25] CA 1989, s 22C(2).
[26] Ibid, s 22C(5)–(7).

(if the local authority is providing accommodation for siblings) enables siblings to live together.[27] Unless it is not reasonably practicable, the placement must be within the local authority's area.[28]

4.32 The provisions in s 22C regarding the nature and location of the child's placement do not apply where the local authority is considering adoption for the child, or has made a decision that the child ought to be placed for adoption.[29] If that is the case, and if a placement with a relative, friend or other connected person is not appropriate, the local authority must instead consider placing the child with a local authority foster parent who has also been approved as a prospective adopter.[30]

Accommodation where the child has no parent or the parents consent: CA 1989, s 20

4.33 Children are accommodated by the local authority if they are provided with accommodation for a period in excess of 24 hours. The CA 1989 does not distinguish between short-term ('respite') accommodation and long-term accommodation.

4.34 For the most part, children who are accommodated by the local authority without a care order are provided with local authority accommodation because their parents are unable to care for them and consent to their accommodation by the local authority. The exceptions are:

✓ children for whom no person has parental responsibility;

✓ children who have been lost or abandoned (including refugee and asylum-seeking children);

✓ children subject to an emergency protection order; and

✓ children remanded to local authority accommodation or detained in connection with criminal proceedings.

4.35 The local authority must provide accommodation for children in need in its area where there is no person with parental responsibility for them, they are lost or abandoned or their parents are unable to provide them with suitable accommodation or care.[31]

---

[27] Ibid, s 22C(8).
[28] Ibid, s 22C (9).
[29] Ibid, s 22C (9A).
[30] Ibid, s 22C (9B). For such a placement (known as a 'foster to adopt' placement), see **6.80**.
[31] Ibid, s 20(1).

4.36 The local authority may provide accommodation for any child within their area, even if the child is not a child in need and/or her parents are able to provide her with accommodation, if they consider that to do so would safeguard or promote the child's welfare.[32]

4.37 The local authority may not keep a child in local authority accommodation (other than under a court order)[33] if any person with parental responsibility, who is able to provide the child with accommodation, objects. A person with parental responsibility may remove the child from local authority accommodation at any time, unless:

- the child is over 16 and wishes to be accommodated; or

- any person who is named in a child arrangements order as a person with whom the child is to live[34] consents to the child being accommodated.

When the child is over 16 and is a child in need the local authority must provide accommodation if her welfare would be seriously prejudiced if it did not do so.[35] It may continue to provide accommodation for young people up to the age of 21 (see **4.112**).

Local authority provision of accommodation

4.38 Where a child has become looked after with parental consent given under CA 1989, s 20, or because the child has no parent, the local authority must be alert to ensure that proper plans are made for the child to be rehabilitated to parental care or for an alternative permanent placement to be found for him. A failure to plan for the future of a looked after child, and/ or to initiate court proceedings if necessary, is likely to amount to a breach of the child's Article 8 right to respect for his private and family life and may lead to a claim for damages under the HRA 1998.[36]

---

[32] Ibid, s 20(2).
[33] For emergency protection orders, see **5.38**. For care orders, see **6.2**.
[34] Or a special guardian, or a person with care of the child under an order made in the exercise of the inherent jurisdiction of the High Court. For special guardianship orders, see **Ch 8**. For orders made under the inherent jurisdiction of the High Court, see **Ch 10**.
[35] CA 1989, s 20(3).
[36] See HRA damages.

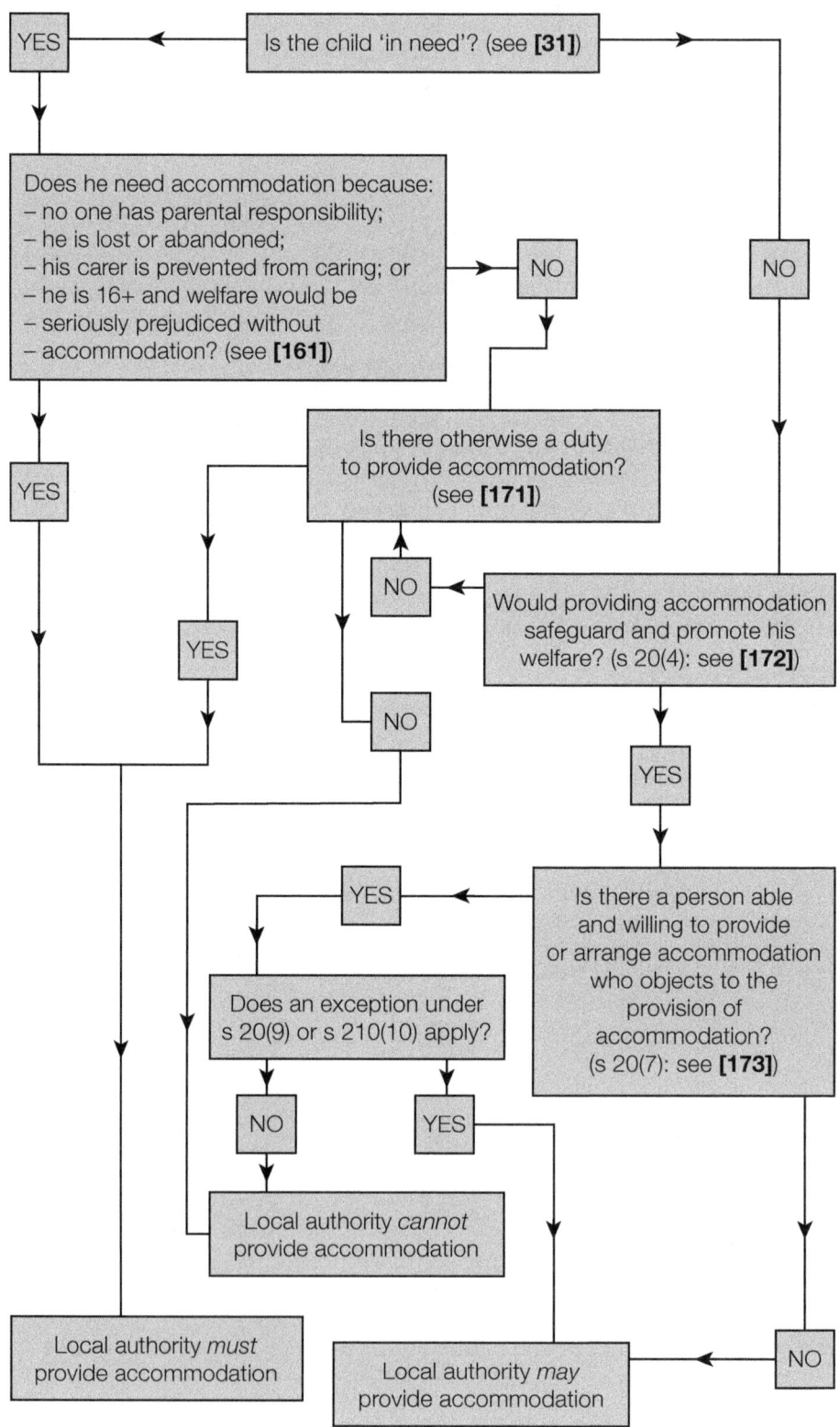

Case Study:

Ali is 14. She lives with her mother, Jo, under a child arrangements order and has fortnightly contact with her father, Malik, who has parental responsibility for her. Jo has been suffering from severe depression and is unable to care for Ali. She has asked the local authority social services department for help. The local authority offers a short-term placement in foster care and Jo accepts. Ali moves to live with local authority foster parents for three months. When Malik finds out he objects to this and wants to know why Ali cannot come to live with him. Jo is adamant that Malik will not be able to look after Ali full time, because of his own work commitments and because his home is too far away for Ali to get to school. Ali would have liked to stay with her father rather than going into care, but is very keen to stay at her school where she is settled and has friends.

Because Jo, who is named in the child arrangements order as the person with whom the child is to live, consents to Ali remaining in local authority accommodation, Malik cannot remove her. His only remedy is to apply to a court for a child arrangements order providing for Ali to live with him.

Accommodation for children in care

4.39 In the CA 1989, the term 'child in the care of a local authority' is used only in relation to those children in respect of whom a court has made a care order under s 31.[37] It does not include other looked after children. Informally the term 'in care' is often used to signify any child accommodated by the local authority. To avoid confusion, this book follows the CA 1989 definition.

> The local authority has parental responsibility for children who are subject to a care order. It does not have parental responsibility for children who are looked after with parental consent

4.40 When a court makes a care order under CA 1989, s 31 (or an interim care order under s 38) parental responsibility for the child is shared between the local authority and any other person with parental responsibility. The local authority has the power to determine the extent to which the child's parents and any other persons may exercise parental responsibility for the child. This means in effect that the parents cannot take any significant decisions in relation to the child without the local authority's agreement, and the local authority has ultimate

---

[37] CA 1989, s 105(1); see **Ch 6** for care and supervision orders.

responsibility for securing the child's welfare. Care orders are considered in detail in **Chapter 6**.

4.41 Children 'in care' may sometimes live at home with a parent or parents under a care order. The local authority has the same obligations towards these children as it does to other children who are subject to care orders but live away from home. The circumstances in which it may be appropriate to place a child in care at home are considered below.

LOOKED AFTER CHILDREN: CARE PLANNING AND REVIEWS

4.42 A local authority which is making arrangements for the placement of a child whom it proposes to look after (whether under a care order or otherwise) must assess the child's needs for services and prepare a care plan for promoting his welfare.[38] Government guidance describes care planning and case reviews as 'a fundamental part of social work with looked after children'.[39]

4.43 When a child comes into care as a result of an order made by a court,[40] a care plan will have been prepared by the local authority under CA 1989, s 31A. When a child becomes looked after other than under a care order (ie with parental consent, or because the child has no one with parental responsibility for him or has been lost or abandoned) the local authority must prepare a placement plan within five working days of the start of the placement.[41] Within 10 working days of the child becoming looked after, the local authority must assess the child's needs and prepare a full care plan for him.[42]

4.44 The child's care plan must include the arrangements made by the local authority to meet his needs, including in relation to health, education, emotional and behavioural development, identity (including religious persuasion, racial origin and cultural and linguistic background), family and social relationships, social presentation and self-care skills.[43] It should be agreed, so far as is reasonably practicable, with the child's parents, any person caring for him before he was accommodated, and the child if he is over 16. Younger children must be consulted about the care plan and their views taken into account.[44]

4.45 The local authority must review the case of each child it is looking after within 20 working days of the date when the child becomes a looked after child.

---

[38] Care Planning, Placement and Case Review (England) Regulations 2010, reg 4(1).
[39] Children Act 1989 Guidance and Regulations, vol 2, para 2.1.
[40] Under CA 1989, s 31; for care orders, see **Ch 6**.
[41] The Care Planning, Placement and Case Review (England) Regulations 2010, reg 9. For the contents of a placement plan, see Sch 2 to the Regulations.
[42] The Care Planning, Placement and Case Review (England) Regulations 2010, reg 4. For the contents of a care plan, see Sch 1 to the Regulations.
[43] Ibid. For the contents of a care plan, see Sch 1 to the Regulations.
[44] Ibid, reg 4(4) and (5); CA 1989, s 22(4)–(5).

A further review must take place within three months, and thereafter on a six-monthly basis.[45] At each review the local authority must consider the effect of any change in the child's circumstances, whether there should be any change in the child's legal status, whether the child has a plan for permanence, arrangements for contact and placement arrangements, the child's education, leisure interests and health, the child's wishes and feelings and whether arrangements need to be made for a time when the child will not be looked after.[46]

4.46 Where reasonably practicable, the local authority must seek the views of, and in most cases invite to all looked after child reviews, the child's parents, the child himself (where appropriate), any other person whose views it considers to be relevant, and the child's Independent Reviewing Officer.[47]

Care plans for children subject to care orders: the role of the court

4.47 A court cannot make a final care order in relation to a child without considering the 'permanence provisions' of the local authority's care plan for the child. The 'permanence provisions' are those parts of the care plan which set out the long-term plan for the child's living arrangements and long-term care, and the way in which the long-term plan for the child's upbringing will meet the child's current and future needs (including needs arising out of any harm he has suffered).[48]

4.48 Care plans are not, however, binding on the local authority. It is accepted that without a crystal ball the local authority cannot be expected to foresee all the possible developments that may occur during the course of a child's journey through care, and the local authority must be entitled to respond to each eventuality as best it can given the child's needs and its own resources.

4.49 An important principle of the CA 1989 is that there should be a line drawn between the responsibilities of the local authority and of the court. While the care plan is an important factor in the court's decision whether or not to make a final care order, once the order is made, responsibility for the child passes to the local authority and the court which made the care order has no jurisdiction to monitor the implementation of the care plan. Instead that responsibility passes to the local authority.

The Independent Reviewing Officer ('IRO')

4.50 Local authorities are obliged to appoint an independent reviewing officer ('IRO') for all looked after children. The IRO is independent of the day-to-day management of the child's case, but not of the local authority. He or she

---

[45] The Care Planning, Placement and Case Review (England) Regulations, reg 33.
[46] CPPCR(E)R 2010, Sch 7.
[47] See para **4.50**.
[48] CA 1989, s 31(3A) and (3B).

will chair review meetings relating to the child, monitor the local authority's implementation of the care plan and, if appropriate, refer the case to CAFCASS[49] and/or assist the child in obtaining his own legal advice. Referral of the case outside the local authority is intended to be a last resort: the IRO is expected to resolve any problems within the local authority where possible.

4.51 The IRO must speak to the child in private prior to the review meeting (so far as is consistent with the child's age and level of understanding) and must ensure that so far as reasonably practicable the views of the child and his parents are taken into account at the review. The IRO must identify the person responsible for implementing any decision taken at the review, and ensure that any failure to implement decisions is brought to the attention of an appropriately senior person within the local authority.[50]

TYPES OF ACCOMMODATION FOR LOOKED AFTER CHILDREN

4.52 The majority of looked after children live in foster placements (74%). 11% live in secure units, children's homes or hostels. 6% are placed with parents or family members, 3% are placed for adoption, 4% are in other placements in the community and 2% are in residential schools or other residential settings.[51] The younger the child, the more likely it is that a foster placement will be available rather than a placement in a children's home.

Foster care

4.53 Children in foster care may be placed with:

✓ a local authority foster parent;

✓ a foster parent identified and approved by an independent fostering agency; or

✓ a member of the extended family or a friend, who has been assessed and approved by the local authority as a foster carer.

In each of these cases, the foster parent(s) provide a home for the child. They do not acquire parental responsibility. If the child is in care parental responsibility is shared between the parents (and/or any other person with parental responsibility)

---

[49] CAFCASS has the power to bring proceedings on behalf of looked after children under HRA 1998, s 7 or by way of judicial review. For these proceedings and other routes to challenging the local authority's decision-making with regards to looked after children, see **Ch 11**.
[50] CPPCR(E)R 2010, reg 36.
[51] Department for Education: Children Looked After in England including Adoption 2016 to 2017.

and the local authority. If he is voluntarily accommodated his parent(s) exercise parental responsibility alone. The effect of this is that a foster parent may only take such steps as are necessary to meet the child's needs on a day-to-day basis. Any significant decision affecting the child must be made by a parent, the local authority or both.

Relative and friend foster placements

4.54 When the local authority wishes to place a looked after child with a relative or friend who does not have parental responsibility, that person must be approved as a foster parent and the fostering regulations apply.[52] However, where the local authority is satisfied that the most appropriate placement for a child is with a relative, friend or other connected person, even though that person is not an approved foster parent, it may approve that person as a foster parent for a temporary period of up to 16 weeks, provided that prior to the placement the local authority has:

- ✓ assessed the suitability of the proposed carer, the accommodation and all other adults living in the placement;

- ✓ considered whether the proposed placement will safeguard the child's welfare and meet her needs;

- ✓ made immediate arrangements for the carer to undergo a full assessment as a local authority foster parent before the 16-week period expires.[53]

Regulation of fostering services

4.55 The provision of fostering services by a local authority or private agency is regulated by:

- ✓ the Care Standards Act 2000;

- ✓ the Care Planning, Placement and Case Reviews (England) Regulations 2010;

- ✓ The Fostering Services (England) Regulations 2011;

- ✓ the *National Minimum Standards for Fostering Services*, issued by the Department of Health (2011); and

- ✓ the *Children Act Guidance and Regulations* Volume 2: Care Planning, Placement and Case Review and Volume 4: Fostering Services.

---

[52] Fostering Services (England) Regulations 2011.
[53] Care Planning, Placement and Case Review (England) Regulations 2010, reg 24.

4.56 The actions of the local authority in relation to the discharge of its fostering functions are under the supervision of Ofsted.[54] If the local authority fails to satisfy the Minimum Standards it will be reported to the Department of Health.

4.57 The following is intended as a guide to the overall structure of the regulation of fostering services. For further information detailed reference should be made to the relevant regulations and guidance.

Local authority foster parents

4.58 Any person with whom a local authority proposes to place a looked after child must be an approved and registered foster parent. The only exceptions are parents and prospective adopters.[55]

4.59 The approval process is detailed and involves a series of interviews, checks and references. At the conclusion of the process the local authority prepares a report which is presented to its fostering panel. The panel will make a recommendation which the local authority fostering service must take into account.[56]

4.60 If the local authority decides to approve the prospective foster parent it must set out in writing the terms of the approval, including any limitations on the number or age of children who may be fostered and the duration of any placement.[57] There is a limit of three foster children in any one placement at any one time, unless a specific exemption is granted or the children are all siblings.[58]

4.61 The local authority then enters into a written agreement with the foster parent.[59] This agreement is known as the 'foster care agreement' and covers arrangements for support and training; review; the procedures for placement of children; and notification of changes in circumstances. The foster parent must agree to care for the child as if he were a member of the foster parent's own family. Corporal punishment is not permitted in a foster placement and the foster parent must formally agree not to administer corporal punishment to any foster child.[60]

4.62 A person who is informed that the local authority proposes not to approve him as a foster carer may request a review by the Independent Review Mechanism (IRM) Panel.[61] The IRM is a review process created by the Independent Review of Determinations (Adoption and Fostering) Regulations 2009. The IRM Panel is independent of the local authority. It has power to make a fresh recommendation

---

[54] Care Standards Act 2000, s 47.
[55] Fostering Services (England) Regulations 2011, reg 2(1); Care Planning, Placement and Case Review (England) Regulations 2010.
[56] FS(E)R 2011; Children Act 1989 Guidance and Regulations, Vol4: Fostering Services
[57] FS(E)R 2011, reg 27(5).
[58] CA 1989, Sch 7.
[59] CPPCR(E)R 2010, reg 22.
[60] FS(E)R 2011, Sch 5.
[61] CA 1989, Sch 2, para 12A and IRD(AF)R 2009, reg 4.

to the local authority but cannot overturn the local authority's decision. In some circumstances, a rejection by the local authority of an IRM Panel's recommendation may ground a successful application for judicial review.[62]

4.63 Subject to a limited discretion, a person must not be approved as a foster parent if he or a member of his household has been convicted of or cautioned for a 'specified offence'. The list includes serious sexual offences and offences against children.[63]

4.64 The local authority must review its foster parents on at least a yearly basis. The review process is less detailed than the initial approval process but the local authority must prepare a written report on the occasion of each review.

Approval of foster parents: the process

✓ Assessment: matters to be covered
 – health
 – marital status
 – other adult members of the household
 – other children in the family
 – accommodation
 – religion, race, cultural and linguistic background
 – employment, activities and interests
 – experience and skills relevant to childcare abilities
 – outcome of previous applications to foster/adopt etc
 – previous convictions and cautions for each adult in the household

✓ Interview of two referees

✓ Presentation of written report to the fostering panel, including
 – assessment of applicant's suitability
 – proposals for any terms and conditions to attach to approval

✓ Decision to approve
 – including any terms and conditions

✓ Foster care agreement between foster parent and local authority

---

Agency foster parents

4.65 Independent fostering agencies are regulated in the same way as local authorities which provide a fostering service, and must comply with the same provisions regarding the approval process. They must also establish a fostering panel, although this may be done jointly with up to two other fostering service providers.

---

[62] *R (ex parte AT and S) v LB Newham* [2008] EWHC 2640 (Admin).
[63] FS(E)R 2011, reg 26.

4.66 A significant difference between the local authority as a fostering service provider and a private (or voluntary) fostering agency is that the private agency does not have parental responsibility for the children placed with its foster carers. A local authority will often make use of independent fostering agencies in its area to provide foster placements. If the local authority places a child in its care with agency foster carers, the local authority retains parental responsibility for the child.

4.67 A person may only be approved as a foster parent by one fostering service provider (whether local authority or independent) at any one time.

4.68 A decision by an independent fostering agency is reviewable by an IRM Panel[64] in the same way as a decision by a local authority acting as a fostering services provider.

Emergency placements

4.69 Ordinarily the local authority must carry out checks before placing a child with foster parents to ensure that the proposed placement is the most suitable way of meeting the child's needs, including medical and educational needs and any cultural or other characteristics of the child.[65] It must also provide the foster parent(s) with information about the child and enter into a written foster placement agreement with them. However, in an emergency a local authority may place a child for up to six working days with any person who has been approved as a foster parent by any fostering services provider.[66] If the local authority wishes to keep the child in foster care after the six day period is up it must terminate the placement unless the terms of the approval have been amended to be consistent with the placement.

Rights and duties of foster parents

4.70 The relationship between the local authority and the foster parent is shaped by two important documents: the foster care agreement, signed by the foster parent at the time of approval, and the foster placement agreement, signed at the beginning of each placement. These should set out the arrangements for managing the practical aspects of each placement, including the financial support to be provided by the local authority and the plans for reviewing and terminating the placement.

4.71 Foster parents must be made aware of the difference in legal status between a child who is subject to a care order and one who has voluntarily been placed in care by his parents. A child who is voluntarily accommodated in foster care may be removed at any time by his parent or any other person with parental responsibility, unless any person named in a child arrangements order

---

[64] See **4.62**.
[65] CA 1989, ss 22–23.
[66] CPPCR(E)R 2010, reg 23

as a person with whom the child is to live objects, or the child is over 16 and wishes to remain in foster care.[67]

4.72 The local authority may only terminate a foster placement (other than an emergency or temporary placement) after carrying out a review. Before terminating the placement, the local authority must make other arrangements for the child's placement, inform the IRO and so far as is reasonably practicable, give notice to the child's parents and others who were notified of the placement, to the foster parent and to the local authority (if different) where the child is placed. The local authority may, however, terminate a placement immediately and without a review if there is an immediate risk of significant harm to the child or a need to protect others from serious injury.[68]

4.73 Foster parents who disagree with a local authority's decision to terminate a placement, or with any other decision relating to them as foster parents, have only a limited number of options available to them. If the local authority's review and complaints procedures do not result in a change of heart the foster parent's most likely remedies will be to make an application for a child arrangements order[69], or for judicial review of the local authority's decision.

4.74 Foster parents who wish to remain in contact with children they have fostered may, if the matter cannot be arranged by agreement between themselves and the parents and/or local authority, apply with the leave of the court for a contact order under s 8 (if the child is not in care) or s 34 (if the child is in care).

4.75 Foster parents have a right to be given information regarding the children placed with them, and the local authority owes a duty of care to its foster carers and their own children: see *W v Essex County Council*.[70]

Funding

4.76 Every local authority must make arrangements for the financial support of children in foster care. The amounts paid to foster parents vary according to the age of the child, any special needs he has and (more controversially) the individual policies of the different local authorities. It is not permissible for a local authority to pay less to an extended family foster parent than it would to one of its own foster parents.[71] The government set national minimum allowances for foster carers, which all local authorities must comply with. The rates for 2018/2019 start at £127 per child per week and vary depending on the age of the child, any special needs the child has, and the location of the placement.

---

[67] CA 1989, s 20.
[68] CPPCR(E)R 2010, reg 14.
[69] See **3.30**.
[70] *W v Essex County Council* [2001] 2 AC 602.
[71] *R v Manchester City Council, ex parte L* [2002] 1 FLR 43.

Children's homes

4.77 A foster parent may offer a home to a maximum of three children unless one of the exceptions (see **4.60**) applies. Any establishment providing a home for more than three children is a children's home. All children's homes must be registered in accordance with the Children's Homes (England) Regulations 2015 and must comply with the minimum standards set out in the Regulations. Failure to register is a criminal offence. Guidance governing children's homes is set out in the Children Act 1989 Guidance and Regulations Volume 5: Children's Homes.[72]

Placement with parents

4.78 The local authority may decide to place a child who is the subject of a care order with:

✓ his parent(s);

✓ any person with parental responsibility; or

✓ a person who is named as a person with whom the child is to live in a child arrangements order which was in force immediately before the care order was made.[73]

4.79 The local authority has a specific duty to consider such a placement, or a placement with another relative or friend of the child, and must facilitate such a placement unless to do so would not be reasonably practicable or consistent with the child's welfare.[74] If a child who is the subject of a care order is placed with a parent, the local authority will retain parental responsibility for the child and all the other duties that come with a care order.[75]

4.80 The placement of a child in care with a parent is governed by the Care Planning, Placement and Case Review (England) Regulations 2010, regs 15–20. The requirements of the Regulations are modified when the child is over 16.

4.81 The decision to place a child in care with a parent or holder of parental responsibility is a significant one. In many cases, the parent with whom it is proposed that the child should be placed is the same parent whose care of the child has been so inadequate that the threshold criteria for a care order have been met.[76] For this reason, the decision to place a child with a parent may only be made by a local authority officer nominated in writing for that purpose.[77]

4.82 A local authority that is proposing to place a child (or allow her to remain placed) with a parent must ordinarily carry out an assessment of the parent's

---

[72] Department for Education
[73] CA 1989, s 23(4).
[74] Ibid, s 23(6).
[75] See **7.2**.
[76] See **6.9**.
[77] CPPCR(E)R 2010, reg 18(1).

suitability before making the placement decision, and must also undertake a formal review of the child's case. If the child is already living with the parent, this does not require the local authority to remove the child from the parent's care while the assessment is being carried out. The matters which the local authority must take into account when assessing the parent's suitability are set out in Sch 3 to the Regulations and include the parent's own physical, emotional and mental health and family history. The local authority must also consider whether it would be appropriate to make an application to discharge the care order.

4.83 If the local authority considers that an immediate placement with a parent is in the child's interests, it may place the child without undertaking a full assessment and review, provided that it holds an interview with the parent and obtains as much information as possible, and then ensures that an assessment and review are carried out, and the approval of the nominated officer is obtained, within 10 working days of the start of the placement.[78]

> The power to place with a parent is often exercised where a teenager's foster placement breaks down, and the young person makes clear their intention to return home. The care order will remain in force until discharged by a court

4.84 This power to make an immediate placement can be contrasted with the position where it is proposed that a child should be placed with a member of the extended family who does not have parental responsibility. In such a case the relative must be approved as a foster parent, at least on a temporary basis,[79] and there is no power to make an immediate placement while the necessary assessments are carried out.

Placement with parents: assessment checklist

The assessment should encompass the following:

✓ the health of the child

✓ the suitability of the person with whom it is proposed that the child should be placed

✓ the suitability of the proposed accommodation, including the proposed sleeping arrangements

✓ the educational and social needs of the child

✓ the suitability of all other members aged 16 and over of the household in which it is proposed that the child will live

---

[78] Ibid, reg 19.
[79] See **4.54**.

4.85 A non-exhaustive list of the factors to be taken into account when assessing suitability (of the proposed carer and his or her household) is set out in Sch 3 to the CPPCR(E)R 2010. Many of these (such as the parent's capacity to provide for the child's needs) are a matter of common sense. In addition to these matters the local authority must also consider the capacity of any member of the household over the age of 18 to provide for the child's needs, and any criminal offences for which they have been convicted or cautioned.

4.86 The local authority must make arrangements to visit any child placed with a parent under the Regulations as frequently as they consider necessary, but at a minimum within one week of the start of the placement, at least every six weeks during the first year of the placement, and at least every three months thereafter. If the child is subject to an interim care order, the child must be visited at least once a week until the first formal review, and then at intervals of not more than four weeks. On each visit the local authority must, so far as is practicable, make arrangements to see the child alone.[80]

4.87 The arrangements for terminating a placement with a parent under the Regulations are the same as those for terminating a placement with foster parents.[81]

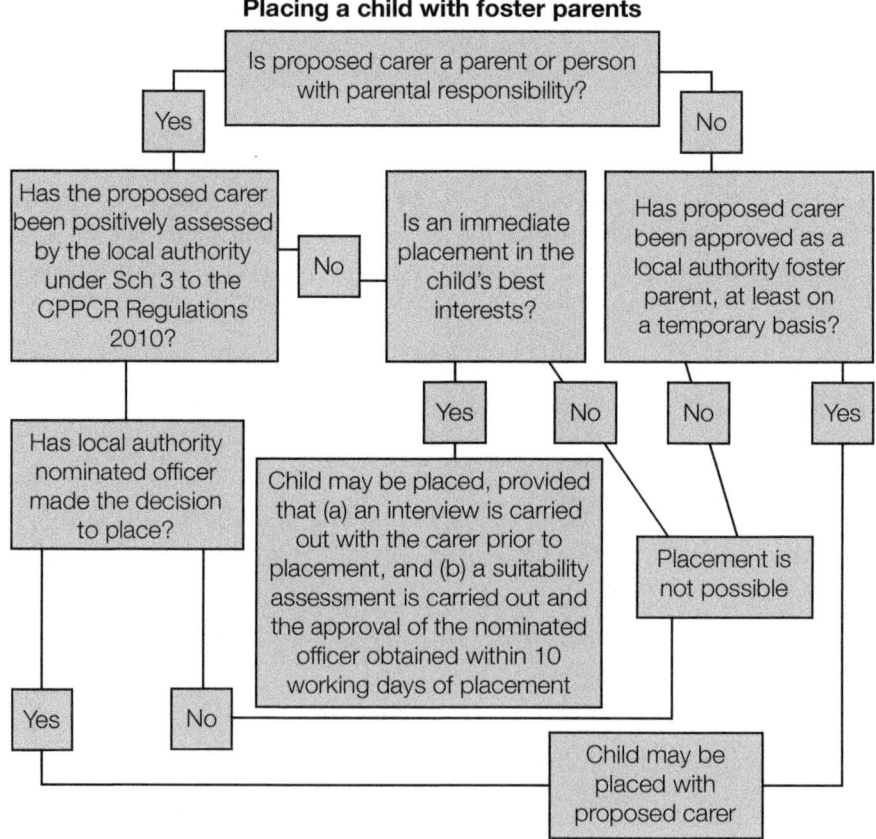

Placing a child with foster parents

---

[80] CPPCR(E)R 2010, reg 28.
[81] See **4.72**.

ACCOMMODATING CHILDREN WHO ARE NOT LOOKED AFTER

4.88 A small minority of children are neither cared for by their parents (or by someone with parental responsibility[82]), nor by the local authority. These children may be:

- ✓ fostered under a private fostering arrangement;

- ✓ accommodated by a voluntary organisation;

- ✓ accommodated (generally by a health authority) in a nursing home, mental nursing home or residential care home;

- ✓ living with a person under an informal, private arrangement that does not fall within the definition of private fostering.

Most of these arrangements are subject to regulation. Private fostering is governed by the Children (Private Arrangements for Fostering) Regulations 2005 (C(PAF)R 2005).[83] Voluntary organisations are covered in the CA 1989, Pt VII. Accommodation by a health authority is also covered in the CA 1989, ss 85–86, but responsibility for children in this position is that of the appropriate health authority.

4.89 The local authority's overall duty to children in its area extends to a duty to monitor private fostering arrangements[84] and the arrangements made by voluntary organisations to accommodate children.[85] Where a health authority is responsible for accommodating a child, it must inform the appropriate local authority which must take such steps as are reasonably practicable to enable it to determine whether the child's welfare is adequately safeguarded, and whether it should exercise any of its own functions under CA 1989.[86]

Private fostering

4.90 Private fostering is defined in s 66 of the CA 1989. A privately fostered child is a child under the age of 16 (other than a looked after child) who is living with and being cared for, for a period of more than 28 days, by a person who is

---

[82] Note that a child arrangements order has the effect of giving parental responsibility, for the duration of the order, to any person named in the order as a person with whom the child is to live: CA 1989, s 12(2).
[83] SI 2005/1533.
[84] C(PAF)R 2005, regs 7 and 8.
[85] CA 1989, s 62.
[86] CA 1989, s 85(1), s 85(4).

not a parent or relative or a person with parental responsibility. The definition does not apply to children in residential schools, hospitals or institutions.

4.91 Parents who intend to enter into a private fostering arrangement have an obligation to notify their local authority of their intentions, and any person who proposes to foster a child privately must also notify the local authority and co-operate with its investigations.

4.92 The local authority must satisfy itself of the suitability of the fostering arrangement in relation to the following key factors:[87]

- ✓ the purpose and intended duration of the fostering arrangement;
- ✓ the child's wishes and feelings about the arrangement;
- ✓ the child's development and arrangements to meet his needs;
- ✓ financial arrangements;
- ✓ the carer's capacity to look after the child;
- ✓ the suitability of other members of the household;
- ✓ arrangements for the child's health care and accommodation; and
- ✓ arrangements for contact with the child's family.

4.93 The local authority has a duty to visit children who are being privately fostered and satisfy itself in relation to their welfare, and may prohibit a person from acting as a private foster carer or impose restrictions on him.[88] Persons who have been convicted of certain specified offences are disqualified from acting as private foster carers.[89] It is a criminal offence to foster a child when disqualified from doing so.[90]

4.94 The 'usual fostering limit' of three children (unless they are siblings) applies to private foster placements as it does to local authority foster placements.

---

[87] C(PAF)R 2005, Sch 3.
[88] CA 1989, s 67.
[89] Ibid, s 68.
[90] Ibid, s 70.

Private fostering arrangements: duties of the local authority

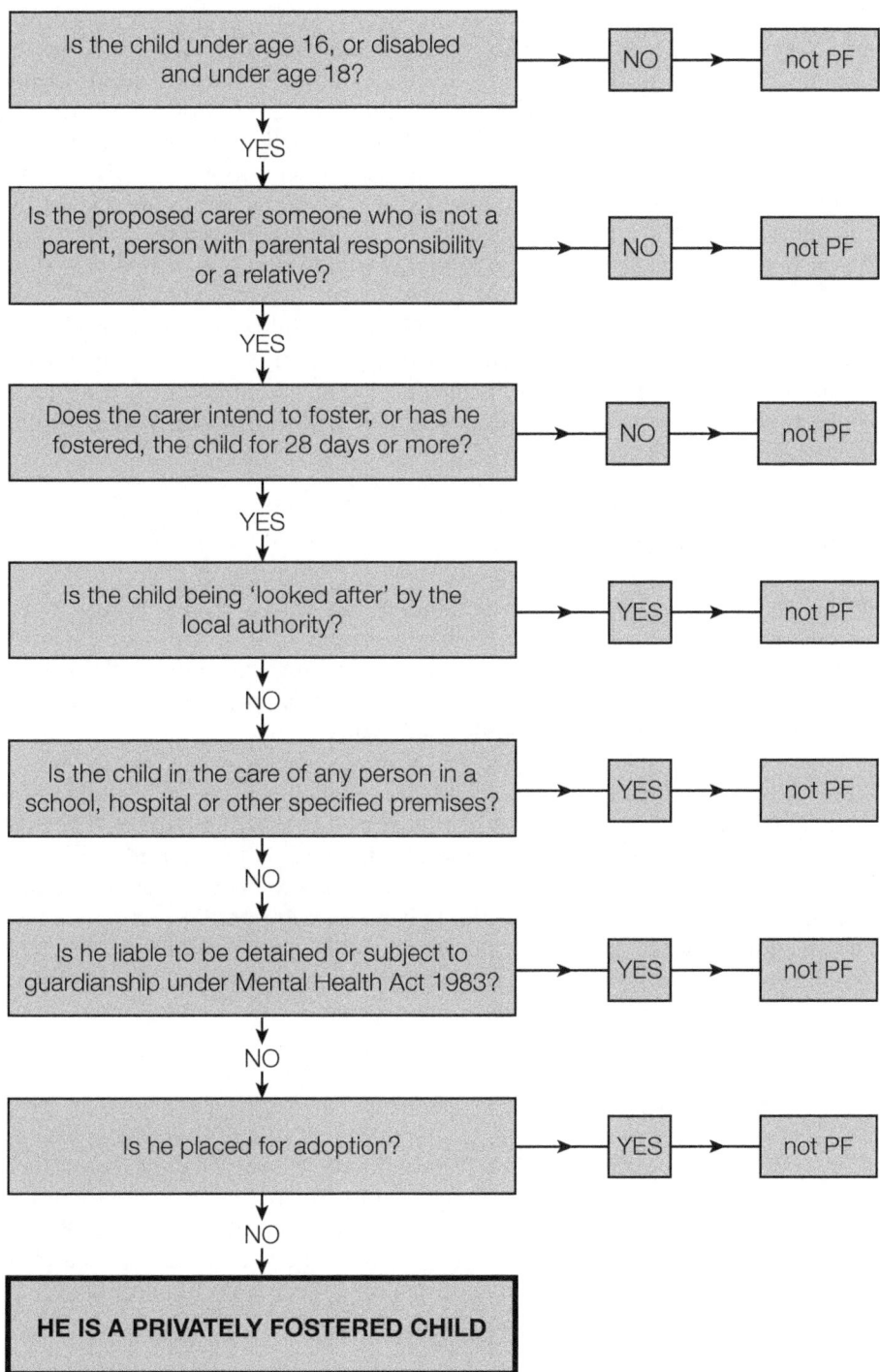

Accommodation by voluntary organisations

4.95 A voluntary organisation may provide accommodation for a child, at the request of a person with parental responsibility. However, the local authority has a continuing duty to satisfy itself that the voluntary organisation is satisfactorily safeguarding and promoting the child's welfare. In particular it must arrange for children who are accommodated by a voluntary organisation to be visited on a regular basis.[91] It has the power at any reasonable time to enter and inspect the accommodation and to examine any child there, and to inspect the records kept by the organisation.[92]

4.96 If the local authority is concerned that a child's welfare is not being satisfactorily safeguarded or promoted by a voluntary organisation it must consider whether it would be in his interests to be accommodated by a parent or other relative and, if not, consider whether the local authority itself should intervene.[93]

Other informal arrangements

4.97 An unascertained number of children live with a relative who is not a parent and who does not have parental responsibility for them. These extended family arrangements, often involving a grandparent, fall outside the private fostering legislation and there is no formal structure in place to monitor the security of the placement or the child's well-being.

4.98 Research indicates that these children are more likely to be children in need and their family units often suffer financial and other hardship.[94] Extended family carers may receive one-off support under the children in need legislation, but are unlikely to be eligible for regular assistance. These carers often face difficulties securing the state benefits that parents are entitled to, and unless they have a residence order giving them parental responsibility they may have problems dealing with schools and health professionals. They may not be eligible for public funding to apply for a child arrangements order.

LEAVING CARE

4.99 For the purposes of the CA 1989 children cease to be children on their eighteenth birthdays. On this date the effect of any care order comes to an end and a child who is being provided with accommodation is no longer a 'looked after child'. The local authority's duties towards the young person, as a child in its area, are concluded. However, it retains limited responsibility for 18- to

---

[91] CA 1989, s 62(1); APCVOO(E)R 2011, reg 16.
[92] CA 1989, s 62(6).
[93] Ibid, s 62(5).
[94] See various research published by the Family Rights Group and available at www.frg.org.uk.

21-year-olds who have been looked after as children, and must take reasonable steps to monitor their welfare as young adults. In the period leading up to the child's eighteenth birthday the local authority must help him to plan for independence.

4.100 The need for support and assistance for these often vulnerable young people is obvious. The educational attainment levels of looked after children are much lower than those of non-looked after children. In March 2017 the percentage of 18-year-old care leavers who were not in education, employment or training was 31%, compared with 12% of all 18-year-olds.[95]

4.101 The local authority has specific obligations towards children leaving care. These were introduced by the Children (Leaving Care) Act 2000 and apply to 16- and 17-year-olds who are or have been looked after by the local authority. They are designed to ease the transition from care to independent living. A distinction is drawn between 'eligible children' and 'relevant children'. The definitions are technical; broadly speaking, eligible children are those who are still being looked after by the local authority; relevant children are those who have recently been looked after.

Eligible children

4.102 An eligible child is a child who:

✓ is aged 16 or 17;

✓ is looked after by the local authority; and

✓ has been looked after by the local authority for a total period of at least 13 weeks that began after he reached the age of 14 and ended after he reached the age of 16. [96]

Relevant children

4.103 A relevant child is a child who:

✓ is aged 16 or 17; and

✓ is not looked after by the local authority; but

✓ was, before he ceased to be looked after, an eligible child; or

---

[95] Department for Education, Children Looked After in England including Adoption: 2016-2017.
[96] CA 1989, Sch 2, para 19B and CPPCR(E)R 2010, reg 40.

✓ on his sixteenth birthday was in hospital or detained in a young offenders' or other similar institution, but was a looked after child immediately prior to his detention or hospital admission and, were it not for that, would have become an eligible child on his sixteenth birthday.[97]

A relevant child who returns to live with his family for a period of six months ceases to be a relevant child; but will become one again if the placement breaks down.[98]

Responsibilities towards eligible and relevant children

4.104 Many of the local authority's responsibilities towards eligible and relevant children are focused on planning and preparatory work for the transition period between adolescence and adulthood. It is important to recognise that in addition to the duties set out below the local authority must carry out for eligible children all the duties it owes to looked after children. If the eligible child is subject to a care order the local authority must continue to exercise parental responsibility for the child until she reaches the age of 18.

4.105 Some of the local authority's obligations are common to both eligible and relevant children. In all cases the local authority must:

✓ prepare a written statement with details of how the child's needs will be assessed, including the timetable for the assessment and the person(s) responsible for carrying it out;

✓ carry out an assessment of the child's needs, taking into account the child's views and those of his parents and/or carers, school and any other interested person;

✓ develop a 'pathway plan' setting out, with dates, the manner in which the local authority proposes to meet the child's needs, and keep it under regular review; and

✓ appoint a personal adviser for the child.[99]

4.106 The role of the personal adviser is to provide practical advice and support, to liaise with the local authority in implementing the pathway plan, and to coordinate the provision of services to the child. He or she must keep a written record of contacts with the child and must ensure that he remains informed about the child's progress and well-being. The personal adviser should participate in the preparation and review of the child's pathway plan.[100]

---

[97] Care Leavers (England) Regulations 2010, reg 3.
[98] Ibid.
[99] CA 1989, Sch 2, para 19B; CA 1989, ss 23A–24D; Care Leavers (England) Regulations 2010, regs 5–9.
[100] Care Leavers (England) Regulations, reg 8.

4.107 The pathway plan must be reviewed when the child or his personal adviser requests it, and in any event not less than every six months.[101]

4.108 Because 'relevant children' are no longer being accommodated by the local authority the local authority has the following main obligations with respect to them in addition to those set out above:

✓ to keep in touch with the child and re-establish contact if it loses touch with her; and

✓ to safeguard and promote her welfare and, unless satisfied that her welfare does not require it, to support her by:
  – maintaining her;
  – providing her with suitable accommodation; and
  – providing support, including in cash.[102]

4.109 Although the local authority has an obligation, if her welfare requires it, to provide accommodation for a relevant child, this will not be a placement in foster care or other local authority accommodation (a child so placed is a 'looked after child'). The accommodation provided for a relevant child, who is *not* 'looked after', will often be housing authority accommodation, a privately rented flat or a 'half-way house'. The local authority's duty is to provide financial support and to check that the proposed accommodation is suitable for the child.

Case Study:

Robbie is aged 16. Last year he spent six months in foster care with his mother's consent, after his relationship with her broke down and he left home. He left the foster home shortly after he turned 16 and went to stay with his father, who had just been released from prison. He has been living with his father for about three months. His relationship with his father is volatile and there have been a number of occasions when arguments between them have become physical and the police have been called.

Robbie is a 'relevant child'. The local authority must maintain him financially and provide him with support. The local authority's obligations towards him include carrying out an assessment of his needs, developing a pathway plan and appointing a personal adviser.

The local authority must also consider whether it should provide Robbie with accommodation in a flat or supported accommodation, and must do so unless satisfied that his welfare does not require it.

---

[101] CL(E)R 2010, reg 7(2).
[102] CA 1989, s 23B.

Former relevant children

4.110 A 'former relevant child' is any person who has been a relevant child, and would be if he were under 19; and has been looked after and immediately before ceasing to be looked after was a relevant child.[103]

4.111 The local authority's responsibilities towards former relevant children including taking reasonable steps to keep in touch; to continue the appointment of a personal advisor; to contribute to expenses, and in some circumstances to provide accommodation.[104] Where a pathway plan provides for education or training to continue beyond the age of 21, most of the local authority's responsibilities will continue until the young person reaches the age of 25.[105]

'Staying Put'

4.112 Where a former relevant child under the age of 21 continues to live in the foster placement in which he was placed as a looked after child, and both the young person and the foster carer want the placement to continue, the local authority must support this by continuing to monitor the placement and to provide advice, assistance and support, including financial support, until the young person reaches the age of 21. This is known as a 'staying put' arrangement.[106] Guidance for local authorities, young people and foster carers is set out in 'Staying Put: Arrangements for Care Leavers aged 18 and above to stay with their former foster carers', Department for Education, May 2013.

---

[103] CA 1989, s 23C.
[104] Ibid; for the provision of accommodation see *R (SO) v LB Barking and Dagenham* [2010] EWCA Civ 1101; [2011] 3 FCR 558.
[105] CA 1989, s 23CA.
[106] CA 1989, s 23CZA.

Chapter 5

REFERRALS, ASSESSMENTS AND EMERGENCY INTERVENTION

Chapter summary

- Introduction
- The initial referral
- The child protection investigation: section 47
- A court 'referral': section 37
- Further child protection measures
- Police protection: section 46
- Emergency protection orders: section 44
- Child assessment orders: section 43
- Recovery orders: section 50
- Child safety orders and parenting orders

INTRODUCTION

5.1 The previous chapter considered the local authority's general responsibility for children in its area, and the assistance that local authorities are under a duty to provide to families and children with varying levels of need.

5.2 This chapter tracks the routes taken by the more serious cases where the balance shifts from the provision of support services to child protection. In the short term, an order of the court may be required to ensure a child's safety or to grant the local authority access to her. In the longer term, if the child protection issues remain live and cannot be resolved by the family working voluntarily with the local authority, these cases may result in the child being placed in the care or under the supervision of the local authority. Care and supervision orders are discussed in **Chapter 6**.

5.3 The guiding document for referrals and assessments is the Department for Education publication, *Working Together to Safeguard Children,* July 2018.[1] The July 2018 publication applies to all organisations and agencies who have functions relating to children and, as statutory guidance, must be complied with unless exceptional circumstances arise.

THE INITIAL REFERRAL

5.4 There are a number of ways in which a child at risk may come to social services' attention. In emergency cases, where there is an obvious and urgent child protection issue, children may have been taken into police protection or made the subject of an emergency protection order by a court. In these cases, the local authority must immediately initiate a full child protection investigation under the Children Act 1989 (CA 1989), s 47.

5.5 In other – generally less urgent – cases, the initial referral may be made by a professional involved with the child: commonly a health visitor, GP, police officer, hospital doctor or teacher. Referrals are sometimes made by family members, friends or neighbours, anonymously or otherwise, directly or via other agencies such as Childline or the NSPCC.

The local authority's response

5.6 The local authority must within one working day of a referral acknowledge receipt to the referrer and make a decision about the next steps and the type of response required. That includes determination of whether, in order of decreasing severity: (i) the child requires immediate protection, (ii) there is reasonable cause to suspect the child is suffering or likely to suffer significant harm and should be assessed (under CA 1989, s 47), (iii) the child is 'in need' and should be assessed (under CA 1989, s 17) or (iv) no further involvement is required, save for onward referral to universal and targeted support services. The maximum timeframe for the assessment to conclude, such that it is possible to reach a decision on next steps, should be no longer than 45 days from the point of referral. If, in discussion with a child, their family and other practitioners, an assessment exceeds 45 working days, the social worker should record the reasons for exceeding the time limit.

---

[1] Available online: https://assets.publishing.service.gov.uk/government/uploads/system/uploads/attachment_data/file/729914/ Working_Together_to_Safeguard_Children-2018.pdf.

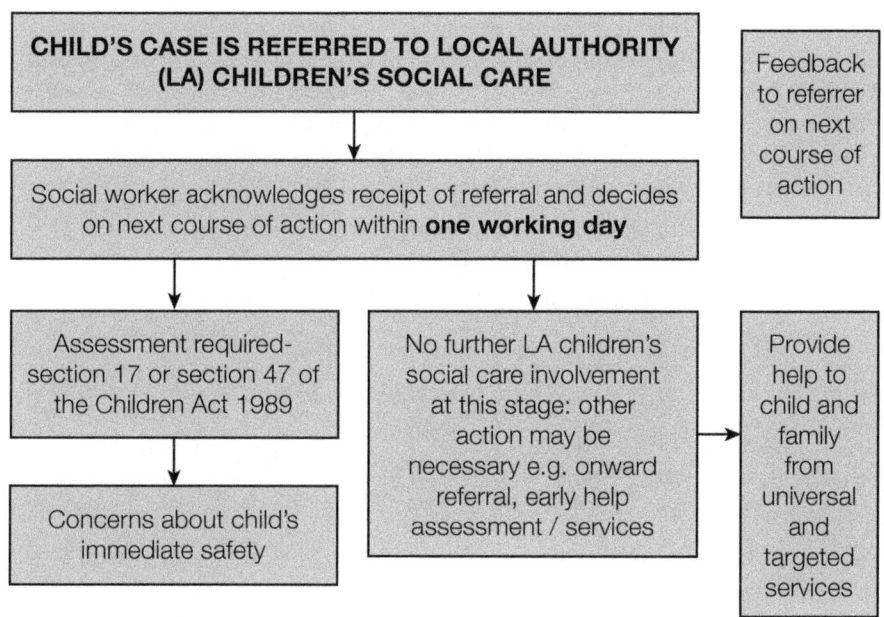

5.7 Any form of emergency action that is planned should take place following a strategy discussion. A strategy discussion should take place whenever there is reasonable cause to suspect that a child is suffering or is likely to suffer significant harm. The discussion may take the form of a multi-agency meeting or phone calls. It should include social care, the police and health, and often other bodies such as the referring agency. At that discussion, available information should be shared, the conduct and timing of any criminal investigation discussed and a decision on the need for a s 47 investigation taken.

THE CHILD PROTECTION INVESTIGATION: SECTION 47

5.8 Section 47 of the CA 1989 sets out the local authority's duty in certain circumstances to carry out a comprehensive child protection investigation. The provisions of s 47 are triggered when a local authority:

✓ has reasonable cause to suspect that a child within its area is suffering, or is likely to suffer, significant harm; or

✓ is informed that a child within its area:
 – is subject to an emergency protection order; or
 – has been taken into police protection.

5.9 The local authority's investigation is designed to establish whether or not it should be taking further steps to protect the child. In many cases, the s 47 investigation is the prelude to an application for a care or supervision order. It is a fairly detailed child protection assessment.

5.10 The structure of the assessment is prescribed by *Working Together to Safeguard Children,* July 2018, which sets out both a framework for assessments generally and specific criteria for a s 47 assessment. The local authority's investigations will focus on three main areas: the child's developmental needs; relevant family and environmental factors; and, the parenting capacity of those with primary responsibility for his care.

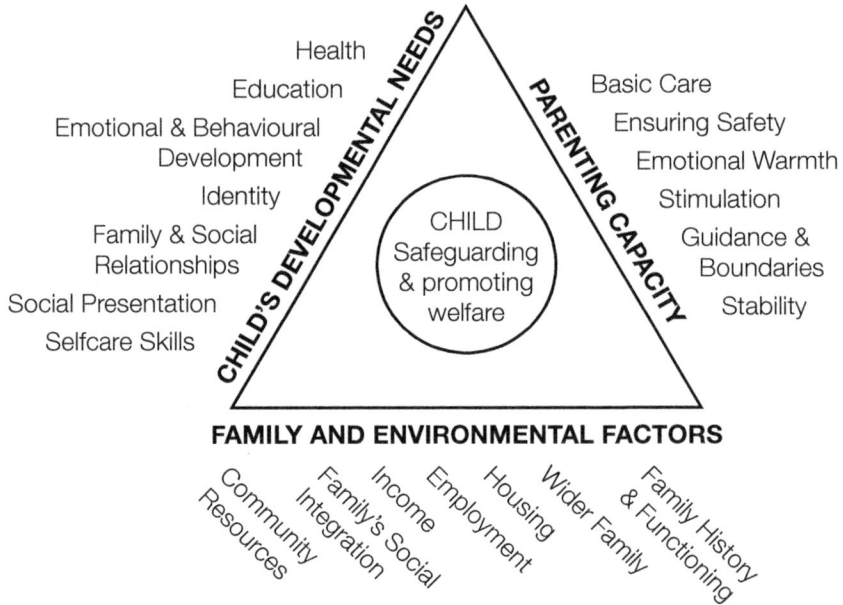

5.11 The framework is designed to cover all assessments of children in need, not just those who are thought to be at risk of significant harm and in need of urgent intervention. The investigation is likely to move more quickly when carried out under s 47 (ie when the child is thought to be at significant risk), but the overall structure of all assessments should be broadly the same.

5.12 The timescales for a s 47 investigation will vary significantly within the 45-working-day maximum. When the trigger for the assessment process is a child in police protection or subject to an emergency protection order, things will have to move quickly. Children can remain in police protection for only 72 hours, and subject to an emergency protection order for a maximum of 15 days, so by the end of that period the local authority must be in possession of the information it needs in order to decide on further action.

5.13 If a local authority carrying out a s 47 investigation is denied access to the child, or is not given information about her whereabouts, it has a specific duty to consider whether an application to the court is necessary (s 47(6)). It must apply for an order (emergency protection order, child assessment order, or care or supervision order) unless satisfied that the child's welfare can be adequately safeguarded without court intervention.[2]

---

[2] CA 1989, s 47(6).

A COURT 'REFERRAL': SECTION 37

5.14 When private law proceedings are under way between parents, or between others concerned with a child, it is not uncommon that allegations are made on one or both sides that raise issues regarding the child's safety or welfare. Alternatively, if a CAFCASS officer has been instructed to report on the family (see **3.69–3.70**), her report may highlight areas of concern. As most family proceedings are heard in private, the local authority will not without more be made aware of any risk to the children that comes to light. Section 37 of the CA 1989 gives power to the court itself, in any family proceedings in which a question arises with respect to the welfare of a child and it seems to the court that an application for a care or supervision order may be appropriate, to direct the appropriate local authority to investigate the child's circumstances.

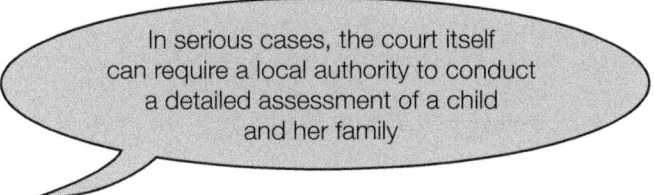

In serious cases, the court itself can require a local authority to conduct a detailed assessment of a child and her family

5.15 It is important to note that the court may only make such a direction where it appears that it may be appropriate for the local authority to make an application for a care or supervision order. The court must not use the procedure to require the local authority to investigate in circumstances in which the concerns are of a relatively minor nature and it is unlikely that the threshold criteria for a care or supervision order (likelihood of future or existence of past significant harm) are met, or where, even if the threshold criteria are met, it is unlikely that a care or supervision order will be necessary. The appropriate course for the court to take where it feels that there may be a role for children's services but a care or supervision order is unlikely to be appropriate is to request a report from the local authority under CA 1989, s 7. When preparing such a report, the social worker is carrying out the same task as an officer of CAFCASS, albeit from a social worker's perspective.

5.16 When a direction is made under s 37 the local authority must carry out an investigation to consider whether or not there is a need to make an application for a care or supervision order (see **Chapter 6**) or whether any other protective or supportive measures are necessary.

5.17 The report must be filed at court within eight weeks, unless otherwise directed.[3] It should focus on the issue of whether or not it would be appropriate to apply for a care or supervision order. It not a general welfare report, although inevitably this issue will require the child's general welfare to be considered. Whilst a s 37 direction requires a local authority to consider applying for a care

---

[3] CA 1989, s 37 (4).

Interim care or interim supervision orders

5.18 When the court makes a direction under s 37, it may at the same time make an interim care order or interim supervision order to cover the period of the local authority's investigation if there are reasonable grounds for believing that the child is suffering or is likely to suffer significant harm. The court's interim order must not extend beyond the first of (i) the disposal of the local authority's application for an interim order or (ii) much more likely, the date by which the local authority is to file its report (ie normally, eight weeks). Generally, the court will fix a date for the next hearing and direct the local authority to file its report in writing shortly before this date. The local authority will be given time to carry out its investigations and if, following those investigations, it decides not to issue proceedings itself, it must give its reasons and specify any other action it proposes to take in respect of the child.[4]

5.19 The s 37 procedure illustrates the delicate allocation of responsibility between the court and the local authority. Although the court can flag up concerns about a child and prompt the initial local authority involvement, the ultimate decision to apply for a care order is the local authority's alone.

Case Study:

A 17-year-old girl, who has left home, makes an application for contact with her 12-year-old sister. The girls' mother has an erratic lifestyle and the younger child is often left alone at home for up to a week at a time. She has not been in school for almost a year. The judge who hears the case at the first hearing dispute resolution appointment is so concerned about her welfare that he makes a s 37 direction requiring the local authority to report back to the court in eight weeks, and makes an interim care order until the reporting date. In the meantime, the local authority carries out an investigation and decides that, in fact, the mother is prepared to modify her lifestyle. It does not believe that there is a need for an order and does not make an application. The interim care order lapses and, unless it has plans to provide support or assistance of any kind, the local authority has no further involvement with the case.

Appointment of a children's guardian

5.20 When the court has made a s 37 direction and has made, or is considering whether to make, an interim care order, the proceedings become 'specified' for

---

[4] CA 1989, ss 37(3), (4) and 38(1) and (4).

the purposes of CA 1989, s 41. This means that the court must appoint an officer of CAFCASS to act as a children's guardian,[5] unless satisfied that it is not necessary to do so in order to safeguard his interests. It has been pointed out that in a case where the local authority is requested to carry out an urgent and intensive investigation, there may not be time for a guardian to play any meaningful role during the assessment process.[6]

5.21 If the local authority subsequently decides not to apply for a care or supervision order, the proceedings cease to be 'specified proceedings'. The role of any guardian appointed under s 41 therefore cannot continue. In an appropriate case, where the court feels that there are still issues that warrant separate representation for the child, the guardian may be 'reappointed' under the Family Procedure Rules 2010 (FPR 2010), r 16.4, known as a 'guardian ad litem'.[7]

FURTHER CHILD PROTECTION MEASURES

5.22 The s 47 assessment may reveal that (i) the concerns are substantiated and the child has suffered or is at risk of significant harm, at which point a child protection conference (see below at **5.24**) should be convened within 15 working days of the strategy discussion at which the s 47 enquiries were initiated, (ii) the concerns are substantiated but it is not thought the child has suffered or is at risk of significant harm, at which point a child protection conference may or may not be convened or (iii) the concerns are not substantiated, but the child is a child 'in need' and both she and her family require support.

Child protection plans

5.23 Central to child protection are child protection plans. Children who are judged to be at continuing risk of significant harm will be made subject to a child protection plan. The aim of a child protection plan is to ensure that the child is safe from harm and prevent her from suffering further harm, promote the child's welfare and development and support the family to safeguard and promote the child's welfare. The allocated social worker under the plan will: be the lead practitioner for inter-agency work with the child and family; develop the outline child protection plan into a more detailed inter-agency plan to be circulated; ensure the plan is aligned and integrated with any associated offender risk management plan; undertake direct work with the child and the family; and, explain the plan to the child in a manner befitting her age and understanding.

---

[5] For 'children's guardian', see **6.89–6.92**.
[6] *Re CE* [1995] 1 FLR 26.
[7] For 'guardian ad litem', see **3.71**.

The child protection conference

5.24 Decisions concerning child protection plans are taken at a child protection conference. Responsibility for convening a conference rests with the local authority, but if the conference is to have before it a full picture of the child's circumstances it is important that a wide variety of professionals should participate. When the decision is taken to convene an initial case conference, the local authority must decide who should be invited to attend. The following should generally be included:

- ✓ the child's parents and, if appropriate, wider family members;
- ✓ social services staff;
- ✓ the child's GP and/or practice nurse;
- ✓ the child's health visitor;
- ✓ the form tutor and/or head teacher of the child's school;
- ✓ a representative from the police; and
- ✓ professionals involved with the parents.

5.25 Parents should be invited to attend case conferences unless there is a good reason why this would put the child or another person at risk: for example, where there is a history of violence perpetrated by one parent against the other. If a parent is excluded from a conference meeting, he should be invited to meet the chair in advance of the meeting and be given an opportunity to put forward his views.

5.26 It is the social worker's responsibility to ensure that the conference has available to it as full a picture as possible of the child's circumstances, the areas of concern, and the family's views. The social worker should provide the conference with a written report including a chronology of significant events and information on the child's health, safety and development and the parenting capacity of the parents and other relevant family members. This report will generally be based on the initial s 47 assessment. It should be made available to the parents prior to the conference.

5.27 The main purpose of the initial child protection conference is to bring together and analyse, in an inter-agency setting, all relevant information and plan how best to safeguard and promote the welfare of the child. As part of that, the conference should establish whether the child should be given a child protection plan and, if so, under which category or categories. A vote is generally taken. The conference will also make recommendations for action that needs to be taken under the child protection plan.

> ### *The initial child protection conference: key functions*
>
> ✓ Should the child be given a child protection plan and, if so, under which category?
>
> ✓ Outline the child protection plan and set a date for production of the full plan
>
> ✓ Appoint a key worker from social services
>
> ✓ Identify the members of the core group and timescales for core group meetings
>
> ✓ Establish how the family are to be involved in the planning process
>
> ✓ Identify what further core and specialist assessments are required
>
> ✓ Consider the need for a contingency plan
>
> ✓ Clarify the purpose of the initial child protection conference, core group and review conference(s)
>
> ✓ Fix a timetable for review conferences

The core group

5.28 A core group is frequently set up. This group will meet more frequently than the full case conference, and on a less formal basis. The core group consists of the parents, foster carers and wider family if appropriate, and key professionals who have regular direct contact with the family, including the key worker and, where relevant, the health visitor and any family support or youth worker.

5.29 The membership of the core group should be established at the initial child protection conference and the first core group meeting should take place within 10 working days. The core group is responsible for developing the child protection plan, implementing the plan, monitoring progress and outcomes, and deciding what steps need to complete the in-depth assessment to inform decisions about the child's safety and welfare. Core group meetings tend to be much more informal than the child protection conference. Where the parents are working amicably with social services, meetings will often take place in the home.

Review conferences

5.30 The first child protection review case conference should take place within three months of the initial conference. Thereafter reviews should take place at least every six months.

Ongoing legal proceedings

5.31 If there are ongoing legal proceedings concerning the family, it is good practice to invite the parents' and the child's legal representatives to the case conferences. In most circumstances, the local authority should invite the children's guardian too. The children's guardian does not need to attend if he feels his attendance might cause the parents to doubt his independence from the local authority, but he should nevertheless be provided with a copy of the conference minutes.

POLICE PROTECTION: SECTION 46

5.32

Police protection: key features

✓   No court order necessary

✓   Officer must have reasonable cause to believe child is likely to suffer significant harm

✓   Maximum duration: 72 hours

✓   Child must be provided with suitable accommodation (refuge or local authority accommodation)

✓   Officer does not acquire parental responsibility

✓   Local authority must be informed as soon as reasonably practicable that the child has been taken into police protection

---

5.33 In an emergency situation, police officers have the power to take a child into their protection, without a court order, for a maximum period of 72 hours. The test is whether the officer has reasonable cause to believe that the child would be likely to suffer significant harm if protective measures were not taken.[8] The police officer may remove the child to suitable accommodation and keep him there, or take reasonable steps to ensure that he is not removed from any place where he is being accommodated. In 2008, guidance was circulated to police offers exercising their powers under CA 1989, s 46: The Duties and Powers of the Police under the Children Act 1989 (Circular 017/2008), which explained when and how police protection powers should be used under CA 1989. That guidance is not referred to in the current, statutory *Working Together* guidance,

---

[8]   CA 1989, s 46(1).

but continues to set out a number of helpful principles that sit alongside the s 46 statutory requirements.

Duties of the officer taking the child into police protection

5.34 A police officer who takes a child into police protection must, as soon as reasonably practicable:

✓ inform the local authority where the child was found, and the local authority where he ordinarily lives (if different), of the steps that have been taken and the location of the child;

✓ speak to the child (if possible) to let him know what steps have been taken and the reasons for them, and to ascertain his wishes and feelings;

✓ find suitable accommodation for the child, either in a refuge or in local authority accommodation; and

✓ inform a designated (child protection) officer.

The police officer must also take whatever steps are practicable to inform the child's parents, any person with parental responsibility and any person with whom he was living of the action that has been taken, the reasons for it, and the plans for the child while he remains in police protection.

Duties of the designated officer

5.35 Once the designated child protection officer has been informed of the situation, she must make enquiries to ensure that the test for keeping the child in police protection continues to be met: ie that there is still reasonable cause for believing that the child is at risk of significant harm. If that appears no longer to be the case the child must be released from police protection. The designated officer must also:

✓ consider whether she should apply on behalf of the appropriate local authority for an emergency protection order;

✓ allow the child's parents, and any other appropriate person,[9] such contact with her as the designated officer feels is in the child's best interests. If the child has been placed in local authority accommodation, this responsibility passes to the local authority.

---

[9] Persons with parental responsibility; any person with whom the child was living; any person in whose favour a 'spends time with' order has been made under s 8 or s 34; and anyone acting on behalf of any of these persons: s 46(10).

5.36 The limitation on the length of time a child may spend in police protection means that the police have the power to act on behalf of the local authority in some limited respects during the period when the child remains in their care, in particular where there is a need to safeguard the child's welfare. The police officer does not, however, acquire parental responsibility for the child and as soon as the local authority is in a position to do so it will take over the child's care from the police. The police officer must, in the meantime, do what is reasonable in all of the circumstances of the case to safeguard and promote the child's welfare.

5.37 When the local authority is informed that a child has been taken into police protection it must:

✓ initiate an investigation into the child's circumstances under s 47; and

✓ consider whether there is a need to apply for an emergency protection order.

EMERGENCY PROTECTION ORDERS: SECTION 44

5.38

Emergency protection orders: key features

✓ For emergency situations where immediate risk of harm

✓ Applicant may be any person; normally a local authority

✓ Initial order for 8 days; may be extended once only for up to 7 days

✓ Authorises the applicant to remove a child from where she is being accommodated or prevent her removal

✓ Applicant has parental responsibility, but this is limited to taking necessary steps to secure the child's short-term welfare

---

5.39 An application for an emergency protection order may be made by any person where there is an urgent need to remove, or prevent the removal of, a child at risk of significant harm. Most professionals facing an emergency situation in relation to a child should be able to enlist the help of social services or, failing that, the police. In extreme situations where for any reason such assistance is not available, any person may make the application, by telephone if necessary. If the application has been made by a person other than the local authority, the local authority will be notified and must consider whether it ought itself to take over the application.[10]

---

[10] Emergency Protection Orders (Transfer of Responsibilities) Regulations 1991, SI 1991/1414, reg 2.

5.40 It is unlikely that a parent would need to make an application for an emergency protection order, as he or she would almost certainly be in a position to apply, if necessary without notice, for one of the s 8 orders (most likely a 'lives with' order or specific issue order). In practice, the application is generally made by a local authority or a person, such as a police officer, acting on its behalf; and in this section references to 'the local authority' include other applicants unless it is clear from the context that this is not the case.

5.41 An emergency protection order gives the applicant parental responsibility for the child. Those persons who already have parental responsibility retain it, but take second place to the local authority for the period of the order. It is a short-term order with two objectives: to remove an immediate risk of harm and to enable the local authority to carry out any assessments necessary to decide what, if any, longer-term measures are needed to protect the child.

Procedure

5.42 The application is made to the Family Court. The respondents are: all those persons the applicant believes to have parental responsibility, or to have had it immediately prior to the care order if the child is in care; and, the child himself. They must be served with the application at least one day in advance of the hearing date. Notice of the proceedings must also be given to parents without parental responsibility; any local authority providing accommodation for the child; any person with whom the child is living; and any person providing refuge accommodation for the child. These people are not automatic respondents but may attend court and apply to become parties.

5.43 An initial emergency protection order lasts for a maximum of eight days; if the eighth day is a public holiday, it will expire at noon on the first day thereafter that is not a public holiday. Public holidays are defined as Christmas Day, Boxing Day, Good Friday, bank holidays and Sundays. The order may be extended on application for up to a further seven days.[11]

5.44 The urgent nature of applications for emergency protection orders, and their limited duration, means that a full investigation of evidence by the court is unlikely to be possible or appropriate. It is rare that such an application will be adjourned for more than a couple of days. The strict rules of evidence do not apply and the court may take account of any oral or written evidence it considers relevant.[12]

5.45 Applications for emergency protection orders are, given their location in CA 1989, Pt V, 'specified proceedings' for the purposes of CA 1989, s 41, and so a children's guardian must be appointed for the child unless the court is satisfied that this is not necessary. Given the limited duration of emergency

---

[11] CA 1989, s 45(5).
[12] Ibid, s 45(7).

protection orders it may not be possible for a guardian to be appointed in time to participate in the proceedings, in which case the court should appoint a solicitor to represent the child.

5.46 An emergency protection order should name the child where possible; if the child's name is not known, the order should describe her in as much detail as possible.[13]

5.47 An emergency protection order may be made in respect of a child who is in care. In such a case, the emergency protection order will take priority and for its duration the care order will take effect subject to the emergency protection order.[14]

5.48 An application for an emergency protection order falls outside of the public law outline (see **6.60**) that governs applications under CA 1989, Pt IV.

Without notice applications

5.49 In cases where giving notice of the application to the child's parents may put her at risk, or there is some other compelling reason why giving notice is not possible or appropriate, the application may be made without notice. The respondents must be served with the application (and order, if granted) within 48 hours.[15] If the court feels that there were insufficient grounds for making the application without notice it may fix a date for a hearing on notice to all parties.[16] The procedure in relation to urgent and out of hours applications (including applications by telephone) to the Family Division of the High Court is set out in the Family Procedure Rules 2010, Practice Direction 12E.

5.50 An emergency protection order made without notice is a 'terrible and drastic' order which requires extremely compelling reasons. The applicant must be prepared to show 'exceptional justification', not only for the order itself but for making the application without notice. In *X Council v B (Emergency Protection Orders)*,[17] Munby J set out 14 points which applicants for an emergency protection order should have in mind; these points are 'required reading' for all lay justices and legal advisers and should be copied and placed before the bench whenever an application is being considered.[18]

---

[13] Ibid, s 44(14).
[14] Ibid, s 91(6).
[15] FPR 2010, r 12.16(4)–(5).
[16] Ibid, r 12.16(6).
[17] *X Council v B (Emergency Protection Orders)* [2004] EWHC 2015 (Fam).
[18] *Re X (Emergency Protection Orders)* [2006] 2 FLR 701.

> ***Application for emergency protection orders: checklist***
>
> ✓ Application in Form C1 with Supplement C11
>
> ✓ What are the plans for (a) the child's accommodation and (b) contact with parents/others?
>
> ✓ Is there a need for a direction regarding any medical or other assessment?
>
> ✓ Identify all respondents (those with parental responsibility; the child)
>
> ✓ Serve respondents with the application at least 1 day prior to hearing
>
> ✓ Child to be served via solicitor or children's guardian (appointed by court upon issue of proceedings)
>
> ✓ Give notice of the proceedings (date, time and place of hearing, but not copies of the application) to:
>   – parents without parental responsibility
>   – any local authority providing accommodation
>   – any person or refuge providing accommodation
>
> *If application made without notice*
>
> ✓ Keep a note of what is said to the court in support of the application and serve it on respondents
>
> ✓ Serve respondents with the application and order as soon as possible (or as directed by the court) and give required notice to others
>
> *If application made by telephone*
>
> ✓ Should take place over tape-recorded conference call with a transcript obtained, or the applicant's legal representative should prepare a note for approval by the judge

Grounds

5.51 There are two alternative grounds for an emergency protection order. They are that:

✓ there are reasonable grounds to believe that the child is likely to suffer significant harm if he is not removed to accommodation provided by the applicant, or kept in the accommodation where he is; or

✓ provided that the applicant is a local authority or authorised person[19]:
   – the local authority is carrying out an investigation of the child's circumstances under s 47 (see **5.8–5.13**) or the authorised person is making enquiries with respect to the child's welfare;
   – the enquiries are being frustrated because access to the child is being denied; and
   – the applicant has reasonable cause to believe that access is required as a matter of urgency.

5.52 Provided that one of the alternative grounds is established, the child's welfare is the paramount consideration when the court is deciding whether or not to grant an emergency protection order, and the 'no order' principle applies: the court may only make the order if satisfied that to do so would be better for the child than making no order at all. The detailed welfare checklist does not apply,[20] although many of the factors on the welfare checklist may well be of relevance.

5.53 It has been emphasised that emergency protection orders are designed for situations where there is an immediate risk of harm. They are not to be used when the risk is longer term and the more appropriate course is the detailed court-directed investigation that would result from an application for a care or supervision order.[21] Similarly, once the order has expired the local authority must decide whether or not to apply for any other order; the court cannot make further orders of its own motion.

5.54 Where the grounds for an order are that the child is living with a particular person who is said to pose a risk, the local authority should explore the possibility of that person leaving the home so that the child can remain living where he is. The local authority may assist the alleged abuser to find alternative accommodation and may assist with funding.[22] Alternatively it may encourage the child's main carer to exclude the alleged abuser from the home via one of the remedies under the Family Law Act 1996. These options should be explored before the local authority applies for an order excluding the alleged abuser from the home (see **5.63–5.67**).

Effect of the order

5.55

Emergency protection order } Parental responsibility to applicant
Applicant can remove / prevent removal of child
Any able person must produce child to applicant[23]

---

[19] An authorised person means any person authorised by the Secretary of State under CA 1989, s 31(9) to bring care proceedings. At present the only authorised person is the NSPCC.
[20] CA 1989, s 1(4).
[21] *Re C and B (Care Order: Future Harm)* [2001] 1 FLR 611.
[22] CA 1989, Sch 2, para 5.
[23] CA 1989, s 44(4).

5.56 The local authority (or other applicant) may only exercise parental responsibility to the extent that is reasonably required in order to safeguard the child's welfare, bearing in mind the duration of the order.[24] The local authority may therefore take action to meet the child's immediate needs by, for example, providing food and accommodation and arranging for any urgent medical treatment to be carried out; but it must not interfere with any longer-term arrangements, for instance by changing the child's school.

5.57 The court may attach supplementary provisions to the order. The available directions fall into four categories.

(1) Provisions to assist the local authority to locate or remove the child.

(2) Regulation of the child's contact with his parents or others.

(3) The exclusion of a named person from the place where the child lives.

(4) Directions permitting, or preventing, any medical or psychiatric examination of the child.

Locating and removing the child

5.58 Where the local authority does not have enough information about a child's whereabouts to locate her, the court may direct any named (or identified) person or persons who appear to have such information to disclose it to the local authority on request.[25]

5.59 An emergency protection order does not of itself authorise the local authority to enter premises without the occupant's permission. Where it is thought that a parent or other occupant is likely to refuse to cooperate with the local authority's social worker, or that a child may be alone in the premises, the court may give permission to the local authority to enter without the occupant's permission and search the premises for the child.[26] The local authority, however, has no means of enforcing such an order and if access to the child continues to be refused, or if it is likely from the outset that an order permitting entry will not be sufficient, the court may issue a warrant authorising a police officer to enter and search the premises, using reasonable force if necessary.[27] Note that without a warrant, a police officer may only enter and search private premises for limited purposes, including 'to save life and limb'.

5.60 The court may direct that a doctor, nurse or health visitor should accompany the social worker and/or police officer.[28]

---

[24] Ibid, s 44(5).
[25] Ibid, s 48(1).
[26] Ibid, s 48(3).
[27] Ibid, s 48(12).
[28] Ibid, s 48(11).

Contact

5.61 The court is given power under s 44(6) to make directions regarding the contact the child is to have with any person during the period of the order, and may impose conditions on that contact. If no specific direction is made, the local authority must allow the child to have 'reasonable contact' with his parents and any person with parental responsibility. It must also allow anyone with whom the child was living before the order, anyone in whose favour a 'spends time with' order under s 8 or contact order under s 34 is in force, and any person acting on behalf of such a person, to have reasonable contact with the child.

5.62 The local authority is not required to draw up detailed care plans in relation to children under emergency protection orders. It is important therefore that thought is given at an early stage to the contact that will be offered; that practical arrangements are put in place; and, that the parents are notified of these arrangements. If it is proposed that no contact should take place between the child and her family for the duration of the order, or that contact should be very limited, the local authority must seek a direction of the court to this effect.

Exclusion requirement: section 44A

5.63 Where it is possible to identify a particular person who poses a risk to the child, an emergency protection order may include a requirement that that person be excluded from the place where the child lives. The alleged abuser may be prevented from living in the child's home, entering the home or coming within a defined area in which the home is situated. The exclusion requirement will generally last for the same period as the emergency protection order, although it may last for a shorter period.

5.64 The court may only include an exclusion requirement in an emergency protection order if there is someone else living in the home who is willing and able to care for the child, and who consents to the exclusion requirement being imposed.

5.65 A power of arrest may be attached to the exclusion requirement. The effect of this is to give the police the power to arrest without a warrant any person whom they have reasonable cause to believe is in breach of the exclusion requirement.

5.66 In place of an order, the court may accept an undertaking from the person whom the local authority seeks to exclude. The undertaking is enforceable in the same way as an exclusion requirement that is part of the order. The only difference is that a power of arrest cannot be attached to an undertaking. If a breach is anticipated and it is likely that the assistance of the police will be needed, an undertaking is unlikely to be acceptable and the court should make an order together with a power of arrest.

Medical examinations and assessments

5.68 As part of its exercise of parental responsibility, the local authority may and should arrange for the child to have any medical treatment that becomes necessary during the period of the emergency protection order. Bearing in mind the duration of an emergency protection order, and the limitations on its exercise of parental responsibility, the local authority would be wise not to arrange any non-essential medical examination during the period of the order without the court's permission. The court may give any directions it deems appropriate regarding a medical or psychiatric examination or assessment, and may direct that no such assessment should be carried out.[29] If a medical or psychiatric assessment is proposed this should be raised with the court as soon as possible and a direction sought.

5.69 As in all situations where the local authority shares parental responsibility, the child's parents should be consulted where possible in relation to all proposed medical treatment. A child who is *Gillick* competent[30] may refuse to submit to an examination or treatment.

Challenging an emergency protection order

5.70 The routes by which an emergency protection order may be challenged are restricted. There is no right of appeal. A party may attend the initial hearing and oppose the making of an emergency protection order; but if he is not successful he cannot then apply for it to be discharged. An application for discharge of the emergency protection order can only be made by a person who did *not* attend the initial hearing and it cannot be made in relation to an emergency protection order that has been extended (ie an order that has lasted eight days, and then be extended for up to a further seven days). An application for discharge can be made as soon as the emergency protection order is made.

Case Study: *Police protection to an emergency protection order*

On Christmas Eve (a Friday) at 9pm, two police officers are called to a fight in a house. They attend and find a woman badly injured, her drunk partner, who readily admits to having beaten her up, and their three-year-old son. Having called an ambulance and arrested the partner it is plain that there is no one available to care for the boy. The officers tell the parents they are taking the

---

[29] Ibid, s 44(6) and (8).
[30] See **2.17**.

> *child into police protection and inform them that they will be told as soon as possible of the address where he will be accommodated and that arrangements will be made for them to see him. The officers take the child to the police station and telephone social services' out-of-hours number. Early on Christmas morning a duty social worker finally manages to arrange an emergency foster placement and arrives to pick up the child. Although the child remains in police protection, he is now staying in accommodation provided by the local authority and therefore social services are responsible for making decisions about his contact with his parents.*
>
> *The designated officer is informed in the early hours of Christmas Day. He speaks to the officers in the case and is of the view that the boy would be at risk of significant harm if he were to return home. The officer is aware that the 72-hour period will expire at 9pm on Monday 27 December, also a bank holiday, and that it is unlikely that the local authority will be able to apply for an emergency protection order before then. Therefore, on Sunday 26 December the designated officer contacts the court on the emergency out-of-hours number. A judge is located and the application is made and granted by telephone. The order is made for a period of four days.*
>
> *The district judge orders that the parents should be notified immediately of the order and that the formal application should be issued. He lists the matter at court on Wednesday afternoon. On Tuesday 28 December, the designated officer manages to contact a local authority solicitor who takes over the case. He prepares the application and issues it on Tuesday afternoon. At the hearing on Wednesday afternoon the emergency protection order is extended for a period of seven days.*

CHILD ASSESSMENT ORDERS: SECTION 43

5.71

> ***Child assessment orders: key features***
>
> ✓ For non-emergency situations where attempts to carry out an assessment are being frustrated
>
> ✓ Applicant is the local authority or authorised person
>
> ✓ Maximum duration: 7 days, with no extension
>
> ✓ The applicant does not acquire parental responsibility

5.72 Child assessment orders, made under CA 1989, s 43, have close connections to emergency protection orders. They are designed to facilitate access to a child where it is suspected that she is at risk but the local authority is having difficulties in carrying out an assessment to establish whether or not this is the case. They do not have the force of emergency protection orders or orders under CA 1989, Pt IV (care and supervision orders): the local authority does not acquire parental responsibility and therefore has limited power if the family does not comply with the order. If there is a failure to co-operate once the order is made, the local authority's only option is to apply for an emergency protection order or, if it is in a position to do so, an interim care order.

5.73 This means that if there is an immediate risk to the child, and his parents have not responded to previous efforts to engage them, an emergency protection order rather than a child assessment order may be necessary. If the court feels it is appropriate, it may treat an application for a child assessment order as an application for an emergency protection order.

5.74 The order lasts for a maximum of seven days, and there is no permitted extension.[31]

Procedure

5.75 While any person may apply for an emergency protection order, the applicant for a child assessment order must be the local authority or an authorised person (currently only officers of the NSPCC). The respondents are:

✓ the child;

✓ any person with parental responsibility; and

✓ (where relevant) any person who had parental responsibility before a care order was made.

5.76 The application, like the application for an emergency protection order, is made in the Family Court. Unlike an application for an emergency protection order, it must be made on notice to all the parties.

5.77 Applications for child assessment orders, like applications for emergency protection orders, are 'specified proceedings' and a children's guardian must be appointed unless the child's interests may otherwise be safeguarded. The observations above (see **5.45**) concerning the short duration of emergency protection orders and the fact that any involvement of a guardian will necessarily be limited are equally relevant to child assessment orders.

5.78 The court may:

✓ make the child assessment order;

✓ refuse to make the order;

✓ treat the application as an application for an emergency protection order and, if appropriate, make that order.

---

[31] CA 1989, s 43(5).

Grounds for the order

5.79 The grounds for a child assessment order are that:

✓ the applicant has reasonable cause to suspect that the child is suffering or is likely to suffer significant harm;

✓ an assessment of the child's health or development, or the way in which he has been treated, is necessary to enable the applicant to establish whether or not he is at risk of significant harm; and

✓ it is unlikely that such an assessment will be carried out satisfactorily without an order.

5.80 The child's welfare is paramount and the 'no order' principle applies. The welfare checklist does not apply, but many of its factors may be relevant.

5.81 The local authority will have to satisfy the court that the proposed assessment is a necessary one. It will need to inform the court of the steps that have already been taken in an attempt to carry out the assessment. If the parents have refused to co-operate with the proposed assessment, the court will need to be satisfied that they are frustrating the local authority's enquiries. It will not be enough to show that there is a dispute about how or by whom an assessment should be carried out.

Effect of the order

5.82 A child assessment order does not give the local authority parental responsibility. It authorises the local authority to carry out the assessment specified in the order. The order may, if necessary, make directions regarding the person who is to carry out the assessment and the place and time where the child is to be produced for the assessment. Because the scope of the order is limited to a specified assessment it is important that what is proposed is set out clearly both in the application and in the order.

RECOVERY ORDERS: SECTION 50

5.83 A recovery order may be made when a child who is in the care of the local authority, in police protection, or subject to an emergency protection order has been abducted, run away or gone missing. Abduction of a child from care is a criminal offence.[32]

5.84 The court's powers to make recovery orders should be considered in tandem with its powers to make directions for the location and recovery of a

---

[32] Ibid, s 49.

child in conjunction with an emergency protection order. Where the grounds for an emergency protection order exist, this may well be the preferred option.

Procedure

5.85 The applicant for a recovery order must be the person who has parental responsibility by virtue of the original order (ie the local authority) or, if the child is in police protection, the designated officer. The application is made in the Family Court. It may be made without notice. In general, the procedure is very similar to that on an application for an emergency protection order.

5.86 The respondents are:

✓ the child;

✓ any person with parental responsibility;

✓ any person with parental responsibility prior to any existing care order;

✓ the person who is said to have abducted or to be keeping the child.

5.87 Notice must be given to:

✓ any local authority providing accommodation for the child;

✓ any person (for example a foster carer) with whom the child was living;

✓ any person providing an authorised refuge where it is said that the child is staying.

Effect of the order

5.88 A recovery order authorises the person with parental responsibility to remove the child from wherever he is being kept. It also operates as a direction to any person who is in a position to do so to produce the child on request, or to disclose any information he possesses about the child's whereabouts to a police officer or an officer of the court. The order may specify premises that a police officer is authorised to enter, by force if necessary, to search for the child. Premises may only be specified if it appears to the court that there are reasonable grounds for believing the child to be on them.

5.89 The person with parental responsibility (usually the local authority) must authorise one of its officers to exercise its powers under the recovery order. Normally an officer of the local authority will attend the property where it is thought the child is being kept together with one or more police officers.

5.90 Under the CA 1989 it is an offence to obstruct an authorised person from implementing a recovery order.[33] The maximum sentence for this offence is a fine. However, a person who resists a police officer acting in the execution of his duty may be arrested without a warrant and sentenced on conviction to a month's imprisonment.

Case Study:

A local authority applies for a care order in respect of a child. At the first hearing in the Family Court, the parents (who have been served with the application) do not attend. The court makes an interim care order on the local authority's care plan for immediate removal. Social workers immediately attend the child's home, but the parents refuse to let them in. The local authority returns to court the same day with an application (without notice) for a recovery order. This is granted and the social worker returns to the home with two police officers. The officers force entry to the house. The child's mother will not give the child up to the officers. When it becomes clear that she cannot be persuaded, she is arrested for obstructing a constable in the execution of his duty and the officer, as he is entitled to do, uses reasonable force to effect the arrest. The child is then recovered.

Older children

5.91 A care order lasts until a child is 18, unless it is previously discharged. This means that, in theory, a child aged 16 or 17 who decides to leave 'home' may be made the subject of a recovery order. If the child refuses to return, it is difficult to see how she can be forced to do so. A local authority facing this situation should think carefully about whether it ought to be making an application under s 50 or whether there is some other way of protecting the child.

5.92 While a person who assists or provides a refuge to a child who has run away from care is guilty of a criminal offence,[34] an exception is made for those who provide registered accommodation in a refuge for children at risk. This means that charities and other groups who provide 'safe houses' for runaway children are not liable to prosecution.[35]

CHILD SAFETY ORDERS AND PARENTING ORDERS

5.93 The Crime and Disorder Act 1998 (CDA 1998), which introduced the now-repealed anti-social behaviour legislation orders (commonly known as ASBOs), gave local authorities the power to apply for orders to assist them in managing the behaviour of young children in their areas.

---

[33] Ibid, s 50(9).
[34] Ibid, s 49(1)(b) and (c).
[35] Ibid, s 51.

5.94 A child safety order can be made in respect of a child under the age of 10 who has committed an act which if older would have constituted an offence, is likely to commit an offence, or has acted in a manner that caused or is likely to cause harassment, alarm or distress. The order places the child under the supervision of a named 'responsible officer' (either a social worker or a member of a youth offending team) and requires her to comply with such requirements as are specified.[36]

5.95 The application is made to the Family Court and the court is required to obtain information about the child's family circumstances before making the order. The power of a magistrates' court to make a care order following a child's failure to comply with a requirement of the order was removed by the Children Act 2004.[37]

5.96 A parenting order may be made in proceedings in any court where:

✓ a child safety order is made;

✓ a parental compensation order is made in relation to a child's behaviour;

✓ a specified injunction or order is granted under the Anti-social Behaviour, Crime and Policing Act 2014 or a sexual harm prevention order is made;

✓ a child is convicted of an offence; or

✓ a parent is convicted of an offence relating to a failure to secure a child's attendance at school.[38]

5.97 A parenting order may be made in such a case provided that the court considers it would be desirable in the interests of addressing the child's anti-social or offending behaviour, or the problems with her school attendance. The order may require the child's parent to attend a specified counselling or guidance programme or to comply with any other requirements contained in the order.

5.98 The maximum duration of a parenting order or a child safety order is 12 months.

---

[36] CDA 1998, s 11.
[37] CA 2004, s 60.
[38] CDA 1998, s 8.

Chapter 6

CARE AND SUPERVISION ORDERS

Chapter summary

- The orders available

- The threshold criteria

- The welfare checklist; the European Convention on Human Rights; a holistic welfare analysis

- Care proceedings: application and procedure

- Representing the child

- Evidence

- The role of the expert witness

- Parental contact with children in care

- Further issues

THE ORDERS AVAILABLE

6.1 Part IV of the Children Act 1989 (CA 1989) deals with care and supervision orders. These two orders are designed for the more serious cases where there is a risk of significant harm to a child. They enable the court to sanction the kind of long-term local authority intervention and monitoring that cannot be provided via any of the supportive services described in CA 1989, Pt III (see **Chapter 4**).

Care orders

6.2

CARE ORDER ⟶ PARENTAL RESPONSIBILITY TO THE LOCAL AUTHORITY

A care order gives the local authority designated in the order[1] parental responsibility for the child. Parental responsibility is shared with the parents, but the local authority is in the driving seat and may restrict the parents' exercise of their parental responsibility. In practical terms, this means that the local authority may if necessary take over responsibility for meeting the child's needs. There are some limitations on the local authority's power to exercise parental responsibility: it cannot change the child's religion or consent to his adoption, or change his surname without the permission of the court. Children subject to a care order may be placed with their parents, with other relatives, in a children's home or in foster care, etc.[2]

6.3 A care order may not be made once the child has reached the age of 17. Once made, it will last until the child is 18, unless it is discharged by the court.[3]

6.4 A child who is the subject of a care order may continue to live at home with her parents. Baker J gave detailed guidance in *Re DE*[4] about how such care orders should be approached. Where a care order is made on the basis of a child living at home, it should be a term of the care plan and a recital to the order that, save in an emergency, the local authority will give not less than 14 days' notice of a removal of the child. Where that notice is given, a parent should consider applying not only for the discharge of the care order but also for an injunction under s 8 of the Human Rights Act 1998 to keep the child at home in the interim. In turn, a court should normally grant an injunction unless the child's welfare requires her immediate removal from the family home.

6.5 The making of a care order automatically discharges any current s 8 order (see **Chapter 3**) and any supervision order or interim care/supervision order made in respect of the child.

6.6 A child who is the subject of a care order is a 'looked after child' for the purposes of the CA 1989 (see **Chapter 4**).

Supervision orders

6.7

SUPERVISION ORDER ━━━▶ ADVISE, ASSIST AND BEFRIEND'

A supervision order does not give the local authority parental responsibility. It imposes a duty on the local authority to 'advise, assist and befriend' the

---

[1] The designated local authority is the authority in which the child ordinarily resides: CA 1989, s 31(8). Disputes may arise where it is not clear which of two local authorities is the 'designated authority' for the purposes of a care order. For guidance see *W (A Child) (Designation of Local Authority)* [2016] EWCA Civ 366 and **6.53**.
[2] See **Ch 4** for the local authority's duties concerning the provision of accommodation.
[3] CA 1989, s 31(3).
[4] *Re DE (A Child)* [2014] EWFC 6.

supervised child. The parents must allow the local authority reasonable contact with the child.[5] However, there are no sanctions for breach of a supervision order; if the local authority has concerns about the parents' lack of co-operation it will have to issue a fresh application for a care order. An initial supervision order lasts for a maximum of one year;[6] it may be extended to a maximum of three years in total but will terminate once the child is 18.

6.8 Proceedings arising out of applications for care and supervision orders are known as care proceedings. On an application for a care order the court may make a supervision order, and vice versa.

THE THRESHOLD CRITERIA

6.9 When a local authority applies for a care or supervision order it must satisfy the court that two initial conditions for state intervention are met. These conditions are:

(1) The child must be suffering, or likely to suffer, significant harm.

(2) The harm or likelihood of harm must be attributable to one of the following:
  (a) the care given to the child, or likely to be given if the order were not made, not being what it would be reasonable to expect a parent to give; or
  (b) the child's being beyond parental control.[7]

Unless both of these conditions are met, the court cannot sanction state intervention in the form of a care or supervision order. The conditions are known as the 'threshold criteria'. If the local authority can prove on the balance of probabilities that the threshold criteria have been established, the court must then go on to decide, applying the welfare checklist,[8] whether it is in the child's best interests that a care or supervision order be made.

Significant harm

6.10 The CA 1989 gives guidance on what is meant by 'harm', although the line between harm and 'significant' harm is not defined. All aspects of a child's development are relevant. Ill-treatment includes sexual abuse and need not be physical ill-treatment.

---

[5] CA 1989, Sch 3, para 8(2)(b).
[6] Ibid, Sch 3, para 6(1), (3).
[7] CA 1989, s 31(2).
[8] Ibid, s 1(3) – see **6.26**.

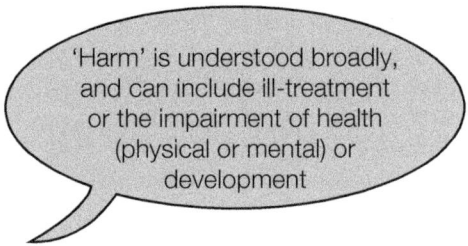

'Harm' is understood broadly, and can include ill-treatment or the impairment of health (physical or mental) or development

6.11 The court should have in mind, when considering the significance of the harm suffered in terms of impaired development, what could reasonably be expected of a similar child.[9] Frequently it will have access to information that places the child on the spectrum of children of a similar age. If the child is not meeting his developmental milestones, or has fallen from his normal position on the percentile chart for his height or weight, it will be necessary to find out why this is and whether it is attributable to the quality of parental care. It is likely that prolonged unauthorised absences from school will give rise to significant harm.

6.12 It is important to be alert to the risk or presence of emotional harm to the child. An abandoned baby is not just at risk of physical injury but is also likely to suffer significant emotional harm as a result of having no knowledge of his parents or background.[10] Witnessing violence is a common cause of emotional harm, even when the child is not directly involved. This has long been acknowledged by professionals and the courts, and is now given statutory endorsement by the Adoption and Children Act 2002, which has extended the definition of harm in s 31 of the CA 1989 to include 'impairment suffered by hearing or seeing the ill-treatment of another'.

6.13 Whether or not the harm alleged is 'significant' is something for the court to decide. Significant should be given its ordinary meaning ('considerable, noteworthy or important') and the child's particular characteristics should be taken into account: a two-year-old left alone with a pan of boiling water within reach is likely to suffer significant harm, but a 13-year-old is not. Similarly, the harm caused to a diabetic child by being fed a bag of sweets is significant; another child will suffer nothing worse than an upset stomach and toothache.

'Likely to suffer'

6.14 The phrase 'likely to suffer' in s 31(1) does *not* mean 'is more likely than not to suffer' or 'has a greater than 50% chance of suffering'. 'Likelihood' in this context means 'a real possibility that it will occur' or 'a real possibility, a possibility that cannot sensibly be ignored having regard to the nature and gravity of the feared harm in the particular case'.[11] It should be remembered

---

[9] Ibid, s 31(10).
[10] *Re M* [1996] 2 FLR 84.
[11] Both *Re B (Care Proceedings: Appeal)* [2013] UKSC 33.

that a comparatively low threshold of likelihood is adopted because some harm is so catastrophic that even a relatively small degree of likelihood should be sufficient to justify the state intervening before it happens.[12]

6.15 However, where the likelihood of harm occurring in the future is based on disputed past events, the court must first decide, on the balance of probabilities, where the truth lies.

> Case Study:
>
> *A toddler is brought to hospital suffering from serious head injuries. The doctors operate but the child dies. The parents say that the child fell down the stairs: the safety gate was faulty. The doctors are suspicious – the injuries suggest a blow rather than a fall – and contact the local authority and the police. An initial criminal investigation results in no further action being taken. Two years later the parents have another child. The local authority is very worried and applies for a care order based on the likelihood of future harm to the new baby.*

6.16 At first glance, it would seem that the court could well decide that the threshold criteria are made out. If there is a real possibility that the first child's death was non-accidental, there must be a real possibility – or 'likelihood' – that the second child will also suffer significant harm. It might be thought that this amounts to a risk that cannot sensibly be ignored. But, the Supreme Court[13] has held that where there is a disputed past event the court must not treat this as grounding a future risk without making a finding of fact about its truth. Therefore, the court must first decide what happened in the past. On the balance of probabilities, was the first incident an accident or the result of deliberate injury perpetrated by a parent? If the court cannot find that it is more probable than not that the first incident was non-accidental (rather than there simply being a real possibility that that is so), there is no past harm on which to base future risk, and the threshold criteria are not met. It should be noted that there is no justification for applying a more stringent test to the evidence where the harm that is alleged to have taken place is extremely serious. The test is the simple balance of probabilities, and while the inherent likelihood or unlikelihood of an allegation is a factor to be taken into account, it is not correct to apply a heightened test where the allegation is particularly unusual or serious.[14]

The relevant date

6.17 The date for determining the occurrence or likelihood of significant harm is the date when proceedings are issued, or, if earlier, the date when there

---

[12] *Re B (Care Proceedings: Appeal)* [2013] UKSC 33, per Lady Hale in her dissenting judgment.
[13] *Re S-B* [2009] UKSC 17.
[14] *Re B* [2008] UKHL 35; [2008] 2 FLR 141; see also *Re S-B* [2009] UKSC 17.

were first put into place arrangements for the protection of the child (such as an emergency protection order or removal into foster care with the parents' consent) as long as these have remained in place continuously up until the date of the hearing.[15]

6.18 The court may take into account evidence that comes to light *after* the local authority has put in place protective measures, if it throws light on the situation at the relevant time. So, if a child living in foster care under an interim order describes to his foster carer an occasion when he was beaten by his father, this evidence may be used to substantiate the threshold criteria. However, this will only be the case if the beating took place *before* the local authority took steps to protect the child by placing him in foster care. If the beating happened after the placement, perhaps during a contact visit, it cannot form part of the 'threshold' evidence. It will come to be considered if the court finds the threshold criteria made out and moves on to consider the welfare checklist, below.

'Attributable to parental care'

6.19 The harm that the child has suffered or is likely to suffer must be attributable to the care that is given to him being below the standard reasonably expected of a parent. This means that there must be a causal link between the care given to the child and the incidence or likelihood of him suffering significant harm. The child's own characteristics will be relevant: a child with complex medical needs may have suffered significant harm, but whether or not this is attributable to the care he has received may be a very difficult question to answer. The person whose care for the child may present a risk need not actually be the child's parent: the unsatisfactory care provided by a grandparent, step-parent or even childminder may fall within the scope of s 31(2).[16]

The standard expected of a reasonable parent

6.20 Parents often feel, once care proceedings are under way and the spotlight is on them and their family, that nothing less than Mary Poppins-style perfection will do. From a social worker's point of view, it can be difficult to know what is outside the bracket of reasonable parenting. Physical chastisement of children falls into this grey area. Terms such as 'acceptable' and 'appropriate' tend to creep in, but can be subjective and need to be used with care.

6.21 Of course, there are times when it is plain that a child has been neglected or hurt or abused, and that her parent is responsible. The threshold criteria are very likely to be met in these cases, and the real question for the court will be whether, perhaps with support from social services or other agencies, the

---

[15] *Re M (A Minor) (Care Order: Threshold Conditions)* [1994] 2 FLR 577.
[16] For cases where care is shared with a non-parent and it is not clear who is responsible for the harm, see *Lancashire County Council v B* [2000] 1 FLR 583.

parent(s) can be helped to provide what has come to be known as 'good enough' parenting.

6.22 Parents who are themselves vulnerable, perhaps because they are very young or have some degree of learning disability or physical impairment that affects their ability to care for their child, may argue that it is not unreasonable of them to provide a lower standard of care than the average parent. But the test is an objective one and the issue is whether the harm is attributable to the care that it would be reasonable to expect *a* parent – not *this* parent – to give. In practice, courts are prepared to brand the inadequate care caused by a parent's youth, drug addiction or even mental illness unreasonable; but it would be a harsh court that found the threshold criteria made out on the basis of a parent's physical disability alone. When the parent is himself vulnerable, the levels of support provided by the local authority, and the parent's willingness to accept this support, will be highly relevant to the court's assessment of the plan for the child's future care.

The child beyond parental control

6.23 A child who is putting herself at risk through no fault of her parents may be the subject of care proceedings, provided that the harm or likelihood of significant harm exists. It is important to remember that not every child who is beyond parental control will have suffered or be at risk of significant harm. Indicators of harm may include persistent truancy, absconding and drug or alcohol abuse.

6.24 Where a child in local authority accommodation is putting herself or others at risk of injury, or regularly absconds and is likely thereby to suffer significant harm, she may be placed in secure accommodation: see **Chapter 9**.

THE WELFARE CHECKLIST; THE EUROPEAN CONVENTION ON HUMAN RIGHTS; A HOLISTIC ANALYSIS

The welfare checklist

6.25 If, and only if, the court finds the threshold criteria have been made out will it go on to decide whether or not to make an order. It is a cardinal principle of the CA 1989 that the court must determine those issues by affording paramount consideration to the child's welfare and must apply the 'welfare checklist' in CA 1989, s 1(3) (see **6.26**). In addition, the court should only make an order if to do so is better for the child than making no order at all (the 'no order' principle).[17] The task for the court is to decide what order, if any, the child's needs and best interests require, and the welfare checklist is a tool designed to highlight particular aspects of the child's situation that will be relevant to this decision.

---

[17] CA 1989, s 1(5).

6.26

> *Welfare checklist*
>
> ✓ The ascertainable wishes and feelings of the child concerned (considered in the light of his age and understanding)
>
> ✓ His physical, emotional and educational needs
>
> ✓ The likely effect on him of any change in his circumstances
>
> ✓ His age, sex, background and any characteristics of his which the court considers relevant
>
> ✓ Any harm which he has suffered or is at risk of suffering
>
> ✓ How capable each of his parents, and any other person in relation to whom the court considers the question to be relevant, is of meeting his needs
>
> ✓ The range of powers available to the court under the CA 1989 in the proceedings in question

6.27 Many of the factors listed in the welfare checklist will be taken into account as a matter of common sense. There are a number of situations commonly considered by the courts where one or more of the factors in the welfare checklist are likely to be relevant.

The European Convention on Human Rights

6.28 The making of an order under CA 1989, Pt IV is an interference in the family's right (both the parents' and the children's rights) to private and family life under European Convention on Human Rights (ECHR), Art 8. Where there is an interference with an Art 8 right, it must be justified as being necessary in a democratic society for the protection of the health and morals and of the rights and freedoms of others (ie it must be *necessary*) and proportionate to the aim of protecting the child concerned (ie it must be *proportionate*). At the same time, the court process must be one that complies with the family's right to a fair trial under ECHR, Art 6. Those rights are brought into domestic law by the Human Rights Act 1998 (HRA 1998).

A holistic welfare analysis

6.29 In the leading 2013 cases of *In the matter of B*[18] and *Re B-S*,[19] the Supreme Court and Court of Appeal have emphasised that the court is required

---

[18] *In the matter of B (A Child)* [2013] UKSC 33.
[19] *Re B-S (Children)* [2013] EWCA CIv 1146.

to undertake a 'global, holistic evaluation' of the competing options before the court. What is required to ensure compliance with ECHR rights is an end to judicial evaluations that are linear in form (ie start with the least interventionist option, and rule that out, before moving in turn through more and more interventionist options, all of which are ruled out, before the final and most serious option – adoption, say – is arrived at) and a focus on 'global, holistic evaluations' in which each competing option is evaluated on to its internal merits and demerits and then held up against and compared with each other option. This process of evaluation is now absolutely central to care proceedings and required in each and every case.

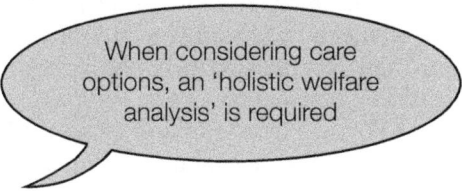

When considering care options, an 'holistic welfare analysis' is required

The birth family

6.30 It has been emphasised several times that local authorities must not lose sight of the importance of the child's natural family, and must work towards reunification of the family where that is possible. As discussed above, the HRA 1998 brought into domestic law the European concept of proportionality: any interference with a person's right to a private and family life must be necessary, and proportionate to the risk to the child. Where a child's rights conflict with an adult's the child's interests will take priority; but the child too has a right to family life, and a right to know and be brought up by his natural parents wherever possible.

6.31 If the child cannot live with a member of her natural family, the court must not forget the importance to her of maintaining a relationship with them. This may be through ongoing direct contact or, at the very least, an exchange of letters and photographs. Even when a child is to be adopted, the adoption agency will collect information about the birth family to help the child ultimately to have some understanding of her birth identity and parentage.

6.32 If adoption is being considered, the Adoption and Children Act 2002 requires the local authority and the court to consider an adoption-specific welfare checklist when coming to a decision relating to the adoption of a child and when considering a care plan that provides for the child to be adopted. The following extracts from the checklist illustrate the focus on the birth family:

'(c) the likely effect on the child (throughout his life) of having ceased to be a member of the original family and become an adopted person ...
(f) the relationship which the child has with relatives... and with any other person in relation to whom the court or agency considers the relationship to be relevant, including

(i) the likelihood of any relationship continuing and the value to the child of its doing so,
(ii) the ability and willingness of any of the child's relatives, or of any such person, to provide the child with a secure environment in which the child can develop, and otherwise meet the child's needs,
(iii) the wishes and feelings of any of the child's relatives, or of any such person, regarding the child.'

Splitting siblings

6.33 When a parent cannot manage to look after all of his children, but may be able to care for one of them, the court must balance the benefits of keeping siblings together against the advantage of being brought up by a natural parent. This is a difficult decision and the court must look at each case individually. Much will depend on the strength of the sibling relationship. In one case, where the plan was that contact between the siblings should continue in any event, the court held that the benefit of keeping one child with his father outweighed the disadvantages of splitting the siblings.[20]

Babies and young children

6.34 A local authority seeking to remove a child at or shortly after birth must be prepared to justify this draconian action, even on an interim basis. It is often difficult to balance the need of most babies for extensive contact with their mothers with the demands placed on local authority resources, particularly where contact between mother and child must be supervised.[21]

6.35 If a final care order is to be made, it is often the case that the younger the child the more likely it is that the court will be prepared to endorse a care plan that provides for the child to be adopted from its natural family. There are two reasons for this: first, the stability that adoption offers in comparison to a childhood spent moving around different foster homes and care homes; and secondly, the fact that the younger the child is, the greater the chances are of a successful adoption. As a rule of thumb, children who are seven and older are significantly less likely to be placed for adoption.

6.36 Although a local authority may (and, where appropriate, should) make plans for issuing legal proceedings before the birth of a child, no application for any order may be made until the child is born. Good practice dictates that (i) a risk assessment of the parents should be commenced immediately upon the social workers being made aware of the pregnancy and completed at least four weeks before the expected delivery date, (ii) the assessment should be disclosed to the parents and, if instructed, their solicitors and (iii) the social work team

---

[20] *Re D* [1999] 1 FLR 134.
[21] See, eg, *Re M* [2003] EWHC 850 (Admin); [2003] 2 FLR 171; *Kirklees Metropolitan District Council v S (Contact to Newborn Babies)* [2006] 1 FLR 333.

should provide to the legal team all relevant documentation necessary to start proceedings no less than seven days before the expected due date.[22] If (iii) has not been possible and the grounds for emergency intervention exist, an emergency protection order may be sought following the child's birth, or the child may be taken into police protection (see **Chapter 5**). Local authorities, hospital staff and other professionals must be aware of the limits of their powers where it is proposed that a newborn baby should be removed from its mother. If none of the orders discussed has been obtained and it is not possible to take the child into police protection, the only circumstances in which a professional may intervene are those in which it is necessary to protect a child from immediate violence at the hands of a parent (in reliance on the wider principle that any person is entitled to intervene to prevent an actual or threatened criminal assault).[23]

Older children

6.37 The older the child is, the greater the importance placed on her wishes and feelings will be given serious consideration. Since the case of *Gillick v West Norfolk and Wisbech Area Health Authority*[24] in 1986 the courts have had to pay careful attention to the views of a child whose level of maturity and understanding means that she is competent to make many decisions for herself.

6.38 The age at which children's views attract great (and near-determinative) weight will vary according to the nature and seriousness of the matter in question and the maturity of the child. In private law proceedings, children tend to achieve this level of competence younger than in care proceedings: it is not uncommon that the views of a child as young as 10 will tip the balance in an application about where the child should live or with whom and when the child should spend time. In care proceedings, however, the stakes tend to be higher and the child may not have the ability to appreciate, for example, any risk of emotional harm. Although children aged (say) 10 to 13 may have clearly expressed views, they may not have the maturity to make an informed judgment in the context of their welfare needs in the long term.

6.39 In practice, a child's age and sense of independence may make it almost impossible for the local authority to effect a care plan that is contrary to her wishes, notwithstanding that it may be in her long-term interests. The local authority may find itself forced to compromise by providing a package of support to the child at home, if the alternative is a foster placement that carries a high risk of breaking down.

---

[22] *Nottingham City Council v LM and Others* [2016] EWHC 11 (Fam); [2016] 2 FKR 1221, FD.
[23] *R(G) v Nottingham City Council* [2008] EWHC 400 (Admin); [2008] 1 FLR 1668.
[24] *Gillick v West Norfolk and Wisbech Area Health Authority* [1986] 1 FLR 224; see **3.18**.

Very young parents

6.40 It is the welfare of the child who is the subject of the proceedings that is paramount, even when one or both of the parents is also a child. Proceedings should be issued on the day of birth and, where the mother is very young (in the case of *Re R*, the mother was 13 when she gave birth), the case should be transferred without delay to the High Court[25] and a separate guardian at litem appointed for the mother immediately. It is not inevitable that babies of very young mothers should be adopted: where there is family or other support for the mother this may well not be the case. However, where the mother's own background or vulnerability makes it likely that the local authority will seek a care order with a plan for adoption, the local authority should begin planning for both mother and baby at an early stage, well before the birth.[26]

Physical and learning disabilities

6.41 A child's special needs may in the end be the factor that determines whether or not his parents can provide him with adequate care. However, it is important to bear in mind the services that a local authority must provide to children in need, a category that includes disabled children (see **Chapter 4**). Local authorities should be prepared to explain what support services have been or may be provided to the family of a disabled child, and why his parents are nevertheless unable to care for him, before seeking a care order.

6.42 Similar considerations may apply, with similar caveats, to particularly gifted children. A parent with learning disabilities may struggle to meet the needs of a very bright child. Again, however, the local authority should proceed with caution: the aim of the court is not to provide the child with a designer family, and the benefits to a child of making a care order must be clear and compelling if they are to outweigh the advantages of being brought up by a natural parent.

6.43 Parents who themselves suffer from learning disabilities may provide their children with care that can be termed inadequate. However, this will not necessarily mean that the threshold criteria are met and the courts and local authorities should be particularly careful to avoid the risks of social engineering when dealing with such parents.[27] Additionally, the court, CAFCASS and the local authority must each carry out its functions in accordance with the Equality Act 2010. The court must take steps to ensure that the parents can participate actively in the proceedings, including the appointment and funding of specialist support. Comprehensive guidance was set out by Sir James Munby P in *Re D (Adoption) (No 3)*.[28]

---

[25] This is likely now to mean a transfer to a High Court judge sitting in the Family Court.
[26] *Re R* [2000] 2 FLR 660.
[27] *Re L* [2007] 1 FLR 2050.
[28] *Re D (Adoption) (No 3)* [2017] 1 FLR 237, FD.

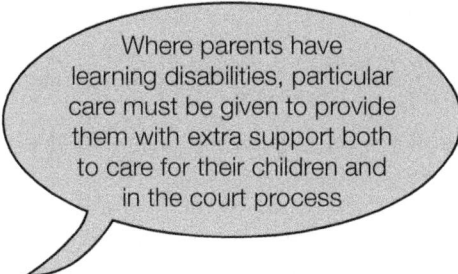

The care plan

6.44 The variety of situations which may lead to an application for a care or supervision order illustrates the need for local authorities to place the child's particular needs and circumstances at the heart of their planning for the child. These needs must inform not only the placement that is to be offered to the child but the educational, therapeutic and other services that will be provided to her and the contact she will have with her birth family. The court will measure the permanence provisions in the local authority's care plan against the pointers contained in the welfare checklist and will be concerned to see that the child's needs, as indicated by the welfare checklist, will be met. The content and structure of the local authority's care plan is discussed more fully below at **6.74–6.77**.

CARE PROCEEDINGS: APPLICATION AND PROCEDURE

The parties

6.45 The applicant for a care or supervision order is almost always the local authority. The only other body at present authorised to bring care proceedings is the NSPCC; in practice, it is far more likely that the NSPCC will refer the case to the local authority.[29] Regardless of who made the application, any care or supervision order will place the child in the care or under the supervision of a local authority.

6.46 The automatic respondents to an application for a care or supervision order are the child and any person who has parental responsibility for him.[30] In addition the local authority is obliged to give notice of the proceedings to:

✓ any person with whom the child is living;

✓ any local authority providing accommodation for the child;

---

[29] The NSPCC has a duty before making an application to consult with the local authority in whose area the child is ordinarily resident: CA 1989, s 31(6).
[30] FPR 2010, r 12.3.

- ✓ any person providing a refuge for the child;
- ✓ any party to pending relevant court proceedings relating to the child; and
- ✓ any parent (ie father) without parental responsibility.[31]

6.47 These persons will be informed of the date and place of the first hearing but will not be served with the application or any papers that have been filed. They may attend the hearing and apply to be joined as parties to the proceedings. The old test for joinder (whether the respondent's position disclosed an arguable case) has been refined in the light of the HRA 1998 and the Art 8 rights of extended family members as well as parents to a private and family life.[32] However, where a person's position or point of view is identical to that of an existing party, it is unlikely that he or she will also be joined to the proceedings.[33]

6.48 A father without parental responsibility is in a stronger position. Although he is not automatically a party and will require the court's permission to take part in the proceedings, this permission will be granted unless there is a good reason for refusing it.[34]

6.49 Once a person has been joined as a party to the proceedings his or her Art 6 right (to a fair trial) are engaged. This does not always extend to the right to see all of the papers filed in the proceedings: in rare cases, where disclosure of all the papers would be an unacceptable infringement of another party's right to a private and family life, the court may order limited confidentiality.[35]

6.50 Where the factors that led to a person being joined as a party cease to apply, the court may order that party's removal from the proceedings.

Intervenors

6.51 Where allegations are made within proceedings against a person who is not a party, or where a non-party's interests may be affected by the proceedings, the court may direct that that person participates in the proceedings to a limited extent, without becoming a full party. He or she may have legal representation but is unlikely to see all the papers in the proceedings or attend for the entirety of the hearing. The judge must determine the extent of the intervenor's participation and the way in which the relevant evidence will be presented. A prime example of a person who may be permitted to intervene is a person against whom serious allegations of abuse have been made, but who is not otherwise a party to the proceedings.

---

[31] Ibid, r 4.4.
[32] *Re J* [2002] EWCA Civ 1346; [2003] 1 FLR 114.
[33] *Re W* [2004] EWHC 3342 (Fam); [2005] 2 FLR 468.
[34] *Re B* [1999] 2 FLR 408.
[35] *Re C* [1996] 1 FLR 797.

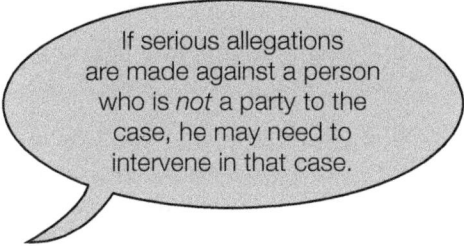

Allocation of proceedings

6.52 Proceedings are issued in the Family Court. When deciding to which level of judge in the Family Court an application for a care or supervision order is allocated, the 'gatekeeping team' (ie normally, a lay justice's legal advisor and district judge, with the team headed by the local designated family judge) will take account of the complexity of the case. At any point in the proceedings, the case can then be re-allocated. Allocation and re-allocation is guided by the *President's Guidance on Allocation and Gatekeeping for Care, Supervision and other Proceedings under Part IV of the Children Act 1989 (Public Law)*, 22 April 2014. Wherever possible, courts will seek to ensure judicial continuity for a set of proceedings, ie that one judge hears all hearings in a case.

The designated local authority

6.53 Any local authority may initiate care proceedings, but if a care order is made the local authority named in the care order must be that where the child is ordinarily resident or, if the child is not ordinarily resident in any local authority, the authority where the circumstances arose that led to the making of the order.[36] In terms of a supervision order, a local authority can only be designated under the order if it agrees or is the one in which the child lives or will live.[37]

6.54 In most cases, the designated local authority is the same as the authority that brings the proceedings. On occasion, it is necessary to determine which is the designated authority. The courts have consistently shown their disapproval of lengthy litigation over what should be a practical and administrative matter.[38] The underlying issue, particularly in a long or complex case, is almost always one of resources.

6.55 Because children will sometimes be placed in foster care outside their 'home' authority, a child's ordinary residence is to be determined by reference

---

[36] CA 1989, s 31(8).
[37] CA 1989, Sch 3, para 9.
[38] See *Northamptonshire County Council v Islington Borough Council* [1999] 2 FLR 881 and *Re W (A Child: Designation of Local Authority)* [2016] EWCA Civ 366.

to where the child was living before being accommodated. Any period in local authority accommodation does not count for the purposes of determining ordinary residence.

6.56 Where the designated local authority is not the authority bringing the proceedings, the two authorities should liaise as soon as possible and, depending on the stage that has been reached, the designated local authority may take over the proceedings. There should be a structured handover with the two authorities working jointly for a period on the case.

The role of the court

6.57 The court cannot make a care or supervision order except on an application by the local authority or other authorised person. It may make a care order on an application for a supervision order, and vice versa. The only exception to the general rule is that the court may make an interim care or supervision order if it has made a s 37 direction requiring the local authority to investigate the child's circumstances (see **5.14–5.17**).

6.58 The court's power under the Crime and Disorder Act 1998 to make a care order on non-compliance with a child safety order was removed by the Children Act 2004 from 1 March 2005: see **5.93–5.98** for child safety orders and parenting orders under the 1998 Act.

6.59 The court's role is investigative. Even where the parties have come to an agreement, it is the duty of the judge to scrutinise that agreement and ensure that the threshold criteria have been made out, the proposed order is necessary, proportionate and in the child's interests, and that the care plan will best meet her needs.

The Public Law Outline

6.60

The Public Law Outline: FPR 2010, PD 12A

Prescribes in detail the steps that must be taken by local authorities prior to issuing care proceedings and by all parties and the court during the proceedings themselves

The Public Law Outline – set out in the Family Procedure Rules 2010, PD 12A – sets out a strict timetable in care proceedings, including detailed provisions as to the number, type and timings of various hearings. Central to the new Public Law Outline is the introduction by the Children and Families Act 2014 of the '26-week target' in care proceedings, which is set out in CA 1989, s 32. Parties and courts are expected to devote significant effort to disposing of a case within the 'target'. Extensions, in appropriate cases, can be granted, with each extension being for a maximum of eight weeks.[39] It has been suggested that there are three categories of case in which an extension of the '26-week target' may be appropriate: (i) cases where this is clear from the outset (such as, extremely complex medical evidence, FDAC-type[40] cases, complicated international cases, and those in which the parents' disabilities require specialist assessment and support), (ii) cases that take an unexpected turn (such as new and serious allegations, death or imprisonment of a proposed carer, or where a realistic carer emerges only late in the day) and (iii) cases afflicted by litigation failure.[41]

> The latest statistics from the Ministry of Justice reveal that, from January to March 2018, 49% of cases were disposed of within 26 weeks and the average time for a case to reach first disposal was 30 weeks.

Attendance of the media at hearings

6.61 Transparency and accountability is at the heart of open justice and is a topic of some importance in the family justice system. In care proceedings, there is a particular tension between the competing ECHR rights of Art 10 (freedom of expression, and the related public interest in the justice system) and Art 8 (right to private and family life). In recent years, there has been a greater emphasis on the former, with changes to the rules and guidance about media attendance at hearings and an emphasis on the publication of (suitably anonymised) judgments.

6.62 Care proceedings are held in private,[42] with members of the public not therefore permitted to be present. Allied to that, there are strict rules on the disclosure of information from the proceedings. By the introduction of FPR 2010, r 27.11(2)(f), however, 'duly accredited representatives of news gathering and reporting organisations' are permitted to attend, unless ordered otherwise. At

---

[39] CA 1989, s 32(8).
[40] FDAC is the Family Drug and Alcohol Court, modelled on their counterparts in the US. FDAC works separately to but alongside the Family Court. It is a 'problem-solving' court based on 'therapeutic jurisprudence' and provides an intensive system in which the court has an active role in helping to resolve the problems that underlie the concerning behaviour.
[41] *Re S (A Child)* [2014] EWCC B44 (Fam).
[42] FPR 2010, r 27.10.

the same time, reporting restriction orders can be made to circumscribe the information that is reported. As noted above, there is now a presumption in many cases that judgments (as anonymised) should be reported.[43] This forms part of a shift in recent years toward greater openness and transparency in the family justice system.

Interim orders

6.63 It can be several months from the application to the final hearing of care proceedings. As set out above, cases will often go very close to, if not exceed, the '26-week target'. The court must decide whether there is a need for the local authority to share parental responsibility for the child during this interim period by means of an interim care order; whether there should be an interim supervision order; or whether the child will be sufficiently protected without an order until the matter is heard. At the same time, the court will need to determine whether the child can remain with, say, her parents or needs to be accommodated in, say, foster care.

6.64 The grounds for an interim order differ from those for a final order in that it is not necessary to prove that the threshold criteria are made out, but only that there are reasonable grounds for believing that this is the case.[44] The reason for this is that at an interim stage it is unlikely that the court will have sufficient evidence before it to make findings of fact on the threshold criteria. At a disputed hearing concerning an interim care or supervision order, the court may well hear oral evidence; but this evidence is likely to be limited and the court should take care not to make a premature determination of issues that are likely to be in dispute at the final hearing. An interim order will, generally, last until discharged or the conclusion of the proceedings.[45]

6.65 An interim order should not be determinative of the ultimate outcome of the proceedings. Even if the 'interim threshold criteria' are made out, the court must apply the welfare checklist to the question of an interim order. This approach should be informed by an understanding of the child's and parent's Art 6 and Art 8 rights under the ECHR. The court may only sanction such interference with the family's Art 8 rights as is necessary to ensure the child's immediate safety or well-being. Where this was not demonstrably the case, and the interim order was effectively determinative of the outcome of the final hearing, the interference with the parents' Art 6 rights to a fair trial was unjustified.[46] In particular, the test for the removal of children from their family

---

[43] *Practice Guidance: Transparency in the Family Courts – Publication of Judgments,* 16 January 2014.
[44] CA 1989, s 38(2). The only exception to this is that if the court makes a 'lives with' order at an interim stage, it must also make an interim supervision order, without considering the threshold criteria, unless satisfied that the child's welfare would be adequately protected without it: s 38(3).
[45] CA 1989, s 38(4).
[46] *Re H* [2003] 1 FCR 350.

at an interim stage is a high one: the local authority must demonstrate that the child's safety demands immediate separation.[47]

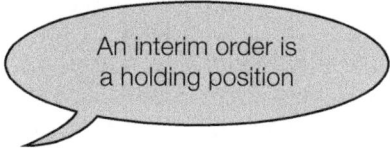
An interim order is a holding position

Exclusion requirements

6.66 When making an interim care order the court may impose an exclusion requirement if the removal of a person who is alleged to pose a risk to the child will enable the child to remain living at home. The grounds for an exclusion requirement under s 38A are that:

✓ there is reasonable cause to believe that if a relevant person is excluded from the place where the child lives, the child will cease to suffer, or be likely to suffer, significant harm; and

✓ there is someone else living in the home who is able to care for the child and consents to the imposition of an exclusion requirement.

An exclusion requirement may incorporate a power of arrest. It will cease to operate if the child is removed from the house by the local authority to alternative accommodation for a period of 24 hours. Additionally, the local authority has a general power to assist an alleged abuser to find alternative accommodation if this would enable a child at risk to remain at home.[48]

Fact-finding or split hearings

6.67 Where there is a significant dispute of fact between the local authority and the parents, it may be necessary to resolve this at an early stage. There may be good reasons for doing so. Courts, however, will permit an earlier hearing or trial to determine a significant factual dispute only where strictly necessary. The Court of Appeal has said that this should happen only in (a) the simplest cases where there is really only one factual issue to be decided and where, if the local authority does not make out its case on that issue, threshold is not met and the proceedings will come to an end and (b) the most complex medical causation cases where death or very serious medical issues have arisen and an accurate medical diagnosis is integral to the future care of the child concerned.[49] Any factual dispute will be determined by the court applying the civil standard of proof, namely that of the balance of probabilities. The burden of proving the facts underpinning the threshold criteria will be on the local authority (see **6.138**).

---

[47] *Re H (A Child) (Interim Care Order)* [2002] EWCA Civ 1932.
[48] CA 1989, Sch 2, para 5.
[49] *Re S (A Child)* [2014] EWCA Civ 25.

6.68 These earlier hearings are sometimes referred to as fact-finding or threshold hearings, because the making (or not) of the finding of fact may determine whether the threshold criteria are made out. It is important to bear in mind that, whilst in some cases the finding of fact will mean the threshold criteria are met (where the allegation is, say, serious sexual abuse), in others the disputed fact, while important, will not in itself meet the threshold criteria. In a third category of case there may be no dispute that the threshold criteria will be satisfied on the basis of either of two possible factual bases, but there is a need to establish which is correct.

Case Study:

(a) *A child tells his teacher that he has been sexually abused by his father. He is taken to the doctor and there is some medical evidence to support the allegation. The father denies it.*

If the court finds on the balance of probabilities that the abuse took place, the threshold criteria will be satisfied. If it does not make such a finding, the threshold is not crossed and the proceedings will come to an immediate end.

(b) *Social workers are told by a grandmother that several years ago her son-in-law used to beat up her daughter. The couple have children who appear happy and well cared for and have never shown signs of witnessing violence. Both parents deny the allegations.*

The court is asked to make a finding on whether the domestic violence occurred. If the court finds that it did not, the proceedings will come to an end. But even if the court finds that there was violence in the relationship, albeit many years ago, it will not automatically find the threshold criteria made out and may require some further evidence, probably from a child psychologist, as to any harm or likelihood of harm to the children.

(c) *A mother has over a period of 12 months attended A & E on several occasions, sometimes with her children, complaining that their father has hit her. The hospital records indicate that the mother appeared to be in pain, but do not disclose any visible injuries. The mother tells a social worker that on several occasions the children have witnessed violence and verbal abuse and have been terrified. When spoken to, the children say that 'daddy always hits mummy', but are unable to give any further details of what they have seen. Two days before the hearing the mother tells her GP that she made up all the allegations.*

If the court finds that violence has occurred and that the children have been involved and frightened by it, the threshold criteria will be made out. However, even if the court finds that no abuse of the mother has taken place, it is likely that the involvement of the children by the mother in her fabricated allegations against their father has caused them significant emotional harm and the court may find the threshold criteria made out on this basis.

6.69 For the difficult situation where it is impossible for the court to determine which of two or more people has caused the harm to the child, see below under 'Further issues' at **6.147–6.150.**

6.70 The fact-finding process and any subsequent welfare hearing are but stages of one hearing; after a fact-finding hearing the case is regarded as part-heard and must proceed before the same judge.

Assessments

6.71 Section 38(6) of the CA 1989 gives the court power, on making an interim care or supervision order, to direct a 'medical or psychiatric examination or other assessment of the child'. This subsection is used fairly widely to order a variety of assessments, from those focusing on the child's specific medical or educational needs to broad multidisciplinary assessments of the family dynamics and the parenting capacity of the adults. Where there is a dispute about whether an assessment is necessary, the court should consider primarily whether the proposed assessment will provide it with the information (or some of the information) required to make its decision at the conclusion of the case.

6.72 The parties should at an early stage put their minds to the consideration of what assessments if any are necessary. Unnecessary duplication of assessments should be avoided and the court may specifically direct that a proposed assessment is *not* to take place. See also the discussion of expert evidence at **6.123–6.129.**

6.73 Any proposed expert assessment will involve consideration of the available resources. The cost of assessing a large family at a flagship multidisciplinary unit can run into the tens of thousands. A residential mother and baby assessment is likely to cost over £1,000 per week. The House of Lords has held that to fall within the bounds of s 38(6), any proposed assessment must be an assessment 'of the child'; it may include assessment of a parent's relationship with the child or behaviour towards him, but the focus must be on the child and not the parent.[50] Arguments based on the local authority's available resources are relevant and a significant amount of parent-focused therapy is likely to place a proposed assessment outside the scope of s 38(6). The House of Lords dismissed the parents' arguments based on their own rights under the ECHR, Art 8, per Lord Scott: 'there is no Article 8 right to be made a better parent at public expense'.

The local authority's care plan

6.74 The local authority must inform the court and the other parties, at both interim and final stages, of its plans for the child. The court may not make a final order unless it has considered the permanence provisions of a care plan.[51]

---

[50] *Re G (Interim Care Order: Residential Assessment)* [2006] 1 FLR 601. See also *Re A (A Child)* [2009] EWHC 865 (Fam).
[51] CA 1989, ss 31(3A)–(3B).

The care plan is a key document in care proceedings: it is only by reference to its plans for the child that a local authority can satisfy the court that a care or supervision order will be better for the child than making no order at all.

6.75 Guidance on the content of care plans is set out in regulations 5–6 of the Care Planning, Placement and Case Review (England) Regulations 2010.

6.76 The Public Law Outline creates an expectation that (save in a very urgent case) the local authority will file an interim care plan together with its application, as part of the pre-proceedings documentation.[52]

6.77 The local authority's implementation of its care plan following a final order, and the court's limited powers to continue to monitor and oversee the care plan, are discussed at **4.47–4.49**.

Parallel planning

6.78 The period from application to the case's conclusion will often be a long one and it is important that, while the court process is underway, time does not stand still as far as long-term planning for the child's future is concerned. Often the issue to be determined in the proceedings will be whether the child's long-term future lies with his parents or other family members, or outside the family. With younger children this may mean an adoptive family; for older children, the only alternative to a placement at home may be long-term local authority accommodation.

6.79 To ensure that, once the final hearing is concluded, there is the minimum of delay before permanent plans for the child are put into place, local authorities are encouraged to pursue a policy of parallel planning. The plans for rehabilitation to the birth family will run in parallel with plans for a placement elsewhere. Ideally, once the final hearing has concluded, the local authority will be in a position immediately to implement its long-term plans. This may mean that the child's case has already been presented to the relevant panels within the local authority that deal with adoption and fostering and some enquiries regarding the availability of alternative carers have been carried out. For details of the family-finding process, in both fostering and adoption contexts, see **Chapters 4** and **7**[53] respectively

Concurrent planning

6.80 Concurrent planning is a specific form of parallel planning (above). In rare cases the local authority may place a child with foster parents who are prepared to adopt her if at the end of the proceedings she cannot be rehabilitated to the birth family. For obvious reasons the foster parents must be carefully prepared and trained and this approach should not be taken without

---

[52] Family Procedure Rules 2010, PD 12A, 1.3 table.
[53] At **7.95** ff.

thorough consideration. An amendment to the Adoption and Children Act 2002 introduced by the Children and Social Work Act 2017 requires the court, when making decisions under the Adoption and Children Act 2002, to have specific regard to the child's relationship with 'any person who is a prospective adopter with whom the child is placed.'[54]

Final order or interim order?

6.81 When should the court make a final order and (subject to the review mechanisms) let go of the case? There is always some uncertainty in the plans for a child's future, especially if the child is very young, and if a final care order is to be made the court must be prepared to leave the resolution of issues that may arise in the future to the local authority. However, if the central features of a care plan cannot be finalised because important information is still outstanding (for example, the result of an assessment that may recommend either adoption or long-term foster care) the court should not make a final care order, even when it is not disputed that this will be the final outcome whatever the care plan. In such a case, the judge should make an interim care order until the outstanding information is available.

6.82 If the court disagrees with a local authority's final care plan, but considers that a care order is necessary, it may make an interim order and invite the local authority to reconsider its plan for the child. In rare cases, it may refuse to make the care order. The court does not have the power to impose conditions on a care order, or to dictate to the local authority where the child should be placed.[55]

Withdrawing the application

6.83 An application for a care order may be withdrawn only with the leave of the court. Where the court considers that the child's welfare demands that the proceedings should continue, and the local authority's contrary view means that the case is not presented as fully as the court feels necessary, the court may use its power to call witnesses itself.[56]

Discharging the order

6.84 An application to discharge a care or supervision order may be made by:

✓ the child;

✓ the local authority; or

✓ any person with parental responsibility.

---

[54] ACA 2002, s 1(4)(f).
[55] *Re T* [1994] 2 FLR 423.
[56] *Re N* [2000] 1 FLR 134.

6.85 If a previous application for discharge has failed, no person may make a further application without the leave of the court until six months have elapsed.[57]

6.86 The procedure is similar to that followed on an application for a care or supervision order. The application is made to the court which made the original order, and the automatic respondents are, in addition to the usual respondents to an application for a care or supervision order, the parties to the original application. Where the child is under a supervision order, her supervisor is also a respondent. Any person may be removed or joined as a party.

6.87 When a child is in care, the local authority is obliged to consider at each 'looked after child review'[58] whether an application should be made to discharge the care order.

6.88 The court may not substitute a care order for a supervision order, but it may substitute a supervision order for a care order. It need not consider the threshold criteria afresh.[59] On discharging an order, the court may make no order in respect of the child, or any s 8 order.

REPRESENTING THE CHILD

The role of the children's guardian

6.89 The child is automatically a respondent to care proceedings. However, the extent to which she will actively participate in those proceedings will vary according to her age and understanding. The court must appoint an officer of CAFCASS[60] to represent the child's interests in care proceedings[61] unless satisfied that it is not necessary to do so in order to safeguard her interests. When acting in this capacity, the officer is known as the children's guardian. He or she acts independently of the local authority and the other parties.

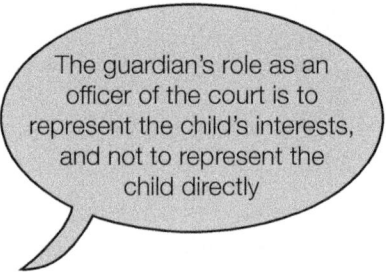

The guardian's role as an officer of the court is to represent the child's interests, and not to represent the child directly

6.90 The guardian will meet the child or children and ascertain their views, and has a duty also to support the child and give advice. Under the Public Law

---

[57] CA 1989, s 91(15).
[58] See **Ch 4**.
[59] CA 1989, s 39(4).
[60] See **Ch 1**.
[61] And other specified proceedings: CA 1989, s 41(6).

Outline,[62] the standard directions given by the court on issue of the application will include a request to CAFCASS to prepare and file an initial case analysis and recommendations. There will frequently be cases where the recommendation of the guardian is at odds with the children's wishes. If the children are very young and their wishes are plainly at odds with their interests, the court is likely to give their wishes little weight. However, when an older child disagrees with her guardian about what is in her interests, the child's solicitor should consider whether she has sufficient understanding to give direct instructions.

6.91 Where the court is asked to make findings of fact, particularly regarding issues of harm, the role of the guardian is not to come down firmly on one side or the other but to assist the court. This may mean flagging up relevant evidence that the other parties have for whatever reason not sought to put before the court. The guardian should be wary of expressing a view on factual issues that are likely to be in dispute (such as the truth or otherwise of a child's allegations of abuse); the role of adjudicating on factual disputes is for the judge alone.

6.92 Over the past few years, there has been an increased emphasis on ensuring the participation of children in family proceedings. It remains rare that it will be in a child's interests to hear the evidence presented or discussed, or to see her parents cross-examined. Steps will be taken, however, to ensure a child's participation in other ways: that could include writing a letter to or coming to meet the judge in chambers. A meeting with the judge is governed by the *Guidelines for Judges Meeting Children who are Subject to Family Proceedings,* April 2010. Equally, many more children give oral evidence in family proceedings than was previously the case. The presumption against them doing so has been removed and important judgments from the Supreme Court and Court of Appeal have emphasised this.[63] The family justice system still, however, lags some way behind its criminal counterpart in the frequency with which children give oral evidence.

The role of the solicitor for the child

6.93 The solicitor for the child is appointed by the children's guardian, or by the court if no guardian has been appointed.[64] His or her role is to represent the child. If the child is too young to give instructions the solicitor takes instructions from the guardian.

6.94 When a solicitor is appointed for an older child who, in the solicitor's opinion, has sufficient understanding to give instructions, he or she must take instructions directly from the child. Where there is a conflict between the child's views and the guardian's, the solicitor must act as an advocate for the child. In such a case, the court must be informed of the conflict as soon as possible. The

---

[62] See **6.60**.
[63] *Re W (Children) (Family Proceedings: Evidence)* [2010] UKSC 12 and *Re E (A Child)* [2016] EWCA Civ 473.
[64] In some cases, CAFCASS will be appoint a 'duty guardian' to provide advice and recommendations at an urgent hearing before a guardian is appointed to the case.

guardian will remain involved in proceedings but, save in exceptional cases in which CAFCASS grants funding for legal representation, will represent himself, as the child's solicitor will separate and represent solely the child.

6.95 The question of when a child becomes able to instruct a solicitor in his own right is a difficult one. The cases on this issue suggest an older threshold age than might be expected. It has been pointed out that what matters, for the purposes of a child being able to instruct his own solicitor, is not so much his chronological age or even his intellectual ability, but whether or not he has the emotional and other resources to analyse the evidence and understand its implications. A 15-year-old, who in two years' time will be too old for the court to make a care order, will nevertheless not always have sufficient understanding to give instructions. The complexity of the issues at stake will be a factor: there will be some cases where it is very unlikely that even a bright teenager will have the necessary maturity and experience to participate directly in the proceedings.

6.96 The decision is initially one for the child's solicitor. However, he or she would be well advised, particularly in cases where it seems that the child may be psychologically or emotionally disturbed, to seek an expert opinion on the child's level of understanding. If there is uncertainty, the court can decide the issue.

EVIDENCE

Fundamental principles

6.97 This is a principle that applies, subject to exceptions, in all areas of the law. In criminal proceedings, for example, the general principle is limited by fairly detailed and stringent rules that restrict, among other matters, the admissibility of hearsay evidence and evidence concerning a defendant's previous criminal history.

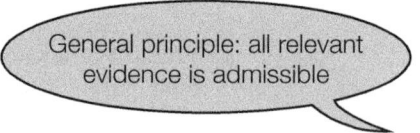

General principle: all relevant evidence is admissible

6.98 In proceedings relating to children there are only a few exceptions to the general rule that relevant evidence should be admitted. The main reason for this is that children cases, particularly in public law, are non-adversarial. The court's primary role is not to adjudicate between the parties to the proceedings but to determine and promote the interests of the child. It is important, therefore, that the court has as full a picture as possible. For example, hearsay evidence that is extremely damaging to one of the adult parties, and would perhaps be inadmissible against that party in criminal proceedings, is admissible in care proceedings.

6.99 One general rule of evidence that is applicable to CA 1989 proceedings, and should be borne in mind, is the rule against opinion evidence. In general, a witness may only give evidence of his opinion (as opposed to evidence of what he saw or heard or did) if the court accepts that he is appropriately qualified to do so, ie that he is an expert in the particular field. The court should be careful to prevent non-experts giving evidence of their opinion on issues that are solely a matter for the court.

6.100 Notwithstanding any statute or other rule of evidence, the court may take into account any statement contained in the guardian's report, and any evidence given in connection with matters referred to in the report, insofar as it is relevant to any question the court is considering.[65] Similarly, any document from the local authority records copied by the guardian is admissible as evidence of any matter referred to by him.[66]

6.101 The standard of proof in all civil proceedings, including family proceedings, is the balance of probabilities. The party seeking a finding from the court – in care proceedings, usually the local authority – must satisfy the court that it is more probable than not that the allegation he makes is true. The court adopts a 'binary' approach with the result that an allegation is either proved or not proved on the balance of probabilities. Where an allegation is not proved, any subsequent assessment of risk to the child will proceed on the basis that the alleged matter did not occur.

Hearsay evidence

6.102 The original rule against hearsay evidence has been almost completely eroded in civil and family proceedings. It remains in criminal proceedings, although weakened by the Criminal Justice Act 2003. It is worth having an understanding of the original rule in order to appreciate the approach the court will take to hearsay evidence.

6.103 Hearsay evidence is evidence of something said by a person who is not himself giving evidence in the proceedings when it is put before the court in order to establish the truth of what was said.

Case Study:

(a) Social worker: 'I went to the house and knocked on the door. A neighbour told me that the family had gone away.'

This is hearsay evidence if, as seems likely, it is put before the court to establish the truth of what was said, namely that the family had gone away.

(b) Social worker: 'I went to the house and knocked on the door. A neighbour shouted out, "Go away you meddling old busybody!"'

This is not hearsay evidence: it is not put before the court to establish the truth of what was said. It is simply direct evidence that the neighbour said it.

---

[65] CA 1989, s 41(11).
[66] Ibid, s 42(2).

6.104 The Children (Admissibility of Hearsay Evidence) Order 1993[67] provides that in family proceedings evidence given in connection with the upbringing, maintenance or welfare of a child will be admissible, notwithstanding that it is hearsay. In practice, this is construed widely and includes most evidence that a party is likely to want to put before the court in care proceedings, including evidence of criminal or dangerous behaviour on the part of the adults insofar as it is relevant to the child's welfare.

6.105 If hearsay evidence does not relate to the upbringing, maintenance or welfare of a child, it can be admitted under the Civil Evidence Act 1995, s 1(1), which provides that in civil proceedings (including family proceedings) evidence shall not be excluded on the ground that it is hearsay. By s 2, the party seeking to rely on hearsay evidence must give notice of this to the other side, but failure to do so does not render the evidence inadmissible and this rule is honoured more in the breach than the observance.

6.106 It is difficult to think of a relevant hearsay statement that would not be admissible in care proceedings, whether by means of its inclusion in the guardian's report or under the Civil Evidence Act 1995 or the Children (Admissibility of Hearsay Evidence) Order 1993. However, whether or not a statement is hearsay is important when the court comes to consider how much weight should be given to it. Second hand or more remote hearsay ('the neighbour told me that her sister heard from her daughter's policeman boyfriend that Bob was a known paedophile') will carry much less weight than direct evidence. In cases where a serious allegation is made and adult witnesses are potentially available to give direct evidence, the court will generally expect the local authority to call them to give evidence rather than to rely on hearsay evidence of what they have said.

Interviewing children

6.107 Statements made by children may sometimes form the central part of a local authority's or other party's evidence. Where children have spoken to a social worker, their guardian, or indeed a parent, about their wishes and feelings about their family or their future, this evidence can often simply be reported directly to the court: indeed, this is one of the important functions of the children's guardian.

6.108 Occasionally, however, children will allege to a party or other person something that, if it is true, will have extremely serious consequences for the child and/or any other person. Often this will be an allegation of serious physical and/or sexual abuse. If this is the case the local authority must take care to ensure that the evidence is put before the court in a careful and responsible way. The *Report of the Inquiry into Child Abuse in Cleveland 1987*[68] stands as a warning as to what may happen when an investigation into allegations of sexual abuse is not undertaken in the proper manner. Equally, as set out at **6.92** there

---

[67] SI 1993/621.
[68] Available through the National Archives.

is an increased recognition of the desirability and ability of children to give oral evidence in family proceedings, as long as this is properly facilitated.

6.109 When an allegation is made that is likely to lead to a criminal investigation, the police and social services may jointly conduct an interview with the child. The guidance for such interviews is set out in *Achieving Best Evidence in Criminal Proceedings, Guidance on interviewing victims and witnesses, and guidance on using special measures,* Ministry of Justice, March 2011.[69] Whilst this document was primarily written for interviews that take place within the context of a criminal investigation, it should be followed by any agency conducting an interview of a child who has made serious allegations that are likely to be considered in court proceedings. It applies, therefore, equally to family proceedings.[70] It covers not only the interview itself but the preparation process. The aim is to ensure that the evidence given by the child in interview is as reliable and uncontaminated as possible.

6.110 The interview should be conducted by a trained and experienced interviewer. Usually there will be a 'lead' interviewer and a second interviewer. It is important that the interview process should not be forced and that if a child is reluctant to answer questions the interviewer should take care not to coerce him.

Interviewing children: key checklist

✓ Preparation
- Is a pre-interview assessment required?
- What inter-agency co-operation has already taken place? Has there been or should there be a strategy discussion between the police, social services and any other agencies?
- To what extent has the child already been questioned by professionals?
- Who should carry out the interview?
- If the child is very young or very traumatized, is an intermediary necessary?
- Consider maximum length of the interview and breaks
- Discussion with the child regarding the purpose and process of the interview

✓ The interview
- Establish rapport with the child, including establishing whether the child understands the difference between truth and lies?
- Give an opportunity for free narrative recall
- Questions from the interviewer (avoid leading questions; open-ended questions elicit the best evidence)
- Closure phase, including summary of the evidence given

---

[69] Available online: www.cps.gov.uk/sites/default/files/documents/legal_guidance/best_evidence_in_criminal_proceedings.pdf.

[70] *Re W and F (Children)* [2015] EWCA Civ 1300, at [33], '*It is accepted that its* [the guidance's] *relevance is not confined to criminal proceedings but extends to proceedings in the family courts.*'

Disclosure

6.111 The local authority has a duty to disclose all relevant information in its possession that might assist a parent or any other person against whom an allegation has been made in rebutting the allegation. The courts are likely to interpret this duty widely: it extends to the disclosure of assessments carried out by the local authority that may not support its case. Local authorities that withhold disclosure of such material are likely to be severely criticised.

6.112 The children's guardian is entitled to, and should, examine and take copies of documents and records held by the local authority that are relevant to the child.[71] These may then be filed as evidence in the proceedings.

Public interest immunity

6.113 A local authority may apply to court for an order permitting it to withhold disclosure of a document on the ground that disclosure would damage the public interest: this is known as public interest immunity. The relevant procedural rules are set out in the Family Procedure Rules 2010, r 21.3. The onus is on the applicant to demonstrate that an application should be granted. That application can be made without telling the other parties, and it will be for the judge to decide whether those other parties should be told. In rare cases, the court may consider appointing a special advocate to see the documents and to represent the interests of parties to whom documents are not disclosed.[72] Most recently, these issues have arisen in the context of police and security service intelligence, for example in cases focused on parents who have allegedly become radicalised by ISIS.[73]

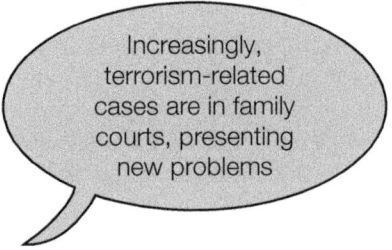

Increasingly, terrorism-related cases are in family courts, presenting new problems

6.114 Where the police or Crown Prosecution Service (CPS) have provided the local authority with information upon the understanding that such information will not be further disclosed, the local authority must not disseminate the information any further without leave of the court. This does not apply to disclosure to the guardian, who has the right to inspect any of the local authority's records; but it does apply to the other parties, who must make an

---

[71] CA 1989, s 42(1).
[72] *Re T (Wardship: Impact of Police Intelligance)* [2009] EWHC 2440 (Fam), [2010] 1 FLR 1048.
[73] *Re C (A Child) (No. 2) (Application for Public Interest Immunity)* [2017] EWHC 692 (Fam).

application for disclosure to the court. If the application is resisted the police and/or CPS should be given the opportunity to make representations.

6.115 In very rare cases the court may order that material should be disclosed in the proceedings, but *not* disclosed to a particular party. This will only happen where there are very powerful arguments against disclosure based on the interests of a child, party, witness or victim.[74]

Confidentiality and disclosure outside the proceedings

6.116 As a general rule, the documents filed in all proceedings relating to children are confidential to those proceedings. Disclosure outside those proceedings to non-parties who may have an interest in the proceedings is strictly controlled. If disclosure is made in contravention of statute or rules, this is likely to amount to a contempt of court.[75] Disclosure of material from proceedings under CA 1989 is governed by the Family Procedure Rules 2010, rr 12.72–12.75, Practice Direction 12G and – in the context of cases about adoption – Practice Direction 14E. The parties may, without the court's permission, disclose information from the proceedings to legal representatives, CAFCASS, expert witnesses (whose instruction has been authorised by the court) and the Legal Aid Agency. Additionally, parties are permitted to disclose information as follows:

Documentation	Disclosable to whom	For what purpose
Any information relating to the proceedings	A lay adviser (McKenzie friend, lay adviser, or provider of pro bono legal services)	Seeking advice or assistance in connection with the case
	Any person	By confidential discussion, to obtain support, advice or assistance in the conduct of proceedings
	Health care or counselling professional	Seeking health care or advice or counselling
	Children's Commissioner	Referral of a case
	A person carrying out an approved research project	Carrying out the research project

---

[74] *Re C* [1996] 1 FLR 797.
[75] A detailed discussion of the statutory provisions governing the publication of confidential information relating to proceedings concerning children is beyond the scope of this work. Reference should be made to Hershman and McFarlane *Children Law and Practice* (Family Law) paras C1206–C1211.

Documentation	Disclosable to whom	For what purpose
	Any person	To engage in mediation or other forms of alternative dispute resolution
	Any person	To make and pursue a complaint against a person or body concerned in the proceedings
	An adoption agency	To enable sharing of information between adoption agencies
	A local authority medical adviser appointed in relation to adoption	To enable the medical adviser to carry out his functions
	European Court of Human Rights	To make an application to the ECtHR
	The Secretary of State, a McKenzie Friend, a lay adviser, the Child Maintenance and Enforcement Commission, or the Upper Tier Tribunal dealing with certain appeals under the Child Support Act 1991	For a purpose connected with that appeal
Text or summary of all or part of a judgment	Police officer	Investigating a crime
	Crown Prosecution Service	Enabling it to carry out its legal functions

6.117 Legal representatives are further permitted to disclose information to those carrying out research, accreditation bodies and insurers, and those determining complaints or assessing quality assurance systems. In some circumstances, the information must be anonymised.[76]

6.118 In every case, the trial judge retains the power to restrict or permit disclosure notwithstanding the provisions of the rules. Any disclosure not permitted by the rules must be explicitly authorised by the court. For example, at the end of (or during) proceedings the police may seek disclosure of documents with a view to their use in criminal proceedings. This application should be made to the trial judge, who must strike a balance between the public interest in protecting the confidentiality of proceedings relating to children, and the public interest in making available to the police documentation that may assist them in carrying out their duties. The Court of Appeal has held that, in cases of

---

[76] FPR 2010, PD 12G, para 2.1.

serious crime, the need to protect children by disclosure to the police is likely to outweigh the public interest in the confidentiality of family proceedings.[77]

6.119 It seems that disclosure will be ordered more readily when a defendant seeks the information: Munby J held that it would be an exceptional case where a family court would deny a defendant access to material that might help him defend himself against a serious criminal charge.[78]

6.120 There may be other occasions when it is in the public interest for information filed or findings made within the care proceedings to be disclosed to a third party. It is fairly common for the local authority to be given leave where a final order has been made to disclose limited documentation to the child's future adoptive parents, in order that they may have some understanding of the child's circumstances. Typically, the guardian's report and any relevant expert reports will be disclosed, edited to remove any material that the prospective adopters do not need to know. Where it is important that particular information remains confidential and not be disclosed to another party, the court should make a clear statement to that effect and should bear in mind that when a large volume of documentary material is to be disclosed, the risks of inadvertent disclosure are significant. The person who is to edit the material should be identified by name, and the chain of possession of the material should be spelled out.[79]

6.121 Otherwise the occasions when disclosure is ordered outside the proceedings will be rare. Factors weighing against disclosure are, chiefly, the risk of harm to the child and the public interest in ensuring that parents, professionals and witnesses are able to speak freely and frankly. In support of this principle, *CA 1989, s 98(2)* provides that an admission made by a party in children proceedings shall not be evidence against him in any criminal proceedings, other than on a charge of perjury. Disclosure outside the proceedings tends to be ordered only where there is a compelling reason to do so, such as the risk of harm to others; but even in such cases disclosure is not automatic and may be refused. The following matters have been the subject of an application to disclose:

✓ a finding in care proceedings that a doctor had sexually abused his daughter (disclosure to the General Medical Council authorised);[80]

✓ evidence in care proceedings that a party was seeking to deceive the immigration authorities (disclosure authorised);

✓ findings of sexual abuse of children (disclosure to the housing association of where the abuser lived authorised, but general disclosure to any future

---

[77] *Re EC* [1996] 2 FLR 725.
[78] *Re Z* [2003] EWHC 61 (Fam); [2003] 1 FLR 1194.
[79] *Re R (Secure Editing of Documents)* [2007] EWHC 876 (Fam); [2007] 2 FLR 759.
[80] *A County Council v W and Others* [1997] 1 FLR 574.

housing association or landlord to whom the abuser might make an application for housing refused).[81]

6.122 The rules of confidentiality should not prevent the sharing of information between agencies, including social services and the police, which are concerned with child protection.

THE ROLE OF THE EXPERT WITNESS

6.123 The courts rely heavily on the evidence of experts, particularly in contested public law children cases. This does not mean, however, that the expert usurps the role of the court in deciding the outcome of the case and the future for the child. The final decision is always that of the judge. An expert may only give his opinion on matters in which he has professional expertise. It is unlikely that expert evidence will assist in determining matters which are factually in dispute, and, in particular, issues that depend on the credibility of a witness are a matter for the judge alone.

6.124 The use of expert evidence is strictly controlled by the court.

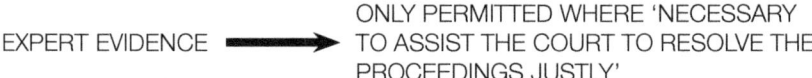

EXPERT EVIDENCE ⟶ ONLY PERMITTED WHERE 'NECESSARY TO ASSIST THE COURT TO RESOLVE THE PROCEEDINGS JUSTLY'

There are very detailed procedural rules for applying for and adducing expert evidence. These are set out in the Family Procedure Rules 2010, Pt 25, and the accompanying practice directions.

6.125 A medical practitioner involved in the treatment of the child is likely to be an important witness, both as to fact and as to the professional opinion upon the child's condition that informed the provision of treatment. Other medical experts, who were not involved in the child's treatment, may be instructed for the proceedings. The roles of the treating clinician and the court-appointed expert are separate and distinct in the court process. It is unusual for a treating clinician to be sent all the court papers and instructed to give a comprehensive expert overview. Nevertheless, their contribution to the case (based upon first-hand knowledge) is likely to be important both to the court appointed experts and to the ultimate decision.

6.126 No person may permit a child who is the subject of proceedings to be medically or psychiatrically examined or assessed in any way by an expert reporting to the court without the court's prior permission.[82] An assessment of the child will in most cases be carried out by an expert instructed jointly by the parties. However, in complex cases where, for example, medical opinion is conflicting or

---

[81] *Re C* [2002] EWHC 234 (Fam); [2002] 2 FLR 375.
[82] CFA 2010, s 13(3).

unclear, the interests of justice may demand that the parents should be permitted to instruct their own expert. A refusal to permit a party to call potentially relevant expert evidence may be a breach of Art 6 of the ECHR (right to a fair trial).

6.127 As noted above, the instruction of experts is governed by the Family Procedure Rules 2010, Pt 25, and the accompanying practice directions. Experts should be instructed at an early stage and their availability both to prepare a report and to attend the final hearing should be confirmed. Once this is done the letter of instruction should be sent out as soon as possible. Letters of instruction to an expert should be agreed between the instructing parties and should:

✓ set out the context in which the expert's opinion is sought (including any ethnic, cultural, religious or linguistic contexts);

✓ set out the questions approved by the court;

✓ list the documentation provided, or provide an indexed and paginated bundle, including an agreed list of essential reading and the procedural rules;

✓ factual background to the case in as neutral a manner as possible, identifying issues where there is a dispute of fact;

✓ remind the expert of his duty to the court, including his duty to provide an opinion that is independent of any party, to confine answers to matters within his expertise and, when expressing an opinion, to take account of all the material facts including any factors arising from ethnic, cultural, religious or linguistic concepts.

6.128 An expert witness, whether jointly instructed or not, must approach the case in an impartial and objective manner and must assist the court. Once he has reported, the party instructing him is under a duty to disclose the report to the court and the other parties, regardless of whether or not it supports that party's case. An expert may be called to give evidence by any party, or by the court.

6.129 Whatever their field of practice or country of origin, experts in family proceedings involving children in England and Wales must comply with the *Standards for Expert Witnesses in Children Proceedings in the Family Court*, and, where relevant, the accompanying appendices, including *UK Health and Social Care Professions and Statutory Regulators with Responsibilities within England and Wales* and *Examples of Professional Bodies/Associations Relating to Non-Statutorily Regulated Work*.[83]

---

[83] Each of these is appended to FPR 2010, PD 25B, which is available online: www.justice.gov.uk/courts/procedure-rules/family/practice_directions/practice-direction-25b-the-duties-of-an-expert,-the-experts-report-and-arrangements-for-an-expert-to-attend-court.

PARENTAL CONTACT WITH CHILDREN IN CARE

6.130 Before making a care order, including an interim order, the court must consider the proposed arrangements for contact and invite the parties to comment on them.[84] In the interim period, contact between the child and his parents, and others who have a significant relationship with him, should be maintained unless there are good reasons for restricting or suspending it.

6.131 The local authority has a duty under CA 1989, s 34(1), both in the interim period and following a final order, to allow the child to have reasonable contact with:

✓ his parents;

✓ any guardian of his;

✓ any person in whose favour a 'lives with' child arrangements order was in force immediately before the care order was made;

✓ any step parent who has parental responsibility (CA 1989, s 4A);

✓ any person with care of the child, prior to the care order, under an order made in the exercise of the High Court's inherent jurisdiction.[85]

6.132 In addition, the local authority's duties under CA 1989, Sch 2, Pt II (looked after children) apply to children subject to an interim or final care order. The local authority must, unless it is not reasonably practicable or consistent with the child's welfare, endeavour to promote contact between the child and any parent, person with parental responsibility, relative, friend or other person connected with him.[86] Any such person who is not a party to the proceedings may apply for leave to make an application for contact.

6.133 The court may make orders specifying the contact that is to take place between the child and any named person and imposing any conditions it feels are appropriate. If it does not do so, the local authority has a discretion regarding the amount of contact it offers, and any conditions imposed on that contact, subject to its duties above.

6.134 The local authority may suspend or terminate contact between the child and any person who would otherwise be entitled to reasonable contact under s 34(1). It may suspend contact without a court order for a period of up to seven days, provided that it is necessary to do so in order to safeguard or promote the child's welfare.[87] The remedy of the person affected is to apply to the court for a contact order.

---

[84] CA 1989, s 34(11).
[85] Ibid, s 34(1).
[86] CA 1989, Sch 2, s 15.
[87] Ibid, s 34(6).

Care and Supervision Orders

6.135 If the local authority wishes to refuse contact for a period in excess of seven days it must apply to the court for an order authorising it to do so. This is a permissive rather than a mandatory order and the local authority may use it as it sees fit. The application may be made at any time, but is commonly made in the run-up to a final hearing where the final care plan provides for the ultimate cessation of contact between the child and his parents. It will be considered by the judge after the decision on the final care order has been made. If granted, the s 34(4) order relieves the local authority of the duty to allow reasonable contact and permits it to phase out contact between child and parents in accordance with its care plan.

6.136 When an application for a contact order under s 34 has been made by any person (other than the local authority) and refused by the court, no further application may be made by the same person within a period of six months unless the court gives leave.[88] Note that this provision applies to interim as well as final orders, and so may have the effect of permitting only one application by any person within the course of the proceedings.

FURTHER ISSUES

6.137 The following issues arise fairly frequently within care proceedings. They often raise questions that are not easily resolved. What follows is intended to flag up the sort of situations where these issues may arise and to point the way towards the most relevant authorities.

Serious allegations and the standard of proof

6.138 The standard of proof in public children law proceedings is the same as in any other civil proceedings: the balance of probabilities. This means that if a court is satisfied that it is more probable than not that an allegation is correct, it will find it proved. This test is to be applied across the spectrum of care proceedings, from the most common cases of physical or emotional neglect to those involving serious sexual abuse, physical injury or death.

6.139 The fact that an allegation is inherently improbable is a factor to be taken into account when reaching a decision on the balance of probabilities. However, each allegation, no matter how serious, must be found proved or disproved on the simple balance of probabilities and there is no place for a heightened standard to apply in such cases.[89] As Peter Jackson J said, quoting the barristers in that case, 'Improbable events occur all the time. Probability itself is a weak prognosticator of occurrence in any given case. Unlikely, even highly unlikely, things do happen. Somebody wins the lottery most weeks; children are struck

---

[88] Ibid, s 91(17).
[89] *Re B* [2008] UKHL 35; [2008] 2 FLR 141; see also *Re S-B* [2009] UKSC 17.

by lightning. The individual probably of any given person enjoying or suffering either fate is extremely low.'[90]

6.140 The standard of proof in criminal cases is, of course, the 'beyond reasonable doubt' or 'sure' test. A criminal jury must be sure that the offence they are considering has been committed. This factor, together with the wider range of evidence that is admissible in a civil trial, means that it is not uncommon for a judge in care proceedings to come to a different result from a jury trying the same allegation in the course of a criminal trial.

> Case Study:
>
> *A mother is charged with causing grievous bodily harm to her child through salt poisoning. At her criminal trial she calls expert evidence to the effect that the child may suffer from a rare condition that prevents his body from processing salt and that would account for the high salt levels found in his body. The jury finds her not guilty, presumably on the basis that there is a reasonable doubt about whether she was responsible for the child's condition. Six months later a judge in care proceedings holds a fact-finding hearing. The same expert gives evidence. At the conclusion of the hearing the judge finds on the balance of probabilities that the mother poisoned the child. The judge comments that she has heard a far wider range of evidence than the jury in the criminal trial and has been particularly influenced by the evidence of the social worker concerning the mother's behaviour towards the child over the past few years.*[91]

6.141 It is also possible (although necessarily much rarer) for a judge in care proceedings to find an allegation not proved, notwithstanding that there is a criminal conviction on the same allegation.[92]

Human rights and the threshold criteria

6.142 The court will commonly find that the threshold criteria are satisfied on the basis of the quality of care provided by only one of the parents. Particularly where the parents are separated and have little to do with each other, this may mean that the other parent plays a very minor role in the threshold stage of the proceedings, and is powerless to resist a determination that the threshold criteria are made out. Bearing in mind that the function of the s 31 threshold requirement is to protect families from intervention unless it is necessary to

---

[90] *Re BR (Proof of Facts)* [2015] EWFC 41.
[91] Judges have repeatedly been reminded of the need in care proceedings to consider any expert medical evidence in the context of the case and the evidence as a whole: see *A County Council v K, D and L* [2005] EWHC 144 (Fam); [2005] 1 FLR 851.
[92] Eg, *Re W (Care Proceedings)* [2008] EWHC 1188 (Fam), [2010] 1 FLR 1176.

protect the child, does this infringe the 'innocent' parent's Art 8 rights to an unacceptable extent?

> Case Study:
>
> *A young child's parents are separated and he lives with his mother who has a heroin addiction. His father has made several unsuccessful attempts to intervene and protect him. Ultimately the local authority issues care proceedings and the court finds, perhaps with all parties' agreement, that the threshold criteria are met on the basis of the mother's care. The father wishes to resist a care order; he hopes to care for the child himself, although he is struggling to cope with the breakdown of a relationship and is also looking after an older teenager who has been in trouble a few times with the police.*
>
> If the child had been living with the father when the local authority became involved, it is unlikely that the threshold criteria would have been met. As it is he starts 'several lengths down', with the threshold for state intervention having already been reached through no fault of his own; and his own circumstances mean that at the welfare stage, there is a real chance that the court may feel the child's needs will be better met elsewhere.

6.143 Similarly, there is no requirement that the threshold criteria should still be satisfied at the time when the order is made. The threshold criteria apply to the situation at the time when the local authority initiates protective measures. So, an interim care order may be made when parents are in the middle of a particularly acrimonious split and are unable to prioritise the children's needs over their own. Several months later this may no longer be the case, and the problems that drew the family to the local authority's attention may have been resolved. Nevertheless, the threshold has been crossed and the court process engaged. The court has no power to revisit the threshold criteria in the light of the circumstances prevailing at the later time, however the court will only make an order if it is necessary, proportionate and required to meet the child's welfare needs in the circumstances that then are known to exist.

Radicalisation

6.144 Since 2014, there has been a marked rise in children cases that have – or are alleged to have – aspects of radicalisation in them. Generally, those cases fall into one of three categories: where children, either with their parents or on their own, are at risk of travelling to ISIS-held territories; where children have been or are at risk of being radicalised; where children have been, or are, at risk of becoming involved in terrorist activities, domestically or abroad.

6.145 Cases involving radicalisation present a number of difficulties for the family justice system and will often require the collaboration of multiple state agencies. Indeed, local authorities – the applicant in care proceedings – may at times feel left 'in the dark' by the non-disclosure to them of detailed information by the police and security services.[93] Applications may be made on the basis of public interest immunity or for proceedings to be held in secret (known as the closed material procedure).

6.146 If involved in such a case, a number of basic principles require remembering:

✓ Radicalisation is normally defined in the family court as 'negatively influencing [a child] with radical fundamentalist thought, which is associated with terrorism';[94]

✓ Cases are allocated to a High Court judge of the Family Division;

✓ Sir James Munby P set out detailed guidance in *Radicalisation cases in the Family Courts*, October 2015, which is available online;[95]

✓ Significant information may not be disclosed by the police and security services;

✓ Perhaps most importantly: the holding of extreme beliefs may not in itself be causative of significant harm so as to satisfy the threshold criteria and permit the court to interfere in the life of the family, let alone a basis for the removal of children from their parents' care.

Uncertain perpetrators

6.147 Cases where it is apparent that a person has caused harm to a child, but it is not clear which of two (or more) persons is responsible, pose a particular difficulty. In the equivalent criminal case, where it is not clear which of two co-defendants is guilty of the offence, although it is obvious that one of them must be, the jury's duty is to acquit both.

6.148 Such an approach would give a very unsatisfactory result in a situation where, for example, the two potential perpetrators are both the child's parents. The court's paramount aim of protecting the child means that it cannot decline to intervene because, although the child is at risk from at least one of her parents, it cannot tell which one.

6.149 In such circumstances, the court's duty is first to establish on the balance of probabilities whether there must be one or more people responsible for the harm caused to the child (ie to exclude any accidental cause). If this is the case, the threshold criteria will be met. There must of course be a nexus linking the harm done to the child to the parental care: a random and unforeseeable attack

---

[93] See, eg, the line of judgments culminating in *C (A Child – Application for Dismissal or Withdrawal of Proceedings) (No. 3)* [2017] EWFC 37.
[94] *Re M (Children)* [2014] EWHC 667 (Fam).
[95] www.judiciary.uk/wp-content/uploads/2015/10/pfd-guidance-radicalisation-cases.pdf.

on the child by a stranger will not establish the threshold criteria; sexual abuse within the family, of which the parent(s) should have been aware even if not perpetrators themselves, will. Cases where the pool of possible perpetrators includes a person outside the family (such as a childminder) pose particular problems: in such a case, the threshold may still be crossed notwithstanding that it is not always obvious that such a nexus exists.[96]

6.150 The court must then identify all possible perpetrators of the harm, asking itself the question whether there is 'a likelihood or a real possibility that one or more of a number of people with access to the child was the perpetrator or a perpetrator of the inflicted injuries'.[97] If the answer to that question is yes, the threshold criteria will be met on that basis, notwithstanding that the court cannot apportion responsibility for the harm between the potential perpetrators. The judge will then do what she can to assist professionals at the subsequent welfare stage, who must proceed on the basis that any one of the identified persons is a possible perpetrator of the harm. However, judges should resist the temptation to apportion likelihood between two possible perpetrators on a percentage basis.[98]

Case Study:

A child is brought to hospital by her parents with serious head injuries. Both parents admit being at home with the child when the injuries occurred. The doctors suspect non-accidental injury and the police and social services are informed. Both parents are charged with causing grievous bodily harm and at a subsequent trial, because the prosecution cannot prove beyond reasonable doubt that either was responsible, both are acquitted. Following the fact-finding hearing in the care proceedings the judge finds that:

(a) *the child's injuries were non-accidental;*

(b) *one or other, or both, of the parents was responsible for causing the injuries by hitting the child against a hard surface; and*

(c) *he cannot make a finding regarding which parent was responsible: it is possible that one may be entirely blameless and the other responsible, or that both share responsibility.*

At the subsequent disposal hearing the parents have separated. Each seeks care of the child (and blames the other for his injuries). The local authority's position is that because neither parent can be exonerated from blame for the child's injuries, the risk of placement with either parent is too high. The care plan is for adoption. Although he recognises the potential injustice to an innocent parent, the judge has no option but to prioritise the child's safety and the care order is made.

---

[96] This was the case in *Lancashire County Council v B* [2000] 1 FLR 583, discussed in *Re S-B* [2009] UKSC 17.
[97] *North Yorkshire County Council v SA* [2003] EWCA Civ 839; [2003] 2 FLR 849.
[98] *Re S-B* [2009] UKSC 17.

Care or supervision order?

6.151 In some cases, the proceedings may conclude with it being clear that the child should remain at home with his parents, but an element of future risk to him remains. In these circumstances, the court must consider whether the risk is such that the child can only adequately be protected by a care order, or whether a supervision order would suffice.

6.152 Factors which have pointed towards a care order have included the following:

(1) Previous violence towards the child: despite a period of calm, the local authority needed to share parental responsibility to enable it to remove the child quickly if the situation deteriorated. Imposing a care order was preferable to relying on the local authority's power to apply for an emergency protection order in the future.[99]

(2) Inability to attach conditions to a supervision order: a care order would ensure that the child remained at a school suitable for his special needs. A condition to that effect, attached to a supervision order, would not be capable of enforcement.[100]

6.153 On the other hand, a supervision order may be more appropriate when the risk to the child is low. If the court makes a 'lives with' child arrangements order within care proceedings, it must also make an interim supervision order unless satisfied that his welfare will be satisfactorily safeguarded without such an order being made.[101] Where the threshold is satisfied on a final basis, it will usually be appropriate to impose a supervision order, whether or not in conjunction with a 'lives with' child arrangements order, as a minimum protective measure and to ensure ongoing local authority involvement.[102]

---

[99] *Re S* [1993] 2 FLR 919.
[100] *Re V* [1996] 1 FLR 776.
[101] CA 1989, s 38(3).
[102] *Re DH* [1994] 1 FLR 679.

Chapter 7

ADOPTION

Chapter summary

- What is adoption?
- Intercountry adoption
- Who can be adopted?
- Who can adopt a child?
- The welfare of the child
- Parental consent
- The effect of giving consent
- Dispensing with parental consent
- Adoption services
- Prospective adopters
- The birth family
- Access to confidential adoption information
- Registration and tracing natural family
- Going behind the adoption curtain: tracing the natural family
- Placing a child for adoption
- Placement with parental consent
- Placement under a placement order
- Care proceedings: how does a plan for adoption develop?
- Contact on placement and after adoption

- Illegal placements and other prohibited steps
- Applying for an adoption order
- Consequences of an adoption order
- Adoptions with an international element

WHAT IS ADOPTION?

7.1 Societies across the world have developed arrangements whereby adults, who are not the natural parents of a child, may act as his parents in their place. In many countries such arrangements may be informal, or arranged within the extended family; in others a formal legal process of 'adoption' may be required. However, even where there is a legal adoption, the resulting status will vary from country to country from a 'full adoption', under which there is a complete and irrevocable severance of all legal ties between the child and his natural family, to 'simple adoption', which is less severe in one or more respects.

7.2 Adoption in England and Wales is entirely regulated by statute law. Until the passing in 1926 of the Adoption of Children Act, while permanent but informal arrangements were made for children, legal adoption was not available in the UK. There is still no procedure for adoption under the common law.

7.3 A UK adoption order is a 'full adoption' and sets out to bring about security and stability for the child by irrevocably[1] altering the rights and duties of the adults involved in order to consolidate the child in his new adoptive family. The current legislation is contained in the Adoption and Children Act 2002 (ACA 2002) and a large body of related subordinate legislation and guidance.

7.4 On the making of an adoption order parental responsibility for a child is given to the adopters. At the same time, the order operates to extinguish permanently the parental responsibility which any person had for the child immediately before the making of the order. An adoption order is irrevocable, save in the very restricted circumstances of ACA 2002, s 55 (revocation upon subsequent legitimation).

7.5 An adopted child is deemed to be the adopter's legitimate child, as if he had been born to either the adoptive couple, or to the single adopter (irrespective of gender). If adopted by a couple,[2] or a single adopter who is the partner of a parent of the child, the child is to be treated as the child of the relationship of the couple in question.[3]

---

[1] Save for revocation upon subsequent legitimation: see ACA 2002, s 55.
[2] The definition of 'couple' is wide, see ibid, s 144(4) and **7.13**.
[3] ACA 2002, s 67(2).

> The effect of an adoption order is that the child is treated in law as if he was born to the adoptive parents

7.6 Adoptive parents are thus treated in law as the child's parents, save that an adoptive parent cannot be guilty of an offence under the Sexual Offences Act 2003 (SOA 2003), ss 64 or 65 (sex with an adult relative),[4] and an adoption order does not of itself confer citizenship or a right to remain in the UK.

7.7 Adoption is the legal process by which a child becomes a permanent and full member of a new family. Long-term placement in local authority foster care has disadvantages which may arise from the possible change of carers, of social workers, or of plans for the child, all of which may erode the child's sense of stability and security. Consequently, in the 1970s and 1980s, long-term fostering fell from favour as the preferred social work option for most children in long-term care.[5] Adoption has become the goal which is sought for most children, especially younger children, who require a permanent family placement away from their natural parents.

In *Re H (Adoption: Parental Agreement)*,[6] Ormrod LJ answered the question: 'What do the adoptive parents gain by an adoption order over and above what they have already got on a long-term fostering basis?' He said:

> 'To that the answer is always the same – and it is always a good one – adoption gives us total security and makes the child part of our family and places us in parental control of the child; long-term fostering leaves us exposed to changes of view of the local authority, it leaves us exposed to applications, and so on by the natural parent. That is a perfectly sensible and reasonable approach; it is far from being only an emotive one.'

7.8 The move towards adoption was given impetus by both Tony Blair and David Cameron during their time as Prime Minister with the consequent introduction of government adoption 'targets'. The government's focus in recent years has been on the need to find a permanent family for those children who wait in care, in addition to the separate category of adoptions which are made within a child's family to reflect the role of a step-parent.

INTERCOUNTRY ADOPTION

7.9 'Intercountry adoption' is a non-legal term used to describe an adoption order in which (initially) the applicant resides in a different country from the child. An intercountry adoption may involve a child who is habitually resident in

---

[4] ACA 2002, s 74 (as amended).
[5] See the seminal work by Rowe and Lambert *Children Who Wait* (Association of British Adoption Agencies, 1974).
[6] *Re H (Adoption: Parental Agreement)* (1982) 3 FLR 386; quoted with approval by House of Lords in *Re C (A Minor) (Adoption Order: Conditions)* [1988] 2 FLR 159 at 168G.

the UK going abroad for adoption, but, more commonly, the arrangement will be that a non-UK resident child is brought here for adoption by UK resident adopters. Strict legal requirements apply whether the child is going out of the UK or being brought in, and whether there has been some form of adoption process in the foreign jurisdiction or none. An international convention (the 1993 Hague Convention on Protection of Children and Co-operation in respect of Intercountry Adoption) regulates the process as between fellow Convention states.[7] In general, subject to the additional requirements and limitations concerning bringing a child into the country, the ordinary domestic adoption law will apply in full to an intercountry adoption.[8]

WHO CAN BE ADOPTED?

7.10 An adoption application may only be made in respect of a person who is under the age of 18 years, but an adoption order may be made after that age if the person is still under 19 years old.[9] Most adoptions relate to younger children, but, given the need to look to the child's welfare throughout his lifetime, an adoption order for a late teenager may sometimes be appropriate.

7.11 An adoption order may be made in respect of a previously adopted child, but not in relation to one who is, or has been, married or in a civil partnership.[10] The child must either be habitually resident in England and Wales, or physically present here, when the adoption application is made. Where the child is habitually resident abroad, the requirements of the Adoptions with a Foreign Element Regulations 2005, Chapter 2[11] must be met before the child can be brought into the UK for adoption.

WHO CAN ADOPT A CHILD?

7.12 A child can be adopted either by a single person or by a couple (whether married or in a civil partnership or not and whether of different gender or the same gender).[12] In each case there are specific requirements that must be satisfied before an adoption order can be made.

Adoption by a couple

7.13 An adoption order may be made in favour of two applicants if they are a married couple, a couple who have entered into a civil partnership or 'two people (whether of different sexes or the same sex) living as partners in an enduring

---

[7] The Hague Convention is ratified and implemented in England and Wales as from June 2003 by the Adoption (Intercountry Aspects) Act 1999.
[8] Further discussion of intercountry adoption is at **7.191**.
[9] ACA 2002, s 49.
[10] Ibid, ss 46(5), 47(8), (8A).
[11] SI 2005/392.
[12] ACA 2002, ss 50, 51 and 144(4).

family relationship'.[13] There is no room for discrimination on the grounds of sexual orientation, or against a couple who have chosen not to formalise their relationship through a marriage or civil partnership. It is important to recognise however that adoption agencies and courts will be anxious to ensure for the sake of the child's stability that the couple's relationship is committed and likely to endure. A couple wishing to adopt must be living 'as partners'. Two close relatives (for example parent and child, or sister and brother) are not a 'couple' for the purposes of the Act and cannot jointly adopt a child.[14]

7.14 Each of the applicant couple must have attained the age of 21 years,[15] except where one is the mother or father of the child (in which case the parent must be over 18 years). While there is no legal upper age limit for an adoptive parent, adoption agencies will not usually place a child with adopters where the age gap between the child and the adopters is more than 45 years unless the child has special needs.[16]

7.15 An application for an adoption order may only be made if one of the following two conditions is satisfied:[17]

(1) at least one of the couple must be domiciled in a part of the British Islands;[18] or

(2) both of the couple have been habitually resident in a part of the British Islands[19] for a period of not less than one year ending with the date of the application.

Different considerations apply in an international case if the application is for a Convention adoption order.[20]

7.16 Where the child was placed for adoption by an adoption agency there is a requirement that he must have had his home with the adopters, or at least one of them, for ten weeks prior to the application.[21] Where the child was not placed for adoption by an adoption agency, the specified period for which he must have lived with the prospective adopters is between six months and five years, depending on their connection with him.[22]

7.17 There is no legal requirement concerning the race of the applicants, but the race, cultural, religious and linguistic factors in a case must be given appropriate regard and weight.[23]

---

[13] Ibid, ss 50, 144(4).
[14] Ibid, s 144(5), (6).
[15] Ibid, s 50(1).
[16] *Adopting a Child* (BAAF, 2008).
[17] ACA 2002, s 49(2), (3).
[18] Ibid.
[19] Ie the UK, the Channel Islands or the Isle of Man (Interpretation Act 1978, Sch 1).
[20] For Convention adoptions, see **7.197**.
[21] ACA 2002, s 42(2).
[22] Ibid, s 42(3)–(5).
[23] For race, culture and religion, see **7.44**.

Parent as an adopter

7.18 A natural parent may make a joint application with her/his spouse or partner to adopt her/his own child. In such a case the age requirement[24] is relaxed so that an adoption order may be made provided that the mother or father has attained the age of 18 years and her/his spouse/partner has attained the age of 21 years.[25] Such an application is only likely to succeed where the identity of the child's other natural parent is unknown or he or she has played and wishes to play no role in the child's life.[26]

7.19 In rare cases a parent may apply to adopt his or her own child alone. The main effect of such an adoption is to extinguish the parental responsibility of the other parent. If the desired result is to exclude a parent as completely as possible from the child's life (and assuming of course that there are good reasons for doing so), this can usually be achieved by a combination of other orders under the Children Act 1989 (CA 1989) and injunctions restricting the parent's involvement with the child. This route will usually be preferable to the drastic and irrevocable route of an adoption.

Step-parent adoption

7.20 As with any other applicant, a child's step-parent may make an application for an adoption order either on his own or as one of a married or unmarried couple. He must satisfy the basic requirements;[27] in particular, he and his spouse/partner must each have attained the age of 21 years, unless his spouse is a parent of the child.

7.21 Adoption by a step-parent together with a natural parent of the child has the artificial effect of changing the legal relationship between the parent and the child from a natural one to an adoptive one. The ACA 2002, s 51(2) seeks to avoid this consequence by permitting a person who is the partner of the child's parent to make an application to adopt on their own. On adoption the child will be treated in law as being the child of the adopter (the non-parent partner) and the other one of the couple (the parent).[28]

7.22 The key consequence of a step-parent adoption is that the legal relationship between the child and the natural parent who is not the step-parent's partner will be extinguished. The courts have shown a reluctance to make step-parent adoption orders where the natural parent had formerly had an established relationship with the other parent and/or the child and is objecting

---

[24] ACA 2002, s 50(1).
[25] Ibid, s 50(2).
[26] See para **7.22**.
[27] For joint applicants' requirements, see **7.13**.
[28] ACA 2002, s 67(2), (3); for effects of adoption, see **7.4**.

to the adoption.[29] However, a step-parent adoption does not breach Art 8 of the ECHR where the absent parent has had very limited contact with the child, and strong family ties exist between the child and her step-parent;[30] the assessment of proportionality will differ with the facts of each case.[31]

7.23 As an alternative to adoption a step-parent may acquire parental responsibility by way of a parental responsibility agreement or court order under CA 1989, s 4A. This provision of the CA 1989 enables an involved and committed step-parent to become a 'third' parent of the child without the need to exclude the child's other natural parent.

Sole applicant

7.24 An adoption application (unless it is a Convention (international) application)[32] may only be made by a sole applicant if either:

(1) he is domiciled in the British Islands;[33] or

(2) he has been habitually resident in the British Islands for a period of not less than one year ending with the date of the application.[34]

7.25 An adoption order may be made on the application of one person, if:

(1) he has attained the age of 21 years;[35] and

(2) he is unmarried or, if married or in a civil partnership, the court is satisfied that:[36]
    (a) his spouse/civil partner cannot be found; or
    (b) he has permanently separated from his spouse/civil partner; or
    (c) his spouse's/civil partner's physical or mental health is such that they are incapable of making an application for an order;

(3) (unless the adoptive placement was made by an adoption agency) the child has his home with the applicant within England and Wales.[37]

---

[29] *Re PJ (Adoption: Practice on Appeal)* [1998] 2 FLR 252.
[30] *Soderbäck v Sweden* [1999] 1 FLR 250.
[31] *Re P (Step-parent Adoption)* [2014] EWCA Civ 1174.
[32] For Convention adoptions, see **7.199**.
[33] ACA 2002, s 49(2).
[34] Ibid, s 49(3).
[35] Ibid, s 51(1).
[36] Ibid, s 51(3) and s 51(3A) inserted by Civil Partnership Act 2004, s 79.
[37] ACA 2002, ss 42, 44.

Previous applicants

7.26 A court may not hear an application for an adoption order where a previous application for adoption made in the British Isles (and Channel Islands) in relation to the same child by the same persons was refused by any court, unless it appears to the court that, because of a change in circumstances or for any other reason, it is proper to hear the application.[38]

THE WELFARE OF THE CHILD

The paramountcy principle

7.27 Whenever a court or adoption agency is coming to a decision relating to the adoption of a child, the paramount consideration must be the child's welfare throughout his life.[39] This amounts to a significant shift in emphasis from the old law, which required the courts only to give 'first consideration' to the need to promote the child's welfare 'throughout his childhood'.[40] The circumstances in which the paramountcy principle applies include those where the issue is whether or not to dispense with, the otherwise necessary, parental consent to placement and/or adoption.[41]

7.28 The court or adoption agency must at all times bear in mind that, in general, any delay in coming to the decision is likely to prejudice the child's welfare.[42]

7.29 The court or adoption agency must also have regard, among other factors, to the adoption 'welfare checklist':[43]

Adoption welfare checklist

✓ the child's ascertainable wishes and feelings regarding the decision (considered in the light of the child's age and understanding);

✓ the child's particular needs;

✓ the likely effect on the child (throughout his life) of having ceased to be a member of the original family and become an adopted person;

✓ the child's age, sex, background and any of the child's characteristics which the court or agency considers relevant;

✓ any harm (within the meaning of the CA 1989) which the child has suffered or is at risk of suffering;

---

[38] Ibid, *s 48*.
[39] Ibid, *s 1(1), (2)*.
[40] *Adoption Act 1976, s 6* (repealed).
[41] Ibid, *s 1(7)*.
[42] Ibid, *s 1(3)*.
[43] Ibid, *s 1(4)*.

> ✓ the relationship which the child has with relatives, with any person who is a prospective adopter with whom the child is placed, and with any person in relation to whom the court or agency considers the question to be relevant including:
> – the likelihood of any such relationship continuing and the value to the child of its doing so;
> – the ability and willingness of any of the child's relatives, or of any such person, to provide the child with a secure environment in which the child can develop and otherwise to meet the child's needs;
> – the wishes and feelings of any of the child's relatives or of any such person regarding the child.

7.30 In placing a child for adoption, any Welsh agency must give due consideration to the child's religious persuasion, racial origin and cultural and linguistic background;[44] and, whereas this provision no longer applies in England, the English court will have regard to these factors, if relevant, as part of the welfare evaluation.[45]

7.31 Finally, the court or agency must always consider the whole range of powers available to it in the child's case; and the court must not make any order under the ACA 2002 unless it considers that making an order would be better for the child than not doing so.[46]

7.32 The welfare provisions of ACA 2002, s 1, while in similar terms and format to CA 1989, s 1, are materially different: welfare of the child 'throughout his life', and a checklist that focuses on terminating and establishing legal relations, are prominent features of the adoption provisions. We would draw particular attention to:

✓ ceasing to be a member of the original family and becoming an adopted person;[47]

✓ relationships which the child has with relatives, any prospective adopter with whom she is placed and any other relevant person.[48]

Ceasing to be a member of the original family and becoming an adopted person

7.33 The ACA 2002, s 1(4)(c) requires the court or agency to project its consideration throughout the child's life. It has a twofold focus:

---

[44] Ibid, s 1(5).
[45] *Re N (Children) (Adoption: Jurisdiction)* [2015] EWCA Civ 1112.
[46] Ibid, s 1(6).
[47] ACA 2002, s 1(4)(c).
[48] Ibid, s 1(4)(f).

(1) ceasing to be a member of the original family; and

(2) becoming an adopted person.

7.34 On adoption the cessation of membership of the original family is total and intended to be so for all time. The original parents' parental responsibility is extinguished and there is a complete severing of all legal ties with the family. The cut-off from his family of origin may have a potentially damaging impact on the child's sense of identity and emotional well-being.

7.35 In considering the likely effect on the child of these changes, the court or adoption agency will be focusing upon the degree of interference with the child's Art 8 rights to family life that would be consequent upon an adoption. This will have to be balanced against the family life that the child is, or will be, enjoying with the adoptive family.

7.36 In *Re M (Adoption or Residence Orders)*,[49] Ward LJ described the issues involved in considering adoption for a child:

> 'The legal nature and effect of an adoption order is ... [that] ... it changes status. The child is treated in law as if she had been born a child of the marriage of the applicants. She ceases in law to be a child of her mother and the sister of her siblings. The old family link is destroyed and new family ties are created. The psychological effect is that the child loses one identity and gains another. Adoption is inconsistent with being a member of both old and new family at the same time. Long-term fostering does enable the child to have the best of both worlds by feeling she belongs to both families though she must reside with ... only one.
>
> The significant advantage of adoption is that it can promote much-needed security and stability, the younger the age of placement, the fuller the advantage. The disadvantage is that it is unlike any other decision made by adults during a child's minority because it is irrevocable. The child cannot at a later stage even in adulthood reverse the process. That is a salutary reminder of the seriousness of the decision. The advantage of the care/child arrangements order is the converse – it can be adapted to meet changing needs, but therein lies its disadvantage – it does not provide absolute certainty and security. Children Act 1989, s 91(14) minimises, if not eliminates, the uncertainty.
>
> In weighing up these considerations, the court must have an eye to the realities of the child's situation, bearing in mind the torture of adolescence through which the child must live, finding and then asserting the independence of growing adulthood. When times are bad – and it would be surprising if there were not such times – it will be the emotional attachment forged between the adopters and the child, not that piece of paper entitled "adoption order", which will prevent a disaffected child searching for a grass which will always seem so much greener in the pastures occupied by the old family.'

---

[49] *Re M (Adoption or Residence Orders)* [1998] 1 FLR 570 at 589.

7.37 More recently there has been a growing awareness among childcare professionals of the possibility of a 'dual identity' for adopted children. The average age of an adopted child in England at the date of adoption is three years and four months;[50] these children are likely to retain memories of their birth family and a sense of birth family identity that, however strong the adoptive relationship, will never be extinguished. The use of 'life story work' and, in appropriate cases, ongoing contact with the birth family after the adoption, have developed in acknowledgement of this awareness. Both are discussed later in this chapter.

Relationship which the child has with relatives and prospective adopters

7.38 The ACA 2002, s 1(4)(f) requires a court or adoption agency to consider the child's existing family relationships to a degree and in a manner which is not expressly required by the companion welfare checklist in CA 1989, s 1(3).

7.39 The court or agency is required to consider 'the relationship which the child has with relatives, with any person who is a prospective adopter with whom the child is placed, and with any person in relation to whom the court or agency considers the question to be relevant'.[51] The pool of relationships is not confined to relatives, but will include any de facto relationships considered to be of importance; on the facts of a particular case this might include foster parents. The reference to prospective adopters, which was inserted by amendment in 2017, is intended to underline the balance between valuable relationships on both sides of the family/adoption divide.

7.40 The welfare checklist applies to any decision relating to adoption and so consideration of existing relationships (particularly between siblings) is likely to be very important in the context of any proposed contact arrangements.[52]

7.41 In the context of ACA 2002, s 1(4)(f) the court or adoption agency must consider:

(1) the likelihood of any such relationship continuing and the value to the child of its doing so;

(2) the ability and willingness of any of the child's relatives, or of any such person, to provide the child with a secure environment in which the child can develop and otherwise to meet the child's needs; and

---

[50] *Children Looked After in England (including adoption), Year Ending 31 March 2017* – available at Dept for Education website.
[51] ACA 2002, s 1(4)(f). A 'relative' in relation to a child means a grandparent, brother, sister, uncle or aunt, whether of the full blood or half-blood or by marriage or civil partnership. For the purposes of ACA 2002, s 1, a 'relative' includes the child's mother and father.
[52] For 'contact after adoption', see **7.163**.

(3) the wishes and feelings of any of the child's relatives or of any such person regarding the child.

7.42 These factors embrace consideration of:

✓ the value to the child of a continuing relationship with his relatives (and any other person who is important to the child);

✓ the value of relationships that the child has formed with the prospective adopters and their family, and

✓ the wishes and feelings of those people.

Within the pool of possible relationships, particular importance is likely to be given to relationships between siblings.

7.43 The ACA 2002, s 1(4)(f)(ii) contains a statutory requirement for an assessment by the adoption agency, and ultimately the court, of the capacity and willingness of relatives or others to provide a long-term home for the child. The type and degree of assessment required will no doubt vary from case to case.

Religion, race and culture

7.44 In placing a child for adoption, an adoption agency in Wales must however give due consideration to the child's religious persuasion, racial origin and cultural and linguistic background;[53] this provision no longer applies in England but the English court will nevertheless continue to focus upon relevant national, linguistic, ethnic and religious factors.[54] The White Paper preceding the *ACA 2002* referred to the common perception that adoptions were being blocked by 'politically correct' social workers who would refuse to place a black child with a white couple (or vice versa). While trans-racial adoptions did and do take place, the new law acknowledges that potential adopters of a child from a different culture or race need to be sufficiently sensitive to assist her to understand and take pride in all the elements of her background.[55]

7.45 It is important that prospective adopters are aware of the child's background and are able, as far as possible, to assist the child to form a sense of her cultural and racial heritage. Where a child's heritage is very mixed, it will rarely be possible for it all to be reflected in the make-up of the adoptive home.

7.46 Issues relating to religion are of importance, but the court must afford paramount consideration to the child's welfare and this may require a placement

---

[53] Ibid, s 1(5).
[54] *Re N (Children) (Adoption: Jurisdiction)* [2015] EWCA Civ 1112.
[55] *Re C (Adoption: Religious Observance)* [2002] 1 FLR 1119.

which does not accord with the parent's religious wishes.[56] The issue demands awareness and sensitivity from practitioners: for a sad case where a mistake about the child's religious identity caused severe distress to both child and adopters some 30 years after the adoption took place, see *Re B (Adoption: Setting Aside)*.[57]

Whole range of powers and 'no order' principle

7.47 The ACA 2002, s 1(6) provides that the court or adoption agency must always consider:

(1) the whole range of powers available to it in the child's case (whether under ACA 2002 or CA 1989); and

(2) the court must not make any order under ACA 2002 unless it considers that making the order would be better for the child than not doing so.

Whole range of powers available

7.48 The requirement in ACA 2002, s 1(6) is upon the court and the adoption agency and applies throughout the course of 'the child's case'. The requirement is dynamic and wide-ranging; it applies 'always' and to the 'whole range of powers available'. The relevant powers available may change from time to time during the life of the child's case.

7.49 The range of options in a particular case may include:

✓ rehabilitation with birth parents;

✓ placement with extended family members or friends;

✓ child arrangements order (with or without a supervision order);

✓ orders coupled with a restriction on further applications under CA 1989, s 91(14);

✓ special guardianship orders under CA 1989, ss 14A–14G;

✓ fostering or other accommodation under a care order; and

✓ adoption:
  – twin-track planning, or concurrent planning;[58]
  – placement agreement or placement order.

---

[56] *Re S; Newcastle City Council v Z* [2005] EWHC 1490 (Fam); *Haringey LBC v C* [2006] EWHC 1620 (Fam); [2007] 1 FLR 1035.
[57] *Re B (Adoption: Setting Aside)* [1995] 1 FLR 1.
[58] *Re D and K (Care Plan)* [1999] 2 FLR 872.

7.50 It is essential to have regard to the nature and effect of each order and the advantages and disadvantages each brings to the safeguarding and promotion of the child's welfare.

'No order' principle

7.51 The ACA 2002, s 1(6) provides that 'the court must not make any order under this Act unless it considers that making the order would be better for the child than not doing so'. While using different phraseology to CA 1989, s 1(5), this statement of the 'no order' principle has a like effect and encapsulates the 'least interventionist' approach and the principle of proportionality under the ECHR.

PARENTAL CONSENT

Overview

7.52 The issue of parental consent may be considered twice: first at the point of placement, or when the adoption agency becomes authorised to place the child (even if a placement does not immediately take place); and secondly when the court comes to consider whether or not to make a final adoption order. However, natural parents and their advisers must be aware that the 'second bite at the cherry' that the Act appears to offer, ie the opportunity to withhold consent first at the placement stage, and then, if that fails, at the final adoption hearing, is largely illusory.

7.53 At the final adoption hearing the court must satisfy itself that the consent of all relevant persons to the adoption has been validly given (and not validly withdrawn) or dispensed with. However, if the parents have already consented to the child's placement, or if the local authority holds a placement order, the parents' participation in the final adoption hearing is severely restricted.

7.54 In agency[59] placement cases, or where a parent has given advance consent to the adoption, the parent may not oppose the making of an adoption order without the court's leave; and the court may not give leave unless there has been a change of circumstances since the consent was given or the placement order was made. It follows that where the child is placed for adoption (by consent or by order), or a parent has given advance consent to adoption, the parent may not then oppose the making of an adoption order at the final hearing unless there has been a change of circumstances. The change of circumstances must be of a nature and degree sufficient to open the door for the court to reconsider the whole question of adoption. The court must decide first whether this is the case as a matter of fact, and then must go on to consider whether or not to exercise

---

[59] An adoption 'agency' is either a local authority or a registered adoption agency (for example Barnardo's).

its discretion to permit the parent to oppose the application. At this second stage the child's welfare is paramount.[60]

7.55 The following section deals with parental consent to adoption. It sets out the steps that the court must go through at the adoption hearing, in relation to parental consent. It must be read in the knowledge that, if the child has been placed for adoption by an agency authorised to do so, the opportunities for parental participation in the court's subsequent decision-making process are limited. The way in which the court (or adoption agency) must approach the issue of consent at the placement stage is considered below at **7.127**.

Consent to adoption

7.56 An adoption order may only be made if the court is satisfied in the case of each parent or guardian of the child:

(1) that the parent or guardian consents to the making of the adoption order:
    – unconditionally; and
    – with full understanding of what is involved;[61] or

(2) that the parent or guardian has given advance consent to adoption under ACA 2002, s 20 (and has not withdrawn that consent) and does not oppose the making of the adoption order;[62] or

(3) that the parent's or guardian's consent should be dispensed with under one of the two statutory grounds available.[63]

7.57 The provisions of ACA 2002, s 1, which require the court to give paramount consideration to the welfare of the child throughout his life, apply to a decision upon whether consent should be dispensed with.[64]

'Parent'

7.58 A 'parent' means 'a parent having parental responsibility for the child under the Children Act 1989'.[65] The following people are therefore included within the meaning of 'parent' for the purposes of the Act:

(1) the child's natural mother (unless parental responsibility has been removed by order of a foreign court or a previous adoption order);

---

[60] *Re P (Adoption: Leave Provisions)* [2007] EWCA Civ 616; [2007] 2 FLR 1069.
[61] ACA 2002, ss 47(2)(a), 52(5).
[62] Ibid, s 47(2)(b).
[63] Ibid, s 47(2)(c); for dispensing with consent to adoption, see **7.74**.
[64] ACA 2002, s 1(7).
[65] Ibid, s 52(6).

(2) the child's natural father:
   (a) if he was married to the child's mother at the time of the child's birth;
   (b) if he subsequently married the child's mother;[66]
   (c) if after 1 December 2003 he is registered as the child's father on the birth certificate;[67]
   (d) if he has obtained an order granting him parental responsibility with respect to the child;[68]
   (e) if, before the commencement of CA 1989, he has obtained an order granting him parental rights and duties in respect of the child[69] as that order will be deemed to be an order under CA 1989, s 4 granting him parental responsibility for the child;[70]
   (f) if he has acquired parental responsibility for the child under a parental responsibility agreement made with the mother;[71]

(3) the child's adoptive parent if he has been the subject of a previous adoption. (In those circumstances, the child's natural parents' consent would not be relevant.)

7.59 The consent of the father without parental responsibility is not required within adoption proceedings.[72] A local authority or adoption agency are only under a duty to make enquiries of a putative father or other relatives if it is in the interests of the child to do so on the basis that the enquiries will genuinely further the prospect of finding a long-term carer for the child.[73]

Guardian

7.60 A child's 'guardian', for the purpose of adoption proceedings, has the same meaning as in the CA 1989, and includes a special guardian.[74] In an international case, whether or not a 'guardian' (which, in that context, might be an institution rather than a person) is a guardian under the ACA 2002 must be determined under English law.[75]

Consent to placement for adoption

7.61 An adoption agency is only authorised to place a child for adoption 'with parental consent' under ACA 2002, s 19 if it is satisfied that each parent

---

[66] Legitimacy Act 1976, s 2 and FLRA 1987.
[67] CA 1989, ss 4(1), 11(1).
[68] Ibid.
[69] FLRA 1987, s 4 (repealed by CA 1989, Sch 15, and converted by CA 1989, Sch 14, para 4).
[70] Ibid.
[71] CA 1989, s 4(1)(b).
[72] ACA 2002, s 52(6); *Re C (A Minor) (Adoption: Parental Agreement: Contact)* [1993] 2 FLR 260.
[73] *Re M and N (Twins; Relinquished Babies; Parentage)* [2017] EWFC 31 (Fam).
[74] ACA 2002, s 144(1).
[75] *Re AMR (Adoption: Procedure)* [1999] 2 FLR 807.

or guardian of a child has consented (and has not withdrawn the consent) to the child being placed for adoption with prospective adopters identified in the consent, or being placed for adoption with any prospective adopters who may be chosen by the agency.[76] Any consent given by a mother is ineffective if given less than six weeks after the child's birth.[77] The ACA 2002, s 19 is subject to the general provisions regarding parental consent in s 52.[78] Consent therefore means consent that is given unconditionally and with full understanding of what is involved.[79]

7.62 Consent to a child being placed for adoption with prospective adopters identified in the consent may be combined with consent to the child subsequently being placed for adoption with any prospective adopters who may be chosen by the agency in circumstances where the child is removed from or returned by the identified adopters.[80]

7.63 Consent to placement for adoption may be withdrawn; however, any attempt to withdraw consent will be ineffective if it occurs after an adoption application has been made.[81]

Advance consent to adoption

7.64 A parent or guardian who consents to the child being placed for adoption by an adoption agency under ACA 2002, s 19 may, at the same or any subsequent time, consent to the making of a future adoption order.[82] A parent giving advance consent may consent to an adoption by named prospective adopters (if any) who are identified in the consent form, or to an adoption by any prospective adopters who may be chosen by the agency.[83]

7.65 Advance consent to adoption may be withdrawn,[84] but any purported withdrawal will be ineffective if it occurs after an adoption application has been made.[85]

7.66 Any consent given by a mother is ineffective if given less than six weeks after the child's birth.[86] The ACA 2002, s 20 is subject to the general provisions regarding parental consent in s 52.[87]

---

[76] ACA 2002, s 19(1).
[77] Ibid, s 52(3).
[78] Ibid, s 19(5).
[79] Ibid, s 52(5).
[80] Ibid, s 19(2).
[81] Ibid, s 52(4).
[82] Ibid, s 20(1).
[83] Ibid, s 20(2).
[84] Ibid, s 20(3).
[85] Ibid, s 52(4).
[86] Ibid, s 52(3).
[87] Ibid, s 20(6).

Consent to making of adoption order

7.67 Before the consent of a parent or guardian can be accepted by the court, the court must be satisfied that the parent or guardian, with full understanding of what is involved, consents unconditionally to the making of an adoption order, whether or not he knows the identity of the applicants.[88]

7.68 In an adoption application, unless the parent has already given advance consent, the consent must be to the specific application that has been made (even if the parent is unaware of the identity of the adopter).[89] Any consent given by a mother is ineffective if given less than six weeks after the child's birth.[90] In a wholly exceptional case, an adoption order may be set aside on appeal on the ground that the parent's consent had been founded upon a basic mistake.[91]

7.69 The consent must be unconditional; however, if the parent or guardian (or other relative/significant person) expresses wishes and feelings about the upbringing of the child, the adoption agency must have regard to those matters when coming to any decision relating to the adoption of the child.[92]

Form and proof of consent

7.70 The parent's or guardian's consent to placement or to adoption (including advance consent) must be given in the form prescribed by the rules or a form to the like effect.[93] It must be appropriately witnessed, in England and Wales by a CAFCASS officer.

Intercountry adoptions: consent

7.71 The provisions set out above apply equally to non-Convention adoption applications relating to a child who has come from another country. (For Convention adoptions, see **7.197**.) The consent of his parent or guardian will either have to be proved or dispensed with before an adoption order may be made. Potential problems at the final hearing can be avoided if the evidence of consent has been obtained in accordance with the rules at the time of the original placement, which will normally have taken place abroad.

---

[88] Ibid, s 52(5).
[89] Ibid, ss 47(2)(a), 52(5); see also FPR 2010, PD 5A: Form A104.
[90] ACA 2002, s 52(3).
[91] *Re M (Minors) (Adoption)* [1991] 1 FLR 458; *Re A (Adoption: Agreement: Procedure)* [2001] 2 FLR 455.
[92] ACA 2002, s 1(1) and (4)(f)(iii).
[93] Ibid, s 52(7); FPR 2010, r 14.10(1) and (2).

THE EFFECT OF GIVING CONSENT

Placement for adoption or advance consent to adoption

7.72 Where a child is placed for adoption with parental consent, the birth parents can validly withdraw their consent to placement and/or advance consent to adoption at any time before an application for an adoption order is made.[94] If consent to placement is withdrawn before an application has been issued, statutory provision is made for the removal and return of the child.[95]

7.73 Where consent to a placement, or advance consent to adoption, has not been withdrawn prior to the issue of an adoption application, the birth parent may only oppose the making of an adoption order with the leave of the court, and the court may only give leave if there has been a change of circumstances.[96]

DISPENSING WITH PARENTAL CONSENT

Grounds for dispensing with parental consent

7.74 A court may dispense with the consent of a parent or guardian to adoption or to the making of a placement order on one or both of two possible grounds,[97] namely that:

(1) the parent or guardian cannot be found or is incapable of giving consent;

(2) the welfare of the child requires the consent to be dispensed with.

Cannot be found or is incapable of giving consent

7.75 In order to satisfy this ground, the applicant must show that every reasonable effort has been made to try and contact the parent. Enquiries should be thorough and should include attempts to contact the extended family of the 'missing parent' where the relevant addresses are known.

7.76 The incapacity of a parent 'incapable of giving consent' may relate to the parent's or guardian's mental or physical condition or circumstances at the date of the decision.

7.77 A parent or other party who lacks capacity (within the meaning of the Mental Capacity Act 2005) to conduct the proceedings will be a 'protected party' and must have a litigation friend to conduct the proceedings on her behalf.[98]

---

[94] ACA 2002, s 52(4).
[95] Ibid, ss 30–41.
[96] Ibid, s 47(5) and (7); for 'change of circumstances', see **7.54**.
[97] Ibid, s 52(1).
[98] FPR 2010, rr 2.3 and 15.2.

Child's welfare requires consent to be dispensed with

7.78 Consent to the making of a placement order or an adoption order may be dispensed with on the ground that the welfare of the child 'requires' the consent to be dispensed with.[99]

7.79 Despite the fact that welfare is brought expressly into the test for dispensing with consent, the consent issue remains separate from the welfare issue; thus the question under ACA 2002, s 52(1) is *not* 'Does the child's welfare require a placement/adoption order?', but is 'Does the child's welfare require the parental consent to be dispensed with?'.

7.80 The child's welfare will be the paramount consideration in determining the issue of dispensing with parental consent. The welfare checklist at ACA 2002, s 1(4) must be applied in determining the consent issue.[100]

7.81 The court must have regard to each element of the welfare checklist. The factors that may indicate that adoption is in the child's best interests must be balanced against those that may point away from adoption, for example s 1(4)(c) (likely effect of ceasing to be a member of the original family) or s 1(4)(f) (relationship with relatives and others).

'Requires'

7.82 The word 'requires' has to be read in the context of adoption and the requirement to have regard to the child's welfare 'throughout his life' with the consequence that the ultimate question relating to consent is 'Does the child's welfare throughout his life require adoption as opposed to something short of adoption?'.[101]

7.83 The 'least interventionist' approach in ACA 2002, s 1(6), together with Art 8 of the ECHR and the principle of proportionality, are likely to be important factors in considering whether a child's welfare 'requires' the court to dispense with parental consent. The Supreme Court has held[102] that adoption should be seen as 'a last resort ...when all else fails' and when 'nothing else will do' to meet the overriding requirements of the child's welfare.

7.84 Commonly encountered factors which may have a bearing on the question of the child's welfare in an appropriate case are: the prospects of rehabilitation to the family, ongoing contact, the child's security, an inherent defect in relation to the parent's ability to care, race, culture and religion, risk of harm to the child, consent given and retracted and, last but not least, the wishes of the child.

---

[99] ACA 2002, s 52(1)(b).
[100] For adoption welfare checklist, see **7.29**.
[101] *Re P* [2008] EWCA Civ 535; [2008] 2 FLR 625.
[102] *Re B (A Child)* [2013] UKSC 33.

Procedure for dispensing with consent

7.85 In a case where the court is asked to dispense with consent, the applicant must give notice of the request in the application form, or at any later stage file a written request setting out the reasons for the request, and must file a statement of facts setting out a summary of the history of the case and any other facts to satisfy the court of the ground(s) for dispensation.[103]

ADOPTION SERVICES

7.86 The range of services that every adoption agency must provide are set out variously in the ACA 2002, the Adoption Agencies Regulations 2005 (AAR 2005)[104] and the Adoption Support Services Regulations 2005.[105] Agencies must also comply with the National Minimum Standards issued by the DFE which apply to local authority and voluntary adoption agencies.

7.87 In general the services provided by a local authority, other (ie non-local authority) adoption agency or adoption support agency will fall into one of four categories:

✓ Provision of information, advice and support to prospective adopters and adoptive families.

✓ Assessment of children and prospective adopters.

✓ Provision of advice and support to birth families.

✓ Maintenance of information relating to adopted children and their birth families.

7.88 Every local authority must set up and maintain an adoption service. Every local authority is therefore also an adoption agency (although not all adoption agencies are local authorities).

PROSPECTIVE ADOPTERS

Advice and information

7.89 Adoption agencies have a duty to provide information to those who are thinking of adopting a child and advice and assistance throughout the adoption process and beyond. They must give prospective adopters clear written information about the assessment and approval process. Agencies must also run

---

[103] FPR 2010, r 14.9(2).
[104] SI 2005/389.
[105] SI 2005/691.

a 'preparation programme' that gives prospective adopters the opportunity to meet with others who have adopted children.

7.90 Following a placement the adoption agency must offer the prospective adopters a wide range of support services, including advice on how to help the child come to terms with his history and background, assistance with managing contact with the birth family and support if the placement runs into difficulties or breaks down.

Assessment

7.91 The assessment process is the most tightly regulated of all an adoption agency's functions. The agency must carry out a detailed system of checks and the prospective adopters must undergo a police check and a medical examination and provide references from at least two referees. Most agencies, including local authorities, use CoramBAAF's 'Form F' as a template for their assessment process. The form is available for purchase from the CoramBAAF website.[106]

Adoption Panel

7.92 Each adoption agency must establish at least one Adoption Panel, which will be made up of a mix of social workers and other professionals, some from within the agency and some who are independent of it. The panel will also include some members who have first-hand experience of adoption in their own lives. The panel are required to give recommendations to the agency on three separate topics:

✓ is a particular child suitable for adoption;

✓ is a particular adult suitable to be a prospective adopter;

✓ the plan to match a particular child with a particular prospective adopter(s).

An agency cannot make a decision about any matter referred to an adoption panel until it has considered the recommendation of the panel. Thereafter the agency may or may not decide in accordance with the panel recommendation.

Independent Review Mechanism

7.93 If an agency informs an applicant that it does not intend to approve him as a prospective adoptive parent, the applicant may ask for a review of the agency's determination via the Independent Review Mechanism (IRM), operated by CoramBAAF[107] on behalf of the Department for Education in

---

[106] https://corambaaf.org.uk/.
[107] Under the Independent Review of Determinations (Adoption and Fostering) Regulations 2009, SI 2009/395; see www.independentreviewmechanism.org.uk.

England and via the IRM for Adoption and Fostering in Wales[108]. The IRM cannot overturn the agency's decision; it can only make a recommendation that the agency should review its determination.

Matching and placement

7.94 Once the plan for adoption for a child has been confirmed, the agency will begin to look for a match between the child and an adoptive family. Depending on the child's situation and needs, that family may be found within the agency's own pool of prospective adopters or located farther afield.

7.95 The Adoption and Children Act Register is an important tool for agencies seeking to place older children, sibling groups, children with special needs or other children who have traditionally been seen as difficult to place. The Register contains details of children waiting for families, and prospective adopters waiting to adopt children. The Register, which is operated by 'Adoption Match' in England and by 'Wales Adoption Register' in Wales, is accessible to adoption agencies and to approved individual adopters.

7.96 Once a potential match has been identified the local authority must present it to its Adoption Panel for approval. If the match is approved, the agency will start the process of introducing the child to the family. Depending on the age of the child, this process can take from a few weeks to a couple of months.

THE BIRTH FAMILY

Counselling and support

7.97 From the time when adoption is identified as the plan for the child, the adoption agency (usually in such cases the local authority) must provide the birth family with a social worker independent of the child's social worker. Via this link the agency must give the birth family support and encourage all members, including siblings, to be involved in the process of providing information to the adoptive family about the child's background and early life. The birth family's views about the adoption must be recorded and parents particularly should have an opportunity to see all information about the birth family that is passed on to the adopters.

7.98 Following the adoption, the agency must make available to the parents a post-adoption service, including counselling if appropriate and assistance with any ongoing direct or indirect contact between the birth family and the child.

---

[108] Under the Independent Review of Determinations (Adoption and Fostering) (Wales) Regulations 2010.

Life story work

7.99 The term 'life story work' describes the important process of informing an adopted child of details of her life prior to coming to live in the adoptive family. A 'life story book' with words and pictures in age-appropriate terms will be prepared, as will a 'later life letter' which sets out details of the child's natural family in more adult terms. An adoption agency is required to provide the adopters with a copy of the child's permanence report and any other information the agency considers relevant before the proposal to match the child with the prospective adopters is presented to the adoption panel.[109] Before the child is placed, the placement plan agreed between the agency and the prospective adopters must indicate the date on which the child's life story book and later life letter are to be passed by the agency to the prospective adopter.[110]

7.100 The birth family should, wherever possible, be given the opportunity to contribute to the life story work done for or with the child, perhaps by providing photographs of the child's early life and important members of the birth family. Involvement of the birth family in this process, where they are able and prepared to participate, is an important part of the post-adoption support services that all adoption agencies must provide.

ACCESS TO CONFIDENTIAL ADOPTION INFORMATION

Confidentiality

7.101 An adoption agency is required to maintain confidentiality with regard to its records.[111] Specified office holders and others have a right of access to the records, and the agency has discretion to provide access for the purpose of carrying out its function as an adoption agency.[112]

REGISTRATION AND TRACING NATURAL FAMILY

Adopted Children Register

7.102 Every adoption must be registered in the Adopted Children Register[113] by the Registrar General in the prescribed form.[114] The Register of Births relating to the adopted child will be marked 'adopted'.[115]

---

[109] AAR 2005, reg 31(1)(a).
[110] Ibid, reg 35 and Sch 5.
[111] Ibid, reg 41.
[112] Ibid, reg 42.
[113] ACA 2002, s 77, Sch 1.
[114] The Adopted Children and Adoption Contact Registers Regulations 2005, SI 2005/924 (ACACRR 2005), reg 2.
[115] ACA 2002, s 77, Sch 1.

7.103 A certified copy of an entry in the Adopted Children Register, if sealed and stamped with the Registrar General's seal, will, without further proof, be received as evidence of the adoption and any other information in the entry as if it were a birth certificate.[116]

GOING BEHIND THE ADOPTION CURTAIN: TRACING THE NATURAL FAMILY

Person adopted before 30 December 2005

7.104 An adopted person over the age of 18 years may apply to the Registrar General for such information as is necessary to enable him to obtain a copy of his birth records.[117] For those who were adopted before 30 December 2005, the procedure for tracing birth records is governed by ACA 2002, Sch 2 and regulations.[118] Where a person who was adopted before 12 November 1975 applies for a record of his birth, the Registrar General is not permitted to disclose the information unless the applicant has attended an interview with an adoption counsellor.[119]

7.105 An applicant (who may be the adopted person or a blood relative) may be entitled to receive 'intermediary services' from an adoption agency or an adoption support agency. Intermediary services are defined[120] as a service for the purpose of:

✓ assisting adopted persons who are over the age of 18 years and who were adopted prior to 30 December 2005 to obtain information in relation to their adoption; and

✓ facilitating contact between such persons and their relatives.

7.106 The potential emotional and psychological impact of reintroducing an adopted person to their natural family after a long period is such that the intermediary agency is charged with a heavy responsibility in deciding whether it is in fact appropriate to proceed with the process and of managing it if they do proceed.

7.107 Before proceeding with any application an intermediary agency must provide information to the applicant about post-adoption counselling services that are available.[121]

---

[116] Ibid, s 77(4).
[117] Ibid, s 79(6).
[118] (In England) the Adoption Information and Intermediary Services (Pre-Commencement Adoptions) Regulations 2005, SI 2005/890 and (in Wales) the Adoption Information and Intermediary Services (Pre-Commencement Adoptions) (Wales) Regulations 2005, SI 2005/2701.
[119] ACA 2002, s 79(6) and Sch 2, para 4.
[120] AIIS(PC)R 2005, reg 4.
[121] Ibid, reg 10.

7.108 An intermediary agency may not disclose any information to an applicant about the adopted person ('the subject') without the subject's consent.[122] If the subject has died or is incapable of giving consent, that information may be given to the applicant.[123]

7.109 An adopted person may put down a written veto (which will be binding on the adoption agencies) to the effect that he does not wish to be contacted by an intermediary agency in relation to an application under those regulations or that he only wishes to be contacted in specified circumstances.[124]

7.110 Where the subject does not consent to disclosure, or is incapable of consent, or there is a veto, the intermediary agency may nevertheless disclose general non-identifying background information to the applicant, if it considers that it is appropriate to do so.[125]

Person adopted after 30 December 2005

7.111 In relation to a person who has been adopted on or after 30 December 2005, the disclosure of information (known as 'section 56 information') relating to his adoption is governed by ACA 2002, ss 56–65 and regulations.[126] The s 56 information that an adoption agency is required to keep (for 100 years) includes:[127]

(1) the case record set up by the Adoption Agencies Regulations 1983 and/or 2005;

(2) any information that has been supplied by a natural parent or relative or other significant person in the adopted person's life, with the intention that the adopted person may, should he wish, be given that information;

(3) any information supplied by the adoptive parents or other persons which is relevant to matters arising after the making of the adoption order;

(4) any information that the adopted person has requested should be kept;

(5) any information given to the adoption agency in respect of an adopted person by the Registrar General under ACA 2002, s 79(5) (information that would enable an adopted person to obtain a certified copy of the record of his birth);

---

[122] Ibid, reg 7.
[123] Ibid.
[124] Ibid, reg 8.
[125] Ibid, reg 9.
[126] (In England) by the Disclosure of Adoption Information (Post-Commencement Adoptions) Regulations 2005, SI 2005/888 (DAI(PCA)R 2005); (in Wales) Access to Information (Post-Commencement Adoptions) (Wales) Regulations 2005, SI 2005/2689.
[127] DAI(PCA)R 2005, reg 4.

(6) any information disclosed to the adoption agency about an entry relating to the adopted person on the Adoption Contact Register.

7.112 An adoption agency is not required to keep information falling within (2)–(4) above if it considers that to do so would be prejudicial to the adopted person's welfare or that it would not be reasonably practicable to keep it.[128]

7.113 Any s 56 information kept by an adoption agency which is about an adopted person or any other person and is, or includes, identifying information about the person in question ('protected information') generally may only be disclosed by the agency to a person (other than that person that the information is about) in pursuance to ACA 2005, ss 56–65.[129]

7.114 An adopted person who has attained the age of 18 years has the right, at his request, to receive from the appropriate adoption agency (in a non-agency case this will mean the local authority to which notice of intention to adopt was given) any information which would enable him to obtain a certified copy of his birth certificate (unless the High Court otherwise orders) or any prescribed information which had been disclosed to his adopters during the adoption process (under ACA 2005, s 54).[130]

7.115 An adoption agency must provide written information about post-adoption counselling in relation to an application for the disclosure of information.[131] If the person requests counselling, the agency has a duty to arrange provision of it.[132]

Adoption Contact Register

7.116 A further register (the Adoption Contact Register – (ACR)) to assist those adoptees and their natural families who wish to express a view about future contact with each other is held by the Registrar General.[133] Part 1 of the ACR contains information provided by the adopted person about his wishes for having contact (or not) with his natural relatives.[134] Part 2 of the ACR contains information about any relative of the adoptee, by blood, half-blood, marriage or civil partnership (but not adoption) who wishes to express a view about contact with the adoptee.[135]

---

[128] Ibid.
[129] ACA 2002, s 57(1).
[130] Ibid, s 60.
[131] DAI(PCA)R 2005, reg 17.
[132] Ibid, reg 17.
[133] ACA 2002, s 80. Useful guidance is given in BAAF Practice Note 20 'The Adoption Contact Register'.
[134] ACA 2002, s 80(2) and (3).
[135] Ibid, s 80.

7.117 The system operates by the Registrar General transmitting to the adopted person whose name appears in Part 1, the name and address of any relative entered in Part 2 who has asked for contact.[136] The register is not open to public inspection.[137]

7.118 This facility is intended to ease the practical problems involved in tracing relatives. Natural family members (not only natural parents) who wish to have the possibility of future contact should be advised of the existence of the register. They may have their name and current address entered upon it at any time after the making of the adoption order, and after the entry of the child's name into the Adopted Children Register. An adopted person can only enter his details in Part 1 if he is over 18 years.

PLACING A CHILD FOR ADOPTION

Background

7.119 Prior to the ACA 2002, the placing of a child for adoption was largely an administrative process conducted by a local authority or adoption agency either with the agreement of the parent(s) or under the authority provided by a care order (interim or full) or an order freeing a child for adoption. The ACA 2002, Chapter 3 establishes a statutory code and legal structure regulating the circumstances in which a child can be placed for adoption and the consequences once such a placement is made. There is provision for substantial court involvement in the process.

7.120 The general effect of the placement provisions in ACA 2002, Chapter 3 is two-fold. First, before a placement for adoption can be made a parent must be fully engaged in the decision-making process, either by giving express consent or by having the opportunity to contest the issue in court proceedings. Secondly, if either a parent consents to placement for adoption, or the court makes a 'placement order', and an adoptive placement is then made, the parent's options for later reversing the progress towards adoption or challenging any eventual adoption application are significantly restricted.

7.121 A central aim of the ACA 2002, Chapter 3 provisions is to bring the parent's opportunity to challenge the crucial adoption decision forward to a stage before any adoptive placement is made. A feature of the earlier law was that in many cases the first opportunity a parent had to challenge a placement in court might be months or years after the placement had been made, by which time the child would be settled in her new family.

7.122 In contrast to the now repealed provisions 'freeing' a child for adoption, where a child is 'placed for adoption' (by agreement or order) the birth parents

---

[136] ACACRR 2005, reg 8.
[137] ACA 2002, s 81(1).

remain the child's parents until any final adoption order but they will be required to share parental responsibility with the prospective adopters and the adoption agency.

'Placement for adoption'

7.123 'Placing a child for adoption' by an adoption agency is defined as 'placing a child for adoption with prospective adopters'. The term includes all situations where the agency has placed or is placing the child with persons who intend to adopt her. A child who is placed or authorised to be placed for adoption by a local authority is a *'looked after child'* under the provisions of CA 1989, Pt III.[138] The local authority will have the continuing responsibility for managing, overseeing and reviewing the child's progress until a future adoption order is made.

7.124 All adoption agencies, whether local authorities or voluntary agencies, must comply with the requirements imposed by Adoption Agency Regulations 2005 (AAR 2005), Pt 6 regarding placement for adoption and conducting statutory reviews.

7.125 Where a local authority are considering adoption for a child, or are satisfied that she should be placed for adoption but are not yet authorised (by consent or court order) to do so, and where there is no appropriate available placement with a family member, they must consider placing the child with a local authority foster parent who is an approved adopter.[139]

In ordinary circumstances, local authority foster parents are able to seek formal approval from the local authority as prospective adopters of children being fostered by them. If they are approved, and the agency leaves the child with them as prospective adopters, the placement will become an adoption placement despite the fact that the child will not have actually moved from the foster home.

Two routes to placement for adoption

7.126 The ACA 2002 establishes two routes by which an adoption agency may be authorised to place a child for adoption:

✓ placement with parental consent;

✓ placement under a placement order.

---

[138] Ibid, s 18(3).
[139] CA 1989, s 22C(9A)–(9C).

PLACEMENT WITH PARENTAL CONSENT

7.127 The ACA 2002, s 19(1) authorises an adoption agency to place a child for adoption where it is satisfied that each parent with parental responsibility or guardian of the child has consented (and has not withdrawn consent) to the child:

✓ being placed for adoption with prospective adopters identified in the consent; or

✓ being placed for adoption with any prospective adopters who may be chosen by the agency.

7.128 'Consent' means consent given unconditionally and with full understanding of what is involved.[140]

7.129 Consent to a child being placed for adoption with prospective adopters identified in the consent (under s 19(1)(a)) may be combined with consent to the child subsequently being placed for adoption with any prospective adopters chosen by the agency (under s 19(1)(b)) if the child were to be removed from or returned by the identified adopters.[141]

7.130 Once a child has been placed for adoption pursuant to a consent given under ACA 2002, s 19, he will continue to be regarded as placed there under that provision until he is removed, notwithstanding that a parent may have withdrawn consent at a later stage.[142]

7.131 The consensual route under ACA 2002, s 19(1) cannot be used where an application for a care or supervision order has been made under CA 1989, s 31 and that application has not been disposed of.[143] Where a care order is made after parental consent to placement has been given, the consent no longer gives the agency authority to place the child for adoption.[144] In any circumstances where a care order has been made or an application is pending, and the appropriate local authority is satisfied that the child ought to be placed for adoption, it must apply for a placement order.[145]

7.132 Once a placement order has been made, it is that order, and not any earlier s 19 parental consent, that provides authority for an agency to place the child for adoption.

---

[140] Ibid, s 52(5) and (6). For parental consent generally, see **7.52**.
[141] Ibid, s 19(2).
[142] Ibid, s 19(4).
[143] Ibid, s 19(3).
[144] Ibid.
[145] Ibid, s 22(2).

Placing a child under six weeks old

7.133 Any consent 'to the making of an adoption order' given by a mother is ineffective if given less than six weeks after the child's birth.[146] By s 18(1) of the Act, an agency does not need a placement order or formal parental consent before placing a child under six weeks old; and so it seems (although this is not explicit in the Act) that the same approach is taken to placement and applies to both parents. However, according to the regulations an adoption agency may place a child who is less than six weeks old for adoption if each parent or guardian of the child has agreed in writing with the agency that the child may be so placed.[147] Once the child is six weeks old this written agreement must be replaced either by each parent's formal consent, given and witnessed according to the requirements of the Act, or by a placement order.

7.134 In practice an adoption agency is unlikely to place a child under six weeks old for adoption unless it is very confident that the necessary parental consent will be forthcoming in due course and will not be withdrawn. If there is any doubt it will be safer to place the child in a short-term foster placement, and move her to an adoptive placement only when the parents have given consent or a placement order has been obtained.

Form of consent

7.135 Consent to placement for adoption and advance consent to adoption must be given using the relevant statutory form, or a form to like effect.[148]

7.136 In England and Wales any consent form must be witnessed by a CAFCASS officer or, where the child is ordinarily resident in Wales, by a Welsh family proceedings officer.[149] Where a parent is prepared to consent to placement, or give advance consent to adoption, the adoption agency must request CAFCASS, or the Welsh Assembly, to appoint an officer for the consent process and must send the information specified in AAR 2005, Sch 2 together with the request.[150]

Advance consent to adoption

7.137 A parent or guardian of a child who consents to the child being placed for adoption under ACA 2002, s 19 may, at the same time or any subsequent time, consent to the making of a future adoption order.[151] In this context, where

---

[146] Ibid, s 52(3).
[147] AAR 2005, reg 35(4); see *A Local Authority v GC* [2008] EWHC 2555 (Fam); [2009] 1 FLR 299.
[148] ACA 2002, s 52(7); FPR 2010, r 14.10(1)(a) and PD 5A: Forms A100–103.
[149] See notes on the relevant Statutory Form.
[150] AAR 2005, reg 20.
[151] ACA 2002, s 20(1).

the placement consent is for placement with identified prospective adopters the additional consent may be advance consent to adoption by them, or it may be consent to adoption by any prospective adopters who may be chosen by the adoption agency.[152]

7.138 Advance consent to adoption may be withdrawn,[153] but any such withdrawal is ineffective if it takes place after an application for an adoption order has been made.[154]

7.139 A parent who gives advance consent to adoption may, at the same time or any subsequent time, give notice to the adoption agency stating that he does not wish to be informed of any application for an adoption order.[155] Such a notice, once given, may subsequently be withdrawn.[156]

Consequences of parental consent to placement for adoption

7.140 The following important and potentially irrevocable consequences flow from a parent giving consent to the placement of a child for adoption:

✓ the parent may only oppose any adoption application with the leave of the court;

✓ the parent's ability to apply for a child arrangements order is restricted;

✓ the parent's ability to have contact with the child will be determined by the adoption agency or subject to a court order under ACA 2002, s 26;

✓ parental responsibility is given to the adoption agency (and in due course to prospective adopters with whom the child is placed);

✓ there are restrictions on a parent's ability to require removal/return of the child.

7.141 Giving consent to placement for adoption has significant consequences for a parent's position in any subsequent adoption application. Where consent to placement has not been withdrawn before an adoption application is made, a parent may only oppose the final adoption order with the leave of the court, and the court may only give leave if there has been a change of circumstances since the s 19 consent was given.[157]

---

[152] Ibid, s 20(2).
[153] Ibid, s 20(3).
[154] Ibid, s 52(4).
[155] Ibid, s 20(4).
[156] Ibid.
[157] Ibid, s 47(4), (5), (7).

7.142 Where a child is placed for adoption following parental consent under ACA 2002, s 19, or an adoption agency is authorised to place for adoption under that section, a parent or guardian may not apply for a child arrangements order unless an application for adoption has been made and the parent has obtained the court's leave to oppose the adoption order.[158] In the same circumstances, a guardian may not apply for a special guardianship order unless he has obtained the court's leave to oppose the adoption.[159]

Restrictions on changing name or removing from UK a child placed for adoption

7.143 Where a child is placed for adoption pursuant to parental consent under ACA 2002, s 19, or a placement order has been made, no person may:

✓ cause the child to be known by a new surname; or

✓ remove the child from the UK,

unless the court gives leave to do so or each parent or guardian of the child gives written consent.[160] A person who provides the child's home may, however, remove the child from the UK for a period of less than one month without the need to obtain parental consent or court leave.[161]

Withdrawal of consent

7.144 Once a parent or guardian has given their consent to the placement of a child for adoption (or advance consent to adoption), the consent may be withdrawn, with the consequence that the agency's authority to place for adoption will cease, at any stage prior to the prospective adopters issuing an adoption application in respect of the child.[162] Consent can only validly be withdrawn by using the statutory form or by notice (which must be in writing) given to the adoption agency.[163] Parental consent cannot be withdrawn if there is a placement order in force or an application for a placement order has been made. If a parent withdraws his consent to placement, the local authority has seven days to make an application for a placement order if the child has not already been placed; 14 days if she has. After that point, if no placement order application has been made, the child must be returned to her parents.[164]

---

[158] Ibid, s 28(1) and s 47(5); for 'leave to oppose adoption', see **7.54**.
[159] Ibid.
[160] Ibid, s 28(2), (3).
[161] Ibid, s 28(4).
[162] Ibid, s 52(4).
[163] Ibid, ss 52(8) and 144(1); Form A107.
[164] Ibid, s 31(2) and 32(2).

Position of a father without parental responsibility

7.145 In relation to the placement of the child it is only the consent of a parent who has parental responsibility for the child that is relevant.[165] The requirements that must be satisfied in the case of a father without parental responsibility are similar to those that apply when the court considers the application to adopt. Where the identity of the father is known to the adoption agency, and the agency considers that it is appropriate to do so, it is required to contact the father in order to counsel him about adoption and explain the procedure for placement/adoption and the legal implications of adoption.[166] The agency must seek to ascertain his wishes and feelings about the child, the plan for placement/ adoption and about contact.[167] They must also ascertain if he wishes to acquire parental responsibility for the child or to apply for a child arrangements order.

7.146 Where an adoption agency is in doubt as to the appropriateness of contacting a father without parental responsibility it may apply to the court for directions on the issue before or after any proceedings have been issued.[168]

7.147 A father who acquires parental responsibility after the agency obtains the mother's consent to placement is deemed to have consented to the child being placed for adoption on the same terms as the mother. This has the advantage of securing the placement for the child; the obvious drawback is that a father who has not managed to acquire parental responsibility before his child reaches the age of six weeks, and whose partner or former partner is determined that the child should be adopted, will have an uphill struggle to contest any subsequent adoption application.

PLACEMENT UNDER A PLACEMENT ORDER

Placement orders

7.148 Given the uncertainty surrounding a consensual placement and the possibility that parental consent may be qualified or withdrawn, it is likely that local authorities will in many cases prefer the security of a placement order. A 'placement order' is 'an order made by the court authorising a local authority to place a child for adoption with any prospective adopters who may be chosen by the authority'.[169]

7.149 While a placement order is in force, parental responsibility for the child is given to the local authority and, while the child is with prospective adopters, also

---

[165] Ibid, s 52(6); for parental consent generally, see **7.52** ff.
[166] AAR 2005, reg 14(3) and (4).
[167] Ibid.
[168] FPR 2010, r 14.21 (application before proceedings) or Pt 19 (application in pending proceedings).
[169] ACA 2002, s 21(1).

to them.[170] In this respect a placement order is similar to a care order, but with the added feature that the prospective adopters share parental responsibility. The local authority may control the way in which any other person exercises parental responsibility; in reality, it is likely that the prospective adopters will make most of the decisions relating to the child, overseen by the local authority, and that the parents' views will carry relatively little weight.

Conditions for making a placement order

7.150 The court may not make a placement order unless:[171]

✓ the child is subject to a care order; or

✓ the court is satisfied that the threshold conditions in CA 1989, s 31(2) (the care or supervision order threshold) are met; or

✓ the child has no parent or guardian; or

✓ each parent or guardian has consented to the child being placed for adoption with any prospective adopters who may be chosen by the local authority and has not withdrawn consent, or

✓ the court is satisfied that the parent's consent should be dispensed with under ACA 2002, s 52.

Provided that one of these conditions is met, the court will go on to apply the welfare test and checklist in ACA 2002, s 1. In contested cases, where a parent does not consent to a placement order, the focus of the hearing will be on whether consent should be dispensed with.

Local authority required to apply for a placement order

7.151 There is a *mandatory* requirement placed upon a local authority to apply for a placement order in the following circumstances:

(1) Where a child is placed for adoption, or is being provided with accommodation, by the local authority, and
    (a) no adoption agency is authorised to place the child for adoption; and
    (b) it considers that the threshold conditions in CA 1989, s 31(2) are met (or that the child has no parent or guardian); and
    (c) it is satisfied that the child ought to be placed for adoption.[172]

---

[170] Ibid, s 25.
[171] Ibid, s 21(2), (3).
[172] Ibid, s 22(1).

(2) Where:
 (a) there is a pending application for a care or supervision order (which has not been disposed of); or
 (b) the child is the subject of a care order and the appropriate local authority is not authorised to place; and
 (c) it is satisfied that the child ought to be placed for adoption.[173]

7.152 The purpose of these provisions is to minimise delay for children waiting in care or subject to care proceedings. They do not apply in respect of a child if any person has given notice to a local authority of intention to adopt the child, unless more than four months have gone by since the notice and no adoption application has been made (or it has been withdrawn or dismissed), or if an adoption application has been made and not disposed of.[174]

Status of child pending determination of placement order application

7.153 If a local authority is under a duty to apply for a placement order, or has applied for one and the application has not been disposed of, the subject child is a 'looked after child' under CA 1989, Pt III.[175]

7.154 Where an application for a placement order has been made and has not been disposed of, and no interim care order is in force, the court may give any directions it considers appropriate for the medical or psychiatric examination or other assessment of the child; but a child who is of sufficient understanding to make an informed decision may refuse to submit to the examination or other assessment.[176] This provision is similar to the court's power to direct assessments under an interim care order.[177]

Consequences of a placement order

7.155 Where a placement order is in force in favour of a local authority the following consequences flow:

(1) The regime for the regulation of contact which applies while an adoption agency is authorised to place a child for adoption applies.

(2) A parent or guardian may not apply for a child arrangements order (and no guardian may apply for a special guardianship order) unless an application

---

[173] Ibid.
[174] Ibid, s 22(5).
[175] Ibid, s 22(4).
[176] Ibid, s 22(6).
[177] CA 1989, s 38(6).

for an adoption order has been made and the parent or guardian has obtained the court's leave to oppose the adoption application.[178]

(3) Unless the court gives leave or each parent or guardian gives written consent, no person may:[179]
   (a) cause the child to be known by a new surname;
   (b) remove the child from the UK (save for a period of less than one month by a person who provides the child's home).

(4) Any existing care order on the child does not have effect at any time when the placement order is in force (but will 'revive' if the placement order is revoked).[180]

(5) Any pre-existing CA 1989, s 8 order or supervision order will cease to have effect on the making of a placement order.[181]

(6) No prohibited steps, specific issue or child arrangements order and no supervision or child assessment orders may be made in respect of the child.[182]

(7) No special guardianship order may be made (unless an adoption application has been made and the court has given leave to a person to apply for a special guardianship order or a guardian has been given leave to oppose the adoption).[183]

Revocation of a placement order

7.156 The child or local authority may apply to revoke a placement order at any time; however other persons (including the parents) may not apply to revoke the order unless they meet each of the following preconditions:

(a) The court gives leave, which it cannot do unless it is satisfied that there has been a 'change of circumstances' since the order was made.

(b) The child has not yet been placed for adoption.

(c) The court considers that the application to revoke has 'a real prospect of success' (having taken into account the child's welfare).[184]

---

[178] ACA 2002, s 28(1).
[179] Ibid, s 28(2) and (3).
[180] Ibid, s 29(1).
[181] Ibid, s 29(2).
[182] Ibid, s 29(3).
[183] Ibid, s 29(5).
[184] *M v Warwickshire CC* [2007] EWCA Civ 1084; [2008] 1 FLR 1093.

A 'change of circumstances' does not need to be 'significant' but must be of a nature and degree sufficient to justify reopening the issue of placement for adoption.[185]

7.157 When determining an application for leave to apply to revoke a placement order the court will adopt a two-stage test deciding: (i) whether there has been a change of circumstances and, if so, (ii) whether to exercise discretion to grant the leave that is sought. At the second stage the court will consider whether the applicant's case has sufficient solidity to justify reopening the adoption issue.[186]

CARE PROCEEDINGS: HOW DOES A PLAN FOR ADOPTION DEVELOP?

7.158 The ACA 2002 has formalised the process by which a child is placed for adoption. Where a plan for adoption develops within ongoing care proceedings, the local authority will not in due course be able to place the child for adoption unless it has been granted a placement order under ACA 2002, s 21. A placement order has a very significant effect upon a parent's ability to challenge any subsequent adoption application. Thus within the compass of care proceedings the plan for the child may develop and, ultimately, the legal rights of the family members may be fundamentally changed by the making of a placement order.

7.159 At the initial stage of a local authority first intervening in a family's care of a child it is unlikely that there will be a ready-made plan for adoption. The process within care proceedings will involve assessment and evaluation of the risks and benefits to the child of remaining with or returning to the natural family. The starting point of any care plan for a child will be a return home to parents, or, if that is not in his best interests, placement within the wider family. Only if the option for family placement is not in accordance with the child's welfare, will an alternative long-term placement be considered appropriate. The priority given to the natural family arises from the duty under domestic law to favour the least interventionist approach[187] and because, under Art 8 of the ECHR, state intervention in family life must be limited to that for which there is a pressing social need, with any plan being proportionate to that need.

7.160 A local authority is under a duty to apply for a placement order if it is 'satisfied that the child ought to be placed for adoption'.[188] In its capacity as an adoption agency, a local authority can only be so 'satisfied' if the question of whether the child is suitable for adoption has been the subject of a decision to that effect taken by a senior 'decision-maker' in the local authority under AAR 2005, reg 19. In order for the local authority to be in a position to consider applying for a placement order within the timescale of ongoing care proceedings,

---

[185] *Re S* [2009] 1 FLR 503.
[186] *Re B-S* [2013] EWCA Civ 1146.
[187] CA 1989, s 1(5) and ACA 2002, s 1(6).
[188] ACA 2002, s 22.

it is necessary for it to plan its assessment process in time to place the case before the decision-maker at an early stage.

7.161 Where adoption is, or may be, the local authority's care plan for a child, the consideration of adoption may run alongside consideration of other options (for example a return home). Two models have developed for this process. In the first, 'parallel' or 'twin-track' planning, the local authority, while working with the family and continuing to assess a family placement, will nevertheless be preparing the paperwork necessary to proceed with an adoption plan without delay if that becomes the final plan for the child. In addition, where a local authority is considering adoption, or is satisfied that adoption is the right plan but are not yet authorised to place for adoption, and where there is no appropriate family placement, the authority must consider placing the child with a local authority foster parent who has been authorised as a prospective adopter.[189]

7.162 The second model, 'concurrent planning', is a more sophisticated and structured option whereby a young child is placed with specialist foster carers who have been selected and trained to work within a programme of rehabilitation of the child to his family, or, if that is not in his interests, to become his adopters in due course. In this model, the main advantage to the child is not having to move from his foster home to his adoptive home.

CONTACT ON PLACEMENT AND AFTER ADOPTION

Contact arrangements when child is authorised for an adoption placement

7.163 On an agency being authorised to place a child for adoption pursuant to parental consent given under ACA 2002, s 19, or pursuant to a placement order, any existing contact orders under CA 1989 (s 8 or s 34) will cease to have effect[190] and the local authority's obligation to afford reasonable contact to his birth family under CA 1989, s 34 is removed. No further application may be made for a Children Act contact order.[191] However, an application for contact may be made during the currency of an agency's authorisation to place for adoption under ACA 2002, s 27.

7.164 The agency must take into account the wishes and feelings of the parent (and, if appropriate, a father without parental responsibility), the advice of the adoption panel and the adoption welfare checklist in ACA 2002, s 1

---

[189] CA 1989, s 22C(9A)–(9B).
[190] ACA 2002, s 26(1), (6).
[191] Ibid, s 26(2).

before making a decision on contact.[192] The contact arrangements must be kept under review and any proposed changes must be canvassed with parents and others.[193]

7.165 The court must consider on an application for a placement order what arrangements are proposed for allowing contact between the child and members of her birth family or any other relevant person. It must invite the parties to comment on those arrangements and may make a s 26 contact order of its own motion.[194]

7.166 When considering whether to make a s 26 order the court must afford paramount consideration to the child's welfare in accordance with ACA 2002, s 1. A s 26 contact order has effect while the adoption agency is authorised to place the child for adoption but may be varied or revoked by the court on an application by the child, the agency or the person named in the order.[195]

7.167 The terms of any s 26 order may be departed from by agreement between the agency and any person for whose contact with the child the order provides, provided that the child (if of sufficient age and understanding) agrees, the prospective adopters agree and relevant persons have been informed of the change.[196]

Adoption agency power to refuse to allow contact

7.168 Unlike the position that applies under a care order, there is no requirement upon an adoption agency with authorisation to place the child to allow contact between the child and any person unless such contact is stipulated in an order under ACA 2002, s 27. Consequently, unless to do so would be in conflict with provision in a s 26 order, the agency may refuse contact without having to seek the court's approval.

7.169 In addition, an adoption agency is permitted to refuse to allow contact that would otherwise be required by virtue of a s 26 order, without first obtaining a court order, if it is satisfied that it is necessary to do so in order to safeguard or promote the child's welfare and the refusal is decided upon as a matter of urgency and does not last for more than seven days.[197] The agency is under a duty to inform relevant individuals as soon as any decision to refuse contact is made.[198]

---

[192] Ibid, s 27(4); AAR 2005, reg 47.
[193] Ibid.
[194] ACA 2002, ss 26, 27.
[195] Ibid, s 27(1).
[196] AAR 2005, reg 47(2).
[197] ACA 2002, s 27(2).
[198] AAR 2005, reg 47.

Application for s 26 contact order

7.170 An application for a s 26 contact order may be made by:[199]

✓ the child;

✓ the agency;

✓ any parent or guardian or relative;

✓ any person in whose favour there was a CA 1989 contact order (which ceased to have effect under s 26(1));

✓ the person with a child arrangements order in force immediately before the adoption agency was authorised to place;

✓ the person who had care of the child by an order under the High Court's inherent jurisdiction before the agency was authorised to place;

✓ any person with the court's leave.

The procedure is governed by FPR 2010, Pt 14; r 14.3 lists the persons who will be respondents to the application.

7.171 It is worth noting that the pool of applicants and respondents to a s 26 contact application is potentially very wide. Any relative of the child – defined in ACA 2002, s 144 to include grandparents, siblings, uncles and aunts, including those of the half blood and relatives by marriage – is entitled to make a s 26 application and there is no leave requirement. Contrast this with the position under the CA 1989, where even grandparents and siblings need leave to make an application for contact under s 8 or s 34. Similarly, the pool of respondents to a s 26 contact application includes those persons 'with whom the child lives or is to live'.

7.172 The court may at any time direct that a child, who is not already a respondent to proceedings, be made a respondent where the child wishes to make an application or has evidence to give to the court, or a legal submission to make, which has not been given or made by any other party, or there are other special circumstances.[200] The court may at any time direct that a person or body be made a respondent or be removed as a respondent.[201]

---

[199] ACA 2002, s 26(3).
[200] FPR 2010, r 14.3(2).
[201] Ibid, r 23(3).

Contact after an adoption order

7.173 In virtually all adoption cases there will be an expectation for some limited indirect contact to continue between the birth family and the adopted child. This can take the form, for example, of letters or short reports sent once or twice each year (possibly with photographs). Direct face-to-face meetings are not usually contemplated, but where the child is older, and particularly where there is benefit in siblings meeting, such contact may take place. The value of some contact post-adoption is that it permits the child to maintain some concept of the complexity of his identity as he moves through childhood and adolescence. In *Down Lisburn Health and Social Services Trust v H*,[202] Baroness Hale reviewed the current approach to (and importance of) post-adoption contact. Once a child is an adult, the provisions of the Adoption Contact Register may apply to facilitate reopening contact with the natural family.[203]

7.174 Where an adoption agency has placed, or was authorised to place, a child for adoption and the court is making or has made an adoption order with respect to the child, the court may make provision for future, post-adoption, contact by an order under ACA 2002, s 51A. The court may make a s 51A order of its own initiative or upon the application of the adopters, the child or any other person who has obtained the court's leave to do so; before granting leave the court must consider the factors listed at s 51A(5). In all other cases where an adoption order has been made, an order for future contact will be a CA 1989, s 8 child arrangements order. It follows that different welfare considerations may apply depending upon whether ACA 2002, s 1 is in play (with respect to a s 51A application) or CA 1989, s 1 in all other cases.

ILLEGAL PLACEMENTS AND OTHER PROHIBITED STEPS

7.175 No person other than an adoption agency, or a person acting pursuant to an order of the High Court, may take any of the steps set out in ACA 2002, s 92(2) relating to the adoption of a child (unless, with respect to some of the steps, the proposed adopter is a relative of the child or a partner of a parent). The nine categories of steps listed in s 92(2) cover in effect any step in the process of arranging for the adoption of a child and apply to arrangements made anywhere in the world. Anyone who breaches s 92(2) is liable to prosecution. To commit an offence, the step must be taken within the jurisdiction of England and Wales.

7.176 Where steps have been taken in breach of s 92(2), the situation thereby created may only continue if the High Court gives authorisation for it to do so.[204]

---

[202] *Down Lisburn Health and Social Services Trust v H* [2006] UKHL 36; [2007] 1 FLR 121.
[203] For Adoption Contact Register, see **7.117**.
[204] ACA 2002, s 92(1).

7.177 In addition to the steps in ACA 2002, s 92(2) no person other than one prescribed by the Restriction on the Preparation of Adoption Reports Regulations 2005[205] may prepare a report for any person about the suitability of a child for adoption, or of a person to adopt a child or about the adoption or placement for adoption of a child.[206] The aim of this provision is to outlaw 'home study' reports prepared to support non-agency adoption applications (frequently intercountry adoptions) by any person other than an experienced adoption social worker employed by an adoption agency.

7.178 Finally, it is illegal to make any payment which is made for, or in consideration of, the adoption of a child (or any related activity) unless the payment is expressly permitted by the legislation.[207]

APPLYING FOR AN ADOPTION ORDER

7.179 An application for an adoption order will be made to the Family Court and will then be allocated to an level in the judiciary. The procedure is governed by the Family Procedure Rules 2010, Pt 14 and associated Practice Directions.

7.180 The applicant will be the prospective adopter(s) and the respondents will be each parent or guardian with parental responsibility for the child (unless they have given notice stating that they do not wish to be informed of any adoption), any person who has a contact order in their favour, any local authority or adoption agency connected with the child's adoption and, in certain circumstances, the child. In addition the court may direct that any person may be added (or removed) as a respondent. Where the child is a party he will normally be represented by a children's guardian and a solicitor for the child must be appointed.

7.181 The court will hold a 'first directions hearing' at which a number of specific issues listed in r 14.8 must be considered with a view to ensuring that the case is properly prepared for a timely final hearing.

7.182 Where a request is being made to dispense with a parent's consent to adoption, a written notice to that effect must be filed and a 'statement of facts' reciting the relevant history must be prepared.

7.183 Where a parent has given advance consent to adoption under ACA 2002, s 20 or the child has been placed for adoption pursuant either to parental consent or under a placement order, the parent or guardian may oppose any adoption application only if the court gives him permission to do so. The court may only consider granting permission to such a parent to oppose the adoption if there

---

[205] SI 2005/1711.
[206] ACA 2002, s 94(1).
[207] Ibid, s 95.

has been 'a change of circumstances' in the intervening period[208] and (giving paramount consideration to the child's welfare) the court considers it is in the child's best interests to permit the parent to oppose the adoption.[209] The result of this provision is that in many cases to which it applies, whilst the parent will be given notice of the adoption application, they will be unable to oppose the application.

7.184 A key statutory requirement is that the court must receive a substantial and comprehensive report upon the child, the natural parents and the adopters before the final hearing can proceed. The report must cover the topics listed in Practice Direction 14C annexed to the Rules. As with any other material filed in the proceedings, these reports are confidential within the proceedings.

7.185 Where a parent opposes the making of the adoption order there will be a full final hearing at which the principal issue is likely to be whether or not the parent's consent to adoption should be dispensed with. In other cases, provided that the application is not opposed by the local authority or adoption agency, and provided that the court is satisfied with the written information that has been provided, the adoption hearing is unlikely to be lengthy.

7.186 Where an adoption order has been made the child will not normally have visited the court or met the judge, it is therefore usual for the child and other family members to attend before the judge/magistrates for on a date some weeks after the adoption order has been made for an informal 'adoption visit' to the court at which, if the court agrees, photographs may be taken. Where it appears likely that there will be an appeal against an adoption order, the party intending to appeal should seek an immediate stay of the order to prevent the child meeting the judge prior to the appeal being heard.[210]

CONSEQUENCES OF AN ADOPTION ORDER

7.187 An adoption order is an order giving parental responsibility for a child to the adopters. The order does not affect parental responsibility so far as it relates to any period prior to the making of the order. Further the making of an adoption order operates to extinguish:

✓ the parental responsibility which any person (other than the adopters) had prior to the adoption;

✓ any order under CA 1989 or in wardship proceedings;

---

[208] Ibid, s 47.
[209] ACA 2002, s 47; *Re P* [2007] 2 FLR 1069. For 'change of circumstances', see **7.158**.
[210] *President's Guidance: Listing Final Hearings in Adoption Cases* (10 April 2018).

✓ any duty to make payments for the child's maintenance or upbringing relating to the period after the adoption.[211]

7.188 An adopted child is treated in law as if he had been born as a child of the adopters, and he is treated as not being the child of any other person.[212] The only matters that are not affected by adoption are the table of kindred and affinity in the Marriage Act 1949 or the Sexual Offences Act 2003 (thus the natural relationships still apply for these purposes), and any provision of the British Nationality Act 1981 and the Immigration Act 1971.

7.189 When an adoption order is made in any court in the UK, the child will automatically become a British citizen if the adopter, or at least one of a couple, is a British citizen on the date of the order.[213] If the applicants wish the child's name to be changed, this can be achieved by stating the child's new name on the adoption application form.

7.190 If provision is to be made for any form of contact between the natural family and the child after an adoption order, this will usually be dealt with without a court order with the plan being spelled out in the local authority report to the court. Alternatively the proposed contact arrangements may be a preliminary recital to any court order. In an exceptional case there may be a need for a court order regulating contact; such an order may be made under CA 1989, s 8 and is a private law contact order. The courts are most unlikely to impose a regime of contact that is not acceptable to the adopters.

ADOPTIONS WITH AN INTERNATIONAL ELEMENT

7.191 The law relating to international adoptions is complex. What follows is no more than a brief overview of the subject.[214]

7.192 An international element may arise in connection with adoption in the following circumstances:

✓ a foreign child has been 'adopted' abroad and brought into England and Wales by his adopters;

✓ a foreign child, who has not been already 'adopted', is brought into England and Wales in order to be adopted here;

✓ an English/Welsh child is to be sent abroad to be adopted in a foreign country.

---

[211] ACA 2002, s 47.
[212] Ibid, s 67.
[213] British Nationality Act 1981, s 1(5).
[214] For a comprehensive description of Adoptions with an International Element, see Hershman and McFarlane, *Children Law and Practice* (Bloomsbury Professional) Division D, Section 7.

Foreign child 'adopted' abroad

7.193 Some foreign adoptions are recognised under English law as being valid adoptions, with the result that the adoption will be seen as valid under English law and the adopters will not need to issue fresh adoption proceedings here. One group of adoptions that are recognised as valid are 'overseas adoptions', being adoptions from one of the 66 states listed in the Adoption (Designation of Overseas Adoptions) Order 1973 (as amended from time to time).[215] Another group of adoptions that are recognised as valid are 'Convention adoptions' made under the 1993 Hague Convention.[216] In addition some foreign adoptions may be recognised under the common law, for which purpose an application for recognition must be made to the English court.[217]

7.194 Where a foreign adoption is neither an 'overseas adoption' nor a Convention adoption, it will be necessary for the adopters to make a fresh application for an adoption order in England and Wales in order for their adoptive status to be recognised. The foreign process may be useful evidence in support of their application.

Foreign child brought into England and Wales for adoption

7.195 Stringent procedures and conditions apply to the process of bringing a child into the UK in order to be adopted here. It is a criminal offence, punishable with up to 12 months' imprisonment, to bring a child into the UK for adoption unless the regulations have been complied with.[218] The key regulations are the Adoptions with a Foreign Element Regulations 2005.[219] In short, they require detailed assessments of the suitability of the adoptive home, and of the child's circumstances, before official approval will be given to any proposed arrangement.[220] Official approval is provided by a certificate issued by the Secretary of State for Education. Once the child has arrived in England and Wales, the adopters must notify their local authority of the fact (they will be regarded in the interim period as private foster parents) and must immediately indicate their intention to apply to adopt the child. The local authority is under a duty to monitor the child's welfare. If an adoption order is made, it will be an ordinary domestic adoption order; all of the conditions described earlier in this chapter will apply to the adoption proceedings just as they would if there were no foreign element.

---

[215] ACA 2002, s 67.
[216] For 'Convention adoptions' see **7.197**.
[217] See, eg: *Re N (Recognition of Foreign Adoption Order)* [2016] EWHC 3085 (Fam).
[218] ACA 2002, s 83.
[219] SI 2005/392.
[220] Detailed guidance on the process can be found at http://education.gov.uk/childrenandyoungpeople/families/adoption/intercountryadoption.

Facilitating the adoption abroad of a child from the UK

7.196 A child who is a Commonwealth citizen or who is habitually resident in the UK must not be removed from the UK for the purpose of adoption unless the prospective adopters have obtained an order under ACA 2002, s 84[221] giving them parental responsibility for the child in order to facilitate a foreign adoption. A breach of this restriction, or being involved in making arrangements to breach it, is a criminal offence and may incur up to 12 months' imprisonment.[222] In order to obtain a s 84 order the applicant must have complied with the Adoptions with a Foreign Element Regulations 2005 and the child must have had his home with each applicant for the preceding 10 weeks. In certain circumstances (which fall short of actual placement for adoption), a local authority may place a child abroad in the home of potential adopters for the purposes of assessment, without either the adopters or the local authority contravening the provisions of ACA 2002, s 55.[223]

Convention adoptions

7.197 The 1993 Hague Convention on Protection of Children and Co-operation with respect to International Adoption has full effect in England and Wales. The Convention is essentially a framework setting out minimum standards for the control and regulation of the flow of children between states for adoption. It has been signed or ratified by a total of 102 states. It establishes a detailed system for co-operation between Member States and seeks to ensure that adoptions in one Member State are recognised as valid in every other Convention state. In the UK the Convention therefore operates to regulate the process in both states and will affect a child coming into the UK from a Convention country, or vice versa. Depending on the process used, a child may be brought to the UK having already been adopted in another Convention country (in which case the adoption is automatically recognised here) or brought into the UK (without being adopted) for the purpose of achieving a UK adoption (in which case the preliminary vetting process will have been carried out in accordance with the Convention).

---

[221] Or similar provisions for Scotland or Northern Ireland.
[222] ACA 2002, s 85.
[223] *A (A Child)* [2009] EWCA Civ 41; [2009] 2 FLR 597.

Chapter 8

SPECIAL GUARDIANSHIP

Chapter summary

- Application and procedure

- Special guardianship orders within care proceedings

- Support services and financial support

- Interaction with other orders

- Variation and discharge

8.1 Special guardianship was introduced by the Adoption and Children Act 2002 (ACA 2002) as a new order designed to meet the needs of children for whom none of the previously available options (primarily adoption, long-term fostering or a child arrangements order) is entirely suitable. It is intended to combine the advantages of a continued legal relationship with the birth family with the security of a long-term placement.

8.2 One important aspect of special guardianship is that there are restrictions on its discharge or revocation. A special guardianship order is revocable, and so can never be as 'secure' as an adoption, but a parent wishing to make an application to discharge the order must first obtain the leave of the court. The legislation is geared towards securing the child's long-term future and the order will almost always be made on the basis that it is intended to last until the child is 18.

8.3 Those who are most likely to apply to become special guardians include wider family members, family friends and foster carers. Parents are specifically excluded.

8.4 In summary, the effect of a special guardianship order is to:

✓ secure the child's long-term placement;

✓ give the special guardian parental responsibility;

✓ maintain the child's links with his or her parent(s); BUT

✓ enable the special guardian to control on a day-to-day basis the parents' exercise of their parental responsibility.

8.5 Section 14C of the Children Act 1989 (CA 1989) sets out the effect of a special guardianship order. The order:

- ✓ gives the special guardian parental responsibility for the child;

- ✓ subject to any other orders in force under the CA 1989, enables the special guardian to exercise parental responsibility to the exclusion of any other person with parental responsibility (other than another special guardian);

- ✓ does not permit the special guardian to do anything which requires the consent of all those with parental responsibility: for example, consent to an adoption or placement for adoption, a change of name or a permanent removal from the jurisdiction.

> Special guardianship offers long-term security to carers, like grandparents and other family members, for whom adoption may not be the right order

8.6 A key feature of a special guardianship order, and that which is likely to make it most attractive to prospective carers in cases where there is a background of parental neglect or abuse, is that the special guardian may exercise parental responsibility to the exclusion of the child's parent(s). This is likely to make the order more suitable in such cases than a child arrangements order, which simply provides for the child to live with the proposed carer.

8.7 The differences between special guardianship orders and adoption orders, in cases where it is intended that the child's placement away from his parents should be permanent, were considered in *Re S (Adoption Order or Special Guardianship Order)*.[1] One key difference is that the child's legal status will be different in a number of respects, depending on which order is made. Essentially, if the child is adopted she will become a permanent member of the adoptive family. If a special guardianship order is made, the special guardian will be responsible for the child's care and upbringing but her legal ties with her birth parents will remain intact.

8.8 The factors pointing towards or against either order in any particular case will vary, and the key question in each case will be which order will best serve the welfare of the particular child.

---

[1] *Re S (Adoption Order or Special Guardianship Order)* [2007] EWCA Civ 54; [2007] 1 FLR 819.

	Adoption	**Special Guardianship**	**Child Arrangements**
Child's legal status	Becomes the child of the adopters	Remains the parents' child	Remains the parents' child
Duration	Lifelong	Until 18	Until 18
Parental responsibility	Held by adopters exclusively.	Shared by Special Guardian and parents, but Special Guardian can make most decisions alone (save for permanent move to another country, or change of surname and – probably – some significant medical treatment issues).	Shared between parents and person caring for the child under a child arrangements order. All significant decisions require consultation; in the event of a disagreement, the court may make an order.
Scope for challenge	Order can be revoked only in very exceptional circumstances.	Parents may apply to discharge, but need the court's leave and must show a significant change of circumstances.	Parents can apply at any time and without leave to discharge the order.
Contact with parents	Parents need the leave of the court to apply.	Parents may apply at any time, without leave.	Parents may apply at any time, without leave.
Financial and other support	Financial assistance may be available at the discretion of the local authority.	Financial support (means tested Special Guardianship Allowance) available. Local authority also obliged to assess need for services including therapeutic support.	Child Arrangements Order Allowance may be payable if child was previously in care. No specific entitlement to support unless child already entitled (eg as a child in need).
	Support services available through local authority or Adoption Support Fund.		

APPLICATION AND PROCEDURE

8.9 The most important feature of the application process is that notice must be given to the relevant local authority[2], which must then prepare a report for the court. The applicant must give the local authority notice of his intention to apply for a special guardianship order at least three months before the application is made. For certain classes of applicant, leave of the court is required.[3] In these cases, the local authority is not obliged to commence preparing a report until the court has granted leave.

8.10 If a placement order is in force, and the applicant already has leave to make the application, the three-month period is waived and notice may be given at any time prior to the application.

'Who may apply for a special guardianship order?'

✓ any guardian of the child

✓ anyone named in a child arrangements order as a person with whom the child is to live

✓ any person with whom the child has lived for a period of at least three years

✓ anyone who has the consent of all persons with parental responsibility, or all persons named in a child arrangements order as persons with whom the child is to live

✓ if the child is in care, any person who has the consent of the local authority

✓ a local authority foster parent with whom the child has lived for at least a year

✓ a relative with whom the child has lived for at least a year

✓ anyone else, with the leave of the court

The local authority's report must deal with:

✓ the suitability of the applicant to be a special guardian;

---

[2] If the child is being looked after by a local authority, that local authority; otherwise, the local authority in whose area the applicant is 'ordinarily resident', which will normally mean 'lives': CA 1989, s 14A(7).
[3] CA 1989, s 14A.

- ✓ the factors set out in the Schedule to the Special Guardianship Regulations 2005 (these include details of the child's and the special guardian's family, medical issues, the wishes and feelings of relevant persons);

- ✓ the implications of making a special guardianship order for the child, his family and the special guardian;

- ✓ an assessment of which of the orders available to the court would best meet the child's long-term interests;

- ✓ any other matter it considers relevant.

In addition, detailed statutory guidance on the form and content of special guardianship order reports was set out by the Department for Education, last updated in January 2017.[4]

8.11 The Special Guardianship (Amendment) Regulations 2016 were produced following concerns about the fragility of a significant number of special guardianship placements made under the 2005 regulations. As a result, the 2016 regulations make explicit that when preparing a special guardianship report, the local authority must include consideration of any harm suffered by the child and any risk of future harm to him, including that posed by his parents, and must also consider the child's likely future needs as well as his current needs. When considering the applicant's suitability to be the child's special guardian, the local authority must have regard to the current and past relationship between the child and special guardian and to the proposed special guardian's parenting capacity, including their understanding of and ability to meet the child's needs and to protect the children from harm (in particular relating to contact), and their ability and suitability to bring up the child until he turns 18.

8.12 The court may make a special guardianship order in family proceedings of its own motion and, to that end, may request the local authority to carry out an investigation and prepare a report. The court is not permitted to make a special guardianship order unless it has received a report dealing with the matters set out above.[5] This means that the issue of special guardianship must be considered at an early stage. If it appears that there is a possibility that the court may wish to make a special guardianship order (for example, in favour of grandparents in care proceedings) the time needed to prepare the report must be factored into the timetable of proceedings.

---

[4] Available online: https://assets.publishing.service.gov.uk/government/uploads/system/uploads/attachment_data/file/ 656593/Special_guardianship_statutory_guidance.pdf.

[5] CA 1989, s 14A(11).

SPECIAL GUARDIANSHIP ORDERS WITHIN CARE PROCEEDINGS

8.13 It is common that a special guardianship order will be one of the options put before the court at the end of care proceedings. The prospective special guardians will not automatically be parties to the proceedings and because of the restrictions on disclosing information from confidential proceedings[6] it can be difficult for them to get a clear picture of what is happening in court. Prospective special guardians are not used granted legal aid and, particularly when their application is not supported by the local authority, may find themselves in a difficult position. In these circumstances the court will usually make directions permitting limited disclosure of information to the applicant special guardians, in order to enable them to decide whether or not they want to proceed with their application.

8.14 The following two case studies illustrate how a special guardianship application may be dealt with during the course of care proceedings, in the first case when the application is supported by the local authority, and in the second case when it is not.

> *Case Study 1: Henry and Yara*
>
> *Henry and Yara are grandparents to Ivan, aged six months. Ivan's father is their son, Frederic. Both Frederic and his partner, Ivan's mother Sue, are heroin addicts and Ivan was taken into care at birth.*
>
> *The social worker came to visit Henry and Yara when Ivan was a few weeks old to discuss whether they would be able to care for him in the long term. Henry and Yara thought about it and decided that they very much wanted to keep Henry in the family. They told the local authority this and the local authority carried out a special guardianship assessment, which was positive. The local authority's position within the care proceedings is that the court should make a special guardianship order in Henry and Yara's favour. Frederic agrees with this but Sue does not. She says that she is undergoing treatment for her drug addiction and wants to care for Ivan, although the evidence suggests that she may recently have relapsed.*
>
> *The final hearing in the care proceedings is next week. Henry and Yara have not been joined as parties to the proceedings, although they attended court at an earlier stage and the Judge invited them in before the hearing started to explain the process to them. The social worker has explained to them that none of the parties require them to give evidence, as the issue is not whether they would be suitable carers for Ivan (everyone agrees that they would) but whether Sue has made enough progress to be able to care for him herself.*

---

[6] See **6.116**.

> *Case Study 2: Mariella*
>
> *Mariella is the maternal aunt of Toby, aged seven. The identity of Toby's father is unknown. Toby's mother, Gloria, has been diagnosed as schizophrenic and her condition has recently worsened; she is currently receiving inpatient treatment. There is considerable doubt about her long-term prognosis and she is not seeking to care for Toby herself. Toby is in temporary foster care, with Gloria's agreement.*
>
> *Mariella has given notice to the local authority of her intention to apply for a special guardianship order and has been assessed. The conclusion of the assessment is negative, primarily because the report-writer considers that Mariella would not be able to prevent her sister Gloria from removing Toby from her care, or to manage contact (there have been difficulties in the past when Mariella has been looking after Toby at Gloria's request). The local authority's plan is that Toby should be placed in long term foster care under a care order. Mariella feels strongly that with enough support from the local authority she would be able to care for Toby and to protect him from the impact of his mother's mental ill-health.*
>
> *The final hearing in the care proceedings is next week. At an earlier hearing the Judge joined Mariella as a party to the proceedings and ordered that she be provided with the documents she needed to prepare her case. Mariella was directed to make a witness statement setting out her reasons for disagreeing with the conclusions of the special guardianship report. Mariella has done this. She will represent herself at the final hearing and give evidence. The Judge will have to decide whether to make the special guardianship order sought by Mariella or the care order sought by the local authority.*

> Whether prospective special guardians need to become parties to the proceedings (attending hearings and receiving court papers) will depend on the circumstances of the case. If they are joined as parties, they frequently represent themselves in court, without a lawyer

SUPPORT SERVICES AND FINANCIAL SUPPORT

8.15 The ACA 2002 imposes on local authorities a duty to make arrangements for the provision within its area of special guardianship support services, and a complaints procedure for those dissatisfied with the support services provided. The services that must be made available include counselling, training, respite care and mediation (for example, in connection with contact arrangements), and services must be provided to special guardians, children and birth families. Details are set out in the 2005 regulations.

8.16 Financial provision is often of critical importance to those, particularly relatives and friends, who are considering whether to apply for a special guardianship order. The provisions governing financial support from a local authority to special guardians are set out in CA 1989, s 14F and Chapter II of the 2005 regulations. The basic point is that, whilst a special guardian may have a right to be assessed for financial support, the payment and extent of financial provision is a decision for a local authority to reach. If there is a dispute about it, the remedy of the special guardians is to seek judicial review.[7] That, of course, cannot be undertaken in the family court; although in practice, if the provision of financial support is the only barrier to otherwise suitable special guardians being in a position to care for the child, the local authority may find itself coming under considerable pressure within family court care proceedings to improve its offer.

8.17 The headline points are that:

✓ non-means tested assistance may be given in cash for specific one-off needs: such as funding a babysitter or paying for petrol for contact;

✓ financial support should be payable in accordance with the 2005 regulations to help secure a suitable special guardianship arrangement where there is otherwise a financial obstacle to the making of that arrangement – in particular, that can include: where the child's needs demand special care; where there are past or likely future legal fees; or where money is required for furniture, domestic equipment, toys, clothing, transport or adaptations to the home;

✓ in determining the amount of financial support provided, a local authority should 'have regard to' the amount that would be paid under fostering allowance;

✓ remuneration is not paid, save for in the case of a former foster parent, in which case it may be, for an initial (and extendable) term of two years.

8.18 It has been held that a blanket policy of a local authority to fix its Special Guardianship Allowance at 66% of the fostering allowance was unlawful.[8]

> A person putting themselves forward during care proceedings to become the child's special guardian would be well advised to discuss and agree with the local authority a package of support before the proceedings come to an end – especially if the child has therapeutic or other needs

---

[7] See **Ch 11**.
[8] *Barrett v Kirklees Metropolitan Council* [2010] EWHC 467 (Admin); [2010] 2 FCR 153.

INTERACTION WITH OTHER ORDERS

8.19 The making of a special guardianship order does not of itself affect any s 8 order; indeed, the special guardian's ability to exercise parental responsibility is circumscribed by any existing Children Act orders. However, the court is expressly required to consider on making the special guardianship order whether any current s 8 order should be varied or discharged.[9]

8.20 A special guardianship order, like a 'lives with' child arrangements order, discharges a care order.[10] However, a care order does not discharge a special guardianship order. The effect of this is that the status of a special guardian continues to be recognised, albeit in a diluted form, notwithstanding the care order. As is the case with parents, the local authority with a care order can determine the extent to which special guardians exercise parental responsibility.[11] Similarly, the local authority's obligations towards the parents of children in care are, generally speaking, extended to special guardians: so, for example, s 34 of the CA 1989 was amended to include special guardians within the categories of persons to whom the local authority must afford reasonable contact with the child.

8.21 If a special guardianship order is in force, no application for a 'lives with' child arrangements order with respect to the child may be made by any person without leave.[12] This important provision indicates the extent to which special guardianship orders are intended to be permanent. Similar restrictions operate in relation to their variation and discharge.

VARIATION AND DISCHARGE

8.22 The court may vary or discharge a special guardianship order on its own motion, or on the application (as of right) of:

✓ the special guardian;

✓ any person with a (current) 'lives with' child arrangements order;

✓ any person with parental responsibility *other than a parent or step-parent* (see below);

✓ a local authority designated in a care order with respect to the child,

and, with leave:

✓ the child;

---

[9] CA 1989, s 14B(1).
[10] Ibid, s 91(5A).
[11] Ibid, s 33(3)(b).
[12] Ibid, s 10(7A).

✓   any parent or guardian;

✓   any step-parent with parental responsibility;

✓   any person who had parental responsibility prior to the making of the special guardianship order, but no longer has it.

> It can be difficult for a parent to get permission to apply to discharge a special guardianship order. The orders are intended to be permanent, to give both the child and the special guardian a sense of security

8.23 Where the applicant for leave is a parent or guardian, step-parent or previous holder of parental responsibility, the court may not grant leave unless there has been 'a significant change in circumstances' since the special guardianship order was made.[13] This ostensibly places parents seeking to discharge a special guardianship order in a significantly worse position than those who are applying to discharge a care order. The Court of Appeal has given guidance on the meaning of 'a significant change in circumstances', taking the view that this, for the time being, should mean the same as 'a change in circumstances' when applying for the revocation of a placement order (ie to stop a plan for adoption) under ACA 2002, s 24.[14]

---

[13] CA 1989, s 14D(5).
[14] *G (A Child)* [2010] EWCA Civ 300, [2010] 2 FLR 696, CA.

Chapter 9

SECURE ACCOMMODATION AND DEPRIVATION OF LIBERTY

Chapter summary

- Introduction
- What is secure accommodation?
- Criteria for a secure accommodation order
- Effect of a secure accommodation order
- Procedure
- The local authority's obligations
- Deprivation of liberty

INTRODUCTION

9.1 The restriction of liberty is an important matter, whether the subject is an adult or a child. By necessity and on a daily basis, children have their liberty restricted: by parents, teachers and others by whom they are cared for. The degree of restriction will depend on their age and development. In this chapter, we are concerned not with restrictions imposed by parents (or those acting on their behalf), but rather by limitations to freedom and liberty imposed by the state, normally, through local authorities. The most intense of those restrictions require court authorisation.

9.2 There are a number of contexts in which the state may restrict a child's liberty. Children who are serving prison sentences and children who have been sectioned under the Mental Health Act 1983 are subject to significant restrictions governed by distinct pieces of legislation. The law there is applicable, with some modification, to both adults and children. This chapter focusses on children whose accommodation is the direct responsibility of a local authority's social services department, and whose behaviour is especially dangerous or difficult so that a local authority seeks to restrict their liberty for their own safety or that of others. Depending on the degree of restriction, the state's actions may engage a child's rights under Art 5 of the European Convention on

Human Rights (ECHR) (right to liberty and security). If so, the state requires authorisation to do so. The statutory scheme to authorise such restrictions is secure accommodation: Children Act 1989 (CA 1989), s 25.

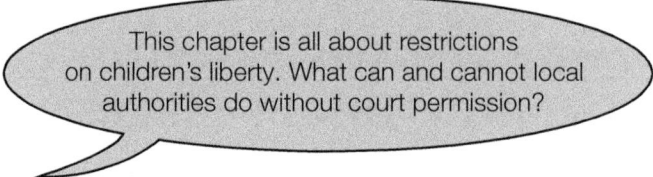

This chapter is all about restrictions on children's liberty. What can and cannot local authorities do without court permission?

9.3 It is important to flag up that the statutory scheme is just that. It applies in relation only to certain types of accommodation and certain children. It is increasingly the case that a type of accommodation or a child will not fall within the power in s 25 of the CA 1989. As such, the courts have had to develop new powers outside of the statutory scheme. Those new powers are commonly known as deprivation of liberty, drawing on the wording of Art 5 of the ECHR.

Significant restrictions on children's liberty } Secure accommodation orders
Deprivation of liberty and the inherent jurisdiction

9.4 This chapter deals first with secure accommodation and secure accommodation orders under CA 1989, s 25. Later on in the chapter, we look at deprivation of liberty and the inherent jurisdiction.

WHAT IS SECURE ACCOMMODATION?

9.5

Secure accommodation: key features

✓ Applies only to children already looked after by the local authority, that is to say children subject to an interim or full care order or (with certain exceptions) provided with local authority accommodation under s 20 of the CA 1989

✓ Criteria:
– history of absconding *and* likely to abscond again *and* likelihood of significant harm if absconds, or
– likely to injure self or others if not kept in secure accommodation

✓ Permissive order: allows the local authority to keep child in secure accommodation; does not require it to do so

✓ Local authority may keep child in secure accommodation without an order for up to 72 hours in any 28-day period

✓ Maximum duration of order is three months on the first application and six months on subsequent applications

9.6 Secure accommodation normally means a registered children's home that is approved as secure accommodation. There are 15 individually managed secure children's homes in England and Wales with 255 beds. The places in those secure children's homes are in very high demand, with the beds shared out between the family and criminal justice system. A children's home designated as secure accommodation is subject to regulation and assessment, and the Secretary of State must approve its use for that purpose.[1]

> On 31 March 2018, there were 204 children accommodated in local authority secure accommodation: 47% were placed by a local authority on welfare grounds, 48% detained or sentenced by the Youth Custody Service and 5% placed by a local authority in the criminal justice context

9.7 Whilst secure accommodation normally means a registered secure children's home, the definition is, in fact, broader than that. In CA 1989, s 25, secure accommodation is defined as 'accommodation provided for the purposes of restricting liberty'. Wall J, fleshing out the statutory definition, described it as accommodation 'designed for, or having as its primary purpose', the restriction of a child's liberty. In that case, therefore, a hospital clinic could not be said to be secure accommodation, because its primary purpose was to achieve treatment, with the restrictions on the child's liberty incidental to that aim.[2] In another case, however, a maternity ward has been found to be secure accommodation, because of the restricted entry to and exit from the ward.[3] So, depending on the facts of the case and the nature of the accommodation, it is possible for accommodation other than a registered secure children's home to be used as secure accommodation.

9.8 Secure accommodation is likely only to be appropriate for older children and teenagers whose behaviour is so extreme that the structure and rules of an ordinary foster placement or children's home are insufficient. In any event, a child under the age of 13 may not be placed in secure accommodation in a children's home without the prior approval of the Secretary of State.[4] From 2010 to 2018, the best represented group of children in secure children's homes were those aged 14 and 15.

---

[1] Children (Secure Accommodation) Regulations 1991, SI 1991/1505, reg 3.
[2] *C (A Minor) (Detention For Medical Treatment), Re* [1997] 2 FLR 180, [1997] 3 FCR 49, [1997] Fam Law 474, Fam D.
[3] *A Metropolitan Borough Council v DB* [1997] 1 FLR 767, [1997] 1 FCR 618, [1997] Fam Law 400, Fam D.
[4] Children (Secure Accommodation) Regulations 1991, SI 1991/1505, reg 4.

9.9 It is important to recognise that the phrasing of s 25 *prevents* a local authority from keeping a child in accommodation whose purpose is restricting her liberty except in the circumstances set out in the statute. It is a prohibitive and not a permissive section and, if the criteria explained below cease to apply, the local authority must release the child immediately even if the order is still in force.

CRITERIA FOR A SECURE ACCOMMODATION ORDER

9.10 Section 25 applies only to children who are already being looked after by the local authority: that is, children who are in care or (with certain exceptions[5]) are accommodated by a local authority exercising its social services functions under s 20 of the CA 1989. The powers in relation to secure accommodation are devolved: the relevant law in Wales is set out in s 119 of the Social Services and Well-being (Wales) Act 2014. The same principles apply.

9.11 There are two alternative grounds for keeping or placing such a child in secure accommodation:

✓ the child has a history of absconding and is likely to abscond from any other description of accommodation and, if he absconds, is likely to suffer significant harm; or

✓ if he is kept in any other description of accommodation he is likely to injure himself or other persons.

9.12 'Likely' in this section means the same as it does in s 31 (see **6.14**). It means that there is a real possibility that cannot sensibly be ignored.

9.13 The court's role in relation to a secure accommodation order differs from the approach taken to other CA 1989 orders. Under s 25 of the CA 1989, the court is required to determine whether the statutory criteria for secure accommodation exist in the particular case and, if they do, then an order must normally be made. Section 1(1) of the CA 1989 does not apply to a secure accommodation application,[6] with the result that the child's welfare is not the court's paramount consideration and the welfare checklist does not apply. The court's role in either granting or refusing a secure accommodation order is therefore a supervisory one rather than one that involves a full assessment of the child's welfare needs.

9.14 The statute says that, if the statutory criteria are satisfied, the court must make the order: CA 1989, s 25(4). However, a recent case has made clear that a secure accommodation order can only be made where necessary and

---

[5] Children (Secure Accommodation) Regulations 1991, SI 1991/1505, reg 5(2)(a).
[6] *M (A Minor), Re* [1995] 1 FLR 418, [1995] Fam 108, [1995] 3 All ER 407, CA.

proportionate.⁷ Once the order is made, the responsibility for ensuring that the power granted by the order is used sparingly, and that the child is only kept in secure accommodation for the minimum period necessary, is that of the local authority.

EFFECT OF A SECURE ACCOMMODATION ORDER

Secure accommodation without an order

9.15 A local authority (or other authority) may keep a child in secure accommodation for a total period of 72 hours, whether or not consecutive, in any 28-day period.⁸

9.16 Special rules apply for calculating and potentially extending the maximum period if it is due to expire between 12 noon the day before a Sunday or bank holiday and 12 noon the day after.⁹

Secure accommodation with an order

9.17 When the child has been remanded to local authority accommodation by a criminal court any secure accommodation order must not extend beyond the period of the remand and, in any event, can last for a maximum of 28 days. If the remand period is longer than 28 days a further order of the court must be sought.¹⁰

9.18 In all other cases the maximum period of a secure accommodation order is three months on the first application, and six months on any subsequent application.¹¹ There is no limit to the number of orders that may be made. However, in 2018, only 11% of those children accommodated in a secure children's home had been in such a placement for over 12 months. The court should make the order only for the minimum period necessary.¹² Interim orders may be made, for no longer than the maximum period for a full order, only when the application for a full order is adjourned.

Age and other restrictions

9.19 The following children may *not* be kept in secure accommodation:

---

[7] *W (A Child)* [2016] EWCA Civ 804, [2016] 4 WLR 159, CA.
[8] Children (Secure Accommodation) Regulations 1991, SI 1991/1505, reg 10(1).
[9] Ibid, reg 10(3).
[10] Ibid, reg 13.
[11] Ibid, regs 11–12.
[12] *W (A Minor) (Secure Accommodation Order), Re* [1993] 1 FLR 692, [1993] 1 FCR 693, [1993] Fam Law 345, Fam D.

✓ a child under the age of 13 may not be kept in secure accommodation in a children's home, unless the Secretary of State has given prior approval;[13]

✓ a child aged 16 and over who is being accommodated by the local authority under s 20(5) of the CA 1989[14] – but, note, a child aged 16 and over who is accommodated by the local authority under s 20(3) may be kept in secure accommodation;

✓ a child subject to a child assessment order under s 43 who is being kept away from home pursuant to that order.[15]

Children looked after by the local authority

9.20 Section 25 applies to children who are being looked after by the local authority. This includes children who are subject to care orders, and children who are accommodated by the local authority in its capacity as a provider of social services. Being accommodated means being provided with accommodation for a period in excess of 24 hours.[16] Children who have been remanded by a criminal court to local authority accommodation become 'looked after' children and therefore fall within the scope of s 25, modified as discussed below.

9.21 The fact that a child who is not in care but is being accommodated has been placed in secure accommodation does not affect the right of any person with parental responsibility to remove her from local authority accommodation, secure or otherwise, at any time.[17]

9.22 The local authority has no power to place a child it is *not* looking after in secure accommodation. Faced with a child who meets the criteria for secure accommodation but whose parents do not agree to accommodation under s 20, the local authority's only option is to apply for a care order or an emergency protection order.

Case Study:

A local authority has been involved for a number of years with a mother and her daughter, now aged 14. The mother has learning difficulties and the child has previously been given a child protection plan under the category of neglect.

---

[13] Children (Secure Accommodation) Regulations 1991, SI 1991/1505, reg 4. There appears to be no prohibition on keeping children of this age in secure accommodation elsewhere: for instance, in a hospital.
[14] Children (Secure Accommodation) Regulations 1991, SI 1991/1505, reg 5(2)(a).
[15] Ibid, reg 5(2)(b).
[16] CA 1989, ss 22(1) and 105(4). The latter category includes children who are lost or abandoned or have no person with parental responsibility for them (s 20(1)); who are accommodated with their parents' consent (s 20(7)); and who are subject to emergency protection orders (s 44).
[17] Subject to the provisions of CA 1989, s 20(9).

The local authority has provided a high level of support to the family and until recently took the view that with this help the mother's parenting was 'good enough' and there was no need to issue proceedings for a care or supervision order. In the last month, the child's behaviour has escalated and she is not attending school, regularly stays out all night and appears to have become involved with drugs and possibly prostitution. She has told her social worker that if she is put in foster care she will run away.

Although the child meets at least the second limb of the s 25 criteria (likely to injure herself or others), the child is not being 'looked after' by the local authority. If the mother objects to the child being accommodated, the local authority must apply for a care order and seek an interim care order at the start of proceedings. At the same time, it may apply for a secure accommodation order. Alternatively, if there is a prospect that a foster placement may succeed, the local authority may apply simply for a care order (and seek an interim are order at the start of proceedings) knowing that if it becomes necessary on an emergency basis to place the child in secure accommodation it may do so for a period of up to 72 hours before it becomes necessary for a court to sanction the placement.

Children accommodated by the health or education authorities

9.23 Section 25 also applies, with modifications, to children who are accommodated by health or local education authorities, and to children who are being accommodated in residential care or nursing homes.

9.24 Regulation 7 of the Children (Secure Accommodation) Regulations 1991 applies s 25 to these children, modifying the section so that instead of referring to children 'looked after by a local authority' it refers to children accommodated by the relevant health or education authority. The provisions are otherwise the same.

Case Study:

A 13-year-old girl is hospitalised suffering from severe anorexia. She has run away from hospital and home on a number of occasions. She agrees to a treatment programme, but on her first night in hospital disappears and is found, disorientated and wearing only pyjamas, at a nearby bus stop the following morning.

The hospital may place the girl on its secure paediatric ward (secured by an electronic pass) for up to 72 hours. If during that time it appears that the criteria for secure accommodation will continue to be met and there is a need to keep the child on the secure ward in the longer term, the hospital must make an application for a secure accommodation order.

Children who are charged or convicted of a criminal offence

9.25 A distinction must be drawn between children who are defendants in pending proceedings, and children who have been convicted and sentenced. Section 25 applies, with modifications, to the former category as these children remain the responsibility of the local authority. It does not apply to the latter category as responsibility for these children passes to the Youth Justice Board.

Children who have been convicted

9.26 Section 25 does *not* apply to children who have been convicted and given a custodial sentence. These children will fall into one of the following categories:

- ✓ children who, following conviction for one of a limited number of very serious offences, are serving long sentences or, following a murder conviction, are detained at Her Majesty's Pleasure;[18]

- ✓ children subject to a detention and training order imposed by a criminal court.

The detention of these children is governed by the relevant criminal statute. Given that secure children's homes often provide beds to both the family and criminal justice systems, these children may in fact be accommodated alongside those children who fall under s 25.

Children who have been charged and/or are on remand

9.27 Section 25 does apply, with an important modification, to children who are looked after by the local authority following arrest and detention by the police prior to a court appearance.[19] Note that s 25 no longer applies to children on remand by a criminal court to local authority accommodation during the course of criminal proceedings.

9.28 The important modification is that it is not necessary that there should be a history of absconding, or a likelihood of significant harm if the child absconds. It is enough simply to prove that the child is 'likely to abscond' (or is 'likely to injure himself or other people' if kept in non-secure accommodation).[20]

---

[18] Children (Secure Accommodation) Regulations 1991, SI 1991/1505, reg 5(1).
[19] Ibid, reg 6(1)(a).
[20] Ibid, reg 6(2).

Children detained under the Mental Health Act 1983

9.29 A child who has been detained in hospital for assessment or treatment under ss 2 or 3 of the Mental Health Act 1983 is not subject to the provisions of s 25. His detention is authorised under the mental health legislation and the provisions of s 25 of the CA 1989 do not apply.

PROCEDURE

9.30 The applicant for a secure accommodation order is the local authority which looks after the child. A child accommodated by a health or education authority, or in a care home or independent hospital, shall, unless the child is looked after by a local authority, be made only by the authority who has made arrangements for the provision of accommodation for the child or the person carrying on the home in which accommodation is provided for the child.[21] The application is made on Form C1 with Supplement Form C20.

9.31 The application is made in the Family Court. The respondents are:

✓ the child;

✓ every person believed to have parental responsibility for the child;

✓ every person believed to have had parental responsibility before the child was placed in care.

Any person may be removed or joined as a respondent.[22]

9.32 Notice of proceedings (in Form C6A) must also be given to:

✓ any local authority providing accommodation for the child;

✓ any person with whom the child is living; and

✓ any person providing an authorised refuge where the child is staying.[23]

9.33 The application must be served and the appropriate notice given at least one day before the hearing date. There is no provision for making applications without notice.[24]

---

[21] Ibid, reg 2.
[22] FPR 2010, r 12.3.
[23] Ibid.
[24] Ibid, r 12.16 (which deals with applications without notice) makes no mention of secure accommodation orders.

Representation of the child

9.34 Although applications under s 25 are not 'specified proceedings' for the purposes of s 41 of the CA 1989, there is authority to the effect that in all but the most exceptional cases a children's guardian should be appointed.[25] Where the child is competent to instruct a solicitor and his instructions are at variance with the guardian's views the solicitor must take instructions directly from the child. See **6.89–6.96** for a full discussion of the roles of the children's guardian and solicitor for the child.

9.35 Because the child's liberty is at stake his rights under Art 5 of the ECHR are engaged (see **9.42** onwards) and his right to a fair trial under Art 6 assumes particular significance. He must be informed promptly of the evidence against him and given the opportunity to answer any allegations made.[26] This may mean that the pre-Human Rights Act authorities which discourage the child's attendance at court should be treated with caution. Equally, not only must the child be legally represented (see s 25(6)), but implicit in that statutory requirement is that, for the legal representation to be effective, the child's solicitor must have had the opportunity to take the child's instructions.[27]

Challenging the order

9.36 Any party may appeal a secure accommodation order.

9.37 Where the criteria for a secure accommodation order cease to apply, but the local authority does not release the child, the appropriate remedy is to issue a writ of habeas corpus.[28] If there is a dispute with the local authority as to whether the criteria continue to apply – with it being alleged either that the local authority has failed properly to carry out its duties to review the placement, or that the local authority has come to an unreasonable decision regarding the continuation of the placement – an application for judicial review should be made.

9.38 Equally, a challenge to any other aspect of the local authority's exercise of its power under a secure accommodation order should be by judicial review.

---

[25] *AS (Secure Accommodation Order), Re* [1999] 1 FLR 103, [1999] 2 FCR 749, [1999] Fam Law 20, Fam D.
[26] *C (Secure Accommodation Order: Representation), Re* [2001] 2 FLR 169, [2001] EWCA Civ 458, [2001] 1 FCR 692, CA.
[27] *AS (Secure Accommodation Order), Re* [1999] 1 FLR 103, [1999] 2 FCR 749, [1999] Fam Law 20, Fam D.
[28] That is a writ challenging the lawfulness of the continued detention.

THE LOCAL AUTHORITY'S OBLIGATIONS

Educational provision

9.39 The local authority has an obligation to make educational provision for all children it is keeping in secure accommodation. While this has always been required as a matter of common sense, it is, since the coming into force of the Human Rights Act 1998, explicitly required by Art 5 of the ECHR. That is because the deprivation of liberty brought about by the period in secure accommodation is permissible in this context only where it is 'for the purpose of educational supervision' (Art 5(1)(d) of the ECHR). That phrase – 'for the purpose of educational supervision' – is interpreted broadly and does not require any form of traditional scholastic education.

Review

9.40 The local authority must keep the secure placement under review. It must appoint at least three persons, including one who is independent of the local authority, to review the placement within one month of it commencing, and at least every three months thereafter.[29] The local authority must be satisfied throughout the duration of the placement that the criteria for keeping the child in secure accommodation continue to apply and that no other accommodation is appropriate.

Release

9.41 As discussed above, a secure accommodation order permits the local authority to keep the child in secure accommodation; it does not oblige it to do so. If the criteria cease to apply the child must be released, regardless of whether or not the order has expired.

DEPRIVATION OF LIBERTY

9.42 The statutory scheme of secure accommodation orders applies in relation only to certain types of accommodation and certain children. There are many children whose welfare requires, in the view of a local authority, that they be subject to significant restrictions on their liberty, in circumstances in which the child herself or the placement in which she is in does not fall within the statutory scheme. Such restrictions, just as they would under a secure accommodation order, engage the child's Art 5 of the ECHR rights. So, they require authorisation.

---

[29] Children (Secure Accommodation) Regulations 1991, SI 1991/1505, reg 15.

The inherent jurisdiction

9.43 The courts have had to develop a non-statutory scheme, using the High Court's powers under its inherent jurisdiction. In the main, the courts have modelled the inherent jurisdiction scheme on the s 25 of the CA 1989 statutory scheme. The law in this area is new and the judges continue to grapple with it. The tests and rules are not as clear-cut as with secure accommodation orders.

Case Study:

A 14-year-old girl diagnosed with autistic spectrum disorder is not able easily to regulate her behaviour and will often become extremely aggressive, both physically and verbally, to other children and to professionals working with her. She is placed, under a care order, in a therapeutic residential placement. There, she is closely monitored, with 1:1 supervision, locked doors to keep her safe and, when required, physical restraint.

The therapeutic residential placement is not a secure children's home or a placement to which s 25 of the CA 1989 applies. So, a secure accommodation order cannot be made. The local authority in whose care the child is in instead needs to apply to the court to authorise the placement – ie to make lawful the restrictions to which she is subject – under the inherent jurisdiction.

Spotting a case in which there is a deprivation of liberty

9.44 Spotting a case in which a secure accommodation order is required will normally be easy: the child will already be or a local authority will wish to place a child in a secure children's home. Identifying a 'deprivation of liberty' case is trickier. The three building blocks, which are known as the *Storck* components,[30] are as follows:

Storck components
(1) The objective component: confinement in a particular restricted place for a not negligible period of time
(2) The subjective component of lack of valid consent
(3) Attribution of responsibility to the state

Where all three *Storck* components are satisfied – ie, a child's liberty is restricted for a not negligible period of time, to which the does child does not consent, and for which the state is responsible – that restriction of liberty will be unlawful unless it is authorised by a court.

---

[30] After the eponymous case, *Storck v Germany* (2006) 43 EHRR 6.

> *Case Study:*
>
> *A 15-year-old boy is thought to be involved in gang activity and 'county line' drug running. He is subject to a care order. The boy is removed by the local authority from his foster placement and placed in a residential home in the countryside. He is not permitted a mobile phone (and his communications are limited to set numbers, for 30 minutes per day, on the landline), he is given very limited money, on all trips from the placement he is accompanied by an escort, is heavily supervised within the home and is provided with a tutor who comes to the home. The boy makes clear that he is very unhappy – he wants, in particular, his mobile phone and to be able to come and go as he wishes.*
>
> The residential home is placing significant restrictions on his liberty which, absent his consent, would constitute a 'deprivation of liberty' within the meaning of Art 5 of the ECHR. Again, the local authority will need to apply to the court to authorise those restrictions so as to make them lawful.

Key points to remember

9.45 This is a comparatively complex area of law. The key question to ask, when looking at whether there is 'confinement in a particular restricted place for a not negligible period of time', is this: is the child under 'continuous supervision and control and not free to leave?'[31] Given that most children are not free to leave (in the sense of being able permanently to depart from their home), cases focus on 'continuous supervision and control'. Courts have to compare the child with whom they are concerned with a child of the same age who is free from disability and state involvement and ask whether the subject child is under 'continuous supervision and control'.

Procedure

9.46 If the three *Storck* components are satisfied – that is to say, if a child is deprived of her liberty – a local authority needs to apply to court for (i) permission to invoke the inherent jurisdiction and (ii) the authorisation of that deprivation of liberty. That application must be dealt with by a High Court judge (or a judge exercising High Court powers) because the authorisation is not statutory, but rather is under the inherent jurisdiction. The application is made on Form C66. There are no regulations or rules made by Parliament setting out the procedure – but, as noted above, where possible, judges have sought to model this process on that used for secure accommodation orders.

---

[31] *P (by his litigation friend, the Official Solicitor) v Cheshire West and Chester Council; P & Q (by their litigation friend, the Official Solicitor) v Surrey County Council* [2014] UKSC 19.

Looking to the future

9.47 As professionals working with children and the family justice system become more familiar with Art 5 of the ECHR and its impact on the lawfulness of the placements of children who are looked after by local authorities, the use of the inherent jurisdiction in 'deprivation of liberty' cases is become more common. At the same time, there is an increasing recognition of the right for children who are unlawfully deprived of their liberty to sue local authorities for breach of their ECHR and other duties. Significant care and thought is required when dealing with cases in which there may be a 'deprivation of liberty', particularly in identifying whether or not the restrictions to which a child is subject to keep her safe meet the test of 'continuous supervision and control and lack of freedom to leave.'

Chapter 10

MEDICAL TREATMENT AND OTHER COMPLEX ISSUES: THE HIGH COURT'S INHERENT JURISDICTION

Chapter summary

- The High Court's inherent jurisdiction – introduction
- Wardship
- Common uses of the wardship jurisdiction
- The inherent jurisdiction outside wardship
- Procedure

THE HIGH COURT'S INHERENT JURISDICTION – INTRODUCTION

10.1 Despite the fact that the determination of very many of the issues that may arise with respect to a child or young person will fall within the Children Act 1989 (CA 1989), the Adoption and Children Act 1989 (ACA 1989), the Child Abduction and Custody Act 1985, the Mental Capacity Act 2002, the Female Genital Mutilation Act 2003, the Forced Marriage (Civil Protection) Act 2007 and other Acts of Parliament, there will inevitably be matters which are not covered by the statutory scheme. As a superior court of record, the High Court has an inherent jurisdiction to hear all matters of criminal and civil law unless that jurisdiction has been limited by statute or case law. It is a 'catch-all' jurisdiction, used particularly to determine issues that arise in difficult or novel situations where statute and case law do not provide an answer. The High Court's inherent jurisdiction to intervene in questions relating to the welfare and upbringing of children has been said to derive from the Crown's 'right and duty ... as *parens patriae* ('parent of the nation') to take care of those who are not able to take care of themselves'.[1]

---

[1] *Re L (an infant)* [1968] 1 All ER 20.

> The High Court has an 'inherent jurisdiction' to make orders to protect children in circumstances where statute law does not provide a remedy. Wardship is an example of the use of this jurisdiction; it is less commonly used than in former times, but still exists

10.2 Historically the way in which the High Court exercised its inherent jurisdiction in relation to children was by making the child a ward of court. The primary effect of wardship is that no important decision in the child's life may be taken without reference to the court. Prior to the implementation of the CA 1989, wardship became the standard way of invoking the High Court's inherent jurisdiction in relation to a child, and in children proceedings the two concepts of wardship and inherent jurisdiction became more or less interchangeable.

10.3 As successive governments have legislated and case law has developed, the High Court's inherent jurisdiction has gradually been eroded. In the field of children's law, the CA 1989 significantly restricted the court's inherent jurisdiction by codifying the law relating to children and providing a statutory scheme to cover most issues arising in public or private law. Section 100 of the CA 1989 expressly restricts the court's inherent jurisdiction in public law proceedings and prevents local authorities from making any application under the court's inherent jurisdiction unless there is no other way in which the desired result could be achieved.

10.4 The High Court retains a residual jurisdiction, which has been used for some time to resolve such complex and sensitive issues as publicity, medical treatment or international child abduction with countries who are not signed up to international conventions. More recently, the jurisdiction has been utilised to protect children who are at risk of radicalisation. This jurisdiction may be exercised within or independently of the wardship jurisdiction.

WARDSHIP

10.5 Since the implementation of the CA 1989, the courts have restricted the use of the wardship jurisdiction to permit it only when no order is available under the Act that will meet the requirements of the case. It has been said that wardship is now an 'exceptional status'[2] requiring exceptional circumstances. Nevertheless, a gap appears to have opened up between public and private law proceedings, where the threshold criteria for local authority intervention has not

---

[2] *Re CT (A Minor) (Child Representation)* [1993] 2 FLR 278.

been met or local authority intervention is otherwise inappropriate, but there is nevertheless a need for judicial supervision in order to protect the child.

Effects of wardship

10.6 A child becomes a ward of court immediately upon issue of an originating summons in wardship. At the first hearing the wardship must be confirmed by court order or it will lapse. The child remains a ward of court until he is 18, unless the wardship is revoked.

10.7 When a child is a ward of court, the High Court itself has parental responsibility for its ward; a status that it shares with all those who also have parental responsibility for her.

10.8 Once a child is a ward, no major step may be taken in her life without the court's consent. 'Major steps' include the following:

✓ psychiatric or psychological examination or treatment;

✓ serious medical treatment;

✓ marriage;

✓ interview by the police;

✓ a change of residence;

✓ a change of school;

✓ a change of name;

✓ placement in secure accommodation;

✓ commencement of adoption proceedings;

✓ publicity relating to the ward.

10.9 From the moment when the child becomes a ward of court she must not leave or be removed from England and Wales without the court's consent (which may be given generally, on conditions, or for specific purposes). There are some exceptions to this rule. When the ward is habitually resident in another part of the UK, or her parents are involved in matrimonial proceedings in a court in another part of the UK, she may move to that part of the UK without the permission of the court.[3]

---

[3] Family Law Act 1986, s 38.

COMMON USES OF THE WARDSHIP JURISDICTION

Medical treatment

10.10 The court's leave is not required for routine medical examinations and treatment for a ward; the consent of a person with parental responsibility will be sufficient. However, where 'serious invasive treatment'[4] or other significant intervention is proposed for a ward, an application must be made to the court.

10.11 Where proceedings are underway in respect of the child the court's leave must be obtained before the child is examined by a psychiatrist or psychologist. A ward may not be admitted to hospital under the *Mental Health Act 1983* without the authorisation of the court, and the court's leave is required to make the application.[5]

10.12 Where the ward's life or health is seriously at risk the courts have been prepared to override major decisions made even by older, *Gillick*-competent wards. The wardship jurisdiction has been used to sanction in-patient treatment for anorexia nervosa in the case of a 16-year-old girl, and to authorise the use of reasonable force if necessary to detain her for the purposes of such treatment.[6] It has also been used to authorise a heart transplant for a 15-year-old who was refusing to consent to the procedure.[7]

Publicity

10.13 Children who are already involved in proceedings have some statutory protection from publicity. The major statutory restriction is s 97(2) of the CA 1989, which prevents publication of any material that is intended or likely to identify any child involved in *CA 1989* proceedings or any address or school of the child. The other sources of statutory protection are set out below.

Protection from publicity: statute

✓ Children Act 1989, s 97(2): no publication of material intended or likely to identify any child involved in Children Act proceedings

✓ Information relating to private children proceedings may not be communicated to any persons other than those permitted under Family Proceedings Rules 2010, r 12.72–75

---

[4] *Re J (A Minor) (Wardship: Medical Treatment)* [1990] 3 All ER 930.
[5] Mental Health Act 1983, s 33.
[6] *Re C (Detention: Medical Treatment)* [1997] 2 FLR 180.
[7] *Re M (Medical Treatment: Consent)* [1999] 2 FCR 577.

> ✓ Administration of Justice Act 1960, s 11: general provision permitting the court to direct confidentiality of any name or other matter relating to court proceedings
>
> ✓ Administration of Justice Act 1960, s 12: contempt of court to publish information relating to proceedings before any court sitting in private where the proceedings concern the exercise of the inherent jurisdiction re minors; are brought under the Children Act 1989; or otherwise relate wholly or mainly to the maintenance or upbringing of a minor
>
> ✓ Children and Young Persons Act 1933, s 39: power to direct in any proceedings in any court that no newspaper shall publish the name, address, school or other material calculated to lead to the identification of any child involved in the proceedings; or any picture of the child

10.14 It has been said that wardship can be used in support of the existing statutory protection where 'conferring on the child the status of ward of court will prove a more effective deterrent than the ordinary sanctions of contempt of court which already protect all family proceedings'.[8] Following the implementation of the Human Rights Act 1998, it seems that the court must only exercise its powers under the inherent jurisdiction when the existing safeguards would be inadequate to protect the child from harm.

10.15 The Human Rights Act 1998 requires courts to balance the child's rights under Art 8 of the ECHR (to a private and family life) with the public interest in freedom of speech and specifically rights deriving from Art 10 (freedom of expression). Each right is liable to be qualified and subject to a test of proportionality, and neither has precedence over the other.

10.16 A distinction has been drawn between cases where the anticipated publicity relates directly to the child's upbringing or to issues involving parental responsibility, and where it does not. The court is more likely to exercise its inherent jurisdiction to restrain publicity in the former category of case.[9] Indeed, the Court of Appeal has said that the court 'should not even consider exercising [its inherent] jurisdiction in cases where the publicity is not directed at the child or the child's carers unless it could have an adverse effect on the court's ability to deal properly with the ... proceedings in question'. The exercise of the jurisdiction now requires the court first to decide whether the child's rights under Art 8 are engaged and, if so, then to conduct the necessary balancing exercise between the competing rights under Arts 8 and 10, considering the proportionality of the potential interference with each right considered independently.[10]

---

[8] *Re CT (A Minor) (Child Representation)* [1993] 2 FLR 278.
[9] *Kelly v BBC* [2001] 1 FLR 197.
[10] *Roddy (a child) (identification: restriction on publication), Re* [2003] EWHC 2927 (Fam); [2004] 2 FLR 949.

Criminal proceedings: limitation of High Court's jurisdiction

10.17 Where a ward is involved in criminal proceedings, either as a defendant or as a witness, the High Court's power to intervene under the wardship jurisdiction is limited. There is no requirement on the police or any other statutory agency to gain the court's permission before interviewing a ward. The decision whether or not to charge a ward is a matter for the police alone and decisions relating to bail are a matter for the criminal court. The wardship court cannot intervene in a prosecution decision to call a ward as a witness.[11]

10.18 Publicity issues surrounding a ward who is involved as a victim in criminal proceedings are a matter for the judge in the criminal proceedings to decide, and not the wardship judge.[12]

Child abduction and forced marriage

10.19 Wardship continues to be an effective process for locating, collecting and, if necessary, repatriating children who have been abducted. The use of the inherent jurisdiction opens up the possibility of using the High Court's extensive powers to locate and/or collect a child. In recent times the wardship jurisdiction has been used to protect teenage girls who are at risk of being forced into a marriage by their families, although such cases are now more properly dealt with under the Forced Marriage Act (Civil Protection) 2007.

Radicalisation

10.20 In recent years the inherent jurisdiction has been deployed to deal with the advent of cases where children are at risk of becoming radicalised and/or suborned into joining terrorist organisations.[13]

THE INHERENT JURISDICTION OUTSIDE WARDSHIP

10.21 It is not necessary to make a child a ward of court in order to invoke the High Court's inherent jurisdiction. There may be good reasons not to do so. A child who is in the care of the local authority cannot be made a ward of court,[14] and the court may not use the wardship jurisdiction to place a child in the local authority's care. However, the local authority is permitted to seek the court's guidance regarding a particular issue relating to a child, and the High Court has the power to make injunctions in support of a care order in relation

---

[11] *Re K (Minors)* [1988] 1 FLR 435.
[12] *Re R (A Minor)* [1994] 2 FLR 637.
[13] *President's Guidance: Radicalisation cases in the Family Courts* (October 2015).
[14] CA 1989, s 101(2)(c).

to specific issues, for example concerning any restriction of the parents' ability to exercise parental responsibility.[15]

10.22 Where the court's guidance or ruling is sought on a discrete issue and there is no likelihood of the court's involvement lasting beyond the resolution of that issue, it may be appropriate to invoke the inherent jurisdiction rather than to make the child a ward of court. Wardship should not be continued beyond the point where it has ceased serving any useful purpose.

Medical treatment and terminal illness under the inherent jurisdiction

10.23 The inherent jurisdiction has for many years provided a forum for the determination of the most anxious issues involving the medical treatment of children, with some, for example the babies Charlie Gard and Alfie Evans, achieving international publicity. What follows is no more than a brief description of the general approach to such cases.

10.24 Other than in an emergency situation, a medical practitioner may not impose treatment on a child without the consent of the parent(s). Without parental consent the medical authorities must apply to the High Court to exercise its inherent jurisdiction to declare the treatment lawful.[16] The position relating to children here differs from that relating to adults, in that while the High Court can in effect 'substitute' its own consent for that of a parent, it cannot do the same in the case of a competent adult. Where an adult, or a young person over the age of 16 years lacks capacity to give their consent as a consequence of mental incapacity, the case may come before the Court of Protection under the Mental Capacity Act 2002.

> Where parents do not consent to proposed medical treatment for a child, it will always be necessary to apply to the court to decide the issue. In some cases involving very serious or risky treatment it may be appropriate to refer the case to the court, even where parents and medical staff agree

10.25 In some circumstances it may be necessary to make an application to the court in relation to proposed medical treatment for a child, even though medical opinion backs the treatment and the parents consent to it. An example is the sterilisation of a child. This may be carried out without court approval

---

[15] Senior Courts Act 1981, s 7.
[16] *Glass v UK* [2004] 1 FLR 1019.

if two medical practitioners are satisfied that it is necessary and in the patient's best interests; but if there is any doubt about the lawfulness of the procedure a declaration from the court should be sought.[17]

Terminal illness

10.26 The position with respect to a terminally ill child is the same as that in the case of a terminally ill adult, save that an adult who retains full mental capacity may decide for herself whether to accept or refuse treatment, whereas a child is dependent on the consent of his parents or a declaration of the court. The following key principles can be distilled from the authorities:

✓ The decision of a competent adult to accept or refuse offered treatment is determinative.

✓ However, medical practitioners are not obliged to administer a specific treatment (other than life-prolonging treatment such as artificial nutrition and hydration) at a patient's (or parent's) request if they feel that such treatment is not in the patient's best interests.[18]

✓ There is no medical guidance that would require a doctor to withhold life-prolonging treatment from a competent patient who requested it. If there were such guidance it would be unlawful and a doctor who acted in such a way would have no defence to a charge of murder.[19]

✓ Once an adult is no longer competent to make his own decisions, or in the case of a child, doctors must act in the patient's best interests. This may include alleviating suffering at expense of prolonging life.[20] Any dispute should be referred to the court.

✓ The withdrawal of life-prolonging treatment from a patient in a PVS (persistent vegetative state) is lawful where it would be:
 – in accordance with good medical practice;
 – appropriate in the clinical judgment of the treating doctors; and
 – in the patient's best interests.[21]

10.27 In many cases, where there is no disagreement about the appropriate treatment (or withdrawal of treatment), an application to the court for a declaration that the proposed course is lawful is not required; in contrast where the way forward is finely balanced, there is a difference of medical opinion, or a

---

[17] *Re S* [2000] 2 FLR 389.
[18] *Re J (A Minor) (Wardship: Medical Treatment)* [1992] 2 FLR 165 (child); *R v GMC (ex parte Burke)* [2005] EWCA Civ 1003 (adult).
[19] *R v GMC (ex parte Burke)* [2005] EWCA Civ 1003.
[20] Eg, *Re C* [1990] 1 FLR 252; *Portsmouth NHS Trust v Wyatt* [2004] EWHC 206; [2005] 1 FLR 21.
[21] *Airedale NHS Trust v Bland* [1993] 1 FLR 1026.

lack of agreement from persons with an interest in the patient's welfare, a court application can and should be made.[22]

Limitations on the use of the inherent jurisdiction with respect to children

10.28 The High Court may only exercise its inherent jurisdiction (whether or not in wardship) with respect to a child who is:

- ✓ under 18; and
- ✓ a British subject; or
- ✓ physically present in England and Wales; or
- ✓ ordinarily resident in England and Wales.

Even if these conditions are met, where the appropriate forum for decision-making regarding the child is another jurisdiction, the High Court will not be able to exercise jurisdiction over the child.

10.29 Examples where the High Court has refused to exercise its inherent jurisdiction, notwithstanding that the jurisdiction exists, include cases where the applicant was attempting to circumvent immigration legislation; where the sole purpose of the proceedings was to generate publicity; and where the proceedings had been issued in an attempt to prevent the arrest of a teenage soldier subject to military law.

Children in care

10.30 The most significant limitation on the High Court's powers under its inherent jurisdiction relates to children who are in the care of a local authority. The courts have always discouraged too much judicial supervision of local authority decision-making with respect to children in their care, although historically it was possible for wardship and a care order to co-exist. A major innovation of the CA 1989 was to transfer responsibility for children in care from the court to the local authority, and to restrict court interference with the local authority's discharge of its duties under a care order.

10.31 Under s 100 of the CA 1989 the court must not exercise its inherent jurisdiction to:

---

[22] *An NHS Trust v Y* [2018] UKSC 46.

- ✓ place a child in the care or under the supervision of a local authority (s 100(2)(a));

- ✓ require a child to be accommodated by or on behalf of a local authority (s 100(2)(b));

- ✓ make a child who is the subject of a care order a ward of court (s 100(2)(c));

- ✓ confer on any local authority power to determine any question in connection with any aspect of parental responsibility for a child (s 100(2)(d)).

10.32 A local authority may only apply for any exercise of the High Court's inherent jurisdiction with the leave of the court, and the court may only grant leave if it is satisfied that:

- ✓ the result which the authority wishes to achieve cannot be achieved through the making of any order which the local authority is entitled to apply for (s 100(4)(a)); and

- ✓ there is reasonable cause to believe that if the court's inherent jurisdiction is not exercised with respect to the child he is likely to suffer significant harm (s 100(4)(b)).

Case Study:

At the conclusion of care proceedings the High Court is proposing to make a final care order in respect of a 9-year-old boy who is living in foster care. The local authority is very concerned that the boy's father, who has been consistently violent towards him, should not have contact and should not be aware of where the boy is living. The local authority is worried that the mother, who is having limited contact with the boy, may pass on information to the father. It seeks leave to invoke the High Court's inherent jurisdiction.

The High Court cannot use its inherent jurisdiction to make an order about contact: the local authority has available to it s 34 of the CA 1989 and must apply under this section for an order giving it leave to refuse contact to the father. However, there is no order available to the local authority that would achieve the desired result of preventing the mother from telling the father where the child is. Its only route is to ask the High Court to grant an injunction forbidding the mother to pass on information that might lead to the father discovering the child's whereabouts.

10.33 The restriction on local authority applications applies whether or not the child is in care. There may be cases where the local authority seeks a declaration from the court on whether a proposed course of action, for example a medical procedure, would be lawful. In such a case the local authority must still overcome the leave restriction in s 100(4) and in particular must satisfy the court that, for example, a child assessment order or specific issue order would not achieve the desired result. It may be that where the child is not in care, and a specific issue order is therefore available,[23] this will be the more appropriate route. Both routes have been used to permit blood transfusions where the child's parents refused to consent to the procedure.[24]

10.34 The courts have consistently (pre- and post-*CA 1989*) discouraged attempts to review, by way of the inherent jurisdiction, a local authority's decision-making under a care order. The appropriate route of challenge to a decision of the local authority is via an application for judicial review, provided that it can be shown that the local authority has acted illegally, improperly or irrationally.

PROCEDURE

10.35 An originating summons in wardship, and an application under the court's inherent jurisdiction, must each be issued in the High Court. Any person with an interest in the child may issue an originating summons. Once a summons in wardship is issued the child immediately becomes a ward of court;[25] an application for a hearing must be made within 21 days, and at that hearing the court must confirm the wardship or it will lapse.

10.36 The court may exercise its inherent jurisdiction, including by making a child a ward of court, of its own motion without an application.

10.37 The originating summons must be accompanied by an affidavit sworn by the plaintiff setting out the grounds for the application. The defendants are those with a genuine interest in the child, including, where the application is made to resolve a specific dispute, the parties to the dispute. The child himself will not be made a party unless there are specific reasons for doing so.

10.38 Applications in wardship or under the inherent jurisdiction may be made without notice. This may be appropriate in cases where there is an emergency and it is not possible or appropriate to give notice. Out of hours the application should be made by telephone to the urgent applications judge, who may be contacted on 020 7947 6000.

---

[23] CA 1989, s 9(1).
[24] *Re S* (A Minor) (Medical Treatment) [1993] 1 FLR 376 (inherent jurisdiction); *Re R* (A Minor) (Blood Transfusion) [1993] 2 FLR 757 (specific issue order).
[25] Senior Courts Act 1981, s 41(2).

Chapter 11

CHALLENGING THE LOCAL AUTHORITY

Chapter summary

- Introduction
- Parental responsibility and consent
- Independent reviewing officer
- Making a complaint
- Powers of the Secretary of State
- Children's Commissioner
- Local Government and Social Care Ombudsman
- Judicial review
- Appeals
- Human Rights Act 1998

INTRODUCTION

11.1 The content of the preceding chapters will have demonstrated the extent of the far-reaching powers conferred by Parliament upon local authorities to order the lives of children for whom they are given statutory responsibilities. These powers in some cases, although reviewable by judicial review[1], are otherwise largely unsupervised by the courts. The potential impact of these powers upon individual families may be devastating. It is thus important for all involved to be aware of the various avenues available for a local authority's actions, or proposed actions, to be questioned or challenged.

11.2 Rather than being embodied in a unified code, the options for challenging a local authority are made up of a cocktail of provisions from various sources. In summary they are:

---

[1] See **11.28**.

- ✓ exercising parental responsibility/ withholding parental consent
- ✓ making representations during the course of the local authority's statutory review process[2]
- ✓ seeking the intervention of the local authority's independent reviewing officer
- ✓ following any general complaints procedure established by the local authority
- ✓ following the complaints procedure established by the local authority under Children Act 1989 (CA 1989), s 26
- ✓ contacting a local councillor, the chair or vice-chair of the children's services committee, or any other councillor
- ✓ seeking the intervention of the local Member of Parliament
- ✓ writing to the appropriate central government department (currently the Department for Education) or the Minister for Children and Families
- ✓ referring the matter to the Children's Commissioner
- ✓ referring the matter to the Local Government and Social Care Ombudsman
- ✓ seeking judicial review of the particular action, or failure to take action, of the local authority
- ✓ applying to the court for an order under CA 1989[3]
- ✓ appealing against the original court order
- ✓ making a claim under the Human Rights Act 1998
- ✓ referring the matter to the European Court of Human Rights

We will now look at some of these options in more detail.

PARENTAL RESPONSIBILITY AND CONSENT

11.3 Whether a child is being looked after by a local authority pursuant to a care order or simply being accommodated, his parents will still have parental

---

[2] For reviews and case planning, see **4.42**.
[3] For applications to discharge a care order, see **6.84**. For private law orders, see **Ch 3**.

responsibility with respect to him. If there is a care order the local authority will also share parental responsibility for the child and has the power to determine the extent to which any other holder of parental responsibility may exercise his parental responsibility for the child.[4]

11.4 Notwithstanding the local authority's general powers under a care order, it may not act without the consent of each person with parental responsibility[5] in respect of arranging for a change of religion, the child's marriage, travel out of the UK for longer than one month, a change of surname, or adoption (or placement for adoption). If a person without parental responsibility objects to the local authority taking any of these steps, it must make an application to the court.

11.5 Where a child is being looked after without a care order, her parents will retain exclusive parental responsibility for her. It is the right of any person with parental responsibility to choose to remove the child from accommodation being provided by the local authority[6].

11.6 Those looking after a child on a day to day basis (for example, foster carers), may do what is reasonable in all the circumstances of the case to safeguard and promote his welfare.[7]

11.7 A child who is of a sufficient age and understanding may refuse to be involved in a certain course of action proposed by a local authority in accordance with the *Gillick* principle.[8]

INDEPENDENT REVIEWING OFFICER

11.8 Once a full care order has been made, the responsibility for developing and implementing the care plan for the child is that of the local authority and not the court. As a result of difficulties that had arisen in past cases where the local authority either failed to implement an agreed plan, or markedly deviated from the plan, the role of 'independent reviewing officer' (IRO) was introduced with the principal aim of monitoring the performance by local authorities of their functions in relation to children who are looked after by them. An IRO must be appointed for every looked after child.

11.9 The IRO must (so far as is reasonably practicable) attend and chair any meetings held in connection with the review of the child's case and has a responsibility for ensuring that the process is conducted in accordance with the

---

[4] CA 1989, s 33(3). Those who have parental responsibility for a child may include a parent, guardian, special guardian or step-parent.
[5] Ibid, s 33(6).
[6] CA 1989, s 20(8) and (9).
[7] CA 1989, s 3(5).
[8] For the *Gillick* principle, see **3.18**.

regulations and that, in particular, the child's views are understood and taken into account.[9]

11.10 If the child wishes to take proceedings under CA 1989 on his own account, the IRO's role is to assist the child to obtain legal advice; or to establish whether an appropriate adult is willing to provide such assistance or bring the proceedings on the child's behalf.[10]

11.11 In addition, if the IRO considers that it is appropriate to do so he/she must refer the case to CAFCASS with a view to that agency taking proceedings under the Human Rights Act 1998, s 7, or for judicial review or any other proceedings in order to bring issues relating to the care plan before a court.[11] Before doing so the IRO must draw the local authority's failure or breach to the attention of persons at an appropriate level of seniority within the local authority and give them an opportunity to address the issue.[12] Guidance for IROs contemplating a referral to CAFCASS is set out in the IRO Handbook[13].

11.12 The power for CAFCASS to initiate court proceedings is sparingly used. Most disputes are resolved either within the local authority, or via negotiation following the intervention of CAFCASS.[14]

MAKING A COMPLAINT

11.13 There are three different complaints procedures relating to local authority decisions:

✓ complaint to the local authority under CA 1989, s 26(3) (by or on behalf of looked after children, their parents and foster carers);

✓ complaint to the local authority under the Local Authority Social Services and National Health Service Complaints (England) Regulations 2009 (in relation to all matters not within the scope of CA 1989, s 26(3); or

✓ complaint in relation to children's homes and voluntary organisations within their own complaints procedures.

The procedure established by s 26(3) includes care and supervision orders, emergency protection orders and other specified orders under CA 1989, Pts IV and V (child protection provisions)[15].

---

[9] CA 1989, s 25B (1).
[10] CPPCR(E)R 2010, reg 45.
[11] CA 1989, s 25B(3); CAFCASS (Reviewed Case Referral) Regulations 2004, SI 2004/2187; *CAFCASS Practice Note: Cases Referred by Independent Reviewing Officers*, December 2017.
[12] CPPCR(E)R 2010, reg 45.
[13] Department for Education, March 2010.
[14] Care Planning and the Role of the Independent Reviewing Officer, University of East Anglia, October 2015.
[15] CA 1989 Representations Procedure (England) Regulations 2006, reg 3.

11.14 The CA 1989, s 26(3) requires local authorities to establish a procedure for considering representations and complaints about the discharge of their functions from the following persons:

- ✓ the child;
- ✓ a parent;
- ✓ any person with parental responsibility;
- ✓ a local authority foster-carer;
- ✓ any other such person who the local authority considers has sufficient interest in the child's welfare to warrant his representation being considered,

in relation to any child being looked after or in need.

11.15 The s 26(3) duty therefore covers not only the accommodation of a child, and the decision whether or not to commence care proceedings, but also day care and services for family support and aftercare provisions. The s 26(3) duty extends to those for whom provision is made by the local authority's Adoption Service under ACA 2002, and children in respect of whom a special guardianship order is in force.

11.16 Voluntary organisations and registered children's homes are also required to have a procedure for considering representations (including complaints) about children's services.

11.17 The s 26(3) procedure involves an independent person in the process with the aim of ensuring that the child, parents and others are sufficiently involved in the process (which is also an important requirement of ECHR law). The procedure does not affect any other rights and is not to be regarded as a formal appeals process. Detailed provision is made by the Children Act 1989 Representations Procedure (England) Regulations 2006. Each local authority should have accessible information available about its complaints procedures. Not that a complaint will not be considered in the circumstances covered by Reg 8, essentially where there are existing or contemplated court, disciplinary or criminal proceedings.

11.18 The local authority must initially consider and try to resolve the representations within 10 working days. An independent person need not be involved at this stage. If the issue cannot be resolved in this way, the local authority must consider the representations with an appropriate independent person and provide a response within 25 working days. If the local authority is unable to comply with the time limit it must notify the complainant of the date by which it will respond (which must be within 65 working days of the start of the representations). If the complainant is dissatisfied with the response, he may request (within 20 working days) that the matter be reconsidered by a panel appointed by the local authority (which must consist of three independent persons). The panel must make its recommendations within a further 35 working days. The local authority, on receipt of the recommendations, must, together with the independent person, consider what action should be taken in relation to the child in the light of the representation/complaint and notify the complainant of this within 15 working days. The procedure is summarised in the following chart:

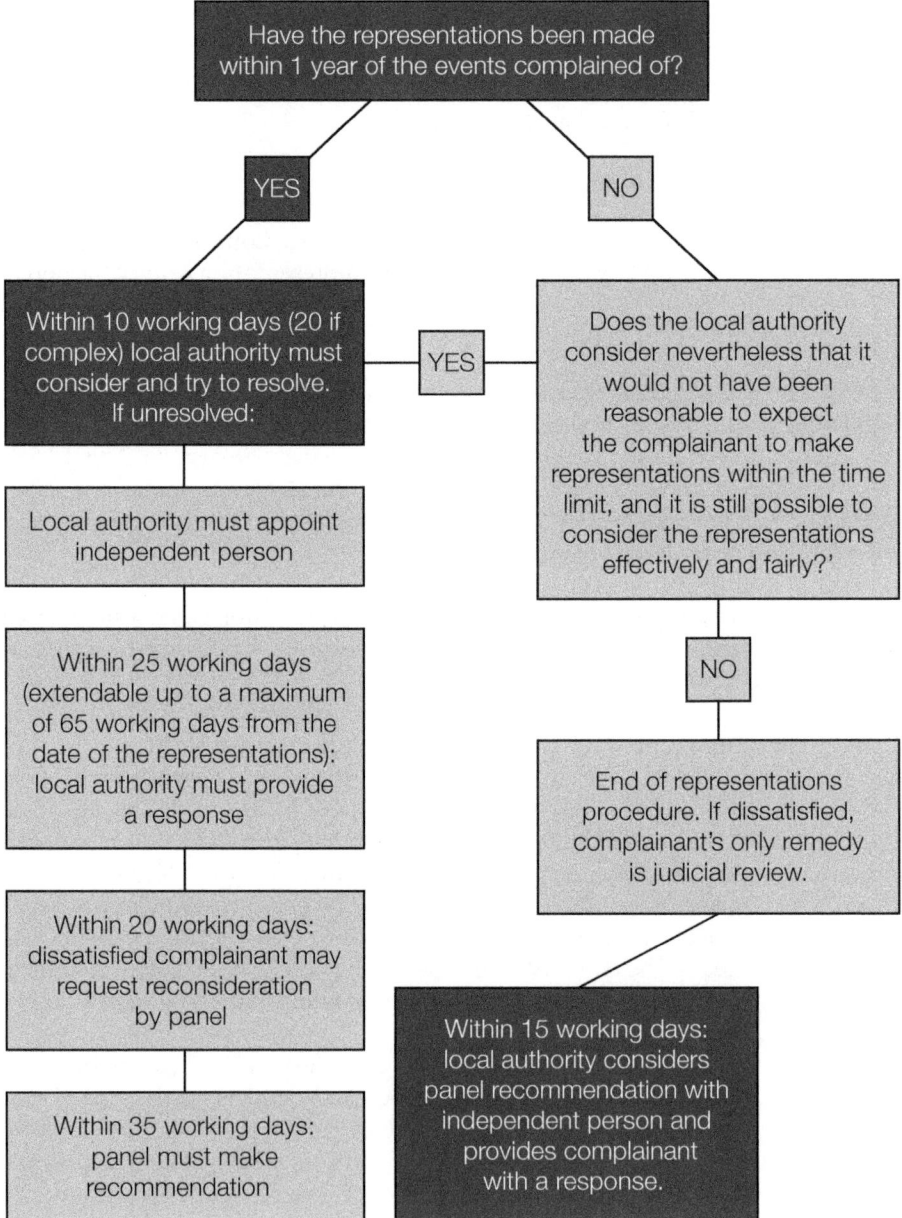

11.19 In relation to matters outside the provisions of CA 1989, s 26(3) local authorities must establish a procedure for considering such representations and complaints made by a qualifying individual.[16]

---

[16] LASSNHSC(E)R 2009

POWERS OF THE SECRETARY OF STATE

11.20 The Local Authority Social Services Act 1970 (LASSA 1970), s 7 requires local authorities to act under any 'general guidance' issued by the Secretary of State. Such guidance is usually in the form of departmental circulars, but may be presented in a formal book of guidance (for example, *Working Together to Safeguard Children*).[17] The Secretary of State for Education and the Minister for Children and Families are the current relevant ministers. A failure of an authority to comply with guidance issued under LASSA 1970, s 7 (which is mandatory) may provide grounds for judicial review.

11.21 The Secretary of State may cause an inspection to take place from time to time in relation to premises provided for a child's accommodation or care.[18]

11.22 If the Secretary of State considers that a local authority has failed without reasonable excuse to comply with any of its duties under the CA 1989, he may make an order declaring the authority to be in default.[19] Such an order may require the authority to comply with a direction within such period as is specified in the order.

CHILDREN'S COMMISSIONER

11.23 There is a Children's Commissioner for England and a separate such officer for Wales. The provisions that apply to each are entirely separate and, in some respects, differ from each other.[20] In England the Commissioner's general function is the promotion of awareness of the views and interests of children in England. In particular he or she may:

(a) encourage persons exercising functions or engaged in activities affecting children to take account of their views and interests;

(b) advise the Secretary of State on the views and interests of children;

(c) consider or research the operation of complaints procedures so far as they relate to children;

(d) consider or research any other matter relating to the interests of children;

(e) publish a report on any matter considered or researched by him.

11.24 Where the Children's Commissioner considers that the case of an individual child raises issues of public policy of relevance to other children, he

---

[17] Department for Education, July 2018.
[18] CA 1989, s 80(1).
[19] Ibid, s 84.
[20] Children Act 2004, Pt 1 governs the Children's Commissioner for England; Care Standards Act 2000, Pt V and Children's Commissioner for Wales Act 2001 (and the Children's Commissioner for Wales Regulations 2001, SI 2001/2787) make provision for Wales.

may hold an inquiry into that case for the purpose of investigating and making recommendations about those issues. He may, however, only hold such an inquiry if to do so would not duplicate the work of another person.

11.25 The Children's Commissioner for Wales has wider powers than his English counterpart and may offer advice and support to specific children, where those children are provided with relevant services in Wales or in respect of whom regulated children's services are provided in Wales.

LOCAL GOVERNMENT AND SOCIAL CARE OMBUDSMAN

11.26 The Ombudsman appointed by Parliament under the Local Government Act 1974, s 23 is an independent and impartial person whose role is to investigate complaints of injustice through maladministration by a local authority. 'Maladministration' means failure to follow agreed policies or procedures, failure to provide information or advice, providing inaccurate information or advice, or causing unjustified delays.[21] The focus of the Ombudsman's investigation will normally be the process of any decision making, rather than the merits of the decision itself.

11.27 A complaint may only be made to the Ombudsman after the matter has been raised with the local authority or organisation in question. If that has not provided a satisfactory outcome, then a referral may be made to the Ombudsman.[22] He does not normally deal with issues where the complainant has or had a right to take legal action and the Ombudsman considers it reasonable to do so. Any conclusion made by the Ombudsman takes the form of a recommendation to the local authority.

JUDICIAL REVIEW

11.28 Judicial review is the process whereby the High Court exercises its supervisory jurisdiction to review the legality and validity of the actions and decisions of persons or bodies exercising administrative powers whether of a legislative, executive or judicial/adjudicatory character. Thus the jurisdiction is over the proceedings and decisions of inferior courts, tribunals and other bodies performing public acts and duties.

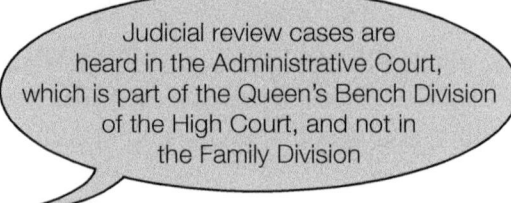

Judicial review cases are heard in the Administrative Court, which is part of the Queen's Bench Division of the High Court, and not in the Family Division

---

[21] Local Government Act 1974, s 26.
[22] See www.lgo.org.uk. Advice line: 0300 061 0614.

11.29 Judicial review is not a system of appeal. A claim for judicial review is a claim for the High Court to review the lawfulness of an enactment, or a decision, action or failure to act in relation to a public function. Judicial review is about the legality and fairness of the process that has been adopted and not about the merits of the decision itself. In general the High Court may quash (that is extinguish) the decision of an inferior body where that body has acted:

- ✓ illegally (an error of law, or an abuse of power or jurisdiction);
- ✓ irrationally (acting on irrelevant matters or unreasonably); or
- ✓ improperly (acting in breach of rules of natural justice and fairness).

11.30 Judicial review proceedings take place within the context of the Human Rights Act 1998 and may be consolidated with a claim under that Act.

11.31 An application for judicial review is a two-stage process, in which the claimant must first obtain permission to make the application. Permission will only be granted if the claimant has:

- ✓ 'sufficient interest' in the matter to which the application relates;
- ✓ a prima facie case;
- ✓ made the application promptly (and in any event within three months from the day when grounds to apply arose);
- ✓ (usually) exhausted alternative remedies of redress; and
- ✓ shown that the decision is one that is capable of challenge by judicial review.

11.32 A favourable result for a judicial review claimant may be a mandatory order, a prohibiting order, a quashing order, a declaration and/or an injunction or damages.[23]

11.33 Judicial review is a highly developed area of public law, detailed consideration of which is well beyond the scope of this work.[24]

APPEALS

11.34 The routes of appeal from and within the Family Court and the High Court are described in **Chapter 1**.

---

[23] Senior Courts Act 1981, s 31.
[24] For further description of judicial review, see Hershman and McFarlane, *Children: Law and Practice* (Family Law) Division K.

11.35 As a general rule, appeals against court decisions about a child's welfare are difficult to sustain if they are not founded upon a point of law, or show that the lower court went outside the band of reasonable conclusions that were open to it. Where a court is exercising its discretion as between two or more reasonable options for a child, it will be very difficult to show to the appeal court that the lower court was 'wrong' for preferring option A over option B. The more finely balanced the case, the less likely there can be an arguable appeal.

> In order to succeed in an appeal it is not enough to show that a different Judge could have made a different decision. An appeal will only succeed if the court below was 'wrong', either by making a mistake about the law, or by reaching a conclusion that could not properly have been reached on the evidence

HUMAN RIGHTS ACT 1998

11.36 The events in Europe in the 1930s and 1940s provided the impetus for the establishment of an international structure to protect the human rights of individual citizens against the actions of the state. The Convention for the Protection of Human Rights and Fundamental Freedoms (ECHR) was signed in November 1950 and ratified by the UK in March 1951. The ECHR structure and law is distinct and separate from European Community Law and the European Court of Justice.

11.37 From October 2000 the Human Rights Act 1998 (HRA 1998) has been fully in force in the UK. The broad effect of the HRA 1998 is to require that UK domestic law is interpreted, and that public authorities act, in a manner that is compatible with the ECHR, with the result that a citizen may rely directly upon the ECHR in proceedings before UK domestic courts. The HRA 1998 does not strictly 'incorporate' the ECHR into UK domestic law. So far as it is possible to do so, primary legislation and subordinate legislation must be read and given effect to in a way that is *compatible* with the Convention rights.[25]

11.38 Whilst it has impact upon many areas of domestic life, the ECHR is a comparatively short document containing brief statements of basic human rights, each set out in a numbered 'article'. Over the past 50 years, the European

---

[25] HRA 1998, s 3(1).

Court of Human Rights (ECtHR) in Strasbourg has interpreted and applied the ECHR to a myriad of different factual circumstances, with the result that there is now a detailed body of case-law.

11.39 In relation to the intervention of public authorities in the lives of children and their families the two key articles of the ECHR are Art 6 (fair trial) and Art 8 (family life). These two articles are considered in summary terms below. Other ECHR articles that may be engaged in a children case are:

✓ Art 2: Right to life;

✓ Art 3: Prohibition of torture, inhuman or degrading treatment or punishment;

✓ Art 5: Right to liberty and security of person;

✓ Art 12: Right to marry and found a family; and

✓ Art 14: Prohibition of discrimination.

Article 6: Right to a fair trial

11.40 Article 6 of the ECHR states:

> '1. In the determination of his civil rights and obligations or of any criminal charge against him, everyone is entitled to a fair and public hearing within a reasonable time by an independent and impartial tribunal established by law. Judgment shall be pronounced publicly but the press and public may be excluded from all or part of the trial in the interest of morals, public order or national security in a democratic society, where the interests of juveniles or the protection of the private life of the parties so require, or to the extent strictly necessary in the opinion of the court in special circumstances where publicity would prejudice the interests of justice.'

The principal features of Art 6 are:

✓ the right to effective access to a court or tribunal;

✓ the tribunal must be independent and impartial;

✓ the hearing must be within a reasonable time;

✓ there must be 'equality of arms' as between the litigants;

✓ the parties must be present and able to participate at the hearing;

✓ a party must know the case against him;

✓ in general the hearing should be in public with a public judgment; and

✓ the judgment should include a reasoned decision.

11.41 Article 6 applies where there is a 'determination' affecting a person's civil rights. There must be a right, recognised by domestic law, involved and there must have been some determination relating to that right.

Article 8: Right to respect for private and family life

11.42 Article 8 of the ECHR states:

> '1. Everyone has the right to respect for his private and family life, his home and his correspondence.
>
> 2. There shall be no interference by a public authority with the exercise of this right except such as is in accordance with the law and is necessary in a democratic society in the interests of national security, public safety or the economic well-being of the country, for the prevention of disorder or crime, for the protection of health or morals, or for the protection of the rights and freedoms of others.'

The preliminary question of whether rights to 'family life' are engaged with respect to a local authority's intervention in relation to children is likely to be answered in the affirmative. Thus, where, for example, a child is removed into care, there will clearly be an interference with rights to family life sufficient to trigger consideration under Art 8. The focus of such consideration will therefore be conducted under Art 8(2) where, in order for the state's interference to be 'justified' (and therefore not in breach of Art 8), the following four conditions must be fulfilled:

(a) the interference must be in accordance with the domestic law (for example under the CA 1989);

(b) the interference must serve a legitimate purpose (for example the protection of children from harm);

(c) the interference must be *'necessary in a democratic society'*; and

(d) the interference must not be discriminatory.

11.43 Of those four conditions (a) and (b) are likely to be met where a local authority is seeking to take a child into care and the key to determining whether or not Art 8 is breached is likely to be (c), namely whether or not the interference is necessary in a democratic society. This latter consideration imports the need to identify some 'pressing social need' and requires a state of affairs which is more than simply that a certain action is 'useful' or 'desirable'; it must be 'necessary'. Further, in determining whether any intervention is 'necessary' not only the need to intervene but also the degree and type of intervention must be considered. The intervention must be 'proportionate' to the need: a sledgehammer is not required to crack a nut.

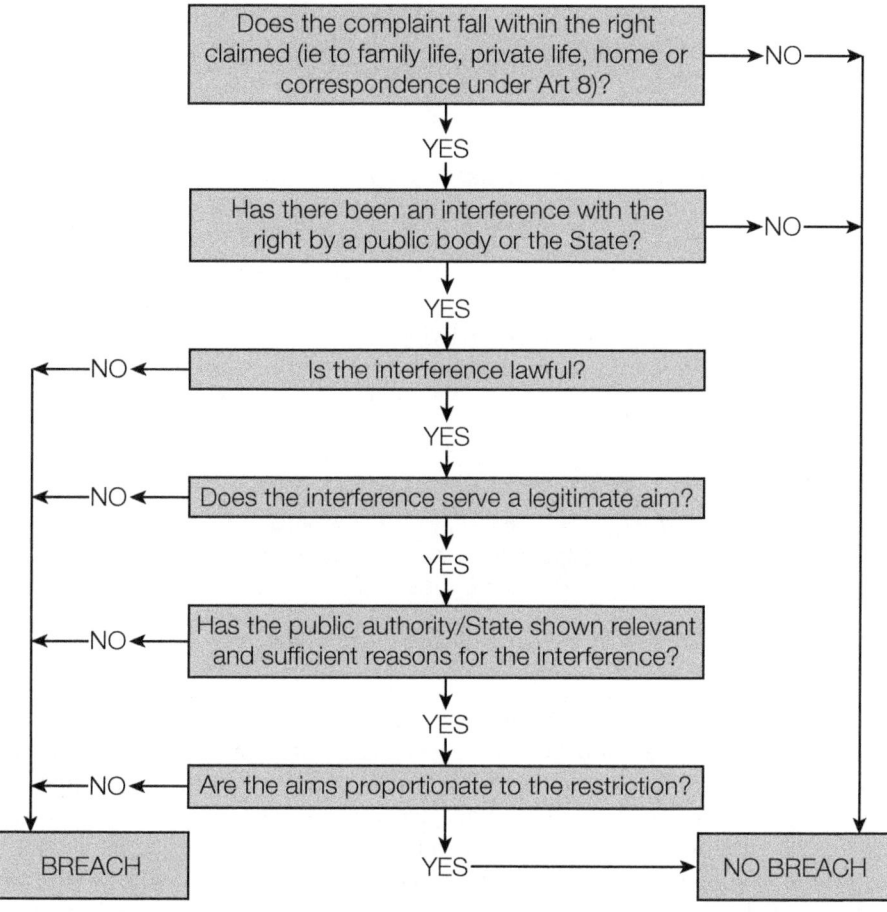

Applying the ECHR in domestic courts under the HRA 1998

11.44 The principal effect of the HRA 1998 is that every action of a local authority (as a public authority) and every decision of a court in family proceedings (and indeed the proceedings themselves) must be compatible with the ECHR. Only where it is impossible to act in a compatible manner, or achieve an interpretation of the law that is compatible, can another course be taken. Where a number of options are all compatible, then a court or an authority will have, so far as the HRA 1998 is concerned, discretion to choose between them.

11.45 Consideration of the ECHR will thus arise during the ordinary process of every care case and every set of family proceedings before a court in England and Wales, without any of the parties having to bring a separate action under the HRA 1998. Where ECHR issues arise in pending proceedings, they should be dealt with within those proceedings. The HRA 1998 does, however, provide the option for separate, free-standing, proceedings to be brought in reliance upon ECHR claims (for example where there are no relevant current proceedings pending before a court). The HRA 1998, s 6 renders it 'unlawful' for a public body (which would include a local authority) to act, or intend to act, in a manner that is incompatible with the ECHR. Where a person claims that a public body (other than a judicial authority) has acted or proposes to act 'unlawfully' in this context, he may bring proceedings under HRA 1998, s 7 in the High Court or a county court.

11.46 Where a local authority designated in a care order has operated the care plan in a manner that may be incompatible with the ECHR rights of the child and family members, it is appropriate for free-standing HRA 1998 proceedings to be brought in order to allow the court to review the matter.[26]

11.47 If the proceedings result in a finding of 'unlawful' activity by the defendant public body, the court has the power to grant such relief or remedy, or make such order, within its powers, as it considers just and appropriate.[27]

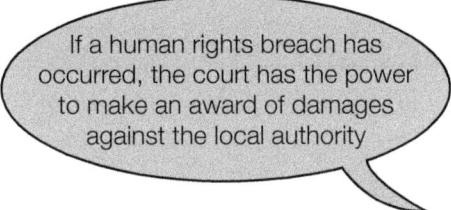

If a human rights breach has occurred, the court has the power to make an award of damages against the local authority

11.48 In recent years there have been a number of HRA 1998 claims brought on behalf of children who have been accommodated in local authority care under CA 1989, s 20 without sufficient steps being taken to ensure that the necessary consents (of those with parental responsibility) have been obtained, and/or in circumstances where the local authority has failed to carry out a proper review of the child's needs and plan for her future. In such a case the amount of damages awarded will depend on a number of factors including the extent to which the local authority has or has not acted in good faith, and the duration of the breach.

Reference to the European Court of Human Rights

11.49 As an option of last resort, a claim that the state (in the guise, for example, of the local authority or the court) has acted in breach of the ECHR may be the subject of an application directly to the ECtHR in Strasbourg. Such an application will normally only be admitted for consideration by the ECtHR if all the legal remedies available within England and Wales have been exhausted. The claim, if it is accepted by the ECtHR as 'admissible', will take a number of years to proceed to final determination. The effect of a final determination in favour of the claimant will be a finding that the state has been in breach of one

---

[26] *Re M (Care: Challenging Decisions by Local Authority)* [2001] 2 FLR 1300 (approved by the House of Lords in *Re S (Care Order: Implementation of Care Plan); Re W (Care Order: Adequacy of Care Plan)* [2002] UKHL 10; [2002] 1 FLR 815).
[27] HRA 1998, s 8.

or more Articles of the ECHR and, in an appropriate case, modest damages may be awarded. It is not within the ECtHR's power to quash the original decision and the result back in England and Wales may be an amendment to the law in due course: an outcome which will not of itself achieve the return of a child 'unlawfully' removed by a local authority some years earlier.

Appendix 1

CHILDREN ACT 1989

(1989 CHAPTER 41)

PART I
INTRODUCTORY

1 Welfare of the child.

(1) When a court determines any question with respect to—

(a) the upbringing of a child; or
(b) the administration of a child's property or the application of any income arising from it,

the child's welfare shall be the court's paramount consideration.

(2) In any proceedings in which any question with respect to the upbringing of a child arises, the court shall have regard to the general principle that any delay in determining the question is likely to prejudice the welfare of the child.

[(2A) A court, in the circumstances mentioned in subsection (4)(a) or (7), is as respects each parent within subsection (6)(a) to presume, unless the contrary is shown, that involvement of that parent in the life of the child concerned will further the child's welfare.

(2B) In subsection (2A) 'involvement' means involvement of some kind, either direct or indirect, but not any particular division of a child's time.][1]

(3) In the circumstances mentioned in subsection (4), a court shall have regard in particular to—

(a) the ascertainable wishes and feelings of the child concerned (considered in the light of his age and understanding);
(b) his physical, emotional and educational needs;
(c) the likely effect on him of any change in his circumstances;
(d) his age, sex, background and any characteristics of his which the court considers relevant;
(e) any harm which he has suffered or is at risk of suffering;
(f) how capable each of his parents, and any other person in relation to whom the court considers the question to be relevant, is of meeting his needs;
(g) the range of powers available to the court under this Act in the proceedings in question.

(4) The circumstances are that—

(a) the court is considering whether to make, vary or discharge a section 8 order, and the making, variation or discharge of the order is opposed by any party to the proceedings; or
(b) the court is considering whether to make, vary or discharge [a special guardianship order or]² an order under Part IV.

(5) Where a court is considering whether or not to make one or more orders under this Act with respect to a child, it shall not make the order or any of the orders unless it considers that doing so would be better for the child than making no order at all.

[(6) In subsection (2A) 'parent' means parent of the child concerned; and, for the purposes of that subsection, a parent of the child concerned—

(a) is within this paragraph if that parent can be involved in the child's life in a way that does not put the child at risk of suffering harm; and
(b) is to be treated as being within paragraph (a) unless there is some evidence before the court in the particular proceedings to suggest that involvement of that parent in the child's life would put the child at risk of suffering harm whatever the form of the involvement.

(7) The circumstances referred to are that the court is considering whether to make an order under section 4(1)(c) or (2A) or 4ZA(1)(c) or (5) (parental responsibility of parent other than mother).]¹

Amendments
1 Inserted by the Children and Families Act 2014, s 11.
2 Inserted by the Adoption and Children Act 2002, s 115(2), (3).

2 Parental responsibility for children.

(1) Where a child's father and mother were married to each other at the time of his birth, they shall each have parental responsibility for the child.

[(1A) Where a child—

(a) has a parent by virtue of section 42 of the Human Fertilisation and Embryology Act 2008; or
(b) has a parent by virtue of section 43 of that Act and is a person to whom section 1(3) of the Family Law Reform Act 1987 applies,

the child's mother and the other parent shall each have parental responsibility for the child.]¹

(2) Where a child's father and mother were not married to each other at the time of his birth—

(a) the mother shall have parental responsibility for the child;
(b) the father [shall have parental responsibility for the child if he has acquired it (and has not ceased to have it)]² in accordance with the provisions of this Act.

[(2A) Where a child has a parent by virtue of section 43 of the Human Fertilisation and Embryology Act 2008 and is not a person to whom section 1(3) of the Family Law Reform Act 1987 applies—
- (a) the mother shall have parental responsibility for the child;
- (b) the other parent shall have parental responsibility for the child if she has acquired it (and has not ceased to have it) in accordance with the provisions of this Act.][1]

(3) References in this Act to a child whose father and mother were, or (as the case may be) were not, married to each other at the time of his birth must be read with section 1 of the Family Law Reform Act 1987 (which extends their meaning).

(4) The rule of law that a father is the natural guardian of his legitimate child is abolished.

(5) More than one person may have parental responsibility for the same child at the same time.

(6) A person who has parental responsibility for a child at any time shall not cease to have that responsibility solely because some other person subsequently acquires parental responsibility for the child.

(7) Where more than one person has parental responsibility for a child, each of them may act alone and without the other (or others) in meeting that responsibility; but nothing in this Part shall be taken to affect the operation of any enactment which requires the consent of more than one person in a matter affecting the child.

(8) The fact that a person has parental responsibility for a child shall not entitle him to act in any way which would be incompatible with any order made with respect to the child under this Act.

(9) A person who has parental responsibility for a child may not surrender or transfer any part of that responsibility to another but may arrange for some or all of it to be met by one or more persons acting on his behalf.

(10) The person with whom any such arrangement is made may himself be a person who already has parental responsibility for the child concerned.

(11) The making of any such arrangement shall not affect any liability of the person making it which may arise from any failure to meet any part of his parental responsibility for the child concerned.

Amendments
1 Inserted by the Human Fertilisation and Embryology Act 2008, s 56, Sch 6, para 26.
2 Substituted by the Adoption and Children Act 2002, s 111(1), (5).

3 Meaning of 'parental responsibility'.

(1) In this Act 'parental responsibility' means all the rights, duties, powers, responsibilities and authority which by law a parent of a child has in relation to the child and his property.

(2) It also includes the rights, powers and duties which a guardian of the child's estate (appointed, before the commencement of section 5, to act generally) would have had in relation to the child and his property.

(3) The rights referred to in subsection (2) include, in particular, the right of the guardian to receive or recover in his own name, for the benefit of the child, property of whatever description and wherever situated which the child is entitled to receive or recover.

(4) The fact that a person has, or does not have, parental responsibility for a child shall not affect—

    (a)   any obligation which he may have in relation to the child (such as a statutory duty to maintain the child); or
    (b)   any rights which, in the event of the child's death, he (or any other person) may have in relation to the child's property.

(5) A person who—

    (a)   does not have parental responsibility for a particular child; but
    (b)   has care of the child,

may (subject to the provisions of this Act) do what is reasonable in all the circumstances of the case for the purpose of safeguarding or promoting the child's welfare.

4 Acquisition of parental responsibility by father.

(1) Where a child's father and mother were not married to each other at the time of his birth[, the father shall acquire parental responsibility for the child if—

    (a)   he becomes registered as the child's father under any of the enactments specified in subsection (1A);
    (b)   he and the child's mother make an agreement (a 'parental responsibility agreement') providing for him to have parental responsibility for the child; or
    (c)   the court, on his application, orders that he shall have parental responsibility for the child.][1]

[(1A) The enactments referred to in subsection (1)(a) are—

    (a)   paragraphs (a), (b) and (c) of section 10(1) and of section 10A(1) of the Births and Deaths Registration Act 1953;
    (b)   paragraphs (a), (b)(i) and (c) of section 18(1), and sections 18(2)(b) and 20(1)(a) of the Registration of Births, Deaths and Marriages (Scotland) Act 1965; and
    (c)   sub-paragraphs (a), (b) and (c) of Article 14(3) of the Births and Deaths Registration (Northern Ireland) Order 1976.

(1B) The [Secretary of State][2] may by order amend subsection (1A) so as to add further enactments to the list in that subsection.][3]

(2) No parental responsibility agreement shall have effect for the purposes of this Act unless—

(a) it is made in the form prescribed by regulations made by the Lord Chancellor; and
(b) where regulations are made by the Lord Chancellor prescribing the manner in which such agreements must be recorded, it is recorded in the prescribed manner.

[(2A) A person who has acquired parental responsibility under subsection (1) shall cease to have that responsibility only if the court so orders.

(3) The court may make an order under subsection (2A) on the application—
(a) of any person who has parental responsibility for the child; or
(b) with the leave of the court, of the child himself,

subject, in the case of parental responsibility acquired under subsection (1)(c), to section 12(4).]¹

(4) The court may only grant leave under subsection (3)(b) if it is satisfied that the child has sufficient understanding to make the proposed application.

Amendments
1 Substituted by the Adoption and Children Act 2002, s 111(1), (2), (4).
2 Substituted by the Transfer of Functions (Children, Young People and Families) Order 2003, SI 2003/3191, art 6, Schedule, para 1.
3 Inserted by the Adoption and Children Act 2002, s 111(1), (3).

[4ZA Acquisition of parental responsibility by second female parent.

(1) Where a child has a parent by virtue of section 43 of the Human Fertilisation and Embryology Act 2008 and is not a person to whom section 1(3) of the Family Law Reform Act 1987 applies, that parent shall acquire parental responsibility for the child if—
(a) she becomes registered as a parent of the child under any of the enactments specified in subsection (2);
(b) she and the child's mother make an agreement providing for her to have parental responsibility for the child; or
(c) the court, on her application, orders that she shall have parental responsibility for the child.

(2) The enactments referred to in subsection (1)(a) are—
(a) paragraphs (a), (b) and (c) of section 10(1B) and of section 10A(1B) of the Births and Deaths Registration Act 1953;
(b) paragraphs (a), (b) and (d) of section 18B(1) and sections 18B(3)(a) and 20(1)(a) of the Registration of Births, Deaths and Marriages (Scotland) Act 1965; and
(c) sub-paragraphs (a), (b) and (c) of Article 14ZA(3) of the Births and Deaths Registration (Northern Ireland) Order 1976.

(3) The Secretary of State may by order amend subsection (2) so as to add further enactments to the list in that subsection.

(4) An agreement under subsection (1)(b) is also a 'parental responsibility agreement', and section 4(2) applies in relation to such an agreement as it applies in relation to parental responsibility agreements under section 4.

(5) A person who has acquired parental responsibility under subsection (1) shall cease to have that responsibility only if the court so orders.

(6) The court may make an order under subsection (5) on the application—

(a) of any person who has parental responsibility for the child; or
(b) with the leave of the court, of the child himself,

subject, in the case of parental responsibility acquired under subsection (1)(c), to section 12(4).

(7) The court may only grant leave under subsection (6)(b) if it is satisfied that the child has sufficient understanding to make the proposed application.][1]

Amendment
1 Inserted by the Human Fertilisation and Embryology Act 2008, s 56, Sch 6, para 27.

[4A Acquisition of parental responsibility by step-parent.

(1) Where a child's parent ('parent A') who has parental responsibility for the child is married to[, or a civil partner of,][1] a person who is not the child's parent ('the step-parent')—

(a) parent A or, if the other parent of the child also has parental responsibility for the child, both parents may by agreement with the step-parent provide for the step-parent to have parental responsibility for the child; or
(b) the court may, on the application of the step-parent, order that the step-parent shall have parental responsibility for the child.

(2) An agreement under subsection (1)(a) is also a 'parental responsibility agreement', and section 4(2) applies in relation to such agreements as it applies in relation to parental responsibility agreements under section 4.

(3) A parental responsibility agreement under subsection (1)(a), or an order under subsection (1)(b), may only be brought to an end by an order of the court made on the application—

(a) of any person who has parental responsibility for the child; or
(b) with the leave of the court, of the child himself.

(4) The court may only grant leave under subsection (3)(b) if it is satisfied that the child has sufficient understanding to make the proposed application.][2]

Amendments
1 Inserted by the Civil Partnership Act 2004, s 75(1), (2).
2 Inserted by the Adoption and Children Act 2002, s 112.

5 Appointment of guardians.

(1) Where an application with respect to a child is made to the court by any individual, the court may by order appoint that individual to be the child's guardian if—

(a) the child has no parent with parental responsibility for him; or
(b) a [parent, guardian or special guardian of the child's was named in a child arrangements order as a person with whom the child was to live and][1] has died while the order was in force[; or][2]

[(c) paragraph (b) does not apply, and the child's only or last surviving special guardian dies.]²

(2) The power conferred by subsection (1) may also be exercised in any family proceedings if the court considers that the order should be made even though no application has been made for it.

(3) A parent who has parental responsibility for his child may appoint another individual to be the child's guardian in the event of his death.

(4) A guardian of a child may appoint another individual to take his place as the child's guardian in the event of his death[; and a special guardian of a child may appoint another individual to be the child's guardian in the event of his death]².

(5) An appointment under subsection (3) or (4) shall not have effect unless it is made in writing, is dated and is signed by the person making the appointment or—

(a) in the case of an appointment made by a will which is not signed by the testator, is signed at the direction of the testator in accordance with the requirements of section 9 of the Wills Act 1837; or

(b) in any other case, is signed at the direction of the person making the appointment, in his presence and in the presence of two witnesses who each attest the signature.

(6) A person appointed as a child's guardian under this section shall have parental responsibility for the child concerned.

(7) Where—

(a) on the death of any person making an appointment under subsection (3) or (4), the child concerned has no parent with parental responsibility for him; or

(b) immediately before the death of any person making such an appointment, a [child arrangements order was in force in which the person was named as a person with whom the child was to live or the person]¹ [was the child's only (or last surviving) special guardian]²,

the appointment shall take effect on the death of that person.

(8) Where, on the death of any person making an appointment under subsection (3) or (4)—

(a) the child concerned has a parent with parental responsibility for him; and

(b) subsection (7)(b) does not apply,

the appointment shall take effect when the child no longer has a parent who has parental responsibility for him.

(9) Subsections (1) and (7) do not apply if the [child arrangements]¹ order referred to in paragraph (b) of those subsections [also named]¹ a surviving parent of the child [as a person with whom the child was to live]³.

(10) Nothing in this section shall be taken to prevent an appointment under subsection (3) or (4) being made by two or more persons acting jointly.

(11) Subject to any provision made by rules of court, no court shall exercise the High Court's inherent jurisdiction to appoint a guardian of the estate of any child.

(12) Where rules of court are made under subsection (11) they may prescribe the circumstances in which, and conditions subject to which, an appointment of such a guardian may be made.

(13) A guardian of a child may only be appointed in accordance with the provisions of this section.

Amendments
1 Substituted by the Children and Families Act 2014, s 12(4), Sch 2, paras 1, 2(1), (2), (3), (4)(a), (b).
2 Inserted by the Adoption and Children Act 2002, s 115(2), (4)(a)(ii), (b), (c).
3 Inserted by the Children and Families Act 2014, s 12(4), Sch 2, paras 1, 2(1), (4)(c).

6 Guardians: revocation and disclaimer.

(1) An appointment under section 5(3) or (4) revokes an earlier such appointment (including one made in an unrevoked will or codicil) made by the same person in respect of the same child, unless it is clear (whether as the result of an express provision in the later appointment or by any necessary implication) that the purpose of the later appointment is to appoint an additional guardian.

(2) An appointment under section 5(3) or (4) (including one made in an unrevoked will or codicil) is revoked if the person who made the appointment revokes it by a written and dated instrument which is signed—

(a) by him; or
(b) at his direction, in his presence and in the presence of two witnesses who each attest the signature.

(3) An appointment under section 5(3) or (4) (other than one made in a will or codicil) is revoked if, with the intention of revoking the appointment, the person who made it—

(a) destroys the instrument by which it was made; or
(b) has some other person destroy that instrument in his presence.

[(3A) An appointment under section 5(3) or (4) (including one made in an unrevoked will or codicil) is revoked if the person appointed is the spouse of the person who made the appointment and either—

(a) a decree of a court of civil jurisdiction in England and Wales dissolves or annuls the marriage, or
(b) the marriage is dissolved or annulled and the divorce or annulment is entitled to recognition in England and Wales by virtue of Part II of the Family Law Act 1986,

unless a contrary intention appears by the appointment.]¹

[(3B) An appointment under section 5(3) or (4) (including one made in an unrevoked will or codicil) is revoked if the person appointed is the civil partner of the person who made the appointment and either–

(a) an order of a court of civil jurisdiction in England and Wales dissolves or annuls the civil partnership, or
(b) the civil partnership is dissolved or annulled and the dissolution or annulment is entitled to recognition in England and Wales by virtue of Chapter 3 of Part 5 of the Civil Partnership Act 2004,

unless a contrary intention appears by the appointment.]²

(4) For the avoidance of doubt, an appointment under section 5(3) or (4) made in a will or codicil is revoked if the will or codicil is revoked.

(5) A person who is appointed as a guardian under section 5(3) or (4) may disclaim his appointment by an instrument in writing signed by him and made within a reasonable time of his first knowing that the appointment has taken effect.

(6) Where regulations are made by the Lord Chancellor prescribing the manner in which such disclaimers must be recorded, no such disclaimer shall have effect unless it is recorded in the prescribed manner.

(7) Any appointment of a guardian under section 5 may be brought to an end at any time by order of the court—

(a) on the application of any person who has parental responsibility for the child;
(b) on the application of the child concerned, with leave of the court; or
(c) in any family proceedings, if the court considers that it should be brought to an end even though no application has been made..

Amendments
1 Inserted by the Law Reform (Succession) Act 1995, s 4(1).
2 Inserted by the Civil Partnership Act 2004, s 76.

7 Welfare reports.

(1) A court considering any question with respect to a child under this Act may—

(a) ask [an officer of the Service]¹ [or a Welsh family proceedings officer]²; or
(b) ask a local authority to arrange for—
　(i) an officer of the authority; or
　(ii) such other person (other than [an officer of the Service]¹ [or a Welsh family proceedings officer]²) as the authority considers appropriate,

to report to the court on such matters relating to the welfare of that child as are required to be dealt with in the report.

(2) The Lord Chancellor may[, after consulting the Lord Chief Justice,]³ make regulations specifying matters which, unless the court orders otherwise, must be dealt with in any report under this section.

(3) The report may be made in writing, or orally, as the court requires.

(4) Regardless of any enactment or rule of law which would otherwise prevent it from doing so, the court may take account of—

(a) any statement contained in the report; and
(b) any evidence given in respect of the matters referred to in the report,

in so far as the statement or evidence is, in the opinion of the court, relevant to the question which it is considering.

(5) It shall be the duty of the authority or [officer of the Service][1] [or a Welsh family proceedings officer][2] to comply with any request for a report under this section.

[(6) The Lord Chief Justice may nominate a judicial office holder (as defined in section 109(4) of the Constitutional Reform Act 2005) to exercise his functions under subsection (2).][3]

Amendments
1   Substituted by the Criminal Justice and Court Services Act 2000, s 74, Sch 7, paras 87, 88.
2   Inserted by the Children Act 2004, s 40, Sch 3, paras 5, 6.
3   Inserted by the Constitutional Reform Act 2005, s 15(1), Sch 4, paras 203, 204.

PART II
ORDERS WITH RESPECT TO CHILDREN IN FAMILY PROCEEDINGS

General

8 [Child arrangements orders][1] and other orders with respect to children.

(1) In this Act—

...[2]

['child arrangements order' means an order regulating arrangements relating to any of the following—
(a) with whom a child is to live, spend time or otherwise have contact, and
(b) when a child is to live, spend time or otherwise have contact with any person;][3]

'a prohibited steps order' means an order that no step which could be taken by a parent in meeting his parental responsibility for a child, and which is of a kind specified in the order, shall be taken by any person without the consent of the court;

...[2] and

'a specific issue order' means an order giving directions for the purpose of determining a specific question which has arisen, or which may arise, in connection with any aspect of parental responsibility for a child.

(2) In this Act 'a section 8 order' means any of the orders mentioned in subsection (1) and any order varying or discharging such an order.

(3) For the purposes of this Act 'family proceedings' means any proceedings—

   (a)   under the inherent jurisdiction of the High Court in relation to children; and
   (b)   under the enactments mentioned in subsection (4),

but does not include proceedings on an application for leave under section 100(3).

(4) The enactments are—

   (a)   Parts I, II and IV of this Act;
   (b)   the Matrimonial Causes Act 1973;
   [(ba) Schedule 5 to the Civil Partnership Act 2004;][4]
   (c)   ...[5]
   [(d)   the Adoption and Children Act 2002;][6]
   (e)   the Domestic Proceedings and Magistrates' Courts Act 1978;
   [(ea) Schedule 6 to the Civil Partnership Act 2004;][4]
   (f)   ...[5]
   (g)   Part III of the Matrimonial and Family Proceedings Act 1984.
   [(h)   the Family Law Act 1996;][7]
   [(i)   sections 11 and 12 of the Crime and Disorder Act 1998.][8]

Amendments
1   Substituted by the Children and Families Act 2014, s 12(4), Sch 2, paras 1, 3.
2   Repealed by the Children and Families Act 2014, s 12(1), (2).
3   Inserted by the Children and Families Act 2014, s 12(1), (3).
4   Inserted by the Civil Partnership Act 2004, s 261(1), Sch 27, para 129.
5   Repealed by the Family Law Act 1996, s 66(3), Sch 10.
6   Substituted by the Adoption and Children Act 2002, s 139(1), Sch 3, paras 54, 55.
7   Inserted by Family Law Act 1996, s 66(1), Sch 8, para 60(1).
8   Inserted by the Crime and Disorder Act 1998, s 119, Sch 8, para 68.

9 Restrictions on making section 8 orders.

(1) No court shall make any section 8 order, other than a [child arrangements order to which subsection (6B) applies][1], with respect to a child who is in the care of a local authority.

(2) No application may be made by a local authority for a [child arrangements][1] order and no court shall make such an order in favour of a local authority.

(3) A person who is, or was at any time within the last six months, a local authority foster parent of a child may not apply for leave to apply for a section 8 order with respect to the child unless—

   (a)   he has the consent of the authority;
   (b)   he is a relative of the child; or
   (c)   the child has lived with him for at least [one year][2] preceding the application.

(4) ...[3]

(5) No court shall exercise its powers to make a specific issue order or prohibited steps order—

(a) with a view to achieving a result which could be achieved by making a [child arrangements]¹ order [or an order under section 51A of the Adoption and Children Act 2002 (post-adoption contact)]⁴; or
(b) in any way which is denied to the High Court (by section 100(2)) in the exercise of its inherent jurisdiction with respect to children.

(6) [No court shall make a [section 8]¹ order]⁵ which is to have effect for a period which will end after the child has reached the age of sixteen unless it is satisfied that the circumstances of the case are exceptional.

[(6A) Subsection (6) does not apply to a child arrangements order to which subsection (6B) applies.

(6B) This subsection applies to a child arrangements order if the arrangements regulated by the order relate only to either or both of the following—

(a) with whom the child concerned is to live, and
(b) when the child is to live with any person.]⁶

(7) No court shall make any section 8 order, other than one varying or discharging such an order, with respect to a child who has reached the age of sixteen unless it is satisfied that the circumstances of the case are exceptional.

Amendments
1 Substituted by the Children and Families Act 2014, s 12(4), Sch 2, paras 1, 4(1)–(5).
2 Substituted by the Adoption and Children Act 2002, s 113(a).
3 Repealed by the Adoption and Children Act 2002, ss 113(b), 139(3), Sch 5.
4 Inserted by the Children and Families Act 2014, s 9(7).
5 Substituted by the Children and Young Persons Act 2008, s 37(1).
6 Inserted by the Children and Families Act 2014, s 12(4), Sch 2, paras 1, 4(1), (6).

10 Power of court to make section 8 orders.

(1) In any family proceedings in which a question arises with respect to the welfare of any child, the court may make a section 8 order with respect to the child if—

(a) an application for the order has been made by a person who—
　(i) is entitled to apply for a section 8 order with respect to the child; or
　(ii) has obtained the leave of the court to make the application; or
(b) the court considers that the order should be made even though no such application has been made.

(2) The court may also make a section 8 order with respect to any child on the application of a person who—

(a) is entitled to apply for a section 8 order with respect to the child; or
(b) has obtained the leave of the court to make the application.

(3) This section is subject to the restrictions imposed by section 9.

(4) The following persons are entitled to apply to the court for any section 8 order with respect to a child—

(a) any parent[, guardian or special guardian]¹ of the child;

[(aa) any person who by virtue of section 4A has parental responsibility for the child;]²
[(b) any person who is named, in a child arrangements order that is in force with respect to the child, as a person with whom the child is to live.]³

(5) The following persons are entitled to apply for a [child arrangements]³ order with respect to a child—

(a) any party to a marriage (whether or not subsisting) in relation to whom the child is a child of the family;
[(aa) any civil partner in a civil partnership (whether or not subsisting) in relation to whom the child is a child of the family;]⁴
(b) any person with whom the child has lived for a period of at least three years;
(c) any person who—
  [(i) in any case where a child arrangements order in force with respect to the child regulates arrangements relating to with whom the child is to live or when the child is to live with any person, has the consent of each of the persons named in the order as a person with whom the child is to live;]³
  (ii) in any case where the child is in the care of a local authority, has the consent of that authority; or
  (iii) in any other case, has the consent of each of those (if any) who have parental responsibility for the child;
[(d) any person who has parental responsibility for the child by virtue of provision made under section 12(2A).]⁵

[(5A) A local authority foster parent is entitled to apply for a [child arrangements order to which subsection (5C) applies]³ with respect to a child if the child has lived with him for a period of at least one year immediately preceding the application.]²

[(5B) A relative of a child is entitled to apply for a [child arrangements order to which subsection (5C) applies]³ with respect to the child if the child has lived with the relative for a period of at least one year immediately preceding the application.]⁶

[(5C) This subsection applies to a child arrangements order if the arrangements regulated by the order relate only to either or both of the following—

(a) with whom the child concerned is to live, and
(b) when the child is to live with any person.]⁵

(6) A person who would not otherwise be entitled (under the previous provisions of this section) to apply for the variation or discharge of a section 8 order shall be entitled to do so if—

(a) the order was made on his application; or
(b) in the case of a [child arrangements]³ order, he is named in [provisions of the order regulating arrangements relating to—]³
  [(i) with whom the child concerned is to spend time or otherwise have contact, or

(ii) when the child is to spend time or otherwise have contact with any person.]³

(7) Any person who falls within a category of person prescribed by rules of court is entitled to apply for any such section 8 order as may be prescribed in relation to that category of person.

[(7A) If a special guardianship order is in force with respect to a child, an application for a [child arrangements order to which subsection (7B) applies]³ may only be made with respect to him, if apart from this subsection the leave of the court is not required, with such leave.]²

[(7B) This subsection applies to a child arrangements order if the arrangements regulated by the order consist of, or include, arrangements which relate to either or both of the following—

(a) with whom the child concerned is to live, and
(b) when the child is to live with any person.]⁵

(8) Where the person applying for leave to make an application for a section 8 order is the child concerned, the court may only grant leave if it is satisfied that he has sufficient understanding to make the proposed application for the section 8 order.

(9) Where the person applying for leave to make an application for a section 8 order is not the child concerned, the court shall, in deciding whether or not to grant leave, have particular regard to—

(a) the nature of the proposed application for the section 8 order;
(b) the applicant's connection with the child;
(c) any risk there might be of that proposed application disrupting the child's life to such an extent that he would be harmed by it; and
(d) where the child is being looked after by a local authority—
    (i) the authority's plans for the child's future; and
    (ii) the wishes and feelings of the child's parents.

(10) The period of three years mentioned in subsection (5)(b) need not be continuous but must not have begun more than five years before, or ended more than three months before, the making of the application.

Amendments
1 Substituted by the Adoption and Children Act 2002, s 139(1), Sch 3, paras 54, 56(a).
2 Inserted by the Adoption and Children Act 2002, s 139(1), Sch 3, paras 54, 56(b), (c), (d).
3 Substituted by the Children and Families Act 2014, s 12(4), Sch 2, paras 1, 5(1), (2), (3)(a), (b), (4), (6), (7).
4 Inserted by the Civil Partnership Act 2004, s 77.
5 Inserted by the Children and Families Act 2014, s 12(4), Sch 2, paras 1, 5(3)(c), (5), (8).
6 Inserted by the Children and Young Persons Act 2008, s 36.

11 General principles and supplementary provisions.

(1) In proceedings in which any question of making a section 8 order, or any other question with respect to such an order, arises, the court shall (in the light of any [provision in rules of court that is of the kind mentioned in subsection (2)(a) or (b))]¹—

(a) draw up a timetable with a view to determining the question without delay; and
(b) give such directions as it considers appropriate for the purpose of ensuring, so far as is reasonably practicable, that that timetable is adhered to.

(2) Rules of court may—
(a) specify periods within which specified steps must be taken in relation to proceedings in which such questions arise; and
(b) make other provision with respect to such proceedings for the purpose of ensuring, so far as is reasonably practicable, that such questions are determined without delay.

(3) Where a court has power to make a section 8 order, it may do so at any time during the course of the proceedings in question even though it is not in a position to dispose finally of those proceedings.

(4) …²

(5) Where—
(a) a [child arrangements]³ order has been made with respect to a child; and
(b) [the child has]³ two parents who each have parental responsibility for him,

the [order, so far as it has the result that there are times when the child lives or is to live with one of the parents,]³ shall cease to have effect if the parents live together for a continuous period of more than six months.

(6) [A child arrangements order made with respect to a child, so far as it provides for the child to spend time or otherwise have contact with one of the child's parents at times when the child is living with the child's other parent,]³ shall cease to have effect if the parents live together for a continuous period of more than six months.

(7) A section 8 order may—
(a) contain directions about how it is to be carried into effect;
(b) impose conditions which must be complied with by any person—
    [(i) who is named in the order as a person with whom the child concerned is to live, spend time or otherwise have contact;]³
    (ii) who is a parent of the child …²;
    (iii) who is not a parent of his but who has parental responsibility for him; or
    (iv) with whom the child is living,
    and to whom the conditions are expressed to apply;
(c) be made to have effect for a specified period, or contain provisions which are to have effect for a specified period;
(d) make such incidental, supplemental or consequential provision as the court thinks fit.

Amendments
1 Substituted by the Children and Families Act 2014, s 14(1), (1), (5).
2 Repealed by the Children and Families Act 2014, s 12(4), Sch 2, paras 1, 6(1), (2), (5)(b).
3 Substituted by the Children and Families Act 2014, s 12(4), Sch 2, paras 1, 6(1), (3), (4), (5)(a).

[11A ...¹ Activity directions

[(1) Subsection (2) applies in proceedings in which the court is considering whether to make provision about one or more of the matters mentioned in subsection (1A) by making—

- (a) a child arrangements order with respect to the child concerned, or
- (b) an order varying or discharging a child arrangements order with respect to the child concerned.

(1A) The matters mentioned in this subsection are—

- (a) with whom a child is to live,
- (b) when a child is to live with any person,
- (c) with whom a child is to spend time or otherwise have contact, and
- (d) when a child is to spend time or otherwise have contact with any person.

(2) The court may make an activity direction in connection with the provision that the court is considering whether to make.

(2A) Subsection (2B) applies in proceedings in which subsection (2) does not apply and in which the court is considering—

- (a) whether a person has failed to comply with a provision of a child arrangements order, or
- (b) what steps to take in consequence of a person's failure to comply with a provision of a child arrangements order.

(2B) The court may make an activity direction in connection with that provision of the child arrangements order.

(3) An activity direction is a direction requiring an individual who is a party to the proceedings concerned to take part in an activity that would, in the court's opinion, help to establish, maintain or improve the involvement in the life of the child concerned of—

- (a) that individual, or
- (b) another individual who is a party to the proceedings.]²

(4) The direction is to specify the activity and the person providing the activity.

(5) The activities that may be so required include, in particular–

- (a) programmes, classes and counselling or guidance sessions of a kind that–
  - (i) may assist a person as regards establishing, maintaining or improving [involvement in a child's life]²;
  - (ii) may, by addressing a person's violent behaviour, enable or facilitate [involvement in a child's life]²;
- (b) sessions in which information or advice is given as regards making or operating arrangements for [involvement in a child's life]², including making arrangements by means of mediation.

(6) No individual may be required by [an]² activity direction–

- (a) to undergo medical or psychiatric examination, assessment or treatment;
- (b) to take part in mediation.

(7) A court may not on the same occasion–

(a) make [an activity direction under subsection (2)]², and
(b) dispose finally of the proceedings as they relate to [the matters mentioned in subsection (1A) in connection with which the activity direction is made]².

[(7A) A court may not on the same occasion—

(a) make an activity direction under subsection (2B), and
(b) dispose finally of the proceedings as they relate to failure to comply with the provision in connection with which the activity direction is made.]³

(8) [Each of subsections (2) and (2B)]² has effect subject to the restrictions in sections 11B and 11E.

(9) In considering whether to make [an]² activity direction, the welfare of the child concerned is to be the court's paramount consideration.]⁴

Amendments
1 Repealed by the Children and Families Act 2014, s 12(4), Sch 2, paras 1, 7(1), (9).
2 Substituted by the Children and Families Act 2014, s 12(4), Sch 2, paras 1, 7(1)–(5), (7), (8).
3 Inserted by the Children and Families Act 2014, s 12(4), Sch 2, paras 1, 7(1), (6).
4 Inserted by the Children and Adoption Act 2006, s 1.

[11B ...¹ Activity directions: further provision

(1) A court may not make [an activity direction under section 11A(2) in connection with any matter mentioned in section 11A(1A)]² unless there is a dispute as regards the provision [about that matter]² that the court is considering whether to make in the proceedings.

(2) A court may not make [an]² activity direction requiring an individual who is a child to take part in an activity unless the individual is a parent of the child in relation to whom the court is considering provision [about a matter mentioned in section 11A(1A)]².

(3) A court may not make [an activity]² direction in connection with the making, variation or discharge of a [child arrangements order]², if the [child arrangements order]² is, or would if made be, an excepted order.

(4) A [child arrangements order]² with respect to a child is an excepted order if–

(a) it is made in proceedings that include proceedings on an application for a relevant adoption order in respect of the child; or
(b) it makes provision as regards contact between the child and a person who would be a parent or relative of the child but for the child's adoption by an order falling within subsection (5).

(5) An order falls within this subsection if it is–

(a) a relevant adoption order;
(b) an adoption order, within the meaning of section 72(1) of the Adoption Act 1976, other than an order made by virtue of section 14 of that Act

on the application of a married couple one of whom is the mother or the father of the child;
(c) a Scottish adoption order, within the meaning of the Adoption and Children Act 2002, other than an order made–
   (i) by virtue of section 14 of the Adoption (Scotland) Act 1978 on the application of a married couple one of whom is the mother or the father of the child, or
   (ii) by virtue of section 15(1)(aa) of that Act; or
   [(iii) by virtue of an application under section 30 of the Adoption and Children (Scotland) Act 2007 where subsection (3) of that section applies; or]³
(d) a Northern Irish adoption order, within the meaning of the Adoption and Children Act 2002, other than an order made by virtue of Article 14 of the Adoption (Northern Ireland) Order 1987 on the application of a married couple one of whom is the mother or the father of the child.

(6) A relevant adoption order is an adoption order, within the meaning of section 46(1) of the Adoption and Children Act 2002, other than an order made–

(a) on an application under section 50 of that Act by a couple (within the meaning of that Act) one of whom is the mother or the father of the person to be adopted, or
(b) on an application under section 51(2) of that Act.

(7) A court may not make [an]² activity direction in relation to an individual unless the individual is habitually resident in England and Wales; and a direction ceases to have effect if the individual subject to the direction ceases to be habitually resident in England and Wales.]⁴

Amendments
1 Repealed by the Children and Families Act 2014, s 12(4), Sch 2, paras 1, 8(7).
2 Substituted by the Children and Families Act 2014, s 12(4), Sch 2, paras 1, 8(2)–(6).
3 Inserted by the Adoption and Children (Scotland) Act 2007 (Consequential Modifications) Order 2011, SI 2011/1740, art 2, Sch 1, para 3(1), (2)
4 Inserted by the Children and Adoption Act 2006, s 1.

[11C ...¹ Activity conditions

(1) This section applies if in any family proceedings the court makes–

[(a) a child arrangements order containing—
   (i) provision for a child to live with different persons at different times,
   (ii) provision regulating arrangements relating to with whom a child is to spend time or otherwise have contact, or
   (iii) provision regulating arrangements relating to when a child is to spend time or otherwise have contact with any person; or
(b) an order varying a child arrangements order so as to add, vary or omit provision of a kind mentioned in paragraph(a)(i), (ii) or (iii).]²

(2) The [child arrangements order]² may impose, or the [child arrangements order]² may be varied so as to impose, a condition [(an 'activity condition')]² requiring an individual falling within subsection (3) to take part in an activity

that [would, in the court's opinion, help to establish, maintain or improve the involvement in the life of the child concerned of—]²

[(a) that individual, or
(b) another individual who is a party to the proceedings.]²

(3) An individual falls within this subsection if he is–

(a) for the purposes of the [child arrangements order]² so made or varied, [a person]² with whom the child concerned lives or is to live;
(b) [a person]² whose contact with the child concerned is provided for in that order; or
(c) a person upon whom that order imposes a condition under section 11(7)(b).

(4) The condition is to specify the activity and the person providing the activity.

(5) Subsections (5) and (6) of section 11A have effect as regards the activities that may be required by [an]² activity condition as they have effect as regards the activities that may be required by [an]² activity direction.

(6) Subsection (2) has effect subject to the restrictions in sections 11D and 11E.]³

Amendment
1 Repealed by the Children and Families Act 2014, s 12(4), Sch 2, paras 1, 9(1), (6).
2 Substituted by the Children and Families Act 2014, s 12(4), Sch 2, paras 1, 9(1)–(5).
3 Inserted by the Children and Adoption Act 2006, s 1.

[11D ...¹ Activity conditions: further provision

(1) A [child arrangements order]² may not impose [an activity]² condition on an individual who is a child unless the individual is a parent of the child concerned.

(2) If a [child arrangements order]² is an excepted order (within the meaning given by section 11B(4)), it may not impose (and it may not be varied so as to impose) [an activity]² condition.

(3) A [child arrangements order]² may not impose [an activity]² condition on an individual unless the individual is habitually resident in England and Wales; and a condition ceases to have effect if the individual subject to the condition ceases to be habitually resident in England and Wales.]³

Amendments
1 Repealed by the Children and Families Act 2014, s 12(4), Sch 2, paras 1, 10(1), (5).
2 Substituted by the Children and Families Act 2014, s 12(4), Sch 2, paras 1, 10(1)-(4).
3 Inserted by the Children and Adoption Act 2006, s 1.

[11E ...¹ Activity directions and conditions: making

(1) Before making [an activity]² direction (or imposing [an activity] 3 condition by means of a [child arrangements order]²), the court must satisfy itself as to the matters falling within subsections (2) to (4).

(2) The first matter is that the activity proposed to be specified is appropriate in the circumstances of the case.

(3) The second matter is that the person proposed to be specified as the provider of the activity is suitable to provide the activity.

(4) The third matter is that the activity proposed to be specified is provided in a place to which the individual who would be subject to the direction (or the condition) can reasonably be expected to travel.

(5) Before making such a direction (or such an order), the court must obtain and consider information about the individual who would be subject to the direction (or the condition) and the likely effect of the direction (or the condition) on him.

(6) Information about the likely effect of the direction (or the condition) may, in particular, include information as to–

(a) any conflict with the individual's religious beliefs;
(b) any interference with the times (if any) at which he normally works or attends an educational establishment.

(7) The court may ask an officer of the Service or a Welsh family proceedings officer to provide the court with information as to the matters in subsections (2) to (5); and it shall be the duty of the officer of the Service or Welsh family proceedings officer to comply with any such request.

(8) In this section 'specified' means specified in [an]² activity direction (or in [an]² activity condition).]³

Amendments
1 Repealed by the Children and Families Act 2014, s 12(4), Sch 2, paras 1, 11(1), (4).
2 Substituted by the Children and Families Act 2014, s 12(4), Sch 2, paras 1, 11(1)-(3).
3 Inserted by the Children and Adoption Act 2006, s 1.

[11F ...¹ Activity directions and conditions: financial assistance

(1) The Secretary of State may by regulations make provision authorising him to make payments to assist individuals falling within subsection (2) in paying relevant charges or fees.

(2) An individual falls within this subsection if he is required by [an activity]² direction or condition to take part in an activity that [is expected to help to establish, maintain or improve the involvement of that or another individual in the life of]² a child, not being a child ordinarily resident in Wales.

(3) The National Assembly for Wales may by regulations make provision authorising it to make payments to assist individuals falling within subsection (4) in paying relevant charges or fees.

(4) An individual falls within this subsection if he is required by [an activity]² direction or condition to take part in an activity that [is expected to help to establish, maintain or improve the involvement of that or another individual in the life of]² a child who is ordinarily resident in Wales.

(5) A relevant charge or fee, in relation to an activity required by [an activity]² direction or condition, is a charge or fee in respect of the activity payable to the person providing the activity.

(6) Regulations under this section may provide that no assistance is available to an individual unless–

- (a) the individual satisfies such conditions as regards his financial resources as may be set out in the regulations;
- (b) the activity in which the individual is required by [an activity]² direction or condition to take part is provided to him in England or Wales;
- (c) where the activity in which the individual is required to take part is provided to him in England, it is provided by a person who is for the time being approved by the Secretary of State as a provider of activities required by [an activity]² direction or condition;
- (d) where the activity in which the individual is required to take part is provided to him in Wales, it is provided by a person who is for the time being approved by the National Assembly for Wales as a provider of activities required by [an activity]² direction or condition.

(7) Regulations under this section may make provision–

- (a) as to the maximum amount of assistance that may be paid to or in respect of an individual as regards an activity in which he is required by [an activity]² direction or condition to take part;
- (b) where the amount may vary according to an individual's financial resources, as to the method by which the amount is to be determined;
- (c) authorising payments by way of assistance to be made directly to persons providing activities required by [an activity]² direction or condition.]³

Amendments
1 Repealed by the Children and Families Act 2014, s 12(4), Sch 2, paras 1, 12(1), (4).
2 Substituted by the Children and Families Act 2014, s 12(4), Sch 2, paras 1, 12(1)–(3).
3 Inserted by the Children and Adoption Act 2006, s 1.

[11G ...¹ Activity directions and conditions: monitoring

(1) This section applies if in any family proceedings the court–

- (a) makes [an activity]² direction in relation to an individual, or
- (b) makes a [child arrangements order]² that imposes, or varies a [child arrangements order]² so as to impose, [an activity]² condition on an individual.

(2) The court may on making the direction (or imposing the condition by means of a [child arrangements order]²) ask an officer of the Service or a Welsh family proceedings officer–

- (a) to monitor, or arrange for the monitoring of, the individual's compliance with the direction (or the condition);
- (b) to report to the court on any failure by the individual to comply with the direction (or the condition).

(3) It shall be the duty of the officer of the Service or Welsh family proceedings officer to comply with any request under subsection (2).]³

Amendments
1 Repealed by the Children and Families Act 2014, s 12(4), Sch 2, paras 1, 13(1), (4).

2   Substituted by the Children and Families Act 2014, s 12(4), Sch 2, paras 1, 13(1)–(3).
3   Inserted by the Children and Adoption Act 2006, s 1.

[11H Monitoring contact [and shared residence][1]

(1) This section applies if in any family proceedings the court makes–

[(a) a child arrangements order containing provision of a kind mentioned in section 11C(1)(a)(i), (ii) or (iii), or
(b) an order varying a child arrangements order so as to add, vary or omit provision of any of those kinds.][2]

(2) The court may ask an officer of the Service or a Welsh family proceedings officer–

(a) to monitor whether an individual falling within subsection (3) complies with [each provision of any of those kinds that is contained in the child arrangements order (or in the child arrangements order as varied);][2]
(b) to report to the court on such matters relating to the individual's compliance as the court may specify in the request.

(3) An individual falls within this subsection if the [child arrangements order][2] so made (or the [child arrangements order][2] as so varied)–

[(za) provides for the child concerned to live with different persons at different times and names the individual as one of those persons;
(a) imposes requirements on the individual with regard to the child concerned spending time or otherwise having contact with some other person;
(b) names the individual as a person with whom the child concerned is to spend time or otherwise have contact; or][2]
(c) imposes a condition under section 11(7)(b) on the individual.

(4) If the [child arrangements order][2] (or the [child arrangements order][2] as varied) includes [an activity][2] condition, a request under subsection (2) is to be treated as relating to the provisions of the order other than [the activity][2] condition.

(5) The court may make a request under subsection (2)–

(a) on making the [child arrangements order][2] (or the order varying the [child arrangements order][2]), or
(b) at any time during the subsequent course of the proceedings as they relate to contact with the child concerned [or to the child's living arrangements][1].

(6) In making a request under subsection (2), the court is to specify the period for which the officer of the Service or Welsh family proceedings officer is to monitor compliance with the order; and the period specified may not exceed twelve months.

(7) It shall be the duty of the officer of the Service or Welsh family proceedings officer to comply with any request under subsection (2).

(8) The court may order any individual falling within subsection (3) to take such steps as may be specified in the order with a view to enabling the officer of the

Service or Welsh family proceedings officer to comply with the court's request under subsection (2).

(9) But the court may not make an order under subsection (8) with respect to an individual who is a child unless he is a parent of the child with respect to whom the order falling within subsection (1) was made.

(10) A court may not make a request under subsection (2) in relation to a [child arrangements]² order that is an excepted order (within the meaning given by section 11B(4)).]³

Amendments
1   Inserted by the Children and Families Act 2014, s 12(4), Sch 2, paras 1, 14(1), (6)(b), (8).
2   Substituted by the Children and Families Act 2014, s 12(4), Sch 2, paras 1, 14(1)–(5), (6)(a), (7).
3   Inserted by the Children and Adoption Act 2006, s 2.

[11I [Child arrangements]¹ orders: warning notices

Where the court makes (or varies) a [child arrangements]¹ order, it is to attach to the [child arrangements]¹ order (or the order varying the [child arrangements]¹ order) a notice warning of the consequences of failing to comply with the [child arrangements]¹ order.]²

Amendment
1   Substituted by the Children and Families Act 2014, s 12(4), Sch 2, paras 1, 15.
2   Inserted by the Children and Adoption Act 2006, s 3.

[11J Enforcement orders

(1) This section applies if a [child arrangements]¹ order with respect to a child has been made.

(2) If the court is satisfied beyond reasonable doubt that a person has failed to comply with [a provision of the child arrangements]¹ order, it may make an order (an 'enforcement order') imposing on the person an unpaid work requirement.

(3) But the court may not make an enforcement order if it is satisfied that the person had a reasonable excuse for failing to comply with the [provision]¹.

(4) The burden of proof as to the matter mentioned in subsection (3) lies on the person claiming to have had a reasonable excuse, and the standard of proof is the balance of probabilities.

(5) The court may make an enforcement order in relation to the [child arrangements order]¹ only on the application of–

(a)   the person who is, for the purposes of the [child arrangements order]¹, [a person]¹ with whom the child concerned lives or is to live;
(b)   [a person]¹ whose contact with the child concerned is provided for in the [child arrangements order]¹;
(c)   any individual subject to a condition under section 11(7)(b) or [an activity]¹ condition imposed by the [child arrangements order]¹; or
(d)   the child concerned.

(6) Where the person proposing to apply for an enforcement order in relation to a [child arrangements]¹ order is the child concerned, the child must obtain the leave of the court before making such an application.

(7) The court may grant leave to the child concerned only if it is satisfied that he has sufficient understanding to make the proposed application.

(8) Subsection (2) has effect subject to the restrictions in sections 11K and 11L.

(9) The court may suspend an enforcement order for such period as it thinks fit.

(10) Nothing in this section prevents a court from making more than one enforcement order in relation to the same person on the same occasion.

(11) Proceedings in which any question of making an enforcement order, or any other question with respect to such an order, arises are to be regarded for the purposes of section 11(1) and (2) as proceedings in which a question arises with respect to a section 8 order.

(12) In Schedule A1–
  (a) Part 1 makes provision as regards an unpaid work requirement;
  (b) Part 2 makes provision in relation to the revocation and amendment of enforcement orders and failure to comply with such orders.

(13) ...²]³

Amendments
1 Substituted by the Children and Families Act 2014, s 12(4), Sch 2, paras 1, 16.
2 Repealed by the Crime and Courts Act 2013, s 17(6), Sch 11, paras 102, 103.
3 Inserted by the Children and Adoption Act 2006, s 4(1).

[11K Enforcement orders: further provision

(1) A court may not make an enforcement order against a person in respect of a failure to comply with a [provision of a child arrangements order]¹ unless it is satisfied that before the failure occurred the person had been given (in accordance with rules of court) a copy of, or otherwise informed of the terms of–

  (a) in the case of a failure to comply with [a provision of a child arrangements order where the order]¹ was varied before the failure occurred, a notice under section 11I relating to the order varying [the child arrangements]¹ order or, where more than one such order has been made, the last order preceding the failure in question;
  (b) in any other case, a notice under section 11I relating to the [child arrangements]¹ order.

(2) A court may not make an enforcement order against a person in respect of any failure to comply with a [provision of a child arrangements]¹ order occurring before the person attained the age of 18.

(3) A court may not make an enforcement order against a person in respect of a failure to comply with a [provision of a child arrangements order where the child arrangements order]¹ is an excepted order (within the meaning given by section 11B(4)).

(4) A court may not make an enforcement order against a person unless the person is habitually resident in England and Wales; and an enforcement order ceases to have effect if the person subject to the order ceases to be habitually resident in England and Wales.]²

Amendments
1 Substituted by the Children and Families Act 2014, s 12(4), Sch 2, paras 1, 17.
2 Inserted by the Children and Adoption Act 2006, s 4(1).

[11L Enforcement orders: making

(1) Before making an enforcement order as regards a person in breach of [a provision of a child arrangements]¹ order, the court must be satisfied that–

(a) making the enforcement order proposed is necessary to secure the person's compliance with the [child arrangements]¹ order or any [child arrangements]¹ order that has effect in its place;

(b) the likely effect on the person of the enforcement order proposed to be made is proportionate to the seriousness of the breach ...².

(2) Before making an enforcement order, the court must satisfy itself that provision for the person to work under an unpaid work requirement imposed by an enforcement order can be made in the local justice area in which the person in breach resides or will reside.

(3) Before making an enforcement order as regards a person in breach of a [provision of a child arrangements]¹ order, the court must obtain and consider information about the person and the likely effect of the enforcement order on him.

(4) Information about the likely effect of the enforcement order may, in particular, include information as to–

(a) any conflict with the person's religious beliefs;

(b) any interference with the times (if any) at which he normally works or attends an educational establishment.

(5) A court that proposes to make an enforcement order may ask an officer of the Service or a Welsh family proceedings officer to provide the court with information as to the matters in subsections (2) and (3).

(6) It shall be the duty of the officer of the Service or Welsh family proceedings officer to comply with any request under this section.

(7) In making an enforcement order in relation to a [child arrangements]¹ order, a court must take into account the welfare of the child who is the subject of the [child arrangements]¹ order.]³

Amendments
1 Substituted by the Children and Families Act 2014, s 12(4), Sch 2, paras 1, 18(2)(a), (b), (3), (4).
2 Repealed by the Children and Families Act 2014, s 12(4), Sch 2, paras 1, 18(2)(c).
3 Inserted by the Children and Adoption Act 2006, s 4(1).

[11M Enforcement orders: monitoring

(1) On making an enforcement order in relation to a person, the court is to ask an officer of the Service or a Welsh family proceedings officer–

(a) to monitor, or arrange for the monitoring of, the person's compliance with the unpaid work requirement imposed by the order;
(b) to report to the court if a report under paragraph 8 of Schedule A1 is made in relation to the person;
(c) to report to the court on such other matters relating to the person's compliance as may be specified in the request;
(d) to report to the court if the person is, or becomes, unsuitable to perform work under the requirement.

(2) It shall be the duty of the officer of the Service or Welsh family proceedings officer to comply with any request under this section.]¹

Amendment
1 Inserted by the Children and Adoption Act 2006, s 4(1).

[11N Enforcement orders: warning notices

Where the court makes an enforcement order, it is to attach to the order a notice warning of the consequences of failing to comply with the order.]¹

Amendment
1 Inserted by the Children and Adoption Act 2006, s 4(1).

[11O Compensation for financial loss

(1) This section applies if a [child arrangements]¹ order with respect to a child has been made.

(2) If the court is satisfied that—
(a) an individual has failed to comply with [a provision of the child arrangements]¹ order, and
(b) a person falling within subsection (6) has suffered financial loss by reason of the breach,

it may make an order requiring the individual in breach to pay the person compensation in respect of his financial loss.

(3) But the court may not make an order under subsection (2) if it is satisfied that the individual in breach had a reasonable excuse for failing to comply with the [particular provision of the child arrangements]¹ order.

(4) The burden of proof as to the matter mentioned in subsection (3) lies on the individual claiming to have had a reasonable excuse.

(5) An order under subsection (2) may be made only on an application by the person who claims to have suffered financial loss.

(6) A person falls within this subsection if he is—
(a) [a person]¹ who is, for the purposes of the [child arrangements order]¹, [a person]¹ with whom the child concerned lives or is to live;
(b) [a person]¹ whose contact with the child concerned is provided for in the [child arrangements order]¹;
(c) an individual subject to a condition under section 11(7)(b) or [an activity]¹ condition imposed by the [child arrangements order]¹; or
(d) the child concerned.

(7) Where the person proposing to apply for an order under subsection (2) is the child concerned, the child must obtain the leave of the court before making such an application.

(8) The court may grant leave to the child concerned only if it is satisfied that he has sufficient understanding to make the proposed application.

(9) The amount of compensation is to be determined by the court, but may not exceed the amount of the applicant's financial loss.

(10) In determining the amount of compensation payable by the individual in breach, the court must take into account the individual's financial circumstances.

(11) An amount ordered to be paid as compensation may be recovered by the applicant as a civil debt due to him.

(12) Subsection (2) has effect subject to the restrictions in section 11P.

(13) Proceedings in which any question of making an order under subsection (2) arises are to be regarded for the purposes of section 11(1) and (2) as proceedings in which a question arises with respect to a section 8 order.

(14) In exercising its powers under this section, a court is to take into account the welfare of the child concerned.][2]

Amendments
1 Substituted by the Children and Families Act 2014, s 12(4), Sch 2, paras 1, 19.
2 Inserted by the Children and Adoption Act 2006, s 5.

[11P Orders under section 11O(2): further provision

(1) A court may not make an order under section 11O(2) requiring an individual to pay compensation in respect of a failure by him to comply with a [provision of a child arrangements order][1] unless it is satisfied that before the failure occurred the individual had been given (in accordance with rules of court) a copy of, or otherwise informed of the terms of—

    (a) in the case of a failure to comply with [a provision of a child arrangements order where the order][1] was varied before the failure occurred, a notice under section 11I relating to the order varying [the child arrangements][1] order or, where more than one such order has been made, the last order preceding the failure in question;
    (b) in any other case, a notice under section 11I relating to the [child arrangements][1] order.

(2) A court may not make an order under section 11O(2) requiring an individual to pay compensation in respect of a failure by him to comply with a [provision of a child arrangements][1] order where the failure occurred before the individual attained the age of 18.

(3) A court may not make an order under section 11O(2) requiring an individual to pay compensation in respect of a failure by him to comply with a [provision of a child arrangements order where the child arrangements order][1] is an excepted order (within the meaning given by section 11B(4)).][2]

Amendments
1   Substituted by the Children and Families Act 2014, s 12(4), Sch 2, paras 1, 20.
2   Inserted by the Children and Adoption Act 2006, s 5.

12 [Child arrangements]¹ orders and parental responsibility.

[(1) Where—

(a) the court makes a child arrangements order with respect to a child,
(b) the father of the child, or a woman who is a parent of the child by virtue of section 43 of the Human Fertilisation and Embryology Act 2008, is named in the order as a person with whom the child is to live, and
(c) the father, or the woman, would not otherwise have parental responsibility for the child,

the court must also make an order under section 4 giving the father, or under section 4ZA giving the woman, that responsibility.

(1A) Where—

(a) the court makes a child arrangements order with respect to a child,
(b) the father of the child, or a woman who is a parent of the child by virtue of section 43 of the Human Fertilisation and Embryology Act 2008, is named in the order as a person with whom the child is to spend time or otherwise have contact but is not named in the order as a person with whom the child is to live, and
(c) the father, or the woman, would not otherwise have parental responsibility for the child,

the court must decide whether it would be appropriate, in view of the provision made in the order with respect to the father or the woman, for him or her to have parental responsibility for the child and, if it decides that it would be appropriate for the father or the woman to have that responsibility, must also make an order under section 4 giving him, or under section 4ZA giving her, that responsibility.]¹

(2) Where the court makes a [child arrangements order and a person who is not a]¹ parent or guardian of the child concerned [is named in the order as a person with whom the child is to live,]² that person shall have parental responsibility for the child while the [order remains in force so far as providing for the child to live with that person]¹.

[(2A) Where the court makes a child arrangements order and—

(a) a person who is not the parent or guardian of the child concerned is named in the order as a person with whom the child is to spend time or otherwise have contact, but
(b) the person is not named in the order as a person with whom the child is to live,

the court may provide in the order for the person to have parental responsibility for the child while paragraphs (a) and (b) continue to be met in the person's case.]²

(3) Where a person has parental responsibility for a child as a result of subsection (2) [or (2A)]², he shall not have the right—

(a) ...³
(b) to agree, or refuse to agree, to the making of an adoption order, or an order under [section 84 of the Adoption and Children Act 2002]⁴, with respect to the child; or
(c) to appoint a guardian for the child.

(4) Where subsection (1) [...⁵]⁶ requires the court to make an order under section 4 [or 4ZA]⁶ [in respect of a]² [parent]⁷ of a child, the court shall not bring that order to an end at any time while the [child arrangements order concerned remains in force so far as providing for the child to live with that parent]².

(5) ...⁸

(6) ...⁸

Amendment
1 Substituted by the Children and Families Act 2014, s 12(4), Sch 2, paras 1, 21(1), (2), (3)(a), (b), (6)(b), (c), (7).
2 Inserted by the Children and Families Act 2014, s 12(4), Sch 2, paras 1, 21(1), (3)(b), (4), (5).
3 Repealed by the Adoption and Children Act 2002, s 139(1), (3), Sch 3, paras 54, 57(a), Sch 5.
4 Substituted by the Adoption and Children Act 2002, s 139(1), Sch 3, paras 54, 57(b).
5 Repealed by the Children and Families Act 2014, s 12(4), Sch 2, paras 1, 21(1), (6)(a).
6 Inserted by the Human Fertilisation and Embryology Act 2008, s 56, Sch 6, para 28(1), (3)(a), (b).
7 Substituted by the Human Fertilisation and Embryology Act 2008, s 56, Sch 6, para 28(3)(c).
8 Repealed by the Children and Young Persons Act 2008, s 42, Sch 4

13 Change of child's name or removal from jurisdiction.

(1) Where a [child arrangements order to which subsection (4) applies]¹ is in force with respect to a child, no person may—

(a) cause the child to be known by a new surname; or
(b) remove him from the United Kingdom;

without either the written consent of every person who has parental responsibility for the child or the leave of the court.

(2) Subsection (1)(b) does not prevent the removal of a child, for a period of less than one month, by [a person named in the child arrangements order as a person with whom the child is to live]¹.

(3) In making a [child arrangements order to which subsection (4) applies,]¹ the court may grant the leave required by subsection (1)(b), either generally or for specified purposes.

[(4) This subsection applies to a child arrangements order if the arrangements regulated by the order consist of, or include, arrangements which relate to either or both of the following—

(a) with whom the child concerned is to live, and
(b) when the child is to live with any person.]²

Amendments
1 Substituted by the Children and Families Act 2014, s 12(4), Sch 2, paras 1, 22(1)–(4).
2 Inserted by the Children and Families Act 2014, s 12(4), Sch 2, paras 1, 22(1), (5).

14 …[1]

…[1]

Amendment
1 Repealed by the Children and Families Act 2014, s 12(4), Sch 2, paras 1, 23.

[Special guardianship

14A Special guardianship orders

(1) A 'special guardianship order' is an order appointing one or more individuals to be a child's 'special guardian' (or special guardians).

(2) A special guardian—

    (a)   must be aged eighteen or over; and
    (b)   must not be a parent of the child in question,

and subsections (3) to (6) are to be read in that light.

(3) The court may make a special guardianship order with respect to any child on the application of an individual who—

    (a)   is entitled to make such an application with respect to the child; or
    (b)   has obtained the leave of the court to make the application,

or on the joint application of more than one such individual.

(4) Section 9(3) applies in relation to an application for leave to apply for a special guardianship order as it applies in relation to an application for leave to apply for a section 8 order.

(5) The individuals who are entitled to apply for a special guardianship order with respect to a child are—

    (a)   any guardian of the child;
    (b)   any individual [who is named in a child arrangements order as a person with whom the child is to live;][1]
    (c)   any individual listed in subsection (5)(b) or (c) of section 10 (as read with subsection (10) of that section);
    (d)   a local authority foster parent with whom the child has lived for a period of at least one year immediately preceding the application[;][2]
    [(e)   a relative with whom the child has lived for a period of at least one year immediately preceding the application.][2]

(6) The court may also make a special guardianship order with respect to a child in any family proceedings in which a question arises with respect to the welfare of the child if—

    (a)   an application for the order has been made by an individual who falls within subsection (3)(a) or (b) (or more than one such individual jointly); or

(b) the court considers that a special guardianship order should be made even though no such application has been made.

(7) No individual may make an application under subsection (3) or (6)(a) unless, before the beginning of the period of three months ending with the date of the application, he has given written notice of his intention to make the application—

(a) if the child in question is being looked after by a local authority, to that local authority, or
(b) otherwise, to the local authority in whose area the individual is ordinarily resident.

(8) On receipt of such a notice, the local authority must investigate the matter and prepare a report for the court dealing with—

(a) the suitability of the applicant to be a special guardian;
(b) such matters (if any) as may be prescribed by the Secretary of State; and
(c) any other matter which the local authority consider to be relevant.

(9) The court may itself ask a local authority to conduct such an investigation and prepare such a report, and the local authority must do so.

(10) The local authority may make such arrangements as they see fit for any person to act on their behalf in connection with conducting an investigation or preparing a report referred to in subsection (8) or (9).

(11) The court may not make a special guardianship order unless it has received a report dealing with the matters referred to in subsection (8).

(12) Subsections (8) and (9) of section 10 apply in relation to special guardianship orders as they apply in relation to section 8 orders.

(13) This section is subject to section 29(5) and (6) of the Adoption and Children Act 2002.]³

Amendments
1 Substituted by the Children and Families Act 2014, s 12(4), Sch 2, paras 1, 24.
2 Inserted by the Children and Young Persons Act 2008, s 38.
3 Inserted by the Adoption and Children Act 2002, s 115(1).

[14B Special guardianship orders: making

(1) Before making a special guardianship order, the court must consider whether, if the order were made—

(a) a [child arrangements order containing contact provision]¹ should also be made with respect to the child, …²
(b) any section 8 order in force with respect to the child should be varied or discharged,
[(c) where [provision contained in a child arrangements order]¹ made with respect to the child is not discharged, any enforcement order relating to [that provision]¹ order should be revoked, and
[(d) where an activity direction has been made—

(i) in proceedings for the making, variation or discharge of a child arrangements order with respect to the child, or
(ii) in other proceedings that relate to such an order,
that direction should be discharged.]¹]³

[(1A) In subsection (1) 'contact provision' means provision which regulates arrangements relating to—

(a) with whom a child is to spend time or otherwise have contact, or
(b) when a child is to spend time or otherwise have contact with any person;

but in paragraphs (a) and (b) a reference to spending time or otherwise having contact with a person is to doing that otherwise than as a result of living with the person.]⁴

(2) On making a special guardianship order, the court may also—

(a) give leave for the child to be known by a new surname;
(b) grant the leave required by section 14C(3)(b), either generally or for specified purposes.]⁵

Amendments
1 Substituted by the Children and Families Act 2014, s 12(4), Sch 2, paras 1, 25(1), (2).
2 Repealed by the Children and Adoption Act 2006, s 15, Sch 2, para 8(a), Sch 3.
3 Inserted by the Children and Adoption Act 2006, s 15(1), Sch 2, para 8(b).
4 Inserted by the Children and Families Act 2014, s 12(4), Sch 2, paras 1, 25(1), (3).
5 Inserted by the Adoption and Children Act 2002, s 115(1).

[14C Special guardianship orders: effect

(1) The effect of a special guardianship order is that while the order remains in force—

(a) a special guardian appointed by the order has parental responsibility for the child in respect of whom it is made; and
(b) subject to any other order in force with respect to the child under this Act, a special guardian is entitled to exercise parental responsibility to the exclusion of any other person with parental responsibility for the child (apart from another special guardian).

(2) Subsection (1) does not affect—

(a) the operation of any enactment or rule of law which requires the consent of more than one person with parental responsibility in a matter affecting the child; or
(b) any rights which a parent of the child has in relation to the child's adoption or placement for adoption.

(3) While a special guardianship order is in force with respect to a child, no person may—

(a) cause the child to be known by a new surname; or
(b) remove him from the United Kingdom,

without either the written consent of every person who has parental responsibility for the child or the leave of the court.

(4) Subsection (3)(b) does not prevent the removal of a child, for a period of less than three months, by a special guardian of his.

(5) If the child with respect to whom a special guardianship order is in force dies, his special guardian must take reasonable steps to give notice of that fact to—

(a) each parent of the child with parental responsibility; and
(b) each guardian of the child,

but if the child has more than one special guardian, and one of them has taken such steps in relation to a particular parent or guardian, any other special guardian need not do so as respects that parent or guardian.

(6) This section is subject to section 29(7) of the Adoption and Children Act 2002.][1]

Amendment
1 Inserted by the Adoption and Children Act 2002, s 115(1).

[14D Special guardianship orders: variation and discharge

(1) The court may vary or discharge a special guardianship order on the application of—

(a) the special guardian (or any of them, if there are more than one);
(b) any parent or guardian of the child concerned;
(c) any individual [who is named in a child arrangements order as a person with whom the child is to live;][1]
(d) any individual not falling within any of paragraphs (a) to (c) who has, or immediately before the making of the special guardianship order had, parental responsibility for the child;
(e) the child himself; or
(f) a local authority designated in a care order with respect to the child.

(2) In any family proceedings in which a question arises with respect to the welfare of a child with respect to whom a special guardianship order is in force, the court may also vary or discharge the special guardianship order if it considers that the order should be varied or discharged, even though no application has been made under subsection (1).

(3) The following must obtain the leave of the court before making an application under subsection (1)—

(a) the child;
(b) any parent or guardian of his;
(c) any step-parent of his who has acquired, and has not lost, parental responsibility for him by virtue of section 4A;
(d) any individual falling within subsection (1)(d) who immediately before the making of the special guardianship order had, but no longer has, parental responsibility for him.

(4) Where the person applying for leave to make an application under subsection (1) is the child, the court may only grant leave if it is satisfied that he has sufficient understanding to make the proposed application under subsection (1).

(5) The court may not grant leave to a person falling within subsection (3)(b)(c) or (d) unless it is satisfied that there has been a significant change in circumstances since the making of the special guardianship order.]²

Amendments
1 Substituted by the Children and Families Act 2014, s 12(4), Sch 2, paras 1, 26.
2 Inserted by the Adoption and Children Act 2002, s 115(1).

[14E Special guardianship orders: supplementary

(1) In proceedings in which any question of making, varying or discharging a special guardianship order arises, the court shall (in the light of any [provision in rules of court that is of the kind mentioned in section 11(2)(a) or (b))]¹—

(a) draw up a timetable with a view to determining the question without delay; and
(b) give such directions as it considers appropriate for the purpose of ensuring, so far as is reasonably practicable, that the timetable is adhered to.

(2) Subsection (1) applies also in relation to proceedings in which any other question with respect to a special guardianship order arises.

(3) The power to make rules in subsection (2) of section 11 applies for the purposes of this section as it applies for the purposes of that.

(4) A special guardianship order, or an order varying one, may contain provisions which are to have effect for a specified period.

(5) Section 11(7) (apart from paragraph (c)) applies in relation to special guardianship orders and orders varying them as it applies in relation to section 8 orders.]²

Amendments
1 Substituted by the Children and Families Act 2014, s 14(1), (6).
2 Inserted by the Adoption and Children Act 2002, s 115(1).

[14F Special guardianship support services

(1) Each local authority must make arrangements for the provision within their area of special guardianship support services, which means—

(a) counselling, advice and information; and
(b) such other services as are prescribed,

in relation to special guardianship.

(2) The power to make regulations under subsection (1)(b) is to be exercised so as to secure that local authorities provide financial support.

(3) At the request of any of the following persons—

(a) a child with respect to whom a special guardianship order is in force;
(b) a special guardian;
(c) a parent;
(d) any other person who falls within a prescribed description,

a local authority may carry out an assessment of that person's needs for special guardianship support services (but, if the Secretary of State so provides in regulations, they must do so if he is a person of a prescribed description, or if his case falls within a prescribed description, or if both he and his case fall within prescribed descriptions).

(4) A local authority may, at the request of any other person, carry out an assessment of that person's needs for special guardianship support services.

(5) Where, as a result of an assessment, a local authority decide that a person has needs for special guardianship support services, they must then decide whether to provide any such services to that person.

(6) If—
- (a) a local authority decide to provide any special guardianship support services to a person, and
- (b) the circumstances fall within a prescribed description,

the local authority must prepare a plan in accordance with which special guardianship support services are to be provided to him, and keep the plan under review.

(7) The Secretary of State may by regulations make provision about assessments, preparing and reviewing plans, the provision of special guardianship support services in accordance with plans and reviewing the provision of special guardianship support services.

(8) The regulations may in particular make provision—
- (a) about the type of assessment which is to be carried out, or the way in which an assessment is to be carried out;
- (b) about the way in which a plan is to be prepared;
- (c) about the way in which, and the time at which, a plan or the provision of special guardianship support services is to be reviewed;
- (d) about the considerations to which a local authority are to have regard in carrying out an assessment or review or preparing a plan;
- (e) as to the circumstances in which a local authority may provide special guardianship support services subject to conditions (including conditions as to payment for the support or the repayment of financial support);
- (f) as to the consequences of conditions imposed by virtue of paragraph (e) not being met (including the recovery of any financial support provided);
- (g) as to the circumstances in which this section may apply to a local authority in respect of persons who are outside that local authority's area;
- (h) as to the circumstances in which a local authority may recover from another local authority the expenses of providing special guardianship support services to any person.

(9) A local authority may provide special guardianship support services (or any part of them) by securing their provision by—
- (a) another local authority; or

(b) a person within a description prescribed in regulations of persons who may provide special guardianship support services,

and may also arrange with any such authority or person for that other authority or that person to carry out the local authority's functions in relation to assessments under this section.

(10) A local authority may carry out an assessment of the needs of any person for the purposes of this section at the same time as an assessment of his needs is made under any other provision of this Act or under any other enactment.

(11) Section 27 (co-operation between authorities) applies in relation to the exercise of functions of a local authority [in England][1] under this section as it applies in relation to the exercise of functions of a local authority under Part 3 [and see sections 164 and 164A of the Social Services and Well-being (Wales) Act 2014 for provision about co-operation between local authorities in Wales and other bodies][1].][2]

Amendments
1 Inserted by the Social Services and Well-being (Wales) Act 2014 (Consequential Amendments) Regulations 2016, SI 2016/413, regs 55, 56.
2 Inserted by the Adoption and Children Act 2002, s 115(1).

[14G ...[1]

...][2]

Amendments
1 Repealed by the Health and Social Care (Community Health and Standards) Act 2003, s 117(2).
2 Inserted by the Adoption and Children Act 2002, s 115(1).

Financial relief

15 Orders for financial relief with respect to children.

(1) Schedule 1 (which consists primarily of the re-enactment, with consequential amendments and minor modifications, of provisions of [section 6 of the Family Law Reform Act 1969][1] the Guardianship of Minors Acts 1971 and 1973, the Children Act 1975 and of sections 15 and 16 of the Family Law Reform Act 1987) makes provision in relation to financial relief for children.

(2) ...[2]

Amendments
1 Inserted by the Courts and Legal Services Act 1990, s 116(1), Sch 16, para 10(1).
2 Repealed by the Crime and Courts Act 2013, s 17(6), Sch 11, paras 102, 105.

Family assistance orders

16 Family assistance orders.

(1) Where, in any family proceedings, the court has power to make an order under this Part with respect to any child, it may (whether or not it makes such an order) make an order requiring—

(a) [an officer of the Service]¹ [or a Welsh family proceedings officer]² to be made available; or
(b) a local authority to make an officer of the authority available,

to advise, assist and (where appropriate) befriend any person named in the order.

(2) The persons who may be named in an order under this section ('a family assistance order') are—

(a) any parent[, guardian or special guardian]³ of the child;
(b) any person with whom the child is living or [who is named in a child arrangements order as a person with whom the child is to live, spend time or otherwise have contact]⁴;
(c) the child himself.

(3) No court may make a family assistance order unless—

(a) ...⁵
(b) it has obtained the consent of every person to be named in the order other than the child.

(4) A family assistance order may direct—

(a) the person named in the order; or
(b) such of the persons named in the order as may be specified in the order,

to take such steps as may be so specified with a view to enabling the officer concerned to be kept informed of the address of any person named in the order and to be allowed to visit any such person.

[(4A) If the court makes a family assistance order with respect to a child and the order is to be in force at the same time as [contact provision contained in a child arrangements order]⁴ made with respect to the child, the family assistance order may direct the officer concerned to give advice and assistance as regards establishing, improving and maintaining contact to such of the persons named in the order as may be specified in the order.]⁶

[(4B) In subsection (4A) 'contact provision' means provision which regulates arrangements relating to—

(a) with whom a child is to spend time or otherwise have contact, or
(b) when a child is to spend time or otherwise have contact with any person.]⁷

(5) Unless it specifies a shorter period, a family assistance order shall have effect for a period of [twelve months]⁸ beginning with the day on which it is made.

[(6) If the court makes a family assistance order with respect to a child and the order is to be in force at the same time as a section 8 order made with respect to the child, the family assistance order may direct the officer concerned to report to the court on such matters relating to the section 8 order as the court may require (including the question whether the section 8 order ought to be varied or discharged).]⁸

(7) A family assistance order shall not be made so as to require a local authority to make an officer of theirs available unless—

(a) the authority agree; or
(b) the child concerned lives or will live within their area.

(8) ...⁹

(9) ...⁹

Amendments
1 Substituted by the Criminal Justice and Court Services Act 2000, s 74, Sch 7, paras 87, 89(a).
2 Inserted by the Children Act 2004, s 40, Sch 3, paras 5, 7.
3 Substituted by the Adoption and Children Act 2002, s 139(1), Sch 3, paras 54, 58.
4 Substituted by the Children and Families Act 2014, s 12(4), Sch 2, paras 1, 27(1)–(3).
5 Repealed by the Children and Adoption Act 2006, ss 6(1), (2), 15(2), Sch 3.
6 Inserted by the Children and Adoption Act 2006, s 6(1), (3).
7 Inserted by the Children and Families Act 2014, s 12(4), Sch 2, paras 1, 27(1), (4).
8 Substituted by the Children and Adoption Act 2006, s 6(1), (4), (5).
9 Repealed by the Criminal Justice and Court Services Act 2000, ss 74, 75, Sch 7, paras 87, 89(b), Sch 8.

[16A Risk assessments

(1) This section applies to the following functions of officers of the Service or Welsh family proceedings officers–

(a) any function in connection with family proceedings in which the court has power to make an order under this Part with respect to a child or in which a question with respect to such an order arises;
(b) any function in connection with an order made by the court in such proceedings.

(2) If, in carrying out any function to which this section applies, an officer of the Service or a Welsh family proceedings officer is given cause to suspect that the child concerned is at risk of harm, he must–

(a) make a risk assessment in relation to the child, and
(b) provide the risk assessment to the court.

(3) A risk assessment, in relation to a child who is at risk of suffering harm of a particular sort, is an assessment of the risk of that harm being suffered by the child.]¹

Amendment
1 Inserted by the Children and Adoption Act 2006, s 7.

PART III
[SUPPORT FOR CHILDREN AND FAMILIES PROVIDED BY LOCAL AUTHORITIES IN ENGLAND]¹

[Application to local authorities in England

16B Application to local authorities in England

(1) This Part applies in relation to local authorities in England.

(2) Accordingly, unless the contrary intention appears, a reference in this Part to a local authority means a local authority in England.]²

Amendments
1 Substituted by the Social Services and Well-being (Wales) Act 2014 (Consequential Amendments) Regulations 2016, SI 2016/413, regs 55, 57(2).
2 Inserted by the Social Services and Well-being (Wales) Act 2014 (Consequential Amendments) Regulations 2016, SI 2016/413, regs 55, 57(1).

Provision of services for children and their families

17 Provision of services for children in need, their families and others.

(1) It shall be the general duty of every local authority (in addition to the other duties imposed on them by this Part)—

(a) to safeguard and promote the welfare of children within their area who are in need; and
(b) so far as is consistent with that duty, to promote the upbringing of such children by their families,

by providing a range and level of services appropriate to those children's needs.

(2) For the purpose principally of facilitating the discharge of their general duty under this section, every local authority shall have the specific duties and powers set out in Part 1 of Schedule 2.

(3) Any service provided by an authority in the exercise of functions conferred on them by this section may be provided for the family of a particular child in need or for any member of his family, if it is provided with a view to safeguarding or promoting the child's welfare.

(4) The [Secretary of State]¹ may by order amend any provision of Part I of Schedule 2 or add any further duty or power to those for the time being mentioned there.

[(4A) Before determining what (if any) services to provide for a particular child in need in the exercise of functions conferred on them by this section, a local authority shall, so far as is reasonably practicable and consistent with the child's welfare–

(a) ascertain the child's wishes and feelings regarding the provision of those services; and
(b) give due consideration (having regard to his age and understanding) to such wishes and feelings of the child as they have been able to ascertain.]²

(5) Every local authority—

(a) shall facilitate the provision by others (including in particular voluntary organisations) of services which [it is a function of the authority]³ to provide by virtue of this section, or section 18, 20, [22A to 22C]³, 23B to 23D, 24A or 24B; and
(b) may make such arrangements as they see fit for any person to act on their behalf in the provision of any such service.

(6) The services provided by a local authority in the exercise of functions conferred on them by this section may include [providing accommodation and]⁴ giving assistance in kind or …⁵ in cash.

(7) Assistance may be unconditional or subject to conditions as to the repayment of the assistance or of its value (in whole or in part).

(8) Before giving any assistance or imposing any conditions, a local authority shall have regard to the means of the child concerned and of each of his parents.

(9) No person shall be liable to make any repayment of assistance or of its value at any time when he is in receipt [of universal credit (except in such circumstances as may be prescribed),]⁶ of income support [under]⁷ [Part VII of the Social Security Contributions and Benefits Act 1992]⁸[, of any element of child tax credit other than the family element, of working tax credit]⁹[, of an income-based jobseeker's allowance or of an income-related employment and support allowance]¹⁰.

(10) For the purposes of this Part a child shall be taken to be in need if—

(a) he is unlikely to achieve or maintain, or to have the opportunity of achieving or maintaining, a reasonable standard of health or development without the provision for him of services by a local authority under this Part;
(b) his health or development is likely to be significantly impaired, or further impaired, without the provision for him of such services; or
(c) he is disabled,

and 'family', in relation to such a child, includes any person who has parental responsibility for the child and any other person with whom he has been living.

(11) For the purposes of this Part, a child is disabled if he is blind, deaf or dumb or suffers from mental disorder of any kind or is substantially and permanently handicapped by illness, injury or congenital deformity or such other disability as may be prescribed; and in this Part—

'development' means physical, intellectual, emotional, social or behavioural development; and
'health' means physical or mental health.

[(12) The Treasury may by regulations prescribe circumstances in which a person is to be treated for the purposes of this Part (or for such of those purposes as are prescribed) as in receipt of any element of child tax credit other than the family element or of working tax credit.]⁹

[(13) The duties imposed on a local authority by virtue of this section do not apply in relation to a child in the authority's area who is being looked after by a local authority in Wales in accordance with Part 6 of the Social Services and Well-being (Wales) Act 2014.]¹¹

Amendments
1 Substituted by the Social Services and Well-being (Wales) Act 2014 (Consequential Amendments) Regulations 2016, SI 2016/413, regs 55, 58(a).
2 Inserted by the Children Act 2004, s 53(1).
3 Substituted by the Children and Young Persons Act 2008, s 8(2), Sch 1, para 1.

4   Inserted by the Adoption and Children Act 2002, s 116(1).
5   Repealed by the Children and Young Persons Act 2008, s 42, Sch 4.
6   Inserted by the Welfare Reform Act 2012, s 31, Sch 2, para 1(a).
7   Substituted by the Tax Credits Act 2002, s 47, Sch 3, paras 15, 16(1), (2)(a).
8   Substituted by the Social Security (Consequential Provisions) Act 1992, s 4, Sch 2, para 108(a).
9   Inserted by the Tax Credits Act 2002, s 47, Sch 3, paras 15, 16(1), (2)(b), (3).
10 Substituted by the Welfare Reform Act 2007, s 28(1), Sch 3, para 6(1), (2).
11 Inserted by the Social Services and Well-being (Wales) Act 2014 (Consequential Amendments) Regulations 2016, SI 2016/413, regs 55, 58(b).

[17ZA   Young carers' needs assessments ...[1]

(1) A local authority ...[1] must assess whether a young carer within their area has needs for support and, if so, what those needs are, if—

 (a) it appears to the authority that the young carer may have needs for support, or
 (b) the authority receive a request from the young carer or a parent of the young carer to assess the young carer's needs for support.

(2) An assessment under subsection (1) is referred to in this Part as a 'young carer's needs assessment'.

(3) In this Part 'young carer' means a person under 18 who provides or intends to provide care for another person (but this is qualified by section 17ZB(3)).

(4) Subsection (1) does not apply in relation to a young carer if the local authority have previously carried out a care-related assessment of the young carer in relation to the same person cared for.

(5) But subsection (1) does apply (and so a young carer's needs assessment must be carried out) if it appears to the authority that the needs or circumstances of the young carer or the person cared for have changed since the last care-related assessment.

(6) 'Care-related assessment' means—

 (a) a young carer's needs assessment;
 (b) an assessment under any of the following—
  (i) section 1 of the Carers (Recognition and Services) Act 1995;
  (ii) section 1 of the Carers and Disabled Children Act 2000;
  (iii) section 4(3) of the Community Care (Delayed Discharges) Act 2003;
  [(iv) Part 1 of the Care Act 2014.][2]

(7) A young carer's needs assessment must include an assessment of whether it is appropriate for the young carer to provide, or continue to provide, care for the person in question, in the light of the young carer's needs for support, other needs and wishes.

(8) A local authority, in carrying out a young carer's needs assessment, must have regard to—

 (a) the extent to which the young carer is participating in or wishes to participate in education, training or recreation, and

(b) the extent to which the young carer works or wishes to work.

(9) A local authority, in carrying out a young carer's needs assessment, must involve—

(a) the young carer,
(b) the young carer's parents, and
(c) any person who the young carer or a parent of the young carer requests the authority to involve.

(10) A local authority that have carried out a young carer's needs assessment must give a written record of the assessment to—

(a) the young carer,
(b) the young carer's parents, and
(c) any person to whom the young carer or a parent of the young carer requests the authority to give a copy.

(11) Where the person cared for is under 18, the written record must state whether the local authority consider him or her to be a child in need.

(12) A local authority …[1] must take reasonable steps to identify the extent to which there are young carers within their area who have needs for support.][3]

Amendments
1 Repealed by the Social Services and Well-being (Wales) Act 2014 (Consequential Amendments) Regulations 2016, SI 2016/413, regs 55, 59.
2 Inserted by the Care Act 2014 and Children and Families Act 2014 (Consequential Amendments) Order 2015, SI 2015/914, art 2, Schedule, paras 43, 44.
3 Inserted by the Children and Families Act 2014, s 96(1).

[17ZB Young carers' needs assessments: supplementary

(1) This section applies for the purposes of section 17ZA.

(2) 'Parent', in relation to a young carer, includes—

(a) a parent of the young carer who does not have parental responsibility for the young carer, and
(b) a person who is not a parent of the young carer but who has parental responsibility for the young carer.

(3) A person is not a young carer if the person provides or intends to provide care—

(a) under or by virtue of a contract, or
(b) as voluntary work.

(4) But in a case where the local authority consider that the relationship between the person cared for and the person under 18 providing or intending to provide care is such that it would be appropriate for the person under 18 to be regarded as a young carer, that person is to be regarded as such (and subsection (3) is therefore to be ignored in that case).

(5) The references in section 17ZA and this section to providing care include a reference to providing practical or emotional support.

(6) Where a local authority—

(a) are required to carry out a young carer's needs assessment, and
(b) are required or have decided to carry out some other assessment of the young carer or of the person cared for;

the local authority may, subject to subsection (7), combine the assessments.

(7) A young carer's needs assessment may be combined with an assessment of the person cared for only if the young carer and the person cared for agree.

(8) The Secretary of State may by regulations make further provision about carrying out a young carer's needs assessment; the regulations may, in particular—

(a) specify matters to which a local authority is to have regard in carrying out a young carer's needs assessment;
(b) specify matters which a local authority is to determine in carrying out a young carer's needs assessment;
(c) make provision about the manner in which a young carer's needs assessment is to be carried out;
(d) make provision about the form a young carer's needs assessment is to take.

(9) The Secretary of State may by regulations amend the list in section 17ZA(6)(b) so as to—

(a) add an entry,
(b) remove an entry, or
(c) vary an entry.][1]

Amendment
1 Inserted by the Children and Families Act 2014, s 96(1).

[17ZC Consideration of young carers' needs assessments

A local authority that carry out a young carer's needs assessment must consider the assessment and decide—

(a) whether the young carer has needs for support in relation to the care which he or she provides or intends to provide;
(b) if so, whether those needs could be satisfied (wholly or partly) by services which the authority may provide under section 17; and
(c) if they could be so satisfied, whether or not to provide any such services in relation to the young carer.][1]

Amendment
1 Inserted by the Children and Families Act 2014, s 96(1).

[17ZD Parent carers' needs assessments ...[1]

(1) A local authority ...[1] must, if the conditions in subsections (3) and (4) are met, assess whether a parent carer within their area has needs for support and, if so, what those needs are.

(2) In this Part 'parent carer' means a person aged 18 or over who provides or intends to provide care for a disabled child for whom the person has parental responsibility.

(3) The first condition is that—

(a) it appears to the authority that the parent carer may have needs for support, or
(b) the authority receive a request from the parent carer to assess the parent carer's needs for support.

(4) The second condition is that the local authority are satisfied that the disabled child cared for and the disabled child's family are persons for whom they may provide or arrange for the provision of services under section 17.

(5) An assessment under subsection (1) is referred to in this Part as a 'parent carer's needs assessment'.

(6) Subsection (1) does not apply in relation to a parent carer if the local authority have previously carried out a care-related assessment of the parent carer in relation to the same disabled child cared for.

(7) But subsection (1) does apply (and so a parent carer's needs assessment must be carried out) if it appears to the authority that the needs or circumstances of the parent carer or the disabled child cared for have changed since the last care-related assessment.

(8) 'Care-related assessment' means—

(a) a parent carer's needs assessment;
(b) an assessment under any of the following—
  (i) section 1 of the Carers (Recognition and Services) Act 1995;
  (ii) section 6 of the Carers and Disabled Children Act 2000;
  (iii) section 4(3) of the Community Care (Delayed Discharges) Act 2003;
  [(iv) Part 1 of the Care Act 2014.]²

(9) A parent carer's needs assessment must include an assessment of whether it is appropriate for the parent carer to provide, or continue to provide, care for the disabled child, in the light of the parent carer's needs for support, other needs and wishes.

(10) A local authority in carrying out a parent carer's needs assessment must have regard to—

(a) the well-being of the parent carer, and
(b) the need to safeguard and promote the welfare of the disabled child cared for and any other child for whom the parent carer has parental responsibility.

(11) In subsection (10) 'well-being' has the same meaning as in Part 1 of the Care Act 2014.

(12) A local authority, in carrying out a parent carer's needs assessment, must involve—

(a) the parent carer,
(b) any child for whom the parent carer has parental responsibility, and
(c) any person who the parent carer requests the authority to involve.

(13) A local authority that have carried out a parent carer's needs assessment must give a written record of the assessment to—

(a) the parent carer, and
(b) any person to whom the parent carer requests the authority to give a copy.

(14) A local authority …¹ must take reasonable steps to identify the extent to which there are parent carers within their area who have needs for support.]³

Amendments
1 Repealed by the Social Services and Well-being (Wales) Act 2014 (Consequential Amendments) Regulations 2016, SI 2016/413, regs 55, 60.
2 Inserted by the Care Act 2014 and Children and Families Act 2014 (Consequential Amendments) Order 2015, SI 2015/914, art 2, Schedule, paras 43, 45.
3 Inserted by the Children and Families Act 2014, s 97(1).

[17ZE Parent carers' needs assessments: supplementary

(1) This section applies for the purposes of section 17ZD.

(2) The references in section 17ZD to providing care include a reference to providing practical or emotional support.

(3) Where a local authority—

(a) are required to carry out a parent carer's needs assessment, and
(b) are required or have decided to carry out some other assessment of the parent carer or of the disabled child cared for,

the local authority may combine the assessments.

(4) The Secretary of State may by regulations make further provision about carrying out a parent carer's needs assessment; the regulations may, in particular—

(a) specify matters to which a local authority is to have regard in carrying out a parent carer's needs assessment;
(b) specify matters which a local authority is to determine in carrying out a parent carer's needs assessment;
(c) make provision about the manner in which a parent carer's needs assessment is to be carried out;
(d) make provision about the form a parent carer's needs assessment is to take.

(5) The Secretary of State may by regulations amend the list in section 17ZD(8)(b) so as to—

(a) add an entry,
(b) remove an entry, or
(c) vary an entry.]¹

Amendment
1 Inserted by the Children and Families Act 2014, s 97(1).

[17ZF Consideration of parent carers' needs assessments

A local authority that carry out a parent carer's needs assessment must consider the assessment and decide—

(a) whether the parent carer has needs for support in relation to the care which he or she provides or intends to provide;
(b) whether the disabled child cared for has needs for support;
(c) if paragraph (a) or (b) applies, whether those needs could be satisfied (wholly or partly) by services which the authority may provide under section 17; and
(d) if they could be so satisfied, whether or not to provide any such services in relation to the parent carer or the disabled child cared for.][1]

Amendment
1 Inserted by the Children and Families Act 2014, s 97(1).

[17ZG Section 17 services: continued provision where EHC plan maintained

(1) This section applies where, immediately before a child in need reaches the age of 18—

(a) a local authority ...[1] is providing services for the child in the exercise of functions conferred by section 17, and
(b) an EHC plan is maintained for the child.

(2) The local authority may continue to provide services for the child in the exercise of those functions after the child reaches the age of 18, but may not continue to do so after the EHC plan has ceased to be maintained[, except in so far as the authority is required to do so under section 17ZH or 17ZI][2].

(3) In this section 'EHC plan' means a plan within section 37(2) of the Children and Families Act 2014.][3]

Amendments
1 Repealed by the Social Services and Well-being (Wales) Act 2014 (Consequential Amendments) Regulations 2016, SI 2016/413, regs 55, 61.
2 Inserted by the Care Act 2014, s 66(2).
3 Inserted by the Children and Families Act 2014, s 50.

[17ZH Section 17 services: transition for children to adult care and support

(1) Subsections (2) to (4) apply where a local authority ...[1] providing services for a child in need in the exercise of functions conferred by section 17—

(a) are required by section 58(1) or 63(1) of the Care Act 2014 to carry out a child's needs assessment or young carer's assessment in relation to the child, or
(b) are required by section 60(1) of that Act to carry out a child's carer's assessment in relation to a carer of the child.

(2) If the local authority carry out the assessment before the child reaches the age of 18 and decide to treat it as a needs or carer's assessment in accordance with section 59(6), 61(6) or 64(7) of the Care Act 2014 (with Part 1 of that Act applying to the assessment as a result), the authority must continue to comply

with section 17 after the child reaches the age of 18 until they reach a conclusion in his case.

(3) If the local authority carry out the assessment before the child reaches the age of 18 but decide not to treat it as a needs or carer's assessment in accordance with section 59(6), 61(6) or 64(7) of the Care Act 2014—

(a) they must carry out a needs or carer's assessment (as the case may be) after the child reaches the age of 18, and
(b) they must continue to comply with section 17 after he reaches that age until they reach a conclusion in his case.

(4) If the local authority do not carry out the assessment before the child reaches the age of 18, they must continue to comply with section 17 after he reaches that age until—

(a) they decide that the duty under section 9 or 10 of the Care Act 2014 (needs or carer's assessment) does not apply, or
(b) having decided that the duty applies and having discharged it, they reach a conclusion in his case.

(5) Subsection (6) applies where a local authority …[1] providing services for a child in need in the exercise of functions conferred by section 17—

(a) receive a request for a child's needs assessment or young carer's assessment to be carried out in relation to the child or for a child's carer's assessment to be carried out in relation to a carer of the child, but
(b) have yet to be required by section 58(1), 60(1) or 63(1) of the Care Act 2014 to carry out the assessment.

(6) If the local authority do not decide, before the child reaches the age of 18, whether or not to comply with the request, they must continue to comply with section 17 after he reaches that age until—

(a) they decide that the duty under section 9 or 10 of the Care Act 2014 does not apply, or
(b) having decided that the duty applies and having discharged it, they reach a conclusion in his case.

(7) A local authority reach a conclusion in a person's case when—

(a) they conclude that he does not have needs for care and support or for support (as the case may be), or
(b) having concluded that he has such needs and that they are going to meet some or all of them, they begin to do so, or
(c) having concluded that he has such needs, they conclude that they are not going to meet any of those needs (whether because those needs do not meet the eligibility criteria or for some other reason).

(8) In this section, 'child's needs assessment', 'child's carer's assessment', 'young carer's assessment', 'needs assessment', 'carer's assessment' and 'eligibility criteria' each have the same meaning as in Part 1 of the Care Act 2014.][2]

Amendments
1   Repealed by the Social Services and Well-being (Wales) Act 2014 (Consequential Amendments) Regulations 2016, SI 2016/413, regs 55, 62.
2   Inserted by the Care Act 2014, s 66(1).

[17ZI Section 17 services: provision after EHC plan no longer maintained

(1) This section applies where a local authority ...[1] providing services for a person in the exercise, by virtue of section 17ZG, of functions conferred by section 17 are required to carry out a needs assessment in that person's case.

(2) If the EHC plan for the person ceases to be maintained before the local authority reach a conclusion in the person's case, they must continue to comply with section 17 until they do reach a conclusion in his case.

(3) The references to the local authority reaching a conclusion in a person's case are to be read with section 17ZH(7).

(4) In this section, 'needs assessment' has the same meaning as in Part 1 of the Care Act 2014.][2]

Amendments
1   Repealed by the Social Services and Well-being (Wales) Act 2014 (Consequential Amendments) Regulations 2016, SI 2016/413, regs 55, 63.
2   Inserted by the Care Act 2014, s 66(1).

[[17A Direct payments

(1) The [Secretary of State][1] may by regulations make provision for and in connection with requiring or authorising the responsible authority in the case of a person of a prescribed description who falls within subsection (2) to make, with that person's consent, such payments to him as they may determine in accordance with the regulations in respect of his securing the provision of the service mentioned in that subsection.

(2) A person falls within this subsection if he is–

    (a)   a person with parental responsibility for a disabled child,
    (b)   a disabled person with parental responsibility for a child, or
    (c)   a disabled child aged 16 or 17,

and a local authority ('the responsible authority') have decided for the purposes of section 17 that the child's needs (or, if he is such a disabled child, his needs) call for the provision by them of a service in exercise of functions conferred on them under that section.

[(3) Regulations under this section may, in particular, make provision—

    (a)   specifying circumstances in which the responsible authority are not required or authorised to make any payments under the regulations to a person, whether those circumstances relate to the person in question or to the particular service mentioned in subsection (2);
    (b)   for any payments required or authorised by the regulations to be made to a person by the responsible authority ('direct payments') to be made to that person ('the payee') as gross payments or alternatively as net payments;

(c) for the responsible authority to make for the purposes of subsection (3A) or (3B) such determination as to—
  (i) the payee's means, and
  (ii) the amount (if any) which it would be reasonably practicable for the payee to pay to the authority by way of reimbursement or contribution,
as may be prescribed;
(d) as to the conditions falling to be complied with by the payee which must or may be imposed by the responsible authority in relation to the direct payments (and any conditions which may not be so imposed);
(e) specifying circumstances in which the responsible authority—
  (i) may or must terminate the making of direct payments,
  (ii) may require repayment (whether by the payee or otherwise) of the whole or part of the direct payments;
(f) for any sum falling to be paid or repaid to the responsible authority by virtue of any condition or other requirement imposed in pursuance of the regulations to be recoverable as a debt due to the authority;
(g) displacing functions or obligations of the responsible authority with respect to the provision of the service mentioned in subsection (2) only to such extent, and subject to such conditions, as may be prescribed;
(h) authorising direct payments to be made to any prescribed person on behalf of the payee;
(j) as to matters to which the responsible authority must, or may, have regard when making a decision for the purposes of a provision of the regulations;
(k) as to steps which the responsible authority must, or may, take before, or after, the authority makes a decision for the purposes of a provision of the regulations;
(l) specifying circumstances in which a person who has fallen within subsection (3D) but no longer does so (whether because of fluctuating capacity, or regaining or gaining of capacity) is to be treated, or may be treated, as falling within subsection (3D) for purposes of this section or for purposes of regulations under this section.

(3A) For the purposes of subsection (3)(b) 'gross payments' means payments—

(a) which are made at such a rate as the authority estimate to be equivalent to the reasonable cost of securing the provision of the service concerned; but
(b) which may be made subject to the condition that the payee pays to the responsible authority, by way of reimbursement, an amount or amounts determined under the regulations.

(3B) For the purposes of subsection (3)(b) 'net payments' means payments—

(a) which are made on the basis that the payee will pay an amount or amounts determined under the regulations by way of contribution towards the cost of securing the provision of the service concerned; and
(b) which are accordingly made at such a rate below that mentioned in subsection (3A)(a) as reflects any such contribution by the payee.

(3C) Regulations made for the purposes of subsection (3)(a) may provide that direct payments shall not be made in respect of the provision of residential accommodation for any person for a period in excess of a prescribed period.

(3D) A person falls within this subsection if the person lacks capacity, within the meaning of the Mental Capacity Act 2005, to consent to the making of direct payments.]²

(4) Regulations under this section shall provide that, where payments are made under the regulations to a person falling within subsection (5)–

(a) the payments shall be made at the rate mentioned in subsection [(3A)(a)]²; and
(b) subsection [(3A)(b)]² shall not apply.

(5) A person falls within this subsection if he is–

(a) a person falling within subsection (2)(a) or (b) and the child in question is aged 16 or 17, or
(b) a person who is in receipt [of universal credit (except in such circumstances as may be prescribed),]³ of income support under Part 7 of the Social Security Contributions and Benefits Act 1992 (c. 4), of any element of child tax credit other than the family element, of working tax credit[, of an income-based jobseeker's allowance or of an income-related employment and support allowance]⁴.

(6) In this section–

...⁵

'disabled' in relation to an adult has the same meaning as that given by section 17(11) in relation to a child;
'prescribed' means specified in or determined in accordance with regulations under this section ...⁵.]⁶]⁷

Amendments
1 Substituted by the Social Services and Well-being (Wales) Act 2014 (Consequential Amendments) Regulations 2016, SI 2016/413, regs 55, 64.
2 Substituted by the Care Act 2014 and Children and Families Act 2014 (Consequential Amendments) Order 2015, SI 2015/914, art 2, Schedule, paras 43, 46(1)–(3).
3 Inserted by the Welfare Reform Act 2012, s 31, Sch 2, para 1(b).
4 Substituted by the Welfare Reform Act 2007, s 28(1), Sch 3, para 6(1), (3).
5 Repealed by the Care Act 2014 and Children and Families Act 2014 (Consequential Amendments) Order 2015, SI 2015/914, art 2, Schedule, paras 43, 46(1), (4).
6 Substituted by the Health and Social Care Act 2001, s 58.
7 Inserted by the Carers and Disabled Children Act 2000, s 7(1).

[17B ...¹

...¹]²

Amendments
1 Repealed by the Social Services and Well-being (Wales) Act 2014 (Consequential Amendments) Regulations 2016, SI 2016/413, regs 55, 65.
2 Inserted by the Carers and Disabled Children Act 2000, s 7(1).

18 Day care for pre-school and other children.

(1) Every local authority shall provide such day care for children in need within their area who are—

(a) aged five or under; and
(b) not yet attending schools,

as is appropriate.

(2) ...[1]

(3) A local authority may provide facilities (including training, advice, guidance and counselling) for those—

(a) caring for children in day care; or
(b) who at any time accompany such children while they are in day care.

(4) In this section 'day care' means any form of care or supervised activity provided for children during the day (whether or not it is provided on a regular basis).

(5) Every local authority shall provide for children in need within their area who are attending any school such care or supervised activities as is appropriate—

(a) outside school hours; or
(b) during school holidays.

(6) ...[1]

(7) In this section 'supervised activity' means an activity supervised by a responsible person.

Amendments
1 Repealed by the Social Services and Well-being (Wales) Act 2014 (Consequential Amendments) Regulations 2016, SI 2016/413, regs 55, 66.

19 Review of provision for day care, child minding etc.

(1) ...[1]

(2) ...[1]

(3) Every local authority in Scotland shall, at least once in every review period, review—

(a) the provision for day care within their area made for children under the age of eight by the local authority and by persons required to register under section 71(1)(b); and
(b) the extent to which the services of child minders are available within their area with respect to children under the age of eight.

(4) In conducting any such review, ...[1] the authority shall have regard to the provision made with respect to children under the age of eight in relevant establishments within their area.

(5) In this section—

['relevant establishment' means—
(a) in relation to Scotland, any establishment which is mentioned in paragraphs 3 and 4 of Schedule 9 (establishments exempt from the registration requirements which apply in relation to the provision of day care in Scotland); and
(b) in relation to England and Wales, any establishment which is mentioned in paragraphs 1 and 2 of Schedule 9A (establishments exempt from the registration requirements which apply in relation to the provision of day care in England and Wales);][2]

'review period' means the period of one year beginning with the commencement of this section and each subsequent period of three years beginning with an anniversary of that commencement.

(6) Where a local authority have conducted a review under this section they shall publish the result of the review—
(a) as soon as is reasonably practicable;
(b) in such form as they consider appropriate; and
(c) together with any proposals they may have with respect to the matters reviewed.

(7) The authorities conducting any review under this section shall have regard to—
(a) any representations made to any one of them by any relevant [Health Authority, Special Health Authority][3][, Primary Care Trust][4] or health board; and
(b) any other representations which they consider to be relevant.

(8) In the application of this section to Scotland, 'day care' has the same meaning as in section 79 and 'health board' has the same meaning as in the National Health Service (Scotland) Act 1978.

Amendments
1   Repealed by the Education Act 2002, s 215(2), Sch 22, Pt 3.
2   Substituted by the Care Standards Act 2000, s 116, Sch 4, para 14(1), (2)(b).
3   Substituted by the Health Authorities Act 1995, s 2(1), Sch 1, para 118(1), (2).
4   Inserted by the Health Act 1999 (Supplementary, Consequential etc. Provisions) Order 2000, SI 2000/90, art 3(1), Sch 1, para 24(1), (2).

Provision of accommodation for children

20 Provision of accommodation for children: general.

(1) Every local authority shall provide accommodation for any child in need within their area who appears to them to require accommodation as a result of—
(a) there being no person who has parental responsibility for him;
(b) his being lost or having been abandoned; or
(c) the person who has been caring for him being prevented (whether or not permanently, and for whatever reason) from providing him with suitable accommodation or care.

(2) Where a local authority provide accommodation under subsection (1) for a child who is ordinarily resident in the area of another local authority, that other local authority may take over the provision of accommodation for the child within—

(a) three months of being notified in writing that the child is being provided with accommodation; or
(b) such other longer period as may be prescribed [in regulations made by the Secretary of State][1].

[(2A) Where a local authority in Wales provide accommodation under section 76(1) of the Social Services and Well-being (Wales) Act 2014 (accommodation for children without parents or who are lost or abandoned etc.) for a child who is ordinarily resident in the area of a local authority in England, that local authority in England may take over the provision of accommodation for the child within—

(a) three months of being notified in writing that the child is being provided with accommodation; or
(b) such other longer period as may be prescribed in regulations made by the Secretary of State.][1]

(3) Every local authority shall provide accommodation for any child in need within their area who has reached the age of sixteen and whose welfare the authority consider is likely to be seriously prejudiced if they do not provide him with accommodation.

(4) A local authority may provide accommodation for any child within their area (even though a person who has parental responsibility for him is able to provide him with accommodation) if they consider that to do so would safeguard or promote the child's welfare.

(5) A local authority may provide accommodation for any person who has reached the age of sixteen but is under twenty-one in any community home which takes children who have reached the age of sixteen if they consider that to do so would safeguard or promote his welfare.

(6) Before providing accommodation under this section, a local authority shall, so far as is reasonably practicable and consistent with the child's welfare—

(a) ascertain the child's wishes [and feelings][2] regarding the provision of accommodation; and
(b) give due consideration (having regard to his age and understanding) to such wishes [and feelings][2] of the child as they have been able to ascertain.

(7) A local authority may not provide accommodation under this section for any child if any person who—

(a) has parental responsibility for him; and
(b) is willing and able to—
 (i) provide accommodation for him; or
 (ii) arrange for accommodation to be provided for him,

objects.

(8) Any person who has parental responsibility for a child may at any time remove the child from accommodation provided by or on behalf of the local authority under this section.

(9) Subsections (7) and (8) do not apply while any person—

[(a) who is named in a child arrangements order as a person with whom the child is to live;]³
[(aa) who is a special guardian of the child; or]⁴
(b) who has care of the child by virtue of an order made in the exercise of the High Court's inherent jurisdiction with respect to children,

agrees to the child being looked after in accommodation provided by or on behalf of the local authority.

(10) Where there is more than one such person as is mentioned in subsection (9), all of them must agree.

(11) Subsections (7) and (8) do not apply where a child who has reached the age of sixteen agrees to being provided with accommodation under this section.

Amendments
1 Inserted by the Social Services and Well-being (Wales) Act 2014 (Consequential Amendments) Regulations 2016, SI 2016/413, regs 55, 67.
2 Inserted by the Children Act 2004, s 53(2).
3 Substituted by the Children and Families Act 2014, s 12(4), Sch 2, paras 1, 28.
4 Inserted by the Adoption and Children Act 2002, s 139(1), Sch 3, paras 54, 59.

21 Provision of accommodation for children in police protection or detention or on remand, etc.

(1) Every local authority shall make provision for the reception and accommodation of children who are removed or kept away from home under Part V.

(2) Every local authority shall receive, and provide accommodation for, children—

(a) in police protection whom they are requested to receive under section 46(3)(f);
(b) whom they are requested to receive under section 38(6) of the Police and Criminal Evidence Act 1984;
(c) who are—
  (i) ...¹
  [(ia) remanded to accommodation provided by or on behalf of a local authority by virtue of paragraph 4 of Schedule 1 or paragraph 6 of Schedule 8 to the Powers of Criminal Courts (Sentencing) Act 2000 (breach etc. of referral orders and reparation orders);]²
  [(ii) remanded to accommodation provided by or on behalf of a local authority by virtue of paragraph 21 of Schedule 2 to the Criminal Justice and Immigration Act 2008 (breach etc. of youth rehabilitation orders); ...³
  [(iia) remanded to accommodation provided by or on behalf of a local authority by virtue of paragraph 10 of the Schedule to the Street Offences Act 1959 (breach of orders under section 1(2A) of that Act);]⁴

(iii) the subject of a youth rehabilitation order imposing a local authority residence requirement or a youth rehabilitation order with fostering,]⁵

and with respect to whom they are the designated authority.

[(2A) In subsection (2)(c)(iii), the following terms have the same meanings as in Part 1 of the Criminal Justice and Immigration Act 2008 (see section 7 of that Act)—

'local authority residence requirement';
'youth rehabilitation order';
'youth rehabilitation order with fostering'.]⁶

(3) Where a child has been—

(a) removed under Part V; or
(b) detained under section 38 of the Police and Criminal Evidence Act 1984,

and he is not being provided with accommodation by a local authority [or by a local authority in Wales]⁷ or in a hospital vested in the [Secretary of State or]⁸ [the Welsh Ministers]⁹ [...¹⁰,]¹¹ [or otherwise made available pursuant to arrangements made by [the Secretary of State, the National Health Service Commissioning Board or a clinical commissioning group under the National Health Service Act 2006 or]¹² a [Local Health Board]¹³]¹⁴ [...¹⁰]¹¹, any reasonable expenses of accommodating him shall be recoverable from the local authority[, or local authority in Wales,]⁷ in whose area he is ordinarily resident.

Amendments

1 Repealed by the Legal Aid, Sentencing and Punishment of Offenders Act 2012, s 105, Sch 12, paras 23, 24.
2 Inserted by the Criminal Justice and Immigration Act 2008, s 6(3), Sch 4, para 105.
3 Repealed by the Policing and Crime Act 2009, s 112(1), (2), Sch 7, para 21, Sch 8, Pt 2.
4 Inserted by the Policing and Crime Act 2009, s 112(1), Sch 7, para 21.
5 Substituted by the Criminal Justice and Immigration Act 2008, s 6(2), Sch 4, paras 33, 34(1), (2)(b).
6 Inserted by the Criminal Justice and Immigration Act 2008, s 6(2), Sch 4, paras 33, 34(1), (3).
7 Inserted by the Social Services and Well-being (Wales) Act 2014 (Consequential Amendments) Regulations 2016, SI 2016/413, regs 55, 68.
8 Substituted by the Health and Social Care Act 2012, s 55(2), Sch 5, paras 47, 48(a).
9 Inserted by the Children and Young Persons Act 2008, s 39, Sch 3, paras 1, 5.
10 Repealed by the Health and Social Care Act 2012, s 55(2), Sch 5, paras 47, 48(b).
11 Inserted by the Health Act 1999 (Supplementary, Consequential etc. Provisions) Order 2000, SI 2000/90, art 3(1), Sch 1, para 24(1), (3).
12 Inserted by the Health and Social Care Act 2012, s 55(2), Sch 5, paras 47, 48(c).
13 Substituted by the References to Health Authorities Order 2007, SI 2007/961, art 3, Schedule, para 20(1), (2)(a).
14 Inserted by the National Health Service and Community Care Act 1990, s 66(1), Sch 9, para 36(1).

Duties of local authorities in relation to children looked after by them

22 General duty of local authority in relation to children looked after by them.

(1) [In this section]¹, any reference to a child who is looked after by a local authority is a reference to a child who is—

(a) in their care; or
(b) provided with accommodation by the authority in the exercise of any functions (in particular those under this Act) which [are social services functions within the meaning of]² the Local Authority Social Services Act 1970[, apart from functions under sections [17,]³ 23B and 24B]⁴.

(2) In subsection (1) 'accommodation' means accommodation which is provided for a continuous period of more than 24 hours.

(3) It shall be the duty of a local authority looking after any child—
(a) to safeguard and promote his welfare; and
(b) to make such use of services available for children cared for by their own parents as appears to the authority reasonable in his case.

[(3A) The duty of a local authority under subsection (3)(a) to safeguard and promote the welfare of a child looked after by them includes in particular a duty to promote the child's educational achievement.]⁵

[(3B) A local authority …⁶ must appoint at least one person for the purpose of discharging the duty imposed by virtue of subsection (3A).

(3C) A person appointed by a local authority under subsection (3B) must be an officer employed by that authority or another local authority …⁶.]⁷

(4) Before making any decision with respect to a child whom they are looking after, or proposing to look after, a local authority shall, so far as is reasonably practicable, ascertain the wishes and feelings of—
(a) the child;
(b) his parents;
(c) any person who is not a parent of his but who has parental responsibility for him; and
(d) any other person whose wishes and feelings the authority consider to be relevant,

regarding the matter to be decided.

(5) In making any such decision a local authority shall give due consideration—
(a) having regard to his age and understanding, to such wishes and feelings of the child as they have been able to ascertain;
(b) to such wishes and feelings of any person mentioned in subsection (4)(b) to (d) as they have been able to ascertain; and
(c) to the child's religious persuasion, racial origin and cultural and linguistic background.

(6) If it appears to a local authority that it is necessary, for the purpose of protecting members of the public from serious injury, to exercise their powers with respect to a child whom they are looking after in a manner which may not be consistent with their duties under this section, they may do so.

(7) If the [Secretary of State]¹ considers it necessary, for the purpose of protecting members of the public from serious injury, to give directions to a local authority with respect to the exercise of their powers with respect to a child

whom they are looking after, [the [Secretary of State]¹]⁸ may give such directions to [the authority]¹.

(8) Where any such directions are given to an authority they shall comply with them even though doing so is inconsistent with their duties under this section.

Amendments
1   Substituted by the Social Services and Well-being (Wales) Act 2014 (Consequential Amendments) Regulations 2016, SI 2016/413, regs 55, 69(a), (d).
2   Substituted by the Local Government Act 2000, s 107(1), Sch 5, para 19.
3   Word inserted by the Adoption and Children Act 2002, s 116(2).
4   Inserted by the Children (Leaving Care) Act 2000, s 2(1), (2).
5   Inserted by the Children Act 2004, s 52.
6   Repealed by the Social Services and Well-being (Wales) Act 2014 (Consequential Amendments) Regulations 2016, SI 2016/413, regs 55, 69(b), (c).
7   Inserted by the Children and Families Act 2014, s 99.
8   Word substituted by the Children and Young Persons Act 2008, s 39, Sch 3, paras 1, 6(b).

[22A Provision of accommodation for children in care

When a child is in the care of a local authority, it is their duty to provide the child with accommodation.]¹

Amendment
1   Substituted by the Children and Young Persons Act 2008, s 8(1).

[22B Maintenance of looked after children

It is the duty of a local authority to maintain a child they are looking after in other respects apart from the provision of accommodation.]¹

Amendment
1   Substituted by the Children and Young Persons Act 2008, s 8(1).

[22C Ways in which looked after children are to be accommodated and maintained

(1) This section applies where a local authority are looking after a child ('C').

(2) The local authority must make arrangements for C to live with a person who falls within subsection (3) (but subject to subsection (4)).

(3) A person ('P') falls within this subsection if—

    (a)   P is a parent of C;
    (b)   P is not a parent of C but has parental responsibility for C; or
    (c)   in a case where C is in the care of the local authority and there was [a child arrangements order]¹ in force with respect to C immediately before the care order was made, P was a person [named in the child arrangements order as a person with whom C was to live]¹.

(4) Subsection (2) does not require the local authority to make arrangements of the kind mentioned in that subsection if doing so—

    (a)   would not be consistent with C's welfare; or
    (b)   would not be reasonably practicable.

(5) If the local authority are unable to make arrangements under subsection (2), they must place C in the placement which is, in their opinion, the most appropriate placement available.

(6) In subsection (5) 'placement' means—

(a) placement with an individual who is a relative, friend or other person connected with C and who is also a local authority foster parent;
(b) placement with a local authority foster parent who does not fall within paragraph (a);
(c) placement in a children's home in respect of which a person is registered under Part 2 of the Care Standards Act 2000 [or Part 1 of the Regulation and Inspection of Social Care (Wales) Act 2016 (anaw 2)][2]; or
(d) subject to section 22D, placement in accordance with other arrangements which comply with any regulations made for the purposes of this section.

(7) In determining the most appropriate placement for C, the local authority must, subject to [subsection (9B) and][3] the other provisions of this Part (in particular, to their duties under section 22)—

(a) give preference to a placement falling within paragraph (a) of subsection (6) over placements falling within the other paragraphs of that subsection;
(b) comply, so far as is reasonably practicable in all the circumstances of C's case, with the requirements of subsection (8); and
(c) comply with subsection (9) unless that is not reasonably practicable.

(8) The local authority must ensure that the placement is such that—

(a) it allows C to live near C's home;
(b) it does not disrupt C's education or training;
(c) if C has a sibling for whom the local authority are also providing accommodation, it enables C and the sibling to live together;
(d) if C is disabled, the accommodation provided is suitable to C's particular needs.

(9) The placement must be such that C is provided with accommodation within the local authority's area.

[(9A) Subsection (9B) applies (subject to subsection (9C)) where the local authority ...[4]—

(a) are considering adoption for C, or
(b) are satisfied that C ought to be placed for adoption but are not authorised under section 19 of the Adoption and Children Act 2002 (placement with parental consent) or by virtue of section 21 of that Act (placement orders) to place C for adoption.

(9B) Where this subsection applies—

(a) subsections (7) to (9) do not apply to the local authority,
(b) the local authority must consider placing C with an individual within subsection (6)(a), and

(c) where the local authority decide that a placement with such an individual is not the most appropriate placement for C, the local authority must consider placing C with a local authority foster parent who has been approved as a prospective adopter.

(9C) Subsection (9B) does not apply where the local authority have applied for a placement order under section 21 of the Adoption and Children Act 2002 in respect of C and the application has been refused.][3]

(10) The local authority may determine—

(a) the terms of any arrangements they make under subsection (2) in relation to C (including terms as to payment); and
(b) the terms on which they place C with a local authority foster parent (including terms as to payment but subject to any order made under section 49 of the Children Act 2004).

(11) The [Secretary of State][5] may make regulations for, and in connection with, the purposes of this section.

[(12) For the meaning of 'local authority foster parent' see section 105(1).][5][6]

Amendments
1 Substituted by the Children and Families Act 2014, s 12(4), Sch 2, paras 1, 29.
2 Inserted by the Regulation and Inspection of Social Care (Wales) Act 2016 (Consequential Amendments) Regulations 2018, SI 2018/195, reg 9.
3 Inserted by the Children and Families Act 2014, s 2.
4 Repealed by the Social Services and Well-being (Wales) Act 2014 (Consequential Amendments) Regulations 2016, SI 2016/413, regs 55, 70(a).
5 Substituted by the Social Services and Well-being (Wales) Act 2014 (Consequential Amendments) Regulations 2016, SI 2016/413, regs 55, 70(b), (c).
6 Inserted by the Children and Young Persons Act 2008, s 8(1).

[22D Review of child's case before making alternative arrangements for accommodation

(1) Where a local authority are providing accommodation for a child ('C') other than by arrangements under section 22C(6)(d), they must not make such arrangements for C unless they have decided to do so in consequence of a review of C's case carried out in accordance with regulations made under section 26.

(2) But subsection (1) does not prevent a local authority making arrangements for C under section 22C(6)(d) if they are satisfied that in order to safeguard C's welfare it is necessary—

(a) to make such arrangements; and
(b) to do so as a matter of urgency.][1]

Amendment
1 Substituted by the Children and Young Persons Act 2008, s 8(1).

[22E Children's homes provided by Secretary of State or Welsh Ministers

Where a local authority place a child they are looking after in a children's home provided, equipped and maintained by the Secretary of State or the Welsh

Ministers under section 82(5), they must do so on such terms as the Secretary of State or the Welsh Ministers (as the case may be) may from time to time determine.]¹

Amendment
1   Substituted by the Social Services and Well-being (Wales) Act 2014 (Consequential Amendments) Regulations 2016, SI 2016/413, regs 55, 71.

[22F Regulations as to children looked after by local authorities

Part 2 of Schedule 2 has effect for the purposes of making further provision as to children looked after by local authorities and in particular as to the regulations which may be made under section 22C(11).]¹

Amendment
1   Substituted by the Children and Young Persons Act 2008, s 8(1).

[22G General duty of local authority to secure sufficient accommodation for looked after children

(1) It is the general duty of a local authority to take steps that secure, so far as reasonably practicable, the outcome in subsection (2).

(2) The outcome is that the local authority are able to provide the children mentioned in subsection (3) with accommodation that—

   (a)   is within the authority's area; and
   (b)   meets the needs of those children.

(3) The children referred to in subsection (2) are those—

   (a)   that the local authority are looking after,
   (b)   in respect of whom the authority are unable to make arrangements under section 22C(2), and
   (c)   whose circumstances are such that it would be consistent with their welfare for them to be provided with accommodation that is in the authority's area.

(4) In taking steps to secure the outcome in subsection (2), the local authority must have regard to the benefit of having—

   (a)   a number of accommodation providers in their area that is, in their opinion, sufficient to secure that outcome; and
   (b)   a range of accommodation in their area capable of meeting different needs that is, in their opinion, sufficient to secure that outcome.

(5) In this section 'accommodation providers' means—

   local authority foster parents; and
   children's homes in respect of which a person is registered under Part 2 of the Care Standards Act 2000.]¹

Amendment
1   Inserted by the Children and Young Persons Act 2008, s 9.

23 ...¹

...¹

Amendment
1 Substituted by the Children and Young Persons Act 2008, s 8(1).

[Educational achievement of previously looked after children

23ZZA Information and advice for promoting educational achievement

(1) A local authority in England must make advice and information available in accordance with this section for the purpose of promoting the educational achievement of each relevant child educated in their area.

(2) The advice and information must be made available to—
- (a) any person who has parental responsibility for the child,
- (b) the member of staff at the child's school designated under section 20A of the Children and Young Persons Act 2008 or by virtue of section 2E of the Academies Act 2010, and
- (c) any other person that the local authority consider appropriate.

(3) A local authority in England may do anything else that they consider appropriate with a view to promoting the educational achievement of relevant children educated in their area.

(4) A local authority in England must appoint at least one person for the purpose of discharging the duty imposed by subsection (1).

(5) The person appointed for that purpose must be an officer employed by the authority or another local authority in England.

(6) In this section—

'relevant child' means—
- (a) a child who was looked after by the local authority or another local authority in England and Wales but ceased to be so looked after as a result of—
    - (i) a child arrangements order which includes arrangements relating to with whom the child is to live, or when the child is to live with any person,
    - (ii) a special guardianship order, or
    - (iii) an adoption order within the meaning given by section 72(1) of the Adoption Act 1976 or section 46(1) of the Adoption and Children Act 2002, or
- (b) a child who appears to the local authority—
    - (i) to have been in state care in a place outside England and Wales because he or she would not otherwise have been cared for adequately, and
    - (ii) to have ceased to be in that state care as a result of being adopted.

(7) For the purposes of this section a child is educated in a local authority's area if—

    (a) the child is receiving early years provision secured by the local authority under section 7(1) of the Childcare Act 2006, or

    (b) the child is of compulsory school age and—

        (i) the child attends a school in the local authority's area, or

        (ii) if the child does not attend school, the child receives all or most of his or her education in the local authority's area.

(8) For the purposes of this section a child is in 'state care' if he or she is in the care of, or accomodated by—

    (a) a public authority,

    (b) a religious organisation, or

    (c) any other organisation the sole or main purpose of which is to benefit society.][1]

Amendment

1 Inserted by the Children and Social Work Act 2017, s 4.

[*Visiting*

23ZA Duty of local authority to ensure visits to, and contact with, looked after children and others

(1) This section applies to—

    (a) a child looked after by a local authority;

    (b) a child who was looked after by a local authority but who has ceased to be looked after by them as a result of prescribed circumstances.

(2) It is the duty of the local authority—

    (a) to ensure that a person to whom this section applies is visited by a representative of the authority ('a representative');

    (b) to arrange for appropriate advice, support and assistance to be available to a person to whom this section applies who seeks it from them.

(3) The duties imposed by subsection (2)—

    (a) are to be discharged in accordance with any regulations made for the purposes of this section by the [Secretary of State][1];

    (b) are subject to any requirement imposed by or under an enactment applicable to the place in which the person to whom this section applies is accommodated.

(4) Regulations under this section for the purposes of subsection (3)(a) may make provision about—

    (a) the frequency of visits;

    (b) circumstances in which a person to whom this section applies must be visited by a representative; and

    (c) the functions of a representative.

(5) In choosing a representative a local authority must satisfy themselves that the person chosen has the necessary skills and experience to perform the functions of a representative.]²

Amendments
1   Substituted by the Social Services and Well-being (Wales) Act 2014 (Consequential Amendments) Regulations 2016, SI 2016/413, regs 55, 72.
2   Inserted by the Children and Young Persons Act 2008, s 15.

[23ZB Independent visitors for children looked after by a local authority

(1) A local authority looking after a child must appoint an independent person to be the child's visitor if—

(a) the child falls within a description prescribed in regulations made by the [Secretary of State]¹; or
(b) in any other case, it appears to them that it would be in the child's interests to do so.

(2) A person appointed under this section must visit, befriend and advise the child.

(3) A person appointed under this section is entitled to recover from the appointing authority any reasonable expenses incurred by that person for the purposes of that person's functions under this section.

(4) A person's appointment as a visitor in pursuance of this section comes to an end if—

(a) the child ceases to be looked after by the local authority;
(b) the person resigns the appointment by giving notice in writing to the appointing authority; or
(c) the authority give him notice in writing that they have terminated it.

(5) The ending of such an appointment does not affect any duty under this section to make a further appointment.

(6) Where a local authority propose to appoint a visitor for a child under this section, the appointment shall not be made if—

(a) the child objects to it; and
(b) the authority are satisfied that the child has sufficient understanding to make an informed decision.

(7) Where a visitor has been appointed for a child under this section, the local authority shall terminate the appointment if—

(a) the child objects to its continuing; and
(b) the authority are satisfied that the child has sufficient understanding to make an informed decision.

(8) If the local authority give effect to a child's objection under subsection (6) or (7) and the objection is to having anyone as the child's visitor, the authority does not have to propose to appoint another person under subsection (1) until the objection is withdrawn.

(9) The [Secretary of State]¹ may make regulations as to the circumstances in which a person is to be regarded for the purposes of this section as independent of the appointing authority.]²

Amendments
1 Substituted by the Social Services and Well-being (Wales) Act 2014 (Consequential Amendments) Regulations 2016, SI 2016/413, regs 55, 73.
2 Inserted by the Children and Young Persons Act 2008, s 16(1).

*Advice and assistance for certain children [and young persons]*¹

[23A The responsible authority and relevant children.

(1) The responsible local authority shall have the functions set out in section 23B in respect of a relevant child.

(2) In subsection (1) 'relevant child' means (subject to subsection (3)) a child who—

   (a) is not being looked after [by any local authority in England or by any local authority in Wales]²;
   (b) was, before last ceasing to be looked after, an eligible child for the purposes of paragraph 19B of Schedule 2; and
   (c) is aged sixteen or seventeen.

(3) The [Secretary of State]² may prescribe—

   (a) additional categories of relevant children; and
   (b) categories of children who are not to be relevant children despite falling within subsection (2).

(4) In subsection (1) the 'responsible local authority' is the one which last looked after the child.

(5) If under subsection (3)(a) the [Secretary of State] 4 prescribes a category of relevant children which includes children who do not fall within subsection (2)(b) (for example, because they were being looked after by a local authority in Scotland), [the [Secretary of State]²]³ may in the regulations also provide for which local authority is to be the responsible local authority for those children.]¹

Amendments
1 Inserted by the Children (Leaving Care) Act 2000, s 2(1), (3), (4).
2 Substituted by the Social Services and Well-being (Wales) Act 2014 (Consequential Amendments) Regulations 2016, SI 2016/413, regs 55, 74.
3 Substituted by the Children and Young Persons Act 2008, s 39, Sch 3, paras 1, 8(1), (3)(b).

[23B Additional functions of the responsible authority in respect of relevant children.

(1) It is the duty of each local authority to take reasonable steps to keep in touch with a relevant child for whom they are the responsible authority, whether he is within their area or not.

(2) It is the duty of each local authority to appoint a personal adviser for each relevant child (if they have not already done so under paragraph 19C of Schedule 2).

(3) It is the duty of each local authority, in relation to any relevant child who does not already have a pathway plan prepared for the purposes of paragraph 19B of Schedule 2—

(a) to carry out an assessment of his needs with a view to determining what advice, assistance and support it would be appropriate for them to provide him under this Part; and
(b) to prepare a pathway plan for him.

(4) ...[1]

(5) ...[1]

(6) ...[1]

(7) ...[1]

(8) The responsible local authority shall safeguard and promote the child's welfare and, unless they are satisfied that his welfare does not require it, support him by—

(a) maintaining him;
(b) providing him with or maintaining him in suitable accommodation; and
(c) providing support of such other descriptions as may be prescribed.

(9) Support under subsection (8) may be in cash.

(10) The [Secretary of State][2] may by regulations make provision about the meaning of 'suitable accommodation' and in particular about the suitability of landlords or other providers of accommodation.

(11) If the local authority have lost touch with a relevant child, despite taking reasonable steps to keep in touch, they must without delay—

(a) consider how to re-establish contact; and
(b) take reasonable steps to do so,

and while the child is still a relevant child must continue to take such steps until they succeed.

(12) Subsections (7) to (9) of section 17 apply in relation to support given under this section as they apply in relation to assistance given under that section.

(13) Subsections (4) and (5) of section 22 apply in relation to any decision by a local authority for the purposes of this section as they apply in relation to the decisions referred to in that section.][3]

Amendments
1 Repealed by the Children and Young Persons Act 2008, s 42, Sch 4.
2 Substituted by the Social Services and Well-being (Wales) Act 2014 (Consequential Amendments) Regulations 2016, SI 2016/413, regs 55, 75.
3 Inserted by the Children (Leaving Care) Act 2000, s 2(1), (4).

[23C Continuing functions in respect of former relevant children.

(1) Each local authority shall have the duties provided for in this section towards—

(a) a person who has been a relevant child for the purposes of section 23A (and would be one if he were under eighteen), and in relation to whom they were the last responsible authority; and

(b) a person who was being looked after by them when he attained the age of eighteen, and immediately before ceasing to be looked after was an eligible child,

and in this section such a person is referred to as a 'former relevant child'.

(2) It is the duty of the local authority to take reasonable steps—

(a) to keep in touch with a former relevant child whether he is within their area or not; and

(b) if they lose touch with him, to re-establish contact.

(3) It is the duty of the local authority—

(a) to continue the appointment of a personal adviser for a former relevant child; and

(b) to continue to keep his pathway plan under regular review.

(4) It is the duty of the local authority to give a former relevant child—

(a) assistance of the kind referred to in section 24B(1), to the extent that his welfare requires it;

(b) assistance of the kind referred to in section 24B(2), to the extent that his welfare and his educational or training needs require it;

(c) other assistance, to the extent that his welfare requires it.

(5) The assistance given under subsection (4)(c) may be in kind or, in exceptional circumstances, in cash.

[(5A) It is the duty of the local authority to pay the relevant amount to a former relevant child who pursues higher education in accordance with a pathway plan prepared for that person.

(5B) The [Secretary of State][1] may by regulations—

(a) prescribe the relevant amount for the purposes of subsection (5A);

(b) prescribe the meaning of 'higher education' for those purposes;

(c) make provision as to the payment of the relevant amount;

(d) make provision as to the circumstances in which the relevant amount (or any part of it) may be recovered by the local authority from a former relevant child to whom a payment has been made.

(5C) The duty set out in subsection (5A) is without prejudice to that set out in subsection (4)(b).][2]

(6) Subject to subsection (7), the duties set out in subsections (2), (3) and (4) subsist until the former relevant child reaches the age of twenty-one.

(7) If the former relevant child's pathway plan sets out a programme of education or training which extends beyond his twenty-first birthday—

(a) the duty set out in subsection (4)(b) continues to subsist for so long as the former relevant child continues to pursue that programme; and

(b) the duties set out in subsections (2) and (3) continue to subsist concurrently with that duty.

(8) For the purposes of subsection (7)(a) there shall be disregarded any interruption in a former relevant child's pursuance of a programme of education or training if the local authority are satisfied that he will resume it as soon as is reasonably practicable.

(9) Section 24B(5) applies in relation to a person being given assistance under subsection (4)(b) [or who is in receipt of a payment under subsection (5A)]² as it applies in relation to a person to whom section 24B(3) applies.

(10) Subsections (7) to (9) of section 17 apply in relation to assistance given under this section as they apply in relation to assistance given under that section.]³

Amendments
1   Substituted by the Social Services and Well-being (Wales) Act 2014 (Consequential Amendments) Regulations 2016, SI 2016/413, regs 55, 76.
2   Inserted by the Children and Young Persons Act 2008, s 21(1)–(3).
3   Inserted by the Children (Leaving Care) Act 2000, s 2(1), (4).

[23CZA Arrangements for certain former relevant children to continue to live with former foster parents

(1) Each local authority ...¹ have the duties provided for in subsection (3) in relation to a staying put arrangement.

(2) A 'staying put arrangement' is an arrangement under which—

(a) a person who is a former relevant child by virtue of section 23C(1)(b), and
(b) a person (a 'former foster parent') who was the former relevant child's local authority foster parent immediately before the former relevant child ceased to be looked after by the local authority,

continue to live together after the former relevant child has ceased to be looked after.

(3) It is the duty of the local authority (in discharging the duties in section 23C(3) and by other means)—

(a) to monitor the staying put arrangement, and
(b) to provide advice, assistance and support to the former relevant child and the former foster parent with a view to maintaining the staying put arrangement.

(4) Support provided to the former foster parent under subsection (3)(b) must include financial support.

(5) Subsection (3)(b) does not apply if the local authority consider that the staying put arrangement is not consistent with the welfare of the former relevant child.

(6) The duties set out in subsection (3) subsist until the former relevant child reaches the age of 21.]²

Amendment
1   Repealed by the Social Services and Well-being (Wales) Act 2014 (Consequential Amendments) Regulations 2016, SI 2016/413, regs 55, 77.
2   Inserted by the Children and Families Act 2014, s 98(1), (2).

[23CZB England: further advice and support

(1) This section applies to a former relevant child if—

 (a) he or she has reached the age of 21 but not the age of 25, and
 (b) a local authority in England had duties towards him or her under section 23C (whether or not some of those duties continue to subsist by virtue of subsection (7) of that section).

(2) If the former relevant child informs the local authority that he or she wishes to receive advice and support under this section, the local authority has the duties provided for in subsections (3) to (6).

(3) The local authority must provide the former relevant child with a personal adviser until the former relevant child—

 (a) reaches the age of 25, or
 (b) if earlier, informs the local authority that he or she no longer wants a personal adviser.

(4) The local authority must—

 (a) carry out an assessment in relation to the former relevant child under subsection (5), and
 (b) prepare a pathway plan for the former relevant child.

(5) An assessment under this subsection is an assessment of the needs of the former relevant child with a view to determining—

 (a) whether any services offered by the local authority (under this Act or otherwise) may assist in meeting his or her needs, and
 (b) if so, what advice and support it would be appropriate for the local authority to provide for the purpose of helping the former relevant child to obtain those services.

(6) The local authority must provide the former relevant child with advice and support that it would be appropriate to provide as mentioned in subsection (5)(b).

(7) Where a former relevant child to whom this section applies is not receiving advice and support under this section, the local authority must offer such advice and support—

 (a) as soon as possible after he or she reaches the age of 21, and
 (b) at least once in every 12 months.

(8) In this section 'former relevant child' has the meaning given by section 23C(1).][1]

Amendment
1   Inserted by the Children and Social Work Act 2017, s 3(1), (2).

[23CA Further assistance to pursue education or training

(1) This section applies to a person if—

(a) he is under the age of twenty-five or of such lesser age as may be prescribed by the [Secretary of State]¹;
(b) he is a former relevant child (within the meaning of section 23C) towards whom the duties imposed by subsections (2), (3) and (4) of that section no longer subsist; and
(c) he has informed the responsible local authority that he is pursuing, or wishes to pursue, a programme of education or training.

[(2) It is the duty of the responsible local authority to provide a personal adviser for a person to whom this section applies.]²

(3) It is the duty of the responsible local authority—

(a) to carry out an assessment of the needs of a person to whom this section applies with a view to determining what assistance (if any) it would be appropriate for them to provide to him under this section; and
(b) to prepare a pathway plan for him.

(4) It is the duty of the responsible local authority to give assistance of a kind referred to subsection (5) to a person to whom this section applies to the extent that his educational or training needs require it.

(5) The kinds of assistance are—

(a) contributing to expenses incurred by him in living near the place where he is, or will be, receiving education or training; or
(b) making a grant to enable him to meet expenses connected with his education and training.

(6) If a person to whom this section applies pursues a programme of education or training in accordance with the pathway plan prepared for him, the duties of the local authority under this section (and under any provision applicable to the pathway plan prepared under this section for that person) subsist for as long as he continues to pursue that programme.

(7) For the purposes of subsection (6), the local authority may disregard any interruption in the person's pursuance of a programme of education or training if they are satisfied that he will resume it as soon as is reasonably practicable.

(8) Subsections (7) to (9) of section 17 apply to assistance given to a person under this section as they apply to assistance given to or in respect of a child under that section, but with the omission in subsection (8) of the words 'and of each of his parents'.

(9) Subsection (5) of section 24B applies to a person to whom this section applies as it applies to a person to whom subsection (3) of that section applies.

(10) Nothing in this section affects the duty imposed by subsection (5A) of section 23C to the extent that it subsists in relation to a person to whom this section applies; but the duty to make a payment under that subsection may be taken into account in the assessment of the person's needs under subsection (3)(a).

(11) In this section 'the responsible local authority' means, in relation to a person to whom this section applies, the local authority which had the duties provided for in section 23C towards him.][3]

Amendments
1. Substituted by the Social Services and Well-being (Wales) Act 2014 (Consequential Amendments) Regulations 2016, SI 2016/413, regs 55, 78.
2. Substituted by the Children and Social Work Act 2017, s 3(1), (3).
3. Inserted by the Children and Young Persons Act 2008, s 22(2).

[Personal advisers and pathway plans

23D Personal advisers.

(1) The [Secretary of State][1] may by regulations require local authorities to appoint a personal adviser for children or young persons of a prescribed description who have reached the age of sixteen but not the age of [twenty-five][2] who are not—

(a) children who are relevant children for the purposes of section 23A;
(b) the young persons referred to in section 23C; or
(c) the children referred to in paragraph 19C of Schedule 2[; or][3]
[(d) persons to whom section 23CA applies.][3]

(2) Personal advisers appointed under or by virtue of this Part shall (in addition to any other functions) have such functions as the [Secretary of State][1] prescribes.

[(3) Where a local authority in England ceases to be under a duty to provide a personal adviser for a person under any provision of this Part, that does not affect any other duty under this Part to provide a personal adviser for the person.

(4) Where a local authority in England has more than one duty under this Part to provide a personal adviser for a person, each duty is discharged by the provision of the same personal adviser (the local authority are not required to provide more than one personal adviser for the person).][4][5]

Amendments
1. Substituted by the Social Services and Well-being (Wales) Act 2014 (Consequential Amendments) Regulations 2016, SI 2016/413, regs 55, 79.
2. Substituted by the Children and Young Persons Act 2008, s 23(1)(a).
3. Inserted by the Children and Young Persons Act 2008, s 23(1)(b).
4. Inserted by the Children and Social Work Act 2017, s 3(1), (4).
5. Inserted by the Children (Leaving Care) Act 2000, s 3.

[23E Pathway plans.

(1) In this Part, a reference to a 'pathway plan' is to a plan setting out—

(a) in the case of a plan prepared under paragraph 19B of Schedule 2—
  (i) the advice, assistance and support which the local authority intend to provide a child under this Part, both while they are looking after him and later; and
  (ii) when they might cease to look after him;

[(aa) in the case of a plan prepared under section 23CZB, the advice and support that the local authority intend to provide;]¹ and

(b) in the case of a plan prepared under section 23B [or 23CA]², the advice, assistance and support which the local authority intend to provide under this Part,

and dealing with such other matters (if any) as may be prescribed [in regulations made by the Secretary of State]³.

[(1ZA) A local authority may carry out an assessment under section 23CZB(5) of a person's needs at the same time as any assessment of the person's needs is made under section 23CA(3).]¹

[(1A) A local authority may carry out an assessment under section 23B(3)[, 23CZB(5)]¹ or 23CA(3) of a person's needs at the same time as any assessment of his needs is made under—

(a) the Chronically Sick and Disabled Persons Act 1970;
(b) Part 4 of the Education Act 1996 [or Part 3 of the Children and Families Act 2014]⁴ (in the case of an assessment under section 23B(3));
(c) the Disabled Persons (Services, Consultation and Representation) Act 1986; or
(d) any other enactment.

(1B) The [Secretary of State]⁵ may by regulations make provision as to assessments for the purposes of section 23B(3)[, 23CZB(5)]¹ or 23CA.

(1C) Regulations under subsection (1B) may in particular make provision about—

(a) who is to be consulted in relation to an assessment;
(b) the way in which an assessment is to be carried out, by whom and when;
(c) the recording of the results of an assessment;
(d) the considerations to which a local authority are to have regard in carrying out an assessment.

(1D) A local authority shall keep each pathway plan prepared by them under section 23B[, 23CZB]¹ or 23CA under review.]²

(2) The [Secretary of State]⁵ may by regulations make provision about pathway plans and their review.]⁶

Amendments
1 Inserted by the Children and Social Work Act 2017, s 3(1), (5)–(10).
2 Inserted by the Children and Young Persons Act 2008, s 22(3)–(5).
3 Inserted by the Social Services and Well-being (Wales) Act 2014 (Consequential Amendments) Regulations 2016, SI 2016/413, regs 55, 80(a).
4 inserted by the Children and Families Act 2014, s 82, Sch 3, para 65(1), (2).
5 Substituted by the Social Services and Well-being (Wales) Act 2014 (Consequential Amendments) Regulations 2016, SI 2016/413, regs 55, 80(b), (c).
6 Inserted by the Children (Leaving Care) Act 2000, s 3.

[24 Persons qualifying for advice and assistance.

[(1) In this Part 'a person qualifying for advice and assistance' means a person to whom subsection (1A) or (1B) applies.

(1A) This subsection applies to a person—

(a) who has reached the age of sixteen but not the age of twenty-one;
(b) with respect to whom a special guardianship order is in force (or, if he has reached the age of eighteen, was in force when he reached that age); and
(c) who was, immediately before the making of that order, looked after by a local authority.

(1B) This subsection applies to a person to whom subsection (1A) does not apply, and who—

(a) is under twenty-one; and
(b) at any time after reaching the age of sixteen but while still a child was, but is no longer, looked after, accommodated or fostered.]¹

(2) In [subsection (1B)(b)]², 'looked after, accommodated or fostered' means—

(a) looked after by a local authority [(without subsequently being looked after by a local authority in Wales)]³;
(b) accommodated by or on behalf of a voluntary organisation;
(c) accommodated in a private children's home;
(d) accommodated for a consecutive period of at least three months—
   (i) by any [Local Health Board]³, Special Health Authority [...⁴ or by a local authority in the exercise of education functions]⁵, or
   (ii) in any care home or independent hospital or in any accommodation provided [pursuant to arrangements made by the Secretary of State, the National Health Service Commissioning Board or a clinical commissioning group under the National Health Service Act 2006 or]⁶ by a National Health Service trust [or an NHS foundation trust]⁷[, or by a local authority in Wales in the exercise of education functions]²; or
(e) privately fostered.

(3) Subsection (2)(d) applies even if the period of three months mentioned there began before the child reached the age of sixteen.

(4) In the case of a person qualifying for advice and assistance by virtue of subsection (2)(a), it is the duty of the local authority which last looked after him to take such steps as they think appropriate to contact him at such times as they think appropriate with a view to discharging their functions under sections 24A and 24B.

(5) In each of sections 24A and 24B, the local authority under the duty or having the power mentioned there ('the relevant authority') is—

[(za) in the case of a person to whom subsection (1A) applies, a local authority determined in accordance with regulations made by the [Secretary of State]⁸;]⁹

(a) in the case of a person qualifying for advice and assistance by virtue of subsection (2)(a), the local authority which last looked after him; or

(b) in the case of any other person qualifying for advice and assistance, the local authority within whose area the person is (if he has asked for help of a kind which can be given under section 24A or 24B).][10]

Amendments
1 Substituted by the Adoption and Children Act 2002, s 139(1), Sch 3, paras 54, 60(a), (b).
2 Inserted by the Social Services and Well-being (Wales) Act 2014 (Consequential Amendments) Regulations 2016, SI 2016/413, regs 55, 81(a), (b).
3 Substituted by the References to Health Authorities Order 2007, SI 2007/961, art 3, Schedule, para 20(1), (2)(b).
4 Repealed by the Health and Social Care Act 2012, s 55(2), Sch 5, paras 47, 49(a).
5 Substituted by the Local Education Authorities and Children's Services Authorities (Integration of Functions) Order 2010, SI 2010/1158, art 5(1), Sch 2, para 37(1), (2).
6 Inserted by the Health and Social Care Act 2012, s 55(2), Sch 5, paras 47, 49(b).
7 Inserted by the Health and Social Care (Community Health and Standards) Act 2003, s 34, Sch 4, paras 75, 76.
8 Substituted by the Social Services and Well-being (Wales) Act 2014 (Consequential Amendments) Regulations 2016, SI 2016/413, regs 55, 81(c).
9 Inserted by the Adoption and Children Act 2002, s 139(1), Sch 3, paras 54, 60(c).
10 Substituted by the Children (Leaving Care) Act 2000, s 4(1).

[24A Advice and assistance.

(1) The relevant authority shall consider whether the conditions in subsection (2) are satisfied in relation to a person qualifying for advice and assistance.

(2) The conditions are that—

(a) he needs help of a kind which they can give under this section or section 24B; and

(b) in the case of a person [to whom section 24(1A) applies, or to whom section 24(1B) applies and][1] who was not being looked after by any local authority [or local authority in Wales][2], they are satisfied that the person by whom he was being looked after does not have the necessary facilities for advising or befriending him.

(3) If the conditions are satisfied—

(a) they shall advise and befriend him if [he is a person to whom section 24(1A) applies, or he is a person to whom section 24(1B) applies and][1] he was being looked after by a local authority [(without subsequently being looked after by a local authority in Wales),][2] or was accommodated by or on behalf of a voluntary organisation; and

(b) in any other case they may do so.

(4) Where as a result of this section a local authority are under a duty, or are empowered, to advise and befriend a person, they may also give him assistance.

(5) The assistance may be in kind [and, in exceptional circumstances, assistance may be given—][3]

[(a) by providing accommodation, if in the circumstances assistance may not be given in respect of the accommodation under section 24B, or

(b) in cash.][3]

(6) Subsections (7) to (9) of section 17 apply in relation to assistance given under this section or section 24B as they apply in relation to assistance given under that section.][4]

Amendments
1   Inserted by the Adoption and Children Act 2002, s 139(1), Sch 3, paras 54, 61.
2   Inserted by the Social Services and Well-being (Wales) Act 2014 (Consequential Amendments) Regulations 2016, SI 2016/413, regs 55, 82.
3   Substituted by the Adoption and Children Act 2002, s 116(3).
4   Substituted by the Children (Leaving Care) Act 2000, s 4(1).

[24B Employment, education and training.

(1) The relevant local authority may give assistance to any person who qualifies for advice and assistance by virtue of [section 24(1A) or][1] section 24(2)(a) by contributing to expenses incurred by him in living near the place where he is, or will be, employed or seeking employment.

(2) The relevant local authority may give assistance to a person to whom subsection (3) applies by—

(a)   contributing to expenses incurred by the person in question in living near the place where he is, or will be, receiving education or training; or
(b)   making a grant to enable him to meet expenses connected with his education or training.

(3) This subsection applies to any person who—

(a)   is under [twenty-five][2]; and
(b)   qualifies for advice and assistance by virtue of [section 24(1A) or][1] section 24(2)(a), or would have done so if he were under twenty-one.

(4) Where a local authority are assisting a person under subsection (2) they may disregard any interruption in his attendance on the course if he resumes it as soon as is reasonably practicable.

(5) Where the local authority are satisfied that a person to whom subsection (3) applies who is in full-time further or higher education needs accommodation during a vacation because his term-time accommodation is not available to him then, they shall give him assistance by—

(a)   providing him with suitable accommodation during the vacation; or
(b)   paying him enough to enable him to secure such accommodation himself.

(6) The [Secretary of State][3] may prescribe the meaning of 'full-time', 'further education', 'higher education' and 'vacation' for the purposes of subsection (5).][4]

Amendments
1   Inserted by the Adoption and Children Act 2002, s 139(1), Sch 3, paras 54, 62.
2   Substituted by the Children and Young Persons Act 2008, s 23(2).
3   Substituted by the Social Services and Well-being (Wales) Act 2014 (Consequential Amendments) Regulations 2016, SI 2016/413, regs 55, 83.
4   Substituted by the Children (Leaving Care) Act 2000, s 4(1).

[24C Information.

(1) Where it appears to a local authority that a person—
- (a) with whom they are under a duty to keep in touch under section 23B, 23C or 24; or
- (b) whom they have been advising and befriending under section 24A; or
- (c) to whom they have been giving assistance under section 24B,

proposes to live, or is living, in the area of another local authority[, or in the area of a local authority in Wales]¹, they must inform that other authority.

[(2) Where a child who is accommodated in England—
- (a) by a voluntary organisation or in a private children's home;
- (b) by or on behalf of any Local Health Board or Special Health Authority;
- (c) by or on behalf of a clinical commissioning group or the National Health Service Commissioning Board;
- (d) by or on behalf of a local authority in the exercise of education functions;
- (e) by or on behalf of a local authority in Wales in the exercise of education functions;
- (f) in any care home or independent hospital; or
- (g) in any accommodation provided by or on behalf of a National Health Service trust or by or on behalf of an NHS Foundation Trust,

ceases to be so accommodated after reaching the age of 16, the person by whom or on whose behalf the child was accommodated or who carries on or manages the home or hospital (as the case may be) must inform the local authority or local authority in Wales within whose area the child proposes to live.]²

(3) Subsection (2) only applies, by virtue of [any of paragraphs (b) to (g)]², if the accommodation has been provided for a consecutive period of at least three months.

[(4) In a case where a child was accommodated by or on behalf of a local authority, or a local authority in Wales, in the exercise of education functions, subsection (2) applies only if the authority who accommodated the child is different from the authority within whose area the child proposes to live.]²]³

Amendments
1. Inserted by the Social Services and Well-being (Wales) Act 2014 (Consequential Amendments) Regulations 2016, SI 2016/413, regs 55, 84(a).
2. Substituted by the Social Services and Well-being (Wales) Act 2014 (Consequential Amendments) Regulations 2016, SI 2016/413, regs 55, 84(b)–(d).
3. Substituted by the Children (Leaving Care) Act 2000, s 4(1).

[24D Representations: sections 23A to 24B.

(1) Every local authority shall establish a procedure for considering representations (including complaints) made to them by—
- (a) a relevant child for the purposes of section 23A or a young person falling within section 23C;
- (b) a person qualifying for advice and assistance; or
- (c) a person falling within section 24B(2),

about the discharge of their functions under this Part in relation to him.

[(1A) Regulations may be made by the [Secretary of State]¹ imposing time limits on the making of representations under subsection (1).]²

(2) In considering representations under subsection (1), a local authority shall comply with regulations (if any) made by the [Secretary of State]¹ for the purposes of this subsection.]³

Amendments
1 Substituted by the Social Services and Well-being (Wales) Act 2014 (Consequential Amendments) Regulations 2016, SI 2016/413, regs 55, 85.
2 Inserted by the Adoption and Children Act 2002, s 117(1).
3 Inserted by the Children (Leaving Care) Act 2000, s 5.

Secure accommodation

25 Use of accommodation for restricting liberty.

(1) Subject to the following provisions of this section, a child who is being looked after by a local authority [[in England or Wales]¹]² may not be placed, and, if placed, may not be kept, in accommodation [in England]² [or Scotland]³ provided for the purpose of restricting liberty ('secure accommodation') unless it appears—

   (a) that—
        (i)   he has a history of absconding and is likely to abscond from any other description of accommodation; and
        (ii) if he absconds, he is likely to suffer significant harm; or
   (b) that if he is kept in any other description of accommodation he is likely to injure himself or other persons.

(2) The [Secretary of State]⁴ may by regulations—

   (a) specify a maximum period—
        (i)   beyond which a child may not be kept in secure accommodation [in England]² [or Scotland]³ without the authority of the court; and
        (ii) for which the court may authorise a child to be kept in secure accommodation [in England]² [or Scotland]³;
   (b) empower the court from time to time to authorise a child to be kept in secure accommodation [in England]² [or Scotland]³ for such further period as the regulations may specify; and
   (c) provide that applications to the court under this section shall be made only by local authorities [[in England or Wales]¹]².

(3) It shall be the duty of a court hearing an application under this section to determine whether any relevant criteria for keeping a child in secure accommodation are satisfied in his case.

(4) If a court determines that any such criteria are satisfied, it shall make an order authorising the child to be kept in secure accommodation and specifying the maximum period for which he may be so kept.

(5) On any adjournment of the hearing of an application under this section, a court may make an interim order permitting the child to be kept during the period of the adjournment in secure accommodation.

[(5A) Where a local authority in England or Wales are authorised under this section to keep a child in secure accommodation in Scotland, the person in charge of the accommodation may restrict the child's liberty to the extent that the person considers appropriate, having regard to the terms of any order made by a court under this section.]³

(6) No court shall exercise the powers conferred by this section in respect of a child who is not legally represented in that court unless, having been informed of his right to apply for [the provision of representation under Part 1 of the Legal Aid, Sentencing and Punishment of Offenders Act 2012]⁵ and having had the opportunity to do so, he refused or failed to apply.

(7) The [Secretary of State]⁴ may by regulations provide that—

(a) this section shall or shall not apply to any description of children specified in the regulations;
(b) this section shall have effect in relation to children of a description specified in the regulations subject to such modifications as may be so specified;
(c) such other provisions as may be so specified shall have effect for the purpose of determining whether a child of a description specified in the regulations may be placed or kept in secure accommodation [in England]² [or Scotland]³;
[(d) a child may only be placed in secure accommodation that is of a description specified in the regulations (and the description may in particular be framed by reference to whether the accommodation, or the person providing it, has been approved by the Secretary of State or the Scottish Ministers).]³

(8) The giving of an authorisation under this section shall not prejudice any power of any court in England and Wales or Scotland to give directions relating to the child to whom the authorisation relates.

[(8A) Sections 168 and 169(1) to (4) of the Children's Hearings (Scotland) Act 2011 (asp 1) (enforcement and absconding) apply in relation to an order under subsection (4) above as they apply in relation to the orders mentioned in section 168(3) or 169(1)(a) of that Act.]³

(9) This section is subject to section 20(8).

Amendments
1 Substituted by the Children and Social Work Act 2017, s 10, Sch 1, paras 1, 2(1), (2)(a), (3)(b).
2 Inserted by the Social Services and Well-being (Wales) Act 2014 (Consequential Amendments) Regulations 2016, SI 2016/413, regs 55, 86(a), (c), (d), (f).
3 Inserted by the Children and Social Work Act 2017, s 10, Sch 1, paras 1, 2(1), (2)(b), (3)(a), (4)–(6).
4 Substituted by the Social Services and Well-being (Wales) Act 2014 (Consequential Amendments) Regulations 2016, SI 2016/413, regs 55, 86(b), (e).
5 Substituted by the Legal Aid, Sentencing and Punishment of Offenders Act 2012, s 39(1), Sch 5, para 38.

[Independent reviewing officers

25A Appointment of independent reviewing officer

(1) If a local authority are looking after a child, they must appoint an individual as the independent reviewing officer for that child's case.

(2) The initial appointment under subsection (1) must be made before the child's case is first reviewed in accordance with regulations made under section 26.

(3) If a vacancy arises in respect of a child's case, the local authority must make another appointment under subsection (1) as soon as is practicable.

(4) An appointee must be of a description prescribed in regulations made by the [Secretary of State]¹.]²

Amendments
1   Substituted by the Social Services and Well-being (Wales) Act 2014 (Consequential Amendments) Regulations 2016, SI 2016/413, regs 55, 87.
2   Inserted by the Children and Young Persons Act 2008, s 10(1).

[25B Functions of the independent reviewing officer

(1) The independent reviewing officer must—

(a)   monitor the performance by the local authority of their functions in relation to the child's case;
(b)   participate, in accordance with regulations made by the [Secretary of State]², in any review of the child's case;
(c)   ensure that any ascertained wishes and feelings of the child concerning the case are given due consideration by the local authority;
(d)   perform any other function which is prescribed in regulations made by the [Secretary of State]¹.

(2) An independent reviewing officer's functions must be performed—

(a)   in such manner (if any) as may be prescribed in regulations made by the [Secretary of State]¹; and
(b)   having regard to such guidance as that authority may issue in relation to the discharge of those functions.

(3) If the independent reviewing officer considers it appropriate to do so, the child's case may be referred by that officer to—

(a)   an officer of the Children and Family Court Advisory and Support Service; …²
(b)   …².

(4) If the independent reviewing officer is not an officer of the local authority, it is the duty of the authority—

(a)   to co-operate with that individual; and
(b)   to take all such reasonable steps as that individual may require of them to enable that individual's functions under this section to be performed satisfactorily.]³

Amendments
1   Substituted by the Social Services and Well-being (Wales) Act 2014 (Consequential Amendments) Regulations 2016, SI 2016/413, regs 55, 88(a).
2   Repealed by the Social Services and Well-being (Wales) Act 2014 (Consequential Amendments) Regulations 2016, SI 2016/413, regs 55, 88(b).
3   Inserted by the Children and Young Persons Act 2008, s 10(1).

[25C Referred cases

(1) In relation to children whose cases are referred to officers under section 25B(3), the Lord Chancellor may by regulations—

(a) extend any functions of the officers in respect of family proceedings (within the meaning of section 12 of the Criminal Justice and Court Services Act 2000) to other proceedings;

(b) require any functions of the officers to be performed in the manner prescribed by the regulations.

(2) ...¹]²

Amendments
1   Repealed by the Social Services and Well-being (Wales) Act 2014 (Consequential Amendments) Regulations 2016, SI 2016/413, regs 55, 89.
2   Inserted by the Children and Young Persons Act 2008, s 10(2).

Supplemental

26 Review of cases and inquiries into representations.

(1) The [Secretary of State]¹ may make regulations requiring the case of each child who is being looked after by a local authority to be reviewed in accordance with the provisions of the regulations.

(2) The regulations may, in particular, make provision—

(a) as to the manner in which each case is to be reviewed;
(b) as to the considerations to which the local authority are to have regard in reviewing each case;
(c) as to the time when each case is first to be reviewed and the frequency of subsequent reviews;
(d) requiring the authority, before conducting any review, to seek the views of—
   (i) the child;
   (ii) his parents;
   (iii) any person who is not a parent of his but who has parental responsibility for him; and
   (iv) any other person whose views the authority consider to be relevant,
   including, in particular, the views of those persons in relation to any particular matter which is to be considered in the course of the review;
(e) requiring the authority ...², in the case of a child who is in their care[—]³

[(i) to keep the section 31A plan for the child under review and, if they are of the opinion that some change is required, to revise the plan, or make a new plan, accordingly,
(ii) to consider]³,
whether an application should be made to discharge the care order;
(f) requiring the authority ...², in the case of a child in accommodation provided by the authority[—]³
 [(i) if there is no plan for the future care of the child, to prepare one,
 (ii) if there is such a plan for the child, to keep it under review and, if they are of the opinion that some change is required, to revise the plan or make a new plan, accordingly,
 (iii) to consider]³,
whether the accommodation accords with the requirements of this Part;
(g) requiring the authority to inform the child, so far as is reasonably practicable, of any steps he may take under this Act;
(h) requiring the authority to make arrangements, including arrangements with such other bodies providing services as it considers appropriate, to implement any decision which they propose to make in the course, or as a result, of the review;
(i) requiring the authority to notify details of the result of the review and of any decision taken by them in consequence of the review to—
 (i) the child;
 (ii) his parents;
 (iii) any person who is not a parent of his but who has parental responsibility for him; and
 (iv) any other person whom they consider ought to be notified;
(j) requiring the authority to monitor the arrangements which they have made with a view to ensuring that they comply with the regulations;
[(k) ...⁴]³

[(2A) ...⁴

(2B) ...⁴

(2C) ...⁴]³

[(2D) ...⁴]⁵

(3) Every local authority shall establish a procedure for considering any representations (including any complaint) made to them by—

(a) any child who is being looked after by them or who is not being looked after by them but is in need;
(b) a parent of his;
(c) any person who is not a parent of his but who has parental responsibility for him;
(d) any local authority foster parent;
(e) such other person as the authority consider has a sufficient interest in the child's welfare to warrant his representations being considered by them,

about the discharge by the authority of any of their [qualifying functions]⁶ in relation to the child.

[(3A) The following are qualifying functions for the purposes of subsection (3)—

(a) functions under this Part,
(b) such functions under Part 4 or 5 as are specified by the [Secretary of State]¹ in regulations.

(3B) The duty under subsection (3) extends to representations (including complaints) made to the authority by—

(a) any person mentioned in section 3(1) of the Adoption and Children Act 2002 (persons for whose needs provision is made by the Adoption Service) and any other person to whom arrangements for the provision of adoption support services (within the meaning of that Act) extend,
(b) such other person as the authority consider has sufficient interest in a child who is or may be adopted to warrant his representations being considered by them,

about the discharge by the authority of such functions under the Adoption and Children Act 2002 as are specified by the [Secretary of State]¹ in regulations.]⁷

[(3C) The duty under subsection (3) extends to any representations (including complaints) which are made to the authority by–

(a) a child with respect to whom a special guardianship order is in force,
(b) a special guardian or a parent of such a child,
(c) any other person the authority consider has a sufficient interest in the welfare of such a child to warrant his representations being considered by them, or
(d) any person who has applied for an assessment under section 14F(3) or (4),

about the discharge by the authority of such functions under section 14F as may be specified by the [Secretary of State]¹ in regulations.]⁸

(4) The procedure shall ensure that at least one person who is not a member or officer of the authority takes part in—

(a) the consideration; and
(b) any discussions which are held by the authority about the action (if any) to be taken in relation to the child in the light of the consideration,

[but this subsection is subject to subsection (5A).]⁷

[(4A) Regulations may be made by the [Secretary of State]¹ imposing time limits on the making of representations under this section.]⁷

(5) In carrying out any consideration of representations under this section a local authority shall comply with any regulations made by the [Secretary of State]¹ for the purpose of regulating the procedure to be followed.

[(5A) Regulations under subsection (5) may provide that subsection (4) does not apply in relation to any consideration or discussion which takes place as part of a procedure for which provision is made by the regulations for the purpose of resolving informally the matters raised in the representations.]⁷

(6) The [Secretary of State][1] may make regulations requiring local authorities to monitor the arrangements that they have made with a view to ensuring that they comply with any regulations made for the purposes of subsection (5).

(7) Where any representation has been considered under the procedure established by a local authority under this section, the authority shall—

(a) have due regard to the findings of those considering the representation; and
(b) take such steps as are reasonably practicable to notify (in writing)—
  (i) the person making the representation;
  (ii) the child (if the authority consider that he has sufficient understanding); and
  (iii) such other persons (if any) as appear to the authority to be likely to be affected,
of the authority's decision in the matter and their reasons for taking that decision and of any action which they have taken, or propose to take.

(8) Every local authority shall give such publicity to their procedure for considering representations under this section as they consider appropriate.

Amendments
1 Substituted by the Social Services and Well-being (Wales) Act 2014 (Consequential Amendments) Regulations 2016, SI 2016/413, regs 55, 90.
2 Repealed by the Adoption and Children Act 2002, ss 118(1)(a), (b), 139(3), Sch 5.
3 Inserted by the Adoption and Children Act 2002, s 118.
4 Repealed by the Children and Young Persons Act 2008, s 42, Sch 4.
5 Inserted by the Children Act 2004, s 40, Sch 3, paras 5, 8(1), (3)
6 Substituted by the Adoption and Children Act 2002, s 117(2), (3).
7 Inserted by the Adoption and Children Act 2002, s 117(2), (4)–(7).
8 Inserted by the Health and Social Care (Community Health and Standards) Act 2003, s 117(1).

[26ZA ...[1]

...[1]][2]

Amendments
1 Repealed by the Education and Inspections Act 2006, s 184, Sch 18, Pt 5.
2 Inserted by the Health and Social Care (Community Health and Standards) Act 2003, s 116(1).

[26ZB ...[1]

...[1]][2]

Amendments
1 Repealed by the Social Services and Well-being (Wales) Act 2014 (Consequential Amendments) Regulations 2016, SI 2016/413, regs 55, 91.
2 Inserted by the Health and Social Care (Community Health and Standards) Act 2003, s 116(2).

[26A Advocacy services

(1) Every local authority shall make arrangements for the provision of assistance to—

(a) persons who make or intend to make representations under section 24D; and
(b) children who make or intend to make representations under section 26.

(2) The assistance provided under the arrangements shall include assistance by way of representation.

[(2A) ...¹]²

(3) The arrangements—

(a) shall secure that a person may not provide assistance if he is a person who is prevented from doing so by regulations made by the [Secretary of State]³; and

(b) shall comply with any other provision made by the regulations in relation to the arrangements.

(4) The [Secretary of State]³ may make regulations requiring local authorities to monitor the steps that they have taken with a view to ensuring that they comply with regulations made for the purposes of subsection (3).

(5) Every local authority shall give such publicity to their arrangements for the provision of assistance under this section as they consider appropriate.]⁴

Amendments
1 Repealed by the Social Services and Well-being (Wales) Act 2014 (Consequential Amendments) Regulations 2016, SI 2016/413, regs 55, 92(a).
2 Inserted by the Health and Social Care (Community Health and Standards) Act 2003, s 116(3).
3 Substituted by the Social Services and Well-being (Wales) Act 2014 (Consequential Amendments) Regulations 2016, SI 2016/413, regs 55, 92(b).
4 Inserted by the Adoption and Children Act 2002, s 119.

27 Co-operation between authorities.

(1) Where it appears to a local authority that any authority ...¹ mentioned in subsection (3) could, by taking any specified action, help in the exercise of any of their functions under this Part, they may request the help of that other authority ...¹, specifying the action in question.

(2) An authority whose help is so requested shall comply with the request if it is compatible with their own statutory or other duties and obligations and does not unduly prejudice the discharge of any of their functions.

(3) The [authorities]² are—

(a) any local authority;
(b) ...³
(c) any local housing authority;
[(ca) the National Health Service Commissioning Board;]⁴
(d) any [clinical commissioning group,]⁴ [[Local Health Board]⁵, Special Health Authority]⁶ ...⁷[, National Health Service trust or NHS foundation trust]⁸;
[(da) any local authority in Wales,]⁹ and
(e) any person authorised by the [Secretary of State]¹⁰ for the purposes of this section.

[(3A) The Secretary of State must not authorise the Welsh Ministers under subsection (3)(e) without their consent.]⁹

(4) ...¹¹

Amendments
1 Repealed by the Courts and Legal Services Act 1990, ss 116(1), 125(7), Sch 16, para 14(a), Sch 20.
2 Substituted by the Courts and Legal Services Act 1990, s 116(1), Sch 16, para 14(b).
3 Repealed by the Local Education Authorities and Children's Services Authorities (Integration of Functions) Order 2010, SI 2010/1158, art 5(2), Sch 3, Pt 2.
4 Inserted by the Health and Social Care Act 2012, s 55(2), Sch 5, paras 47, 51(a), (b)(i).
5 Substituted by the References to Health Authorities Order 2007, SI 2007/961, art 3, Schedule, para 20(1), (2)(d).
6 Substituted by the Health Authorities Act 1995, s 2(1), Sch 1, para 118(1), (5).
7 Repealed by the Health and Social Care Act 2012, s 55(2), Sch 5, paras 47, 51(b)(ii).
8 Substituted by the Health and Social Care (Community Health and Standards) Act 2003, s 34, Sch 4, paras 75, 78.
9 Inserted by the Social Services and Well-being (Wales) Act 2014 (Consequential Amendments) Regulations 2016, SI 2016/413, regs 55, 93(a), (c).
10 Substituted by the Social Services and Well-being (Wales) Act 2014 (Consequential Amendments) Regulations 2016, SI 2016/413, regs 55, 93(b).
11 Repealed by the Education Act 1993, s 307(1), (3), Sch 19, para 147, Sch 21, Pt II.

28 ...¹

...¹

Amendment
1 Repealed by the Local Education Authorities and Children's Services Authorities (Integration of Functions) Order 2010, SI 2010/1158, art 5(2), Sch 3, Pt 2.

29 Recoupment of cost of providing services etc.

(1) Where a local authority provide any service under section 17 or 18, other than advice, guidance or counselling, they may recover from a person specified in subsection (4) such charge for the service as they consider reasonable.

(2) Where the authority are satisfied that that person's means are insufficient for it to be reasonably practicable for him to pay the charge, they shall not require him to pay more than he can reasonably be expected to pay.

(3) No person shall be liable to pay any charge under subsection (1) [for a service provided under section 17 or section 18(1) or (5)]¹ at any time when he is in receipt [of universal credit (except in such circumstances as may be prescribed),]² of income support or [under]³ [Part VII of the Social Security Contributions and Benefits Act 1992]⁴[, of any element of child tax credit other than the family element, of working tax credit]⁵[, of an income-based jobseeker's allowance or of an income-related employment and support allowance]⁶.

[(3A) No person shall be liable to pay any charge under subsection (1) for a service provided under section 18(2) or (6) at any time when he is in receipt [of universal credit (except in such circumstances as may be prescribed),]² of income support under Part VII of the Social Security Contributions and Benefits Act 1992[, of an income-based jobseeker's allowance or of an income-related employment and support allowance]⁶.]¹

[(3B) No person shall be liable to pay any charge under subsection (1) for a service provided under section 18(2) or (6) at any time when—

(a) he is in receipt of guarantee state pension credit under section 1(3)(a) of the State Pension Credit Act 2002, or

(b) he is a member of a [couple]⁸ (within the meaning of that Act) the other member of which is in receipt of guarantee state pension credit.]⁷

(4) The persons are—

(a) where the service is provided for a child under sixteen, each of his parents;

(b) where it is provided for a child who has reached the age of sixteen, the child himself; and

(c) where it is provided for a member of the child's family, that member.

(5) Any charge under subsection (1) may, without prejudice to any other method of recovery, be recovered summarily as a civil debt.

(6) Part III of Schedule 2 makes provision in connection with contributions towards the maintenance of children who are being looked after by local authorities and consists of the re-enactment with modifications of provisions in Part V of the Child Care Act 1980.

(7) Where a local authority provide any accommodation under section 20(1) for a child who was (immediately before they began to look after him) ordinarily resident within the area of another local authority [or the area of a local authority in Wales]⁹, they may recover from that other authority any reasonable expenses incurred by them in providing the accommodation and maintaining him.

(8) Where a local authority provide accommodation under section 21(1) or (2) (a) or (b) for a child who is ordinarily resident within the area of another local authority [or the area of a local authority in Wales]⁹ and they are not maintaining him in—

(a) a community home provided by them;

(b) a controlled community home; or

(c) a hospital vested in the [Secretary of State or]¹⁰ [the Welsh Ministers]¹¹ ...¹² [or any other hospital made available pursuant to arrangements made by [the Secretary of State, the National Health Service Commissioning Board or a clinical commissioning group under the National Health Service Act 2006 or by]¹³ ...¹² a [Local Health Board]¹⁴]¹⁵ ...¹²,

they may recover from that other authority any reasonable expenses incurred by them in providing the accommodation and maintaining him.

(9) [Except where subsection (10) [or subsection (11)]⁹ applies, where]¹⁶ a local authority comply with any request under section 27(2) [or section 164A(2) of the Social Services and Well-being (Wales) Act 2014 (duty of other persons to co-operate and provide information)]⁹ in relation to a child or other person who is not ordinarily resident within their area, they may recover from the local authority [or a local authority in Wales]⁹ in whose area the child or person is ordinarily resident any [reasonable expenses]¹⁷ incurred by them in respect of that person.

[(10) Where a local authority ('authority A') comply with any request under section 27(2) from another local authority ('authority B') in relation to a child or other person—

(a) whose responsible authority is authority B for the purposes of section 23B or 23C; or

(b) whom authority B are advising or befriending or to whom they are giving assistance by virtue of section 24(5)(a),

authority A may recover from authority B any reasonable expenses incurred by them in respect of that person.]¹⁶

[(11) Where a local authority ('authority A') comply with any request under section 164A(2) of the Social Services and Well-being (Wales) Act 2014 (duty of other persons to co-operate and provide information) from a local authority in Wales ('authority B') in relation to a person, and authority B are the responsible local authority for that person (within the meaning of section 104(5)(b) (except for category 4 young persons) or (d) of that Act), then authority A may recover from authority B any reasonable expenses incurred by them in respect of that person.]⁹

Amendments
1 Inserted by the Local Government Act 2000, s 103.
2 Inserted by the Welfare Reform Act 2012, s 31, Sch 2, para 1(c).
3 Substituted by the Tax Credits Act 2002, s 47, Sch 3, paras 15, 18(a).
4 Substituted by the Social Security (Consequential Provisions) Act 1992, s 4, Sch 2, para 108(b).
5 Inserted by the Tax Credits Act 2002, s 47, Sch 3, paras 15, 18(b).
6 Substituted by the Welfare Reform Act 2007, s 28(1), Sch 3, para 6(1), (4).
7 Inserted by State Pension Credit Act 2002 c. 16 Sch.2(3) para.30.
8 Substituted by the Civil Partnership Act 2004 (Overseas Relationships and Consequential, etc. Amendments) Order 2005, SI 2005/3129, art 4(4), Sch 4, para 9.
9 Inserted by the Social Services and Well-being (Wales) Act 2014 (Consequential Amendments) Regulations 2016, SI 2016/413, regs 55, 94.
10 Substituted by the Health and Social Care Act 2012, s 55(2), Sch 5, paras 47, 52(a).
11 Inserted by the Children and Young Persons Act 2008, s 39, Sch 3, paras 1, 20.
12 Repealed by the Health and Social Care Act 2012, s 55(2), Sch 5, paras 47, 52(b), (d).
13 Inserted by the Health and Social Care Act 2012, s 55(2), Sch 5, paras 47, 52(c).
14 Substituted by the References to Health Authorities Order 2007, SI 2007/961, art 3, Schedule, para 20(1), (2)(e).
15 Inserted by the National Health Service and Community Care Act 1990, s 66(1), Sch 9, para 36(3)
16 Inserted by the Children (Leaving Care) Act 2000, s 7(1), (3).
17 Substituted by the Courts and Legal Services Act 1990, s 116(1), Sch 16, para 15.

30 Miscellaneous.

(1) Nothing in this Part shall affect any duty imposed on a local authority by or under any other enactment.

(2) Any question arising under section 20(2), 21(3) or 29(7) to (9) as to the ordinary residence of a child shall be determined by agreement between the local authorities concerned or, in default of agreement, by the [Secretary of State]¹ [but see subsection (2C)]².

[(2A) ...³

(2B) ...³]⁴

[(2C) Any question arising as to whether a child is ordinarily resident—

(a) in the area of a local authority under section 20(2), 21(3) or 29(7) to (9), or

(b) in the area of a local authority in Wales under section 76(2), 77(4) or (5), or 193(3) to (6) of the Social Services and Well-being (Wales) Act 2014,

shall be determined by the local authority and local authority in Wales concerned, or in default of agreement, by the Secretary of State.

(2D) The Secretary of State must consult the Welsh Ministers before making a determination under subsection (2C).][2]

(3) ...[5]

(4) The [Secretary of State][1] may make regulations for determining, as respects any [education][6] functions specified in the regulations, whether a child who is being looked after by a local authority is to be treated, for purposes so specified, as a child of parents of sufficient resources or as a child of parents without resources.

Amendments
1 Substituted by the Social Services and Well-being (Wales) Act 2014 (Consequential Amendments) Regulations 2016, SI 2016/413, regs 55, 95(a)(i), (d).
2 Inserted by the Social Services and Well-being (Wales) Act 2014 (Consequential Amendments) Regulations 2016, SI 2016/413, regs 55, 95(a)(ii), (c).
3 Repealed by the Social Services and Well-being (Wales) Act 2014 (Consequential Amendments) Regulations 2016, SI 2016/413, regs 55, 95(b).
4 Inserted by the Children and Young Persons Act 2008, s 39, Sch 3, paras 1, 21(1), (3).
5 Repealed by the Local Education Authorities and Children's Services Authorities (Integration of Functions) Order 2010, SI 2010/1158, art 5(1), (2), Sch 2, para 37(1) (6)(a), Sch 3, Pt 2.
6 Substituted by the Local Education Authorities and Children's Services Authorities (Integration of Functions) Order 2010, SI 2010/1158, art 5(1), Sch 2, para 37(1), (6)(b).

31 ...[1]

...[1]

Amendment
1 Repealed by the Social Services and Well-being (Wales) Act 2014 (Consequential Amendments) Regulations 2016, SI 2016/413, regs 55, 96.

PART IV
CARE AND SUPERVISION

General

31 Care and supervision orders.

(1) On the application of any local authority or authorised person, the court may make an order—

(a) placing the child with respect to whom the application is made in the care of a designated local authority; or
(b) putting him under the supervision of a designated local authority ...[1].

(2) A court may only make a care order or supervision order if it is satisfied—

(a) that the child concerned is suffering, or is likely to suffer, significant harm; and

(b) that the harm, or likelihood of harm, is attributable to—
  (i) the care given to the child, or likely to be given to him if the order were not made, not being what it would be reasonable to expect a parent to give to him; or
  (ii) the child's being beyond parental control.

(3) No care order or supervision order may be made with respect to a child who has reached the age of seventeen (or sixteen, in the case of a child who is married).

[(3A) A court deciding whether to make a care order—
  (a) is required to consider the permanence provisions of the section 31A plan for the child concerned, but
  (b) is not required to consider the remainder of the section 31A plan, subject to section 34(11).

[(3B) For the purposes of subsection (3A), the permanence provisions of a section 31A plan are—
  (a) such of the plan's provisions setting out the long-term plan for the upbringing of the child concerned as provide for any of the following—
    (i) the child to live with any parent of the child's or with any other member of, or any friend of, the child's family;
    (ii) adoption;
    (iii) long-term care not within sub-paragraph (i) or (ii);
  (b) such of the plan's provisions as set out any of the following—
    (i) the impact on the child concerned of any harm that he or she suffered or was likely to suffer;
    (ii) the current and future needs of the child (including needs arising out of that impact);
    (iii) the way in which the long-term plan for the upbringing of the child would meet those current and future needs.]²

(3C) The Secretary of State may by regulations amend this section for the purpose of altering what for the purposes of subsection (3A) are the permanence provisions of a section 31A plan.]³]⁴

(4) An application under this section may be made on its own or in any other family proceedings.

(5) The court may—
  (a) on an application for a care order, make a supervision order;
  (b) on an application for a supervision order, make a care order.

(6) Where an authorised person proposes to make an application under this section he shall—
  (a) if it is reasonably practicable to do so; and
  (b) before making the application,

consult the local authority appearing to him to be the authority in whose area the child concerned is ordinarily resident.

(7) An application made by an authorised person shall not be entertained by the court if, at the time when it is made, the child concerned is—

(a) the subject of an earlier application for a care order, or supervision order, which has not been disposed of; or

(b) subject to—
  (i) a care order or supervision order;
  [(ii) a youth rehabilitation order within the meaning of Part 1 of the Criminal Justice and Immigration Act 2008; or][5]
  [(iii) a compulsory supervision order or interim compulsory supervision order as defined by sections 83 and 86 of the Children's Hearings (Scotland) Act 2011.][6]

(8) The local authority designated in a care order must be—

(a) the authority within whose area the child is ordinarily resident; or
(b) where the child does not reside in the area of a local authority, the authority within whose area any circumstances arose in consequence of which the order is being made.

(9) In this section—

'authorised person' means —
  (a) the National Society for the Prevention of Cruelty to Children and any of its officers; and
  (b) any person authorised by order of the Secretary of State to bring proceedings under this section and any officer of a body which is so authorised;

'harm' means ill-treatment or the impairment of health or development [including, for example, impairment suffered from seeing or hearing the ill-treatment of another][7];

'development' means physical, intellectual, emotional, social or behavioural development;

'health' means physical or mental health; and

'ill-treatment' includes sexual abuse and forms of ill-treatment which are not physical.

(10) Where the question of whether harm suffered by a child is significant turns on the child's health or development, his health or development shall be compared with that which could reasonably be expected of a similar child.

(11) In this Act—

'a care order' means (subject to section 105(1)) an order under subsection (1)(a) and (except where express provision to the contrary is made) includes an interim care order made under section 38; and

'a supervision order' means an order under subsection (1)(b) and (except where express provision to the contrary is made) includes an interim supervision order made under section 38.

Amendments
1 Repealed by the Criminal Justice and Court Services Act 2000, s 75, Sch 8.
2 Substituted by the Children and Social Work Act 2017, s 8.
3 Substituted by the Children and Families Act 2014, s 15(1).

4 Inserted by the Adoption and Children Act 2002, s 121(1).
5 Substituted by the Criminal Justice and Immigration Act 2008, s 6(2), Sch 4, paras 33, 35.
6 Substituted by the Children's Hearings (Scotland) Act 2011 (Consequential and Transitional Provisions and Savings) Order 2013, SI 2013/1465, art 17(1), Sch 1, para 2(1), (2).
7 Inserted by the Adoption and Children Act 2002, s 120.

[31A Care orders: care plans

(1) Where an application is made on which a care order might be made with respect to a child, the appropriate local authority must, within such time as the court may direct, prepare a plan ('a care plan') for the future care of the child.

(2) While the application is pending, the authority must keep any care plan prepared by them under review and, if they are of the opinion some change is required, revise the plan, or make a new plan, accordingly.

(3) A care plan must give any prescribed information and do so in the prescribed manner.

(4) For the purposes of this section, the appropriate local authority, in relation to a child in respect of whom a care order might be made, is the local authority proposed to be designated in the order.

(5) In section 31(3A) and this section, references to a care order do not include an interim care order.

(6) A plan prepared, or treated as prepared, under this section is referred to in this Act as a 'section 31A plan'.][1]

Amendment
1 Inserted by the Adoption and Children Act 2002, s 121(2).

32 Period within which application for order under this Part must be disposed of.

(1) A court [in which an application for an order under this Part is proceeding][1] shall (in the light of any [provision in rules of court that is of the kind mentioned in subsection (2)(a) or (b))][1]—

    (a) draw up a timetable with a view to [disposing of the application—][2]
        [(i) without delay, and
        (ii) in any event within twenty-six weeks beginning with the day on which the application was issued; and][2]
    (b) give such directions as it considers appropriate for the purpose of ensuring, so far as is reasonably practicable, that that timetable is adhered to.

(2) Rules of court may—

    (a) specify periods within which specified steps must be taken in relation to such proceedings; and
    (b) make other provision with respect to such proceedings for the purpose of ensuring, so far as is reasonably practicable, that they are disposed of without delay.

[(3) A court, when drawing up a timetable under subsection (1)(a), must in particular have regard to—

(a) the impact which the timetable would have on the welfare of the child to whom the application relates; and
(b) the impact which the timetable would have on the conduct of the proceedings.

(4) A court, when revising a timetable drawn up under subsection (1)(a) or when making any decision which may give rise to a need to revise such a timetable (which does not include a decision under subsection (5)), must in particular have regard to—

(a) the impact which any revision would have on the welfare of the child to whom the application relates; and
(b) the impact which any revision would have on the duration and conduct of the proceedings.

(5) A court in which an application under this Part is proceeding may extend the period that is for the time being allowed under subsection (1)(a)(ii) in the case of the application, but may do so only if the court considers that the extension is necessary to enable the court to resolve the proceedings justly.

(6) When deciding whether to grant an extension under subsection (5), a court must in particular have regard to—

(a) the impact which any ensuing timetable revision would have on the welfare of the child to whom the application relates, and
(b) the impact which any ensuing timetable revision would have on the duration and conduct of the proceedings;

and here 'ensuing timetable revision' means any revision, of the timetable under subsection (1)(a) for the proceedings, which the court considers may ensue from the extension.

(7) When deciding whether to grant an extension under subsection (5), a court is to take account of the following guidance: extensions are not to be granted routinely and are to be seen as requiring specific justification.

(8) Each separate extension under subsection (5) is to end no more than eight weeks after the later of—

(a) the end of the period being extended; and
(b) the end of the day on which the extension is granted.

(9) The Lord Chancellor may by regulations amend subsection (1)(a)(ii), or the opening words of subsection (8), for the purpose of varying the period for the time being specified in that provision.

(10) Rules of court may provide that a court—

(a) when deciding whether to exercise the power under subsection (5), or
(b) when deciding how to exercise that power,

must, or may or may not, have regard to matters specified in the rules, or must take account of any guidance set out in the rules.]³

Amendments
1 Substituted by the Children and Families Act 2014, s 14(1), (7).
2 Substituted by the Children and Families Act 2014, s 14(1), (2).
3 Inserted by the Children and Families Act 2014, s 14(1), (3).

Care orders

33 Effect of care order.

(1) Where a care order is made with respect to a child it shall be the duty of the local authority designated by the order to receive the child into their care and to keep him in their care while the order remains in force.

(2) Where—

- (a) a care order has been made with respect to a child on the application of an authorised person; but
- (b) the local authority designated by the order was not informed that that person proposed to make the application,

the child may be kept in the care of that person until received into the care of the authority.

(3) While a care order is in force with respect to a child, the local authority designated by the order shall—

- (a) have parental responsibility for the child; and
- (b) have the power (subject to the following provisions of this section) to determine the extent to which[—]¹
  - [(i) a parent, guardian or special guardian of the child; or
  - (ii) a person who by virtue of section 4A has parental responsibility for the child,]¹

may meet his parental responsibility for him.

(4) The authority may not exercise the power in subsection (3)(b) unless they are satisfied that it is necessary to do so in order to safeguard or promote the child's welfare.

(5) Nothing in subsection (3)(b) shall prevent [a person mentioned in that provision who has care of the child]¹ from doing what is reasonable in all the circumstances of the case for the purpose of safeguarding or promoting his welfare.

(6) While a care order is in force with respect to a child, the local authority designated by the order shall not—

- (a) cause the child to be brought up in any religious persuasion other than that in which he would have been brought up if the order had not been made; or
- (b) have the right—
  - (i) …²
  - (ii) to agree or refuse to agree to the making of an adoption order, or an order under [section 84 of the Adoption and Children Act 2002]¹, with respect to the child; or
  - (iii) to appoint a guardian for the child.

(7) While a care order is in force with respect to a child, no person may—

(a) cause the child to be known by a new surname; or
(b) remove him from the United Kingdom,

without either the written consent of every person who has parental responsibility for the child or the leave of the court.

(8) Subsection (7)(b) does not—

(a) prevent the removal of such a child, for a period of less than one month, by the authority in whose care he is; or
(b) apply to arrangements for such a child to live outside England and Wales (which are governed by paragraph 19 of Schedule 2 [in England, and section 124 of the Social Services and Well-being (Wales) Act 2014 in Wales]³).

(9) The power in subsection (3)(b) is subject (in addition to being subject to the provisions of this section) to any right, duty, power, responsibility or authority which [a person mentioned in that provision]¹ has in relation to the child and his property by virtue of any other enactment.

Amendments
1 Substituted by the Adoption and Children Act 2002, s 139(1), Sch 3, paras 54, 63(a), (b), (c)(ii), (d).
2 Repealed by the Adoption and Children Act 2002, s 139(1), (3), Sch 3, paras 54, 63(c)(i), Sch 5.
3 Inserted by the Social Services and Well-being (Wales) Act 2014 (Consequential Amendments) Regulations 2016, SI 2016/413, regs 55, 97.

34 Parental contact etc. with children in care.

(1) Where a child is in the care of a local authority, the authority shall (subject to the provisions of this section [and their duty under section 22(3)(a)]¹ [or, where the local authority is in Wales, under section 78(1)(a) of the Social Services and Well-being (Wales) Act 2014]²) allow the child reasonable contact with—

(a) his parents;
(b) any guardian [or special guardian]³ of his;
[(ba) any person who by virtue of section 4A has parental responsibility for him;]³
(c) where there was a [child arrangements]⁴ order in force with respect to the child immediately before the care order was made, [any person named in the child arrangements order as a person with whom the child was to live]⁴; and
(d) where, immediately before the care order was made, a person had care of the child by virtue of an order made in the exercise of the High Court's inherent jurisdiction with respect to children, that person.

(2) On an application made by the authority or the child, the court may make such order as it considers appropriate with respect to the contact which is to be allowed between the child and any named person.

(3) On an application made by—

(a) any person mentioned in paragraphs (a) to (d) of subsection (1); or

(b) any person who has obtained the leave of the court to make the application,

the court may make such order as it considers appropriate with respect to the contact which is to be allowed between the child and that person.

(4) On an application made by the authority or the child, the court may make an order authorising the authority to refuse to allow contact between the child and any person who is mentioned in paragraphs (a) to (d) of subsection (1) and named in the order.

(5) When making a care order with respect to a child, or in any family proceedings in connection with a child who is in the care of a local authority, the court may make an order under this section, even though no application for such an order has been made with respect to the child, if it considers that the order should be made.

(6) An authority may refuse to allow the contact that would otherwise be required by virtue of subsection (1) or an order under this section if—

(a) they are satisfied that it is necessary to do so in order to safeguard or promote the child's welfare; and
(b) the refusal—
   (i) is decided upon as a matter of urgency; and
   (ii) does not last for more than seven days.

[(6A) Where (by virtue of an order under this section, or because subsection (6) applies) a local authority in England are authorised to refuse to allow contact between the child and a person mentioned in any of paragraphs (a) to (c) of paragraph 15(1) of Schedule 2, paragraph 15(1) of that Schedule does not require the authority to endeavour to promote contact between the child and that person.][1]

[(6B) Where (by virtue of an order under this section, or because subsection (6) applies) a local authority in Wales is authorised to refuse contact between the child and a person mentioned in any of paragraphs (a) to (c) of section 95(1) of the Social Services and Well-being (Wales) Act 2014, section 95(1) of that Act does not require the authority to promote contact between the child and that person.][2]

(7) An order under this section may impose such conditions as the court considers appropriate.

(8) The Secretary of State may by regulations make provision as to—

[(za) what a local authority in England must have regard to in considering whether contact between a child and a person mentioned in any of paragraphs (a) to (d) of subsection (1) is consistent with safeguarding and promoting the child's welfare;][1]
(a) the steps to be taken by a local authority who have exercised their powers under subsection (6);
(b) the circumstances in which, and conditions subject to which, the terms of any order under this section may be departed from by agreement

between the local authority and the person in relation to whom the order is made;
(c) notification by a local authority of any variation or suspension of arrangements made (otherwise than under an order under this section) with a view to affording any person contact with a child to whom this section applies.

(9) The court may vary or discharge any order made under this section on the application of the authority, the child concerned or the person named in the order.

(10) An order under this section may be made either at the same time as the care order itself or later.

(11) Before [making, varying or discharging an order under this section or]¹ making a care order with respect to any child the court shall—
(a) consider the arrangements which the authority have made, or propose to make, for affording any person contact with a child to whom this section applies; and
(b) invite the parties to the proceedings to comment on those arrangements.

Amendments
1   Inserted by the Children and Families Act 2014, s 8.
2   Inserted by the Social Services and Well-being (Wales) Act 2014 (Consequential Amendments) Regulations 2016, SI 2016/413, regs 55, 98.
3   Inserted by the Adoption and Children Act 2002, s 139(1), Sch 3, paras 54, 64.
4   Substituted by the Children and Families Act 2014, s 12(4), Sch 2, paras 1, 31.

Supervision orders

35 Supervision orders.

(1) While a supervision order is in force it shall be the duty of the supervisor—
(a) to advise, assist and befriend the supervised child;
(b) to take such steps as are reasonably necessary to give effect to the order; and
(c) where—
 (i) the order is not wholly complied with; or
 (ii) the supervisor considers that the order may no longer be necessary, to consider whether or not to apply to the court for its variation or discharge.

(2) Parts I and II of Schedule 3 make further provision with respect to supervision orders.

36 Education supervision orders.

(1) On the application of any [local authority]¹, the court may make an order putting the child with respect to whom the application is made under the supervision of a designated [local authority]¹.

(2) In this Act 'an education supervision order' means an order under subsection (1).

(3) A court may only make an education supervision order if it is satisfied that the child concerned is of compulsory school age and is not being properly educated.

(4) For the purposes of this section, a child is being properly educated only if he is receiving efficient full-time education suitable to his age, ability and aptitude and any special educational needs he may have.

(5) Where a child is—

(a) the subject of a school attendance order which is in force under [section 437 of the Education Act 1996]² and which has not been complied with; or

[(b) is not attending regularly within the meaning of section 444 of that Act—
  (i) a school at which he is a registered pupil,
  (ii) any place at which education is provided for him in the circumstances mentioned in subsection (1) [or (1A)]³ of section 444ZA of that Act, or
  (iii) any place which he is required to attend in the circumstances mentioned in subsection [(1B) or]³ (2) of that section,]⁴

then, unless it is proved that he is being properly educated, it shall be assumed that he is not.

(6) An education supervision order may not be made with respect to a child who is in the care of a local authority.

(7) The [local authority]¹ designated in an education supervision order must be—

(a) the authority within whose area the child concerned is living or will live; or
(b) where—
  (i) the child is a registered pupil at a school; and
  (ii) the authority mentioned in paragraph (a) and the authority within whose area the school is situated agree,
  the latter authority.

(8) Where a [local authority]¹ propose to make an application for an education supervision order they shall, before making the application, consult the ...⁵ appropriate local authority [if different]⁶.

(9) The appropriate local authority is—

(a) in the case of a child who is being provided with accommodation by, or on behalf of, a local authority, that authority; and
(b) in any other case, the local authority within whose area the child concerned lives, or will live.

(10) Part III of Schedule 3 makes further provision with respect to education supervision orders.

Amendments
1 Substituted by the Local Education Authorities and Children's Services Authorities (Integration of Functions) Order 2010, SI 2010/1158, art 5(1), Sch 2, para 37(1), (7)(a), (b), (c)(i).

2 Substituted by the Education Act 1996, s 582(1), Sch 37, para 85(a).
3 Inserted by the Education and Skills Act 2008, s 169(1), Sch 1, para 43.
4 Substituted by the Education Act 2005, s 117, Sch 18, para 1.
5 Repealed by the Education Act 1993, s 307(1), (3), Sch 19, para 147, Sch 21, Pt II.
6 Inserted by the Local Education Authorities and Children's Services Authorities (Integration of Functions) Order 2010, SI 2010/1158, art 5(1), Sch 2, para 37(1), (7)(c)(ii).

Powers of court

37 Powers of court in certain family proceedings.

(1) Where, in any family proceedings in which a question arises with respect to the welfare of any child, it appears to the court that it may be appropriate for a care or supervision order to be made with respect to him, the court may direct the appropriate authority to undertake an investigation of the child's circumstances.

(2) Where the court gives a direction under this section the local authority concerned shall, when undertaking the investigation, consider whether they should—

 (a) apply for a care order or for a supervision order with respect to the child;
 (b) provide services or assistance for the child or his family; or
 (c) take any other action with respect to the child.

(3) Where a local authority undertake an investigation under this section, and decide not to apply for a care order or supervision order with respect to the child concerned, they shall inform the court of—

 (a) their reasons for so deciding;
 (b) any service or assistance which they have provided, or intend to provide, for the child and his family; and
 (c) any other action which they have taken, or propose to take, with respect to the child.

(4) The information shall be given to the court before the end of the period of eight weeks beginning with the date of the direction, unless the court otherwise directs.

(5) The local authority named in a direction under subsection (1) must be—

 (a) the authority in whose area the child is ordinarily resident; or
 (b) where the child [is not ordinarily resident]¹ in the area of a local authority, the authority within whose area any circumstances arose in consequence of which the direction is being given.

(6) If, on the conclusion of any investigation or review under this section, the authority decide not to apply for a care order or supervision order with respect to the child—

 (a) they shall consider whether it would be appropriate to review the case at a later date; and
 (b) if they decide that it would be, they shall determine the date on which that review is to begin.

Amendment
1 Substituted by the Courts and Legal Services Act 1990, s 116(1), Sch 16, para 16.

38 Interim orders.

(1) Where—

(a) in any proceedings on an application for a care order or supervision order, the proceedings are adjourned; or
(b) the court gives a direction under section 37(1),

the court may make an interim care order or an interim supervision order with respect to the child concerned.

(2) A court shall not make an interim care order or interim supervision order under this section unless it is satisfied that there are reasonable grounds for believing that the circumstances with respect to the child are as mentioned in section 31(2).

(3) Where, in any proceedings on an application for a care order or supervision order, a court makes a [child arrangements order with respect to the living arrangements of]¹ the child concerned, it shall also make an interim supervision order with respect to him unless satisfied that his welfare will be satisfactorily safeguarded without an interim order being made.

[(3A) For the purposes of subsection (3), a child arrangements order is one made with respect to the living arrangements of the child concerned if the arrangements regulated by the order consist of, or include, arrangements which relate to either or both of the following—

(a) with whom the child is to live, and
(b) when the child is to live with any person.]²

(4) An interim order made under or by virtue of this section shall have effect for such period as may be specified in the order, but shall in any event cease to have effect on whichever of the following events first occurs—

(a) ...³
(b) ...³
(c) in a case which falls within subsection (1)(a), the disposal of the application;
(d) in a case which falls within subsection (1)(b), the disposal of an application for a care order or supervision order made by the authority with respect to the child;
[(da) in a case which falls within subsection (1)(b) and in which—
  (i) no direction has been given under section 37(4), and
  (ii) no application for a care order or supervision order has been made with respect to the child,
the expiry of the period of eight weeks beginning with the date on which the order is made;]⁴
(e) in a case which falls within subsection (1)(b) and in which—
  (i) the court has given a direction under section 37(4), but

(ii) no application for a care order or supervision order has been made with respect to the child,

the expiry of the period fixed by that direction.

(5) ...³

(6) Where the court makes an interim care order, or interim supervision order, it may give such directions (if any) as it considers appropriate with regard to the medical or psychiatric examination or other assessment of the child; but if the child is of sufficient understanding to make an informed decision he may refuse to submit to the examination or other assessment.

(7) A direction under subsection (6) may be to the effect that there is to be—

(a) no such examination or assessment; or
(b) no such examination or assessment unless the court directs otherwise.

[(7A) A direction under subsection (6) to the effect that there is to be a medical or psychiatric examination or other assessment of the child may be given only if the court is of the opinion that the examination or other assessment is necessary to assist the court to resolve the proceedings justly.

(7B) When deciding whether to give a direction under subsection (6) to that effect the court is to have regard in particular to—

(a) any impact which any examination or other assessment would be likely to have on the welfare of the child, and any other impact which giving the direction would be likely to have on the welfare of the child,
(b) the issues with which the examination or other assessment would assist the court,
(c) the questions which the examination or other assessment would enable the court to answer,
(d) the evidence otherwise available,
(e) the impact which the direction would be likely to have on the timetable, duration and conduct of the proceedings,
(f) the cost of the examination or other assessment, and
(g) any matters prescribed by Family Procedure Rules.]⁵

(8) A direction under subsection (6) may be—

(a) given when the interim order is made or at any time while it is in force; and
(b) varied at any time on the application of any person falling within any class of person prescribed by rules of court for the purposes of this subsection.

(9) Paragraphs 4 and 5 of Schedule 3 shall not apply in relation to an interim supervision order.

(10) Where a court makes an order under or by virtue of this section it shall, in determining the period for which the order is to be in force, consider whether any party who was, or might have been, opposed to the making of the order was in a position to argue his case against the order in full.

Amendments

1 Substituted by the Children and Families Act 2014, s 12(4), Sch 2, paras 1, 32(1), (2).
2 Inserted by the Children and Families Act 2014, s 12(4), Sch 2, paras 1, 32(1), (3).
3 Repealed by the Children and Families Act 2014, s 14(1), (4)(a), (c).
4 Inserted by the Children and Families Act 2014, s 14(1), (4)(b).
5 Inserted by the Children and Families Act 2014, s.13(11).

[38A Power to include exclusion requirement in interim care order.

(1) Where—

- (a) on being satisfied that there are reasonable grounds for believing that the circumstances with respect to a child are as mentioned in section 31(2)(a) and (b)(i), the court makes an interim care order with respect to a child, and
- (b) the conditions mentioned in subsection (2) are satisfied,

the court may include an exclusion requirement in the interim care order.

(2) The conditions are—

- (a) that there is reasonable cause to believe that, if a person ('the relevant person') is excluded from a dwelling-house in which the child lives, the child will cease to suffer, or cease to be likely to suffer, significant harm, and
- (b) that another person living in the dwelling-house (whether a parent of the child or some other person)—
  - (i) is able and willing to give to the child the care which it would be reasonable to expect a parent to give him, and
  - (ii) consents to the inclusion of the exclusion requirement.

(3) For the purposes of this section an exclusion requirement is any one or more of the following—

- (a) a provision requiring the relevant person to leave a dwelling-house in which he is living with the child,
- (b) a provision prohibiting the relevant person from entering a dwelling-house in which the child lives, and
- (c) a provision excluding the relevant person from a defined area in which a dwelling-house in which the child lives is situated.

(4) The court may provide that the exclusion requirement is to have effect for a shorter period than the other provisions of the interim care order.

(5) Where the court makes an interim care order containing an exclusion requirement, the court may attach a power of arrest to the exclusion requirement.

(6) Where the court attaches a power of arrest to an exclusion requirement of an interim care order, it may provide that the power of arrest is to have effect for a shorter period than the exclusion requirement.

(7) Any period specified for the purposes of subsection (4) or (6) may be extended by the court (on one or more occasions) on an application to vary or discharge the interim care order.

(8) Where a power of arrest is attached to an exclusion requirement of an interim care order by virtue of subsection (5), a constable may arrest without warrant any person whom he has reasonable cause to believe to be in breach of the requirement.

(9) Sections 47(7), (11) and (12) and 48 of, and Schedule 5 to, the Family Law Act 1996 shall have effect in relation to a person arrested under subsection (8) of this section as they have effect in relation to a person arrested under section 47(6) of that Act.

(10) If, while an interim care order containing an exclusion requirement is in force, the local authority have removed the child from the dwelling-house from which the relevant person is excluded to other accommodation for a continuous period of more than 24 hours, the interim care order shall cease to have effect in so far as it imposes the exclusion requirement.][1]

Amendment
1 Inserted by the Family Law Act 1996, s 52, Sch 6, para 1.

[38B Undertakings relating to interim care orders.

(1) In any case where the court has power to include an exclusion requirement in an interim care order, the court may accept an undertaking from the relevant person.

(2) No power of arrest may be attached to any undertaking given under subsection (1).

(3) An undertaking given to a court under subsection (1)—

   (a) shall be enforceable as if it were an order of the court, and
   (b) shall cease to have effect if, while it is in force, the local authority have removed the child from the dwelling-house from which the relevant person is excluded to other accommodation for a continuous period of more than 24 hours.

(4) This section has effect without prejudice to the powers of the High Court and [family court][1] apart from this section.

(5) In this section 'exclusion requirement' and 'relevant person' have the same meaning as in section 38A.][2]

Amendments
1 Substituted by the Crime and Courts Act 2013, s 17(6), Sch 11, paras 102, 106.
2 Inserted by the Family Law Act 1996, s 52, Sch 6, para 1.

39 Discharge and variation etc. of care orders and supervision orders.

(1) A care order may be discharged by the court on the application of—

   (a) any person who has parental responsibility for the child;
   (b) the child himself; or
   (c) the local authority designated by the order.

(2) A supervision order may be varied or discharged by the court on the application of—

(a) any person who has parental responsibility for the child;
(b) the child himself; or
(c) the supervisor.

(3) On the application of a person who is not entitled to apply for the order to be discharged, but who is a person with whom the child is living, a supervision order may be varied by the court in so far as it imposes a requirement which affects that person.

[(3A) On the application of a person who is not entitled to apply for the order to be discharged, but who is a person to whom an exclusion requirement contained in the order applies, an interim care order may be varied or discharged by the court in so far as it imposes the exclusion requirement.

(3B) Where a power of arrest has been attached to an exclusion requirement of an interim care order, the court may, on the application of any person entitled to apply for the discharge of the order so far as it imposes the exclusion requirement, vary or discharge the order in so far as it confers a power of arrest (whether or not any application has been made to vary or discharge any other provision of the order).][1]

(4) Where a care order is in force with respect to a child the court may, on the application of any person entitled to apply for the order to be discharged, substitute a supervision order for the care order.

(5) When a court is considering whether to substitute one order for another under subsection (4) any provision of this Act which would otherwise require section 31(2) to be satisfied at the time when the proposed order is substituted or made shall be disregarded.

Amendment
1 Inserted by the Family Law Act 1996, s 52, Sch 6, para 2.

40 Orders pending appeals in cases about care or supervision orders.

(1) Where—

(a) a court dismisses an application for a care order; and
(b) at the time when the court dismisses the application, the child concerned is the subject of an interim care order,

the court may make a care order with respect to the child to have effect subject to such directions (if any) as the court may see fit to include in the order.

(2) Where—

(a) a court dismisses an application for a care order, or an application for a supervision order; and
(b) at the time when the court dismisses the application, the child concerned is the subject of an interim supervision order,

the court may make a supervision order with respect to the child to have effect subject to such directions (if any) as the court may see fit to include in the order.

(3) Where a court grants an application to discharge a care order or supervision order, it may order that—

(a) its decision is not to have effect; or
(b) the care order, or supervision order, is to continue to have effect but subject to such directions as the court sees fit to include in the order.

(4) An order made under this section shall only have effect for such period, not exceeding the appeal period, as may be specified in the order.

(5) Where—

(a) an appeal is made against any decision of a court under this section; or
(b) any application is made to the appellate court in connection with a proposed appeal against that decision,

the appellate court may extend the period for which the order in question is to have effect, but not so as to extend it beyond the end of the appeal period.

(6) In this section 'the appeal period' means—

(a) where an appeal is made against the decision in question, the period between the making of that decision and the determination of the appeal; and
(b) otherwise, the period during which an appeal may be made against the decision.

[*Representation of child*][1]

41 Representation of child and of his interests in certain proceedings.

(1) For the purpose of any specified proceedings, the court shall appoint [an officer of the Service][1] [or a Welsh family proceedings officer][2] for the child concerned unless satisfied that it is not necessary to do so in order to safeguard his interests.

(2) The [officer of the Service][1] [or Welsh family proceedings officer][2] shall—

(a) be appointed in accordance with rules of court; and
(b) be under a duty to safeguard the interests of the child in the manner prescribed by such rules.

(3) Where—

(a) the child concerned is not represented by a solicitor; and
(b) any of the conditions mentioned in subsection (4) is satisfied,

the court may appoint a solicitor to represent him.

(4) The conditions are that—

(a) no [officer of the Service][1] [or Welsh family proceedings officer][2] has been appointed for the child;
(b) the child has sufficient understanding to instruct a solicitor and wishes to do so;
(c) it appears to the court that it would be in the child's best interests for him to be represented by a solicitor.

(5) Any solicitor appointed under or by virtue of this section shall be appointed, and shall represent the child, in accordance with rules of court.

(6) In this section 'specified proceedings' means any proceedings—

   (a) on an application for a care order or supervision order;

   (b) in which the court has given a direction under section 37(1) and has made, or is considering whether to make, an interim care order;

   (c) on an application for the discharge of a care order or the variation or discharge of a supervision order;

   (d) on an application under section 39(4);

   (e) in which the court is considering whether to make a [child arrangements order with respect to the living arrangements of][3] a child who is the subject of a care order;

   (f) with respect to contact between a child who is the subject of a care order and any other person;

   (g) under Part V;

   (h) on an appeal against—

      (i) the making of, or refusal to make, a care order, supervision order or any order under section 34;

      (ii) the making of, or refusal to make, a [child arrangements order with respect to the living arrangements of][3] a child who is the subject of a care order; or

      (iii) the variation or discharge, or refusal of an application to vary or discharge, an order of a kind mentioned in sub-paragraph (i) or (ii);

      (iv) the refusal of an application under section 39(4); or

      (v) the making of, or refusal to make, an order under Part V;

  [(hh) on an application for the making or revocation of a placement order (within the meaning of section 21 of the Adoption and Children Act 2002);][4] or

   (i) which are specified for the time being, for the purposes of this section, by rules of court.

[(6A) The proceedings which may be specified under subsection (6)(i) include (for example) proceedings for the making, varying or discharging of a section 8 order.][4]

[(6B) For the purposes of subsection (6), a child arrangements order is one made with respect to the living arrangements of a child if the arrangements regulated by the order consist of, or include, arrangements which relate to either or both of the following—

   (a) with whom the child is to live, and

   (b) when the child is to live with any person.][5]

(7) ...[6]

(8) ...[6]

(9) ...[6]

(10) Rules of court may make provision as to—

(a) the assistance which any [officer of the Service]¹ [or Welsh family proceedings officer]² may be required by the court to give to it;
(b) the consideration to be given by any [officer of the Service]¹ [or Welsh family proceedings officer]², where an order of a specified kind has been made in the proceedings in question, as to whether to apply for the variation or discharge of the order;
(c) the participation of [officers of the Service]¹ [or Welsh family proceedings officers]² in reviews, of a kind specified in the rules, which are conducted by the court.

(11) Regardless of any enactment or rule of law which would otherwise prevent it from doing so, the court may take account of—

(a) any statement contained in a report made by [an officer of the Service]¹ [or a Welsh family proceedings officer]² who is appointed under this section for the purpose of the proceedings in question; and
(b) any evidence given in respect of the matters referred to in the report,

in so far as the statement or evidence is, in the opinion of the court, relevant to the question which the court is considering.

(12) ...⁶

Amendments
1 Substituted by the Criminal Justice and Court Services Act 2000, s 74, Sch 7, paras 87, 91(a)–(c), (e).
2 Inserted by the Children Act 2004, s 40, Sch 3, paras 5, 9.
3 Substituted by the Children and Families Act 2014, s 12(4), Sch 2, paras 1, 33(1), (2).
4 Inserted by the Adoption and Children Act 2002, s 122(1).
5 Inserted by the Children and Families Act 2014, s 12(4), Sch 2, paras 1, 33(1), (3).
6 Repealed by the Criminal Justice and Court Services Act 2000, ss 74, 75, Sch 7, paras 87, 91(d), Sch 8.

42 [Right of officer of the Service to have access to local authority records.]¹

(1) Where [an officer of the Service]¹ [or Welsh family proceedings officer]² has been appointed [under section 41]¹ he shall have the right at all reasonable times to examine and take copies of—

(a) any records of, or held by, a local authority [or an authorised person]³ which were compiled in connection with the making, or proposed making, by any person of any application under this Act with respect to the child concerned; ...⁴
(b) any ...⁴ records of, or held by, a local authority which were compiled in connection with any functions which [are social services functions within the meaning of]⁵ the Local Authority Social Services Act 1970 [or for the purposes of the Social Services and Well-being (Wales) Act 2014]⁶, so far as those records relate to that child[; or]³
[(c) any records of, or held by, an authorised person which were compiled in connection with the activities of that person, so far as those records relate to that child.]³

(2) Where [an officer of the Service]¹ [or Welsh family proceedings officer]² takes a copy of any record which he is entitled to examine under this section, that

copy or any part of it shall be admissible as evidence of any matter referred to in any—

(a) report which he makes to the court in the proceedings in question; or
(b) evidence which he gives in those proceedings.

(3) Subsection (2) has effect regardless of any enactment or rule of law which would otherwise prevent the record in question being admissible in evidence.

[(4) In this section 'authorised person' has the same meaning as in section 31.][3]

Amendments
1 Substituted by the Criminal Justice and Court Services Act 2000, s 74, Sch 7, paras 87, 92.
2 Inserted by the Children Act 2004, s 40, Sch 3, paras 5, 10.
3 Inserted by the Courts and Legal Services Act 1990, s 116(1), Sch 16, para 18.
4 Repealed by the Courts and Legal Services Act 1990, s 125(7), Sch 20.
5 Substituted by the Local Government Act 2000, s 107(1), Sch 5, para 20.
6 Inserted by the Social Services and Well-being (Wales) Act 2014 (Consequential Amendments) Regulations 2016, SI 2016/413, regs 55, 99.

PART V
PROTECTION OF CHILDREN

43 Child assessment orders.

(1) On the application of a local authority or authorised person for an order to be made under this section with respect to a child, the court may make the order if, but only if, it is satisfied that—

(a) the applicant has reasonable cause to suspect that the child is suffering, or is likely to suffer, significant harm;
(b) an assessment of the state of the child's health or development, or of the way in which he has been treated, is required to enable the applicant to determine whether or not the child is suffering, or is likely to suffer, significant harm; and
(c) it is unlikely that such an assessment will be made, or be satisfactory, in the absence of an order under this section.

(2) In this Act 'a child assessment order' means an order under this section.

(3) A court may treat an application under this section as an application for an emergency protection order.

(4) No court shall make a child assessment order if it is satisfied—

(a) that there are grounds for making an emergency protection order with respect to the child; and
(b) that it ought to make such an order rather than a child assessment order.

(5) A child assessment order shall—

(a) specify the date by which the assessment is to begin; and
(b) have effect for such period, not exceeding 7 days beginning with that date, as may be specified in the order.

(6) Where a child assessment order is in force with respect to a child it shall be the duty of any person who is in a position to produce the child—

(a) to produce him to such person as may be named in the order; and
(b) to comply with such directions relating to the assessment of the child as the court thinks fit to specify in the order.

(7) A child assessment order authorises any person carrying out the assessment, or any part of the assessment, to do so in accordance with the terms of the order.

(8) Regardless of subsection (7), if the child is of sufficient understanding to make an informed decision he may refuse to submit to a medical or psychiatric examination or other assessment.

(9) The child may only be kept away from home—

(a) in accordance with directions specified in the order;
(b) if it is necessary for the purposes of the assessment; and
(c) for such period or periods as may be specified in the order.

(10) Where the child is to be kept away from home, the order shall contain such directions as the court thinks fit with regard to the contact that he must be allowed to have with other persons while away from home.

(11) Any person making an application for a child assessment order shall take such steps as are reasonably practicable to ensure that notice of the application is given to—

(a) the child's parents;
(b) any person who is not a parent of his but who has parental responsibility for him;
(c) any other person caring for the child;
[(d) any person named in a child arrangements order as a person with whom the child is to spend time or otherwise have contact;][1]
(e) any person who is allowed to have contact with the child by virtue of an order under section 34; and
(f) the child,

before the hearing of the application.

(12) Rules of court may make provision as to the circumstances in which—

(a) any of the persons mentioned in subsection (11); or
(b) such other person as may be specified in the rules,

may apply to the court for a child assessment order to be varied or discharged.

(13) In this section 'authorised person' means a person who is an authorised person for the purposes of section 31.

Amendment
1   Substituted by the Children and Families Act 2014, s 12(4), Sch 2, paras 1, 34.

44 Orders for emergency protection of children.

(1) Where any person ('the applicant') applies to the court for an order to be made under this section with respect to a child, the court may make the order if, but only if, it is satisfied that—

- (a) there is reasonable cause to believe that the child is likely to suffer significant harm if—
    - (i) he is not removed to accommodation provided by or on behalf of the applicant; or
    - (ii) he does not remain in the place in which he is then being accommodated;
- (b) in the case of an application made by a local authority—
    - (i) enquiries are being made with respect to the child under section 47(1)(b); and
    - (ii) those enquiries are being frustrated by access to the child being unreasonably refused to a person authorised to seek access and that the applicant has reasonable cause to believe that access to the child is required as a matter of urgency; or
- (c) in the case of an application made by an authorised person—
    - (i) the applicant has reasonable cause to suspect that a child is suffering, or is likely to suffer, significant harm;
    - (ii) the applicant is making enquiries with respect to the child's welfare; and
    - (iii) those enquiries are being frustrated by access to the child being unreasonably refused to a person authorised to seek access and the applicant has reasonable cause to believe that access to the child is required as a matter of urgency.

(2) In this section—

- (a) 'authorised person' means a person who is an authorised person for the purposes of section 31; and
- (b) 'a person authorised to seek access' means—
    - (i) in the case of an application by a local authority, an officer of the local authority or a person authorised by the authority to act on their behalf in connection with the enquiries; or
    - (ii) in the case of an application by an authorised person, that person.

(3) Any person—

- (a) seeking access to a child in connection with enquiries of a kind mentioned in subsection (1); and
- (b) purporting to be a person authorised to do so,

shall, on being asked to do so, produce some duly authenticated document as evidence that he is such a person.

(4) While an order under this section ('an emergency protection order') is in force it—

- (a) operates as a direction to any person who is in a position to do so to comply with any request to produce the child to the applicant;

(b) authorises—
  (i) the removal of the child at any time to accommodation provided by or on behalf of the applicant and his being kept there; or
  (ii) the prevention of the child's removal from any hospital, or other place, in which he was being accommodated immediately before the making of the order; and
(c) gives the applicant parental responsibility for the child.

(5) Where an emergency protection order is in force with respect to a child, the applicant—

(a) shall only exercise the power given by virtue of subsection (4)(b) in order to safeguard the welfare of the child;
(b) shall take, and shall only take, such action in meeting his parental responsibility for the child as is reasonably required to safeguard or promote the welfare of the child (having regard in particular to the duration of the order); and
(c) shall comply with the requirements of any regulations made by the Secretary of State for the purposes of this subsection.

(6) Where the court makes an emergency protection order, it may give such directions (if any) as it considers appropriate with respect to—

(a) the contact which is, or is not, to be allowed between the child and any named person;
(b) the medical or psychiatric examination or other assessment of the child.

(7) Where any direction is given under subsection (6)(b), the child may, if he is of sufficient understanding to make an informed decision, refuse to submit to the examination or other assessment.

(8) A direction under subsection (6)(a) may impose conditions and one under subsection (6)(b) may be to the effect that there is to be—

(a) no such examination or assessment; or
(b) no such examination or assessment unless the court directs otherwise.

(9) A direction under subsection (6) may be—

(a) given when the emergency protection order is made or at any time while it is in force; and
(b) varied at any time on the application of any person falling within any class of person prescribed by rules of court for the purposes of this subsection.

(10) Where an emergency protection order is in force with respect to a child and—

(a) the applicant has exercised the power given by subsection (4)(b)(i) but it appears to him that it is safe for the child to be returned; or
(b) the applicant has exercised the power given by subsection (4)(b)(ii) but it appears to him that it is safe for the child to be allowed to be removed from the place in question,

he shall return the child or (as the case may be) allow him to be removed.

(11) Where he is required by subsection (10) to return the child the applicant shall—

(a) return him to the care of the person from whose care he was removed; or
(b) if that is not reasonably practicable, return him to the care of—
   (i) a parent of his;
   (ii) any person who is not a parent of his but who has parental responsibility for him; or
   (iii) such other person as the applicant (with the agreement of the court) considers appropriate.

(12) Where the applicant has been required by subsection (10) to return the child, or to allow him to be removed, he may again exercise his powers with respect to the child (at any time while the emergency protection order remains in force) if it appears to him that a change in the circumstances of the case makes it necessary for him to do so.

(13) Where an emergency protection order has been made with respect to a child, the applicant shall, subject to any direction given under subsection (6), allow the child reasonable contact with—

(a) his parents;
(b) any person who is not a parent of his but who has parental responsibility for him;
(c) any person with whom he was living immediately before the making of the order;
[(d) any person named in a child arrangements order as a person with whom the child is to spend time or otherwise have contact;][1]
(e) any person who is allowed to have contact with the child by virtue of an order under section 34; and
(f) any person acting on behalf of any of those persons.

(14) Wherever it is reasonably practicable to do so, an emergency protection order shall name the child; and where it does not name him it shall describe him as clearly as possible.

(15) A person shall be guilty of an offence if he intentionally obstructs any person exercising the power under subsection (4)(b) to remove, or prevent the removal of, a child.

(16) A person guilty of an offence under subsection (15) shall be liable on summary conviction to a fine not exceeding level 3 on the standard scale.

Amendment
1 Substituted by the Children and Families Act 2014, s 12(4), Sch 2, paras 1, 35.

[44A Power to include exclusion requirement in emergency protection order.

(1) Where—

(a) on being satisfied as mentioned in section 44(1)(a), (b) or (c), the court makes an emergency protection order with respect to a child, and
(b) the conditions mentioned in subsection (2) are satisfied,

the court may include an exclusion requirement in the emergency protection order.

(2) The conditions are—

(a) that there is reasonable cause to believe that, if a person ('the relevant person') is excluded from a dwelling-house in which the child lives, then—
   (i) in the case of an order made on the ground mentioned in section 44(1)(a), the child will not be likely to suffer significant harm, even though the child is not removed as mentioned in section 44(1)(a)(i) or does not remain as mentioned in section 44(1)(a)(ii), or
   (ii) in the case of an order made on the ground mentioned in paragraph (b) or (c) of section 44(1), the enquires referred to in that paragraph will cease to be frustrated, and
(b) that another person living in the dwelling-house (whether a parent of the child or some other person)—
   (i) is able and willing to give to the child the care which it would be reasonable to expect a parent to give him, and
   (ii) consents to the inclusion of the exclusion requirement.

(3) For the purposes of this section an exclusion requirement is any one or more of the following—

(a) a provision requiring the relevant person to leave a dwelling-house in which he is living with the child,
(b) a provision prohibiting the relevant person from entering a dwelling-house in which the child lives, and
(c) a provision excluding the relevant person from a defined area in which a dwelling-house in which the child lives is situated.

(4) The court may provide that the exclusion requirement is to have effect for a shorter period than the other provisions of the order.

(5) Where the court makes an emergency protection order containing an exclusion requirement, the court may attach a power of arrest to the exclusion requirement.

(6) Where the court attaches a power of arrest to an exclusion requirement of an emergency protection order, it may provide that the power of arrest is to have effect for a shorter period than the exclusion requirement.

(7) Any period specified for the purposes of subsection (4) or (6) may be extended by the court (on one or more occasions) on an application to vary or discharge the emergency protection order.

(8) Where a power of arrest is attached to an exclusion requirement of an emergency protection order by virtue of subsection (5), a constable may arrest without warrant any person whom he has reasonable cause to believe to be in breach of the requirement.

(9) Sections 47(7), (11) and (12) and 48 of, and Schedule 5 to, the Family Law Act 1996 shall have effect in relation to a person arrested under subsection (8) of this section as they have effect in relation to a person arrested under section 47(6) of that Act.

(10) If, while an emergency protection order containing an exclusion requirement is in force, the applicant has removed the child from the dwelling-house from which the relevant person is excluded to other accommodation for a continuous period of more than 24 hours, the order shall cease to have effect in so far as it imposes the exclusion requirement.]¹

Amendment
1 Inserted by the Family Law Act 1996, s 52, Sch 6, para 3.

[44B Undertakings relating to emergency protection orders.

(1) In any case where the court has power to include an exclusion requirement in an emergency protection order, the court may accept an undertaking from the relevant person.

(2) No power of arrest may be attached to any undertaking given under subsection (1).

(3) An undertaking given to a court under subsection (1)—
   (a) shall be enforceable as if it were an order of the court, and
   (b) shall cease to have effect if, while it is in force, the applicant has removed the child from the dwelling-house from which the relevant person is excluded to other accommodation for a continuous period of more than 24 hours.

(4) This section has effect without prejudice to the powers of the High Court and [family court]¹ apart from this section.

(5) In this section 'exclusion requirement' and 'relevant person' have the same meaning as in section 44A.]²

Amendments
1 Substituted by the Crime and Courts Act 2013, s 17(6), Sch 11, paras 102, 107.
2 Inserted by the Family Law Act 1996, s 52, Sch 6, para 3.

45 Duration of emergency protection orders and other supplemental provisions.

(1) An emergency protection order shall have effect for such period, not exceeding eight days, as may be specified in the order.

(2) Where—
   (a) the court making an emergency protection order would, but for this subsection, specify a period of eight days as the period for which the order is to have effect; but
   (b) the last of those eight days is a public holiday (that is to say, Christmas Day, Good Friday, a bank holiday or a Sunday),

the court may specify a period which ends at noon on the first later day which is not such a holiday.

(3) Where an emergency protection order is made on an application under section 46(7), the period of eight days mentioned in subsection (1) shall begin with the first day on which the child was taken into police protection under section 46.

(4) Any person who—

(a) has parental responsibility for a child as the result of an emergency protection order; and
(b) is entitled to apply for a care order with respect to the child,

may apply to the court for the period during which the emergency protection order is to have effect to be extended.

(5) On an application under subsection (4) the court may extend the period during which the order is to have effect by such period, not exceeding seven days, as it thinks fit, but may do so only if it has reasonable cause to believe that the child concerned is likely to suffer significant harm if the order is not extended.

(6) An emergency protection order may only be extended once.

(7) Regardless of any enactment or rule of law which would otherwise prevent it from doing so, a court hearing an application for, or with respect to, an emergency protection order may take account of—

(a) any statement contained in any report made to the court in the course of, or in connection with, the hearing; or
(b) any evidence given during the hearing,

which is, in the opinion of the court, relevant to the application.

(8) Any of the following may apply to the court for an emergency protection order to be discharged—

(a) the child;
(b) a parent of his;
(c) any person who is not a parent of his but who has parental responsibility for him; or
(d) any person with whom he was living immediately before the making of the order.

[(8A) On the application of a person who is not entitled to apply for the order to be discharged, but who is a person to whom an exclusion requirement contained in the order applies, an emergency protection order may be varied or discharged by the court in so far as it imposes the exclusion requirement.

(8B) Where a power of arrest has been attached to an exclusion requirement of an emergency protection order, the court may, on the application of any person entitled to apply for the discharge of the order so far as it imposes the exclusion requirement, vary or discharge the order in so far as it confers a power of arrest (whether or not any application has been made to vary or discharge any other provision of the order).]¹

(9) ...²

[(10) No appeal may be made against—

(a) the making of, or refusal to make, an emergency protection order;
(b) the extension of, or refusal to extend, the period during which such an order is to have effect;

(c) the discharge of, or refusal to discharge, such an order; or
(d) the giving of, or refusal to give, any direction in connection with such an order.][3]

(11) Subsection (8) does not apply—

(a) where the person who would otherwise be entitled to apply for the emergency protection order to be discharged—
   (i) was given notice (in accordance with rules of court) of the hearing at which the order was made; and
   (ii) was present at that hearing; or
(b) to any emergency protection order the effective period of which has been extended under subsection (5).

(12) A court making an emergency protection order may direct that the applicant may, in exercising any powers which he has by virtue of the order, be accompanied by a registered medical practitioner, registered nurse or [registered midwife][4], if he so chooses.

[(13) The reference in subsection (12) to a registered midwife is to such a midwife who is also registered in the Specialist Community Public Health Nurses' Part of the register maintained under article 5 of the Nursing and Midwifery Order 2001.][5]

Amendments
1 Inserted by the Family Law Act 1996, s 52, Sch 6, para 4.
2 Repealed by the Children and Young Persons Act 2008, s 42, Sch 4.
3 Substituted by the Courts and Legal Services Act 1990, s 116(1), Sch 16, para 19.
4 Substituted by Nursing and Midwifery Order (2001) 2002/253 Sch.5 para.10(a).
5 Inserted by the Health Act 1999 (Consequential Amendments) (Nursing and Midwifery) Order 2004, SI 2004/1771, art 3, Schedule, para 4(a).

46 Removal and accommodation of children by police in cases of emergency.

(1) Where a constable has reasonable cause to believe that a child would otherwise be likely to suffer significant harm, he may—

(a) remove the child to suitable accommodation and keep him there; or
(b) take such steps as are reasonable to ensure that the child's removal from any hospital, or other place, in which he is then being accommodated is prevented.

(2) For the purposes of this Act, a child with respect to whom a constable has exercised his powers under this section is referred to as having been taken into police protection.

(3) As soon as is reasonably practicable after taking a child into police protection, the constable concerned shall—

(a) inform the local authority within whose area the child was found of the steps that have been, and are proposed to be, taken with respect to the child under this section and the reasons for taking them;
(b) give details to the authority within whose area the child is ordinarily resident ('the appropriate authority') of the place at which the child is being accommodated;

(c) inform the child (if he appears capable of understanding)—
  (i) of the steps that have been taken with respect to him under this section and of the reasons for taking them; and
  (ii) of the further steps that may be taken with respect to him under this section;
(d) take such steps as are reasonably practicable to discover the wishes and feelings of the child;
(e) secure that the case is inquired into by an officer designated for the purposes of this section by the chief officer of the police area concerned; and
(f) where the child was taken into police protection by being removed to accommodation which is not provided—
  (i) by or on behalf of a local authority; or
  (ii) as a refuge, in compliance with the requirements of section 51, secure that he is moved to accommodation which is so provided.

(4) As soon as is reasonably practicable after taking a child into police protection, the constable concerned shall take such steps as are reasonably practicable to inform—

(a) the child's parents;
(b) every person who is not a parent of his but who has parental responsibility for him; and
(c) any other person with whom the child was living immediately before being taken into police protection,

of the steps that he has taken under this section with respect to the child, the reasons for taking them and the further steps that may be taken with respect to him under this section.

(5) On completing any inquiry under subsection (3)(e), the officer conducting it shall release the child from police protection unless he considers that there is still reasonable cause for believing that the child would be likely to suffer significant harm if released.

(6) No child may be kept in police protection for more than 72 hours.

(7) While a child is being kept in police protection, the designated officer may apply on behalf of the appropriate authority for an emergency protection order to be made under section 44 with respect to the child.

(8) An application may be made under subsection (7) whether or not the authority know of it or agree to its being made.

(9) While a child is being kept in police protection—

(a) neither the constable concerned nor the designated officer shall have parental responsibility for him; but
(b) the designated officer shall do what is reasonable in all the circumstances of the case for the purpose of safeguarding or promoting the child's welfare (having regard in particular to the length of the period during which the child will be so protected).

(10) Where a child has been taken into police protection, the designated officer shall allow—

(a) the child's parents;
(b) any person who is not a parent of the child but who has parental responsibility for him;
(c) any person with whom the child was living immediately before he was taken into police protection;
[(d) any person named in a child arrangements order as a person with whom the child is to spend time or otherwise have contact;]¹
(e) any person who is allowed to have contact with the child by virtue of an order under section 34; and
(f) any person acting on behalf of any of those persons,

to have such contact (if any) with the child as, in the opinion of the designated officer, is both reasonable and in the child's best interests.

(11) Where a child who has been taken into police protection is in accommodation provided by, or on behalf of, the appropriate authority, subsection (10) shall have effect as if it referred to the authority rather than to the designated officer.

Amendment
1 Substituted by the Children and Families Act 2014, s 12(4), Sch 2, paras 1, 36.

47 Local authority's duty to investigate.

(1) Where a local authority—

(a) are informed that a child who lives, or is found, in their area—
   (i) is the subject of an emergency protection order; or
   (ii) is in police protection; ...¹
   [(iii) ...¹; or]²
(b) have reasonable cause to suspect that a child who lives, or is found, in their area is suffering, or is likely to suffer, significant harm,

the authority shall make, or cause to be made, such enquiries as they consider necessary to enable them to decide whether they should take any action to safeguard or promote the child's welfare. [...¹]²

(2) Where a local authority have obtained an emergency protection order with respect to a child, they shall make, or cause to be made, such enquiries as they consider necessary to enable them to decide what action they should take to safeguard or promote the child's welfare.

(3) The enquiries shall, in particular, be directed towards establishing—

[(a) whether the authority should—
   (i) make any application to court under this Act;
   (ii) exercise any of their other powers under this Act;
   (iii) exercise any of their powers under section 11 of the Crime and Disorder Act 1998 (child safety orders); or
   (iv) (where the authority is a local authority in Wales) exercise any of their powers under the Social Services and Well-being (Wales) Act 2014;

with respect to the child;]³
- (b) whether, in the case of a child—
  - (i) with respect to whom an emergency protection order has been made; and
  - (ii) who is not in accommodation provided by or on behalf of the authority,

  it would be in the child's best interests (while an emergency protection order remains in force) for him to be in such accommodation; and
- (c) whether, in the case of a child who has been taken into police protection, it would be in the child's best interests for the authority to ask for an application to be made under section 46(7).

(4) Where enquiries are being made under subsection (1) with respect to a child, the local authority concerned shall (with a view to enabling them to determine what action, if any, to take with respect to him) take such steps as are reasonably practicable—

- (a) to obtain access to him; or
- (b) to ensure that access to him is obtained, on their behalf, by a person authorised by them for the purpose,

unless they are satisfied that they already have sufficient information with respect to him.

(5) Where, as a result of any such enquiries, it appears to the authority that there are matters connected with the child's education which should be investigated, they shall consult [the local authority (as defined in section 579(1) of the Education 1996), if different, specified in subsection (5ZA).]⁴

[(5ZA) The local authority referred to in subsection (5) is—

- (a) the local authority who —
  - (i) maintain any school at which the child is a pupil, or
  - (i) make arrangements for the provision of education for the child otherwise than at school pursuant to section 19 of the Education Act 1996, or
- (b) in a case where the child is a pupil at a school which is not maintained by a local authority, the local authority in whose area the school is situated.]⁴

[(5A) For the purposes of making a determination under this section as to the action to be taken with respect to a child, a local authority shall, so far as is reasonably practicable and consistent with the child's welfare-

- (a) ascertain the child's wishes and feelings regarding the action to be taken with respect to him; and
- (b) give due consideration (having regard to his age and understanding) to such wishes and feelings of the child as they have been able to ascertain.]⁵

(6) Where, in the course of enquiries made under this section—

- (a) any officer of the local authority concerned; or

(b) any person authorised by the authority to act on their behalf in connection with those enquiries—
   (i) is refused access to the child concerned; or
   (ii) is denied information as to his whereabouts,

the authority shall apply for an emergency protection order, a child assessment order, a care order or a supervision order with respect to the child unless they are satisfied that his welfare can be satisfactorily safeguarded without their doing so.

(7) If, on the conclusion of any enquiries or review made under this section, the authority decide not to apply for an emergency protection order, a child assessment order, a care order or a supervision order they shall—

(a) consider whether it would be appropriate to review the case at a later date; and
(b) if they decide that it would be, determine the date on which that review is to begin.

(8) Where, as a result of complying with this section, a local authority conclude that they should take action to safeguard or promote the child's welfare they shall take that action (so far as it is both within their power and reasonably practicable for them to do so).

(9) Where a local authority are conducting enquiries under this section, it shall be the duty of any person mentioned in subsection (11) to assist them with those enquiries (in particular by providing relevant information and advice) if called upon by the authority to do so.

(10) Subsection (9) does not oblige any person to assist a local authority where doing so would be unreasonable in all the circumstances of the case.

(11) The persons are—

(a) any local authority;
(b) ...[6]
(c) any local housing authority;
[(ca) the National Health Service Commissioning Board;][7]
(d) any [clinical commissioning group,][7] [[Local Health Board][8], Special Health Authority][9] ...[10][, National Health Service trust or NHS foundation trust][11]; and
(e) any person authorised by the Secretary of State for the purposes of this section.

(12) Where a local authority are making enquiries under this section with respect to a child who appears to them to be ordinarily resident within the area of another authority, they shall consult that other authority, who may undertake the necessary enquiries in their place.

Amendments
1 Repealed by the Policing and Crime Act 2009, s 112(2), Sch 8, Pt 13.
2 Inserted by the Crime and Disorder Act 1998, s 15(4).
3 Substituted by the Social Services and Well-being (Wales) Act 2014 (Consequential Amendments) Regulations 2016, SI 2016/413, regs 55, 100.

4 Substituted by the Local Education Authorities and Children's Services Authorities (Integration of Functions) Order 2010, SI 2010/1158, art 5(1), Sch 2, para 37(1), (8)(a).
5 Inserted by the Children Act 2004, s 53(3).
6 Repealed by the Local Education Authorities and Children's Services Authorities (Integration of Functions) Order 2010, SI 2010/1158, art 5(1), (2), Sch 2, para 37(1), (8)(b), Sch 3, Pt 2.
7 Inserted by the Health and Social Care Act 2012, s 55(2), Sch 5, paras 47, 53(a), (b)(i).
8 Substituted by the References to Health Authorities Order 2007, SI 2007/961, art 3, Schedule, para 20(1), (2)(f).
9 Substituted by the Health Authorities Act 1995, s 2(1), Sch 1, para 118(1), (7).
10 Repealed by the Health and Social Care Act 2012, s 55(2), Sch 5, paras 47, 53(b)(ii).
11 Substituted by the Health and Social Care (Community Health and Standards) Act 2003, s 34, Sch 4, paras 75, 79.

48 Powers to assist in discovery of children who may be in need of emergency protection.

(1) Where it appears to a court making an emergency protection order that adequate information as to the child's whereabouts—

(a) is not available to the applicant for the order; but
(b) is available to another person,

it may include in the order a provision requiring that other person to disclose, if asked to do so by the applicant, any information that he may have as to the child's whereabouts.

(2) No person shall be excused from complying with such a requirement on the ground that complying might incriminate him or his spouse [or civil partner][1] of an offence; but a statement or admission made in complying shall not be admissible in evidence against either of them in proceedings for any offence other than perjury.

(3) An emergency protection order may authorise the applicant to enter premises specified by the order and search for the child with respect to whom the order is made.

(4) Where the court is satisfied that there is reasonable cause to believe that there may be another child on those premises with respect to whom an emergency protection order ought to be made, it may make an order authorising the applicant to search for that other child on those premises.

(5) Where—

(a) an order has been made under subsection (4);
(b) the child concerned has been found on the premises; and
(c) the applicant is satisfied that the grounds for making an emergency protection order exist with respect to him,

the order shall have effect as if it were an emergency protection order.

(6) Where an order has been made under subsection (4), the applicant shall notify the court of its effect.

(7) A person shall be guilty of an offence if he intentionally obstructs any person exercising the power of entry and search under subsection (3) or (4).

(8) A person guilty of an offence under subsection (7) shall be liable on summary conviction to a fine not exceeding level 3 on the standard scale.

(9) Where, on an application made by any person for a warrant under this section, it appears to the court—

(a) that a person attempting to exercise powers under an emergency protection order has been prevented from doing so by being refused entry to the premises concerned or access to the child concerned; or
(b) that any such person is likely to be so prevented from exercising any such powers,

it may issue a warrant authorising any constable to assist the person mentioned in paragraph (a) or (b) in the exercise of those powers, using reasonable force if necessary.

(10) Every warrant issued under this section shall be addressed to, and executed by, a constable who shall be accompanied by the person applying for the warrant if—

(a) that person so desires; and
(b) the court by whom the warrant is issued does not direct otherwise.

(11) A court granting an application for a warrant under this section may direct that the constable concerned may, in executing the warrant, be accompanied by a registered medical practitioner, registered nurse or [registered midwife]² if he so chooses.

[(11A) The reference in subsection (11) to a registered midwife is to such a midwife who is also registered in the Specialist Community Public Health Nurses' Part of the register maintained under article 5 of the Nursing and Midwifery Order 2001.]³

(12) An application for a warrant under this section shall be made in the manner and form prescribed by rules of court.

(13) Wherever it is reasonably practicable to do so, an order under subsection (4), an application for a warrant under this section and any such warrant shall name the child; and where it does not name him it shall describe him as clearly as possible.

Amendments
1   Inserted by the Civil Partnership Act 2004, s 261(1), Sch 27, para 130.
2   Substituted by Nursing and Midwifery Order (2001) 2002/253 Sch.5 para.10(b).
3   Inserted by the Health Act 1999 (Consequential Amendments) (Nursing and Midwifery) Order 2004, SI 2004/1771, art 3, Schedule, para 4(b).

49 Abduction of children in care etc.

(1) A person shall be guilty of an offence if, knowingly and without lawful authority or reasonable excuse, he—

(a) takes a child to whom this section applies away from the responsible person;
(b) keeps such a child away from the responsible person; or

(c) induces, assists or incites such a child to run away or stay away from the responsible person.

(2) This section applies in relation to a child who is—

(a) in care;
(b) the subject of an emergency protection order; or
(c) in police protection,

and in this section 'the responsible person' means any person who for the time being has care of him by virtue of the care order, the emergency protection order, or section 46, as the case may be.

(3) A person guilty of an offence under this section shall be liable on summary conviction to imprisonment for a term not exceeding six months, or to a fine not exceeding level 5 on the standard scale, or to both.

50 Recovery of abducted children etc.

(1) Where it appears to the court that there is reason to believe that a child to whom this section applies—

(a) has been unlawfully taken away or is being unlawfully kept away from the responsible person;
(b) has run away or is staying away from the responsible person; or
(c) is missing,

the court may make an order under this section ('a recovery order').

(2) This section applies to the same children to whom section 49 applies and in this section 'the responsible person' has the same meaning as in section 49.

(3) A recovery order—

(a) operates as a direction to any person who is in a position to do so to produce the child on request to any authorised person;
(b) authorises the removal of the child by any authorised person;
(c) requires any person who has information as to the child's whereabouts to disclose that information, if asked to do so, to a constable or an officer of the court;
(d) authorises a constable to enter any premises specified in the order and search for the child, using reasonable force if necessary.

(4) The court may make a recovery order only on the application of—

(a) any person who has parental responsibility for the child by virtue of a care order or emergency protection order; or
(b) where the child is in police protection, the designated officer.

(5) A recovery order shall name the child and—

(a) any person who has parental responsibility for the child by virtue of a care order or emergency protection order; or
(b) where the child is in police protection, the designated officer.

(6) Premises may only be specified under subsection (3)(d) if it appears to the court that there are reasonable grounds for believing the child to be on them.

(7) In this section—

'an authorised person' means —
- (a) any person specified by the court;
- (b) any constable;
- (c) any person who is authorised—
    - (i) after the recovery order is made; and
    - (ii) by a person who has parental responsibility for the child by virtue of a care order or an emergency protection order,
  to exercise any power under a recovery order; and

'the designated officer' means the officer designated for the purposes of section 46.

(8) Where a person is authorised as mentioned in subsection (7)(c)—
- (a) the authorisation shall identify the recovery order; and
- (b) any person claiming to be so authorised shall, if asked to do so, produce some duly authenticated document showing that he is so authorised.

(9) A person shall be guilty of an offence if he intentionally obstructs an authorised person exercising the power under subsection (3)(b) to remove a child.

(10) A person guilty of an offence under this section shall be liable on summary conviction to a fine not exceeding level 3 on the standard scale.

(11) No person shall be excused from complying with any request made under subsection (3)(c) on the ground that complying with it might incriminate him or his spouse [or civil partner][1] of an offence; but a statement or admission made in complying shall not be admissible in evidence against either of them in proceedings for an offence other than perjury.

(12) Where a child is made the subject of a recovery order whilst being looked after by a local authority, any reasonable expenses incurred by an authorised person in giving effect to the order shall be recoverable from the authority.

(13) A recovery order shall have effect in Scotland as if it had been made by the Court of Session and as if that court had had jurisdiction to make it.

(14) In this section 'the court', in relation to Northern Ireland, means a magistrates' court within the meaning of the Magistrates' Courts (Northern Ireland) Order 1981.

Amendment
1   Inserted by the Civil Partnership Act 2004, s 261(1), Sch 27, para 131.

51 Refuges for children at risk.

(1) Where it is proposed to use a voluntary home or [private][1] children's home to provide a refuge for children who appear to be at risk of harm, the Secretary of State may issue a certificate under this section with respect to that home.

(2) Where a local authority or voluntary organisation arrange for a foster parent to provide such a refuge, the Secretary of State may issue a certificate under this section with respect to that foster parent.

(3) In subsection (2) 'foster parent' means a person who is, or who from time to time is, a local authority foster parent or a foster parent with whom children are placed by a voluntary organisation.

(4) The Secretary of State may by regulations—
- (a) make provision as to the manner in which certificates may be issued;
- (b) impose requirements which must be complied with while any certificate is in force; and
- (c) provide for the withdrawal of certificates in prescribed circumstances.

(5) Where a certificate is in force with respect to a home, none of the provisions mentioned in subsection (7) shall apply in relation to any person providing a refuge for any child in that home.

(6) Where a certificate is in force with respect to a foster parent, none of those provisions shall apply in relation to the provision by him of a refuge for any child in accordance with arrangements made by the local authority or voluntary organisation.

(7) The provisions are—
- (a) section 49;
- [(b) articles 9, 10 and 11 of the Children's Hearing (Scotland) Act 2011 (Consequential and Transitional Provisions and Savings) Order 2013, so far as they apply to anything done in England and Wales;][2]
- (c) section 32(3) of the Children and Young Persons Act 1969 (compelling, persuading, inciting or assisting any person to be absent from detention, etc.), so far as it applies in relation to anything done in England and Wales;
- (d) section 2 of the Child Abduction Act 1984.

Amendments
1 Substituted by the Care Standards Act 2000, s 116, Sch 4, para 14(1), (7).
2 Substituted by the Children's Hearings (Scotland) Act 2011 (Consequential and Transitional Provisions and Savings) Order 2013, SI 2013/1465, art 17(1), Sch 1, para 2(1), (3).

52 Rules and regulations.

(1) Without prejudice to section 93 or any other power to make such rules, rules of court may be made with respect to the procedure to be followed in connection with proceedings under this Part.

(2) The rules may, in particular make provision—
- (a) as to the form in which any application is to be made or direction is to be given;
- (b) prescribing the persons who are to be notified of—
  - (i) the making, or extension, of an emergency protection order; or
  - (ii) the making of an application under section 45(4) or (8) or 46(7); and

(c) as to the content of any such notification and the manner in which, and person by whom, it is to be given.

(3) The Secretary of State may by regulations provide that, where—

(a) an emergency protection order has been made with respect to a child;
(b) the applicant for the order was not the local authority within whose area the child is ordinarily resident; and
(c) that local authority are of the opinion that it would be in the child's best interests for the applicant's responsibilities under the order to be transferred to them,

that authority shall (subject to their having complied with any requirements imposed by the regulations) be treated, for the purposes of this Act, as though they and not the original applicant had applied for, and been granted, the order.

(4) Regulations made under subsection (3) may, in particular, make provision as to—

(a) the considerations to which the local authority shall have regard in forming an opinion as mentioned in subsection (3)(c); and
(b) the time at which responsibility under any emergency protection order is to be treated as having been transferred to a local authority.

Appendix 2

ADOPTION AND CHILDREN ACT 2002

(2002 CHAPTER 38)

PART 1
ADOPTION

Chapter 1
Introductory

1 Considerations applying to the exercise of powers

(1) [Subsections (2) to (4) apply]¹ whenever a court or adoption agency is coming to a decision relating to the adoption of a child.

(2) The paramount consideration of the court or adoption agency must be the child's welfare, throughout his life.

(3) The court or adoption agency must at all times bear in mind that, in general, any delay in coming to the decision is likely to prejudice the child's welfare.

(4) The court or adoption agency must have regard to the following matters (among others)—

- (a) the child's ascertainable wishes and feelings regarding the decision (considered in the light of the child's age and understanding),
- (b) the child's particular needs,
- (c) the likely effect on the child (throughout his life) of having ceased to be a member of the original family and become an adopted person,
- (d) the child's age, sex, background and any of the child's characteristics which the court or agency considers relevant,
- (e) any harm (within the meaning of the Children Act 1989 (c. 41)) which the child has suffered or is at risk of suffering,
- (f) the relationship which the child has with relatives, [with any person who is a prospective adopter with whom the child is placed,]² and with any other person in relation to whom the court or agency considers the relationship to be relevant, including—
  - (i) the likelihood of any such relationship continuing and the value to the child of its doing so,
  - (ii) the ability and willingness of any of the child's relatives, or of any such person, to provide the child with a secure environment in which the child can develop, and otherwise to meet the child's needs,

(iii) the wishes and feelings of any of the child's relatives, or of any such person, regarding the child.

(5) [In placing a child for adoption, an adoption agency in Wales][1] must give due consideration to the child's religious persuasion, racial origin and cultural and linguistic background.

(6) [Incoming to a decision relating to the adoption of a child, a court or adoption agency][1] must always consider the whole range of powers available to it in the child's case (whether under this Act or the Children Act 1989); and the court must not make any order under this Act unless it considers that making the order would be better for the child than not doing so.

(7) In this section, 'coming to a decision relating to the adoption of a child', in relation to a court, includes—

(a) coming to a decision in any proceedings where the orders that might be made by the court include an adoption order (or the revocation of such an order), a placement order (or the revocation of such an order) or an order under section 26 [or 51A][3] (or the revocation or variation of such an order),

(b) coming to a decision about granting leave in respect of any action (other than the initiation of proceedings in any court) which may be taken by an adoption agency or individual under this Act,

but does not include coming to a decision about granting leave in any other circumstances.

(8) For the purposes of this section—

(a) references to relationships are not confined to legal relationships,
(b) references to a relative, in relation to a child, include the child's mother and father.

[(9) In this section 'adoption agency in Wales' means an adoption agency that is—

(a) a local authority in Wales, or
(b) a registered adoption society whose principal office is in Wales.][4]

Amendments
1 Substituted by the Children and Families Act 2014, s 3(1), (2), (3)(a), (b).
2 Inserted by the Children and Social Work Act 2017, s 9.
3 Inserted by the Children and Families Act 2014, s 9(2).
4 Inserted by the Children and Families Act 2014, s 3(1), (3)(c).

Chapter 3
Placement for adoption and adoption orders

Placement of children by adoption agency for adoption

18 Placement for adoption by agencies

(1) An adoption agency may—

(a) place a child for adoption with prospective adopters, or

(b) where it has placed a child with any persons (whether under this Part or not), leave the child with them as prospective adopters,

but, except in the case of a child who is less than six weeks old, may only do so under section 19 or a placement order.

(2) An adoption agency may only place a child for adoption with prospective adopters if the agency is satisfied that the child ought to be placed for adoption.

(3) A child who is placed or authorised to be placed for adoption with prospective adopters by a local authority is looked after by the authority.

(4) If an application for an adoption order has been made by any persons in respect of a child and has not been disposed of—

(a) an adoption agency which placed the child with those persons may leave the child with them until the application is disposed of, but
(b) apart from that, the child may not be placed for adoption with any prospective adopters.

'Adoption order' includes a Scottish or Northern Irish adoption order.

(5) References in this Act (apart from this section) to an adoption agency placing a child for adoption—

(a) are to its placing a child for adoption with prospective adopters, and
(b) include, where it has placed a child with any persons (whether under this Act or not), leaving the child with them as prospective adopters;

and references in this Act (apart from this section) to a child who is placed for adoption by an adoption agency are to be interpreted accordingly.

(6) References in this Chapter to an adoption agency being, or not being, authorised to place a child for adoption are to the agency being or (as the case may be) not being authorised to do so under section 19 or a placement order.

(7) This section is subject to sections 30 to 35 (removal of children placed by adoption agencies).

19 Placing children with parental consent

(1) Where an adoption agency is satisfied that each parent or guardian of a child has consented to the child—

(a) being placed for adoption with prospective adopters identified in the consent, or
(b) being placed for adoption with any prospective adopters who may be chosen by the agency,

and has not withdrawn the consent, the agency is authorised to place the child for adoption accordingly.

(2) Consent to a child being placed for adoption with prospective adopters identified in the consent may be combined with consent to the child subsequently

being placed for adoption with any prospective adopters who may be chosen by the agency in circumstances where the child is removed from or returned by the identified prospective adopters.

(3) Subsection (1) does not apply where—

(a) an application has been made on which a care order might be made and the application has not been disposed of, or

(b) a care order or placement order has been made after the consent was given.

(4) References in this Act to a child placed for adoption under this section include a child who was placed under this section with prospective adopters and continues to be placed with them, whether or not consent to the placement has been withdrawn.

(5) This section is subject to section 52 (parental etc. consent).

20 Advance consent to adoption

(1) A parent or guardian of a child who consents to the child being placed for adoption by an adoption agency under section 19 may, at the same or any subsequent time, consent to the making of a future adoption order.

(2) Consent under this section—

(a) where the parent or guardian has consented to the child being placed for adoption with prospective adopters identified in the consent, may be consent to adoption by them, or

(b) may be consent to adoption by any prospective adopters who may be chosen by the agency.

(3) A person may withdraw any consent given under this section.

(4) A person who gives consent under this section may, at the same or any subsequent time, by notice given to the adoption agency—

(a) state that he does not wish to be informed of any application for an adoption order, or

(b) withdraw such a statement.

(5) A notice under subsection (4) has effect from the time when it is received by the adoption agency but has no effect if the person concerned has withdrawn his consent.

(6) This section is subject to section 52 (parental etc. consent).

21 Placement orders

(1) A placement order is an order made by the court authorising a local authority to place a child for adoption with any prospective adopters who may be chosen by the authority.

(2) The court may not make a placement order in respect of a child unless—

(a) the child is subject to a care order,

(b) the court is satisfied that the conditions in section 31(2) of the 1989 Act (conditions for making a care order) are met, or
(c) the child has no parent or guardian.

(3) The court may only make a placement order if, in the case of each parent or guardian of the child, the court is satisfied—

(a) that the parent or guardian has consented to the child being placed for adoption with any prospective adopters who may be chosen by the local authority and has not withdrawn the consent, or
(b) that the parent's or guardian's consent should be dispensed with.

This subsection is subject to section 52 (parental etc. consent).

(4) A placement order continues in force until—

(a) it is revoked under section 24,
(b) an adoption order is made in respect of the child, or
(c) the child marries[, forms a civil partnership]¹ or attains the age of 18 years.

'Adoption order' includes a Scottish or Northern Irish adoption order.

Amendment
1 Inserted by the Civil Partnership Act 2004, s 79(1), (2).

22 Applications for placement orders

(1) A local authority must apply to the court for a placement order in respect of a child if—

(a) the child is placed for adoption by them or is being provided with accommodation by them,
(b) no adoption agency is authorised to place the child for adoption,
(c) the child has no parent or guardian or the authority consider that the conditions in section 31(2) of the 1989 Act are met, and
(d) the authority are satisfied that the child ought to be placed for adoption.

(2) If—

(a) an application has been made (and has not been disposed of) on which a care order might be made in respect of a child, or
(b) a child is subject to a care order and the appropriate local authority are not authorised to place the child for adoption,

the appropriate local authority must apply to the court for a placement order if they are satisfied that the child ought to be placed for adoption.

(3) If—

(a) a child is subject to a care order, and
(b) the appropriate local authority are authorised to place the child for adoption under section 19,

the authority may apply to the court for a placement order.

(4) If a local authority—
- (a) are under a duty to apply to the court for a placement order in respect of a child, or
- (b) have applied for a placement order in respect of a child and the application has not been disposed of,

the child is looked after by the authority.

(5) Subsections (1) to (3) do not apply in respect of a child—
- (a) if any persons have given notice of intention to adopt, unless the period of four months beginning with the giving of the notice has expired without them applying for an adoption order or their application for such an order has been withdrawn or refused, or
- (b) if an application for an adoption order has been made and has not been disposed of.

'Adoption order' includes a Scottish or Northern Irish adoption order.

(6) Where—
- (a) an application for a placement order in respect of a child has been made and has not been disposed of, and
- (b) no interim care order is in force,

the court may give any directions it considers appropriate for the medical or psychiatric examination or other assessment of the child; but a child who is of sufficient understanding to make an informed decision may refuse to submit to the examination or other assessment.

(7) The appropriate local authority—
- (a) in relation to a care order, is the local authority in whose care the child is placed by the order, and
- (b) in relation to an application on which a care order might be made, is the local authority which makes the application.

23 Varying placement orders

(1) The court may vary a placement order so as to substitute another local authority for the local authority authorised by the order to place the child for adoption.

(2) The variation may only be made on the joint application of both authorities.

24 Revoking placement orders

(1) The court may revoke a placement order on the application of any person.

(2) But an application may not be made by a person other than the child or the local authority authorised by the order to place the child for adoption unless—
- (a) the court has given leave to apply, and
- (b) the child is not placed for adoption by the authority.

(3) The court cannot give leave under subsection (2)(a) unless satisfied that there has been a change in circumstances since the order was made.

(4) If the court determines, on an application for an adoption order, not to make the order, it may revoke any placement order in respect of the child.

(5) Where—

(a) an application for the revocation of a placement order has been made and has not been disposed of, and
(b) the child is not placed for adoption by the authority,

the child may not without the court's leave be placed for adoption under the order.

25 Parental responsibility

(1) This section applies while—

(a) a child is placed for adoption under section 19 or an adoption agency is authorised to place a child for adoption under that section, or
(b) a placement order is in force in respect of a child.

(2) Parental responsibility for the child is given to the agency concerned.

(3) While the child is placed with prospective adopters, parental responsibility is given to them.

(4) The agency may determine that the parental responsibility of any parent or guardian, or of prospective adopters, is to be restricted to the extent specified in the determination.

26 Contact

(1) On an adoption agency being authorised to place a child for adoption, or placing a child for adoption who is less than six weeks old[—]¹

[(a) any contact provision in a child arrangements order under section 8 of the 1989 Act ceases to have effect,
(b) any order under section 34 of that Act (parental etc contact with children in care) ceases to have effect, and
(c) any activity direction made in proceedings for the making, variation or discharge of a child arrangements order with respect to the child, or made in other proceedings that relate to such an order, is discharged.]¹

(2) While an adoption agency is so authorised or a child is placed for adoption—

(a) no application may be made for[—]¹
   [(i) a child arrangements order under section 8 of the 1989 Act containing contact provision, or
   (ii) an order under section 34 of that Act, but]¹
(b) the court may make an order under this section requiring the person with whom the child lives, or is to live, to allow the child to visit or stay with the person named in the order, or for the person named in the order and the child otherwise to have contact with each other.

(3) An application for an order under this section may be made by—

(a) the child or the agency,

(b) any parent, guardian or relative,
(c) any person in whose favour there was provision ...² which ceased to have effect by virtue of subsection [(1)(a) or an order which ceased to have effect by virtue of subsection (1)(b)]¹,
(d) if a [child arrangements]¹ order was in force immediately before the adoption agency was authorised to place the child for adoption or (as the case may be) placed the child for adoption at a time when he was less than six weeks old, [any person named in the order as a person with whom the child was to live]¹,
(e) if a person had care of the child immediately before that time by virtue of an order made in the exercise of the High Court's inherent jurisdiction with respect to children, that person,
(f) any person who has obtained the court's leave to make the application.

(4) When making a placement order, the court may on its own initiative make an order under this section.

(5) ...³

[(5A) In this section 'contact provision' means provision which regulates arrangements relating to—

(a) with whom a child is to spend time or otherwise have contact, or
(b) when a child is to spend time or otherwise have contact with any person;

but in paragraphs (a) and (b) a reference to spending time or otherwise having contact with a person is to doing that otherwise than as a result of living with the person.

(6) In this section 'activity direction' has the meaning given by section 11A of the 1989 Act.]¹

Amendments
1 Substituted by the Children and Families Act 2014, s 12(4), Sch 2, paras 59, 60(1)-(3), (4)(b), (5), (7).
2 Repealed by the Children and Families Act 2014, s 12(4), Sch 2, paras 59, 60(1), (4)(a).
3 Repealed by the Children and Families Act 2014, s 9(3).

27 Contact: supplementary

(1) An order under section 26—

(a) has effect while the adoption agency is authorised to place the child for adoption or the child is placed for adoption, but
(b) may be varied or revoked by the court on an application by the child, the agency or a person named in the order.

(2) The agency may refuse to allow the contact that would otherwise be required by virtue of an order under that section if—

(a) it is satisfied that it is necessary to do so in order to safeguard or promote the child's welfare, and
(b) the refusal is decided upon as a matter of urgency and does not last for more than seven days.

(3) Regulations may make provision as to—

(a) the steps to be taken by an agency which has exercised its power under subsection (2),
(b) the circumstances in which, and conditions subject to which, the terms of any order under section 26 may be departed from by agreement between the agency and any person for whose contact with the child the order provides,
(c) notification by an agency of any variation or suspension of arrangements made (otherwise than under an order under that section) with a view to allowing any person contact with the child.

(4) Before making a placement order the court must—

(a) consider the arrangements which the adoption agency has made, or proposes to make, for allowing any person contact with the child, and
(b) invite the parties to the proceedings to comment on those arrangements.

(5) An order under section 26 may provide for contact on any conditions the court considers appropriate.

28 Further consequences of placement

(1) Where a child is placed for adoption under section 19 or an adoption agency is authorised to place a child for adoption under that section—

(a) a parent or guardian of the child may not apply for a [child arrangements order regulating the child's living arrangements][1] unless an application for an adoption order has been made and the parent or guardian has obtained the court's leave under subsection (3) or (5) of section 47,
(b) if an application has been made for an adoption order, a guardian of the child may not apply for a special guardianship order unless he has obtained the court's leave under subsection (3) or (5) of that section.

(2) Where—

(a) a child is placed for adoption under section 19 or an adoption agency is authorised to place a child for adoption under that section, or
(b) a placement order is in force in respect of a child,

then (whether or not the child is in England and Wales) a person may not do either of the following things, unless the court gives leave or each parent or guardian of the child gives written consent.

(3) Those things are—

(a) causing the child to be known by a new surname, or
(b) removing the child from the United Kingdom.

(4) Subsection (3) does not prevent the removal of a child from the United Kingdom for a period of less than one month by a person who provides the child's home.

[(5) For the purposes of subsection (1)(a), a child arrangements order regulates a child's living arrangements if the arrangements regulated by the order consist of, or include, arrangements which relate to either or both of the following—

(a) with whom the child is to live, and
(b) when the child is to live with any person.]²

Amendments
1 Substituted by the Children and Families Act 2014, s 12(4), Sch 2, paras 59, 61(1), (2).
2 Inserted by the Children and Families Act 2014, s 12(4), Sch 2, paras 59, 61(1), (3).

29 Further consequences of placement orders

(1) Where a placement order is made in respect of a child and either—

(a) the child is subject to a care order, or
(b) the court at the same time makes a care order in respect of the child,

the care order does not have effect at any time when the placement order is in force.

(2) On the making of a placement order in respect of a child, any order mentioned in section 8(1) of the 1989 Act, and any supervision order in respect of the child, ceases to have effect.

(3) Where a placement order is in force—

(a) no prohibited steps order ...¹ or specific issue order, and
(b) no supervision order or child assessment order,

may be made in respect of the child.

(4) [Where a placement order is in force, a child arrangements order may be made with respect to the child's living arrangements only if—]²

(a) an application for an adoption order has been made in respect of the child, and
(b) the [child arrangements]² order is applied for by a parent or guardian who has obtained the court's leave under subsection (3) or (5) of section 47 or by any other person who has obtained the court's leave under this subsection.

[(4A) For the purposes of subsection (4), a child arrangements order is one made with respect to a child's living arrangements if the arrangements regulated by the order consist of, or include, arrangements which relate to either or both of the following—

(a) with whom the child is to live, and
(b) when the child is to live with any person.]³

(5) Where a placement order is in force, no special guardianship order may be made in respect of the child unless—

(a) an application has been made for an adoption order, and
(b) the person applying for the special guardianship order has obtained the court's leave under this subsection or, if he is a guardian of the child, has obtained the court's leave under section 47(5).

(6) Section 14A(7) of the 1989 Act applies in respect of an application for a special guardianship order for which leave has been given as mentioned in subsection (5)(b) with the omission of the words 'the beginning of the period of three months ending with'.

(7) Where a placement order is in force—

    (a) section 14C(1)(b) of the 1989 Act (special guardianship: parental responsibility) has effect subject to any determination under section 25(4) of this Act,

    (b) section 14C(3) and (4) of the 1989 Act (special guardianship: removal of child from UK etc.) does not apply.

Amendments
1 Repealed by the Children and Families Act 2014, s 12(4), Sch 2, paras 59, 62(1), (2).
2 Substituted by the Children and Families Act 2014, s 12(4), Sch 2, paras 59, 62(1), (3).
3 Inserted by the Children and Families Act 2014, s 12(4), Sch 2, paras 59, 62(1), (4).

Preliminaries to adoption

42 Child to live with adopters before application

(1) An application for an adoption order may not be made unless—

    (a) if subsection (2) applies, the condition in that subsection is met,

    (b) if that subsection does not apply, the condition in whichever is applicable of subsections (3) to (5) applies.

(2) If—

    (a) the child was placed for adoption with the applicant or applicants by an adoption agency or in pursuance of an order of the High Court, or

    (b) the applicant is a parent of the child,

the condition is that the child must have had his home with the applicant or, in the case of an application by a couple, with one or both of them at all times during the period of ten weeks preceding the application.

(3) If the applicant or one of the applicants is the partner of a parent of the child, the condition is that the child must have had his home with the applicant or, as the case may be, applicants at all times during the period of six months preceding the application.

(4) If the applicants are local authority foster parents, the condition is that the child must have had his home with the applicants at all times during the period of one year preceding the application.

(5) In any other case, the condition is that the child must have had his home with the applicant or, in the case of an application by a couple, with one or both of them for not less than three years (whether continuous or not) during the period of five years preceding the application.

(6) But subsections (4) and (5) do not prevent an application being made if the court gives leave to make it.

(7) An adoption order may not be made unless the court is satisfied that sufficient opportunities to see the child with the applicant or, in the case of an application by a couple, both of them together in the home environment have been given—

(a) where the child was placed for adoption with the applicant or applicants by an adoption agency, to that agency,
(b) in any other case, to the local authority within whose area the home is.

(8) In this section and sections 43 and 44(1)—

(a) references to an adoption agency include a Scottish or Northern Irish adoption agency,
(b) references to a child placed for adoption by an adoption agency are to be read accordingly.

43 Reports where child placed by agency

Where an application for an adoption order relates to a child placed for adoption by an adoption agency, the agency must—

(a) submit to the court a report on the suitability of the applicants and on any other matters relevant to the operation of section 1, and
(b) assist the court in any manner the court directs.

44 Notice of intention to adopt

(1) This section applies where persons (referred to in this section as 'proposed adopters') wish to adopt a child who is not placed for adoption with them by an adoption agency.

(2) An adoption order may not be made in respect of the child unless the proposed adopters have given notice to the appropriate local authority of their intention to apply for the adoption order (referred to in this Act as a 'notice of intention to adopt').

(3) The notice must be given not more than two years, or less than three months, before the date on which the application for the adoption order is made.

(4) Where—

(a) if a person were seeking to apply for an adoption order, subsection (4) or (5) of section 42 would apply, but
(b) the condition in the subsection in question is not met,

the person may not give notice of intention to adopt unless he has the court's leave to apply for an adoption order.

(5) On receipt of a notice of intention to adopt, the local authority must arrange for the investigation of the matter and submit to the court a report of the investigation.

(6) In particular, the investigation must, so far as practicable, include the suitability of the proposed adopters and any other matters relevant to the operation of section 1 in relation to the application.

(7) If a local authority receive a notice of intention to adopt in respect of a child whom they know was (immediately before the notice was given) looked after by another local authority, they must, not more than seven days after the receipt of the notice, inform the other local authority in writing that they have received the notice.

(8) Where—
(a) a local authority have placed a child with any persons otherwise than as prospective adopters, and
(b) the persons give notice of intention to adopt,

the authority are not to be treated as leaving the child with them as prospective adopters for the purposes of section 18(1)(b).

(9) In this section, references to the appropriate local authority, in relation to any proposed adopters, are—
(a) in prescribed cases, references to the prescribed local authority,
(b) in any other case, references to the local authority for the area in which, at the time of giving the notice of intention to adopt, they have their home,

and 'prescribed' means prescribed by regulations.

45 Suitability of adopters

(1) Regulations under section 9 may make provision as to the matters to be taken into account by an adoption agency in determining, or making any report in respect of, the suitability of any persons to adopt a child.

(2) In particular, the regulations may make provision for the purpose of securing that, in determining the suitability of a couple to adopt a child, proper regard is had to the need for stability and permanence in their relationship.

The making of adoption orders

46 Adoption orders

(1) An adoption order is an order made by the court on an application under section 50 or 51 giving parental responsibility for a child to the adopters or adopter.

(2) The making of an adoption order operates to extinguish—
(a) the parental responsibility which any person other than the adopters or adopter has for the adopted child immediately before the making of the order,
(b) any order under the 1989 Act or the Children (Northern Ireland) Order 1995 (S.I. 1995/755 (N.I. 2)),
(c) any order under the Children (Scotland) Act 1995 (c. 36) other than an excepted order,
[(ca) any child assessment order or child protection order within the meaning given in section 202(1) of the Children's Hearing (Scotland) Act 2011,][1] and

(d) any duty arising by virtue of an agreement or an order of a court to make payments, so far as the payments are in respect of the adopted child's maintenance or upbringing for any period after the making of the adoption order.

'Excepted order' means an order under section 9, 11(1)(d) or 13 of the Children (Scotland) Act 1995 or an exclusion order within the meaning of section 76(1) of that Act.

(3) An adoption order—

(a) does not affect parental responsibility so far as it relates to any period before the making of the order, and
(b) in the case of an order made on an application under section 51(2) by the partner of a parent of the adopted child, does not affect the parental responsibility of that parent or any duties of that parent within subsection (2)(d).

(4) Subsection (2)(d) does not apply to a duty arising by virtue of an agreement—

(a) which constitutes a trust, or
(b) which expressly provides that the duty is not to be extinguished by the making of an adoption order.

(5) An adoption order may be made even if the child to be adopted is already an adopted child.

(6) Before making an adoption order, the court must consider whether there should be arrangements for allowing any person contact with the child; and for that purpose the court must consider any existing or proposed arrangements and obtain any views of the parties to the proceedings.

Amendment
1 Inserted by the Children's Hearings (Scotland) Act 2011 (Consequential and Transitional Provisions and Savings) Order 2013, SI 2013/1465, s 17(1), Sch 1, para 9.

47 Conditions for making adoption orders

(1) An adoption order may not be made if the child has a parent or guardian unless one of the following three conditions is met; but this section is subject to section 52 (parental etc. consent).

(2) The first condition is that, in the case of each parent or guardian of the child, the court is satisfied—

(a) that the parent or guardian consents to the making of the adoption order,
(b) that the parent or guardian has consented under section 20 (and has not withdrawn the consent) and does not oppose the making of the adoption order, or
(c) that the parent's or guardian's consent should be dispensed with.

(3) A parent or guardian may not oppose the making of an adoption order under subsection (2)(b) without the court's leave.

(4) The second condition is that—

- (a) the child has been placed for adoption by an adoption agency with the prospective adopters in whose favour the order is proposed to be made,
- (b) either—
  - (i) the child was placed for adoption with the consent of each parent or guardian and the consent of the mother was given when the child was at least six weeks old, or
  - (ii) the child was placed for adoption under a placement order, and
- (c) no parent or guardian opposes the making of the adoption order.

(5) A parent or guardian may not oppose the making of an adoption order under the second condition without the court's leave.

(6) The third condition is that the child[—]¹

- [(a) is the subject of a Scottish permanence order which includes provision granting authority for the child to be adopted, or
- (b) is free for adoption by virtue of an order made, under Article 17(1) or 18(1) of the Adoption (Northern Ireland) Order 1987 (S.I. 1987/2203 (N.I. 22)).]¹

(7) The court cannot give leave under subsection (3) or (5) unless satisfied that there has been a change in circumstances since the consent of the parent or guardian was given or, as the case may be, the placement order was made.

(8) An adoption order may not be made in relation to a person who is or has been married.

[(8A) An adoption order may not be made in relation to a person who is or has been a civil partner.]²

(9) An adoption order may not be made in relation to a person who has attained the age of 19 years.

[(10) In this section, 'Scottish permanence order' means a permanence order under section 80 of the Adoption and Children (Scotland) Act 2007 (asp 4) (including a deemed permanence order having effect by virtue of article 13(1), 14(2), 17(1) or 19(2) of the Adoption and Children (Scotland) Act 2007 (Commencement No. 4, Transitional and Savings Provisions) Order 2009 (S.S.I. 2009/267)).]³

Amendments
1 Substituted by the Adoption and Children (Scotland) Act 2007 (Consequential Modifications) Order 2011, SI 2011/1740, art 2, Sch 1, para 6(1), (2)(a).
2 Inserted by the Civil Partnership Act 2004, s 79(1), (3).
3 Inserted by the Adoption and Children (Scotland) Act 2007 (Consequential Modifications) Order 2011, SI 2011/1740, art 2, Sch 1, para 6(1), (2)(b).

48 Restrictions on making adoption orders

(1) The court may not hear an application for an adoption order in relation to a child, where a previous application to which subsection (2) applies made in relation to the child by the same persons was refused by any court, unless it

appears to the court that, because of a change in circumstances or for any other reason, it is proper to hear the application.

(2) This subsection applies to any application—

(a) for an adoption order or a Scottish or Northern Irish adoption order, or
(b) for an order for adoption made in the Isle of Man or any of the Channel Islands.

49 Applications for adoption

(1) An application for an adoption order may be made by—

(a) a couple, or
(b) one person,

but only if it is made under section 50 or 51 and one of the following conditions is met.

(2) The first condition is that at least one of the couple (in the case of an application under section 50) or the applicant (in the case of an application under section 51) is domiciled in a part of the British Islands.

(3) The second condition is that both of the couple (in the case of an application under section 50) or the applicant (in the case of an application under section 51) have been habitually resident in a part of the British Islands for a period of not less than one year ending with the date of the application.

(4) An application for an adoption order may only be made if the person to be adopted has not attained the age of 18 years on the date of the application.

(5) References in this Act to a child, in connection with any proceedings (whether or not concluded) for adoption, (such as 'child to be adopted' or 'adopted child') include a person who has attained the age of 18 years before the proceedings are concluded.

50 Adoption by couple

(1) An adoption order may be made on the application of a couple where both of them have attained the age of 21 years.

(2) An adoption order may be made on the application of a couple where—

(a) one of the couple is the mother or the father of the person to be adopted and has attained the age of 18 years, and
(b) the other has attained the age of 21 years.

51 Adoption by one person

(1) An adoption order may be made on the application of one person who has attained the age of 21 years and is not married [or a civil partner][1].

(2) An adoption order may be made on the application of one person who has attained the age of 21 years if the court is satisfied that the person is the partner of a parent of the person to be adopted.

(3) An adoption order may be made on the application of one person who has attained the age of 21 years and is married if the court is satisfied that—

    (a)   the person's spouse cannot be found,
    (b)   the spouses have separated and are living apart, and the separation is likely to be permanent, or
    (c)   the person's spouse is by reason of ill-health, whether physical or mental, incapable of making an application for an adoption order.

[(3A) An adoption order may be made on the application of one person who has attained the age of 21 years and is a civil partner if the court is satisfied that–

    (a)   the person's civil partner cannot be found,
    (b)   the civil partners have separated and are living apart, and the separation is likely to be permanent, or
    (c)   the person's civil partner is by reason of ill-health, whether physical or mental, incapable of making an application for an adoption order.][1]

(4) An adoption order may not be made on an application under this section by the mother or the father of the person to be adopted unless the court is satisfied that—

    (a)   the other natural parent is dead or cannot be found,
    [(b)   by virtue of the provisions specified in subsection (5), there is no other parent, or][2]
    (c)   there is some other reason justifying the child's being adopted by the applicant alone,

and, where the court makes an adoption order on such an application, the court must record that it is satisfied as to the fact mentioned in paragraph (a) or (b) or, in the case of paragraph (c), record the reason.

[(5) The provisions referred to in subsection (4)(b) are—

    (a)   section 28 of the Human Fertilisation and Embryology Act 1990 (disregarding subsections (5A) to (5I) of that section), or
    (b)   sections 34 to 47 of the Human Fertilisation and Embryology Act 2008 (disregarding sections 39, 40 and 46 of that Act).][3]

Amendments
1   Inserted by the Civil Partnership Act 2004, s 79(1), (4), (5).
2   Substituted by the Human Fertilisation and Embryology Act 2008, s 56, Sch 6, para 39(1), (2).
3   Inserted by the Human Fertilisation and Embryology Act 2008, s 56, Sch 6, para 39(1), (3).

[*Post-adoption contact*

51A Post-adoption contact

(1) This section applies where—

    (a)   an adoption agency has placed or was authorised to place a child for adoption, and
    (b)   the court is making or has made an adoption order in respect of the child.

(2) When making the adoption order or at any time afterwards, the court may make an order under this section—

(a) requiring the person in whose favour the adoption order is or has been made to allow the child to visit or stay with the person named in the order under this section, or for the person named in that order and the child otherwise to have contact with each other, or

(b) prohibiting the person named in the order under this section from having contact with the child.

(3) The following people may be named in an order under this section—

(a) any person who (but for the child's adoption) would be related to the child by blood (including half-blood), marriage or civil partnership;

(b) any former guardian of the child;

(c) any person who had parental responsibility for the child immediately before the making of the adoption order;

(d) any person who was entitled to make an application for an order under section 26 in respect of the child (contact with children placed or to be placed for adoption) by virtue of subsection (3)(c), (d) or (e) of that section;

(e) any person with whom the child has lived for a period of at least one year.

(4) An application for an order under this section may be made by—

(a) a person who has applied for the adoption order or in whose favour the adoption order is or has been made,

(b) the child, or

(c) any person who has obtained the court's leave to make the application.

(5) In deciding whether to grant leave under subsection (4)(c), the court must consider—

(a) any risk there might be of the proposed application disrupting the child's life to such an extent that he or she would be harmed by it (within the meaning of the 1989 Act),

(b) the applicant's connection with the child, and

(c) any representations made to the court by—

(i) the child, or

(ii) a person who has applied for the adoption order or in whose favour the adoption order is or has been made.

(6) When making an adoption order, the court may on its own initiative make an order of the type mentioned in subsection (2)(b).

(7) The period of one year mentioned in subsection (3)(e) need not be continuous but must not have begun more than five years before the making of the application.

(8) Where this section applies, an order under section 8 of the 1989 Act may not make provision about contact between the child and any person who may be named in an order under this section.][1]

Amendment
1 Inserted by the Children and Families Act 2014, s 9(1).

[51B Orders under section 51A: supplementary

(1) An order under section 51A—

- (a) may contain directions about how it is to be carried into effect,
- (b) may be made subject to any conditions the court thinks appropriate,
- (c) may be varied or revoked by the court on an application by the child, a person in whose favour the adoption order was made or a person named in the order, and
- (d) has effect until the child's 18th birthday, unless revoked.

(2) Subsection (3) applies to proceedings—

- (a) on an application for an adoption order in which—
  - (i) an application is made for an order under section 51A, or
  - (ii) the court indicates that it is considering making such an order on its own initiative;
- (b) on an application for an order under section 51A;
- (c) on an application for such an order to be varied or revoked.

(3) The court must (in the light of any rules made by virtue of subsection (4))—

- (a) draw up a timetable with a view to determining without delay whether to make, (or as the case may be) vary or revoke an order under section 51A, and
- (b) give directions for the purpose of ensuring, so far as is reasonably practicable, that that timetable is adhered to.

(4) Rules of court may—

- (a) specify periods within which specified steps must be taken in relation to proceedings to which subsection (3) applies, and
- (b) make other provision with respect to such proceedings for the purpose of ensuring, so far as is reasonably practicable, that the court makes determinations about orders under section 51A without delay.]¹

Amendment
1 Inserted by the Children and Families Act 2014, s 9(1).

Placement and adoption: general

52 Parental etc. consent

(1) The court cannot dispense with the consent of any parent or guardian of a child to the child being placed for adoption or to the making of an adoption order in respect of the child unless the court is satisfied that—

- (a) the parent or guardian cannot be found or [lacks capacity (within the meaning of the Mental Capacity Act 2005) to give consent]¹, or
- (b) the welfare of the child requires the consent to be dispensed with.

(2) The following provisions apply to references in this Chapter to any parent or guardian of a child giving or withdrawing—

(a) consent to the placement of a child for adoption, or
(b) consent to the making of an adoption order (including a future adoption order).

(3) Any consent given by the mother to the making of an adoption order is ineffective if it is given less than six weeks after the child's birth.

(4) The withdrawal of any consent to the placement of a child for adoption, or of any consent given under section 20, is ineffective if it is given after an application for an adoption order is made.

(5) 'Consent' means consent given unconditionally and with full understanding of what is involved; but a person may consent to adoption without knowing the identity of the persons in whose favour the order will be made.

(6) 'Parent' (except in subsections (9) and (10) below) means a parent having parental responsibility.

(7) Consent under section 19 or 20 must be given in the form prescribed by rules, and the rules may prescribe forms in which a person giving consent under any other provision of this Part may do so (if he wishes).

(8) Consent given under section 19 or 20 must be withdrawn—

(a) in the form prescribed by rules, or
(b) by notice given to the agency.

(9) Subsection (10) applies if—

(a) an agency has placed a child for adoption under section 19 in pursuance of consent given by a parent of the child, and
(b) at a later time, the other parent of the child acquires parental responsibility for the child.

(10) The other parent is to be treated as having at that time given consent in accordance with this section in the same terms as those in which the first parent gave consent.

Amendment
1   Substituted by the Mental Capacity Act 2005, s 67(1), Sch 6, para 45.

Chapter 4
Status of adopted children

66 Meaning of adoption in Chapter 4

(1) In this Chapter 'adoption' means—

(a) adoption by an adoption order or a Scottish or Northern Irish adoption order,
(b) adoption by an order made in the Isle of Man or any of the Channel Islands,

(c) an adoption effected under the law of a Convention country outside the British Islands, and certified in pursuance of Article 23(1) of the Convention (referred to in this Act as a 'Convention adoption'),
(d) an overseas adoption, or
(e) an adoption recognised by the law of England and Wales and effected under the law of any other country;

and related expressions are to be interpreted accordingly.

(2) But references in this Chapter to adoption do not include an adoption effected before the day on which this Chapter comes into force (referred to in this Chapter as 'the appointed day').

(3) Any reference in an enactment to an adopted person within the meaning of this Chapter includes a reference to an adopted child within the meaning of Part 4 of the Adoption Act 1976 (c. 36).

67 Status conferred by adoption

(1) An adopted person is to be treated in law as if born as the child of the adopters or adopter.

(2) An adopted person is the legitimate child of the adopters or adopter and, if adopted by—

(a) a couple, or
(b) one of a couple under section 51(2),

is to be treated as the child of the relationship of the couple in question.

(3) An adopted person—

(a) if adopted by one of a couple under section 51(2), is to be treated in law as not being the child of any person other than the adopter and the other one of the couple, and
(b) in any other case, is to be treated in law, subject to subsection (4), as not being the child of any person other than the adopters or adopter;

but this subsection does not affect any reference in this Act to a person's natural parent or to any other natural relationship.

(4) In the case of a person adopted by one of the person's natural parents as sole adoptive parent, subsection (3)(b) has no effect as respects entitlement to property depending on relationship to that parent, or as respects anything else depending on that relationship.

(5) This section has effect from the date of the adoption.

(6) Subject to the provisions of this Chapter and Schedule 4, this section—

(a) applies for the interpretation of enactments or instruments passed or made before as well as after the adoption, and so applies subject to any contrary indication, and
(b) has effect as respects things done, or events occurring, on or after the adoption.

68 Adoptive relatives

(1) A relationship existing by virtue of section 67 may be referred to as an adoptive relationship, and—

- (a) an adopter may be referred to as an adoptive parent or (as the case may be) as an adoptive father or adoptive mother,
- (b) any other relative of any degree under an adoptive relationship may be referred to as an adoptive relative of that degree.

(2) Subsection (1) does not affect the interpretation of any reference, not qualified by the word 'adoptive', to a relationship.

(3) A reference (however expressed) to the adoptive mother and father of a child adopted by—

- (a) a couple of the same sex, or
- (b) a partner of the child's parent, where the couple are of the same sex,

is to be read as a reference to the child's adoptive parents.

Chapter 6
Adoptions with a foreign element

Bringing children into and out of the United Kingdom

83 Restriction on bringing children in

(1) This section applies where a person who is habitually resident in the British Islands (the 'British resident')—

- (a) brings, or causes another to bring, a child who is habitually resident outside the British Islands into the United Kingdom for the purpose of adoption by the British resident, or
- (b) at any time brings, or causes another to bring, into the United Kingdom a child adopted by the British resident under an external adoption effected within the period of [twelve][1] months ending with that time.

The references to adoption, or to a child adopted, by the British resident include a reference to adoption, or to a child adopted, by the British resident and another person.

(2) But this section does not apply if the child is intended to be adopted under a Convention adoption order.

(3) An external adoption means an adoption, other than a Convention adoption, of a child effected under the law of any country or territory outside the British Islands, whether or not the adoption is—

- (a) an adoption within the meaning of Chapter 4, or
- (b) a full adoption (within the meaning of section 88(3)).

(4) Regulations may require a person intending to bring, or to cause another to bring, a child into the United Kingdom in circumstances where this section applies—

(a) to apply to an adoption agency (including a Scottish or Northern Irish adoption agency) in the prescribed manner for an assessment of his suitability to adopt the child, and
(b) to give the agency any information it may require for the purpose of the assessment.

(5) Regulations may require prescribed conditions to be met in respect of a child brought into the United Kingdom in circumstances where this section applies.

(6) In relation to a child brought into the United Kingdom for adoption in circumstances where this section applies, regulations may—

(a) provide for any provision of Chapter 3 to apply with modifications or not to apply,
(b) if notice of intention to adopt has been given, impose functions in respect of the child on the local authority to which the notice was given.

(7) If a person brings, or causes another to bring, a child into the United Kingdom at any time in circumstances where this section applies, he is guilty of an offence if—

(a) he has not complied with any requirement imposed by virtue of subsection (4), or
(b) any condition required to be met by virtue of subsection (5) is not met,

before that time, or before any later time which may be prescribed.

(8) A person guilty of an offence under this section is liable—

(a) on summary conviction to imprisonment for a term not exceeding six months, or a fine not exceeding the statutory maximum, or both,
(b) on conviction on indictment, to imprisonment for a term not exceeding twelve months, or a fine, or both.

(9) In this section, 'prescribed' means prescribed by regulations and 'regulations' means regulations made by the Secretary of State, after consultation with the Assembly.

Amendment
1 Substituted by the Children and Adoption Act 2006, s 14(1).

84 Giving parental responsibility prior to adoption abroad

(1) The High Court may, on an application by persons who the court is satisfied intend to adopt a child under the law of a country or territory outside the British Islands, make an order giving parental responsibility for the child to them.

(2) An order under this section may not give parental responsibility to persons who the court is satisfied meet those requirements as to domicile, or habitual residence, in England and Wales which have to be met if an adoption order is to be made in favour of those persons.

(3) An order under this section may not be made unless any requirements prescribed by regulations are satisfied.

(4) An application for an order under this section may not be made unless at all times during the preceding ten weeks the child's home was with the applicant or, in the case of an application by two people, both of them.

(5) Section 46(2) to (4) has effect in relation to an order under this section as it has effect in relation to adoption orders.

(6) Regulations may provide for any provision of this Act which refers to adoption orders to apply, with or without modifications, to orders under this section.

(7) In this section, 'regulations' means regulations made by the Secretary of State, after consultation with the Assembly.

85 Restriction on taking children out

(1) A child who—
- (a) is a Commonwealth citizen, or
- (b) is habitually resident in the United Kingdom,

must not be removed from the United Kingdom to a place outside the British Islands for the purpose of adoption unless the condition in subsection (2) is met.

(2) The condition is that—
- (a) the prospective adopters have parental responsibility for the child by virtue of an order under section 84, or
- (b) the child is removed under the authority of an order under [section 59 of the Adoption and Children (Scotland) Act 2007 (asp 4)][1] or Article 57 of the Adoption (Northern Ireland) Order 1987 (S.I. 1987/2203 (N.I. 22)).

(3) Removing a child from the United Kingdom includes arranging to do so; and the circumstances in which a person arranges to remove a child from the United Kingdom include those where he—
- (a) enters into an arrangement for the purpose of facilitating such a removal of the child,
- (b) initiates or takes part in any negotiations of which the purpose is the conclusion of an arrangement within paragraph (a), or
- (c) causes another person to take any step mentioned in paragraph (a) or (b).

An arrangement includes an agreement (whether or not enforceable).

(4) A person who removes a child from the United Kingdom in contravention of subsection (1) is guilty of an offence.

(5) A person is not guilty of an offence under subsection (4) of causing a person to take any step mentioned in paragraph (a) or (b) of subsection (3) unless it is proved that he knew or had reason to suspect that the step taken would contravene subsection (1).

But this subsection only applies if sufficient evidence is adduced to raise an issue as to whether the person had the knowledge or reason mentioned.

(6) A person guilty of an offence under this section is liable—

(a) on summary conviction to imprisonment for a term not exceeding six months, or a fine not exceeding the statutory maximum, or both,

(b) on conviction on indictment, to imprisonment for a term not exceeding twelve months, or a fine, or both.

(7) In any proceedings under this section—

(a) a report by a British consular officer or a deposition made before a British consular officer and authenticated under the signature of that officer is admissible, upon proof that the officer or the deponent cannot be found in the United Kingdom, as evidence of the matters stated in it, and

(b) it is not necessary to prove the signature or official character of the person who appears to have signed any such report or deposition.

Amendment
1 Substituted by the Adoption and Children (Scotland) Act 2007 (Consequential Modifications) Order 2011, SI 2011/1740, art 2, Sch 1, para 6(1), (3).

86 Power to modify sections 83 and 85

(1) Regulations may provide for section 83 not to apply if—

(a) the adopters or (as the case may be) prospective adopters are natural parents, natural relatives or guardians of the child in question (or one of them is), or

(b) the British resident in question is a partner of a parent of the child,

and any prescribed conditions are met.

(2) Regulations may provide for section 85(1) to apply with modifications, or not to apply, if—

(a) the prospective adopters are parents, relatives or guardians of the child in question (or one of them is), or

(b) the prospective adopter is a partner of a parent of the child,

and any prescribed conditions are met.

(3) On the occasion of the first exercise of the power to make regulations under this section—

(a) the statutory instrument containing the regulations is not to be made unless a draft of the instrument has been laid before, and approved by a resolution of, each House of Parliament, and

(b) accordingly section 140(2) does not apply to the instrument.

(4) In this section, 'prescribed' means prescribed by regulations and 'regulations' means regulations made by the Secretary of State after consultation with the Assembly.

Overseas adoptions

87 Overseas adoptions

(1) In this Act, 'overseas adoption' —

(a) means an adoption of a description specified in an order made by the Secretary of State, being a description of adoptions effected under the law of any country or territory outside the British Islands, but
(b) does not include a Convention adoption.

(2) Regulations may prescribe the requirements that ought to be met by an adoption of any description effected after the commencement of the regulations for it to be an overseas adoption for the purposes of this Act.

(3) At any time when such regulations have effect, the Secretary of State must exercise his powers under this section so as to secure that subsequently effected adoptions of any description are not overseas adoptions for the purposes of this Act if he considers that they are not likely within a reasonable time to meet the prescribed requirements.

(4) In this section references to this Act include the Adoption Act 1976 (c. 36).

(5) An order under this section may contain provision as to the manner in which evidence of any overseas adoption may be given.

(6) In this section—

'adoption' means an adoption of a child or of a person who was a child at the time the adoption was applied for,
'regulations' means regulations made by the Secretary of State after consultation with the Assembly.

Miscellaneous

88 Modification of section 67 for Hague Convention adoptions

(1) If the High Court is satisfied, on an application under this section, that each of the following conditions is met in the case of a Convention adoption, it may direct that section 67(3) does not apply, or does not apply to any extent specified in the direction.

(2) The conditions are—

(a) that under the law of the country in which the adoption was effected, the adoption is not a full adoption,
(b) that the consents referred to in Article 4(c) and (d) of the Convention have not been given for a full adoption or that the United Kingdom is not the receiving State (within the meaning of Article 2 of the Convention),
(c) that it would be more favourable to the adopted child for a direction to be given under subsection (1).

(3) A full adoption is an adoption by virtue of which the child is to be treated in law as not being the child of any person other than the adopters or adopter.

(4) In relation to a direction under this section and an application for it, sections 59 and 60 of the Family Law Act 1986 (c. 55) (declarations under Part 3 of that Act as to marital status) apply as they apply in relation to a direction under that Part and an application for such a direction.

89 Annulment etc. of overseas or Hague Convention adoptions

(1) The High Court may, on an application under this subsection, by order annul a Convention adoption or Convention adoption order on the ground that the adoption is contrary to public policy.

(2) The High Court may, on an application under this subsection—

(a) by order provide for an overseas adoption or a determination under section 91 to cease to be valid on the ground that the adoption or determination is contrary to public policy or that the authority which purported to authorise the adoption or make the determination was not competent to entertain the case, or
(b) decide the extent, if any, to which a determination under section 91 has been affected by a subsequent determination under that section.

(3) The High Court may, in any proceedings in that court, decide that an overseas adoption or a determination under section 91 is to be treated, for the purposes of those proceedings, as invalid on either of the grounds mentioned in subsection (2)(a).

(4) Subject to the preceding provisions, the validity of a Convention adoption, Convention adoption order or overseas adoption or a determination under section 91 cannot be called in question in proceedings in any court in England and Wales.

90 Section 89: supplementary

(1) Any application for an order under section 89 or a decision under subsection (2)(b) or (3) of that section must be made in the prescribed manner and within any prescribed period.

'Prescribed' means prescribed by rules.

(2) No application may be made under section 89(1) in respect of an adoption unless immediately before the application is made—

(a) the person adopted, or
(b) the adopters or adopter,

habitually reside in England and Wales.

(3) In deciding in pursuance of section 89 whether such an authority as is mentioned in section 91 was competent to entertain a particular case, a court is bound by any finding of fact made by the authority and stated by the authority to be so made for the purpose of determining whether the authority was competent to entertain the case.

91 Overseas determinations and orders

(1) Subsection (2) applies where any authority of a Convention country (other than the United Kingdom) or of the Channel Islands, the Isle of Man or any British overseas territory has power under the law of that country or territory—

(a) to authorise, or review the authorisation of, an adoption order made in that country or territory, or
(b) to give or review a decision revoking or annulling such an order or a Convention adoption.

(2) If the authority makes a determination in the exercise of that power, the determination is to have effect for the purpose of effecting, confirming or terminating the adoption in question or, as the case may be, confirming its termination.

(3) Subsection (2) is subject to section 89 and to any subsequent determination having effect under that subsection.

[91A Power to charge

(1) This section applies to adoptions to which–
(a) section 83 applies, or
(b) regulations made under section 1 of the Adoption (Intercountry Aspects) Act 1999 apply.

(2) The Secretary of State may charge a fee to adopters for services provided or to be provided by him in relation to adoptions to which this section applies.

(3) The Assembly may charge a fee to adopters for services provided or to be provided by it as the Central Authority in relation to adoptions to which this section applies by virtue of subsection (1)(b).

(4) The Secretary of State and the Assembly may determine the level of fee as he or it sees fit, and may in particular–
(a) charge a flat fee or charge different fees in different cases or descriptions of case, and
(b) in any case or description of case, waive a fee.

(5) But the Secretary of State and the Assembly must each secure that, taking one financial year with another, the income from fees under this section does not exceed the total cost to him or, as the case may be, to it of providing the services in relation to which the fees are imposed.

(6) In this section–
references to adoptions and adopters include prospective adoptions and prospective adopters,
'Central Authority' is to be construed in accordance with section 2 of the Adoption (Intercountry Aspects) Act 1999,
'financial year' means a period of twelve months ending with 31st March.][1]

Amendment
1 Inserted by the Children and Adoption Act 2006, s 13.

Chapter 7
Miscellaneous

Restrictions

92 Restriction on arranging adoptions etc.

(1) A person who is neither an adoption agency nor acting in pursuance of an order of the High Court [or the family court][1] must not take any of the steps mentioned in subsection (2).

(2) The steps are—

- (a) asking a person other than an adoption agency to provide a child for adoption,
- (b) asking a person other than an adoption agency to provide prospective adopters for a child,
- (c) offering to find a child for adoption,
- (d) offering a child for adoption to a person other than an adoption agency,
- (e) handing over a child to any person other than an adoption agency with a view to the child's adoption by that or another person,
- (f) receiving a child handed over to him in contravention of paragraph (e),
- (g) entering into an agreement with any person for the adoption of a child, or for the purpose of facilitating the adoption of a child, where no adoption agency is acting on behalf of the child in the adoption,
- (h) initiating or taking part in negotiations of which the purpose is the conclusion of an agreement within paragraph (g),
- (i) causing another person to take any of the steps mentioned in paragraphs (a) to (h).

(3) Subsection (1) does not apply to a person taking any of the steps mentioned in paragraphs (d), (e), (g), (h) and (i) of subsection (2) if the following condition is met.

(4) The condition is that—

- (a) the prospective adopters are parents, relatives or guardians of the child (or one of them is), or
- (b) the prospective adopter is the partner of a parent of the child.

(5) References to an adoption agency in subsection (2) include a prescribed person outside the United Kingdom exercising functions corresponding to those of an adoption agency, if the functions are being exercised in prescribed circumstances in respect of the child in question.

(6) The Secretary of State may, after consultation with the Assembly, by order make any amendments of subsections (1) to (4), and any consequential amendments of this Act, which he considers necessary or expedient.

(7) In this section—

- (a) 'agreement' includes an arrangement (whether or not enforceable),
- (b) 'prescribed' means prescribed by regulations made by the Secretary of State after consultation with the Assembly.

Amendment
1   Inserted by the Crime and Courts Act 2013, s 17(6), Sch 11, paras 102, 155.

93 Offence of breaching restrictions under section 92

(1) If a person contravenes section 92(1), he is guilty of an offence; and, if that person is an adoption society, the person who manages the society is also guilty of the offence.

(2) A person is not guilty of an offence under subsection (1) of taking the step mentioned in paragraph (f) of section 92(2) unless it is proved that he knew or had reason to suspect that the child was handed over to him in contravention of paragraph (e) of that subsection.

(3) A person is not guilty of an offence under subsection (1) of causing a person to take any of the steps mentioned in paragraphs (a) to (h) of section 92(2) unless it is proved that he knew or had reason to suspect that the step taken would contravene the paragraph in question.

(4) But subsections (2) and (3) only apply if sufficient evidence is adduced to raise an issue as to whether the person had the knowledge or reason mentioned.

(5) A person guilty of an offence under this section is liable on summary conviction to imprisonment for a term not exceeding six months, or [a fine][1], or both.

Amendment
1   Substituted by the Legal Aid, Sentencing and Punishment of Offenders Act 2012 (Fines on Summary Conviction) Regulations 2015, SI 2015/664, reg 4(1), Sch 4, para 32(1), (2).

94 Restriction on reports

(1) A person who is not within a prescribed description may not, in any prescribed circumstances, prepare a report for any person about the suitability of a child for adoption or of a person to adopt a child or about the adoption, or placement for adoption, of a child.

'Prescribed' means prescribed by regulations made by the Secretary of State after consultation with the Assembly.

(2) If a person—
   (a)   contravenes subsection (1), or
   (b)   causes a person to prepare a report, or submits to any person a report which has been prepared, in contravention of that subsection,

he is guilty of an offence.

(3) If a person who works for an adoption society—
   (a)   contravenes subsection (1), or
   (b)   causes a person to prepare a report, or submits to any person a report which has been prepared, in contravention of that subsection,

the person who manages the society is also guilty of the offence.

(4) A person is not guilty of an offence under subsection (2)(b) unless it is proved that he knew or had reason to suspect that the report would be, or had been, prepared in contravention of subsection (1).

But this subsection only applies if sufficient evidence is adduced to raise an issue as to whether the person had the knowledge or reason mentioned.

(5) A person guilty of an offence under this section is liable on summary conviction to imprisonment for a term not exceeding six months, or a fine not exceeding level 5 on the standard scale, or both.

95 Prohibition of certain payments

(1) This section applies to any payment (other than an excepted payment) which is made for or in consideration of—

    (a)   the adoption of a child,
    (b)   giving any consent required in connection with the adoption of a child,
    (c)   removing from the United Kingdom a child who is a Commonwealth citizen, or is habitually resident in the United Kingdom, to a place outside the British Islands for the purpose of adoption,
    (d)   a person (who is neither an adoption agency nor acting in pursuance of an order of the High Court [or family court][1]) taking any step mentioned in section 92(2),
    (e)   preparing, causing to be prepared or submitting a report the preparation of which contravenes section 94(1).

(2) In this section and section 96, removing a child from the United Kingdom has the same meaning as in section 85.

(3) Any person who—

    (a)   makes any payment to which this section applies,
    (b)   agrees or offers to make any such payment, or
    (c)   receives or agrees to receive or attempts to obtain any such payment,

is guilty of an offence.

(4) A person guilty of an offence under this section is liable on summary conviction to imprisonment for a term not exceeding six months, or [a fine][2], or both.

Amendments
1   Inserted by the Crime and Courts Act 2013, s 17(6), Sch 11, paras 102, 156.
2   Substituted by the Legal Aid, Sentencing and Punishment of Offenders Act 2012 (Fines on Summary Conviction) Regulations 2015, SI 2015/664, reg 4(1), Sch 4, para 32(1), (3).

Appendix 3

FAMILY PROCEDURE RULES 2010

SI 2010/2955

PART 1
OVERRIDING OBJECTIVE

1.1 The overriding objective

(1) These rules are a new procedural code with the overriding objective of enabling the court to deal with cases justly, having regard to any welfare issues involved.

(2) Dealing with a case justly includes, so far as is practicable—

- (a) ensuring that it is dealt with expeditiously and fairly;
- (b) dealing with the case in ways which are proportionate to the nature, importance and complexity of the issues;
- (c) ensuring that the parties are on an equal footing;
- (d) saving expense; and
- (e) allotting to it an appropriate share of the court's resources, while taking into account the need to allot resources to other cases.

1.2 Application by the court of the overriding objective

The court must seek to give effect to the overriding objective when it—

- (a) exercises any power given to it by these rules; or
- (b) interprets any rule.

1.3 Duty of the parties

The parties are required to help the court to further the overriding objective.

1.4 Court's duty to manage cases

(1) The court must further the overriding objective by actively managing cases.

[(2) Active case management includes—

- (a) setting timetables or otherwise controlling the progress of the case;
- (b) identifying at an early stage—
  - (i) the issues; and
  - (ii) who should be a party to the proceedings;
- (c) deciding promptly—

(i) which issues need full investigation and hearing and which do not; and
(ii) the procedure to be followed in the case;
(d) deciding the order in which issues are to be resolved;
(e) controlling the use of expert evidence;
(f) encouraging the parties to use [a non-court dispute resolution]¹ procedure if the court considers that appropriate and facilitating the use of such procedure;
(g) helping the parties to settle the whole or part of the case;
(h) encouraging the parties to co-operate with each other in the conduct of proceedings;
(i) considering whether the likely benefits of taking a particular step justify the cost of taking it;
(j) dealing with as many aspects of the case as it can on the same occasion;
(k) dealing with the case without the parties needing to attend at court;
(l) making use of technology; and
(m) giving directions to ensure that the case proceeds quickly and efficiently.]²

Amendments
1 Substituted by the Family Procedure (Amendment) (No.5) Rules 2012, SI 2012/3061, rr 2, 3.
2 Substituted by the Family Procedure (Amendment No. 3) Rules 2014, SI 2014/843, rr 2, 3.

PART 12
[CHILDREN PROCEEDINGS]¹ EXCEPT PARENTAL ORDER PROCEEDINGS AND PROCEEDINGS FOR APPLICATIONS IN ADOPTION, PLACEMENT AND RELATED PROCEEDINGS

Chapter 1
Interpretation and application of this Part

12.1 Application of this Part

(1) The rules in this Part apply to—

(a) emergency proceedings;
(b) private law proceedings;
(c) public law proceedings;
(d) proceedings relating to the exercise of the court's inherent jurisdiction (other than applications for the court's permission to start such proceedings);
(e) proceedings relating to child abduction and the recognition and enforcement of decisions relating to custody under the European Convention;
(f) proceedings relating to the Council Regulation or the 1996 Hague Convention in respect of children; and
(g) any other proceedings which may be referred to in a practice direction.

(Part 18 sets out the procedure for making an application for permission to bring proceedings.)

(Part 31 sets out the procedure for making applications for recognition and enforcement of judgments under the Council Regulation or the 1996 Hague Convention.)

(2) The rules in Chapter 7 of this Part also apply to family proceedings which are not within paragraph (1) but which otherwise relate wholly or mainly to the maintenance or upbringing of a minor.

Amendment
1   Substituted by the Family Procedure (Amendment) (No.5) Rules 2012, SI 2012/3061, rr 2, 5(a).

12.2 Interpretation

In this Part—

'the 2006 Act' means the Childcare Act 2006;
['activity condition' has the meaning given to it by section 11C(2) of the 1989 Act;
'activity direction' has the meaning given to it by section 11A(3) of the 1989 Act;][1]
'advocate' means a person exercising a right of audience as a representative of, or on behalf of, a party;
'care proceedings' means proceedings for a care order under section 31(1)(a) of the 1989 Act;
['Case Management Order' means an order in the form referred to in Practice Direction 12A;][2]
'child assessment order' has the meaning assigned to it by section 43(2) of the 1989 Act;
...[3]
...[3]
'contribution order' has the meaning assigned to it by paragraph 23(2) of Schedule 2 to the 1989 Act;
'education supervision order' has the meaning assigned to it by section 36(2) of the 1989 Act;
'emergency proceedings' means proceedings for—
  (a) the disclosure of information as to the whereabouts of a child under section 33 of the 1986 Act;
  (b) an order authorising the taking charge of and delivery of a child under section 34 of the 1986 Act;
  (c) an emergency protection order;
  (d) an order under section 44(9)(b) of the 1989 Act varying a direction in an emergency protection order given under section 44(6) of that Act;
  (e) an order under section 45(5) of the 1989 Act extending the period during which an emergency protection order is to have effect;
  (f) an order under section 45(8) of the 1989 Act discharging an emergency protection order;
  (g) an order under section 45(8A) of the 1989 Act varying or discharging an emergency protection order in so far as it imposes an exclusion requirement on a person who is not entitled to apply for the order to be discharged;

(h) an order under section 45(8B) of the 1989 Act varying or discharging an emergency protection order in so far as it confers a power of arrest attached to an exclusion requirement;
(i) warrants under sections 48(9) and 102(1) of the 1989 Act and under section 79 of the 2006 Act; or
(j) a recovery order under section 50 of the 1989 Act;

'emergency protection order' means an order under section 44 of the 1989 Act;

'enforcement order' has the meaning assigned to it by section 11J(2) of the 1989 Act;

'financial compensation order' means an order made under section 11O(2) of the 1989 Act;

'interim order' means an interim care order or an interim supervision order referred to in section 38(1) of the 1989 Act;

['Part 4 proceedings' means proceedings for—
(a) a care order, or the discharge of such an order, under section 39(1) of the 1989 Act;
(b) an order giving permission to change a child's surname or remove a child from the United Kingdom under section 33(7) of the 1989 Act;
(c) a supervision order, the discharge or variation of such an order under section 39(2) of the 1989 Act, or the extension of such an order under paragraph 6(3) of Schedule 3 to that Act;
(d) an order making provision regarding contact under section 34(2) to (4) of the 1989 Act or an order varying or discharging such an order under section 34(9) of that Act;
(e) an education supervision order, the extension of an education supervision order under paragraph 15(2) of Schedule 3 to the 1989 Act, or the discharge of such an order under paragraph 17(1) of Schedule 3 to that Act;
(f) an order varying directions made with an interim care order or interim supervision order under section 38(8)(b) of the 1989 Act;
(g) an order under section 39(3) of the 1989 Act varying a supervision order in so far as it affects a person with whom the child is living but who is not entitled to apply for the order to be discharged;
(h) an order under section 39(3A) of the 1989 Act varying or discharging an interim care order in so far as it imposes an exclusion requirement on a person who is not entitled to apply for the order to be discharged;
(i) an order under section 39(3B) of the 1989 Act varying or discharging an interim care order in so far as it confers a power of arrest attached to an exclusion requirement; or
(j) the substitution of a supervision order for a care order under section 39(4) of the 1989 Act;][1]

'private law proceedings' means proceedings for—
[(a) a section 8 order except a child arrangements order to which section 9(6B) of the 1989 Act applies with respect to a child who is in the care of a local authority;][2]
(b) a parental responsibility order under sections 4(1)(c), 4ZA(1)(c) or 4A(1)(b) of the 1989 Act or an order terminating parental responsibility under sections 4(2A), 4ZA(5) or 4A(3) of that Act;

(c) an order appointing a child's guardian under section 5(1) of the 1989 Act or an order terminating the appointment under section 6(7) of that Act;
(d) an order giving permission to change a child's surname or remove a child from the United Kingdom under sections 13(1) or 14C(3) of the 1989 Act;
(e) a special guardianship order except where that order relates to a child who is subject of a care order;
(f) an order varying or discharging such an order under section 14D of the 1989 Act;
(g) an enforcement order;
(h) a financial compensation order;
(i) an order under paragraph 9 of Schedule A1 to the 1989 Act following a breach of an enforcement order;
(j) an order under Part 2 of Schedule A1 to the 1989 Act revoking or amending an enforcement order; or
(k) an order that a warning notice be attached to a [child arrangements order][2];

'public law proceedings' means [Part 4 proceedings and][1] proceedings for—
[(a) a child arrangements order to which section 9(6B) of the 1989 Act applies with respect to a child who is in the care of a local authority;][2]
(b) a special guardianship order relating to a child who is the subject of a care order;
(c) a secure accommodation order under section 25 of the 1989 Act 20;
(d) ...[3]
(e) ...[3]
(f) ...[3]
(g) ...[3]
(h) ...[3]
(i) ...[3]
(j) ...[3]
(k) ...[3]
(l) ...[3]
(m) ...[3]
(n) a child assessment order, or the variation or discharge of such an order under section 43(12) of the 1989 Act;
(o) an order permitting the local authority to arrange for any child in its care to live outside England and Wales under paragraph 19(1) of Schedule 2 to the 1989 Act;
(p) a contribution order, or revocation of such an order under paragraph 23(8) of Schedule 2 to the 1989 Act;
(q) an appeal under paragraph 8(1) of Schedule 8 to the 1989 Act;

'special guardianship order' has the meaning assigned to it by section 14A(1) of the 1989 Act;

'supervision order' has the meaning assigned to it by section 31(11) of the 1989 Act;

'supervision proceedings' means proceedings for a supervision order under section 31(1)(b) of the 1989 Act;

'warning notice' means a notice attached to an order pursuant to section 8(2) of the Children and Adoption Act 2006.

(The 1980 Hague Convention, the 1996 Hague Convention, the Council Regulation, and the European Convention are defined in rule 2.3.)

Amendments
1   Inserted by the Family Procedure (Amendment No. 3) Rules 2014, SI 2014/843, rr 2, 15(a), (d), (f)(i).
2   Substituted by the Family Procedure (Amendment No. 3) Rules 2014, SI 2014/843, rr 2, 15(b), (e), (f)(ii).
3   Repealed by the Family Procedure (Amendment No. 3) Rules 2014, SI 2014/843, rr 2, 15(c).

Chapter 2
General rules

12.3 Who the parties are

(1) In relation to the proceedings set out in column 1 of the following table, column 2 sets out who may make the application and column 3 sets out who the respondents to those proceedings will be.

Proceedings for	*Applicants*	*Respondents*
A parental responsibility order (section 4(1)(c), 4ZA(1)(c), or section 4A(1)(b) of the 1989 Act).	The child's father; the step parent; or the child's parent (being a woman who is a parent by virtue of section 43 of the Human Fertilisation and Embryology Act 2008 and who is not a person to whom section 1(3) of the Family Law Reform Act 1987 applies) (sections 4(1)(c), 4ZA(1)(c) and 4A(1)(b) of the 1989 Act).	Every person whom the applicant believes to have parental responsibility for the child; where the child is the subject of a care order, every person whom the applicant believes to have had parental responsibility immediately prior to the making of the care order; in the case of an application to extend, vary or discharge an order, the parties to the proceedings leading to the order which it is sought to have extended, varied or discharged; in the case of specified proceedings, the child.

Proceedings for	Applicants	Respondents
An order terminating a parental responsibility order or agreement (section 4(2A), 4ZA(5) or section 4A(3) of the 1989 Act).	Any person who has parental responsibility for the child; or with the court's permission, the child (section 4(3), 4ZA(6) and section 4A(3) of the 1989 Act).	As above.
An order appointing a guardian (section 5(1) of the 1989 Act).	An individual who wishes to be appointed as guardian (section 5(1) of the 1989 Act).	As above.
An order terminating the appointment of a guardian (section 6(7) of the 1989 Act).	Any person who has parental responsibility for the child; or with the court's permission, the child (section 6(7) of the 1989 Act).	As above.
A section 8 order.	Any person who is entitled to apply for a section 8 order with respect to the child (section 10(4) to (7) of the 1989 Act); or with the court's permission, any person (section 10(2)(b) of the 1989 Act).	As above.
An enforcement order (section 11J of the 1989 Act).	A person who is, for the purposes of the [child arrangements order][1], a person with whom the child concerned lives or is to live; any person whose contact with the child concerned is provided for in the [child arrangements order][1];	The person the applicant alleges has failed to comply with the [child arrangements order][1].

Proceedings for	Applicants	Respondents
	any individual subject to a condition under section 11(7)(b) of the 1989 Act or [an activity]¹ condition imposed by a [child arrangements order]¹; or	
	with the court's permission, the child (section 11J(5) of the 1989 Act).	
A financial compensation order (section 11O of the 1989 Act).	Any person who is, for the purposes of the [child arrangements order]¹, a person with whom the child concerned lives or is to live;	The person the applicant alleges has failed to comply with the [child arrangements order]¹.
	any person whose contact with the child concerned is provided for in the [child arrangements order]¹;	
	any individual subject to a condition under section 11(7)(b) of the 1989 Act or [an activity]¹ condition imposed by a [child arrangements order]¹; or	
	with the court's permission, the child (section 11O(6) of the 1989 Act).	
An order permitting the child's name to be changed or the removal of the child from the United Kingdom (section 13(1), 14C(3) or 33(7) of the 1989 Act).	Any person (section 13(1), 14C(3), 33(7) of the 1989 Act).	As for a parental responsibility order.

Proceedings for	Applicants	Respondents
A special guardianship order (section 14A of the 1989 Act).	Any guardian of the child; any individual [who is named in a child arrangements order as a person with whom the child is to live]¹; any individual listed in subsection (5)(b) or (c) of section 10 (as read with subsection (10) of that section) of the 1989 Act; a local authority foster parent with whom the child has lived for a period of at least one year immediately preceding the application; or any person with the court's permission (section 14A(3) of the 1989 Act) (more than one such individual can apply jointly (section 14A(3) and (5) of that Act)).	As above, and if a care order is in force with respect to the child, the child.
Variation or discharge of a special guardianship order (section 14D of the 1989 Act).	The special guardian (or any of them, if there is more than one); any individual [who is named in a child arrangements order as a person with whom the child is to live;]¹ the local authority designated in a care order with respect to the child; any individual within section 14D(1)(d) of the 1989 Act who has parental responsibility for the child;	As above.

Proceedings for	Applicants	Respondents
	the child, any parent or guardian of the child and any step-parent of the child who has acquired, and has not lost, parental responsibility by virtue of section 4A of that Act with the court's permission; or

any individual within section 14D(1)(d) of that Act who immediately before the making of the special guardianship order had, but no longer has, parental responsibility for the child with the court's permission. | |
| A secure accommodation order (section 25 of the 1989 Act). | The local authority which is looking after the child; or

the Health Authority, [Secretary of State, National Health Service Commissioning Board, clinical commissioning group,][2] National Health Service Trust established under section 25 of the National Health Service Act 2006 or section 18(1) of the National Health Service (Wales) Act 2006, National Health Service Foundation Trust or any local authority providing [or arranging][3] accommodation for the child (unless the child is looked after by a local authority). | As above. |

Proceedings for	Applicants	Respondents
A care or supervision order (section 31 of the 1989 Act).	Any local authority; the National Society for the Prevention of Cruelty to Children and any of its officers (section 31(1) of the 1989 Act); or any authorised person.	As above.
An order varying directions made with an interim care or interim supervision order (section 38(8)(b) of the 1989 Act).	The parties to proceedings in which directions are given under section 38(6) of the 1989 Act; or any person named in such a direction.	As above.
An order discharging a care order (section 39(1) of the 1989 Act).	Any person who has parental responsibility for the child; the child; or the local authority designated by the order (section 39(1) of the 1989 Act).	As above.
An order varying or discharging an interim care order in so far as it imposes an exclusion requirement (section 39(3A) of the 1989 Act).	A person to whom the exclusion requirement in the interim care order applies who is not entitled to apply for the order to be discharged (section 39(3A) of the 1989 Act).	As above.
An order varying or discharging an interim care order in so far as it confers a power of arrest attached to an exclusion requirement (section 39(3B) of the 1989 Act).	Any person entitled to apply for the discharge of the interim care order in so far as it imposes the exclusion requirement (section 39(3B) of the 1989 Act).	As above.

Proceedings for	Applicants	Respondents
An order substituting a supervision order for a care order (section 39(4) of the 1989 Act).	Any person entitled to apply for a care order to be discharged under section 39(1) (section 39(4) of the 1989 Act).	As above.
A child assessment order (section 43(1) of the 1989 Act).	Any local authority; the National Society for the Prevention of Cruelty to Children and any of its officers; or any person authorised by order of the Secretary of State to bring the proceedings and any officer of a body who is so authorised (section 43(1) and (13) of the 1989 Act).	As above.
An order varying or discharging a child assessment order (section 43(12) of the 1989 Act).	The applicant for an order that has been made under section 43(1) of the 1989 Act; or the persons referred to in section 43(11) of the 1989 Act (section 43(12) of that Act).	As above.
An emergency protection order (section 44(1) of the 1989 Act).	Any person (section 44(1) of the 1989 Act).	As for a parental responsibility order.
An order extending the period during which an emergency protection order is to have effect (section 45(4) of the 1989 Act).	Any person who – has parental responsibility for a child as the result of an emergency protection order; and is entitled to apply for a care order with respect to the child (section 45(4) of the 1989 Act).	As above.

Proceedings for	Applicants	Respondents
An order discharging an emergency protection order (section 45(8) of the 1989 Act).	The child; a parent of the child; any person who is not a parent of the child but who has parental responsibility for the child; or any person with whom the child was living before the making of the emergency protection order (section 45(8) of the 1989 Act).	As above.
An order varying or discharging an emergency protection order in so far as it imposes the exclusion requirement (section 45(8A) of the 1989 Act).	A person to whom the exclusion requirement in the emergency protection order applies who is not entitled to apply for the emergency protection order to be discharged (section 45(8A) of the 1989 Act).	As above.
An order varying or discharging an emergency protection order in so far as it confers a power of arrest attached to an exclusion requirement (section 45(8B) of the 1989 Act).	Any person entitled to apply for the discharge of the emergency protection order in so far as it imposes the exclusion requirement (section 45(8B) of the 1989 Act).	As above.
An emergency protection order by the police (section 46(7) of the 1989 Act).	The officer designated officer for the purposes of section 46(3)(e) of the 1989 Act (section 46(7) of the 1989 Act).	As above.

Proceedings for	Applicants	Respondents
A warrant authorising a constable to assist in exercise of certain powers to search for children and inspect premises (section 48 of the 1989 Act).	Any person attempting to exercise powers under an emergency protection order who has been or is likely to be prevented from doing so by being refused entry to the premises concerned or refused access to the child concerned (section 48(9) of the 1989 Act).	As above.
A warrant authorising a constable to assist in exercise of certain powers to search for children and inspect premises (section 102 of the 1989 Act).	Any person attempting to exercise powers under the enactments mentioned in section 102(6) of the 1989 Act who has been or is likely to be prevented from doing so by being refused entry to the premises concerned or refused access to the child concerned (section 102(1) of that Act).	As above.
An order revoking an enforcement order (paragraph 4 of Schedule A1 to the 1989 Act).	The person subject to the enforcement order.	The person who was the applicant for the enforcement order; and where the child was a party to the proceedings in which the enforcement order was made, the child.
An order amending an enforcement order (paragraphs 5 to 7 of Schedule A1 to the 1989 Act).	The person subject to the enforcement order.	The person who was the applicant for the enforcement order. (Rule 12.33 makes provision about applications under paragraph 5 of Schedule A1 to the 1989 Act.)

Proceedings for	Applicants	Respondents
An order following breach of an enforcement order (paragraph 9 of Schedule A1 to the 1989 Act).	Any person who is, for [the purposes of the child arrangements order]¹, the person with whom the child lives or is to live; any person whose contact with the child concerned is [provided for in the child arrangements order]¹; any individual subject to a condition under section 11(7)(b) of the 1989 Act or [an activity condition imposed by a child arrangements order;]¹ or with the court's permission, the child (paragraph 9 of Schedule A1 to the 1989 Act).	The person the applicant alleges has failed to comply with the unpaid work requirement imposed by an enforcement order; and where the child was a party to the proceedings in which the enforcement order was made, the child.
An order permitting the local authority to arrange for any child in its care to live outside England and Wales (Schedule 2, paragraph 19(1), to the 1989 Act).	The local authority (Schedule 2, paragraph 19(1), to the 1989 Act).	As for a parental responsibility order.
A contribution order (Schedule 2, paragraph 23(1), to the 1989 Act).	The local authority (Schedule 2, paragraph 23(1), to the 1989 Act).	As above and the contributor.
An order revoking a contribution order (Schedule 2, paragraph 23(8), to the 1989 Act).	The contributor; or the local authority.	As above.

Proceedings for	Applicants	Respondents
An order relating to contact with the child in care and any named person (section 34(2) of the 1989 Act) or permitting the local authority to refuse contact (section 34(4) of that Act).	The local authority; or the child (section 34(2) or 34(4) of the 1989 Act).	As above; and the person whose contact with the child is the subject of the application.
An order relating to contact with the child in care (section 34(3) of the 1989 Act).	The child's parents; any guardian or special guardian of the child; any person who by virtue of section 4A of the 1989 Act has parental responsibility for the child; [where there was a child arrangements order in force with respect to the child immediately before the care order was made, any person named in that order as a person with whom the child was to live;][1] a person who by virtue of an order made in the exercise of the High Court's inherent jurisdiction with respect to children had care of the child immediately before the care order was made (section 34(3)(a) of the 1989 Act); or with the court's permission, any person (section 34(3)(b) of that Act).	As above; and the person whose contact with the child is the subject of the application.

Proceedings for	Applicants	Respondents
An order varying or discharging an order for contact with a child in care under section 34 (section 34((9) of the 1989 Act).	The local authority; the child; or any person named in the order (section 34(9) of the 1989 Act).	As above; and the person whose contact with the child is the subject of the application.
An education supervision order (section 36 of the 1989 Act).	Any local authority (section 36(1) of the 1989 Act).	As above; and the child.
An order varying or discharging a supervision order (section 39(2) of the 1989 Act).	Any person who has parental responsibility for the child; the child; or the supervisor (section 39(2) of the 1989 Act).	As above; and the supervisor.
An order varying a supervision order in so far as it affects the person with whom the child is living (section 39(3) of the 1989 Act).	The person with whom the child is living who is not entitled to apply for the order to be discharged (section 39(3) of the 1989 Act).	As above; and the supervisor.
An order varying a direction under section 44(6) of the 1989 Act in an emergency protection order (section 44(9)(b) of that Act).	The parties to the application for the emergency protection order in respect of which it is sought to vary the directions; the children's guardian; the local authority in whose area the child is ordinarily resident; or any person who is named in the directions.	As above, and the parties to the application for the order in respect of which it is sought to vary the directions; any person who was caring for the child prior to the making of the order; and any person [named in a child arrangements order as a person with whom the child is to spend time or otherwise have contact and who][1] is affected by the direction which it is sought to have varied.

Proceedings for	Applicants	Respondents
A recovery order (section 50 of the 1989 Act).	Any person who has parental responsibility for the child by virtue of a care order or an emergency protection order; or

where the child is in police protection the officer designated for the purposes of section 46(3)(e) of the 1989 Act (section 50(4) of the 1989 Act). | As above; and

the person whom the applicant alleges to have effected or to have been or to be responsible for the taking or keeping of the child. |
| An order discharging an education supervision order (Schedule 3, paragraph 17(1), to the 1989 Act). | The child concerned;

a parent of the child; or

the local authority concerned (Schedule 3, paragraph 17(1), to the 1989 Act). | As above; and

the local authority concerned; and

the child. |
| An order extending an education supervision order (Schedule 3, paragraph 15(2), to the 1989 Act). | The local authority in whose favour the education supervision order was made (Schedule 3, paragraph 15(2), to the 1989 Act). | As above; and

the child. |
| An appeal under paragraph (8) of Schedule 8 to the 1989 Act. | A person aggrieved by the matters listed in paragraph 8(1) of Schedule 8 to the 1989 Act. | The appropriate local authority. |
| An order for the disclosure of information as to the whereabouts of a child under section 33 of the 1986 Act. | Any person with a legitimate interest in proceedings for an order under Part 1 of the 1986 Act; or

a person who has registered an order made elsewhere in the United Kingdom or a specified dependent territory. | Any person alleged to have information as to the whereabouts of the child. |

Proceedings for	Applicants	Respondents
An order authorising the taking charge of and delivery of a child under section 34 of the 1986 Act.	The person to whom the child is to be given up under section 34(1) of the 1986 Act.	As above; and the person who is required to give up the child in accordance with section 34(1) of the 1986 Act.
An order relating to the exercise of the court's inherent jurisdiction (including wardship proceedings).	A local authority (with the court's permission); any person with a genuine interest in or relation to the child; or the child (wardship proceedings only).	The parent or guardian of the child; any other person who has an interest in or relationship to the child; and the child (wardship proceedings only and with the court's permission as described at rule 12.37).
A warrant under section 79 of the 2006 Act authorising any constable to assist Her Majesty's Chief Inspector for Education, Children's Services and Skills in the exercise of powers conferred on him by section 77 of the 2006 Act.	Her Majesty's Chief Inspector for Education, Children's Services and Skills.	Any person preventing or likely to prevent Her Majesty's Chief Inspector for Education, Children's Services and Skills from exercising powers conferred on him by section 77 of the 2006 Act.
An order in respect of a child under the 1980 Hague Convention.	Any person, institution or body who claims that a child has been removed or retained in breach of rights of custody or claims that there has been a breach of rights of access in relation to the child.	The person alleged to have brought the child into the United Kingdom; the person with whom the child is alleged to be; any parent or guardian of the child who is within the United Kingdom and is not otherwise a party;

Proceedings for	Applicants	Respondents
		any person in whose favour a decision relating to custody has been made if that person is not otherwise a party; and
		any other person who appears to the court to have sufficient interest in the welfare of the child.
An order concerning the recognition and enforcement of decisions relating to custody under the European Convention.	Any person who has a court order giving that person rights of custody in relation to the child.	As above.
An application for the High Court to request transfer of jurisdiction under Article 15 of the Council Regulation or Article 9 of the 1996 Hague Convention (rule 12.65).	Any person with sufficient interest in the welfare of the child and who would be entitled to make a proposed application in relation to that child, or who intends to seek the permission of the court to make such application if the transfer is agreed.	As directed by the court in accordance with rule 12.65.
An application under rule 12.71 for a declaration as to the existence, or extent, of parental responsibility under Article 16 of the 1996 Convention.	Any interested person including a person who holds, or claims to hold, parental responsibility for the child under the law of another State which subsists in accordance with Article 16 of the 1996 Hague Convention following the child becoming habitually resident in a territorial unit of the United Kingdom	Every person whom the applicant believes to have parental responsibility for the child; any person whom the applicant believes to hold parental responsibility for the child under the law of another State which subsists in accordance with Article 16 of the 1996 Hague Convention following the child becoming habitually resident in a territorial unit of the United Kingdom; and

Proceedings for	Applicants	Respondents
		where the child is the subject of a care order, every person whom the applicant believes to have had parental responsibility immediately prior to the making of the care order
A warning notice.	The person who is, for the purposes of the [child arrangements order]¹, the person with whom the child concerned lives or is to live; the person whose contact with the child concerned is provided for in the [child arrangements order]¹; any individual subject to a condition under section 11(7)(b) of the 1989 Act or [an activity]¹ condition imposed by the [child arrangements order]²; or with the court's permission, the child.	Any person who was a party to the proceedings in which the [child arrangements order]¹ was made. (Rule 12.33 makes provision about applications for warning notices).

(2) The court will direct that a person with parental responsibility be made a party to proceedings where that person requests to be one.

(3) Subject to rule 16.2, the court may at any time direct that—

(a) any person or body be made a party to proceedings; or
(b) a party be removed.

(4) If the court makes a direction for the addition or removal of a party under this rule, it may give consequential directions about—

(a) the service of a copy of the application form or other relevant documents on the new party;
(b) the management of the proceedings.

(5) In this rule—

'a local authority foster parent' has the meaning assigned to it by section 23(3) of the 1989 Act; and 'care home', 'independent hospital', 'local authority' and ['clinical commissioning group']² have the meanings assigned to them by section 105 of the 1989 Act.

(Part 16 contains the rules relating to the representation of children.)

Amendments
1   Substituted by the Family Procedure (Amendment No. 3) Rules 2014, SI 2014/843, rr 2, 16.
2   Substituted by National Treatment Agency (Abolition) and the Health and Social Care Act 2012 (Consequential, Transitional and Saving Provisions) Order 2013/235 Sch.2(1) para.156(a)(i), (b).
3   Inserted by National Treatment Agency (Abolition) and the Health and Social Care Act 2012 (Consequential, Transitional and Saving Provisions) Order 2013/235 Sch.2(1) para.156(a)(ii).

12.4 Notice of proceedings to person with foreign parental responsibility

(1) This rule applies where a child is subject to proceedings to which this Part applies and —

(a) a person holds or is believed to hold parental responsibility for the child under the law of another State which subsists in accordance with Article 16 of the 1996 Hague Convention following the child becoming habitually resident in a territorial unit of the United Kingdom; and

(b) that person is not otherwise required to be joined as a respondent under rule 12.3.

(2) The applicant shall give notice of the proceedings to any person to whom the applicant believes paragraph (1) applies in any case in which a person whom the applicant believed to have parental responsibility under the 1989 Act would be a respondent to those proceedings in accordance with rule 12.3.

(3) The applicant and every respondent to the proceedings shall provide such details as they possess as to the identity and whereabouts of any person they believe to hold parental responsibility for the child in accordance with paragraph (1) to the court officer, upon making, or responding to the application as appropriate.

(4) Where the existence of a person who is believed to have parental responsibility for the child in accordance with paragraph (1) only becomes apparent to a party at a later date during the proceedings, that party must notify the court officer of those details at the earliest opportunity.

(5) Where a person to whom paragraph (1) applies receives notice of proceedings, that person may apply to the court to be joined as a party using the Part 18 procedure.

12.5 What the court will do when the application has been issued

[(1)]¹ When ...² proceedings [other than public law proceedings]¹ have been issued the court will consider—

(a) setting a date for—
    (i) a directions appointment;
    (ii) in private law proceedings, a First Hearing Dispute Resolution Appointment; [or]¹

(iii) ...²
(iv) the hearing of the application ...²,
and if the court sets a date it will do so in accordance with rule 12.13 and [Practice Direction 12B]³;
(b) giving any of the directions listed in rule 12.12 or, where Chapter 6, section 1 applies, rule 12.48; and
(c) doing anything else which is set out in [Practice Direction 12B]³ or any other practice direction.

[(Practice Direction 12A sets out details relating to the Case Management Hearing. Practice Direction 12B supplementing this Part sets out details relating to the First Hearing Dispute Resolution Appointment.)]³

[(2) When Part 4 proceedings and in so far as practicable other public law proceedings have been issued the court will—

(a) set a date for the Case Management Hearing in accordance with Practice Direction 12A;
(b) set a date for the hearing of an application for an interim order if necessary;
(c) give any directions listed in rule 12.12; and
(d) do anything else which is set out in Practice Direction 12A.]¹

Amendments
1 Inserted by the Family Procedure (Amendment No. 3) Rules 2014, SI 2014/843, rr 2, 17(a), (c), (d), (i).
2 Repealed by the Family Procedure (Amendment No. 3) Rules 2014, SI 2014/843, rr 2, 17(b), (e), (f).
3 Substituted by the Family Procedure (Amendment No. 3) Rules 2014, SI 2014/843, rr 2, 17(g), (h), (j).

12.6 Children's guardian, solicitor and reports under section 7 of the 1989 Act

[Within a day of the issue of Part 4 proceedings or the transfer of Part 4 Proceedings to the court and as]¹ soon as practicable after the issue of [other]² proceedings or the transfer of the [other]² proceedings to the court, the court will—

(a) in specified proceedings, appoint a children's guardian under rule 16.3(1) unless—
 (i) such an appointment has already been made by the court which made the transfer and is subsisting; or
 (ii) the court considers that such an appointment is not necessary to safeguard the interests of the child;
(b) where section 41(3) of the 1989 Act applies, consider whether a solicitor should be appointed to represent the child, and if so, appoint a solicitor accordingly;
(c) consider whether to ask an officer of the service or a Welsh family proceedings officer for advice relating to the welfare of the child;
(d) consider whether a report relating to the welfare of the child is required, and if so, request such a report in accordance with section 7 of the 1989 Act.

(Part 16 sets out the rules relating to representation of children.)

Amendments
1 Substituted by the Family Procedure (Amendment No. 3) Rules 2014, SI 2014/843, rr 2, 18(a).
2 Inserted by the Family Procedure (Amendment No. 3) Rules 2014, SI 2014/843, rr 2, 18(b), (c).

12.7 What a court officer will do

(1) As soon as practicable after the issue of proceedings the court officer will return to the applicant the copies of the application together with the forms referred to in Practice Direction 5A.

(2) As soon as practicable after the issue of proceedings or the transfer of proceedings to the court or at any other stage in the proceedings the court officer will—

(a) give notice of any hearing set by the court to the applicant; and
(b) do anything else set out in Practice Directions 12A or 12B or any other practice direction.

[12.8 Service

(1) After the issue of proceedings under this Part, the documents specified in paragraph (5) must be served on the respondent or respondents.

(2) In section 8 private law proceedings, service under paragraph (1) will be effected by the court officer, unless—

(a) the applicant requests to do so; or
(b) the court directs the applicant to do so.

(3) In this Rule, 'section 8 private law proceedings' are proceedings for a section 8 order except proceedings for a child arrangements order to which section 9(6B) of the 1989 Act applies with respect to a child who is in the care of a local authority.

(4) In any other proceedings to which this Part applies, service under paragraph (1) must be effected by the applicant.

(5) The documents are—

(a) the application together with the documents referred to in Practice Direction 12C; and
(b) notice of any hearing set by the court.

(6) Service under this rule must be carried out in accordance with Practice Direction 12C.

(7) The general rules about service in Part 6 apply but are subject to this rule.

[(Practice Direction 12C (Service of Application in Children Proceedings) provides that in Part 4 proceedings (except proceedings for an interim order) the minimum number of days prior to the Case Management Hearing for service of the application and accompanying documents is 7 days. The Court has discretion to extend or shorten this time (see rule 4.1(3)(a)).][1]][2]

Amendments
1 Inserted by the Family Procedure (Amendment No. 3) Rules 2014, SI 2014/843, rr 2, 20.
2 Substituted by the Family Procedure (Amendment No. 3) Rules 2014, SI 2014/843, rr 2, 19.

12.9 ...[1]

...[1]

Amendment
1 Repealed by the Family Procedure (Amendment No.3) Rules 2013, SI 2013/3204, rr 2, 47.

12.10 ...[1]

...[1]

Amendment
1 Repealed by the Family Procedure (Amendment No.3) Rules 2013, SI 2013/3204, rr 2, 47.

12.11 ...[1]

...[1]

Amendment
1 Repealed by the Family Procedure (Amendment No.3) Rules 2013, SI 2013/3204, rr 2, 47.

12.12 Directions

(1) This rule does not apply to proceedings under Chapter 6 of this Part.

(2) At any stage in the proceedings, the court may give directions about the conduct of the proceedings including—

- (a) the management of the case;
- (b) the timetable for steps to be taken between the giving of directions and the final hearing;
- (c) the joining of a child or other person as a party to the proceedings in accordance with rules 12.3(2) and (3);
- (d) the attendance of the child;
- (e) the appointment of a children's guardian or of a solicitor under section 41(3) of the 1989 Act;
- (f) the appointment of a litigation friend;
- (g) the service of documents;
- (h) the filing of evidence including experts' reports; and
- (i) the exercise by an officer of the Service, Welsh family proceedings officer or local authority officer of any duty referred to in rule 16.38(1)

(3) Paragraph (4) applies where—

- (a) an officer of the Service or a Welsh family proceedings officer has filed a report or a risk assessment as a result of exercising a duty referred to in rule 16.38(1)(a); or
- (b) a local authority officer has filed a report as a result of exercising a duty referred to in rule 16.38(1)(b).

(4) The court may—

- (a) give directions setting a date for a hearing at which that report or risk assessment will be considered; and
- (b) direct that the officer who prepared the report or risk assessment attend any such hearing.

(5) The court may exercise the powers in paragraphs (2) and (4) on an application or of its own initiative.

(6) Where the court proposes to exercise its powers of its own initiative the procedure set out in rule 4.3(2) to (6) applies.

(7) Directions of a court which are still in force immediately prior to the transfer of proceedings to another court will continue to apply following the transfer subject to—

    (a)   any changes of terminology which are required to apply those directions to the court to which the proceedings are transferred; and

    (b)   any variation or revocation of the direction.

(8) The court or court officer will—

    (a)   take a note of the giving, variation or revocation of a direction under this rule; and

    (b)   as soon as practicable serve a copy of the note on every party.

(Rule 12.48 provides for directions in proceedings under the 1980 Hague Convention and the European Convention.)

12.13 Setting dates for hearings and setting or confirming the timetable and date for the final hearing

(1) At the—

    (a)   transfer to a court of proceedings;

    (b)   postponement or adjournment of any hearing; or

    (c)   conclusion of any hearing at which the proceedings are not finally determined,

the court will set a date for the proceedings to come before the court again for the purposes of giving directions or for such other purposes as the court directs.

(2) At any hearing the court may—

    (a)   confirm a date for the final hearing or the week within which the final hearing is to begin (where a date or period for the final hearing has already been set);

    (b)   set a timetable for the final hearing unless a timetable has already been fixed, or the court considers that it would be inappropriate to do so; or

    (c)   set a date for the final hearing or a period within which the final hearing of the application is to take place.

(3) The court officer will notify the parties of—

    (a)   the date of a hearing fixed in accordance with paragraph (1);

    (b)   the timetable for the final hearing; and

    (c)   the date of the final hearing or the period in which it will take place.

(4) Where the date referred to in paragraph (1) is set at the transfer of proceedings, the date will be as soon as possible after the transfer.

(5) The requirement in paragraph (1) to set a date for the proceedings to come before the court again is satisfied by the court setting or confirming a date for the final hearing.

12.14 Attendance at hearings

(1) This rule does not apply to proceedings under Chapter 6 of this Part except for proceedings for a declaration under rule 12.71.

(2) Unless the court directs otherwise and subject to paragraph (3), the persons who must attend a hearing are—

(a) any party to the proceedings;
(b) any litigation friend for any party or legal representative instructed to act on that party's behalf; and
(c) any other person directed by the court or required by Practice Directions 12A or 12B or any other practice direction to attend.

(3) Proceedings or any part of them will take place in the absence of a child who is a party to the proceedings if—

(a) the court considers it in the interests of the child, having regard to the matters to be discussed or the evidence likely to be given; and
(b) the child is represented by a children's guardian or solicitor.

(4) When considering the interests of the child under paragraph (3) the court will give—

(a) the children's guardian;
(b) the solicitor for the child; and
(c) the child, if of sufficient understanding,

an opportunity to make representations.

(5) Subject to paragraph (6), where at the time and place appointed for a hearing, the applicant appears but one or more of the respondents do not, the court may proceed with the hearing.

(6) The court will not begin to hear an application in the absence of a respondent unless the court is satisfied that—

(a) the respondent received reasonable notice of the date of the hearing; or
(b) the circumstances of the case justify proceeding with the hearing.

(7) Where, at the time and place appointed for a hearing one or more of the respondents appear but the applicant does not, the court may—

(a) refuse the application; or
(b) if sufficient evidence has previously been received, proceed in the absence of the applicant.

(8) Where at the time and place appointed for a hearing neither the applicant nor any respondent appears, the court may refuse the application.

(9) Paragraphs (5) to (8) do not apply to a hearing where the court—

(a) is considering—
  (i) whether to make [an activity]¹ direction or to attach [an activity]¹ condition to a [child arrangements order]¹; or
  (ii) an application for a financial compensation order, an enforcement order or an order under paragraph 9 of Schedule A1 to the 1989 Act following a breach of an enforcement order; and
(b) has yet to obtain sufficient evidence from, or in relation to, the person who may be the subject of the direction, condition or order to enable it to determine the matter.

(10) Nothing in this rule affects the provisions of Article 18 of the Council Regulation in cases to which that provision applies.

(The Council Regulation makes provision in Article 18 for the court to stay proceedings where the respondent is habitually resident in another Member State of the European Union and has not been adequately served with the proceedings as required by that provision.)

Amendments
1 Substituted by the Family Procedure (Amendment No. 3) Rules 2014, SI 2014/843, rr 2, 21.

12.15 Steps taken by the parties

If—

(a) the parties or any children's guardian agree proposals for the management of the proceedings (including a proposed date for the final hearing or a period within which the final hearing is to take place); and
(b) the court considers that the proposals are suitable,

it may approve them without a hearing and give directions in the terms proposed.

[(Practice Direction 12A gives guidance as to the application of this rule to Part 4 proceedings in the light of the period that is for the time being allowed under section 32(1)(a)(ii) of the 1989 Act)]¹

Amendment
1 Inserted by the Family Procedure (Amendment No. 3) Rules 2014, SI 2014/843, rr 2, 22.

12.16 Applications without notice

(1) This rule applies to—

(a) proceedings for a section 8 order;
(b) emergency proceedings; and
(c) proceedings relating to the exercise of the court's inherent jurisdiction (other than an application for the court's permission to start such proceedings and proceedings for collection, location and passport orders where Chapter 6 applies).

(2) An application in proceedings referred to in paragraph (1) may ...¹ be made without notice in which case the applicant must file the application—

(a) where the application is made by telephone, the next business day after the making of the application; or

(b) in any other case, at the time when the application is made.

(3) ...¹

(4) Where—

(a) a section 8 order;
(b) an emergency protection order;
(c) an order for the disclosure of information as to the whereabouts of a child under section 33 of the 1986 Act; or
(d) an order authorising the taking charge of and delivery of a child under section 34 of the 1986 Act,

is made without notice, the applicant must serve a copy of the application on each respondent within 48 hours after the order is made.

(5) Within 48 hours after the making of an order without notice, the applicant must serve a copy of the order on—

(a) the parties, unless the court directs otherwise;
(b) any person who has actual care of the child or who had such care immediately prior to the making of the order; and
(c) in the case of an emergency protection order and a recovery order, the local authority in whose area the child lives or is found.

(6) Where the court refuses to make an order on an application without notice it may direct that the application is made on notice in which case the application will proceed in accordance with rules 12.3 to 12.15.

(7) Where the hearing takes place outside the hours during which the court office is normally open, the court or court officer will take a note of the proceedings.

(Practice Direction 12E (Urgent Business) provides further details of the procedure for out of hours applications. See also Practice Direction 12D (Inherent Jurisdiction (including Wardship Proceedings)).)

(Rule 12.47 provides for without-notice applications in proceedings under Chapter 6, section 1 of this Part, (proceedings under the 1980 Hague Convention and the European Convention).)

Amendment
1 Repealed by the Family Procedure (Amendment No.3) Rules 2013, SI 2013/3204, rr 2, 48.

12.17 Investigation under section 37 of the 1989 Act

(1) This rule applies where a direction is given to an appropriate authority by the court under section 37(1) of the 1989 Act.

(2) On giving the direction the court may adjourn the proceedings.

(3) As soon as practicable after the direction is given the court will record the direction.

(4) As soon as practicable after the direction is given the court officer will—

(a) serve the direction on—
(i) the parties to the proceedings in which the direction is given; and

(ii) the appropriate authority where it is not a party;
(b) serve any documentary evidence directed by the court on the appropriate authority.

(5) Where a local authority informs the court of any of the matters set out in section 37(3)(a) to (c) of the 1989 Act it will do so in writing.

(6) Unless the court directs otherwise, the court officer will serve a copy of any report to the court under section 37 of the 1989 Act on the parties.

(Section 37 of the 1989 Act refers to the appropriate authority and section 37(5) of that Act sets out which authority should be named in a particular case.)

12.18 Disclosure of a report under section 14A(8) or (9) of the 1989 Act

(1) In proceedings for a special guardianship order, the local authority must file the report under section 14A(8) or (9) of the 1989 Act within the timetable fixed by the court.

(2) The court will consider whether to give a direction that the report under section 14A(8) or (9) of the 1989 Act be disclosed to each party to the proceedings.

(3) Before giving a direction for the report to be disclosed, the court must consider whether any information should be deleted from the report.

(4) The court may direct that the report must not be disclosed to a party.

(5) The court officer must serve a copy of the report in accordance with any direction under paragraph (2).

(6) In paragraph (3), information includes information which a party has declined to reveal under rule 29.1(1).

12.19 Additional evidence

(1) This rule applies to proceedings for a section 8 order or a special guardianship order.

(2) Unless the court directs otherwise, a party must not—
   (a) file or serve any document other than in accordance with these rules or any practice direction;
   (b) in completing a form prescribed by these rules or any practice direction, give information or make a statement which is not required or authorised by that form; or
   (c) file or serve at a hearing—
       (i) any witness statement of the substance of the oral evidence which the party intends to adduce; or
       (ii) any copy of any document (including any experts' report) which the party intends to rely on.

(3) Where a party fails to comply with the requirements of this rule in relation to any witness statement or other document, the party cannot seek to rely on that statement or other document unless the court directs otherwise.

12.20 ...¹

...¹

Amendment
1 Repealed by the Family Procedure (Amendment) (No.5) Rules 2012, SI 2012/3061, rr 2, 4.

12.21 Hearings

(1) The court may give directions about the order of speeches and the evidence at a hearing.

(2) Subject to any directions given under paragraph (1), the parties and the children's guardian must adduce their evidence at a hearing in the following order—

- (a) the applicant;
- (b) any party with parental responsibility for the child;
- (c) other respondents;
- (d) the children's guardian;
- (e) the child, if the child is a party to proceedings and there is no children's guardian.

Chapter 3
Special provisions about public law proceedings

[12.22 Timetable for the proceedings

In public law proceedings other than Part 4 proceedings, in so far as practicable the court will draw up the timetable for the proceedings or revise that timetable with a view to disposing of the application without delay and in any event within 26 weeks beginning with the date on which the application is issued.

(In relation to Part 4 proceedings, section 32(1)(a) of the 1989 Act requires the court to draw up a timetable with a view to disposing of the application without delay and in any event within 26 weeks beginning with the day on which the application is issued.)]¹

Amendment
1 Substituted by the Family Procedure (Amendment No. 3) Rules 2014, SI 2014/843, rr 2, 23.

[12.23 Application of rules 12.24 to 12.26C

Rules 12.24 to 12.26C apply to Part 4 proceedings and in so far as practicable other public law proceedings.]¹

Amendment
1 Substituted by the Family Procedure (Amendment No. 3) Rules 2014, SI 2014/843, rr 2, 24.

12.24 Directions

The court will direct the parties to—

- (a) monitor compliance with the court's directions; and
- (b) tell the court or court officer about—

(i) any failure to comply with a direction of the court; and
(ii) any other delay in the proceedings.

[12.25 The Case Management Hearing and the Issues Resolution Hearing

(1) The court will conduct the Case Management Hearing with the objective of—

(a) confirming the level of judge to which the proceedings have been allocated;
(b) drawing up a timetable for the proceedings including the time within which the proceedings are to be resolved;
(c) identifying the issues; and
(d) giving directions in accordance with rule 12.12 and Practice Direction 12A to manage the proceedings.

(2) The court may hold a further Case Management Hearing only where this hearing is necessary to fulfil the objectives of the Case Management Hearing set out in paragraph (1).

(3) The court will conduct the Issues Resolution Hearing with the objective of—

(a) identifying the remaining issues in the proceedings;
(b) as far as possible resolving or narrowing those issues; and
(c) giving directions to manage the proceedings to the final hearing in accordance with rule 12.12 and Practice Direction 12A.

(4) Where it is possible for all the issues in the proceedings to be resolved at the Issues Resolution Hearing, the court may treat the Issues Resolution Hearing as a final hearing and make orders disposing of the proceedings.

(5) The court may set a date for the Case Management Hearing, a further Case Management Hearing and the Issues Resolution Hearing at the times referred to in Practice Direction 12A.

(6) The matters which the court will consider at the hearings referred to in this rule are set out in Practice Direction 12A.

(Rule 25.6 (experts: when to apply for the court's permission) provides that unless the court directs otherwise, parties must apply for the court's permission as mentioned in section 13(1), (3) and (5) of the 2014 Act as soon as possible and in Part 4 proceedings and in so far as practicable other public law proceedings no later than the Case Management Hearing.)][1]

Amendment
1 Substituted by the Family Procedure (Amendment No. 3) Rules 2014, SI 2014/843, rr 2, 25.

[12.26 Discussion between advocates

(1) When setting a date for the Case Management Hearing or the Issues Resolution Hearing the court will direct a discussion between the parties' advocates to—

(a) discuss the provisions of a draft of the Case Management Order; and
(b) consider any other matter set out in Practice Direction 12A.

(2) Where there is a litigant in person the court will give directions about how that person may take part in the discussions between the parties' advocates.

(3) Unless the court directs otherwise—

(a) any discussion between advocates must take place no later than 2 days before the Case Management Hearing; and

(b) a draft of the Case Management Order must be filed with the court no later than 11a.m. on the day before the Case Management Hearing.

(4) Unless the court directs otherwise—

(a) any discussion between advocates must take place no later than 7 days before the Issues Resolution Hearing; and

(b) a draft of the Case Management Order must be filed with the court no later than 11a.m. on the day before the Issues Resolution Hearing.

(5) For the purposes of this rule 'advocate' includes a litigant in person.][1]

Amendment
1 Substituted by the Family Procedure (Amendment No. 3) Rules 2014, SI 2014/843, rr 2, 26.

[12.26A Application for extension of the time limit for disposing of the application

(1) An application requesting the court to grant an extension must state—

(a) the reasons for the request;
(b) the period of extension being requested; and
(c) a short explanation of—
 (i) why it is necessary for the request to be granted to enable the court to resolve the proceedings justly;
 (ii) the impact which any ensuing timetable revision would have on the welfare of the child to whom the application relates;
 (iii) the impact which any ensuing timetable revision would have on the duration and conduct of the proceedings; and
 (iv) the reasons for the grant or refusal of any previous request for extension.

(2) Part 18 applies to an application requesting the grant of an extension.

(3) In this rule

'ensuing timetable revision' has the meaning given to it by section 32(6) of the 1989 Act;

'extension' means an extension of the period for the time being allowed under section 32(1)(a)(ii) of the 1989 Act which is to end no more than 8 weeks after the later of the times referred to in section 32(8) of that Act.][1]

Amendment
1 Inserted by the Family Procedure (Amendment No. 3) Rules 2014, SI 2014/843, rr 2, 27.

[12.26B Disapplication of rule 4.1(3)(a) court's power to extend or shorten the time for compliance with a rule

Rule 4.1(3)(a) does not apply to any period that is for the time being allowed under section 32(1)(a)(ii) of the 1989 Act.][1]

Amendment
1 Inserted by the Family Procedure (Amendment No. 3) Rules 2014, SI 2014/843, rr 2, 27.

[12.26C Extension of time limit: reasons for court's decision

(1) When refusing or granting an extension of the period that is for the time being allowed under section 32(1)(a)(ii) in the case of the application, the court will announce its decision and—

(a) the reasons for that decision; and
(b) where an extension is granted or refused, a short explanation of the impact which the decision would have on the welfare of the child.

(2) The court office will supply a copy of the order granting or refusing the extension including the reasons for the court's decision and the period of any extension and short explanation given under paragraph (1)(b) to—

(a) the parties; and
(b) any person who has actual care of the child who is the subject of the proceedings.]¹

Amendment
1 Inserted by the Family Procedure (Amendment No. 3) Rules 2014, SI 2014/843, rr 2, 27.

12.27 Matters prescribed for the purposes of the Act

(1) Proceedings for an order under any of the following provisions of the 1989 Act—

(a) a secure accommodation order under section 25;
(b) an order giving permission to change a child's surname or remove a child from the United Kingdom under section 33(7);
(c) an order permitting the local authority to arrange for any child in its care to live outside England and Wales under paragraph 19(1) of Schedule 2;
(d) the extension or further extension of a supervision order under paragraph 6(3) of Schedule 3;
(e) appeals against the determination of proceedings of a kind set out in sub-paragraphs (a) to (d);

are specified for the purposes of section 41 of that Act in accordance with section 41(6)(i) of that Act.

(2) The persons listed as applicants in the table set out in rule 12.3 to proceedings for the variation of directions made with interim care or interim supervision orders under section 38(8) of the 1989 Act are the prescribed class of persons for the purposes of that section.

(3) The persons listed as applicants in the table set out in rule 12.3 to proceedings for the variation of a direction made under section 44(6) of the 1989 Act in an emergency protection order are the prescribed class of persons for the purposes of section 44(9) of that Act.

12.28 Exclusion requirements: interim care orders and emergency protection orders

(1) This rule applies where the court includes an exclusion requirement in an interim care order or an emergency protection order.

(2) The applicant for an interim care order or emergency protection order must—

  (a) prepare a separate statement of the evidence in support of the application for an exclusion requirement;
  (b) serve the statement personally on the relevant person with a copy of the order containing the exclusion requirement (and of any power of arrest which is attached to it);
  (c) inform the relevant person of that person's right to apply to vary or discharge the exclusion requirement.

(3) Where a power of arrest is attached to an exclusion requirement in an interim care order or an emergency protection order, the applicant will deliver—

  (a) a copy of the order; and
  (b) a statement showing that the relevant person has been served with the order or informed of its terms (whether by being present when the order was made or by telephone or otherwise),

to the officer for the time being in charge of the police station for the area in which the dwellinghouse in which the child lives is situated (or such other police station as the court may specify).

(4) Rules 10.6(2) and 10.10 to 10.17 will apply, with the necessary modifications, for the service, variation, discharge and enforcement of any exclusion requirement to which a power of arrest is attached as they apply to an order made on an application under Part 4 of the 1996 Act.

(5) The relevant person must serve the parties to the proceedings with any application which that person makes for the variation or discharge of the exclusion requirement.

(6) Where an exclusion requirement ceases to have effect whether—

  (a) as a result of the removal of a child under section 38A(10) or 44A(10) of the 1989 Act;
  (b) because of the discharge of the interim care order or emergency protection order; or
  (c) otherwise,

the applicant must inform—
  (i) the relevant person;
  (ii) the parties to the proceedings;
  (iii) any officer to whom a copy of the order was delivered under paragraph (3); and
  (iv) (where necessary) the court.

(7) Where the court includes an exclusion requirement in an interim care order or an emergency protection order of its own motion, paragraph (2) will apply with the omission of any reference to the statement of the evidence.

(8) In this rule, 'the relevant person' has the meaning assigned to it by sections 38A(2) and 44A(2) of the 1989 Act.

12.29 Notification of consent

(1) Consent for the purposes of the following provisions of the 1989 Act—

    (a)   section 16(3);
    (b)   section 38A(2)(b)(ii) or 44A(2)(b)(ii); or
    (c)   paragraph 19(3)(c) or (d) of Schedule 2,

must be given either—

    (i)   orally to the court; or
    (ii)   in writing to the court signed by the person giving consent.

(2) Any written consent for the purposes of section 38A(2) or 44A(2) of the 1989 Act must include a statement that the person giving consent—

    (a)   is able and willing to give to the child the care which it would be reasonable to expect a parent to give; and
    (b)   understands that the giving of consent could lead to the exclusion of the relevant person from the dwelling-house in which the child lives.

12.30 Proceedings for secure accommodation orders: copies of reports

In proceedings under section 25 of the 1989 Act, the court will, if practicable, arrange for copies of all written reports filed in the case to be made available before the hearing to—

    (a)   the applicant;
    (b)   the parent or guardian of the child to whom the application relates;
    (c)   any legal representative of the child;
    (d)   the children's guardian; and
    (e)   the child, unless the court directs otherwise,

and copies of the reports may, if the court considers it desirable, be shown to any person who is entitled to notice of any hearing in accordance with Practice Direction 12C.

Chapter 4
Special provisions about private law proceedings

12.31 The First Hearing Dispute Resolution Appointment

(1) The court may set a date for the First Hearing Dispute Resolution Appointment after the proceedings have been issued.

(2) The court officer will give notice of any of the dates so fixed to the parties.

(Provisions relating to the timing of and issues to be considered at the First Hearing Dispute Resolution Appointment are contained in Practice Direction 12B.)

12.32 Answer

A respondent must file and serve on the parties an answer to the application for an order in private law proceedings within 14 days beginning with the date on which the application is served.

12.33 Applications for warning notices or applications to amend enforcement orders by reason of change of residence

(1) This rule applies in relation to an application ...[1] for—

   (a) a warning notice to be attached to a [child arrangements][2] order; or

   (b) an order under paragraph 5 of Schedule A1 to the 1989 Act to amend an enforcement order by reason of change of residence.

(2) The application must be made without notice.

(3) The court may deal with the application without a hearing.

(4) If the court decides to deal with the application at a hearing, rules 12.5, 12.7 and 12.8 will apply.

Amendments
1 Repealed by the Family Procedure (Amendment No.3) Rules 2013, SI 2013/3204, rr 2, 49.
2 Substituted by the Family Procedure (Amendment No. 3) Rules 2014, SI 2014/843, rr 2, 28.

12.34 Service of a risk assessment

(1) Where an officer of the Service or a Welsh family proceedings officer has filed a risk assessment with the court, subject to paragraph (2), the court officer will as soon as practicable serve copies of the risk assessment on each party.

(2) Before serving the risk assessment, the court must consider whether, in order to prevent a risk of harm to the child, it is necessary for—

   (a) information to be deleted from a copy of the risk assessment before that copy is served on a party; or

   (b) service of a copy of the risk assessment (whether with information deleted from it or not) on a party to be delayed for a specified period,

and may make directions accordingly.

12.35 Service of enforcement orders or orders amending or revoking enforcement orders

(1) Paragraphs (2) and (3) apply where [the court][1] makes—

   (a) an enforcement order; or

   (b) an order under paragraph 9(2) of Schedule A1 to the 1989 Act (enforcement order made following a breach of an enforcement order).

(2) As soon as practicable after an order has been made, a copy of it must be served by the court officer on—

   (a) the parties, except the person against whom the order is made;

   (b) the officer of the Service or the Welsh family proceedings officer who is to comply with a request under section 11M of the 1989 Act 2 to monitor compliance with the order; and

   (c) the responsible officer.

(3) Unless the court directs otherwise, the applicant must serve a copy of the order personally on the person against whom the order is made.

(4) The court officer must send a copy of an order made under paragraph 4, 5, 6 or 7 of Schedule A1 to the 1989 Act (revocation or amendment of an enforcement order) to—

(a) the parties;
(b) the officer of the Service or the Welsh family proceedings officer who is to comply with a request under section 11M of the 1989 Act to monitor compliance with the order;
(c) the responsible officer; and
(d) in the case of an order under paragraph 5 of Schedule A1 to the 1989 Act (amendment of enforcement order by reason of change of residence), the responsible officer in the former local justice area.

(5) In this rule, 'responsible officer' has the meaning given in paragraph 8(8) of Schedule A1 to the 1989 Act.

Amendment
1   Substituted by the Family Procedure (Amendment No.3) Rules 2013, SI 2013/3204, rr 2, 50.

Chapter 5
Special provisions about inherent jurisdiction proceedings

12.36 Where to start proceedings

(1) An application for proceedings under the Inherent Jurisdiction of the court must be started in the High Court.

(2) Wardship proceedings, except applications for an order that a child be made or cease to be a ward of court, may be transferred to the [family court]¹ unless the issues of fact or law make them more suitable for hearing in the High Court.

(The question of suitability for hearing in the High Court is explained in Practice Direction 12D (Inherent Jurisdiction (including Wardship Proceedings)).)

Amendment
1   Substituted by the Family Procedure (Amendment No.3) Rules 2013, SI 2013/3204, rr 2, 51.

12.37 Child as respondent to wardship proceedings

(1) A child who is the subject of wardship proceedings must not be made a respondent to those proceedings unless the court gives permission following an application under paragraph (2).

(2) Where nobody other than the child would be a suitable respondent to wardship proceedings, the applicant may apply without notice for permission to make the wardship application—

(a) without notice; or
(b) with the child as the respondent.

12.38 Registration requirements

The court officer will send a copy of every application for a child to be made a ward of court to the principal registry for recording in the register of wards.

12.39 Notice of child's whereabouts

(1) Every respondent, other than a child, must file with the acknowledgment of service a notice stating—

 (a) the respondent's address; and
 (b) either—
  (i) the whereabouts of the child; or
  (ii) that the respondent is unaware of the child's whereabouts if that is the case.

(2) Unless the court directs otherwise, the respondent must serve a copy of that notice on the applicant.

(3) Every respondent other than a child must immediately notify the court in writing of—

 (a) any subsequent changes of address; or
 (b) any change in the child's whereabouts,

and, unless the court directs otherwise, serve a copy of that notice on the applicant.

(4) In this rule a reference to the whereabouts of a child is a reference to—

 (a) the address at which the child is living;
 (b) the person with whom the child is living; and
 (c) any other information relevant to where the child may be found.

12.40 Enforcement of orders in wardship proceedings

The High Court may secure compliance with any direction relating to a ward of court by an order addressed to the tipstaff.

(The role of the tipstaff is explained in Practice Direction 12D (Inherent Jurisdiction (including Wardship Proceedings)).)

12.41 Child ceasing to be ward of court

(1) A child who, by virtue of section 41(2) of the Senior Courts Act 1981, automatically becomes a ward of court on the making of a wardship application will cease to be a ward on the determination of the application unless the court orders that the child be made a ward of court.

(2) Nothing in paragraph (1) affects the power of the court under section 41(3) of the Senior Courts Act 1981 to order that any child cease to be a ward of court.

12.42 Adoption of a child who is a ward of court

An application for permission—

 (a) to start proceedings to adopt a child who is a ward of court;
 (b) to place such a child for adoption with parental consent; or
 (c) to start proceedings for a placement order in relation to such a child,

may be made without notice in accordance with Part 18.

[12.42A Application for a writ of habeas corpus for release in relation to a minor

(1) Part 87 of the CPR applies in respect of an application for a writ of habeas corpus for release in relation to a minor—

  (a) as if—
      (i) for rule 87.2(1)(a) of the CPR there were substituted—

          '(a) an application notice; and'; and

      (ii) for rule 87.2(4) of the CPR there were substituted—

          '(4) The application notice must be filed in the Family Division of the High Court.'; and

  (b) subject to any additional necessary modifications.

(2) Rules 12.5 to 12.8, 12.12 to 12.16, 12.21 and 12.39 do not apply to an application to which this rule applies.

(The term 'application notice' is defined in rule 2.3(1).)][1]

Amendment
1 Inserted by the Family Procedure (Amendment No. 4) Rules 2014, SI 2014/3296, rr 2, 10.

Chapter 6
Proceedings under the 1980 Hague Convention, the European Convention, the Council Regulation, and the 1996 Hague Convention

Scope

12.43 Scope

This Chapter applies to —

  (a) [children proceedings][1] under the 1980 Hague Convention or the European Convention; and
  (b) applications relating to the Council Regulation or the 1996 Hague Convention in respect of children.

Amendment
1 Substituted by the Family Procedure (Amendment) (No.5) Rules 2012, SI 2012/3061, rr 2, 5(b).

Section 1 – Proceedings under the 1980 Hague Convention

12.44 Interpretation

In this section—

  'the 1985 Act' means the Child Abduction and Custody Act 1985;
  'Central Authority' means, in relation to England and Wales, the Lord Chancellor;
  'Contracting State' has the meaning given in—
    (a) section 2 of the 1985 Act in relation to the 1980 Hague Convention; and
    (b) section 13 of the 1985 Act in relation to the European Convention; and

'decision relating to custody' has the same meaning as in the European Convention.

('the 1980 Hague Convention' and the 'the European Convention' are defined in rule 2.3)

12.45 Where to start proceedings

Every application under the 1980 Hague Convention or the European Convention must be—

(a) made in the High Court and issued in the principal registry; and
(b) heard by a Judge of the High Court unless the application is;
  (i) to join a respondent; or
  (ii) to dispense with service or extend the time for acknowledging service.

12.46 Evidence in support of application

Where the party making an application under this section does not produce the documents referred to in Practice Direction 12F, the court may—

(a) fix a time within which the documents are to be produced;
(b) accept equivalent documents; or
(c) dispense with production of the documents if the court considers it has sufficient information.

12.47 Without-notice applications

(1) This rule applies to applications—

(a) commencing or in proceedings under this section;
(b) for interim directions under section 5 or 19 of the 1985 Act;
(c) for the disclosure of information about the child and for safeguarding the child's welfare, under rule 12.57;
(d) for the disclosure of relevant information as to where the child is, under section 24A of the 1985 Act; or
(e) for a collection order, location order or passport order.

(2) Applications under this rule may be made without notice, in which case the applicant must file the application—

(a) where the application is made by telephone, the next business day after the making of the application; or
(b) in any other case, at the time when the application is made.

(3) Where an order is made without notice, the applicant must serve a copy of the order on the other parties as soon as practicable after the making of the order, unless the court otherwise directs.

(4) Where the court refuses to make an order on an application without notice, it may direct that the application is made on notice.

(5) Where any hearing takes place outside the hours during which the court office is usually open—

(a) if the hearing takes place by telephone, the applicant's solicitors will, if practicable, arrange for the hearing to be recorded; and
(b) in all other cases, the court or court officer will take a note of the proceedings.

(Practice Direction 12E (Urgent Business) provides further details of the procedure for out of hours applications. See also Practice Direction 12D (Inherent Jurisdiction (including Wardship Proceedings)).)

12.48 Directions

(1) As soon as practicable after an application to which this section applies has been made, the court may give directions as to the following matters, among others—

(a) whether service of the application may be dispensed with;
(b) whether the proceedings should be transferred to another court under rule 12.54;
(c) expedition of the proceedings or any part of the proceedings (and any direction for expedition may specify a date by which the court must issue its final judgment in the proceedings or a specified part of the proceedings);
(d) the steps to be taken in the proceedings and the time by which each step is to be taken;
(e) whether the child or any other person should be made a party to the proceedings;
(f) if the child is not made a party to the proceedings, the manner in which the child's wishes and feelings are to be ascertained, having regard to the child's age and maturity and in particular whether an officer of the Service or a Welsh family proceedings officer should report to the court for that purpose;
(g) where the child is made a party to the proceedings, the appointment of a children's guardian for that child unless a children's guardian has already been appointed;
(h) the attendance of the child or any other person before the court;
(i) the appointment of a litigation friend for a child or for any protected party, unless a litigation friend has already been appointed;
(j) the service of documents;
(k) the filing of evidence including expert evidence; and
(l) whether the parties and their representatives should meet at any stage of the proceedings and the purpose of such a meeting.

(Rule 16.2 provides for when the court may make the child a party to the proceedings and rule 16.4 for the appointment of a children's guardian for the child who is made a party. Rule 16.5 (without prejudice to rule 16.6) requires a child who is a party to the proceedings but not the subject of those proceedings to have a litigation friend.)

(2) Directions of a court which are in force immediately prior to the transfer of proceedings to another court under rule 12.54 will continue to apply following the transfer subject to—

(a) any changes of terminology which are required to apply those directions to the court to which the proceedings are transferred; and
(b) any variation or revocation of the directions.

(3) The court or court officer will—

(a) take a note of the giving, variation or revocation of directions under this rule; and
(b) as soon as practicable serve a copy of the directions order on every party.

12.49 Answer

(1) Subject to paragraph (2) and to any directions given under rule 12.48, a respondent must file and serve on the parties an answer to the application within 7 days beginning with the date on which the application is served.

(2) The court may direct a longer period for service where the respondent has been made a party solely on one of the following grounds—

(a) a decision relating to custody has been made in the respondent's favour; or
(b) the respondent appears to the court to have sufficient interest in the welfare of the child.

12.50 Filing and serving written evidence

(1) The respondent to an application to which this section applies may file and serve with the answer a statement verified by a statement of truth, together with any further evidence on which the respondent intends to rely.

(2) The applicant may, within 7 days beginning with the date on which the respondent's evidence was served under paragraph (1), file and serve a statement in reply verified by a statement of truth, together with any further evidence on which the applicant intends to rely.

12.51 Adjournment

The court will not adjourn the hearing of an application to which this section applies for more than 21 days at at any one time.

12.52 Stay of proceedings upon notification of wrongful removal etc.

(1) In this rule and in rule 12.53—

(a) 'relevant authority' means —
 (i) the High Court;
 (ii) [the family court][1];
 ...[2]
 (iv) the Court of Session;
 (v) a sheriff court;
 [(vi) a children's hearing within the meaning of the Children's Hearings (Scotland) Act 2011;][3]

(vii) the High Court in Northern Ireland;
(viii) a county court in Northern Ireland;
(ix) a court of summary jurisdiction in Northern Ireland;
(x) the Royal Court of Jersey;
(xi) a court of summary jurisdiction in Jersey;
(xii) the High Court of Justice of the Isle of Man;
(xiii) a court of summary jurisdiction in the Isle of Man; or
(xiv) the Secretary of State; and
(b) 'rights of custody' has the same meaning as in the 1980 Hague Convention.

(2) Where a party to proceedings under the 1980 Hague Convention knows that an application relating to the merits of rights of custody is pending in or before a relevant authority, that party must file within the proceedings under the 1980 Hague Convention a concise statement of the nature of that application, including the relevant authority in or before which it is pending.

(3) On receipt of a statement filed in accordance with paragraph (2) above, a court officer will notify the relegant authority in or before which the application is pending and will subsequently notify the relevant authority of the result of the proceedings.

(4) On receipt by the relevant authority of a notification under paragraph (3) from the High Court or equivalent notification from the Court of Session, the High Court in Northern Ireland or the High Court of Justice of the Isle of Man—

(a) all further proceedings in the action will be stayed(GL) unless and until the proceedings under the 1980 Hague Convention in the High Court, Court of Session, the High Court in Northern Ireland or the High Court of Justice of the Isle of Man are dismissed; and
(b) the parties to the action will be notified by the court officer of the stay(GL) and dismissal.

Amendments
1 Substituted by the Family Procedure (Amendment No.3) Rules 2013, SI 2013/3204, rr 2, 52(a).
2 Repealed by the Family Procedure (Amendment No.3) Rules 2013, SI 2013/3204, rr 2, 52(b).
3 Substituted by the Children's Hearings (Scotland) Act 2011 (Consequential and Transitional Provisions and Savings) Order 2013, SI 2013/1465, art 17(1), Sch 1, para 28.

12.53 Stay of proceedings where application made under s.16 of the 1985 Act (registration of decisions under the European Convention)

(1) A person who—
    (a) is a party to—
        (i) proceedings under section 16 of the 1985 Act; or
        (ii) proceedings as a result of which a decision relating to custody has been registered under section 16 of the 1985 Act; and
    (b) knows that an application is pending under—
        (i) section 20(2) of the 1985 Act;
        (ii) Article 21(2) of the Child Abduction and Custody (Jersey) Law 2005; or
        (iii) section 42(2) of the Child Custody Act 1987 (an Act of Tynwald),

must file within the proceedings under section 16 of the 1985 Act a concise statement of the nature of the pending application.

(2) On receipt of a statement filed in accordance with paragraph (1) above, a court officer will notify the relevant authority in or before which the application is pending and will subsequently notify the relevant authority of the result of the proceedings.

(3) On receipt by the relevant authority of a notification under paragraph (2) from the High Court or equivalent notification from the Court of Session, the High Court in Northern Ireland or the High Court of Justice of the Isle of Man, the court officer will notify the parties to the action.

12.54 Transfer of proceedings

(1) At any stage in proceedings under the 1985 Act the court may—

- (a) of its own initiative; or
- (b) on the application of a party with a minimum of two days' notice;

order that the proceedings be transferred to a court listed in paragraph (4).

(2) Where the court makes an order for transfer under paragraph (1)—

- (a) the court will state its reasons on the face of the order;
- (b) a court officer will send a copy of the order, the application and the accompanying documents (if any) and any evidence to the court to which the proceedings are transferred; and
- (c) the costs of the proceedings both before and after the transfer will be at the discretion of the court to which the proceedings are transferred.

(3) Where proceedings are transferred to the High Court from a court listed in paragraph (4), a court officer will notify the parties of the transfer and the proceedings will continue as if they had been commenced in the High Court.

(4) The listed courts are the Court of Session, the High Court in Northern Ireland, the Royal Court of Jersey or the High Court of Justice of the Isle of Man.

12.55 Revocation and variation of registered decisions

(1) This rule applies to decisions which—

- (a) have been registered under section 16 of the 1985 Act; and
- (b) are subsequently varied or revoked by an authority in the Contracting State in which they were made.

(2) The court will, on cancelling the registration of a decision which has been revoked, notify—

- (a) the person appearing to the court to have care of the child;
- (b) the person on whose behalf the application for registration of the decision was made; and
- (c) any other party to the application.

(3) The court will, on being informed of the variation of a decision, notify—
   (a) the party appearing to the court to have care of the child; and
   (b) any party to the application for registration of the decision;

and any such person may apply to make representations to the court before the registration is varied.

(4) Any person appearing to the court to have an interest in the proceedings may apply for the registration of a decision for the cancellation or variation of the decision referred to in paragraph (1).

12.56 The central index of decisions registered under the 1985 Act

A central index of decisions registered under section 16 of the 1985 Act, together with any variation of those decisions made under section 17 of that Act, will be kept by the principal registry.

12.57 Disclosure of information in proceedings under the European Convention

At any stage in proceedings under the European Convention the court may, if it has reason to believe that any person may have relevant information about the child who is the subject of those proceedings, order that person to disclose such information and may for that purpose order that the person attend before it or file affidavit[GL] evidence.

Section 2 – Applications relating to the Council Regulation

12.58 Interpretation

(1) In this section—

...[1]

'Contracting State' means a State party to the 1996 Hague Convention;
['domestic Central Authority' means—
   (a) where the matter relates to the Council Regulation, the Lord Chancellor;
   (b) where the matter relates to the 1996 Hague Convention in England, the Lord Chancellor;
   (c) where the matter relates to the 1996 Hague Convention in Wales, the Welsh Ministers;][2]
'judgment' has the meaning given in Article 2(4) of the Council Regulation;
'Member State' means a Member State bound by the Council Regulation or a country which has subsequently adopted the Council Regulation;
'parental responsibility' has the meaning given in —
   (a) Article 2(7) of the Council Regulation in relation to proceedings under that Regulation; and
   (b) Article 1(2) of the 1996 Hague Convention in relation to proceedings under that Convention; and
'seised' has the meaning given in Article 16 of the Council Regulation.

(2) In rules 12.59 to 12.70, references to the court of another member State or Contracting State include authorities within the meaning of 'court' in Article

2(1) of the Council Regulation, and authorities of Contracting States which have jurisdiction to take measures directed to the protection of the person or property of the child within the meaning of the 1996 Hague Convention.

Amendments
1   Repealed by the Family Procedure (Amendment No. 3) Rules 2012, SI 2012/2046, rr 2, 4(a).
2   Inserted by the Family Procedure (Amendment No. 3) Rules 2012, SI 2012/2046, rr 2, 4(b).

12.59 Procedure under Article 11(6) of the Council Regulation where the court makes a nonreturn order under Article 13 of the 1980 Hague Convention

(1) Where the court makes an order for the non-return of a child under Article 13 of the 1980 Hague Convention, it must immediately transmit the documents referred to in Article 11(6) of the Council Regulation—

(a)   directly to the court with jurisdiction or the central authority in the Member State where the child was habitually resident immediately before the wrongful removal to, or wrongful retention in, England and Wales; or

(b)   to the [domestic Central Authority][1] for onward transmission to the court with jurisdiction or the central authority in the other Member State mentioned in subparagraph (a).

(2) The documents required by paragraph (1) must be transmitted by a method which, in the case of direct transmission to the court with jurisdiction in the other Member State, ensures and, in any other case, will not prevent, their receipt by that court within one month of the date of the non-return order.

Amendment
1   Substituted by the Family Procedure (Amendment No. 3) Rules 2012, SI 2012/2046, rr 2, 5.

12.60 Procedure under Article 11(7) of the Council Regulation where the court receives a nonreturn order made under Article 13 of the 1980 Hague Convention by a court in another Member State

(1) This rule applies where the court receives an order made by a court in another Member State for the non-return of a child.

(2) In this rule, the order for non-return of the child and the papers transmitted with that order from the court in the other Member State are referred to as 'the non-return order'.

(3) Where, at the time of receipt of the non-return order, the court is already seised of a question of parental responsibility in relation to the child, —

(a)   the court officer shall immediately —
  (i)   serve copies of the non-return order on each party to the proceedings in which a question of parental responsibility in relation to the child is at issue; and
  (ii) where the non-return order was received directly from the court or the central authority in the other Member State, transmit to the [domestic Central Authority][1] a copy of the non-return order.

(b)   the court shall immediately invite the parties to the 1980 Hague Convention proceedings to file written submissions in respect of the question of custody by a specified date, or to attend a hearing to consider the future conduct of the proceedings in the light of the nonreturn order.

(4) Where, at the time of receipt of the non-return order, the court is not already seised of the question of parental responsibility in relation to the child, it shall immediately—

(a) open a court file in respect of the child and assign a court reference to the file;
(b) serve a copy of the non-return order on each party to the proceedings before the court in the Member State which made that order;
(c) invite each party to file, within 3 months of notification to that party of receipt of the non-return order, submissions in the form of—
   (i) an application for an order under—
      (aa) the 1989 Act; or
      (bb) (in the High Court only) an application under the inherent jurisdiction in respect of the child; or
   (ii) where permission is required to make an application for the order in question, an application for that permission;
(d) where the non-return order was received directly from the court or central authority in the other Member State, transmit to the [domestic Central Authority][1] a copy of the non-return order.

(5) In a case to which paragraph (4) applies where no application is filed within the 3 month period provided for by paragraph (4)(c) the court must close its file in respect of the child.

(Enforcement of a subsequent judgment requiring the return of the child, made under Article 11(8) by a court examining custody of the child under Article 11(7), is dealt with in Part 31 below.)

Amendment
1 Substituted by the Family Procedure (Amendment No. 3) Rules 2012, SI 2012/2046, rr 2, 5.

12.61 Transfer of proceedings under Article 15 of the Council Regulation or under Article 8 of the 1996 Hague Convention

(1) Where the court is considering the transfer of proceedings to the court of another Member State or Contracting State under rules 12.62 to 12.64 it will—

(a) fix a date for a hearing for the court to consider the question of transfer; and
(b) give directions as to the manner in which the parties may make representations.

(2) The court may, with the consent of all parties, deal with the question of transfer without a hearing.

(3) Directions which are in force immediately prior to the transfer of proceedings to a court in another Member State or Contracting State under rules 12.62 to 12.64 will continue to apply until the court in that other State accepts jurisdiction in accordance with the provisions of the Council Regulation or the 1996 Hague

Convention (as appropriate), subject to any variation or revocation of the directions.

(4) The court or court officer will—

(a) take a note of the giving, variation or revocation of directions under this rule; and
(b) as soon as practicable serve a copy of the directions order on every party.

(5) A register of all applications and requests for transfer of jurisdiction to or from another Member State or Contracting State will be kept by the principal registry.

12.62 Application by a party for transfer of the proceedings

(1) A party may apply to the court under Article 15(1) of the Council Regulation or under Article 8(1) of the 1996 Hague Convention—

(a) to stay(GL) the proceedings or a specified part of the proceedings and to invite the parties to introduce a request before a court of another Member State or Contracting State; or
(b) to make a request to a court of another Member State or another Contracting State to assume jurisdiction for the proceedings, or a specified part of the proceedings.

(2) An application under paragraph (1) must be made—

(a) to the court in which the relevant parental responsibility proceedings are pending; and
(b) using the Part 18 procedure.

(3) The applicant must file the application notice and serve it on the respondents—

(a) where the application is also made under Article 11 of the Council Regulation, not less than 5 days, and
(b) in any other case, not less than 42 days,

before the hearing of the application.

12.63 Application by a court of another Member State or another Contracting State for transfer of the proceedings

(1) This rule applies where a court of another Member State or another Contracting State makes an application under Article 15(2)(c) of the Council Regulation or under Article 9 of the 1996 Hague Convention that the court having jurisdiction in relation to the proceedings transfer the proceedings or a specific part of the proceedings to the applicant court.

(2) When the court receives the application, the court officer will—

(a) as soon as practicable, notify the [domestic Central Authority][1] of the application; and
(b) serve the application, and notice of the hearing on all other parties in England and Wales not less than 5 days before the hearing of the application.

Amendment
1 Substituted by the Family Procedure (Amendment No. 3) Rules 2012, SI 2012/2046, rr 2, 5.

12.64 Exercise by the court of its own initiative of powers to seek to transfer the proceedings

(1) The court having jurisdiction in relation to the proceedings may exercise its powers of its own initiative under Article 15 of the Council Regulation or Article 8 of the 1996 Hague Convention in relation to the proceedings or a specified part of the proceedings.

(2) Where the court proposes to exercise its powers, the court officer will give the parties not less than 5 days' notice of the hearing.

12.65 Application to High Court to make request under Article 15 of the Council Regulation or Article 9 of the 1996 Hague Convention to request transfer of jurisdiction

(1) An application for the court to request transfer of jurisdiction in a matter concerning a child from another Member State or another Contracting State under Article 15 of the Council Regulation, or Article 9 of the 1996 Hague Convention (as the case may be) must be made to the principal registry and heard in the High Court.

(2) An application must be made without notice to any other person and the court may give directions about joining any other party to the application.

(3) Where there is agreement between the court and the court or competent authority to which the request under paragraph (1) is made to transfer the matter to the courts of England and Wales, the court will consider with that other court or competent authority the specific timing and conditions for the transfer.

(4) Upon receipt of agreement to transfer jurisdiction from the court or other competent authority in the Member State, or Contracting State to which the request has been made, the court officer will serve on the applicant a notice that jurisdiction has been accepted by the courts of England and Wales.

(5) The applicant must attach the notice referred to in paragraph (3) to any subsequent application in relation to the child.

(6) Nothing in this rule requires an application with respect to a child commenced following a transfer of jurisdiction to be made to or heard in the High Court.

(7) Upon allocation, the court to which the proceedings are allocated must immediately fix a directions hearing to consider the future conduct of the case.

12.66 Procedure where the court receives a request from the authorities of another Member State or Contracting State to assume jurisdiction in a matter concerning a child

(1) Where any court other than the High Court receives a request to assume jurisdiction in a matter concerning a child from a court or other authority

which has jurisdiction in another Member State or Contracting State, that court must immediately refer the request to a Judge of the High Court for a decision regarding acceptance of jurisdiction to be made.

(2) Upon the High Court agreeing to the request under paragraph (1), the court officer will notify the parties to the proceedings before the other Member State or Contracting State of that decision, and the case must be allocated as if the application had been made in England and Wales.

(3) Upon allocation, the court to which the proceedings are allocated must immediately fix a directions hearing to consider the future conduct of the case.

(4) The court officer will serve notice of the directions hearing on all parties to the proceedings in the other Member State or Contracting State no later than 5 days before the date of that hearing.

12.67 Service of the court's order or request relating to transfer of jurisdiction under the Council Regulation or the 1996 Hague Convention

The court officer will serve an order or request relating to transfer of jurisdiction on all parties, the Central Authority of the other Member State or Contracting State, and the [domestic Central Authority][1].

Amendment
1 Substituted by the Family Procedure (Amendment No. 3) Rules 2012, SI 2012/2046, rr 2, 5.

12.68 Questions as to the court's jurisdiction or whether the proceedings should be stayed

(1) If at any time after issue of the application it appears to the court that under any of Articles 16 to 18 of the Council Regulation it does not or may not have jurisdiction to hear an application, or that under Article 19 of the Council Regulation or Article 13 of the 1996 Hague Convention it is or may be required to stay$^{(GL)}$ the proceedings or to decline jurisdiction, the court must—

(a) stay(GL) the proceedings; and
(b) fix a date for a hearing to determine jurisdiction or whether there should be a stay$^{(GL)}$ or other order.

(2) The court officer will serve notice of the hearing referred to at paragraph (1)(b) on the parties to the proceedings.

(3) The court must, in writing—

(a) give reasons for its decision under paragraph (1); and
(b) where it makes a finding of fact, state such finding.

(4) The court may with the consent of all the parties deal with any question as to the jurisdiction of the court, or as to whether the proceedings should be stayed$^{(GL)}$, without a hearing.

12.69 Request for consultation as to contemplated placement of child in England and Wales

(1) This rule applies to a request made —

(a) under Article 56 of the Council Regulation, by a court in another Member State; or

(b) under Article 33 of the 1996 Hague Convention by a court in another Contracting State for consultation on or consent to the contemplated placement of a child in England and Wales.

(2) Where the court receives a request directly from a court in another Member State or Contracting State, the court shall, as soon as practicable after receipt of the request, notify the [domestic Central Authority][1] of the request and take the appropriate action under paragraph (4).

(3) Where it appears to the court officer that no proceedings relating to the child are pending before a court in England and Wales, the court officer must inform the [domestic Central Authority][1] of that fact and forward to the Central Authority all documents relating to the request sent by the court in the other Member State or Contracting State.

(4) Where the court receives a request forwarded by the [domestic Central Authority][1], the court must, as soon as practicable after receipt of the request, either—

(a) where proceedings relating to the child are pending before the court, fix a directions hearing; or

(b) where proceedings relating to the child are pending before another court in England and Wales, send a copy of the request to that court.

Amendment
1 Substituted by the Family Procedure (Amendment No. 3) Rules 2012, SI 2012/2046, rr 2, 5.

12.70 Request made by court in England and Wales for consultation as to contemplated placement of child in another Member State or Contracting State

(1) This rule applies where the court is contemplating the placement of a child in another Member State under Article 56 of the Council Regulation or another Contracting State under Article 33 of the 1996 Hague Convention, and proposes to send a request for consultation with or for the consent of the central authority or other authority having jurisdiction in the other State in relation to the contemplated placement.

(2) In this rule, a reference to 'the request' includes a reference to a report prepared for purposes of Article 33 of the 1996 Hague Convention where the request is made under that Convention.

(3) Where the court sends the request directly to the central authority or other authority having jurisdiction in the other State, it shall at the same time send a copy of the request to the [domestic Central Authority][1].

(4) The court may send the request to the [domestic Central Authority][1] for onward transmission to the central authority or other authority having jurisdiction in the other Member State.

(5) The court should give consideration to the documents which should accompany the request.

(See Chapters 1 to 3 of this Part generally, for the procedure governing applications for an order under paragraph 19(1) of Schedule 2 to the 1989 Act permitting a local authority to arrange for any child in its care to live outside England and Wales.)

(Part 14 sets out the procedure governing applications for an order under section 84 (giving parental responsibility prior to adoption abroad) of the Adoption and Children Act 2002.)

Amendment
1   Substituted by the Family Procedure (Amendment No. 3) Rules 2012, SI 2012/2046, rr 2, 5.

12.71 Application for a declaration as to the extent, or existence, of parental responsibility in relation to a child under Article 16 of the 1996 Hague Convention

(1) Any interested person may apply for a declaration —

(a) that a person has, or does not have, parental responsibility for a child; or
(b) as to the extent of a person's parental responsibility for a child,

where the question arises by virtue of the application of Article 16 of the 1996 Hague Convention.

(2) An application for a declaration as to the extent, or existence of a person's parental responsibility for a child by virtue of Article 16 of the 1996 Hague Convention must be made in the principal registry and heard in the High Court.

(3) An application for a declaration referred to in paragraph (1) may not be made where the question raised is otherwise capable of resolution in any other family proceedings in respect of the child.

Chapter 7
Communication of information: children proceedings

12.72 Interpretation

...[1] In this Chapter 'independent reviewing officer' means a person appointed in respect of a child in accordance with regulation 2A of the Review of Children's Cases Regulations 1991, or regulation 3 of the Review of Children's Cases (Wales) Regulations 2007.

Amendment
1   Repealed by the Family Procedure (Amendment) Rules 2012, SI 2012/679, rr 2, 22.

12.73 Communication of information: general

(1) For the purposes of the law relating to contempt of court, information relating to proceedings held in private (whether or not contained in a document filed with the court) may be communicated—

(a) where the communication is to—
   (i) a party;
   (ii) the legal representative of a party;

(iii) a professional legal adviser;
(iv) an officer of the service or a Welsh family proceedings officer;
(v) the welfare officer;
(vi) [the Director of Legal Aid Casework (within the meaning of section 4 of the Legal Aid, Sentencing and Punishment of Offenders Act 2012)][1];
(vii) an expert whose instruction by a party has been authorised by the court for the purposes of the proceedings;
(viii) a professional acting in furtherance of the protection of children;
(ix) an independent reviewing officer appointed in respect of a child who is, or has been, subject to proceedings to which this rule applies;
(b) where the court gives permission; or
(c) subject to any direction of the court, in accordance with rule 12.75 and Practice Direction 12G.

(2) Nothing in this Chapter permits the communication to the public at large, or any section of the public, of any information relating to the proceedings.

(3) Nothing in rule 12.75 and Practice Direction 12G permits the disclosure of an unapproved draft judgment handed down by any court.

Amendment
1 Substituted by the Legal Aid, Sentencing and Punishment of Offenders Act 2012 (Consequential, Transitional and Saving Provisions) Regulations 2013, SI 2013/534, reg 14(1), (2), Schedule, para 22(a).

12.74 ...[1]

...[1]

Amendment
1 Repealed by the Family Procedure (Amendment) (No.5) Rules 2012, SI 2012/3061, rr 2, 4.

12.75 Communication of information for purposes connected with the proceedings

(1) A party or the legal representative of a party, on behalf of and upon the instructions of that party, may communicate information relating to the proceedings to any person where necessary to enable that party—

(a) by confidential discussion, to obtain support, advice or assistance in the conduct of the proceedings;
[(b) to attend a mediation information and assessment meeting, or to engage in mediation or other forms of non-court dispute resolution;][1]
(c) to make and pursue a complaint against a person or body concerned in the proceedings; or
(d) to make and pursue a complaint regarding the law, policy or procedure relating to a category of proceedings to which this Part applies.

(2) Where information is communicated to any person in accordance with paragraph (1)(a) of this rule, no further communication by that person is permitted.

(3) When information relating to the proceedings is communicated to any person in accordance with paragraphs (1)(b),(c) or (d) of this rule—

(a) the recipient may communicate that information to a further recipient, provided that—
   (i) the party who initially communicated the information consents to that further communication; and
   (ii) the further communication is made only for the purpose or purposes for which the party made the initial communication; and
(b) the information may be successively communicated to and by further recipients on as many occasions as may be necessary to fulfil the purpose for which the information was initially communicated, provided that on each such occasion the conditions in subparagraph (a) are met.

Amendment
1 Substituted by the Family Procedure (Amendment No. 3) Rules 2014, SI 2014/843, rr 2, 29.

PRACTICE DIRECTION 12A
CARE, SUPERVISION AND OTHER PART 4 PROCEEDINGS: GUIDE TO CASE MANAGEMENT

The key stages of the court process

1.1 The Public Law Outline set out in the Table below contains an outline of—

(1) the order of the different stages of the process;

(2) the matters to be considered at the main case management hearings;

(3) the latest timescales within which the main stages of the process should take place in order to resolve the proceedings within 26 weeks.

1.2 In the Public Law Outline –

(1) 'CMH' means the Case Management Hearing;

(2) 'FCMH' means Further Case Management Hearing;

(3) 'ICO' means interim care order;

(4) 'IRH' means the Issues Resolution Hearing;

(5) 'LA' means the Local Authority which is applying for a care or supervision order or a final order in other Part 4 proceedings;

(6) 'OS' means the Official Solicitor.

1.3 In applying the provisions of FPR Part 12 and the Public Law Outline the court and the parties must also have regard to –

(1) all other relevant rules and Practice Directions and in particular –
- FPR Part 1 (Overriding Objective);
- FPR Part 4 (General Case Management Powers);

- FPR Part 15 (Representation of Protected Parties) and Practice Direction 15B (Adults Who May Be Protected Parties and Children Who May Become Protected Parties in Family Proceedings);
- FPR Part 18 (Procedure for Other Applications in Proceedings);
- FPR Part 22 (Evidence);
- FPR Part 24 (Witnesses, depositions generally and taking of evidence in Member States of the European Union);
- FPR Part 25 (Experts) and the Experts Practice Directions;
- FPR 27.6 and Practice Direction 27A (Court Bundles);
- FPR 30 (Appeals) and Practice Direction 30A (Appeals);

(2) the Allocation Rules;

(3) the Justices' Clerks Rules;

(4) President's Guidance issued from time to time on –

- Distribution of business of the family court;
- Judicial continuity and deployment;
- Prescribed templates and orders;

(5) International instruments –

- The Council Regulation (EC) No 2201/2003 (Brussels 2 revised);
- The 1996 Hague Convention;

(6) Guidance relating to protected parties and others with a disability –

- Protected Parties in Family Proceedings: Checklist For the Appointment of a Litigation Friend (including the Official Solicitor) (published in Family Law (January 2014);
- The Mental Capacity Act 2005 (Transfer of Proceedings) Order 2007 SI 2007/1899, relating to young people over 16 where they are likely to lack decision-making capacity at age 18.

Public Law Outline

PRE-PROCEEDINGS	
PRE-PROCEEDINGS CHECKLIST	
Annex Documents are the documents specified in the Annex to the Application Form which are to be attached to that form and filed with the court: - Social Work Chronology - Social Work Statement and Genogram - The current assessments relating to the child and/or the family and friends of the child to which the	Checklist documents (already existing on the LA's files) are – (a) Evidential documents including – - Previous court orders including foreign orders and judgments/reasons - Any assessment materials relevant to the key issues including capacity to litigate, section 7 and 37 reports

Family Procedure Rules 2010

PRE-PROCEEDINGS	
PRE-PROCEEDINGS CHECKLIST	
Social Work Statement refers and on which the LA relies • Care Plan • Index of Checklist Documents	• Single, joint or inter-agency materials (e.g., health andeducation/Home Office and Immigration Tribunal documents); (b) Decision-making records including – • Records of key discussions with the family • Key LA minutes and records for the child • Pre-existing care plans (e.g., child in need plan, looked after child plan and child protection plan) • Letters Before Proceedings Only Checklist documents in *(a) are to be served* with the application form Checklist Documents in *(b) are to be disclosed on request* by any party Checklist documents are *not* to be – • filed with the court unless the court directs otherwise; and • older than 2 years before the date of issue of the proceedings unless reliance is placed on the same in the LA's evidence

STAGE 1 – ISSUE AND ALLOCATION

DAY 1 AND DAY 2 (see interpretation section)

On Day 1 (Day of issue):

- The LA files the Application Form and Annex Documents and sends copies to Cafcass/CAFCASS Cymru
- The LA notifies the court of the need for an urgent preliminary case management hearing or an urgent contested ICO hearing where this is known or expected
- Court officer issues application

Within a day of issue (Day 2):

- Court considers jurisdiction in a case with an international element
- Court considers initial allocation to specified level of judge, in accordance with the Allocation Rules and any President's Guidance on the distribution of business

STAGE 1 – ISSUE AND ALLOCATION
DAY 1 AND DAY 2 (see interpretation section)
<ul><li>LA serves the Application Form, Annex Documents and evidential Checklist Documents on the parties together with the notice of date and time of CMH and any urgent hearing</li><li>Court gives standard directions on Issue and Allocation including:<ul><li>Checking compliance with Pre-Proceedings Checklist including service of any missing Annex Documents</li><li>Appointing Children's Guardian (to be allocated by Cafcass/ CAFCASS Cymru)</li><li>Appointing solicitor for the child only if necessary</li><li>Appointing (if the person to be appointed consents) a litigation friend for any protected party or any non subject child who is a party, including the OS where appropriate</li><li>Identifying whether a request has been made or should be made to a Central Authority or other competent authority in a foreign state or a consular authority in England and Wales in a case with an international element</li><li>Filing and service of a LA Case Summary</li><li>Filing and service of a Case Analysis by the Children's Guardian</li><li>Filing and Serving the Parents' Response</li><li>Sending a request for disclosure to, e.g., the police or health service body</li><li>Filing and serving an application for permission relating to experts under Part 25 on a date prior to the advocates meeting for the CMH</li><li>Directing the solicitor for the child to arrange an advocates' meeting no later than 2 business days before the CMH</li><li>Listing the CMH</li></ul></li><li>Court considers any request for an urgent preliminary case management hearing or an urgent contested ICO hearing and where necessary lists the hearing and gives additional directions.</li><li>Court officer sends copy Notice of Hearing of the CMH and any urgent hearing by email to Cafcass/ CAFCASS Cymru.</li></ul>

STAGE 2 – CASE MANAGEMENT HEARING	
ADVOCATES' MEETING (including any litigants in person)	**CASE MANAGEMENT HEARING**
No later than 2 business days before CMH (or FCMH if it is necessary)	CMH: Not before day 12 and not later than day 18 A FCMH is to be held only if necessary, it is to be listed as soon as possible and in any event no later than day 25

STAGE 2 – CASE MANAGEMENT HEARING	
ADVOCATES' MEETING (including any litigants in person)	**CASE MANAGEMENT HEARING**
<ul><li>Consider information on the Application Form and Annex documents, the LA Case Summary, and the Case Analysis</li><li>Identify the parties' positions to be recited in the draft Case Management Order</li><li>Identify the parties' positions about jurisdiction, in particular arising out of any international element</li><li>If necessary, identify proposed experts and draft questions in accordance with Part 25 and the Experts Practice Directions</li><li>Identify any disclosure that in the advocates' views is necessary</li><li>Immediately notify the court of the need for a contested ICO hearing and any issue about allocation</li><li>LA advocate to file a draft Case Management Order in prescribed form with court by 11a.m. on the business day before the CMH and/ or FCMH</li></ul>	<ul><li>Court gives detailed case management directions, including: – Considering jurisdiction in a case with an international element; – Confirming allocation – Drawing up the timetable for the child and the timetable for the proceedings and considering if an extension is necessary – Identifying additional parties, intervenors and representation (including confirming that Cafcass/CAFCASS Cymru have allocated a Children's Guardian and that a litigation friend is appointed for any protected party or non-subject child) – Giving directions for the determination of any disputed issue about litigation capacity – Identifying the key issues – Identifying the evidence necessary to enable the court to resolve the key issues – Deciding whether there is a real issue about threshold to be resolved – Determining any application made under Part 25 and otherwise ensuring compliance with Part 25 where it is necessary for expert(s) to be instructed – Identifying any necessary disclosure and if appropriate giving directions – Giving directions for any concurrent or proposed placement order proceedings – Ensuring compliance with the court's directions</li></ul>

STAGE 2 – CASE MANAGEMENT HEARING	
ADVOCATES' MEETING (including any litigants in person)	**CASE MANAGEMENT HEARING**
	– If a FCMH is necessary, directing an advocates' meeting and Case Analysis if required – Directing filing of any threshold agreement, final evidence and Care Plan and responses to those documents for the IRH – Directing a Case Analysis for the IRH – Directing an advocates' meeting for the IRH – Listing (any FCMH) IRH, Final Hearing (including early Final Hearing) as appropriate – Giving directions for special measures and/or interpreters and intermediaries – Issuing the Case Management Order

STAGE 3 – ISSUES RESOLUTION HEARING	
ADVOCATES' MEETING (including any litigants in person)	**IRH**
No later than 7 business days before the IRH	As directed by the court, in accordance with the timetable for the proceedings

• Review evidence and the positions of the parties
• Identify the advocates' views of –
  – the remaining key issues and how the issues may be resolved or narrowed at the IRH including by the making of final orders
  – the further evidence which is required to be heard to enable the key issues to be resolved or narrowed at the IRH
  – the evidence that is relevant and the witnesses that are required at the final hearing
	• Court identifies the key issue(s) (if any) to be determined and the extent to which those issues can be resolved or narrowed at the IRH
	• Court considers whether the IRH can be used as a final hearing
	• Court resolves or narrows the issues by hearing evidence
	• Court identifies the evidence to be heard on the issues which remain to be resolved at the final hearing
	• Court gives final case management directions including:
	  – Any extension of the timetable for the proceedings which is necessary

STAGE 3 – ISSUES RESOLUTION HEARING	
ADVOCATES' MEETING (including any litigants in person)	**IRH**

– the need for a contested hearing and/or time for oral evidence to be given at the IRH
 • LA advocate to –
   – notify the court immediately of the outcome of the discussion at the meeting
     ○ Final evidence and Care Plan
   – file a draft Case Management Order with the court by 11a.m. on the business day before the IRH
     ○ Witness templates
	– Filing of the threshold agreement or a statement of facts/issues remaining to be determined
	 – Filing of:
	   ○ Case Analysis for Final Hearing (if required)
	   ○ Skeleton arguments
	 – Judicial reading list/reading time, including time estimate and an estimate for judgment writing time
	 – Ensuring Compliance with PD27A (the Bundles Practice Direction)
	 – Listing the Final Hearing
	 • Court issues Case Management Order

Flexible powers of the court

2.1 Attention is drawn to the flexible powers of the court either following the issue of the application or at any other stage in the proceedings.

2.2 The court may give directions without a hearing including setting a date for the Final Hearing or a period within which the Final Hearing will take place. The steps, which the court will ordinarily take at the various stages of the proceedings provided for in the Public Law Outline, may be taken by the court at another stage in the proceedings if the circumstances of the case merit this approach.

2.3 The flexible powers of the court include the ability for the court to cancel or repeat a particular hearing. For example, if the issue on which the case turns can with reasonable practicability be crystallised and resolved by taking evidence at an IRH then such a flexible approach must be taken in accordance with the overriding objective and to secure compliance with section 1(2) of the 1989 Act and resolving the proceedings within 26 weeks or the period for the time being specified by the court.

2.4 Where a party has requested an urgent hearing a) to enable the court to give immediate directions or orders to facilitate any case management issue which is to be considered at the CMH, or b) to decide whether an ICO is necessary, the court may list such a hearing at any appropriate time before the CMH and give directions for that hearing. It is anticipated that an urgent preliminary case management hearing will only be necessary to consider issues such as jurisdiction, parentage, party status, capacity to litigate, disclosure and whether there is, or should be, a request to a Central Authority or other competent authority in a foreign state or consular authority in England and Wales in an international case. It is not intended that any urgent hearing will delay the CMH.

2.5 Where it is anticipated that oral evidence may be required at the CMH, FCMH or IRH, the court must be notified in accordance with Stages 2 and 3 of the Public Law Outline well in advance and directions sought for the conduct of the hearing.

2.6 It is expected that full case management will take place at the CMH. It follows that the parties must be prepared to deal with all relevant case management issues, as identified in Stage 2 of the Public Law Outline. A FCMH should only be directed where necessary and must not be regarded as a routine step in proceedings.

Compliance with pre-proceedings checklist

3.1 It is recognised that in a small minority of cases the circumstances are such that the safety and welfare of the child may be jeopardised if the start of proceedings is delayed until all of the documents appropriate to the case and referred to in the Pre-proceedings Checklist are available. The safety and welfare of the child should never be put in jeopardy by delaying issuing proceedings whether because of lack of documentation or otherwise. (Nothing in this Practice Direction affects an application for an emergency protection order under section 44 of the 1989 Act). Also, where an application for an interim order is urgent, then the hearing of that application is NOT expected to be postponed until the Case Management Hearing. The Case Management Hearing is still to be held not before day 12 and not later than day 18 in accordance with the Public Law Outline and guidance in this Practice Direction. If an urgent preliminary Case Management Hearing or an urgent contested ICO hearing is held before the CMH, the court should not dispense with the CMH unless all of the parties have been sufficiently prepared and the court has been able to deal with all case management issues which would have come before it at the CMH.

3.2 The court recognises that the preparation may need to be varied to suit the circumstances of the case. In cases where any of the Annex Documents required to be attached to the Application Form are not available at the time of issue of the application, the court will consider making directions on issue about when any missing documentation is to be filed. The expectation is that there must be a good reason why one or more of the documents are not available. Further directions relating to any missing documentation will also be made at the Case Management Hearing.

Allocation

4.1 The court considers the allocation of proceedings in accordance with the Allocation Rules and any Guidance issued by the President on distribution of business of the family court. The justices' clerk or assistant justices' clerk (with responsibility for gatekeeping and allocation of proceedings) will discuss initial allocation with a district judge (with responsibility for allocation and gatekeeping of proceedings) as provided for in any Guidance issued by the President on distribution of business of the family court. The expectation is that, wherever possible, any question relating to allocation of the proceedings will be considered at the CMH.

The timetable for the child and the timetable for proceedings

5.1   The timetable for the proceedings –

(1) The court will draw up a timetable for the proceedings with a view to disposing of the application –

   (a)   without delay; and
   (b)   in any event within 26 weeks beginning with the day on which the application was issued in accordance with section 32(1)(a)(ii) of the Children Act 1989.

(2) The court, when drawing up or revising a timetable under paragraph (1), will in particular have regard to –

   (a)   the impact which the timetable or any revised timetable would have on the welfare of the child to whom the application relates; and
   (b)   the impact which the timetable or any revised timetable would have on the duration and conduct of the proceedings.

5.2   The impact which the timetable for the proceedings, any revision or extension of that timetable would have on the welfare of the child to whom the application relates are matters to which the court is to have particular regard. The court will use the Timetable for the Child to assess the impact of these matters on the welfare of the child and to draw up and revise the timetable for the proceedings.

5.3   The 'Timetable for the Child is the timetable set by the court which takes into account dates which are important to the child's welfare and development.

5.4   The timetable for the proceedings is set having particular regard to the Timetable for the Child and the Timetable for the Child needs to be reviewed regularly. Where adjustments are made to the Timetable for the Child, the timetable for the proceedings will have to be reviewed consistently with resolving the proceedings within 26 weeks or the period for the time being specified by the court.

5.5   Examples of the dates the court will record and take into account when setting the Timetable for the Child are the dates of –

(1) any formal review by the Local Authority of the case of a looked after child (within the meaning of section 22(1) of the 1989 Act);

(2) any significant educational steps, including the child taking up a place at a new school and, where applicable, any review by the Local Authority of a statement of the child's special educational needs;

(3) any health care steps, including assessment by a paediatrician or other specialist;

(4) any review of Local Authority plans for the child, including any plans for permanence through adoption, Special Guardianship or placement with parents or relatives;

(5) any change or proposed change of the child's placement;

(6) any significant change in the child's social or family circumstances; or

(7) any timetable for the determination of an issue in a case with an international element.

5.6 To identify the Timetable for the Child, the applicant is required to provide the information needed about the significant steps in the child's life in the Application Form and the Social Work Statement and to update this information regularly taking into account information received from others involved in the child's life such as the parties, members of the child's family, the person who is caring for the child, the children's guardian, the Independent Reviewing Officer, the child's key social worker and any Central Authority or competent authority in a foreign state or a consular authority in England and Wales in a case with an international element.

5.7 Where more than one child is the subject of the proceedings, the court should consider and will set a Timetable for the Child for each child. The children may not all have the same timetable, and the court will consider the appropriate progress of the proceedings in relation to each child.

5.8 Where there are parallel care proceedings and criminal proceedings against a person connected with the child for a serious offence against the child, linked directions hearings should where practicable take place as the case progresses. The timing of the proceedings in a linked care and criminal case should appear in the Timetable for the Child. The time limit of resolving the proceedings within 26 weeks applies unless a longer timetable has been set by the court in order to resolve the proceedings justly in accordance with section 32(1)(a)(ii) and (5) of the 1989 Act. Early disclosure and listing of hearings is necessary in proceedings in a linked care and criminal case.

Extensions to the timetable for proceedings

6.1 The court is required to draw up a timetable for proceedings with a view to disposing of the application without delay and in any event within 26 weeks. If proceedings can be resolved earlier, then they should be. A standard timetable and process is expected to be followed in respect of the giving of standard directions on issue and allocation and other matters which should be carried out by the court on issue, including setting and giving directions for the Case Management Hearing.

6.2 Having regard to the circumstances of the particular case, the court may consider that it is necessary to extend the time by which the proceedings are to be resolved beyond 26 weeks to enable the court to resolve the proceedings justly (see section 32 (5) of the 1989 Act). When making this decision, the court is to take account of the guidance that extensions are not to be granted routinely and are to be seen as requiring specific justification (see section 32(7) of the 1989 Act). The decision and reason(s) for extending a case should be recorded in writing (in the Case Management Order) and orally stated in court, so that all parties are aware of the reasons for delay in the case (see FPR 12.26C). The Case Management Order must contain a record of this information, as well as the impact of the court's decision on the welfare of the child.

6.3 The court may extend the period within which proceedings are intended to be resolved on its own initiative or on application. Applications for an extension should, wherever possible, only be made so that they are considered at any hearing for which a date has been fixed or for which a date is about to be fixed. Where a date for a hearing has been fixed, a party who wishes to make an application at that hearing but does not have sufficient time to file an application notice should as soon as possible inform the court (if possible in writing) and, if possible, the other parties of the nature of the application and the reason for it. The party should then make the application orally at the hearing.

6.4 If the court agrees an extension is necessary, an initial extension to the time limit may be granted for up to eight weeks (or less if directed) in order to resolve the case justly (see section 32(8) of the 1989 Act). If more time is necessary, in order to resolve the proceedings justly, a further extension of up to eight weeks may be agreed by the court. There is no limit on the number of extensions that may be granted in a particular case.

6.5 If the court considers that the timetable for the proceedings will require an extension beyond the next eight week period in order to resolve the proceedings justly, the Case Management Order should –

(1) state the reason(s) why it is necessary to have a further extension;

(2) fix the date of the next effective hearing (which might be in a period shorter than a further eight weeks); and

(3) indicate whether it is appropriate for the next application for an extension of the timetable to be considered on paper.

6.6 The expectation is that, subject to paragraph 6.5, extensions should be considered at a hearing and that a court will not approve proposals for the management of a case under FPR 12.15 where the consequence of those proposals is that the case is unlikely to be resolved within 26 weeks or other period for the time being allowed for resolution of the proceedings. In accordance with FPR 4.1(3)(e), the court may hold a hearing and receive evidence by telephone or by using any other method of direct oral communication. When deciding whether to extend the timetable, the court must have regard to the impact of any ensuing timetable revision on the welfare of the child (see section 32(6) of the 1989 Act).

Interpretation

7.1 'Allocation Rules' mean any rules relating to composition of the court and distribution of business made under section 31D of the Matrimonial and Family Proceedings Act 1984;

'Care Plan' is a separate document from the evidence that is filed by the local authority. It is a 'section 31A plan' referred to in section 31A of the 1989 Act which complies with guidance as to content issued by the Secretary of State;

'Case Analysis' means a written or, if there is insufficient time for a written, an oral outline of the case from the perspective of the child's best interests prepared by the children's guardian or Welsh family proceedings officer for the CMH or FCMH (where one is necessary) and IRH or as otherwise directed by the court, incorporating an analysis of the key issues that need to be resolved in the case including –

(a) a threshold analysis;
(b) a case management analysis, including an analysis of the timetable for the proceedings, an analysis of the Timetable for the Child and the evidence which any party proposes is necessary to resolve the issues;
(c) a parenting capability analysis;
(d) a child impact analysis, including an analysis of the ascertainable wishes and feelings of the child and the impact on the welfare of the child of any application to adjourn a hearing or extend the timetable for the proceedings;
(e) an early permanence analysis including an analysis of the proposed placements and contact framework; by reference to a welfare and proportionality analysis.
(f) whether and if so what communication it is proposed there should be during the proceedings with the child by the court;

'Case Management Order' is the prescribed form of order referred to in any Guidance issued by the President from time to time on prescribed templates and orders;

'Day' means 'business day'. 'Day 1' is the day of issue and 'Day 2' is the next business day following the day of issue of proceedings. 'Day 12', 'Day 18' and 'Day 25' are respectively the 11th, 17th and the 24th business days after the day of issue of proceedings (Day 1). '26 weeks' means 26 calendar weeks beginning on the day of issue of proceedings (Day 1);

'Experts Practice Directions' mean –

(a) Practice Direction 25A (Experts – Emergencies and Pre Proceedings Instructions);
(b) Practice Direction 25B (The Duties of An Expert, The Expert's Report and Arrangements For An Expert To Attend Court);
(c) Practice Direction 25C (Children's Proceedings - The Use Of Single Joint Experts and The Process Leading to An Expert Being Instructed or Expert Evidence Being Put Before the Court);

(d) Practice Direction 25E (Discussions Between Experts in Family Proceedings);

'Genogram' means a family tree, setting out in diagrammatic form the child's family and extended family members and their relationship with the child;

'Index of Checklist Documents' means a list of Checklist Documents referred to in the Public Law Outline Pre-Proceedings Checklist which is divided into two parts with Part A being the documents referred to in column 2, paragraph (a) of the Pre- Proceedings Checklist and Part B being those referred to in column 2, paragraph (b) of the Pre-proceedings Checklist;

'International instruments'

'the Council Regulation (EC) No 2201/2003 (Brussels 2 revised)' means Council Regulation (EC) No 2201/2003' of 27 November 2003 on jurisdiction and the recognition and enforcement of judgments in matrimonial matters and in matters of parental responsibility;

'Justices' Clerks Rules' means any rules made under section 310 of the Matrimonial and Family Proceedings Act 1984 enabling functions of the family court or judge of that court to be carried out by a justices' clerk or assistant to a justices' clerk;

'The 1996 Hague Convention' means the Convention on Jurisdiction, Applicable Law, Recognition, Enforcement and Co-operation in Respect of Parental Responsibility and Measures for the Protection of Children;

'Letter Before Proceedings' means any letter from the Local Authority containing written notification to the parents and others with parental responsibility for the child of the Local Authority's likely intention to apply to court for a care or supervision order and any related subsequent correspondence confirming the Local Authority's position;

'Local Authority Case Summary' means a document prepared by the Local Authority legal representative for each case management hearing in the form referred to in any Guidance issued by the President from time to time on prescribed templates and orders;

'Parents' Response' means a document from either or both of the parents containing –

(a) in no more than two pages, the parents' response to the Threshold Statement, and
(b) the parents' placement proposals including the identity and whereabouts of all relatives and friends they propose be considered by the court;
(c) Information which may be relevant to a person's capacity to litigate including information about any referrals to mental health services and adult services;

'Section 7 report' means any report under section 7 of the 1989 Act;

'Section 37 report' means any report by the Local Authority to the court as a result of a direction under section 37 of the 1989 Act;

'Social Work Chronology' means a schedule containing –

(a) a succinct summary of the length of involvement of the local authority with the family and in particular with the child;
(b) a succinct summary of the significant dates and events in the child's life in chronological order- i.e. a running record up to the issue of the proceedings; providing such information under the following headings-
  (i) serial number;
  (ii) date;
  (iii) event-detail;
  (iv) witness or document reference (where applicable);

'Social Work Statement' means a statement prepared by the Local Authority limited to the following evidence–

Summary

(a) The order sought;
(b) Succinct summary of reasons with reference as appropriate to the Welfare Checklist;

Family

(c) Family members and relationships especially the primary carers and significant adults/other children;
(d) Genogram;

Threshold

(e) Precipitating events;
(f) Background circumstances –
  (i) summary of children's services involvement cross-referenced to the chronology;
  (ii) previous court orders and emergency steps;
  (iii) previous assessments;
(g) Summary of significant harm and or likelihood of significant harm which the LA will seek to establish by evidence or concession;

Parenting capability

(h) Assessment of child's needs;
(i) Assessment of parental capability to meet needs;
(j) Analysis of why there is a gap between parental capability and the child's needs;
(k) Assessment of other significant adults who may be carers;

Child impact

(l) Wishes and feelings of the child(ren);
(m) Timetable for the Child;
(n) Delay and timetable for the proceedings;

Permanence and contact

(o) Parallel planning;

(p) Realistic placement options by reference to a welfare and proportionality analysis;
(q) Contact framework;

Case Management

(r) Evidence and assessments necessary and outstanding;
(s) Any information about any person's litigation capacity, mental health issues, disabilities or vulnerabilities that is relevant to their capability to participate in the proceedings; and
(t) Case management proposals.

'Standard Directions on Issue and Allocation' means directions given by the court on issue and upon allocation in the prescribed form referred to in any Guidance issued by the President from time to time on prescribed templates and orders;

'Threshold Statement' means a written outline by the legal representative of the LA in the application form of the facts which the LA will seek to establish by evidence or concession to satisfy the threshold criteria under s 31(2) of the 1989 Act limited to no more than 2 pages;

'Welfare Checklist' means the list of matters which is set out in section 1(3) of the 1989 Act and to which the court is to have particular regard in accordance with section (1)(3) and (4).

PRACTICE DIRECTION 12J
CHILD ARRANGEMENTS AND CONTACT ORDERS: DOMESTIC ABUSE AND HARM

This Practice Direction supplements FPR Part 12, and incorporates and supersedes the President's Guidance in Relation to Split Hearings (May 2010) as it applies to proceedings for child arrangements orders.

Summary

1 This Practice Direction applies to any family proceedings in the Family Court or the High Court under the relevant parts of the Children Act 1989 or the relevant parts of the Adoption and Children Act 2002 in which an application is made for a child arrangements order, or in which any question arises about where a child should live, or about contact between a child and a parent or other family member, where the court considers that an order should be made.

2 The purpose of this Practice Direction is to set out what the Family Court or the High Court is required to do in any case in which it is alleged or admitted, or there is other reason to believe, that the child or a party has experienced domestic abuse perpetrated by another party or that there is a risk of such abuse.

3 For the purpose of this Practice Direction –

'domestic abuse' includes any incident or pattern of incidents of controlling, coercive or threatening behaviour, violence or abuse between those aged 16 or over who are or have been intimate partners or family members regardless of gender or sexuality. This can encompass, but is not limited to, psychological, physical, sexual, financial, or emotional abuse. Domestic abuse also includes culturally specific forms of abuse including, but not limited to, forced marriage, honour-based violence, dowry-related abuse and transnational marriage abandonment;

'abandonment' refers to the practice whereby a husband, in England and Wales, deliberately abandons or 'strands' his foreign national wife abroad, usually without financial resources, in order to prevent her from asserting matrimonial and/or residence rights in England and Wales. It may involve children who are either abandoned with, or separated from, their mother;

'coercive behaviour' means an act or a pattern of acts of assault, threats, humiliation and intimidation or other abuse that is used to harm, punish, or frighten the victim;

'controlling behaviour' means an act or pattern of acts designed to make a person subordinate and/or dependent by isolating them from sources of support, exploiting their resources and capacities for personal gain, depriving them of the means needed for independence, resistance and escape and regulating their everyday behaviour;

'development' means physical, intellectual, emotional, social or behavioural development;

'harm' means ill-treatment or the impairment of health or development including, for example, impairment suffered from seeing or hearing the ill-treatment of another, by domestic abuse or otherwise;

'health' means physical or mental health;

'ill-treatment' includes sexual abuse and forms of ill-treatment which are not physical; and

'judge' includes salaried and fee-paid judges and lay justices sitting in the Family Court and, where the context permits, can include a justices' clerk or assistant to a justices' clerk in the Family Court.

General principles

4 Domestic abuse is harmful to children, and/or puts children at risk of harm, whether they are subjected to domestic abuse, or witness one of their parents being violent or abusive to the other parent, or live in a home in which domestic abuse is perpetrated (even if the child is too young to be conscious of the behaviour). Children may suffer direct physical, psychological and/or emotional harm from living with domestic abuse, and may also suffer harm indirectly where the domestic abuse impairs the parenting capacity of either or both of their parents.

5 The court must, at all stages of the proceedings, and specifically at the First Hearing Dispute Resolution Appointment ('FHDRA'), consider whether domestic abuse is raised as an issue, either by the parties or by Cafcass or CAFCASS Cymru or otherwise, and if so must –

- identify at the earliest opportunity (usually at the FHDRA) the factual and welfare issues involved;
- consider the nature of any allegation, admission or evidence of domestic abuse, and the extent to which it would be likely to be relevant in deciding whether to make a child arrangements order and, if so, in what terms;
- give directions to enable contested relevant factual and welfare issues to be tried as soon as possible and fairly;
- ensure that where domestic abuse is admitted or proven, any child arrangements order in place protects the safety and wellbeing of the child and the parent with whom the child is living, and does not expose either of them to the risk of further harm; and
- ensure that any interim child arrangements order (i.e. considered by the court before determination of the facts, and in the absence of admission) is only made having followed the guidance in paragraphs 25–27 below.

In particular, the court must be satisfied that any contact ordered with a parent who has perpetrated domestic abuse does not expose the child and/or other parent to the risk of harm and is in the best interests of the child.

6 In all cases it is for the court to decide whether a child arrangements order accords with Section 1(1) of the Children Act 1989; any proposed child arrangements order, whether to be made by agreement between the parties or otherwise must be carefully scrutinised by the court accordingly. The court must not make a child arrangements order by consent or give permission for an application for a child arrangements order to be withdrawn, unless the parties are present in court, all initial safeguarding checks have been obtained by the court, and an officer of Cafcass or CAFCASS Cymru has spoken to the parties separately, except where it is satisfied that there is no risk of harm to the child and/or the other parent in so doing.

7 In proceedings relating to a child arrangements order, the court presumes that the involvement of a parent in a child's life will further the child's welfare, unless there is evidence to the contrary. The court must in every case consider carefully whether the statutory presumption applies, having particular regard to any allegation or admission of harm by domestic abuse to the child or parent or any evidence indicating such harm or risk of harm.

8 In considering, on an application for a child arrangements order by consent, whether there is any risk of harm to the child, the court must consider all the evidence and information available. The court may direct a report under Section 7 of the Children Act 1989 to be provided either orally or in writing, before it makes its decision; in such a case, the court must ask for information about any advice given by the officer preparing the report to the parties and whether they, or the child, have been referred to any other agency, including local authority children's services. If the report is not in writing, the court must make a note of its substance on the court file and a summary of the same shall be set out in a Schedule to the relevant order.

Before the FHDRA

9 Where any information provided to the court before the FHDRA or other first hearing (whether as a result of initial safeguarding enquiries by Cafcass or CAFCASS Cymru or on form C1A or otherwise) indicates that there are issues of domestic abuse which may be relevant to the court's determination, the court must ensure that the issues are addressed at the hearing, and that the parties are not expected to engage in conciliation or other forms of dispute resolution which are not suitable and/or safe.

10 If at any stage the court is advised by any party (in the application form, or otherwise), by Cafcass or CAFCASS Cymru or otherwise that there is a need for special arrangements to protect the party or child attending any hearing, the court must ensure so far as practicable that appropriate arrangements are made for the hearing (including the waiting arrangements at court prior to the hearing, and arrangements for entering and exiting the court building) and for all subsequent hearings in the case, unless it is advised and considers that these are no longer necessary. Where practicable, the court should enquire of the alleged victim of domestic abuse how best she/he wishes to participate.

First hearing/ FHDRA

11 At the FHDRA, if the parties have not been provided with the safeguarding letter/report by Cafcass/CAFCASS Cymru, the court must inform the parties of the content of any safeguarding letter or report or other information which has been provided by Cafcass or CAFCASS Cymru, unless it considers that to do so would create a risk of harm to a party or the child.

12 Where the results of Cafcass or CAFCASS Cymru safeguarding checks are not available at the FHDRA, and no other reliable safeguarding information is available, the court must adjourn the FHDRA until the results of safeguarding checks are available. The court must not generally make an interim child arrangements order, or orders for contact, in the absence of safeguarding information, unless it is to protect the safety of the child, and/or safeguard the child from harm (see further paragraphs 25–27 below).

13 There is a continuing duty on the Cafcass Officer/Welsh FPO which requires them to provide a risk assessment for the court under section 16A Children Act 1989 if they are given cause to suspect that the child concerned is at risk of harm. Specific provision about service of a risk assessment under section 16A of the 1989 Act is made by rule 12.34 of the FPR 2010.

14 The court must ascertain at the earliest opportunity, and record on the face of its order, whether domestic abuse is raised as an issue which is likely to be relevant to any decision of the court relating to the welfare of the child, and specifically whether the child and/or parent would be at risk of harm in the making of any child arrangements order.

Admissions

15 Where at any hearing an admission of domestic abuse toward another person or the child is made by a party, the admission must be recorded in writing by the judge and set out as a Schedule to the relevant order. The court office must arrange for a copy of any order containing a record of admissions to be made available as soon as possible to any Cafcass officer or officer of CAFCASS Cymru or local authority officer preparing a report under section 7 of the Children Act 1989.

Directions for a fact-finding hearing

16 The court should determine as soon as possible whether it is necessary to conduct a fact-finding hearing in relation to any disputed allegation of domestic abuse –

(a) in order to provide a factual basis for any welfare report or for assessment of the factors set out in paragraphs 36 and 37 below;
(b) in order to provide a basis for an accurate assessment of risk;
(c) before it can consider any final welfare-based order(s) in relation to child arrangements; or
(d) before it considers the need for a domestic abuse-related Activity (such as a Domestic Violence Perpetrator Programme (DVPP)).

17 In determining whether it is necessary to conduct a fact-finding hearing, the court should consider –

(a) the views of the parties and of Cafcass or CAFCASS Cymru;
(b) whether there are admissions by a party which provide a sufficient factual basis on which to proceed;
(c) if a party is in receipt of legal aid, whether the evidence required to be provided to obtain legal aid provides a sufficient factual basis on which to proceed;
(d) whether there is other evidence available to the court that provides a sufficient factual basis on which to proceed;
(e) whether the factors set out in paragraphs 36 and 37 below can be determined without a fact-finding hearing;
(f) the nature of the evidence required to resolve disputed allegations;
(g) whether the nature and extent of the allegations, if proved, would be relevant to the issue before the court; and
(h) whether a separate fact-finding hearing would be necessary and proportionate in all the circumstances of the case.

18 Where the court determines that a finding of fact hearing is not necessary, the order must record the reasons for that decision.

19 Where the court considers that a fact-finding hearing is necessary, it must give directions as to how the proceedings are to be conducted to ensure that the matters in issue are determined as soon as possible, fairly and proportionately, and within the capabilities of the parties. In particular it should consider –

(a) what are the key facts in dispute;
(b) whether it is necessary for the fact-finding to take place at a separate (and earlier) hearing than the welfare hearing;
(c) whether the key facts in dispute can be contained in a schedule or a table (known as a Scott Schedule) which sets out what the applicant complains of or alleges, what the respondent says in relation to each individual allegation or complaint; the allegations in the schedule should be focused on the factual issues to be tried; and if so, whether it is practicable for this schedule to be completed at the first hearing, with the assistance of the judge;
(d) what evidence is required in order to determine the existence of coercive, controlling or threatening behaviour, or of any other form of domestic abuse;
(e) directing the parties to file written statements giving details of such behaviour and of any response;
(f) whether documents are required from third parties such as the police, health services or domestic abuse support services and giving directions for those documents to be obtained;
(g) whether oral evidence may be required from third parties and if so, giving directions for the filing of written statements from such third parties;
(h) where (for example in cases of abandonment) third parties from whom documents are to be obtained are abroad, how to obtain those documents in good time for the hearing, and who should be responsible for the costs of obtaining those documents;
(i) whether any other evidence is required to enable the court to decide the key issues and giving directions for that evidence to be provided;
(j) what evidence the alleged victim of domestic abuse is able to give and what support the alleged victim may require at the fact-finding hearing in order to give that evidence;
(k) in cases where the alleged victim of domestic abuse is unable for reasons beyond their control to be present at the hearing (for example, abandonment cases where the abandoned spouse remains abroad), what measures should be taken to ensure that that person's best evidence can be put before the court. Where video-link is not available, the court should consider alternative technological or other methods which may be utilised to allow that person to participate in the proceedings;
(l) what support the alleged perpetrator may need in order to have a reasonable opportunity to challenge the evidence; and
(m) whether a pre-hearing review would be useful prior to the fact-finding hearing to ensure directions have been complied with and all the required evidence is available.

20 Where the court fixes a fact-finding hearing, it must at the same time fix a Dispute Resolution Appointment to follow. Subject to the exception in paragraph 31 below, the hearings should be arranged in such a way that they are conducted by the same judge or, wherever possible, by the same panel of lay justices; where it is not possible to assemble the same panel of justices, the resumed hearing should be listed before at least the same chairperson of the lay justices. Judicial continuity is important.

Reports under Section 7

21 In any case where a risk of harm to a child resulting from domestic abuse is raised as an issue, the court should consider directing that a report on the question of contact, or any other matters relating to the welfare of the child, be prepared under section 7 of the Children Act 1989 by an Officer of Cafcass or a Welsh family proceedings officer (or local authority officer if appropriate), unless the court is satisfied that it is not necessary to do so in order to safeguard the child's interests.

22 If the court directs that there shall be a fact-finding hearing on the issue of domestic abuse, the court will not usually request a section 7 report until after that hearing. In that event, the court should direct that any judgment is provided to Cafcass/CAFCASS Cymru; if there is no transcribed judgment, an agreed list of findings should be provided, as set out at paragraph 29.

23 Any request for a section 7 report should set out clearly the matters the court considers need to be addressed.

Representation of the child

24 Subject to the seriousness of the allegations made and the difficulty of the case, the court must consider whether it is appropriate for the child who is the subject of the application to be made a party to the proceedings and be separately represented. If the court considers that the child should be so represented, it must review the allocation decision so that it is satisfied that the case proceeds before the correct level of judge in the Family Court or High Court.

Interim orders before determination of relevant facts

25 Where the court gives directions for a fact-finding hearing, or where disputed allegations of domestic abuse are otherwise undetermined, the court should not make an interim child arrangements order unless it is satisfied that it is in the interests of the child to do so and that the order would not expose the child or the other parent to an unmanageable risk of harm (bearing in mind the impact which domestic abuse against a parent can have on the emotional well-being of the child, the safety of the other parent and the need to protect against domestic abuse including controlling or coercive behaviour).

26 In deciding any interim child arrangements question the court should–
  (a) take into account the matters set out in section 1(3) of the Children Act 1989 or section 1(4) of the Adoption and Children Act 2002 ('the welfare check-list'), as appropriate; and

(b) give particular consideration to the likely effect on the child, and on the care given to the child by the parent who has made the allegation of domestic abuse, of any contact and any risk of harm, whether physical, emotional or psychological, which the child and that parent is likely to suffer as a consequence of making or declining to make an order.

27 Where the court is considering whether to make an order for interim contact, it should in addition consider –

    (a) the arrangements required to ensure, as far as possible, that any risk of harm to the child and the parent who is at any time caring for the child is minimised and that the safety of the child and the parties is secured; and in particular:
        (i) whether the contact should be supervised or supported, and if so, where and by whom; and
        (ii) the availability of appropriate facilities for that purpose;
    (b) if direct contact is not appropriate, whether it is in the best interests of the child to make an order for indirect contact; and
    (c) whether contact will be beneficial for the child.

The fact-finding hearing or other hearing of the facts where domestic abuse is alleged

28 While ensuring that the allegations are properly put and responded to, the fact-finding hearing or other hearing can be an inquisitorial (or investigative) process, which at all times must protect the interests of all involved. At the fact-finding hearing or other hearing –

- each party can be asked to identify what questions they wish to ask of the other party, and to set out or confirm in sworn evidence their version of the disputed key facts; and
- the judge should be prepared where necessary and appropriate to conduct the questioning of the witnesses on behalf of the parties, focusing on the key issues in the case.

29 The court should, wherever practicable, make findings of fact as to the nature and degree of any domestic abuse which is established and its effect on the child, the child's parents and any other relevant person. The court must record its findings in writing in a Schedule to the relevant order, and the court office must serve a copy of this order on the parties. A copy of any record of findings of fact or of admissions must be sent by the court office to any officer preparing a report under Section 7 of the 1989 Act.

30 At the conclusion of any fact-finding hearing, the court must consider, notwithstanding any earlier direction for a section 7 report, whether it is in the best interests of the child for the court to give further directions about the preparation or scope of any report under section 7; where necessary, it may adjourn the proceedings for a brief period to enable the officer to make representations about the preparation or scope of any further enquiries. Any section 7 report should address the factors set out in paragraphs 36 and 37 below, unless the court directs otherwise.

31 Where the court has made findings of fact on disputed allegations, any subsequent hearing in the proceedings should be conducted by the same judge or by at least the same chairperson of the justices. Exceptions may be made only where observing this requirement would result in delay to the planned timetable and the judge or chairperson is satisfied, for reasons which must be recorded in writing, that the detriment to the welfare of the child would outweigh the detriment to the fair trial of the proceedings.

In all cases where domestic violence or abuse has occurred

32 The court should take steps to obtain (or direct the parties or an Officer of Cafcass or a Welsh family proceedings officer to obtain) information about the facilities available locally (to include local domestic abuse support services) to assist any party or the child in cases where domestic abuse has occurred.

33 Following any determination of the nature and extent of domestic abuse, whether or not following a fact-finding hearing, the court must, if considering any form of contact or involvement of the parent in the child's life, consider –

(a) whether it would be assisted by any social work, psychiatric, psychological or other assessment (including an expert safety and risk assessment) of any party or the child and if so (subject to any necessary consent) make directions for such assessment to be undertaken and for the filing of any consequent report. Any such report should address the factors set out in paragraphs 36 and 37 below, unless the court directs otherwise;

(b) whether any party should seek advice, treatment or other intervention as a precondition to any child arrangements order being made, and may (with the consent of that party) give directions for such attendance.

34 Further or as an alternative to the advice, treatment or other intervention referred to in paragraph 33(b) above, the court may make an Activity Direction under section 11A and 11B Children Act 1989. Any intervention directed pursuant to this provision should be one commissioned and approved by Cafcass. It is acknowledged that acceptance on a DVPP is subject to a suitability assessment by the service provider, and that completion of a DVPP will take time in order to achieve the aim of risk-reduction for the long-term benefit of the child and the parent with whom the child is living.

Factors to be taken into account when determining whether to make child arrangements orders in all cases where domestic violence or abuse has occurred

35 When deciding the issue of child arrangements the court should ensure that any order for contact will not expose the child to an unmanageable risk of harm and will be in the best interests of the child.

36 In the light of any findings of fact or admissions or where domestic abuse is otherwise established, the court should apply the individual matters in the welfare checklist with reference to the domestic abuse which has occurred and any expert risk assessment obtained. In particular, the court should in every case consider any harm which the child and the parent with whom the child is living has suffered as a consequence of that domestic abuse, and any harm which the child and the parent with whom the child is living is at risk of suffering, if a child arrangements order is made. The court should make an order for contact only if it is satisfied that the physical and emotional safety of the child and the parent with whom the child is living can, as far as possible, be secured before during and after contact, and that the parent with whom the child is living will not be subjected to further domestic abuse by the other parent.

37 In every case where a finding or admission of domestic abuse is made, or where domestic abuse is otherwise established, the court should consider the conduct of both parents towards each other and towards the child and the impact of the same. In particular, the court should consider –

(a) the effect of the domestic abuse on the child and on the arrangements for where the child is living;
(b) the effect of the domestic abuse on the child and its effect on the child's relationship with the parents;
(c) whether the parent is motivated by a desire to promote the best interests of the child or is using the process to continue a form of domestic abuse against the other parent;
(d) the likely behaviour during contact of the parent against whom findings are made and its effect on the child; and
(e) the capacity of the parents to appreciate the effect of past domestic abuse and the potential for future domestic abuse.

Directions as to how contact is to proceed

38 Where any domestic abuse has occurred but the court, having considered any expert risk assessment and having applied the welfare checklist, nonetheless considers that direct contact is safe and beneficial for the child, the court should consider what, if any, directions or conditions are required to enable the order to be carried into effect and in particular should consider –

(a) whether or not contact should be supervised, and if so, where and by whom;
(b) whether to impose any conditions to be complied with by the party in whose favour the order for contact has been made and if so, the nature of those conditions, for example by way of seeking intervention (subject to any necessary consent);
(c) whether such contact should be for a specified period or should contain provisions which are to have effect for a specified period; and
(d) whether it will be necessary, in the child's best interests, to review the operation of the order; if so the court should set a date for the review consistent with the timetable for the child, and must give directions to ensure that at

the review the court has full information about the operation of the order. Where a risk assessment has concluded that a parent poses a risk to a child or to the other parent, contact via a supported contact centre, or contact supervised by a parent or relative, is not appropriate.

39 Where the court does not consider direct contact to be appropriate, it must consider whether it is safe and beneficial for the child to make an order for indirect contact.

The reasons of the court

40 In its judgment or reasons the court should always make clear how its findings on the issue of domestic abuse have influenced its decision on the issue of arrangements for the child. In particular, where the court has found domestic abuse proved but nonetheless makes an order which results in the child having future contact with the perpetrator of domestic abuse, the court must always explain, whether by way of reference to the welfare check-list, the factors in paragraphs 36 and 37 or otherwise, why it takes the view that the order which it has made will not expose the child to the risk of harm and is beneficial for the child.

This Practice Direction is issued by the President of the Family Division, as the nominee of the Lord Chief Justice, with the agreement of the Lord Chancellor.

PART 14
PROCEDURE FOR APPLICATIONS IN ADOPTION, PLACEMENT AND RELATED PROCEEDINGS

14.1 Application of this Part and interpretation

(1) The rules in this Part apply to the following proceedings—

(a) adoption proceedings;
(b) placement proceedings; and
(c) proceedings for—
  (i) the making of [an]¹ order under section 26 [or an order under section 51A(2)(a)]² of the 2002 Act 3;
    [(aa) the making of an order under section 51A(2)(b) of the 2002 Act;]²
  (ii) the variation or revocation of[—]¹
    [(aa) an order under section 27 of the 2002 Act; or
    (bb) an order under section 51A(2) of the 2002 Act in accordance with section 51B(1)(c);]²
  (iii) an order giving permission to change a child's surname or remove a child from the United Kingdom under section 28(2) and (3) of the 2002 Act;
  (iv) a section 84 order;
  (v) a section 88 direction;

(vi) a section 89 order; or
(vii) any other order that may be referred to in a practice direction.

(2) In this Part—

'Central Authority' means—
(a) in relation to England, the Secretary of State; and
(b) in relation to Wales, the Welsh Ministers;

'Convention adoption order' means an adoption order under the 2002 Act which, by virtue of regulations under section 1 of the Adoption (Intercountry Aspects) Act 19996 (regulations giving effect to the Convention on Protection of Children and Co-operation in Respect of Intercountry Adoption, concluded at the Hague on 29th May 1993), is made as a Convention adoption order;

'guardian' means—
(a) a guardian (other than the guardian of the estate of a child) appointed in accordance with section 5 of the 1989 Act 7; and
(b) a special guardian within the meaning of section 14A of the 1989 Act 8;

['provision for contact' has the meaning given to it in rule 13.1(2);][1]

'section 88 direction' means a direction given by the High Court under section 88 of the 2002 Act that section 67(3) of that Act (status conferred by adoption) does not apply or does not apply to any extent specified in the direction.

Amendments
1 Substituted by the Family Procedure (Amendment No. 3) Rules 2014, SI 2014/843, rr 2, 31(a)(i), (c), (d).
2 Inserted by the Family Procedure (Amendment No. 3) Rules 2014, SI 2014/843, rr 2, 31(a)(ii), (b).

[14.2 [Assignment of][1] a serial number

(1) This rule applies where—
(a) any application in proceedings is made by a person who intends to adopt a child; or
(b) an adoption order in respect of the child has been made and an application is made for—
  (i) a contact order under section 51A(2)(a) of the 2002 Act;
  (ii) an order prohibiting contact with the child under section 51A(2)(b) of the 2002 Act; or
  (iii) the variation or revocation of an order under section 51A(2) of the 2002 Act in accordance with section 51B(1)(c).

[(2) In a case under paragraph (1)(a), a serial number must be assigned to identify the person intending to adopt the child in connection with the proceedings in order for the person's identity to be kept confidential in those proceedings.

(3) In a case under paragraph (1)(b), a serial number must be assigned to the person in whose favour the adoption order has been made to keep the identity of the person confidential in proceedings referred to in paragraph (1)(b).][1]

(4) The court may at any time direct that a serial number assigned to a person under paragraph (2) or (3) must be removed.

(5) [When]¹ a serial number has been assigned to a person under paragraph (2) or (3)—

  (a) the court officer will ensure that any notice sent in accordance with these rules does not contain information which discloses, or is likely to disclose, the identity of that person to any other party to that application who is not already aware of that person's identity; and
  (b) the proceedings on the application will be conducted with a view to securing that the person is not seen by or made known to any party who is not already aware of the person's identity except with the person's consent.]²

Amendments
1 Substituted by Family Procedure (Amendment No. 3) Rules 2016/1013 rule 2.
2 Substituted by the Family Procedure (Amendment No. 3) Rules 2014, SI 2014/843, rr 2, 32.

14.3 Who the parties are

(1) In relation to the proceedings set out in column 1 of the following table, column 2 sets out who the application may be made by and column 3 sets out who the respondents to those proceedings will be.

Proceedings for	Applicants	Respondents
An adoption order (section 46 of the 2002 Act).	The prospective adopters (sections 50 and 51 of the 2002 Act).	Each parent who has parental responsibility for the child unless that parent has given notice under section 20(4)(a) of the 2002 Act (statement of wish not to be informed of any application for an adoption order) which has effect;
		any guardian of the child unless that guardian has given notice under section 20(4)(a) of the 2002 Act (statement of wish not to be informed of any application for an adoption order) which has effect;
		any person in whose favour there is provision for contact;
		any adoption agency having parental responsibility for the child under section 25 of the 2002 Act;
		any adoption agency which has taken part at any stage in the arrangements for adoption of the child;

Proceedings for	Applicants	Respondents
		any local authority to whom notice under section 44 of the 2002 Act (notice of intention to adopt or apply for a section 84 order) has been given;
		any local authority or voluntary organisation which has parental responsibility for, is looking after or is caring for, the child; and
		the child where –
		– permission has been granted to a parent or guardian to oppose the making of the adoption order (section 47(3) or 47(5) of the 2002 Act);
		– the child opposes the making of an adoption order;
		– a children and family reporter recommends that it is in the best interests of the child to be a party to the proceedings and that recommendation is accepted by the court;
		– the child is already an adopted child;
		– any party to the proceedings or the child is opposed to the arrangements for allowing any person contact with the child, or a person not being allowed contact with the child after the making of the adoption order;
		– the application is for a Convention adoption order or a section 84 order;
		– the child has been brought into the United Kingdom in the circumstances where section 83(1) of the 2002 Act applies (restriction on bringing children in);
		– the application is for an adoption order other than a Convention adoption order

Proceedings for	Applicants	Respondents
		and the prospective adopters intend the child to live in a country or territory outside the British Islands after the making of the adoption order; or
		– the prospective adopters are relatives of the child.
A section 84 order.	The prospective adopters asking for parental responsibility prior to adoption abroad.	As for an adoption order.
A placement order (section 21 of the 2002 Act).	A local authority (section 22 of the 2002 Act).	Each parent who has parental responsibility for the child:
		any guardian of the child;
		any person in whose favour an order under the 1989 Act is in force in relation to the child;
		any adoption agency or voluntary organisation which has parental responsibility for, is looking after, or is caring for, the child;
		the child; and
		the parties or any persons who are or have been parties to proceedings for a care order in respect of the child where those proceedings have led to the application for the placement order.
An order varying a placement order (section 23 of the 2002 Act).	The joint application of the local authority authorised by the placement order to place the child for adoption and the local authority which is to be substituted for that authority (section 23 of the 2002 Act).	The parties to the proceedings leading to the placement order which it is sought to have varied except the child who was the subject of those proceedings; and
		any person in whose favour there is provision for contact.

Proceedings for	Applicants	Respondents
An order revoking a placement order (section 24 of the 2002 Act).	The child; the local authority authorised to place the child for adoption; or where the child is not placed for adoption by the authority, any other person who has the permission of the court to apply (section 24 of the 2002 Act).	The parties to the proceedings leading to the placement order which it is sought to have revoked; and any person in whose favour there is provision for contact.
[An order under section 26 of the 2002 Act.]¹	The child; the adoption agency; any parent, guardian or relative; any person in whose favour there was provision for contact under the 1989 Act which ceased to have effect on an adoption agency being authorised to place a child for adoption, or placing a child for adoption who is less than six weeks old (section 26(1) of the 2002 Act); [if a child arrangements order was in force immediately before the adoption agency was authorised to place the child for adoption or (as the case may be) placed the child for adoption at a time when he or she was less than six weeks old, any person	The adoption agency authorised to place the child for adoption or which has placed the child for adoption; the person with whom the child lives or is to live; each parent with parental responsibility for the child; any guardian of the child; and the child where – – the adoption agency authorised to place the child for adoption or which has placed the child for adoption or a parent with parental responsibility for the child opposes the making of [the order]¹ under section 26 of the 2002 Act; – the child opposes the making of [the order]¹ under section 26 of the 2002 Act; – existing provision for contact is to be revoked; – relatives of the child do not agree to the arrangements for allowing any person contact with the child, or a person not being allowed contact with the child; or

Proceedings for	Applicants	Respondents
	named in the order as a person with whom the child was to live;]¹ a person who by virtue of an order made in the exercise of the High Court's inherent jurisdiction with respect to children had care of the child immediately before that time; or any person who has the permission of the court to make the application (section 26 of the 2002 Act).	– the child is suffering or is at risk of suffering harm within the meaning of the 1989 Act.
An order varying or revoking [an order under section 26 of the 2002 Act]¹ (section 27 of the 2002 Act).	The child; the adoption agency; or any person named in [the order]¹ (section 27(1) of the 2002 Act).	The parties to the proceedings leading to [the order]¹ which it is sought to have varied or revoked; and any person named in [the order]¹.
An order permitting the child's name to be changed or the removal of the child from the United Kingdom (section 28(2) and (3) of the 2002 Act).	Any person including the adoption agency or the local authority authorised to place, or which has placed, the child for adoption (section 28(2) of the 2002 Act).	The parties to proceedings leading to any placement order; the adoption agency authorised to place the child for adoption or which has placed the child for adoption; any prospective adopters with whom the child is living; each parent with parental responsibility for the child; and any guardian of the child.
[A contact order under section 51A(2)(a) of the 2002 Act.	The child; or any person who has obtained the court's leave to make the application.	A person who has applied for the adoption order or in whose favour the adoption order is or has been made; and

Proceedings for	Applicants	Respondents
		Any adoption agency having parental responsibility for the child under section 25 of the 2002 Act.]²
[An order prohibiting the person named in the order from having contact with the child (section 51A(2)(b) of the 2002 Act).	A person who has applied for the adoption order or in whose favour the adoption order is or has been made; the child; or any person who has obtained the court's leave to make the application.	A person against whom an application is made who— (but for the child's adoption) would be related to the child by blood (including half-blood), marriage or civil partnership; is a former guardian of the child; is a person who had parental responsibility for the child immediately before the making of the adoption order; is a person who was entitled to make an application for an order under section 26 of the 2002 Act in respect of the child (contact with children placed or to be placed for adoption) by virtue of subsection (3)(c), (d) or (e) of that section; is a person with whom the child has lived for a period of at least one year; and any adoption agency having parental responsibility for the child under section 25 of the 2002 Act.]²
[The variation or revocation of a contact order or an order prohibiting contact under section 51A(2) of the 2002 Act (section 51B(1)(c) of that Act).	The child; a person in whose favour the adoption order was made; or a person named in the order.	The parties to the proceedings leading to the contact order or an order prohibiting contact which it is sought to have varied or revoked; and any person named in the contact order or the order prohibiting contact.]²
A section 88 direction.	The adopted child; the adopters; any parent; or any other person.	The adopters; the parents; the adoption agency; the local authority to whom notice under section 44 of the

Proceedings for	Applicants	Respondents
		2002 Act (notice of intention to apply for a section 84 order) has been given; and
		the Attorney-General.
A section 89 order.	The adopters; the adopted person; any parent; the relevant Central Authority; the adoption agency; the local authority to whom notice under section 44 of the 2002 Act (notice of intention to adopt or apply for a section 84 order) has been given; the Secretary of State for the Home Department; or any other person.	The adopters; the parents; the adoption agency; and the local authority to whom notice under section 44 of the 2002 Act (notice of intention to adopt or apply for a section 84 order) has been given.

(2) The court may at any time direct that a child, who is not already a respondent to proceedings, be made a respondent to proceedings where—

    (a) the child—
        (i) wishes to make an application; or
        (ii) has evidence to give to the court or a legal submission to make which has not been given or made by any other party; or
    (b) there are other special circumstances.

(3) The court may at any time direct that—

    (a) any other person or body be made a respondent to proceedings; or
    (b) a party be removed.

(4) If the court makes a direction for the addition or removal of a party, it may give consequential directions about—

    (a) serving a copy of the application form on any new respondent;
    (b) serving relevant documents on the new party; and
    (c) the management of the proceedings.

Amendments
1 Substituted by the Family Procedure (Amendment No. 3) Rules 2014, SI 2014/843, rr 2, 34.
2 Inserted by the Family Procedure (Amendment No. 3) Rules 2014, SI 2014/843, rr 2, 33.

14.4 Notice of proceedings to person with foreign parental responsibility

(1) This rule applies where a child is subject to proceedings to which this Part applies and –

 (a) a parent of the child holds or is believed to hold parental responsibility for the child under the law of another State which subsists in accordance with Article 16 of the 1996 Hague Convention following the child becoming habitually resident in a territorial unit of the United Kingdom; and
 (b) that parent is not otherwise required to be joined as a respondent under rule 14.3.

(2) The applicant shall give notice of the proceedings to any parent to whom the applicant believes paragraph (1) applies in any case in which a person who was a parent with parental responsibility under the 1989 Act would be a respondent to the proceedings in accordance with rule 14.3.

(3) The applicant and every respondent to the proceedings shall provide such details as they possess as to the identity and whereabouts of any parent they believe to hold parental responsibility for the child in accordance with paragraph (1) to the court officer, upon making, or responding to the application as appropriate.

(4) Where the existence of such a parent only becomes apparent to a party at a later date during the proceedings, that party must notify the court officer of those details at the earliest opportunity.

(5) Where a parent to whom paragraph (1) applies receives notice of proceedings, that parent may apply to the court to be joined as a party using the Part 18 procedure.

14.5 Who is to serve

(1) The general rules about service in Part 6 are subject to this rule.

(2) In proceedings to which this Part applies, a document which has been issued or prepared by a court officer will be served by the court officer except where—

 (a) a practice direction provides otherwise; or
 (b) the court directs otherwise.

(3) Where a court officer is to serve a document, it is for the court to decide which of the methods of service specified in rule 6.23 is to be used.

14.6 What the court or a court officer will do when the application has been issued

(1) As soon as practicable after the application has been issued in proceedings—

 (a) the court will—
  (i) if section 48(1) of the 2002 Act (restrictions on making adoption orders) applies, consider whether it is proper to hear the application;
  (ii) subject to paragraph (4), set a date for the first directions hearing;

(iii) appoint a children's guardian in accordance with rule 16.3(1);
(iv) appoint a reporting officer in accordance with rule 16.30;
(v) consider whether a report relating to the welfare of the child is required, and if so, request such a report in accordance with rule 16.33;
(vi) set a date for the hearing of the application; and
(vii) do anything else that may be set out in a practice direction; and

(b) a court officer will—
(i) subject to receiving confirmation in accordance with paragraph (2)(b)(ii), give notice of any directions hearing set by the court to the parties and to any children's guardian, reporting officer or children and family reporter;
(ii) serve a copy of the application form (but, subject to sub-paragraphs (iii) and (iv), not the documents attached to it) on the persons referred to in Practice Direction 14A;
(iii) send a copy of the certified copy of the entry in the register of live-births or Adopted Children Register and any health report attached to an application for an adoption order to—
(aa) any children's guardian, reporting officer or children and family reporter; and
(bb) the local authority to whom notice under section 44 of the 2002 Act (notice of intention to adopt or apply for a section 84 order) has been given;
(iv) if notice under rule 14.9(2) has been given (request to dispense with consent of parent or guardian), in accordance with that rule inform the parent or guardian of the request and send a copy of the statement of facts to—
(aa) the parent or guardian;
(bb) any children's guardian, reporting officer or children and family reporter;
(cc) any local authority to whom notice under section 44 of the 2002 Act (notice of intention to adopt or apply for a section 84 order) has been given; and
(dd) any adoption agency which has placed the child for adoption; and
(v) do anything else that may be set out in a practice direction.

(2) In addition to the matters referred to in paragraph (1), as soon as practicable after an application for an adoption order or a section 84 order has been issued the court or the court officer will—

(a) where the child is not placed for adoption by an adoption agency—
(i) ask either the Service or the Assembly to file any relevant form of consent to an adoption order or a section 84 order; and
(ii) ask the local authority to prepare a report on the suitability of the prospective adopters if one has not already been prepared; and
(b) where the child is placed for adoption by an adoption agency, ask the adoption agency to—
(i) file any relevant form of consent to—

(aa) the child being placed for adoption;
(bb) an adoption order;
(cc) a future adoption order under section 20 of the 2002 Act; or
(dd) a section 84 order;
    (ii) confirm whether a statement has been made under section 20(4)(a) of the 2002 Act (statement of wish not to be informed of any application for an adoption order) and if so, to file that statement;
    (iii) file any statement made under section 20(4)(b) of the 2002 Act (withdrawal of wish not to be informed of any application for an adoption order) as soon as it is received by the adoption agency; and
    (iv) prepare a report on the suitability of the prospective adopters if one has not already been prepared.

(3) In addition to the matters referred to in paragraph (1), as soon as practicable after an application for a placement order has been issued—

(a) the court will consider whether a report giving the local authority's reasons for placing the child for adoption is required, and if so, will direct the local authority to prepare such a report; and
(b) the court or the court officer will ask either the Service or the Assembly to file any form of consent to the child being placed for adoption.

(4) Where it considers it appropriate the court may, instead of setting a date for a first directions hearing, give the directions provided for by rule 14.8.

14.7 Date for first directions hearing

Unless the court directs otherwise, the first directions hearing must be within 4 weeks beginning with the date on which the application is issued.

14.8 The first directions hearing

(1) At the first directions hearing in the proceedings the court will—

(a) fix a [timetable for the proceedings including a]¹ timetable for the filing of—
    (i) any report relating to the suitability of the applicants to adopt a child;
    (ii) any report from the local authority;
    (iii) any report from a children's guardian, reporting officer or children and family reporter;
    (iv) if a statement of facts has been filed, any amended statement of facts;
    (v) any other evidence, and
    (vi) give directions relating to the reports and other evidence;
(b) consider whether the child or any other person should be a party to the proceedings and, if so, give directions in accordance with rule 14.3(2) or (3) joining that child or person as a party;

(c) give directions relating to the appointment of a litigation friend for any protected party or child who is a party to, but not the subject of, proceedings unless a litigation friend has already been appointed;
(d) consider [in accordance with rule 29.17][2] whether the case needs to be transferred to another court and, if so, give directions to transfer the proceedings to another court ...[3];
(e) give directions about—
   (i) tracing parents or any other person the court considers to be relevant to the proceedings;
   (ii) service of documents;
   (iii) subject to paragraph (2), disclosure as soon as possible of information and evidence to the parties; and
   (iv) the final hearing.

([Under Part 3][4] the court may also direct that the case be adjourned if it considers that [non-court dispute resolution][4] is appropriate.)

(2) Rule 14.13(2) applies to any direction given under paragraph (1)(e)(iii) as it applies to a direction given under rule 14.13(1).

(3) In addition to the matters referred to in paragraph (1), the court will give any of the directions listed in Practice Direction 14B in proceedings for—

(a) a Convention adoption order;
(b) a section 84 order;
(c) a section 88 direction;
(d) a section 89 order; or
(e) an adoption order where section 83(1) of the 2002 Act applies (restriction on bringing children in).

(4) The parties or their legal representatives must attend the first directions hearing unless the court directs otherwise.

(5) Directions may also be given at any stage in the proceedings—

(a) of the court's own initiative; or
(b) on the application of a party or any children's guardian or, where the direction concerns a report by a reporting officer or children and family reporter, the reporting officer or children and family reporter.

(6) For the purposes of giving directions or for such purposes as the court directs—

(a) the court may set a date for a further directions hearing or other hearing; and
(b) the court officer will give notice of any date so fixed to the parties and to any children's guardian, reporting officer or children and family reporter.

(7) After the first directions hearing the court will monitor compliance by the parties with the court's timetable and directions.

Amendments
1 Inserted by the Family Procedure (Amendment No. 3) Rules 2014, SI 2014/843, rr 2, 35(a).

2   Inserted by the Family Procedure (Amendment No.3) Rules 2013, SI 2013/3204, rr 2, 59(a).
3   Repealed by the Family Procedure (Amendment No.3) Rules 2013, SI 2013/3204, rr 2, 59(b).
4   Substituted by the Family Procedure (Amendment No. 3) Rules 2014, SI 2014/843, rr 2, 35(b).

14.9 Requesting the court to dispense with the consent of any parent or guardian

(1) This rule applies where the applicant wants to ask the court to dispense with the consent of any parent or guardian of a child to—

(a)   the child being placed for adoption;
(b)   the making of an adoption order except a Convention adoption order; or
(c)   the making of a section 84 order.

(2) The applicant requesting the court to dispense with the consent must—

(a)   give notice of the request in the application form or at any later stage by filing a written request setting out the reasons for the request; and
(b)   file a statement of facts setting out a summary of the history of the case and any other facts to satisfy the court that—
   (i)   the parent or guardian cannot be found or is incapable of giving consent; or
   (ii) the welfare of the child requires the consent to be dispensed with.

(3) If a serial number has been assigned to the applicant under rule 14.2, the statement of facts supplied under paragraph (2)(b) must be framed so that it does not disclose the identity of the applicant.

(4) On receipt of the notice of the request—

(a)   a court officer will—
   (i)   inform the parent or guardian of the request unless the parent or guardian cannot be found; and
   (ii) send a copy of the statement of facts filed in accordance with paragraph (2)(b) to—
      (aa) the parent or guardian unless the parent or guardian cannot be found;
      (bb) any children's guardian, reporting officer or children and family reporter;
      (cc) any local authority to whom notice under section 44 of the 2002 Act (notice of intention to adopt or apply for a section 84 order) has been given; and
      (dd) any adoption agency which has placed the child for adoption; and
(b)   if the applicant considers that the parent or guardian is incapable of giving consent, the court will consider whether to—
   (i)   appoint a litigation friend for the parent or guardian under rule 15.6(1); or
   (ii) give directions for an application to be made under rule 15.6(3),
   (iii) unless a litigation friend is already appointed for that parent or guardian.

14.10 Consent

(1) Consent of any parent or guardian of a child—

- (a) under section 19 of the 2002 Act, to the child being placed for adoption; and
- (b) under section 20 of the 2002 Act, to the making of a future adoption order,

must be given in the form referred to in Practice Direction 5A or a form to the like effect.

(2) Subject to paragraph (3), consent—

- (a) to the making of an adoption order; or
- (b) to the making of a section 84 order,

may be given in the form referred to in Practice Direction 5A or a form to the like effect or otherwise as the court directs.

(3) Any consent to a Convention adoption order must be in a form which complies with the internal law relating to adoption of the Convention country of which the child is habitually resident.

(4) Any form of consent executed in Scotland must be witnessed by a Justice of the Peace or a Sheriff.

(5) Any form of consent executed in Northern Ireland must be witnessed by a Justice of the Peace.

(6) Any form of consent executed outside the United Kingdom must be witnessed by—

- (a) any person for the time being authorised by law in the place where the document is executed to administer an oath for any judicial or other legal purpose;
- (b) a British Consular officer;
- (c) a notary public; or
- (d) if the person executing the document is serving in any of the regular armed forces of the Crown, an officer holding a commission in any of those forces.

14.11 Reports by the adoption agency or local authority

(1) The adoption agency or local authority must file the report on the suitability of the applicant to adopt a child within the timetable fixed by the court.

(2) A local authority that is directed to prepare a report on the placement of the child for adoption must file that report within the timetable fixed by the court.

(3) The reports must cover the matters specified in Practice Direction 14C.

(4) The court may at any stage request a further report or ask the adoption agency or local authority to assist the court in any other manner.

(5) A court officer will send a copy of any report referred to in this rule to any children's guardian, reporting officer or children and family reporter.

(6) A report to the court under this rule is confidential.

14.12 Health reports

(1) Reports by a registered medical practitioner ('health reports') made not more than 3 months earlier on the health of the child and of each applicant must be attached to an application for an adoption order or a section 84 order except where—

    (a)   the child was placed for adoption with the applicant by an adoption agency;
    (b)   the applicant or one of the applicants is a parent of the child; or
    (c)   the applicant is the partner of a parent of the child.

(2) Health reports must contain the matters set out in Practice Direction 14D.

(3) A health report is confidential.

14.13 Confidential reports to the court and disclosure to the parties

(1) The court will consider whether to give a direction that a confidential report be disclosed to each party to the proceedings.

(2) Before giving such a direction the court will consider whether any information should be deleted including information which—

    (a)   discloses, or is likely to disclose, the identity of a person who has been assigned a serial number under rule 14.2(2) [or (3)]1; or
    (b)   discloses the particulars referred to in rule 29.1(1) where a party has given notice under rule 29.1(2) (disclosure of personal details).

(3) The court may direct that the report will not be disclosed to a party.

Amendment
1   Inserted by the Family Procedure (Amendment No. 3) Rules 2014, SI 2014/843, rr 2, 36.

14.14 Communication of information relating to proceedings

For the purposes of the law relating to contempt of court, information (whether or not it is recorded in any form) relating to proceedings held in private may be communicated—

    (a)   where the court gives permission;
    (b)   unless the court directs otherwise, in accordance with Practice Direction 14E; or
    (c)   where the communication is to—
        (i)   a party;
        (ii)   the legal representative of a party;
        (iii)   a professional legal adviser;
        (iv)   an officer of the service or a Welsh family proceedings officer;

(v) a welfare officer;
(vi) [the Director of Legal Aid Casework (within the meaning of section 4 of the Legal Aid, Sentencing and Punishment of Offenders Act 2012)][1];
(vii) an expert whose instruction by a party has been authorised by the court for the purposes of the proceedings; or
(viii) a professional acting in furtherance of the protection of children.

Amendment
1 Substituted by the Legal Aid, Sentencing and Punishment of Offenders Act 2012 (Consequential, Transitional and Saving Provisions) Regulations 2013, SI 2013/534, reg 14(1), (2), Schedule, para 22(b).

14.15 Notice of final hearing

A court officer will give notice to the parties, any children's guardian, reporting officer or children and family reporter and to any other person to whom a practice direction may require such notice to be given—

(a) of the date and place where the application will be heard; and
(b) of the fact that, unless the person wishes or the court requires, the person need not attend.

14.16 The final hearing

(1) Any person who has been given notice in accordance with rule 14.15 may attend the final hearing and, subject to paragraph (2), be heard on the question of whether an order should be made.

(2) A person whose application for the permission of the court to oppose the making of an adoption order under section 47(3) or (5) of the 2002 Act has been refused is not entitled to be heard on the question of whether an order should be made.

(3) Any member or employee of a party which is a local authority, adoption agency or other body may address the court at the final hearing if authorised to do so.

(4) The court may direct that any person must attend a final hearing.

(5) Paragraphs (6) and (7) apply to—

(a) an adoption order;
(b) a section 84 order; or
(c) a section 89 order.

(6) Subject to paragraphs (7) and (8), the court cannot make an order unless the applicant and the child personally attend the final hearing.

(7) The court may direct that the applicant or the child need not attend the final hearing.

(8) In a case of adoption by a couple under section 50 of the 2002 Act, the court may make an adoption order after personal attendance of one only of the applicants if there are special circumstances.

(9) The court cannot make a placement order unless a legal representative of the applicant attends the final hearing.

14.17 Proof of identity of the child

(1) Unless the contrary is shown, the child referred to in the application will be deemed to be the child referred to in the form of consent—

- (a) to the child being placed for adoption;
- (b) to the making of an adoption order; or
- (c) to the making of a section 84 order,

where the conditions in paragraph (2) apply.

(2) The conditions are—

- (a) the application identifies the child by reference to a full certified copy of an entry in the registers of live-births;
- (b) the form of consent identifies the child by reference to a full certified copy of an entry in the registers of live-births attached to the form; and
- (c) the copy of the entry in the registers of live-births referred to in sub-paragraph (a) is the same or relates to the same entry in the registers of live-births as the copy of the entry in the registers of live-births attached to the form of consent.

(3) Where the child is already an adopted child paragraph (2) will have effect as if for the references to the registers of live-births there were substituted references to the Adopted Children Register.

(4) Subject to paragraph (7), where the precise date of the child's birth is not proved to the satisfaction of the court, the court will determine the probable date of birth.

(5) The probable date of the child's birth may be specified in the placement order, adoption order or section 84 order as the date of the child's birth.

(6) Subject to paragraph (7), where the child's place of birth cannot be proved to the satisfaction of the court—

- (a) the child may be treated as having been born in [the registration district and sub-district in which the court sits]1 where it is probable that the child may have been born in—
  - (i) the United Kingdom;
  - (ii) the Channel Islands; or
  - (iii) the Isle of Man; or
- (b) in any other case, the particulars of the country of birth may be omitted from the placement order, adoption order or section 84 order.

(7) A placement order identifying the probable date and place of birth of the child will be sufficient proof of the date and place of birth of the child in adoption proceedings and proceedings for a section 84 order.

Amendment
1 Substituted by the Family Procedure (Amendment No.3) Rules 2013, SI 2013/3204, rr 2, 60.

14.18 Disclosing information to an adopted adult

(1) The adopted person has the right, on request, to receive from the court which made the adoption order a copy of the following—

(a) the application form for an adoption order (but not the documents attached to that form);
(b) the adoption order and any other orders relating to the adoption proceedings;
(c) orders [containing any provision for contact]¹ with the child after the adoption order was made; and
(d) any other document or order referred to in Practice Direction 14F.

(2) The court will remove any protected information from any copy of a document or order referred to in paragraph (1) before the copies are given to the adopted person.

(3) This rule does not apply to an adopted person under the age of 18 years.

(4) In this rule 'protected information' means information which would be protected information under section 57(3) of the 2002 Act if the adoption agency gave the information and not the court.

Amendment
1 Substituted by the Family Procedure (Amendment No. 3) Rules 2014, SI 2014/843, rr 2, 37.

14.19 Translation of documents

(1) Where a translation of any document is required for the purposes of proceedings for a Convention adoption order the translation must—

(a) unless the court directs otherwise, be provided by the applicant; and
(b) be signed by the translator to certify that the translation is accurate.

(2) This rule does not apply where the document is to be served in accordance with the Service Regulation.

14.20 Application for recovery orders

[(1) An application for any of the orders referred to in section 41(2) of the 2002 Act (recovery orders) may be made without notice, in which case the applicant must file the application—

(a) where the application is made by telephone, the next business day after the making of the application; or
(b) in any other case, at the time when the application is made.]¹

(2) Where the court refuses to make an order on an application without notice it may direct that the application is made on notice in which case the application will proceed in accordance with rules 14.1 to 14.17.

(3) The respondents to an application under this rule are—

(a) in a case where—
    (i) placement proceedings;
    (ii) adoption proceedings; or

(iii) proceedings for a section 84 order,
are pending, all parties to those proceedings;
(b) any adoption agency authorised to place the child for adoption or which has placed the child for adoption;
(c) any local authority to whom notice under section 44 of the 2002 Act (notice of intention to adopt or apply for a section 84 order) has been given;
(d) any person having parental responsibility for the child;
(e) any person in whose favour there is provision for contact;
(f) any person who was caring for the child immediately prior to the making of the application; and
(g) any person whom the applicant alleges to have effected, or to have been or to be responsible for, the taking or keeping of the child.

Amendment
1 Substituted by the Family Procedure (Amendment No.3) Rules 2013, SI 2013/3204, rr 2, 61.

14.21 Inherent jurisdiction and fathers without parental responsibility

Where no proceedings have started an adoption agency or local authority may ask the High Court for directions on the need to give a father without parental responsibility notice of the intention to place a child for adoption.

14.22 Timing of applications for section 89 order

An application for a section 89 order must be made within 2 years beginning with the date on which—

(a) the Convention adoption or Convention adoption order; or
(b) the overseas adoption or determination under section 91 of the 2002 Act,

to which it relates was made.

14.23 Custody of documents

All documents relating to proceedings under the 2002 Act must, while they are in the custody of the court, be kept in a place of special security.

14.24 Documents held by the court not to be inspected or copied without the court's permission

Subject to the provisions of these rules, any practice direction or any direction given by the court—

(a) no document or order held by the court in proceedings under the 2002 Act will be open to inspection by any person; and
(b) no copy of any such document or order, or of an extract from any such document or order, will be taken by or given to any person.

14.25 Orders

(1) An order takes effect from the date when it is made, or such later date as the court may specify.

(2) In proceedings in Wales a party may request that an order be drawn up in Welsh as well as English.

[(Rule 37.9 makes provision for the court to endorse an order prohibiting contact under section 51A(2)(b) of the 2002 Act with a penal notice on the application of the person entitled to enforce the order.)]¹

Amendment
1   Inserted by the Family Procedure (Amendment No. 3) Rules 2014, SI 2014/843, rr 2, 38.

14.26 Copies of orders

(1) Within 7 days beginning with the date on which the final order was made in proceedings, or such shorter time as the court may direct, a court officer will send—

- (a) a copy of the order to the applicant;
- (b) a copy, which is sealed^(GL), authenticated with the stamp of the court or certified as a true copy, of—
    - (i) an adoption order;
    - (ii) a section 89 order; or
    - (iii) an order quashing or revoking an adoption order or allowing an appeal against an adoption order,

    to the Registrar General;
- (c) a copy of a Convention adoption order to the relevant Central Authority;
- (d) a copy of a section 89 order relating to a Convention adoption order or a Convention adoption to the—
    - (i) relevant Central Authority;
    - (ii) adopters;
    - (iii) adoption agency; and
    - (iv) local authority;
- (e) unless the court directs otherwise, [a copy of an]¹ under section 26 of the 2002 Act or a [variation or revocation of such]¹ order under section 27 of the 2002 Act to the—
    - (i) person with whom the child is living;
    - (ii) adoption agency; and
    - (iii) local authority; ...²
- [(ee) unless the court directs otherwise, a copy of a contact order under section 51A(2)(a) of the 2002 Act, an order prohibiting contact under section 51A(2)(b) of that Act or a variation or revocation of such orders under section 51B(1)(c) of that Act to the parties to the proceedings; and]³
- (f) a notice of the making or refusal of—
    - (i) the final order; or
    - (ii) an order quashing or revoking an adoption order or allowing an appeal against an order in proceedings,

    to every respondent and, with the permission of the court, any other person.

(2) The court officer will also send notice of the making of an adoption order or a section 84 order to—

(a) any court in Great Britain which appears to the court officer to have made any such order as is referred to in section 46(2) of the 2002 Act (order relating to parental responsibility for, and maintenance of, the child); and
(b) the principal registry, if it appears to the court officer that a parental responsibility agreement has been recorded at the principal registry.

(3) A copy of any final order may be sent to any other person with the permission of the court.

(4) The court officer will send a copy of any order made during the course of the proceedings to the following persons or bodies, unless the court directs otherwise—
(a) all the parties to those proceedings;
(b) any children and family reporter appointed in those proceedings;
(c) any adoption agency or local authority which has prepared a report on the suitability of an applicant to adopt a child;
(d) any local authority which has prepared a report on placement for adoption.

(5) If an order has been drawn up in Welsh as well as English in accordance with rule 14.25(2) any reference in this rule to sending an order is to be taken as a reference to sending both the Welsh and English orders.

Amendments
1   Substituted by the Family Procedure (Amendment No. 3) Rules 2014, SI 2014/843, rr 2, 39(a).
2   Repealed by the Family Procedure (Amendment No. 3) Rules 2014, SI 2014/843, rr 2, 39(b).
3   Inserted by the Family Procedure (Amendment No. 3) Rules 2014, SI 2014/843, rr 2, 39(b).

14.27 Amendment and revocation of orders

(1) Subject to paragraph (2), an application under—
(a) section 55 of the 2002 Act (revocation of adoptions on legitimation); or
(b) paragraph 4 of Schedule 1 to the 2002 Act (amendment of adoption order and revocation of direction),

may be made without serving a copy of the application notice.

(2) The court may direct that an application notice be served on such persons as it thinks fit.

(3) Where the court makes an order granting the application, a court officer will send the Registrar General a notice—
(a) specifying the amendments; or
(b) informing the Registrar General of the revocation,

giving sufficient particulars of the order to enable the Registrar General to identify the case.

14.28 ...[1]

...[1]

Amendment
1   Repealed by the Family Procedure (Amendment No.3) Rules 2013, SI 2013/3204, rr 2, 62.

[PART 25
EXPERTS AND ASSESSORS][1]

[25.1 ...[2]

...[2]][1]

Amendments
1 Substituted by the Family Procedure (Amendment) (No.5) Rules 2012, SI 2012/3061, r 6, Schedule.
2 Repealed by the Family Procedure (Amendment No. 3) Rules 2014, SI 2014/843, rr 2, 44.

[25.2 Interpretation

(1) In this Part—

...[1]

'children proceedings' means—
(a) proceedings referred to in rules 12.1 and 14.1 and any other proceedings which relate wholly or mainly to the maintenance or upbringing of a minor;
(b) applications for permission to start proceedings mentioned in paragraph (a);and
(c) applications made in the course of proceedings mentioned in paragraph (a);

'expert' means a person who provides expert evidence for use in proceedings; [(Section 13(8) of the 2014 Act provides for what is not included in reference to providing expert evidence or putting expert evidence before the court in children proceedings)][2]

...[1]

'single joint expert' means a person who provides expert evidence for use in proceedings on behalf of two or more of the parties (including the applicant) to the proceedings.

[(2) The meaning of 'children proceedings' in paragraph (1) is the prescribed meaning for the purposes of section 13(9) of the 2014 Act.][3]

(Regulation 3 of the Restriction on the Preparation of Adoption Reports Regulations 2005 (S.I. 2005/1711) sets out which persons are within a prescribed description for the purposes of section 94(1) of the 2002 Act.)][4]

Amendments
1 Repealed by the Family Procedure (Amendment No. 3) Rules 2014, SI 2014/843, rr 2, 45(a), (c).
2 Inserted by the Family Procedure (Amendment No. 3) Rules 2014, SI 2014/843, rr 2, 45(b).
3 Substituted by the Family Procedure (Amendment No. 3) Rules 2014, SI 2014/843, rr 2, 45(d).
4 Substituted by the Family Procedure (Amendment) (No.5) Rules 2012, SI 2012/3061, r 6, Schedule.

[25.3 Experts–overriding duty to the court

(1) It is the duty of experts to help the court on matters within their expertise.

(2) This duty overrides any obligation to the person from whom experts have received instructions or by whom they are paid.

(Particular duties of an expert are set out in Practice Direction 25B (The Duties of an Expert, the Expert's Report and Arrangements for an Expert to Attend Court.)]¹

Amendment
1   Substituted by the Family Procedure (Amendment) (No.5) Rules 2012, SI 2012/3061, r 6, Schedule.

[25.4 Control of expert evidence in proceedings other than children proceedings

(1) This rule applies to proceedings other than children proceedings.

(2) A person may not without the permission of the court put expert evidence (in any form) before the court.

(3) The court may give permission as mentioned in paragraph (2) only if the court is of the opinion that the expert evidence is necessary to assist the court to resolve the proceedings.

(Provision relating to the control of expert evidence in children proceedings is contained in section 13 of the 2014 Act.)]¹

Amendment
1   Substituted by the Family Procedure (Amendment No. 3) Rules 2014, SI 2014/843, rr 2, 46.

[25.5 Further provisions about the court's power to restrict expert evidence

[(1) When deciding whether to give permission as mentioned in section 13(1), (3) or (5) of the 2014 Act or to give a direction under 38(6) of the 1989 Act in children proceedings, the court is to have regard in particular to any failure to comply with rule 25.6 or any direction of the court about expert evidence.]¹

[(1A) The matter referred to in paragraph (1) is a prescribed matter for the purposes of section 13(7)(h) of the 2014 Act and section 38(7B) of the 1989 Act.]²

(2) When deciding whether to give permission as mentioned in rule 25.4(1) in proceedings other than children proceedings, the court is to have regard in particular to—

    (a)   the issues to which the expert evidence would relate;
    (b)   the questions which the court would require the expert to answer;
    (c)   the impact which giving permission would be likely to have on the timetable, duration and conduct of the proceedings;
    (d)   any failure to comply with rule 25.6 or any direction of the court about expert evidence; and
    (e)   the cost of the expert evidence.]³

Amendments
1   Substituted by the Family Procedure (Amendment No. 3) Rules 2014, SI 2014/843, rr 2, 47(a).
2   Inserted by the Family Procedure (Amendment No. 3) Rules 2014, SI 2014/843, rr 2, 47(b).
3   Substituted by the Family Procedure (Amendment) (No.5) Rules 2012, SI 2012/3061, r 6, Schedule.

[25.6 When to apply for the court's permission

Unless the court directs otherwise, parties must apply for the court's permission as mentioned in section 13(1), (3) or (5) of the 2014 Act or rule 25.4(2) as soon as possible and—

(a) in Part 4 proceedings referred to in rule 12.2 and in so far as practicable other public law proceedings referred to in that rule, no later than a Case Management Hearing;
(b) in private law proceedings referred to in rule 12.2, no later than the First Hearing Dispute Resolution Appointment;
(c) in adoption proceedings and placement proceedings, no later than the first directions hearing;
(d) in proceedings for a financial remedy, no later than the first appointment; and
(e) in a defended case referred to in rule 7.1(3), no later than any Case Management Hearing directed by the court under rule 7.20.]¹

Amendment
1 Substituted by the Family Procedure (Amendment No. 3) Rules 2014, SI 2014/843, rr 2, 48.

[25.7 What an application notice requesting the court's permission must include

(1) Part 18 applies to an application for the court's permission as mentioned in [section 13(1), (3) or (5) of the 2014 Act or]¹ rule 25.4[(2)]¹.

(2) In any proceedings—

(a) the application notice requesting the court's permission as mentioned in [section 13(1), (3) or (5) of the 2014 Act or]1 rule 25.4[(2)]1 must state—
  (i) the field in which the expert evidence is required;
  (ii) where practicable, the name of the proposed expert;
  (iii) the issues to which the expert evidence is to relate;
  (iv) whether the expert evidence could be obtained from a single joint expert;
  (v) the other matters set out in Practice Direction 25C or 25D, as the case may be; and
(b) a draft of the order sought is to be attached to the application notice requesting the court's permission and that draft order must set out the matters specified in Practice Direction 25C or 25D, as the case may be.

(3) In children proceedings, an application notice requesting the court's permission as mentioned in [section 13(1), (3) or (5) of the 2014 Act]² must, in addition to the matters specified in paragraph (2)(a), state the questions which the expert is to be required to answer.]³

Amendments
1 Inserted by the Family Procedure (Amendment No. 3) Rules 2014, SI 2014/843, rr 2, 49(a), (b).
2 Substituted by the Family Procedure (Amendment No. 3) Rules 2014, SI 2014/843, rr 2, 49(c).
3 Substituted by the Family Procedure (Amendment) (No.5) Rules 2012, SI 2012/3061, r 6, Schedule.

[25.8 Where permission is granted

(1) In any proceedings, where the court grants permission as mentioned in [section 13(1), (3) or (5) of the 2014 Act or]¹ rule 25.4[(2)]¹—

(a) it will grant permission only in relation to the expert named or the field identified in the application notice requesting the court's permission; and

(b) the court will give directions specifying the date by which the expert is to provide a written report.

(2) In children proceedings, in addition to the directions in paragraph (1)(b), the court will give directions—

(a) approving the questions which the expert is required to answer;
(b) specifying the date by which the expert is to receive the letter of instruction.]²

Amendments
1 Inserted by the Family Procedure (Amendment No. 3) Rules 2014, SI 2014/843, rr 2, 50.
2 Substituted by the Family Procedure (Amendment) (No.5) Rules 2012, SI 2012/3061, r 6, Schedule.

[25.9 General requirement for expert evidence to be given in a written report

(1) Expert evidence is to be given in a written report unless the court directs otherwise.

(2) The court will not direct an expert to attend a hearing unless it is necessary to do so in the interests of justice.]¹

Amendment
1 Substituted by the Family Procedure (Amendment) (No.5) Rules 2012, SI 2012/3061, r 6, Schedule.

[25.10 Written questions to experts

(1) A party may put written questions about an expert's report to—

(a) an expert instructed by another party; or
(b) a single joint expert appointed under rule 25.11.

(2) Unless the court directs otherwise or a practice direction provides otherwise, written questions under paragraph (1)—

(a) must be proportionate;
(b) may be put once only;
(c) must be put within 10 days beginning with the date on which the expert's report was served;
(d) must be for the purpose only of clarification of the report; and
(e) must be copied and sent to the other parties at the same time as they are sent to the expert.

(3) An expert's answers to questions put in accordance with paragraph (1)—

(a) must be given within the timetable specified by the court; and
(b) are treated as part of the expert's report.

(4) Where—

(a) a party has put a written question to an expert instructed by another party; and
(b) the expert does not answer that question,

the court may make one or both of the following orders in relation to the party who instructed the expert—

(i) that the party may not rely on the evidence of that expert; or
(ii) that the party may not recover the fees and expenses of that expert from any other party.]¹

Amendment
1 Substituted by the Family Procedure (Amendment) (No.5) Rules 2012, SI 2012/3061, r 6, Schedule.

[25.11 Court's power to direct that evidence is to be given by a single joint expert

(1) Where two or more parties wish to put expert evidence before the court on a particular issue, the court may direct that the evidence on that issue is to be given by a single joint expert.

(2) Where the parties who wish to put expert evidence before the court ('the relevant parties') cannot agree who should be the single joint expert, the court may—

(a) select the expert from a list prepared or identified by the relevant parties; or
(b) direct that the expert be selected in such other manner as the court may direct.]¹

Amendment
1 Substituted by the Family Procedure (Amendment) (No.5) Rules 2012, SI 2012/3061, r 6, Schedule.

[25.12 Instructions to a single joint expert

(1) Where the court gives a direction under rule 25.11(1) for a single joint expert to be used, the instructions are to be contained in a jointly agreed letter unless the court directs otherwise.

(2) Where the instructions are to be contained in a jointly agreed letter, in default of agreement the instructions may be determined by the court on the written request of any relevant party copied to the other relevant parties.

(3) Where the court permits the relevant parties to give separate instructions to a single joint expert, each instructing party must, when giving instructions to the expert, at the same time send a copy of the instructions to the other relevant parties.

(4) The court may give directions about—

(a) the payment of the expert's fees and expenses; and
(b) any inspection, examination or assessments which the expert wishes to carry out.

(5) The court may, before an expert is instructed, limit the amount that can be paid by way of fees and expenses to the expert.

(6) Unless the court directs otherwise, the relevant parties are jointly and severally liable for the payment of the expert's fees and expenses.]¹

Amendment
1 Substituted by the Family Procedure (Amendment) (No.5) Rules 2012, SI 2012/3061, r 6, Schedule.

[25.13 Power of court to direct a party to provide information

(1) Subject to paragraph (2), where a party has access to information which is not reasonably available to another party, the court may direct the party who has access to the information to—

 (a) prepare and file a document recording the information; and
 (b) serve a copy of that document on the other party.

(2) In proceedings under Part 14 (procedure for applications in adoption, placement and related proceedings), a court officer will send a copy of the document recording the information to the other party.][1]

Amendment
1 Substituted by the Family Procedure (Amendment) (No.5) Rules 2012, SI 2012/3061, r 6, Schedule.

[25.14 Contents of report

(1) An expert's report must comply with the requirements set out in Practice Direction 25B.

(2) At the end of an expert's report there must be a statement that the expert understands and has complied with the expert's duty to the court.

(3) The instructions to the expert are not privileged against disclosure.

(Rule 21.1 explains what is meant by disclosure.)][1]

Amendment
1 Substituted by the Family Procedure (Amendment) (No.5) Rules 2012, SI 2012/3061, r 6, Schedule.

[25.15 Use by one party of expert's report disclosed by another

Where a party has disclosed an expert's report, any party may use that expert's report as evidence at any hearing where an issue to which the report relates is being considered.][1]

Amendment
1 Substituted by the Family Procedure (Amendment) (No.5) Rules 2012, SI 2012/3061, r 6, Schedule.

[25.16 Discussions between experts

(1) The court may, at any stage, direct a discussion between experts for the purpose of requiring the experts to—

 (a) identify and discuss the expert issues in the proceedings; and
 (b) where possible, reach an agreed opinion on those issues.

(2) The court may specify the issues which the experts must discuss.

(3) The court may direct that following a discussion between the experts they must prepare a statement for the court setting out those issues on which—

 (a) they agree; and
 (b) they disagree, with a summary of their reasons for disagreeing.][1]

Amendment

1 Substituted by the Family Procedure (Amendment) (No.5) Rules 2012, SI 2012/3061, r 6, Schedule.

[25.17 Expert's right to ask court for directions

(1) Experts may file written requests for directions for the purpose of assisting them in carrying out their functions.

(2) Experts must, unless the court directs otherwise, provide copies of the proposed requests for directions under paragraph (1)—

    (a) to the party instructing them, at least 7 days before they file the requests; and

    (b) to all other parties, at least 4 days before they file them.

(3) The court, when it gives directions, may also direct that a party be served with a copy of the directions.][1]

Amendment

1 Substituted by the Family Procedure (Amendment) (No.5) Rules 2012, SI 2012/3061, r 6, Schedule.

[25.18 Copies of orders and other documents

Unless the court directs otherwise, a copy of any order or other document affecting an expert filed with the court after the expert has been instructed, must be served on the expert by the party who instructed the expert or, in the case of a single joint expert, the party who was responsible for instructing the expert, within 2 days of that party receiving the order or other document.][1]

Amendment

1 Substituted by the Family Procedure (Amendment) (No.5) Rules 2012, SI 2012/3061, r 6, Schedule.

[25.19 Action after final hearing

(1) Within 10 business days after the final hearing, the party who instructed the expert or, in the case of a single joint expert, the party who was responsible for instructing the expert, must inform the expert in writing about the court's determination and the use made by the court of the expert's evidence.

(2) Unless the court directs otherwise, the party who instructed the expert or, in the case of the single joint expert, the party who was responsible for instructing the expert, must send to the expert a copy of the court's final order[, any transcript or written record of the court's decision, and its reasons for reaching its decision, within 10 business days from the date when the party received the order and any such transcript or record][1] ...[2]

    (a) ...[2]
    (b) ...[2]

within 10 business days from the date when that party received the order and transcript or reasons.][3]

Amendments

1 Inserted by the Family Procedure (Amendment No. 3) Rules 2014, SI 2014/843, rr 2, 51(a).

2 Repealed by the Family Procedure (Amendment No. 3) Rules 2014, SI 2014/843, rr 2, 51(b).
3 Substituted by the Family Procedure (Amendment) (No.5) Rules 2012, SI 2012/3061, r 6, Schedule.

[25.20 Assessors

(1) This rule applies where the court appoints one or more persons under section 70 of the Senior Courts Act 1981 ...[1] as an assessor.

(2) An assessor will assist the court in dealing with a matter in which the assessor has skill and experience.

(3) The assessor will take such part in the proceedings as the court may direct and in particular the court may direct an assessor to—

(a) prepare a report for the court on any matter at issue in the proceedings; and
(b) attend the whole or any part of the hearing to advise the court on any such matter.

(4) If the assessor prepares a report for the court before the hearing has begun—

(a) the court will send a copy to each of the parties; and
(b) the parties may use it at the hearing.

(5) Unless the court directs otherwise, an assessor will be paid at the daily rate payable for the time being to a fee-paid deputy district judge of the principal registry and an assessor's fees will form part of the costs of the proceedings.

(6) The court may order any party to deposit in the court office a specified sum in respect of an assessor's fees and, where it does so, the assessor will not be asked to act until the sum has been deposited.

(7) Paragraphs (5) and (6) do not apply where the remuneration of the assessor is to be paid out of money provided by Parliament.][2]

Amendments
1 Repealed by the Family Procedure (Amendment No. 2) Rules 2014, SI 2014/667, rr 2, 18.
2 Substituted by the Family Procedure (Amendment) (No.5) Rules 2012, SI 2012/3061, r 6, Schedule.

PRACTICE DIRECTION 25B
THE DUTIES OF AN EXPERT, THE EXPERT'S REPORT AND ARRANGEMENTS FOR AN EXPERT TO ATTEND COURT

This Practice Direction supplements FPR Part 25

Scope of this Practice Direction

1.1 This Practice Direction focuses on the duties of an expert including the contents of the expert's report and, where an expert is to attend court, the arrangements for such attendance. Other Practice Directions supporting FPR

Part 25 deal with different aspects of experts in family proceedings. The relevant Practice Directions are –

(a) Practice Direction 25A (Experts – Emergencies and Pre proceedings Instructions);
(b) Practice Direction 25C (Children Proceedings – The Use of Single Joint Experts and the Process Leading to an Expert Being Instructed or Expert Evidence Being Put Before the Court);
(c) Practice Direction 25D (Financial Remedy Proceedings and Other Family Proceedings (except Children Proceedings) – The Use of Single Joint Experts and the Process Leading to Expert Evidence Being Put Before The Court);and
(d) Practice Direction 25E (Discussions Between Experts in Family Proceedings).

1.2 Practice Direction 15B (Adults Who May Be Protected Parties and Children Who May Become Protected Parties In Family Proceedings) gives guidance relating to proceedings where an adult party may not have capacity to conduct the litigation or to instruct an expert.

1.3 In accordance with FPR 25.2(1), 'children proceedings' means-

(a) proceedings referred to in FPR 12.1 and 14.1 and any other proceedings which relate wholly or mainly to the maintenance or upbringing of a minor;
(b) applications for permission to start proceedings mentioned in paragraph (a);
(c) applications made in the course of proceedings mentioned in paragraph (a).

The meaning of 'expert'

2.1 In accordance with FPR 25.2(1), 'expert' means a person who provides expert evidence for use in family proceedings. Section 13(8) of the 2014 Act expressly refers to evidence that is not expert evidence. For example, evidence given by a children's guardian is not expert evidence.

2.2 An expert includes a reference to an expert team which can include ancillary workers in addition to experts. In an expert team, an 'ancillary' worker may be, for example, a play therapist or similar who undertakes work with the child or family for the purpose of the expert assessment. It is perfectly possible that such workers will be experts in their own right and in their own field, but it would be cumbersome to name everyone in that position in an order giving permission for an expert to be instructed, a child to be medically or psychiatrically examined or otherwise assessed or expert evidence to be put before the court or in a letter of instruction to an expert. The purpose of the term 'expert team' is to enable a multi-disciplinary team to undertake the assessment without the order having to name everyone who may be involved. The final expert's report must, however, give information about those persons who have taken part in the assessment and their respective roles and who is responsible for the report.

The expert's overriding duty

3.1 An expert in family proceedings has an overriding duty to the court that takes precedence over any obligation to the person from whom the expert has received instructions or by whom the expert is paid.

Particular duties of the expert

4.1 An expert shall have regard to the following, among other, duties –
  (a) to assist the court in accordance with the overriding duty;
  (aa) in children proceedings, to comply with the Standards for Expert Witnesses in Children Proceedings in the Family Court which are set out in the Annex to this Practice Direction;
  (b) to provide advice to the court that conforms to the best practice of the expert's profession;
  (c) to answer the questions about which the expert is required to give an opinion (in children proceedings, those questions will be set out in the order of the court giving permission for an expert to be instructed, a child to be examined or otherwise assessed or expert evidence to be put before the court);
  (d) to provide an opinion that is independent of the party or parties instructing the expert;
  (e) to confine the opinion to matters material to the issues in the case and in relation only to the questions that are within the expert's expertise (skill and experience);
  (f) where a question has been put which falls outside the expert's expertise, to state this at the earliest opportunity and to volunteer an opinion as to whether another expert is required to bring expertise not possessed by those already involved or, in the rare case, as to whether a second opinion is required on a key issue and, if possible, what questions should be asked of the second expert;
  (g) in expressing an opinion, to take into consideration all of the material facts including any relevant factors arising from ethnic, cultural, religious or linguistic contexts at the time the opinion is expressed;
  (h) to inform those instructing the expert without delay of any change in the opinion and of the reason for the change.

The requirement for the court's permission

5.1 The general rule in family proceedings is that the court's permission is required to put expert evidence (in any form) before the court (see section 13(5) of the 2014 Act for children proceedings and FPR 25.4(2) for other family proceedings.). The court is under a duty to restrict expert evidence to that which in the opinion of the court is necessary to assist the court to resolve the proceedings. The overriding objective in FPR1.1 applies when the court is exercising this duty. In children proceedings, the court's permission is required to instruct an expert and for a child to be medically or psychiatrically examined or otherwise assessed for the purposes of the provision of expert evidence in the proceedings section 13(1) and (3) of the 2014 Act.

Preliminary enquiries which the expert should expect to receive

6.1 In good time for the information requested to be available for –

(a) the court hearing when the court will decide whether to give permission for the expert evidence to be put before the court (or also in children proceedings, for the expert to be instructed or the child to be examined or otherwise assessed); or
(b) the advocates' meeting or discussion where one takes place before such a hearing,

the party or parties intending to instruct the expert shall approach the expert with some information about the case.

6.2 The details of the information to be given to the expert are set out in Practice Direction 25C, paragraph 3.2 and Practice Direction 25D paragraph 3.3 and include the nature of the proceedings, the questions for the expert, the time when the expert's report is likely to be required, the timing of any hearing at which the expert may have to give evidence and how the expert's fees will be funded.

6.3 Children proceedings are confidential which means in thos eproceedings parties raising preliminary enquiries of an expert who has not ye tbeen instructed can only tell the expert information which he or she will need about the case to be able to answer the preliminary questions raised.

Balancing the needs of the court and those of the expert

7.1 It is essential that there should be proper co-ordination between the court and the expert when drawing up the case management timetable: the needs of the court should be balanced with the needs of the expert whose forensic work is undertaken as an adjunct to his or her main professional duties.

The expert's response to preliminary enquiries

8.1 In good time for the court hearing when the court will decide whether or not to give permission for the expert evidence to be put before the court (or also in children proceedings, for the expert to be instructed or the child to be examined or otherwise assessed) or for the advocates' meeting or discussion where one takes place before that hearing, the party or parties intending to instruct the expert will need confirmation from the expert –

(a) that acceptance of the proposed instructions will not involve the expert in any conflict of interest;
(b) that the work required is within the expert's expertise;
(c) that the expert is available to do the relevant work within the suggested time scale;
(d) when the expert is available to give evidence, of the dates and times to avoid and, where a hearing date has not been fixed, of the amount of notice the expert will require to make arrangements to come to court (or to give evidence by telephone conference or video link) without undue disruption to his or her normal professional routines;
(e) of the cost, including hourly or other charging rates, and likely hours to be spent attending experts' meetings, attending court and writing the report (to include any examinations and interviews);
(f) of any representations which the expert wishes to make to the court about being named or otherwise identified in any public judgment given by the court.

Content of the expert's report

9.1 The expert's report shall be addressed to the court and prepared and filed in accordance with the court's timetable and must –

(a) give details of the expert's qualifications and experience;
(b) include a statement identifying the document(s) containing the material instructions and the substance of any oral instructions and, as far as necessary to explain any opinions or conclusions expressed in the report, summarising the facts and instructions which are material to the conclusions and opinions expressed;
(c) state who carried out any test, examination or interview which the expert has used for the report and whether or not the test, examination or interview has been carried out under the expert's supervision;
(d) give details of the qualifications of any person who carried out the test, examination or interview;
(e) answer the questions about which the expert is to give an opinion and which relate to the issues in the case;
(f) in expressing an opinion to the court –
  (i) take into consideration all of the material facts including any relevant factors arising from ethnic, cultural, religious or linguistic contexts at the time the opinion is expressed, identifying the facts, literature and any other material, including research material, that the expert has relied upon in forming an opinion;
  (ii) describe the expert's own professional risk assessment process and process of differential diagnosis, highlighting factual assumptions, deductions from the factual assumptions, and any unusual, contradictory or inconsistent features of the case;
  (iii) indicate whether any proposition in the report is an hypothesis (in particular a controversial hypothesis), or an opinion deduced in accordance with peer-reviewed and tested technique, research and experience accepted as a consensus in the scientific community;

(iv) indicate whether the opinion is provisional (or qualified, as the case may be), stating the qualification and the reason for it, and identifying what further information is required to give an opinion without qualification;

(g) where there is a range of opinion on any question to be answered by the expert –
  (i) summarise the range of opinion;
  (ii) identify and explain, within the range of opinions, any 'unknown cause', whether arising from the facts of the case (for example, because there is too little information to form a scientific opinion) or from limited experience or lack of research, peer review or support in the relevant field of expertise;
  (iii) give reasons for any opinion expressed: the use of a balance sheet approach to the factors that support or undermine an opinion can be of great assistance to the court;

(h) contain a summary of the expert's conclusions and opinions;

(i) contain a statement that the expert–
  (i) has no conflict of interest of any kind, other than any conflict disclosed in his or her report;
  (ii) does not consider that any interest disclosed affects his or her suitability as an expert witness on any issue on which he or she has given evidence;
  (iii) will advise the instructing party if, between the date of the expert's report and the final hearing, there is any change in circumstances which affects the expert's answers to (i) or (ii) above;
  (iv) understands their duty to the court and has complied with that duty; and
  (v) is aware of the requirements of FPR Part 25 and this practice direction;
  (vi) in children proceedings, has complied with the Standards for Expert Witnesses in Children Proceedings in the Family Court which are set out in the Annex to this Practice Direction;

(j) be verified by a statement of truth in the following form –

'I confirm that I have made clear which facts and matters referred to in this report are within my own knowledge and which are not. Those that are within my own knowledge I confirm to be true. The opinions I have expressed represent my true and complete professional opinions on the matters to which they refer.'

Where the report relates to children proceedings the form of statement of truth must include –

'I also confirm that I have complied with the Standards for Expert Witnesses in Children Proceedings in the Family Court which are set out in the Annex to Practice Direction 25B- The Duties of an Expert, the Expert's Report and Arrangements for an Expert to Attend Court'

(FPR Part 17 deals with statements of truth. Rule 17.6 sets out the consequences of verifying a document containing a false statement without an honest belief in its truth.)

Arrangements for experts to give evidence

Preparation

10.1 Where the court has directed the attendance of an expert witness, the party who instructed the expert or party responsible for the instruction of the expert shall, by a date specified by the court prior to the hearing at which the expert is to give oral evidence ('the specified date') or, where in care or supervision proceedings an Issues Resolution Hearing ('the IRH') is to be held, by the IRH, ensure that –

(a) a date and time (if possible, convenient to the expert) are fixed for the court to hear the expert's evidence, substantially in advance of the hearing at which the expert is to give oral evidence and no later than a specified date prior to that hearing or, where an IRH is to be held, than the IRH;

(b) if the expert's oral evidence is not required, the expert is notified as soon as possible;

(c) the witness template accurately indicates how long the expert is likely to be giving evidence, in order to avoid the inconvenience of the expert being delayed at court;

(d) consideration is given in each case to whether some or all of the experts participate by telephone conference or video link, or submit their evidence in writing, to ensure that minimum disruption is caused to professional schedules and that costs are minimised.

Experts attending court

10.2 Where expert witnesses are to be called, all parties shall, by the specified date or, where an IRH is to be held, by the IRH, ensure that –

(a) the parties' advocates have identified (whether at an advocates' meeting or by other means) the issues which the experts are to address;

(b) wherever possible, a logical sequence to the evidence is arranged, with experts of the same discipline giving evidence on the same day;

(c) the court is informed of any circumstance where all experts agree but a party nevertheless does not accept the agreed opinion, so that directions can be given for the proper consideration of the experts' evidence and opinion;

(d) in the exceptional case the court is informed of the need for a witness summons.

Annex
Standards for Expert Witnesses in Children Proceedings in the Family Court

Subject to any order made by the court, expert witnesses involved in family proceedings (involving children) in England and Wales, whatever their field of practice or country of origin, must comply with the standards (1–11).

1. The expert's area of competence is appropriate to the issue(s) upon which the court has identified that an opinion is required, and relevant experience is evidenced in their CV.

2. The expert has been active in the area of work or practice, (as a practitioner or an academic who is subject to peer appraisal), has sufficient experience of the issues relevant to the instant case, and is familiar with the breadth of current practice or opinion.

3. The expert has working knowledge of the social, developmental, cultural norms and accepted legal principles applicable to the case presented at initial enquiry, and has the cultural competence skills to deal with the circumstances of the case.

4. The expert is up-to-date with Continuing Professional Development appropriate to their discipline and expertise, and is in continued engagement with accepted supervisory mechanisms relevant to their practice.

5. If the expert's current professional practice is regulated by a UK statutory body (See Appendix 1) they are in possession of a current licence to practise or equivalent.

6. If the expert's area of professional practice is not subject to statutory registration (e.g. child psychotherapy, systemic family therapy, mediation, and experts in exclusively academic appointments) the expert should demonstrate appropriate qualifications and/ or registration with a relevant professional body on a case by case basis. Registering bodies usually provide a code of conduct and professional standards and should be accredited by the Professional Standards Authority for Health and Social Care (See Appendix 2). If the expertise is academic in nature (e.g. regarding evidence of cultural influences) then no statutory registration is required (even if this includes direct contact or interviews with individuals) but consideration should be given to appropriate professional accountability.

7. The expert is compliant with any necessary safeguarding requirements, information security expectations, and carries professional indemnity insurance.

8. If the expert's current professional practice is outside the UK they can demonstrate that they are compliant with the FJC 'Guidelines for the instruction of medical experts from overseas in family cases'[1].

9. The expert has undertaken appropriate training, updating or quality assurance activity – including actively seeking feedback from cases in which they have provided evidence- relevant to the role of expert in the family courts in England and Wales within the last year.

10. The expert has a working knowledge of, and complies with, the requirements of Practice Directions relevant to providing reports for and giving evidence to the family courts in England and Wales. This includes compliance with the requirement to identify where their opinion on the instant case lies in relation to other accepted mainstream views and the overall spectrum of opinion in the UK.

Footnote
1   December 2011. See www.judiciary.gov.uk/about-the-judiciary/advisory-bodies/fjc.

Expectations in relation to experts' fees

11. The expert should state their hourly rate in advance of agreeing to accept instruction, and give an estimate of the number of hours the report is likely to take. This will assist the legal representative to apply expeditiously to the Legal Aid Agency if prior authority is to be sought in a publicly funded case.

Appendix 1 to the standards
UK Health and Social Care Professions and Statutory Regulators with responsibilities within England and Wales

The Professional Standards Authority for Health and Social Care (PSA)[1] (formerly the Council for Healthcare Regulatory Excellence) oversees statutory bodies that regulate health and social care professionals in the UK. It assesses their performance, conducts audits, scrutinises their decisions and reports to Parliament. It also sets standards for organisations holding voluntary registers for health and social care occupations and accredits those that meet them. It shares good practice and knowledge, conducts research and introduces new ideas to the sector including the concept of right-touch regulation. It monitors policy developments in the UK and internationally and provides advice on issues relating to professional standards in health and social care.

The General Medical Council[2] (GMC) is the independent regulator for doctors in the UK. The GMC's statutory purpose is to protect, promote and maintain the health and safety of the public by ensuring proper standards in the practice of medicine through the Medical Register.

The General Dental Council[3] regulates dental professionals in the UK. All dentists, dental nurses, dental technicians, clinical dental technicians, dental hygienists, dental therapists and orthodontic therapists must be registered with the GDC to work in the UK.

The Nursing and Midwifery Council[4] regulates nurses and midwives in the UK, setting standards for work, education and a code of conduct for all registered nurses and midwives.

Care Council for Wales: The Care Council for Wales is the social care workforce regulator in Wales responsible for promoting and securing high standards across the social services and social care workforce. It regulates social workers in Wales and managers of care services, including residential care homes for children, care homes for adults and domiciliary care for both adults and children. It also regulates social work students and residential child care workers.

The General Optical Council[5] is the regulator for the optical professions in the UK. Its purpose is to protect the public by promoting high standards of education, performance and conduct amongst opticians.

The General Pharmacy Council[6] is the independent regulator for pharmacists, pharmacy technicians and pharmacy premises in Great Britain. Its role is to protect, promote and maintain the health, safety and wellbeing of members of the public by upholding standards and public trust in pharmacy.

The General Chiropractic Council[7] is a UK-wide statutory body with regulatory powers established by the Chiropractors Act 1994. Its duties are to protect the public by establishing and operating a scheme of statutory regulation for chiropractors, to set the standards of chiropractic education, conduct and practice and to ensure the development of the profession of chiropractic, using a model of continuous improvement in practice.

The General Osteopathic Council[8] regulates the practice of osteopathy in the United Kingdom. By law osteopaths must be registered with the Council in order to practise in the UK. It works with the public and osteopathic profession to promote patient safety by registering qualified professionals and sets, maintain and develop standards of osteopathic practice and conduct.

The Health and Care Professions Council[9] regulates health and social care professionals with protected titles. Further information is set out in the table below.

Profession	Protected title(s)
Arts therapist An art, music or drama therapist encourages people to express their feelings and emotions through art, such as painting and drawing, music or drama.	• Art psychotherapist • Art therapist • Dramatherapist • Music therapist
Biomedical scientist A biomedical scientist analyses specimens from patients to provide data to help doctors diagnose and treat disease.	• Biomedical scientist
Chiropodist/Podiatrist A chiropodist/podiatrist diagnoses and treats disorders, diseases and deformities of the feet.	• Chiropodist • Podiatrist
Clinical scientist A clinical scientist oversees specialist tests for diagnosing and managing disease. They advise doctors on using tests and interpreting data and they also carry out research to understand diseases.	• Clinical scientist
Dietician A dietician uses the science of nutrition to devise eating plans for patients to treat medical conditions, and to promote good health.	• Dietician
Hearing aid dispenser Hearing aid dispensers assess, fit and provide aftercare for hearing aids.	• Hearing aid dispenser
Occupational therapist An occupational therapist uses specific activities to limit the effects of disability and promote independence in all aspects of daily life.	• Occupational therapist

Profession	Protected title(s)
Operating department practitioner Operating department practitioners participate in the assessment of the patient prior to surgery and provide individualised care.	• Operating department practitioner
Orthoptist Orthoptists specialise in diagnosing and treating visual problems involving eye movement and alignment.	• Orthoptist
Paramedic Paramedics provide specialist care and treatment to patients who are either acutely ill or injured. They can administer a range of drugs and carry out certain surgical techniques.	• Paramedic
Physiotherapist Physiotherapists deal with human function and movement and help people to achieve their full physical potential. They use physical approaches to promote, maintain and restore wellbeing.	• Physiotherapist • Physical therapist
Practitioner psychologist Psychology is the scientific study of people, the mind and behaviour. Psychologists attempt to understand the role of mental functions in individual and social behaviour.	• Practitioner psychologist • Registered psychologist • Clinical psychologist • Counselling psychologist • Educational psychologist • Forensic psychologist • Health psychologist • Occupational psychologist • Sport and exercise psychologist
Prosthetist/Orthotist Prosthetists and orthotists are responsible for all aspects of supplying prostheses and orthoses for patients. A prosthesis is a device that replaces a missing body part. An orthosis is a device fixed to the body.	• Prosthetist • Orthotist
Radiographer Therapeutic radiographers plan and deliver treatment using radiation. Diagnostic radiographers produce and interpret high-quality images of the body to diagnose injuries and diseases.	• Radiographer • Diagnostic radiographer • Therapeutic radiographer

Profession	Protected title(s)
Social workers in England	• Social worker
Speech and language therapist Speech and language therapists assess, treat and help to prevent speech, language and swallowing difficulties.	• Speech and language therapist • Speech therapist

Footnotes
1   www.professionalstandards.org.uk
2   www.gmc-uk.org
3   www.gdc-uk.org
4   www.nmc-uk.org
5   www.optical.org
6   www.pharmacyregulation.org/about-us
7   www.gcc-uk.org/page.cfm
8   www.osteopathy.org.uk
9   www.hpc-uk.org/aboutregistration/protectedtitles

Appendix 2 to the standards
Examples of professional bodies / associations relating to non- statutorily regulated work

Resolution UK
www.resolution.org.uk/
Resolution's members are family lawyers committed to the constructive resolution of family disputes. Members follow a Code of Practice that promotes a non-confrontational approach to family problems, encourage solutions that consider the needs of the whole family and in particular the best interests of children.

Association of Child Psychotherapists (Psychoanalytic)
www.childpsychotherapy.org.uk
The Association of Child Psychotherapists is the professional organisation for Child and Adolescent Psychoanalytic Psychotherapy in the UK. The Association recognises and monitors five training schools in Child and Adolescent Psychotherapy (e.g. the Tavistock and Portman NHS Foundation Trust). Child Psychotherapists who have qualified in one of these trainings (minimum 4 years in-service clinical training, doctoral or doctoral equivalent) are eligible for full membership of the Association and are able to work as autonomous professionals within the NHS or in independent practice. Child Psychotherapists are appointed at similar grades to Clinical Psychologists.

The UK Council for Psychotherapy (UKCP)
www.psychotherapy.org.uk
The UKCP is a membership organisation with over 75 training and listing organisations, and over 7,000 individual practitioners. UKCP holds the national register of psychotherapists and psychotherapeutic counsellors, listing those practitioner members who meet exacting standards and training requirements. Organisational members / associations are grouped together in modality colleges representing all the main traditions in the practice of psychotherapy in the UK including

- Association for Cognitive Analytic Therapy
- Association for Family Therapy and Systemic Practice
- Gestalt Psychotherapy and Training Institute
- Institute of Transactional Analysis
- Institute for Arts in Therapy and Education

The British Association for Counselling & Psychotherapy (BACP)
www.bacp.co.uk
BACP is a membership organisation and a registered charity that sets standards for a wide variety of therapeutic practice and provides information for therapists, clients of therapy, and the general public. It has over 37,000 members and is the largest professional body representing counselling and psychotherapy in the UK. BACP accredits training courses for counsellors and psychotherapists and is dedicated to ensuring its members practice responsibly, ethically and to the highest of standards.

The British Association for Behavioural and Cognitive Psychotherapies (BABCP)
www.babcp.com
The BABCP is the lead organisation for Cognitive Behavioural Therapy in the UK. It is a multi-disciplinary interest group for people involved in the practice and theory of behavioural and cognitive psychotherapy. The BABCP maintain standards for practitioners of Behavioural & Cognitive Psychotherapy by providing the opportunity for members who meet minimum criteria to become accredited.

British Psychoanalytic Council
www.psychoanalytic-council.org
Psychoanalytic or psychodynamic psychotherapy draws on theories and practices of analytical psychology and psychoanalysis. It is a therapeutic process which helps patients understand and resolve their problems by increasing awareness of their inner world and its influence over relationships both past and present. It differs from most other therapies in aiming for deep seated change in personality and emotional development. Psychoanalytic and psychodynamic psychotherapy aim to help people with serious psychological disorders to understand and change complex, deep-seated and often unconsciously based emotional and relationship problems thereby reducing symptoms and alleviating distress.

NAGALRO
www.nagalro.com
Professional association for Family Court Advisers, Children's Guardians and Independent Social Workers.

British Association of Social Workers (BASW)
www.basw.co.uk
UK professional association of social workers.

Confederation of Independent Social Work Agencies UK (CISWA)
www.ciswa-uk.org
CISWA-UK is a not for profit organisation which brings independent social work providers together with the aim of improving the professionalism and expertise of agencies providing services to children and families.

PRACTICE DIRECTION 25C
CHILDREN PROCEEDINGS – THE USE OF SINGLE JOINT EXPERTS AND THE PROCESS LEADING TO AN EXPERT BEING INSTRUCTED OR EXPERT EVIDENCE BEING PUT BEFORE THE COURT

This Practice Direction supplements FPR Part 25

Scope of this Practice Direction

1.1 This Practice Direction applies to children proceedings and contains guidance on –

(a) the use of single joint experts;
(b) how to prepare for the hearing at which the court will consider whether to give permission for an expert to be instructed, a child to be medically or psychiatrically examined or otherwise assessed for the purposes of provision of expert evidence in the proceedings or for putting expert evidence (in any form) before the court including –
  (i) preliminary enquiries of experts;
  (ii) the content of an application for the court's permission in addition to matters mentioned in FPR25.7;
  (iii) matters to be set out in the draft order to be attached to the application for permission; and
(c) the letter of instruction to the expert.

1.2 'Children proceedings' includes proceedings under Schedule 1 to the 1989 Act as those proceedings are proceedings which relate wholly or mainly to the maintenance or upbringing of a minor referred to in FPR25.2(1).

Single joint experts

2.1 section 13(1),(3) and (5) of the 2014 Act applies to a single joint expert ('SJE') in addition to an expert instructed by one party. This means that the court's permission is required to put expert evidence from an SJE (in any form) before the court section 13(5) of the 2014 Act. The court's permission is also required to instruct an SJE and for a child to be medically or psychiatrically examined or otherwise assessed for the purposes of provision of evidence from an SJE substitute section 13(1) and (3) of the 2014 Act. Wherever possible, expert evidence should be obtained from an SJE instructed by both or all the parties. To that end, a party wishing to instruct an expert should as soon as possible after the start of the proceedings first give the other party or parties a list of the names of one or more experts in the relevant speciality whom they consider suitable to be instructed.

2.2 Within 5 business days after receipt of the list of proposed experts, the other party or parties should indicate any objection to one or more of the named experts and, if so, supply the name(s) of one or more experts whom they consider suitable.

2.3 Each party should disclose whether they have already consulted any of the proposed experts about the issue(s) in question.

2.4 Where the parties cannot agree on the identity of the expert, each party should think carefully before seeking the permission of the court to instruct their own expert because of the costs implications. Disagreements about the use and identity of an expert may be better managed by the court in the context of the application for the court's permission to instruct the expert and for directions for the use of an SJE (see paragraph 2.6 below).

Instructing separate experts

2.5 If the parties seek the permission of the court to instruct separate experts –

(a) they should agree in advance that the reports will be disclosed; and
(b) the instructions to each expert should comply, so far as appropriate, with paragraphs 4.1 and 6.1 below (Letter of instruction).

Where two or more parties wish to instruct an SJE

2.6 If two or more parties wish to instruct an SJE, before applying to the court for permission and directions for the use of an SJE, the parties should –

(a) so far as appropriate, comply with the guidance in paragraphs 3.2 (Preliminary enquiries of the expert) and paragraphs 3.10 and 3.11 below;
(b) receive the expert's confirmation in response to preliminary enquiries referred to in paragraph 8.1 of Practice Direction 25B;
(c) have agreed in what proportion the SJE's fee is to be shared between them (at least in the first instance) and when it is to be paid; and
(d) if applicable, have obtained agreement for public funding.

2.7 The instructions to the SJE should comply, so far as appropriate, with paragraphs 4.1 and 6.1 below (Letter of instruction).

Preparation for the permission hearing

3.1 Paragraphs 3.2 to 3.11 give guidance on how to prepare for the hearing at which the court will consider whether to give permission for an expert to be instructed, a child to be examined or otherwise assessed or expert evidence to be put before the court. The purpose of the preparation is to ensure that the court has the information required to enable it to exercise its powers under section 13(1), (3), (5) and (7) of the 2014 Act and FPR 25.5.

Preliminary enquiries of the expert

3.2 In good time for the information requested to be available for the hearing at which the court will consider whether to give permission for an expert to be instructed, a child to be examined or otherwise assessed or expert evidence to be put before the court or for the advocates' meeting or discussion where one takes place before that hearing, the party or parties intending to instruct the expert shall approach the expert with the following information –

(a) the nature of the proceedings and the issues likely to require determination by the court;
(b) the issues in the proceedings to which the expert evidence is to relate;
(c) the questions about which the expert is to be asked to give an opinion (including any ethnic, cultural, religious or linguistic contexts) and which relate to the issues in the case;
(d) the date when the court is to be asked to give permission for the instruction (or if – unusually – permission has already been given, the date and details of that permission);
(e) whether permission is to be asked of the court for the instruction of another expert in the same or any related field (that is, to give an opinion on the same or related questions);
(f) the volume of reading which the expert will need to undertake;
(g) whether or not permission has been applied for or given for the expert to examine the child;
(h) whether or not it will be necessary for the expert to conduct interviews – and, if so, with whom;
(i) the likely timetable of legal and social work steps;
(j) in care and supervision proceedings, any dates in the Timetable for the Child which would be relevant to the proposed timetable for the assessment;
(k) when the expert's report is likely to be required;
(l) whether and, if so, what date has been fixed by the court for any hearing at which the expert may be required to give evidence (in particular the Final Hearing); and whether it may be possible for the expert to give evidence by telephone conference or video link: see paragraphs 10.1 and 10.2 (Arrangements for experts to give evidence) of Practice Direction 25B;
(m) the possibility of making, through their instructing solicitors, representations to the court about being named or otherwise identified in any public judgment given by the court;
(n) whether the instructing party has public funding and the legal aid rates of payment which are applicable.

Confidentiality of children proceedings and making preliminary enquiries of an expert

3.3 For the purposes of the law of contempt of court, information relating to children proceedings (whether or not contained in a document filed with the court or recorded in any form) may be communicated only to an expert whose instruction by a party has been permitted by the court (see FPR 12.73(1)(a)(vii) and 14.14(c)(vii)) as children proceedings are confidential.

3.4 Before permission is obtained from the court to instruct an expert in children proceedings, the party seeking permission needs to make the enquiries of the expert referred to above in order to provide the court with information to enable it to decide whether to give permission. In practice, enquiries may need to be made of more than one expert for this purpose. This will in turn require each expert to be given sufficient information about the case to decide whether or not he or she is in a position to accept instructions. Such preliminary enquiries, and the disclosure of information about the case which is a necessary part of such enquiries, will not require the court's permission and will not amount to a contempt of court.

Expert's response to preliminary enquiries

3.5 In good time for the hearing at which the court will consider whether to give permission for an expert to be instructed, a child to be examined or otherwise assessed or expert evidence to be put before the court, the party or parties intending to instruct the expert must obtain the confirmations from the expert referred to in paragraph 8.1 of Practice Direction 25B. These confirmations include that the work is within the expert's expertise, the expert is available to do the work within the relevant timescale and the expert's costs.

3.6 Where the parties cannot agree who should be the single joint expert before the hearing at which the court will consider whether to give permission for an expert to be instructed, a child to be examined or otherwise assessed or expert evidence to be put before the court, they should obtain the above confirmations in respect of all experts whom they intend to put to the court for the purposes of FPR 25.11(2)(a) as candidates for the appointment.

The application for the court's permission mentioned in in section 13(1), (3) and (5) of the 2014 Act

Timing and oral applications for the court's permission mentioned in in section 13(1), (3) and (5) of the 2014 Act

3.7 An application for the court's permission for an expert to be instructed, a child to be examined or otherwise assessed or expert evidence to be put before the court should be made as soon as it becomes apparent that it is necessary to make it. FPR 25.6 makes provision about the time by which applications for the court's permission should be made.

3.8 Applications should, wherever possible, be made so that they are considered at any directions hearing or other hearing for which a date has been fixed or for which a date is about to be fixed. It should be noted that one application notice can be used by a party to make more than one application for an order or direction at a hearing held during the course of proceedings. An application for the court's permission for an expert to be instructed, a child to be examined or otherwise assessed or expert evidence to be put before the court may therefore be included in an application notice requesting other orders to be made at such a hearing.

3.9 Where a date for a hearing has been fixed, a party who wishes to make an application at that hearing but does not have sufficient time to file an application notice should as soon as possible inform the court (if possible in writing) and, if possible, the other parties of the nature of the application and the reason for it. The party should provide the court and the other party with as much as possible of the information referred to in FPR 25.7 and paragraph 3.10 below. That party should then make the application orally at the hearing. An oral application of this kind should be the exception and reserved for genuine cases where circumstances are such that it has only become apparent shortly before the hearing that an expert opinion is necessary.

The application

3.10 In addition to the matters specified in FPR 25.7(2)(a)and (3), an application for the court's permission for an expert to be instructed, a child to be examined or otherwise assessed or expert evidence to be put before the court, must state –

(a) the discipline, qualifications and expertise of the expert (by way of C.V. where possible);
(b) the expert's availability to undertake the work;
(c) the timetable for the report;
(d) the responsibility for instruction;
(e) whether the expert evidence can properly be obtained by only one party (for example, on behalf of the child);
(f) why the expert evidence proposed cannot properly be given by an officer of the service, Welsh family proceedings officer or the local authority (social services undertaking a core assessment) in accordance with their respective statutory duties or any other party to the proceedings or an expert already instructed in the proceedings;
(g) the likely cost of the report on an hourly or other charging basis;
(h) the proposed apportionment (at least in the first instance) of any jointly instructed expert's fee; when it is to be paid; and, if applicable, whether public funding has been approved.

The terms of the draft order to be attached to the application for the court's permission

3.11 FPR 25.7(2)(b) provides that a draft of the order giving the court's permission as mentioned in section 13(1), (3) and (5) of the 2014 Act is to be attached to the application for the court's permission. That draft order must set out the following matters –

(a) the issues in the proceedings to which the expert evidence is to relate and which the court is to identify;
(b) the questions relating to the issues in the case which the expert is to answer and which the court is to approve ensuring that they –
    (i) are within the ambit of the expert's area of expertise;

    (ii)   do not contain unnecessary or irrelevant detail;
    (iii) are kept to a manageable number and are clear, focused and direct;
(c) the party who is responsible for drafting the letter of instruction and providing the documents to the expert;
(d) the timetable within which the report is to be prepared, filed and served;
(e) the disclosure of the report to the parties and to any other expert;
(f) the organisation of, preparation for and conduct of any experts' discussion (see Practice Direction 25E – Discussions between Experts in Family Proceedings);
(g) the preparation of a statement of agreement and disagreement by the experts following an experts' discussion;
(h) making available to the court at an early opportunity the expert reports in electronic form;
(i) the attendance of the expert at court to give oral evidence (alternatively, the expert giving his or her evidence in writing or remotely by video link), whether at or for the Final Hearing or another hearing; unless agreement about the opinions given by the expert is reached at or before the Issues Resolution Hearing ('IRH') or, if no IRH is to be held, by a date specified by the court prior to the hearing at which the expert is to give oral evidence.

Letter of instruction

4.1 The party responsible for instructing the expert shall prepare (in agreement with the other parties where appropriate), a letter of instruction to the expert and shall –

(a) set out the context in which the expert's opinion is sought (including any ethnic, cultural, religious or linguistic contexts);
(b) set out the questions approved by the court and which the expert is required to answer and any other linked questions ensuring that they –
    (i)   are within the ambit of the expert's area of expertise;
    (ii)   do not contain unnecessary or irrelevant detail;
    (iii) are kept to a manageable number and are clear, focused and direct; and
    (iv)   reflect what the expert has been requested to do by the court
    (Annex A to this Practice Direction sets out suggested questions in letters of instruction to (1) child mental health professionals or paediatricians, and (2) adult psychiatrists and applied psychologists, in Children Act 1989 proceedings);
(c) list the documentation provided,or provide for the expert an indexed and paginated bundle which shall include–
    (i)   an agreed list of essential reading; and
    (ii)   a copy of this Practice Direction and Practice Directions 25B and E and where appropriate Practice Direction 15B;
(d) identify any materials provided to the expert which have not been produced either as original medical (or other professional) records or

in response to an instruction from a party, and state the source of that material (such materials may contain an assumption as to the standard of proof, the admissibility or otherwise of hearsay evidence, and other important procedural and substantive questions relating to the different purposes of other enquiries, for example, criminal or disciplinary proceedings);
(e) identify all requests to third parties for disclosure and their responses in order to avoid partial disclosure, which tends only to prove a case rather than give full and frank information;
(f) identify the relevant people concerned with the proceedings (for example, the treating clinicians) and inform the expert of his or her right to talk to them provided that an accurate record is made of the discussions;
(g) identify any other expert instructed in the proceedings and advise the expert of their right to talk to the other experts provided that an accurate record is made of the discussions;
(h) subject to any public funding requirement for prior authority, define the contractual basis upon which the expert is retained and in particular the funding mechanism including how much the expert will be paid (an hourly rate and overall estimate should already have been obtained), when the expert will be paid, and what limitation there might be on the amount the expert can charge for the work which they will have to do. In cases where the parties are publicly funded, there may also be a brief explanation of the costs and expenses excluded from public funding by Funding Code criterion 1.3 and the detailed assessment process.

Adult who is a protected party

5.1 Where the adult is a protected party, that party's representative shall be involved in any instruction of an expert, including the instruction of an expert to assess whether the adult, although a protected party, is competent to give evidence (see Practice Direction 15B – Adults Who May Be Protected Parties and Children Who May Become Protected Parties in Family Proceedings).

Asking the court to settle the letter of instruction to a single joint expert

6.1 Where possible, the written request for the court to consider the letter of instruction referred to in rule 25.12(2) should be set out in an e-mail to the court and copied by e-mail to the other instructing parties. The request should be sent to the relevant court or (by prior arrangement only) directly to the judge dealing with the proceedings. Where a legal adviser has been appointed as the case manager, the request should also be sent to the appointed legal adviser. The court will settle the letter of instruction, usually without a hearing to avoid delay; and will send (where practicable, by e-mail) the settled letter to the lead solicitor for transmission forthwith to the expert, and copy it to the other instructing parties for information.

Annex A

(drafted by the Family Justice Council)

Suggested questions in letters of instruction to child mental health professional or paediatrician in Children Act 1989 proceedings

A. The Child(ren)

1. Please describe the child(ren)'s current health, development and functioning (according to your area of expertise), and identify the nature of any significant changes which have occurred

- Behavioural
- Emotional
- Attachment organisation
- Social/peer/sibling relationships
- Cognitive/educational
- Physical
    — Growth, eating, sleep
    — Non-organic physical problems (including wetting and soiling)
    — Injuries
    — Paediatric conditions

2. Please comment on the likely explanation for/aetiology of the child(ren)'s problems/difficulties/injuries

- History/experiences (including intrauterine influences, and abuse and neglect)
- Genetic/innate/developmental difficulties
- Paediatric/psychiatric disorders

3. Please provide a prognosis and risk if difficulties not addressed above.

4. Please describe the child(ren)'s needs in the light of the above

- Nature of care-giving
- Education
- Treatment

in the short and long term (subject, where appropriate, to further assessment later).

B. The parents/primary carers

5. Please describe the factors and mechanisms which would explain the parents' (or primary carers) harmful or neglectful interactions with the child(ren) (if relevant).

6. What interventions have been tried and what has been the result?

7. Please assess the ability of the parents or primary carers to fulfil the child(ren)'s identified needs now.

8. What other assessments of the parents or primary carers are indicated?

- Adult mental health assessment
- Forensic risk assessment
- Physical assessment
- Cognitive assessment

9. What, if anything, is needed to assist the parents or primary carers now, within the child(ren)'s timescales and what is the prognosis for change?

- Parenting work
- Support
- Treatment/therapy

C. *Alternatives*

10. Please consider the alternative possibilities for the fulfilment of the child(ren)'s needs

- What sort of placement
- Contact arrangements

Please consider the advantages, disadvantages and implications of each for the child(ren).

Suggested questions in letters of instruction to adult psychiatrists and applied psychologists in Children Act 1989 proceedings

1. Does the parent/adult have – whether in his/her history or presentation – a mental illness/disorder (including substance abuse) or other psychological/emotional difficulty and, if so, what is the diagnosis?

2. How do any/all of the above (and their current treatment if applicable) affect his/her functioning, including interpersonal relationships?

3. If the answer to Q1 is yes, are there any features of either the mental illness or psychological/emotional difficulty or personality disorder which could be associated with risk to others, based on the available evidence base (whether published studies or evidence from clinical experience)?

4. What are the experiences/antecedents/aetiology which would explain his/her difficulties, if any, (taking into account any available evidence base or other clinical experience)?

5. What treatment is indicated, what is its nature and the likely duration?

6. What is his/her capacity to engage in/partake of the treatment/therapy?

7. Are you able to indicate the prognosis for, time scales for achieving, and likely durability of, change?

8. What other factors might indicate positive change?

(It is assumed that this opinion will be based on collateral information as well as interviewing the adult).

PART 30
APPEALS

30.1 Scope and interpretation

(1) The rules in this Part apply to appeals to—

    (a)   the High Court; and

    (b)   [the family court][1].

(2) This Part does not apply to an appeal in detailed assessment proceedings against a decision of an authorised court officer.

(Rules [47.21 to 47.24][1] of the CPR deal with appeals against a decision of an authorised court officer in detailed assessment proceedings.)

(3) In this Part—

'appeal court' means the court to which an appeal is made;
'appeal notice' means an appellant's or respondent's notice;
'appellant' means a person who brings or seeks to bring an appeal;
['costs judge' means —
    (a)   the Chief Taxing Master;
    (b)   a taxing master of the Senior Courts; or
    (c)   a person appointed to act as deputy for the person holding office referred to in paragraph (b) or to act as temporary additional officer for any such office;
'district judge' means —
    (a)   the Senior District Judge of the Family Division
    (b)   a district judge of the Principal Registry of the Family Division;
    (c)   a person appointed to act as deputy for the person holding office referred to in paragraph (b) or to act as temporary additional officer for any such office;
    (d)   a district judge;
    (e)   a deputy district judge appointed under section 102 of the Senior Courts Act 1981 or section 8 of the County Courts Act 1984; or
    (f)   a District Judge (Magistrates' Courts);][2]
'lower court' means the court from which, or the person from whom, the appeal lies; and
'respondent' means—
    (a)   a person other than the appellant who was a party to the proceedings in the lower court and who is affected by the appeal; and
    (b)   a person who is permitted by the appeal court to be a party to the appeal.

(4) This Part is subject to any rule, enactment or practice direction which sets out special provisions with regard to any particular category of appeal.

Amendments
1   Substituted by the Family Procedure (Amendment No. 2) Rules 2014, SI 2014/667, rr 2, 21(a), (b).
2   Inserted by the Family Procedure (Amendment No. 2) Rules 2014, SI 2014/667, rr 2, 21(c).

30.2 Parties to comply with the practice direction

All parties to an appeal must comply with Practice Direction 30A.

30.3 Permission

[(1) Paragraphs (1B) and (2) of this rule set out when permission to appeal is, or is not, required under these rules to appeal against a decision or order of the family court.

(1A) This rule does not apply where the route of appeal from a decision or order of the family court is to the Court of Appeal, namely where the appeal is against a decision or order made by a circuit judge or Recorder—

- (a) in proceedings under—
    - (i) Part 4 of the 1989 Act (care and supervision);
    - (ii) Part 5 of the 1989 Act (protection of children);
    - (iii) paragraph 19(1) of Schedule 2 to the 1989 Act (approval by the court of local authority arrangements to assist children to live abroad); or
    - (iv) the 2002 Act (adoption, placement etc.);
- (b) in exercise of the family court's jurisdiction in relation to contempt of court where that decision or order was made in, or in connection with, proceedings referred to in sub-paragraph (a); or
- (c) where that decision or order was itself made on an appeal to the family court.

(Appeals in the cases referred to in this paragraph are outside the scope of these rules. The CPR make provision requiring permission to appeal in those cases.)

(1B) Permission to appeal is required under these rules—

- (a) unless paragraph (2) applies, where the appeal is against a decision made by a circuit judge, Recorder, district judge or costs judge; or
- (b) as provided by Practice Direction 30A.][1]

(2) Permission to appeal is not required where the appeal is against—

- (a) a committal order; ...[2]
- (b) a secure accommodation order under section 25 of the 1989 Act[; or][3]
- [(c) a refusal to grant habeas corpus for release in relation to a minor.][4]

(3) An application for permission to appeal may be made—

- (a) to the lower court at the hearing at which the decision to be appealed was made; or
- (b) to the appeal court in an appeal notice.

(Rule 30.4 sets out the time limits for filing an appellant's notice at the appeal court. Rule 30.5 sets out the time limits for filing a respondent's notice at the appeal court. Any application for permission to appeal to the appeal court must be made in the appeal notice (see rules 30.4(1) and 30.5(3).)

(4) Where the lower court refuses an application for permission to appeal, a further application for permission to appeal may be made to the appeal court.

(5) [Subject to paragraph (5A), where][5] the appeal court, without a hearing, refuses permission to appeal, the person seeking permission may request the decision to be reconsidered at a hearing.

[(5A) Where a judge of the High Court or [in the family court, a judge of the High Court or][6] a Designated Family Judge refuses permission to appeal without a hearing and considers that the application is totally without merit, the judge may make an order that the person seeking permission may not request the decision to be reconsidered at a hearing.

(5B) Rule 4.3(5) will not apply to an order that the person seeking permission may not request the decision to be reconsidered at a hearing made under paragraph (5A).][7]

(6) A request under paragraph (5) must be filed within 7 days beginning with the date on which the notice that permission has been refused was served.

(7) Permission to appeal may be given only where—

(a) the court considers that the appeal would have a real prospect of success; or
(b) there is some other compelling reason why the appeal should be heard.

(8) An order giving permission may—

(a) limit the issues to be heard; and
(b) be made subject to conditions.

(9) ...[8]

Amendments
1   Substituted by the Access to Justice Act 1999 (Destination of Appeals) (Family Proceedings) (Amendment) Order 2016, SI 2016/891, art 3.
2   Repealed by the Family Procedure (Amendment No. 4) Rules 2014, SI 2014/3296, rr 2, 11(a).
3   Substituted by the Family Procedure (Amendment No. 4) Rules 2014, SI 2014/3296, rr 2, 11(b).
4   Inserted by the Family Procedure (Amendment No. 4) Rules 2014, SI 2014/3296, rr 2, 11(c).
5   Substituted by the Family Procedure (Amendment) Rules 2013, SI 2013/530, rr 2, 5(a).
6   Inserted by the Family Procedure (Amendment No. 2) Rules 2014, SI 2014/667, rr 2, 22(a).
7   Inserted by the Family Procedure (Amendment) Rules 2013, SI 2013/530, rr 2, 5(b).
8   Repealed by the Family Procedure (Amendment No. 2) Rules 2014, SI 2014/667, rr 2, 22(b).

30.4 Appellant's notice

(1) Where the appellant seeks permission from the appeal court it must be requested in the appellant's notice.

(2) Subject to paragraph (3), the appellant must file the appellant's notice at the appeal court within —

(a) such period as may be directed by the lower court (which may be longer or shorter than the period referred to in sub-paragraph (b)); or
(b) where the court makes no such direction, 21 days after the date of the decision of the lower court against which the appellant wishes to appeal.

[(3) Where the appeal is against —

(a) a case management decision; or
(b) an order under section 38(1) of the 1989 Act,

the appellant must file the appellant's notice within 7 days beginning with the date of the decision of the lower court.]¹

(4) Unless the appeal court orders otherwise, an appellant's notice must be served on each respondent and the persons referred to in paragraph (5)—

(a) as soon as practicable; and
(b) in any event not later than 7 days,

after it is filed.

(5) The persons referred to in paragraph (4) are—

(a) any children's guardian, welfare officer, or children and family reporter;
(b) a local authority who has prepared a report under section 14A(8) or (9) of the 1989 Act;
(c) an adoption agency or local authority which has prepared a report on the suitability of the applicant to adopt a child; [and]²
(d) a local authority which has prepared a report on the placement of the child for adoption [.]²
(e) ...²

Amendments
1 Substituted by the Family Procedure (Amendment No. 2) Rules 2014, SI 2014/667, rr 2, 23(a).
2 Repealed by the Family Procedure (Amendment No. 2) Rules 2014, SI 2014/667, rr 2, 23(b).

30.5 Respondent's notice

(1) A respondent may file and serve a respondent's notice.

(2) A respondent who—

(a) is seeking permission to appeal from the appeal court; or
(b) wishes to ask the appeal court to uphold the order of the lower court for reasons different from or additional to those given by the lower court,

must file a respondent's notice.

(3) Where the respondent seeks permission from the appeal court it must be requested in the respondent's notice.

(4) [Subject to paragraph (4A), a respondent's notice]¹ must be filed within—

(a) such period as may be directed by the lower court; or
(b) where the court makes no such direction, 14 days beginning with the date referred to in paragraph (5).

[(4A) Where the appeal is against a case management decision, a respondent's notice must be filed within—

(a) such period as may be directed by the lower court; or
(b) where the court makes no such direction, 7 days beginning with the date referred to in paragraph (5).]²

(5) The date referred to in paragraph (4) is—

(a) the date on which the respondent is served with the appellant's notice where—
 (i) permission to appeal was given by the lower court; or
 (ii) permission to appeal is not required;
(b) the date on which the respondent is served with notification that the appeal court has given the appellant permission to appeal; or
(c) the date on which the respondent is served with notification that the application for permission to appeal and the appeal itself are to be heard together.

(6) Unless the appeal court orders otherwise, a respondent's notice must be served on the appellant, any other respondent and the persons referred to in rule 30.4(5)—

(a) as soon as practicable; and
(b) in any event not later than 7 days,

after it is filed.

(7) Where there is an appeal against an order under section 38(1) of the 1989 Act—

(a) a respondent may not, in that appeal, bring an appeal from the order or ask the appeal court to uphold the order of the lower court for reasons different from or additional to those given by the lower court; and
(b) paragraphs (2) and (3) do not apply.

Amendments
1 Substituted by the Family Procedure (Amendment No. 2) Rules 2014, SI 2014/667, rr 2, 24(a).
2 Inserted by the Family Procedure (Amendment No. 2) Rules 2014, SI 2014/667, rr 2, 24(b).

30.6 Grounds of appeal

The appeal notice must state the grounds of appeal.

30.7 Variation of time

(1) An application to vary the time limit for filing an appeal notice must be made to the appeal court.

(2) The parties may not agree to extend any date or time limit set by—

(a) these rules;
(b) Practice Direction 30A; or
(c) an order of the appeal court or the lower court.

(Rule 4.1(3)(a) provides that the court may extend or shorten the time for compliance with a rule, practice direction or court order (even if an application for extension is made after the time for compliance has expired).)

(Rule 4.1(3)(c) provides that the court may adjourn or bring forward a hearing.)

30.8 Stay

Unless the appeal court or the lower court orders otherwise, an appeal does not operate as a stay(GL) of any order or decision of the lower court.

30.9 Amendment of appeal notice

An appeal notice may not be amended without the permission of the appeal court.

30.10 Striking out appeal notices and setting aside or imposing conditions on permission to appeal

(1) The appeal court may—

- (a) strike out(GL) the whole or part of an appeal notice;
- (b) set aside(GL) permission to appeal in whole or in part;
- (c) impose or vary conditions upon which an appeal may be brought.

(2) The court will only exercise its powers under paragraph (1) where there is a compelling reason for doing so.

(3) Where a party was present at the hearing at which permission was given that party may not subsequently apply for an order that the court exercise its powers under paragraphs (1)(b) or (1)(c).

30.11 Appeal court's powers

(1) In relation to an appeal the appeal court has all the powers of the lower court.

(Rule 30.1(4) provides that this Part is subject to any enactment that sets out special provisions with regard to any particular category of appeal.)

(2) The appeal court has power to—

- (a) affirm, set aside(GL) or vary any order or judgment made or given by the lower court;
- (b) refer any application or issue for determination by the lower court;
- (c) order a new hearing;
- (d) make orders for the payment of interest;
- (e) make a costs order.

(3) The appeal court may exercise its powers in relation to the whole or part of an order of the lower court.

(Rule 4.1 contains general rules about the court's case management powers.)

(4) If the appeal court—

- (a) refuses an application for permission to appeal;
- (b) strikes out an appellant's notice; or
- (c) dismisses an appeal,

and it considers that the application, the appellant's notice or the appeal is totally without merit, the provisions of paragraph (5) must be complied with.

(5) Where paragraph (4) applies—

- (a) the court's order must record the fact that it considers the application, the appellant's notice or the appeal to be totally without merit; and

(b) the court must at the same time consider whether it is appropriate to make a civil restraint order.

30.12 Hearing of appeals

(1) Every appeal will be limited to a review of the decision of the lower court unless—

(a) an enactment or practice direction makes different provision for a particular category of appeal; or
(b) the court considers that in the circumstances of an individual appeal it would be in the interests of justice to hold a re-hearing.

(2) Unless it orders otherwise, the appeal court will not receive—

(a) oral evidence; or
(b) evidence which was not before the lower court.

(3) The appeal court will allow an appeal where the decision of the lower court was—

(a) wrong; or
(b) unjust because of a serious procedural or other irregularity in the proceedings in the lower court.

(4) The appeal court may draw any inference of fact which it considers justified on the evidence.

(5) At the hearing of the appeal a party may not rely on a matter not contained in that party's appeal notice unless the appeal court gives permission.

30.13 Assignment of appeals to the Court of Appeal

(1) Where the court from or to which an appeal is made or from which permission to appeal is sought ('the relevant court') considers that—

(a) an appeal which is to be heard by a county court or the High Court would raise an important point of principle or practice; or
(b) there is some other compelling reason for the Court of Appeal to hear it,

the relevant court may order the appeal to be transferred to the Court of Appeal.

[(2) Paragraph (1) does not allow an application for permission to appeal to be transferred to the Court of Appeal.][1]

Amendment
1 Substituted by the Family Procedure (Amendment No. 2) Rules 2014, SI 2014/667, rr 2, 25.

30.14 Reopening of final appeals

(1) The High Court will not reopen a final determination of any appeal unless—

(a) it is necessary to do so in order to avoid real injustice;
(b) the circumstances are exceptional and make it appropriate to reopen the appeal; and

(c) there is no alternative effective remedy.

(2) In paragraphs (1), (3), (4) and (6), 'appeal' includes an application for permission to appeal.

(3) This rule does not apply to appeals to [the family court][1].

(4) Permission is needed to make an application under this rule to reopen a final determination of an appeal.

(5) There is no right to an oral hearing of an application for permission unless, exceptionally, the judge so directs.

(6) The judge will not grant permission without directing the application to be served on the other party to the original appeal and giving that party an opportunity to make representations.

(7) There is no right of appeal or review from the decision of the judge on the application for permission, which is final.

(8) The procedure for making an application for permission is set out in Practice Direction 30A.

Amendment
1 Substituted by the Family Procedure (Amendment No. 2) Rules 2014, SI 2014/667, rr 2, 26.

Appendix 4

FRAMEWORK FOR THE ASSESSMENT OF CHILDREN IN NEED AND THEIR FAMILIES

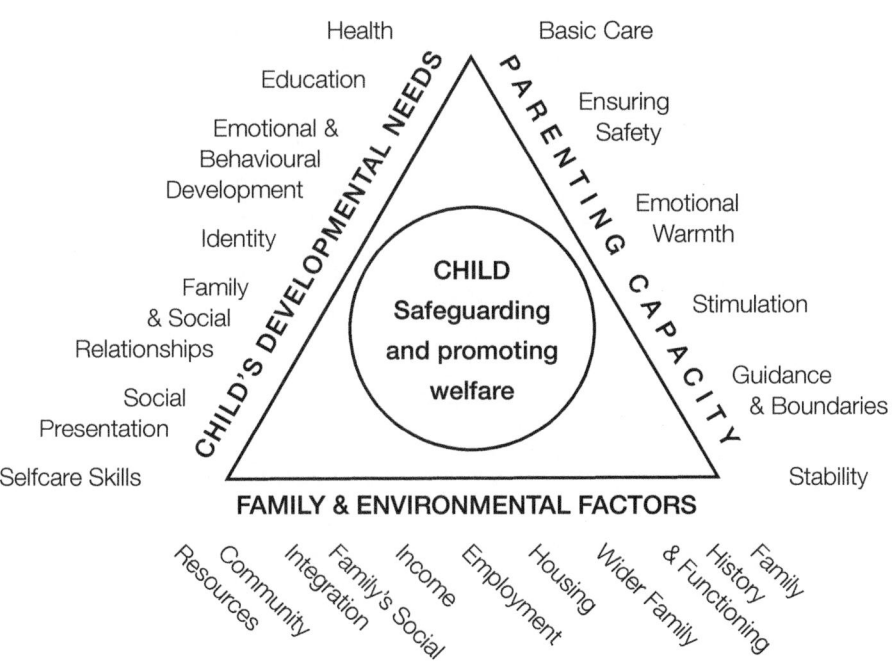

Appendix 5

SCHEDULE OF ITEMS IN RELATION TO THE EXERCISE OF PARENTAL RESPONSIBILITY

Disclaimer: In *A v A* [2004] EWHC 142 (Fam), at the conclusion of a high-conflict private law case, Wall J approved the following schedule which had been drawn up by the parents, with the assistance of the child's guardian, as a parental responsibility 'road map' intended to reduce future conflict. The statute does not provide specific guidance on which issues relating to parental responsibility require consultation and which do not. So, this schedule is only one example of an approach taken in a particular case. We include it here as a useful starting point for those seeking to set some ground rules for the exercise of parental responsibility by parents/carers who do not live together.

(1) Decisions that could be taken independently and without any consultation or notification to the other parent:
   How the children are to spend their time during contact
   Personal care for the children
   Activities undertaken
   Religious and spiritual pursuits
   Continuance of medicine prescribed by GP.

(2) Decisions where one parent would always need to inform the other parent of the decision, but did not need to consult or take the other parent's views into account:
   Medical treatment in an emergency
   Booking holidays or to take the children abroad in contact time
   Planned visits to the GP and the reasons for this.

(3) Decisions that you would need to both inform and consult the other parent prior to making the decision:
   Schools the children are to attend, including admissions applications. With reference to which senior school C should attend this is to be decided taking into account C's own views and in consultation and with advice from her teachers
   Contact rotas in school holidays
   Planned medical and dental treatment
   Stopping medication prescribed for the children
   Attendance at school functions so they can be planned to avoid meetings wherever possible
   Age that children should be able to watch videos, ie videos recommended for children over 12 and 18.

Appendix 6

KEY EXTRACTS FROM IMPORTANT JUDGMENTS

PUBLIC CHILDREN LAW, INCLUDING ADOPTION

Hedley J in *Re L (Care: Threshold Criteria)* [2007] 1 FLR 2050:

50. .... Basically it is the tradition of the UK, recognised in law, that children are best brought up within natural families. Lord Templeman, in *Re KD (A Minor Ward) (Termination of Access)* [1988] 1 AC 806, [1988] 2 FLR 139, at 812 and 141 respectively, said this:

> 'The best person to bring up a child is the natural parent. It matters not whether the parent is wise or foolish, rich or poor, educated or illiterate, provided the child's moral and physical health are not in danger. Public authorities cannot improve on nature.'

There are those who may regard that last sentence as controversial but undoubtedly it represents the present state of the law in determining the starting point. It follows inexorably from that, that society must be willing to tolerate very diverse standards of parenting, including the eccentric, the barely adequate and the inconsistent. It follows too that children will inevitably have both very different experiences of parenting and very unequal consequences flowing from it. It means that some children will experience disadvantage and harm, while others flourish in atmospheres of loving security and emotional stability. These are the consequences of our fallible humanity and it is not the provenance of the state to spare children all the consequences of defective parenting. In any event, it simply could not be done.

Lord Wilson *In the matter of B (A Child)* [2013] UKSC 33:

32. Judge Cryan's care order in relation to Amelia with a view to her adoption represented an interference with the exercise by Amelia, by M and by F of their rights to respect for their family life. It was therefore lawful only if, within the meaning of article 8(2) of the Convention, it was not only in accordance with the law but also "necessary" in a democratic society for the protection of the right of A to grow up free from harm. In *Johansen v Norway* (1997) 23 EHRR 33 the European Commission of Human Rights observed, at para 83, that "the notion of necessity implies that the interference corresponds to a pressing social need and, in particular, that it is proportional to the legitimate aim pursued.

33. In a number of its judgments the European Court of Human Rights, "the ECtHR", has spelt out the stark effects of the proportionality requirement in its application to a determination that a child should be adopted. Only a year ago, in YC v United Kingdom (2012) 55 EHRR 967, it said:

> "134 The Court reiterates that in cases concerning the placing of a child for adoption, which entails the permanent severance of family ties, the best interests of the child are paramount. In identifying the child's best interests in a particular case, two considerations must be borne in mind: first, it is in the child's best interests that his ties with his family be maintained except in cases where the family has proved particularly unfit; and secondly, it is in the child's best interests to ensure his development in a safe and secure environment. It is clear from the foregoing that family ties may only be severed in very exceptional circumstances and that everything must be done to preserve personal relations and, where appropriate, to 'rebuild' the family. It is not enough to show that a child could be placed in a more beneficial environment for his upbringing. However, where the maintenance of family ties would harm the child's health and development, a parent is not entitled under article 8 to insist that such ties be maintained."

Although in that paragraph it did not in terms refer to proportionality, the court had prefaced it with a reference to the need to examine whether the reasons adduced to justify the measures were relevant and sufficient, in other words whether they were proportionate to them.

34. In my view it is important not to take any one particular sentence out of its context in the whole of para 134 of the YC case: for each of its propositions is interwoven with the others. But the paragraph well demonstrates the high degree of justification which article 8 demands of a determination that a child should be adopted or placed in care with a view to adoption. Yet, while in every such case the trial judge should, as Judge Cryan expressly did, consider the proportionality of adoption to the identified risks, he is likely to find that domestic law runs broadly in parallel with the demands of article 8. Thus domestic law makes clear that:

(a) it is not enough that it would be better for the child to be adopted than to live with his natural family (*In re S-B (Children) (Care Proceedings: Standard of Proof)* [2009] UKSC 17, [2010] 1 AC 678, para 7); and

(b) a parent's consent to the making of an adoption order can be dispensed with only if the child's welfare so requires (section 52(1)(b) of the Adoption and Children Act 2002); there is therefore no point in making a care order with a view to adoption unless there are good grounds for considering that this statutory test will be satisfied.

The same thread therefore runs through both domestic law and Convention law, namely that the interests of the child must render it necessary to make an adoption order. The word "requires" in section 52(1)(b) "was plainly chosen as best conveying the essence of the Strasbourg jurisprudence" (*Re P (Placement Orders: Parental Consent)*[2008] EWCA Civ 535, [2008] 2 FLR 625, para 125).

Sir James Munby, President of the Family Division in *Re B-S (Children)* [2013] EWCA Civ 1146:

17. Before proceeding any further, it is necessary for us to go back to first principles and to emphasise a number of essential considerations that judges *must* always have in mind, and we emphasise this, at *every* stage of the process. Regrettably, the continuing lack of attention to what has been said in previous judgments necessitates our use of plain, even strong, language.

18. We start with Article 8 of the European Convention for the Protection of Human Rights and Fundamental Freedoms. There is no need for us to go through the jurisprudence of the Strasbourg court. The relevant passages from three key decisions, *K and T v Finland* (2001) 36 EHRR 255, *R and H v United Kingdom* (2012) 54 EHRR 2, [2011] 2 FLR 1236 [1], and *YC v United Kingdom* (2012) 55 EHRR 967, are set out by the Supreme Court in In re B (A Child) (Care Proceedings: Threshold Criteria) [2013] UKSC 33, [2013] 1 WLR 1911. The overarching principle remains as explained by Hale LJ, as she then was, in *Re C and B* [2001] 1 FLR 611, para 34:

> "Intervention in the family may be appropriate, but the aim should be to reunite the family when the circumstances enable that, and the effort should be devoted towards that end. Cutting off all contact and the relationship between the child or children and their family is only justified by the overriding necessity of the interests of the child."

To this we need only add what the Strasbourg court said in *YC v United Kingdom* (2012) 55 EHRR 967, para 134:

> "family ties may only be severed in very exceptional circumstances and ... everything must be done to preserve personal relations and, where appropriate, to 'rebuild' the family. It is not enough to show that a child could be placed in a more beneficial environment for his upbringing."

19. In this connection it is to be remembered, as Baroness Hale pointed out in *Down Lisburn Health and Social Services Trust and another v H and another* [2006] UKHL 36, para 34, that the United Kingdom is unusual in Europe in permitting the total severance of family ties without parental consent.

20. Section 52(1)(b) of the 2002 Act provides, as we have seen, that the consent of a parent with capacity can be dispensed with only if the welfare of the child "requires" this. "Require" here has the Strasbourg meaning of necessary, "the connotation of the imperative, what is demanded rather than what is merely optional or reasonable or desirable": *Re P (Placement Orders: Parental Consent)* [2008] EWCA Civ 535, [2008] 2 FLR 625, paras 120, 125. This is a stringent and demanding test.

21. Just how stringent and demanding has been spelt out very recently by the Supreme Court in In re B (A Child) (Care Proceedings: Threshold Criteria) [2013] UKSC 33, [2013] 1 WLR 1911. The significance of Re B was rightly emphasised in two judgments of this court handed down on 30 July 2013: *Re P (A Child)* [2013] EWCA Civ 963, para 102 (Black LJ), and *Re G (A Child)* [2013] EWCA Civ 965, paras 29-31 (McFarlane LJ). As Black LJ put it in Re P, Re B is a forceful reminder of just what is required.

22. The language used in Re B is striking. Different words and phrases are used, but the message is clear. Orders contemplating non-consensual adoption – care orders with a plan for adoption, placement orders and adoption orders – are "a very extreme thing, a last resort", only to be made where "nothing else will do", where "no other course [is] possible in [the child's] interests", they are "the most extreme option", a "last resort – when all else fails", to be made "only in exceptional circumstances and where motivated by overriding requirements pertaining to the child's welfare, in short, where nothing else will do": see Re B paras 74, 76, 77, 82, 104, 130, 135, 145, 198, 215.

23. Behind all this there lies the well-established principle, derived from s 1(5) of the 1989 Act, read in conjunction with s 1(3)(g), and now similarly embodied in s 1(6)

of the 2002 Act, that the court should adopt the 'least interventionist' approach. As Hale J, as she then was, said in Re O (Care or Supervision Order) [1996] 2 FLR 755, 760:

> "the court should begin with a preference for the less interventionist rather than the more interventionist approach. This should be considered to be in the better interests of the children ... unless there are cogent reasons to the contrary."

24. Linked with this is the vitally important point made by Wall LJ in Re P (Placement Orders: Parental Consent) [2008] EWCA Civ 535, [2008] 2 FLR 625, para 126:

> "Section 52(1) is concerned with adoption – the making of either a placement order or an adoption order – and what therefore has to be shown is that the child's welfare 'requires' adoption as opposed to something short of adoption. A child's circumstances may 'require' statutory intervention, perhaps may even 'require' the indefinite or long-term removal of the child from the family and his or her placement with strangers, but that is not to say that the same circumstances will necessarily 'require' that the child be adopted. They may or they may not. The question, at the end of the day, is whether what is 'required' is adoption."

...

34. First, there must be proper evidence both from the local authority and from the guardian. The evidence must address *all* the options which are realistically possible and must contain an analysis of the arguments for and against each option. As Ryder LJ said in Re R (Children) [2013] EWCA Civ 1018, para 20, what is required is:

> "evidence of the lack of alternative options for the children and an analysis of the evidence that is accepted by the court sufficient to drive it to the conclusion that nothing short of adoption is appropriate for the children."

The same judge indicated in Re S, K v The London Borough of Brent [2013] EWCA Civ 926, para 21, that what is needed is:

> "An assessment of the benefits and detriments of each option for placement and in particular the nature and extent of the risk of harm involved in each of the options".

McFarlane LJ made the same point in Re G (A Child) [2013] EWCA Civ 965, para 48, when he identified:

> "the need to take into account the negatives, as well as the positives, of any plan to place a child away from her natural family".

We agree with all of this.

...

41. The second thing that is essential, and again we emphasise that word, is an adequately reasoned judgment by the judge. We have already referred to Ryder LJ's criticism of the judge in Re S, K v The London Borough of Brent [2013] EWCA Civ 926. That was on 29 July 2013. The very next day, in Re P (A Child) [2013]

EWCA Civ 963, appeals against the making of care and placement orders likewise succeeded because, as Black LJ put it (para 107):

> "the judge ... failed to carry out a proper balancing exercise in order to determine whether it was necessary to make a care order with a care plan of adoption and then a placement order or, if she did carry out that analysis, it is not apparent from her judgments. Putting it another way, she did not carry out a proportionality analysis."

She added (para 124): "there is little acknowledgment in the judge's judgments of the fact that adoption is a last resort and little consideration of what it was that justified it in this case."

42. The judge must grapple with the factors at play in the particular case and, to use Black LJ's phrase (para 126), give "proper focussed attention to the specifics".

43. In relation to the nature of the judicial task we draw attention to what McFarlane LJ said in *Re G (A Child)* [2013] EWCA Civ 965, paras 49-50:

> "In most child care cases a choice will fall to be made between two or more options. The judicial exercise should not be a linear process whereby each option, other than the most draconian, is looked at in isolation and then rejected because of internal deficits that may be identified, with the result that, at the end of the line, the only option left standing is the most draconian and that is therefore chosen without any particular consideration of whether there are internal deficits within that option.
>
> The linear approach ... is not apt where the judicial task is to undertake a global, holistic evaluation of each of the options available for the child's future upbringing before deciding which of those options best meets the duty to afford paramount consideration to the child's welfare."

We need not quote the next paragraph in McFarlane LJ's judgment, which explains in graphic and compelling terms the potential danger of adopting a linear approach.

44. We emphasise the words "global, holistic evaluation". This point is crucial. The judicial task is to evaluate *all* the options, undertaking a global, holistic and (see *Re G* para 51) multi-faceted evaluation of the child's welfare which takes into account *all* the negatives and the positives, *all* the pros and cons, of each option. To quote McFarlane LJ again (para 54):

> "What is required is a balancing exercise in which each option is evaluated to the degree of detail necessary to analyse and weigh its own internal positives and negatives and each option is then compared, side by side, against the competing option or options."

45. McFarlane LJ added this important observation (para 53) which we respectfully endorse:

> "a process which acknowledges that long-term public care, and in particular adoption contrary to the will of a parent, is 'the most draconian option', yet does not engage with the very detail of that option which renders it 'draconian' cannot be a full or effective process of evaluation. Since the phrase was first coined some years ago, judges now routinely make reference to the 'draconian' nature of permanent separation of parent and child and

they frequently do so in the context of reference to 'proportionality'. Such descriptions are, of course, appropriate and correct, but there is a danger that these phrases may inadvertently become little more than formulaic judicial window-dressing if they are not backed up with a substantive consideration of what lies behind them and the impact of that on the individual child's welfare in the particular case before the court. If there was any doubt about the importance of avoiding that danger, such doubt has been firmly swept away by the very clear emphasis in *Re B* on the duty of the court actively to evaluate proportionality in every case."

PRIVATE CHILDREN LAW AND PARENTAL RESPONSIBILITY

McFarlane LJ in *Re W (Children)* [2012] EWCA Civ 999:

72. Having determined the issues in this appeal, I return briefly to the concept of parental responsibility and the potential for it to be given greater prominence in the resolution of private law disputes as to the arrangements for the welfare of children.

73. The observations that I now make are part of a wider context in which the family courts seek to encourage parents to see the bigger picture in terms of the harmful impact upon their children of sustained disputes over the contact which is most neatly encapsulated in the words of Black LJ in T v T [2010] EWCA Civ 1366:

"[The parents] must put aside their differences ... if the adults do not manage to resolve things by communicating with each other, the children inevitably suffer and the adults may also pay the price when the children are old enough to be aware of what has been going on. ... It is a tremendous privilege to be involved in bringing up a child. Childhood is over all too quickly and, whilst I appreciate that both sides think that they are motivated only by concern for the children, it is still very sad to see it being allowed to slip away whilst energy is devoted to adult wrangles and to litigation. What is particularly unfair is that the legacy of a childhood tainted in that way is likely to remain with the children into their own adult lives."

74. In describing the statutory legal context within which decisions as to the private law arrangements for a child are to be made, I have stressed that it is the parents, rather than the court or more generally the state, who are the primary decision makers and actors for determining and delivering the upbringing that the welfare of their child requires. I have stressed that, along with the rights, powers and authority of a parent, come duties and responsibilities which must be discharged in a manner which respects similarly held rights, powers, duties and responsibilities of the other parent where parental responsibility is shared.

75. In all aspects of life, whilst some duties and responsibilities may be a pleasure to discharge, others may well be unwelcome and a burden. Whilst parenting in many respects brings joy, even in families where life is comparatively harmonious, the responsibility of being a parent can be tough. Where parents separate the burden for each and every member of the family group can be, and probably will be, heavy. It is not easy, indeed it is tough, to be a single parent with the care of a child. Equally, it is tough to be the parent of a child for whom you no longer have the day

to day care and with whom you no longer enjoy the ordinary stuff of everyday life because you only spend limited time with your child. Where all contact between a parent and a child is prevented, the burden on that parent will be of the highest order. Equally, for the parent who has the primary care of a child, to send that child off to spend time with the other parent may, in some cases, be itself a significant burden; it may, to use modern parlance, be "a very big ask". Where, however, it is plainly in the best interests of a child to spend time with the other parent then, tough or not, part of the responsibility of the parent with care must be the duty and responsibility to deliver what the child needs, hard though that may be.

76. Where parental responsibility is shared by a child's parents, the statute is plain (CA 1989, s 3) that each of those parents, and both of them, share 'duties' and 'responsibilities' in relation to the child, as well as 'rights ... powers ... and authority'. Where all are agreed, as in the present case, that it is in the best interests of a child to have a meaningful relationship with both parents, the courts are entitled to look to each parent to use their best endeavours to deliver what their child needs, hard or burdensome or downright tough that may be. The statute places the primary responsibility for delivering a good outcome for a child upon each of his or her parents, rather than upon the courts or some other agency.

77. Where there are significant difficulties in the way of establishing safe and beneficial contact, the parents share the primary responsibility of addressing those difficulties so that, in time, and maybe with outside help, the child can benefit from being in a full relationship with each parent. In the present case the emotional and psychological make up of the two parents, both separately and in combination, prevented easy contact taking place. Dr G advised that both parents needed to access support or therapy to enable them to approach matters in a different way. F engaged in the necessary work, but M declined to. It may have been in F's interests to do so, and M may have taken a contrary view; be that as it may, the only interests that either parent should have had in mind were those of each of their two children.

78. Parents, both those who have primary care and those who seek to spend time with their child, have a responsibility to do their best to meet their child's needs in relation to the provision of contact, just as they do in every other regard. It is not, at face value, acceptable for a parent to shirk that responsibility and simply to say 'no' to reasonable strategies designed to improve the situation in this regard.

79. The observations that I have made will be, I suspect, very familiar thoughts to family judges, lawyers, mediators and others. My intention in setting them out in this judgment is to give them a degree of prominence so that they may be brought to the attention of parents who have separated at an early stage in the discussion of the arrangements for their child.

80. Whether or not a parent has parental responsibility is not simply a matter that achieves the ticking of a box on a form. It is a significant matter of status as between parent and child and, just as important, as between each of the parents. By stressing the 'responsibility' which is so clearly given prominence in CA 1989, s 3 and the likely circumstance that that responsibility is shared with the other parent, it is to be hoped that some parents may be encouraged more readily to engage with the difficulties that undoubtedly arise when contemplating post-separation contact than may have hitherto been the case.

INDEX

[all references are to paragraph number]

Access to information	
adoption, and	7.101

Accommodation
see also **Secure accommodation**

child has no parent or parents	
consent	4.33–4.38
children in care	4.39–4.41
children in need	4.17
general duty	4.26–4.32
'looked after children'	4.26

Adopted Children Register

contact preferences	7.116–7.118
generally	7.102–7.103
tracing the natural family	7.104–7.115

Adoption

advance consent to adoption	
effect	7.72–7.73
form	7.70
generally	7.64–7.66
proof	7.70
agencies	
adoption by couples	7.16
advance consent to adoption	7.64
ceasing to be a member of original family	7.33
consent to making of adoption order	7.69
consent to placement for adoption	7.61–7.62
paramountcy principle	7.27–7.31
parental consent	7.52–7.55
relationship with relatives and prospective adopters	7.38–7.43
religion, race and culture	7.44
services provided	7.86–7.197
welfare of child	7.27–7.48
whole range of powers	7.48
applicants	2.24
becoming an adopted person	7.33–7.37
care orders, and	6.31–6.32
ceasing to be a member of original family	7.33–7.37
child arrangements order, and	7.49
child's welfare	2.20
consent to adoption	
advance, in	7.64–7.66
criteria	7.56
effect	7.72–7.73
form	7.70
generally	7.56–7.57
guardian	7.60

Adoption—*continued*

consent to adoption—*continued*	
'parent'	7.58–7.59
proof	7.70
welfare of child, and	7.57
consent to intercountry adoption	7.71
consent to making an adoption order	7.67–7.69
consent to placement for adoption	
criteria	7.56
effect	7.72–7.73
form	7.70
generally	7.61–7.63
proof	7.70
cultural background	7.44–7.45
dispensing with parental consent	
grounds	7.74–7.84
parent cannot be found or incapable of giving consent	7.75–7.77
procedure	7.85
'requires'	7.82–7.84
welfare of child, for	7.78–7.81
fostering, and	7.49
generally	2.19–2.22
inter-country applications	
generally	7.9
introduction	2.25
meaning	
generally	7.1–7.8
introduction	2.20
'no order' principle	7.51
paramountcy principle	7.27–7.32
parental consent	
adoption, to	7.56–7.60
advance, in	7.64–7.66
dispensing with	7.74–7.
effect	7.72–7.73
form and proof	7.70
intercountry applications, in	7.71
making an adoption order, to	7.67–7.69
overview	7.52–7.55
placement for adoption, to	7.61–7.63
persons entitled to adopt	
couples	7.13–7.17
generally	7.12
introduction	2.24
parents	7.18–7.19
previous applicants	7.26
sole applicant	7.24–7.25
step-parents	7.20–7.23

Adoption—*continued*
persons who can be adopted 7.10–7.11
placement agreement, and 7.49
placement for adoption
  background 7.119–7.122
  contact, and 7.163–7.174
  introduction 2.22
  meaning 7.123–7.125
  order, by 7.148–7.157
  parental consent, with 7.127–7.147
  routes 7.126
placement orders
  application by local
    authority 7.151–7.152
  care proceedings, and 7.158–7.162
  conditions 7.150
  consequences 7.155
  generally 7.148–7.149
  revocation 7.156–7.157
  status of child pending determination
    of application 7.153–7.154
placement with extended family, and 7.49
placement with parental consent
  advance, in 7.137–7.139
  change of name, and 7.143
  child under six weeks old 7.133–7.134
  consequences 7.140–7.142
  father without parental
    responsibility, and 7.145–7.147
  form 7.135–7.136
  generally 7.127–7.132
  removal from UK, and 7.143
  withdrawal of consent 7.144
racial origin 7.44–7.45
range of powers available 7.47–7.50
rehabilitation with birth parents, and 7.49
relationship with care proceedings 2.23
relationship child has with relatives
  and prospective adopters 7.38–7.43
religious persuasion 7.46
services
  see also **Adoption services**
  application for order 7.179–7.186
  birth family 7.97–7.100
  care proceedings 7.158–7.162
  categories 7.87
  confidentiality 7.101
  consequences of order 7.187–7.190
  contact on placement and after
    adoption 7.163–7.174
  establishment 7.88
  generally 7.86–7.88
  illegal placements 7.175–7.178
  international adoptions 7.191–7.197
  minimum standards 7.86
  placement for adoption 7.119–7.157
  placement with order 7.148–7.157
  placement with parental
    consent 7.127–7.147
  prohibited steps 7.175–7.178
  prospective adopters 7.89–7.96
  registration 7.102–7.103
  tracing the natural family 7.104–7.118
special guardianship orders, and 7.49, 8.7

Adoption—*continued*
statutory basis 2.19–2.22
twin-track planning, and 7.49
welfare of child
  becoming an adopted person 7.33–7.37
  ceasing to be a member of
    original family 7.33–7.37
  cultural background 7.44–7.45
  introduction 2.20
  'no order' principle 7.51
  paramountcy principle 7.27–7.32
  racial origin 7.44–7.45
  range of powers available 7.47–7.50
  relationship with relatives and
    prospective adopters 7.38–7.43
  religious persuasion 7.46
  whole range of powers available 7.47–7.50
Adoption agencies
adoption by couples 7.16
advance consent to adoption 7.64
ceasing to be a member of original
  family 7.33
consent to making of adoption order 7.69
consent to placement for adoption 7.61–7.62
paramountcy principle 7.27–7.31
parental consent 7.52–7.55
relationship with relatives and
  prospective adopters 7.38–7.43
religion, race and culture 7.44
services provided
  see also **Adoption services**
  generally 7.86–7.197
welfare of child
  ceasing to be a member of
    original family 7.33
  paramountcy principle 7.27–7.31
  range of powers 7.48
  relationship with relatives and
    prospective adopters 7.38–7.43
  religion, race and culture 7.44
  whole range of powers 7.48
Adoption and Children Act 2002
generally 2.19–2.25
register 7.95
special guardianship 8.1
Adoption Contact Register
generally 7.116–7.118
Adoption Panel
generally 7.92
Adoption services
access to adoption information 7.101
Adopted Children Register
  contact preferences 7.116–7.118
  generally 7.102–7.103
  tracing the natural family 7.104–7.115
Adoption and Children Act Register 7.95
Adoption Contact Register 7.116–7.118
adoption orders
  applications 7.179–7.186
  consequences 7.187–7.190
Adoption Panel 7.92
advice and information 7.89–7.90
application for order 7.179–7.186
assessment 7.91

Index

Adoption services—*continued*
  birth family
    counselling   7.97–7.98
    life story work   7.99–7.100
    support   7.97–7.98
  care proceedings   7.158–7.162
  categories   7.87
  confidentiality   7.101
  consequences of order   7.187–7.190
  contact after adoption   7.173–7.174
  contact on placement
    application for order   7.170–7.172
    authorised for placement,
      when   7.163–7.167
    power to refuse   7.168–7.169
  establishment   7.88
  generally   7.86–7.88
  illegal placements   7.175–7.178
  Independent Review Mechanism   7.93
  international adoptions
    foreign child 'adopted'
      abroad   7.193–7.194
    foreign child brought into England
      and Wales for adoption   7.195
    generally   7.191–7.192
    Hague Convention 1993, under   7.197
    UK child adopted abroad   7.196
  matching   7.94–7.96
  minimum standards   7.86
  placement for adoption
    background   7.119–7.122
    contact, and   7.163–7.174
    meaning   7.123–7.125
    order, by   7.148–7.157
    parental consent, with   7.127–7.147
    routes   7.126
  placement orders
    application by local authority   7.151–7.152
    care proceedings, and   7.158–7.162
    conditions   7.150
    consequences   7.155
    generally   7.148–7.149
    revocation   7.156–7.157
    status of child pending determination
      of application   7.153–7.154
  placement with parental consent
    advance, in   7.137–7.139
    change of name, and   7.143
    child under six weeks old   7.133–7.134
    consequences   7.140–7.142
    father without parental
      responsibility, and   7.145–7.147
    form   7.135–7.136
    generally   7.127–7.132
    removal from UK, and   7.143
    withdrawal of consent   7.144
  prohibited steps   7.175–7.178
  prospective adopters, to
    Adoption and Children Act Register   7.95
    Adoption Panel   7.92
    advice and information   7.89–7.90
    assessment   7.91
    Independent Review Mechanism   7.93
    matching   7.94–7.96

Adoption services—*continued*
    registration   7.102–7.103
  tracing the natural family
    post-29 December 2005
      adoption   7.111–7.115
    pre-30 December 2005
      adoption   7.104–7.110
Advance consent to adoption
  effect   7.72–7.73
  form   7.70
  generally   7.64–7.66
  proof   7.70
Advice and information
  adoption, and   7.89–7.90
After school care
  local authority services, and   4.12
Allocation of cases
  exclusions   1.8
  generally   1.8–1.10
  guidance   1.7
  introduction   1.6
Appeals
  challenging the local authority   11.34–11.35
  emergency protection orders, and   5.70
  generally   1.11–1.15
Appointment of guardian
  court referrals, and   5.20–5.21
  emergency protection orders, and   5.45
  parental responsibility, and   3.24–3.26
Assessment
  adoption, and   7.91
Assistance in kind or cash
  local authority services, and   4.17

Birth family
  care orders, and   6.30–6.32
Butler-Sloss Inquiry (1988)
  child sexual abuse   2.1

CAFCASS
  generally   1.27
  referrals, and   5.14
Care orders
  see also **Care proceedings**
  adoption, and   6.31–6.32
  allocation   6.52
  assessments   6.71–6.73
  attendance of media at hearings   6.61–6.62
  'attributable to parental care'
    child beyond control   6.23–6.24
    expected standard   6.20–6.22
    generally   6.19
  birth family, and   6.30–6.32
  care plan   6.74–6.77
  child beyond parental control   6.23–6.24
  concurrent planning   6.80
  designated local authority   6.53–6.56
  discharge   6.84–6.88
  disclosure
    confidentiality   6.116–6.122
    generally   6.111–6.112
    public interest immunity   6.113–6.115
  evidence
    admissibility   6.97

Care orders—*continued*
  evidence—*continued*
    confidentiality   6.116–6.122
    disclosure   6.111–6.112
    expert witnesses   6.123–6.129
    general principles   6.97–6.101
    hearsay   6.102–6.106
    interviews with children   6.107–6.110
    public interest immunity   6.113–6.115
    serious allegations, and   6.138–6.141
    standard of proof   6.101
    use outside proceedings   6.116–6.122
  exclusion requirements   6.66
  expected standard of care   6.20–6.22
  expert witnesses   6.123–6.129
  fact-finding hearings   6.67–6.70
  final orders   6.81–6.82
  generally   6.2–6.6
  guardian's role   6.89–6.92
  hearsay evidence   6.102–6.106
  human rights, and
    generally   6.28
    threshold criteria   6.142–6.143
  inherent jurisdiction of the High
    Court, and
    generally   10.30–10.34
    introduction   10.21–10.22
  interim orders   6.63–6.65
  intervenors   6.51
  introduction   6.1
  'likely to suffer'   6.14–6.16
  local authority care plan   6.74–6.77
  local authority support
    generally   2.10–2.16
    legislative basis   2.7
  parallel planning   6.78–6.79
  parental contact with child in
    care   6.130–6.136
  parties
    applicants   6.45
    date and place of initial hearing   6.47
    joinder   6.47–6.49
    removal of party from proceedings   6.50
    respondents   6.46
  proceedings
    allocation   6.52
    assessments   6.71–6.73
    attendance of media at
      hearings   6.61–6.62
    available orders   6.57
    care plan   6.74–6.77
    concurrent planning   6.80
    designated local authority   6.53–6.56
    discharge of order   6.84–6.88
    evidence   6.97–6.129
    exclusion requirements   6.66
    fact-finding hearings   6.67–6.70
    final orders   6.81–6.82
    guardian's role   6.89–6.92
    interim orders   6.63–6.65
    intervenors   6.51
    local authority's care plan   6.74–6.77
    parallel planning   6.78–6.79
    parties   6.45–6.50

Care orders—*continued*
  proceedings—*continued*
    Public Law Online   6.60
    representation of child   6.89–6.96
    role of court   6.57–6.59
    solicitor's role   6.93–6.96
    threshold hearings   6.67–6.70
    timetable   6.50
    withdrawal of application   6.83
  Public Law Online   6.60
  radicalisation   6.144–6.146
  relevant date   6.17–6.18
  representation of child
    guardian   6.89–6.92
    solicitor   6.93–6.96
  significant harm   6.10–6.13
  solicitor's role   6.93–6.96
  special guardianship, and   8.20
  splitting siblings   6.33
  standard of proof
    generally   6.101
    serious allegations, and   6.138–6.141
  substitution   6.88
  supervision orders, and   6.151–6.163
  threshold criteria
    'attributable to parental care'   6.19–6.24
    human rights, and   6.142–6.143
    introduction   6.9
    'likely to suffer'   6.14–6.16
    significant harm   6.10–6.13
  threshold hearings   6.67–6.70
  timetable   6.50
  uncertain perpetrators   6.147–6.150
  welfare checklist
    babies   6.34–6.36
    birth family   6.30–6.32
    care plan   6.44
    generally   6.25–6.27
    holistic analysis   6.29
    human rights, and   6.28
    learning disabilities   6.41–6.43
    older children   6.37–6.39
    physical disabilities   6.41–6.43
    splitting siblings   6.33
    very young parents   6.40
    young children   6.34–6.36
  withdrawal of application   6.83
Care proceedings
  adoption, and   7.158–7.162
  special guardianship, and   8.13–8.14
Challenging the local authority
  appeals   11.34–11.35
  Children's Commissioner   11.23–11.25
  complaint procedures   11.13–11.19
  emergency protection orders, and   5.70
  human rights
    application in domestic
      courts   11.44–11.48
    generally   11.36–11.39
    reference to ECtHR   11.49
    right to a fair trial   11.40–11.41
    right to respect for private and
      family life   11.42–11.43
  independent reviewing officer   11.8–11.12

Index

Challenging the local authority—*continued*
- introduction — 11.1–11.2
- judicial review — 11.28–11.33
- Local Government and Social Care Ombudsman — 11.26–11.27
- parental consent — 11.3–11.7
- parental responsibility — 11.3–11.7
- powers of the Secretary of State — 11.20–11.22
- secure accommodation orders, and — 9.36–9.38
- sources — 11.2
- special guardianship, and — 8.8

Charging for services
- local authority services, and — 4.18

Child abduction
- allocation of cases, and — 1.8
- wardship, and — 10.19

Child arrangements orders
- applications — 3.64–3.67
- child parties — 3.71
- children age 16 and over — 3.32
- conditions — 3.33
- domestic abuse — 3.40–3.43
- enforcement — 3.47–3.52
- generally — 3.30
- guardians ad litem — 3.71
- interim orders — 3.44–3.46
- 'lives with' orders — 3.53–3.55
- procedure
  - applications — 3.64–3.67
  - child parties — 3.71
  - guardians ad litem — 3.71
  - respondents — 3.68
  - welfare reports — 3.69–3.70
- respondents — 3.68
- special guardianship, and — 8.20–8.21
- 'spends time with' orders
  - domestic abuse — 3.40–3.43
  - generally — 3.34–3.39
- types — 3.31
- welfare reports — 3.69–3.70

Child Arrangements Programme (CAP)
- parental responsibility, and — 3.4

Child assessment orders
- applications — 5.75–5.76
- duration — 5.73
- effect — 5.82
- generally — 5.72–5.74
- grounds — 5.79–5.81
- orders available — 5.78
- procedure — 5.75–5.78
- purpose — 5.72
- 'specified proceedings', as — 5.77

Child protection
- Adoption and Children Act 2002 — 2.19–2.25
- background — 2.1–2.2
- Children Act 1989 — 2.4–2.18
- Family Justice Council — 2.34
- government guidance — 2.32
- Human Rights Act 1998 — 2.26–2.29
- inherent jurisdiction of the High Court — 2.35–2.37
- introduction — 2.1–2.2
- sources of law — 2.3

Child protection—*continued*
- statutory rules — 2.31
- UN Convention on the Rights of the Child — 2.30
- Wales — 2.33
- wardship — 2.35–2.37

Child protection conference
- attendees — 5.24
- core group — 5.28–5.29
- generally — 5.24–5.27
- ongoing legal proceedings, and — 5.31
- parental involvement — 5.25
- purpose — 5.27
- reviews — 5.30
- social worker's report — 5.26

Child protection investigation
- child protection conference
  - attendees — 5.24
  - core group — 5.28–5.29
  - generally — 5.24–5.27
  - ongoing legal proceedings, and — 5.31
  - parental involvement — 5.25
  - purpose — 5.27
  - reviews — 5.30
  - social worker's report — 5.26
- child protection plans — 5.23
- court referral, and — 5.16
- generally — 5.8–5.13
- introduction — 5.6–5.7
- outcome — 5.22

Child protection plans
- generally — 5.23

Child safety orders
- applications — 5.95
- duration — 5.98
- generally — 5.93
- grounds — 5.94
- parenting orders, and — 5.96–5.97
- procedure — 5.95–5.98

Childline
- referrals, and — 5.5

Children Act 1989
- background — 2.1–2.2
- care orders
  - generally — 2.10–2.16
  - legislative basis — 2.7
- child protection — 2.7–2.9
- child's welfare — 2.6
- emergency powers
  - generally — 2.17–2.18
  - legislative basis — 2.7
- local authority support
  - generally — 2.8–2.9
  - legislative basis — 2.7
- paramouncy of child — 2.6
- parental responsibility — 2.4–2.5
- structure — 2.7–2.8
- supervision orders
  - generally — 2.10–2.16
  - legislative basis — 2.7
- welfare of child — 2.6

Children in care
see also **Care orders**
- accommodation, and — 4.39–4.41

Children in care—*continued*
  emergency protection orders, and 5.47
  inherent jurisdiction of the High
    Court, and
      generally 10.30–10.34
      introduction 10.21–10.22
Children in need
  accommodation 4.17
  'appropriate' provision 4.16
  assessment 4.13
  assistance in kind or cash 4.17
  charging for services 4.18
  definition 4.13
  general duty of authority 4.15
  services 4.14–4.18
Children proceedings
  allocation of cases 1.8
  private law 1.16–1.19
  public law 1.16–1.19
Children with disabilities
  'disabled' 4.19
  generally 4.19
  register of disabled children 4.19
  support for parents 4.22
Children with special needs
  education, health and care plan 4.21
  generally 4.20
Children's Commissioner
  challenging the local authority,
    and 11.23–11.25
Child's welfare
  care orders, and
    babies 6.34–6.36
    birth family 6.30–6.32
    care plan 6.44
    generally 6.25–6.27
    holistic analysis 6.29
    human rights, and 6.28
    learning disabilities 6.41–6.43
    older children 6.37–6.39
    physical disabilities 6.41–6.43
    splitting siblings 6.33
    very young parents 6.40
    young children 6.34–6.36
  generally 2.6
Complaint procedures
  challenging the local authority,
    and 11.13–11.19
Confidentiality
  adoption, and 7.101
Consent to adoption
  advance, in
    effect 7.72–7.73
    form 7.70
    generally 7.64–7.66
    proof 7.70
  challenging the local authority,
    and 11.3–11.7
  criteria 7.56
  dispensing with
    grounds 7.74–7.84
    parent cannot be found or incapable
      of giving consent 7.75–7.77
    procedure 7.85

Consent to adoption—*continued*
  dispensing with—*continued*
    'requires' 7.82–7.84
    welfare of child, for 7.78–7.81
  effect 7.72–7.73
  form 7.70
  generally 7.56–7.57
  guardian 7.60
  intercountry applications, in 7.71
  making an adoption order 7.67–7.69
  overview 7.52–7.55
  'parent' 7.58–7.59
  placement, and
    criteria 7.56
    effect 7.72–7.73
    form 7.70
    generally 7.61–7.63
    proof 7.70
  proof 7.70
  welfare of child, and 7.57
Contact
  adoption, after 7.173–7.174
  placement for adoption, on
    application for order 7.170–7.172
    authorised for placement,
      when 7.163–7.167
    power to refuse 7.168–7.169
  section 8 orders, and 3.31
  special guardianship, and 8.8
Court of Appeal
  appeals 1.12
Court referrals
  see also **Referrals**
  appointment of CAFCASS
    guardian 5.20–5.21
  filing report 5.17
  generally 5.14–5.17
  interim care or supervision orders 5.18–5.19
  local authority investigation 5.16
Criminal proceedings
  wardship, and 10.17–10.18

Deprivation of liberty
  secure accommodation orders, *and*
    future issues 9.47
    identification cases of 9.44
    inherent jurisdiction 9.43
    introduction 9.42
    key points 9.45
    procedure 9.46
Disabled children
  local authority services, and 4.8
DNA testing
  parental responsibility, and 3.9–3.11
Domestic abuse
  section 8 orders, and
    generally 3.47
    'spends time with' orders, and 3.40–3.43

Education authorities
  secure accommodation orders, and 9.23–9.24
Educational provision
  secure accommodation orders, and 9.39

Index

Emergency powers
generally 2.17–2.18
legislative basis 2.7
Emergency protection orders
appeals, and 5.70
applications
  checklist 5.50
  generally 5.42–5.48
  grounds 5.51–5.54
  without notice 5.49–5.50
appointment of guardian 5.45
challenges to 5.70
child in care 5.47
contact, and 5.61–5.62
directions 5.57
discharge 5.70
duration 5.43
effect 5.55–5.57
exclusion requirement 5.63–5.67
generally 5.39–5.41
Gillick-competence, and 5.69
grounds 5.51–5.54
locating the child 5.58–5.60
medical examinations and
  assessments 5.68–5.69
name of child 5.46
opposition to 5.70
parental responsibility, and 5.69
procedure
  applications 5.42–5.48
  without notice applications 5.49–5.50
reasonable contact, and 5.61–5.62
referrals, and 5.4
removal of the child 5.58–5.60
'specified proceedings', as 5.45
supplementary provisions 5.57
without notice applications 5.49–5.50
Enforcement
section 8 orders, and 3.47–3.52

Family centres
local authority services, and 4.11
Family Court
allocation of cases
  exclusions 1.8
  generally 1.8–1.10
  guidance 1.7
  introduction 1.6
appeals 1.11–1.15
background 1.4
excluded areas of work 1.8
generally 1.3–1.4
judiciary 1.5
jurisdiction within the UK, and 1.1
procedure
  Practice Directions 1.26
  Rules 1.20–1.25
relationship with High Court 1.8–1.10
structure 1.5–1.7
Family Justice Council
generally 2.34
Family Procedure Rules 2010
confidentiality 1.22–1.25
generally 1.20–1.21

Family Procedure Rules 2010—*continued*
overriding objective 1.20
transparency 1.22–1.25
Financial support
special guardianship, and
  generally 8.16–8.18
  introduction 8.8
Forced marriage
wardship, and 10.19
Foreign adoptions
foreign child 'adopted' abroad 7.193–7.194
foreign child brought into England
  and Wales for adoption 7.195
generally 7.191–7.192
Hague Convention 1993, under 7.197
UK child adopted abroad 7.196
Foster care
agency parents 4.65–4.68
approval process 4.65–4.84
children's homes 4.77
duties of parents 4.70–4.75
emergency placements 4.69
friends 4.54
funding 4.76
generally 4.53
introduction 4.52
local authority foster parents 4.58–4.64
placement with parent 4.78–4.
regulatory framework 4.55–4.57
relatives 4.54
rights of parents 4.70–4.75
types 4.53

Gillick competency
emergency protection orders, and 5.69
parental responsibility, and 3.18
GPs
referrals, and 5.5
Guardians
see also **Special guardianship**
parental responsibility, and
  appointment 3.24–3.26
  disclaimer 3.25
  generally 3.21–3.23
  responsibilities 3.27
  special guardians 3.28–3.29
Guidance
allocation of cases 1.7
generally 2.32
powers of the Secretary of State 11.20–11.22
referrals and assessments 5.3
taking child into police protection 5.33
transparency in the family courts 1.25

Health authorities
secure accommodation orders,
  and 9.23–9.24
Health visitors
referrals, and 5.5
Her Majesty's Courts and Tribunals Service (HMCTS)
generally 1.28
Human rights
application in domestic courts 11.44–11.48

Human rights—*continued*
  care orders, and
    generally   6.28
    threshold criteria   6.142–6.143
  challenging the local authority, and
    application in domestic
      courts   11.44–11.48
    generally   11.36–11.39
    reference to ECtHR   11.49
    right to a fair trial   11.40–11.41
    right to respect for private and
      family life   11.42–11.43
  deprivation of liberty, and
    future issues   9.47
    identification cases of   9.44
    inherent jurisdiction   9.43
    introduction   9.42
    key points   9.45
    procedure   9.46
  generally   2.26–2.29
  reference to ECtHR   11.49
  right to fair trial
    generally   11.40–11.41
    introduction   2.28
  right to family and private life
    generally   11.42–11.43
    introduction   2.27

Independent Review Mechanism
  adoption, and   7.93
Independent reviewing officers
  challenging the local authority,
    and   11.8–11.12
Information sharing
  local authority services, and   4.6
Inherent jurisdiction of the
    High Court
  applications   10.35–10.38
  children in care
    generally   10.30–10.34
    introduction   10.21–10.22
  deprivation of liberty, and   9.43
  generally   2.35–2.37
  introduction   10.1–10.4
  limitations on use   10.28–10.29
  medical treatment   10.23–10.25
  procedure   10.35–10.38
  terminal illness   10.26–10.27
  wardship
    applications   10.35–10.38
    child abduction   10.19
    criminal proceedings   10.17–10.18
    effects   10.6–10.9
    forced marriage   10.19
    generally   10.5
    medical treatment   10.10–10.12
    procedure   10.35–10.38
    publicity   10.13–10.16
    radicalisation   10.20
    uses   10.10–10.20
Inter-agency working
  local authority services, and   4.5–4.6
Intercountry adoption
  foreign child 'adopted' abroad   7.193–7.194

Intercountry adoption—*continued*
  foreign child brought into England
    and Wales for adoption   7.195
  generally   7.191–7.192
  Hague Convention 1993, under   7.197
  parental consent, and   7.71
  UK child adopted abroad   7.196
International child abduction
  allocation of cases   1.8

Judicial review
  challenging the local authority,
    and   11.28–11.33

Leaving care
  duties of local authority   4.101
  eligible children   4.102
  former relevant children   4.110–4.111
  generally   4.99–4.101
  relevant children   4.103
  responsibilities of local
    authority   4.104–4.109
  'staying put'   4.112
Legal aid
  private law proceedings, and   3.3
Leisure facilities
  local authority services, and   4.12
'Lives with' orders
  children age 16 and over   3.32
  conditions   3.32
  generally   3.53–3.55
  introduction   3.30–3.31
  procedure
    applications   3.64–3.67
    child parties   3.71
    guardians ad litem   3.71
    respondents   3.68
    welfare reports   3.69–3.70
  special guardianship, and   8.20–8.21
Local authorities
  accommodation
    child has no parent or parents
      consent   4.33–4.38
    children in care   4.39–4.41
    children in need   4.17
    general duty   4.26–4.32
    'looked after children'   4.26
  after school care   4.12
  assistance in kind or cash   4.17
  charging for services   4.18
  children in care
    accommodation   4.39–4.41
  children in need
    accommodation   4.17
    'appropriate' provision   4.16
    assessment   4.13
    assistance in kind or cash   4.17
    charging for services   4.18
    definition   4.13
    general duty of authority   4.15
    services   4.14–4.18
  children who are not looked after
    generally   4.88–4.89
    private fostering   4.90–4.98

Index

Local authorities—*continued*
  children with disabilities
    'disabled'   4.19
    generally   4.19
    register of disabled children   4.19
    support for parents   4.22
  children with special needs
    education, health and care plan   4.21
    generally   4.20
  delegation of duties   4.10
  disabled children   4.8
  family centres   4.11
  foster care
    agency parents   4.65–4.68
    approval process   4.65–4.84
    children's homes   4.77
    duties of parents   4.70–4.75
    emergency placements   4.69
    friends   4.54
    funding   4.76
    generally   4.53
    introduction   4.52
    local authority foster parents   4.58–4.64
    placement with parent   4.78–4.
    regulatory framework   4.55–4.57
    relatives   4.54
    rights of parents   4.70–4.75
    types   4.53
  information sharing   4.6
  inter-agency working   4.5–4.6
  introduction   4.1–4.4
  leaving care
    duties of local authority   4.101
    eligible children   4.102
    former relevant children   4.110–4.111
    generally   4.99–4.101
    relevant children   4.103
    responsibilities of local authority   4.104–4.109
    'staying put'   4.112
  leisure facilities   4.12
  local safeguarding partners   4.5–4.6
  looked after children
    accommodation   4.26, 4.52
    care plans   4.42–4.44
    care plans for children subject to care order   4.47–4.49
    foster care   4.52–4.77
    independent reviewing officer   4.50–4.51
    introduction   4.42–4.46
    reviews   4.45–4.46
  meaning   4.4
  placement with parents
    assessment checklist   4.85–4.87
    generally   4.78–4.84
  private fostering
    accommodation by voluntary organisations   4.95–4.96
    duties of local authority   4.95–4.
    generally   4.90–4.94
    introduction   4.88–4.89
    other informal arrangements   4.97–4.98
  provision of services
    accommodation   4.26–4.41

Local authorities—*continued*
  provision of services—*continued*
    all children, to   4.10–4.12
    children in need, for   4.14–4.18
    children who are not looked after, to   4.88–4.98
    children with special needs and disabilities, to   4.19–4.22
    delegation   4.10
    family centres   4.11
    foster care   4.52–4.77
    generally   2.8–2.9
    introduction   4.7–4.9
    leaving care, on   4.99–4.112
    legislative basis   2.7
    looked after children   4.42–4.87
    placement with parents   4.78–4.87
    private fostering   4.90–4.98
    structure   4.7
    types   4.7
    young carers, to   4.23–4.25
  referral, and
    see also **Referrals**
    court, by   5.14–5.21
    initial referral   5.4–5.13
    introduction   5.1–5.3
  safeguarding partners   4.5–4.6
  school facilities   4.12
  section 27 duty   4.2
  social services, and   4.2
  support for children and families
    accommodation   4.26–4.41
    all children, to   4.10–4.12
    children in need, for   4.14–4.18
    children who are not looked after, to   4.88–4.98
    children with special needs and disabilities, to   4.19–4.22
    delegation   4.10
    family centres   4.11
    foster care   4.52–4.77
    generally   2.8–2.9
    introduction   4.7–4.9
    leaving care, on   4.99–4.112
    legislative basis   2.7
    looked after children   4.42–4.87
    placement with parents   4.78–4.87
    private fostering   4.90–4.98
    structure   4.7
    types   4.7
    young carers, to   4.23–4.25
  voluntary groups, and   4.10–4.11
  young carer services   4.23–4.25

Local Government and Social Care Ombudsman
  challenging the local authority, and   11.26–11.27

Local safeguarding partners
  local authority services, and   4.5–4.6

Looked after children
  accommodation   4.26, 4.52
  care plans   4.42–4.44
  care plans for children subject to care order   4.47–4.49

Looked after children—*continued*
foster care 4.52–4.77
independent reviewing officer 4.50–4.51
introduction 4.42–4.46
reviews 4.45–4.46
secure accommodation orders,
 and 9.20–9.22

Medical examinations and assessments
emergency protection orders, and 5.68–5.69
Medical treatment
inherent jurisdiction of the High
 Court, and 10.23–10.25

NSPCC
referrals, and 5.5

Overseas adoptions
foreign child 'adopted' abroad 7.193–7.194
foreign child brought into England
 and Wales for adoption 7.195
generally 7.191–7.192
Hague Convention 1993, under 7.197
UK child adopted abroad 7.196

Paramouncy of child
generally 2.6
Parental consent to adoption
advance, in
 effect 7.72–7.73
 form 7.70
 generally 7.64–7.66
 proof 7.70
challenging the local authority,
 and 11.3–11.7
criteria 7.56
dispensing with
 grounds 7.74–7.84
 parent cannot be found or incapable
  of giving consent 7.75–7.77
 procedure 7.85
 'requires' 7.82–7.84
 welfare of child, for 7.78–7.81
effect 7.72–7.73
form 7.70
generally 7.56–7.57
guardian 7.60
intercountry applications, in 7.71
making an adoption order 7.67–7.69
overview 7.52–7.55
'parent' 7.58–7.59
placement, and
 criteria 7.56
 effect 7.72–7.73
 form 7.70
 generally 7.61–7.63
 proof 7.70
proof 7.70
welfare of child, and 7.57
Parental responsibility
challenging the local authority,
 and 11.3–11.7
child, and 3.18–3.20

Parental responsibility—*continued*
child arrangements orders
 children age 16 and over 3.32
 conditions 3.33
 domestic abuse 3.40–3.43
 enforcement 3.47–3.52
 generally 3.30
 interim orders 3.44–3.46
 'lives with' orders 3.53–3.55
 'spends time with' orders 3.34–3.43
 types 3.31
contact orders, and 3.31
definition 3.12–3.14
DNA testing 3.9–3.11
domestic abuse
 generally 3.47
 'spends time with' orders, and 3.40–3.43
emergency protection orders, and 5.69
enforcement 3.47–3.52
generally 2.4–2.5
Gillick competency 3.18
guardians
 appointment 3.24–3.26
 disclaimer 3.25
 generally 3.21–3.23
 responsibilities 3.27
 special guardians 3.28–3.29
introduction 3.1–3.4
'lives with' orders
 children age 16 and over 3.32
 conditions 3.32
 generally 3.53–3.55
 introduction 3.30–3.31
meaning 3.12–3.14
'parent'
 generally 3.5–3.8
 testing 3.9–3.11
parenting plans 3.61
private law proceedings, and 3.2
prohibited steps orders
 children age 16 and over 3.32
 conditions 3.33
 generally 3.57–3.60
 introduction 3.30
relevant persons 3.15–3.17
removal of child from jurisdiction 3.62–3.63
residence orders, and 3.31
section 8 orders
 applications 3.64–3.67
 child arrangements 3.30–3.31
 child parties 3.71
 children age 16 and over 3.32
 conditions 3.33
 enforcement 3.47–3.52
 generally 3.30–3.33
 guardians ad litem 3.71
 interim orders 3.44–3.46
 'lives with' orders 3.53–3.55
 parenting plans 3.61
 procedure 3.64–3.71
 prohibited steps 3.57–3.60
 removal of child from
  jurisdiction 3.62–3.63
 respondents 3.68

Parental responsibility—*continued*
  section 8 orders—*continued*
    specific issue   3.57–3.60
    'spends time with' orders   3.34–3.43
    types   3.30
    welfare reports   3.69–3.70
  shared 'lives with' orders
    children age 16 and over   3.32
    conditions   3.32
    generally   3.53–3.55
    introduction   3.30–3.31
  special guardianship, and   3.28–3.29, 8.6
  specific issue orders
    children age 16 and over   3.32
    conditions   3.33
    generally   3.57–3.60
    introduction   3.30
  'spends time with' orders
    children age 16 and over   3.32
    conditions   3.33
    domestic abuse   3.40–3.43
    generally   3.34–3.39
    interim orders   3.44–3.46
    introduction   3.30–3.31
  step-parents   3.16–3.17

Parenting orders
  generally   5.96–5.97

Parenting plans
  section 8 orders, and   3.61

Placement agreement
  generally   7.49

Placement for adoption
  background   7.119–7.122
  consent
    criteria   7.56
    effect   7.72–7.73
    form   7.70
    generally   7.61–7.63
    proof   7.70
  contact, and   7.163–7.174
  extended family, with   7.49
  introduction   2.22
  meaning   7.123–7.125
  order, by
    application by local authority   7.151–7.152
    care proceedings, and   7.158–7.162
    conditions   7.150
    consequences   7.155
    generally   7.148–7.149
    revocation   7.156–7.157
    status of child pending determination of application   7.153–7.154
  parental consent, with
    advance, in   7.137–7.139
    change of name, and   7.143
    child under six weeks old   7.133–7.134
    consequences   7.140–7.142
    father without parental responsibility, and   7.145–7.147
    form   7.135–7.136
    generally   7.127–7.132
    removal from UK, and   7.143
    withdrawal of consent   7.144

Placement for adoption—*continued*
  parents, with
    assessment checklist   4.85–4.87
    generally   4.78–4.84
  routes   7.126
  special guardianship, and   8.10

Placement orders
  application by local authority   7.151–7.152
  care proceedings, and   7.158–7.162
  conditions   7.150
  consequences   7.155
  generally   7.148–7.149
  revocation   7.156–7.157
  status of child pending determination of application   7.153–7.154

Placement with extended family
  generally   7.49

Placement with parental consent
  advance, in   7.137–7.139
  change of name, and   7.143
  child under six weeks old   7.133–7.134
  consequences   7.140–7.142
  father without parental responsibility, and   7.145–7.147
  form   7.135–7.136
  generally   7.127–7.132
  removal from UK, and   7.143
  withdrawal of consent   7.144

Placement with parents
  assessment checklist   4.85–4.87
  generally   4.78–4.84

Police protection
  guidance   5.33
  introduction   5.33
  referrals, and   5.4–5.5
  taking child into protection
    duties of designated officer   5.35–5.37
    duties of officer   5.34
    generally   5.33
  Working Together guidance   5.33

Practice Directions
  generally   1.26

Private fostering
  accommodation by voluntary organisations   4.95–4.96
  duties of local authority   4.95–4.
  generally   4.90–4.94
  introduction   4.88–4.89
  other informal arrangements   4.97–4.98

Private law children proceedings
  generally   1.16–1.19
  legal aid   3.3
  parental responsibility, and   3.1–3.2
  statutory provisions   3.4

Prohibited steps orders
  children age 16 and over   3.32
  conditions   3.33
  generally   3.57–3.60
  introduction   3.30

Public law children proceedings
  generally   1.16–1.19
  parental responsibility, and   3.1–3.2

Public Law Online
  generally   6.60

Radicalisation
  wardship, and   10.20
Recovery orders
  applications   5.85
  effect   5.88–5.90
  generally   5.83–5.84
  notice   5.87
  older children, and   5.91–5.92
  procedure   5.85–5.87
  respondents   5.86
  use   5.84
Referrals
  CAFCASS report, after   5.14
  child-related agencies, through   5.5
  court, by
    appointment of CAFCASS
      guardian   5.20–5.21
    filing report   5.17
    generally   5.14–5.17
    interim care or supervision
      orders   5.18–5.19
    local authority investigation   5.16
  emergency, in   5.4
  emergency protection order, under   5.4
  GP, by   5.5
  health visitor, by   5.5
  initial referral
    child protection investigation   5.8–5.13
    generally   5.4–5.5
    local authority's response   5.6–5.7
  introduction   5.1–5.3
  local authority's response   5.6–5.7
  police, by   5.4–5.5
  s 47 investigation   5.8–5.13
  strategy discussion   5.7
Removal of child
  emergency protection orders, and   5.58–5.60
  section 8 orders, and   3.62–3.63
Representation of child
  care orders, and
    guardian   6.89–6.92
    solicitor   6.93–6.96
  secure accommodation orders,
    and   9.34–9.35
Residence orders
  section 8 orders, and   3.31

Safeguarding partners
  local authority services, and   4.5–4.6
School facilities
  local authority services, and   4.12
Section 8 orders
  applications   3.64–3.67
  child arrangements orders
    children age 16 and over   3.32
    conditions   3.33
    domestic abuse   3.40–3.43
    enforcement   3.47–3.52
    generally   3.30
    interim orders   3.44–3.46
    'lives with' orders   3.53–3.55
    'spends time with' orders   3.34–3.43
    types   3.31
  child parties   3.71

Section 8 orders—*continued*
  children age 16 and over   3.32
  conditions   3.33
  contact orders, and   3.31
  domestic abuse
    generally   3.47
    'spends time with' orders,
      and   3.40–3.43
  enforcement   3.47–3.52
  generally   3.30–3.33
  guardians ad litem   3.71
  interim orders   3.44–3.46
  'lives with' orders
    children age 16 and over   3.32
    conditions   3.32
    generally   3.53–3.55
    introduction   3.30–3.31
  parenting plans   3.61
  parties
    applicants   3.64–3.67
    children   3.71
    guardians ad litem   3.71
    respondents   3.68
  procedure
    applications   3.64–3.67
    child parties   3.71
    guardians ad litem   3.71
    respondents   3.68
    welfare reports   3.69–3.70
  prohibited steps orders
    children age 16 and over   3.32
    conditions   3.33
    generally   3.57–3.60
    introduction   3.30
  removal of child from jurisdiction   3.62–3.63
  residence orders, and   3.31
  respondents   3.68
  shared 'lives with' orders
    children age 16 and over   3.32
    conditions   3.32
    generally   3.53–3.55
    introduction   3.30–3.31
  special guardianship, and   3.28–3.29, 8.19
  specific issue orders
    children age 16 and over   3.32
    conditions   3.33
    generally   3.57–3.60
    introduction   3.30
  'spends time with' orders
    children age 16 and over   3.32
    conditions   3.33
    domestic abuse   3.40–3.43
    generally   3.34–3.39
    interim orders   3.44–3.46
    introduction   3.30–3.31
  types   3.30
  welfare reports   3.69–3.70
Secure accommodation orders
  see also **Accommodation**
  age restrictions   9.19
  applicants   9.30
  applications   9.300–9.31
  challenges to   9.36–9.38
  court's role   9.13

Index

Secure accommodation orders—*continued*
 criminal offences
  child charged   9.27–9.28
  child convicted   9.26
  child detained under Mental Health
   Act 1983   9.29
  child on remand   9.27–9.28
  introduction   9.25
 criteria   9.10–9.14
 deprivation of liberty
  future issues   9.47
  identification cases of   9.44
  inherent jurisdiction   9.43
  introduction   9.42
  key points   9.45
  procedure   9.46
 education authorities, and   9.23–9.24
 educational provision   9.39
 effect   9.15–9.18
 grounds   9.11
 health authorities, and   9.23–9.24
 introduction   9.1–9.4
 'likely'   9.12
 local authority's obligations
  educational provision   9.39
  release   9.41
  review   9.40
 looked after children   9.20–9.22
 notice of proceedings   9.32
 procedure   9.30–9.
 proportionality   9.14
 registered children's homes.   9.6
 release   9.41
 representation of child   9.34–9.35
 respondents   9.31
 restriction of liberty, and   9.1–9.3
 review   9.40
 role of court   9.13
 'secure accommodation'   9.5–9.9
 service of applications   9.33
Shared 'lives with' orders
 children age 16 and over   3.32
 conditions   3.32
 generally   3.53–3.55
 introduction   3.30–3.31
Social services
 local authority services, and   4.2
Sources of law
 Adoption and Children Act 2002   2.19–2.25
 background   2.1–2.2
 Children Act 1989   2.4–2.18
 Family Justice Council   2.34
 government guidance   2.32
 Human Rights Act 1998   2.26–2.29
 inherent jurisdiction of the High
  Court   2.35–2.37
 introduction   2.3
 statutory rules   2.31
 UN Convention on the Rights of the
  Child   2.30
 Wales   2.33
 wardship   2.35–2.37
Special guardianship
 adoption orders, and   8.7

Special guardianship—*continued*
 allowances   8.16–8.18
 applicants
  generally   8.10
  introduction   8.3
 applications   8.9–8.12
 care orders, and   8.20
 care proceedings, within   8.13–8.14
 challenges   8.8
 child arrangements orders, and   8.20–8.21
 child's legal status   8.8
 contact with parents   8.8
 discharge
  generally   8.22–8.23
  introduction   8.2
 duration   8.8
 effect   8.4–8.5
 factors   8.8
 financial support
  generally   8.16–8.18
  introduction   8.8
 generally   8.1–8.8
 interaction with other orders   8.19–8.21
 'lives with' orders, and   8.20–8.21
 notice of application   8.9
 parental responsibility, and   3.28–3.29, 8.6
 parents, and   8.3
 placement for adoption, and   8.10
 procedure   8.9–8.12
 purpose   8.1
 revocation   8.2
 section 8 orders, and   8.19
 support services   8.15
 variation   8.22–8.23
Specific issue orders
 children age 16 and over   3.32
 conditions   3.33
 generally   3.57–3.60
 introduction   3.30
'Specified proceedings'
 child assessment orders, and   5.77
 emergency protection orders, and   5.45
 interim care orders, and   5.21
'Spends time with' orders
 children age 16 and over   3.32
 conditions   3.33
 domestic abuse   3.40–3.43
 generally   3.34–3.39
 interim orders   3.44–3.46
 introduction   3.30–3.31
 procedure
  applications   3.64–3.67
  child parties   3.71
  guardians ad litem   3.71
  respondents   3.68
  welfare reports   3.69–3.70
Step-parents
 parental responsibility, and   3.16–3.18
Strategy discussion
 referrals, and   5.7
Supervision orders
 see also **Care orders**
 allocation of proceedings   6.52
 assessments   6.71

Supervision orders—*continued*	
care plan	6.44, 6.74
designated local authority	6.53
discharge	6.84
generally	6.7–6.8
interim orders	6.63
introduction	6.1
local authority support	
generally	2.10–2.16
legislative basis	2.7
parties	6.45
role of court	6.57
substitution	6.88
threshold criteria	6.9
use	6.151–6.153
Supreme Court	
appeals	1.13
Taking child into protection	
duties of designated officer	5.35–5.37
duties of officer	5.34
guidance	5.33
introduction	5.33
Terminal illness	
inherent jurisdiction of the High Court, and	10.26–10.27
UN Convention on the Rights of the Child	
generally	2.30
Wales	
generally	2.33
Wardship	
applications	10.35–10.38
child abduction	10.19
criminal proceedings	10.17–10.18
effects	10.6–10.9
forced marriage	10.19
generally	10.5
introduction	2.35–2.37
medical treatment	10.10–10.12
procedure	10.35–10.38
publicity	10.13–10.16
radicalisation	10.20
uses	10.10–10.20
Welfare of child	
adoption, and	7.57
care orders, and	
babies	6.34–6.36
birth family	6.30–6.32
care plan	6.44
generally	6.25–6.27
holistic analysis	6.29
human rights, and	6.28
learning disabilities	6.41–6.43
older children	6.37–6.39
physical disabilities	6.41–6.43
splitting siblings	6.33
very young parents	6.40
young children	6.34–6.36
generally	2.6
Without notice applications	
emergency protection orders, and	5.49–5.50
Young carers	
local authority services, and	4.23–4.25